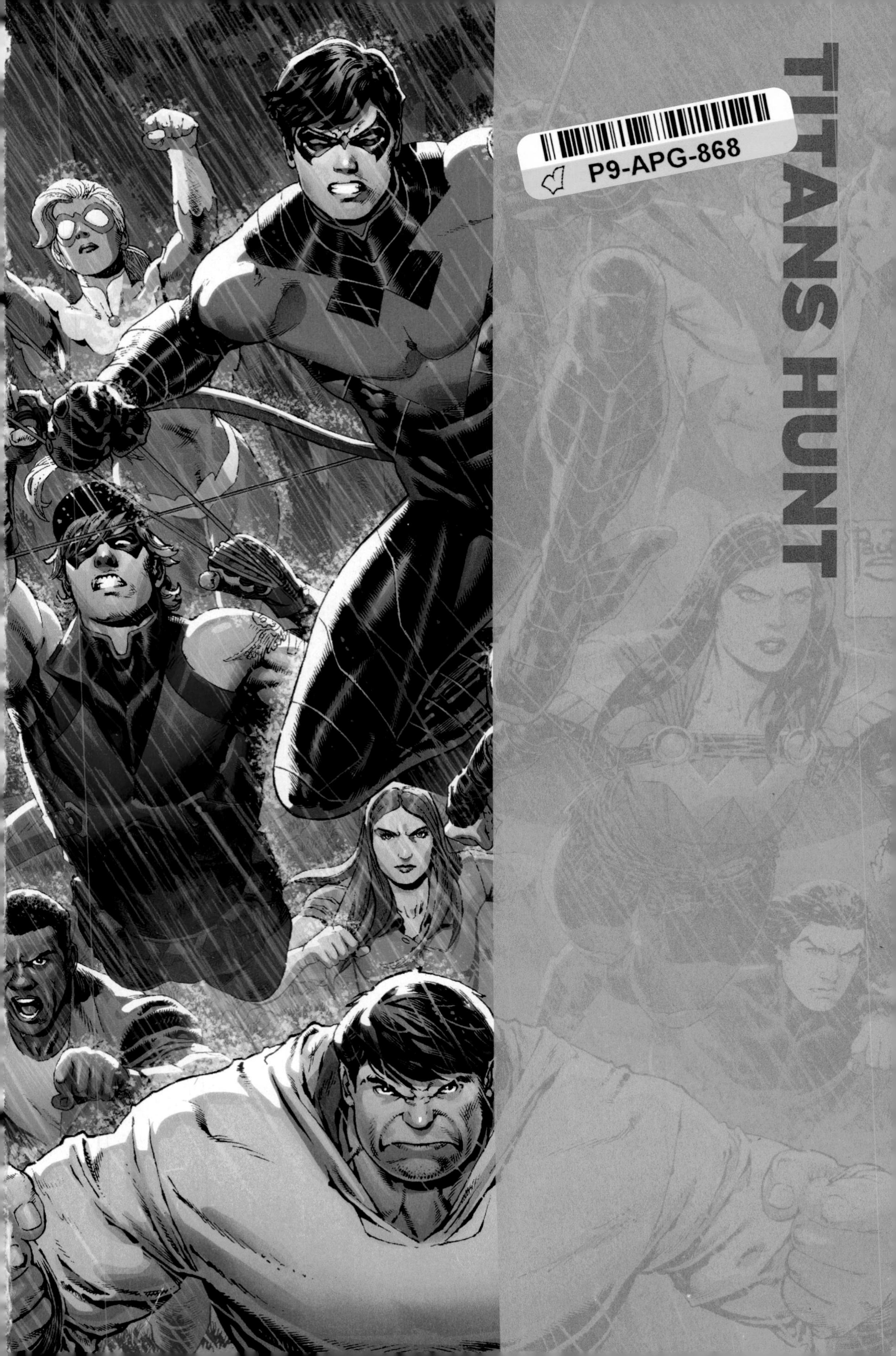
TITANS HUNT

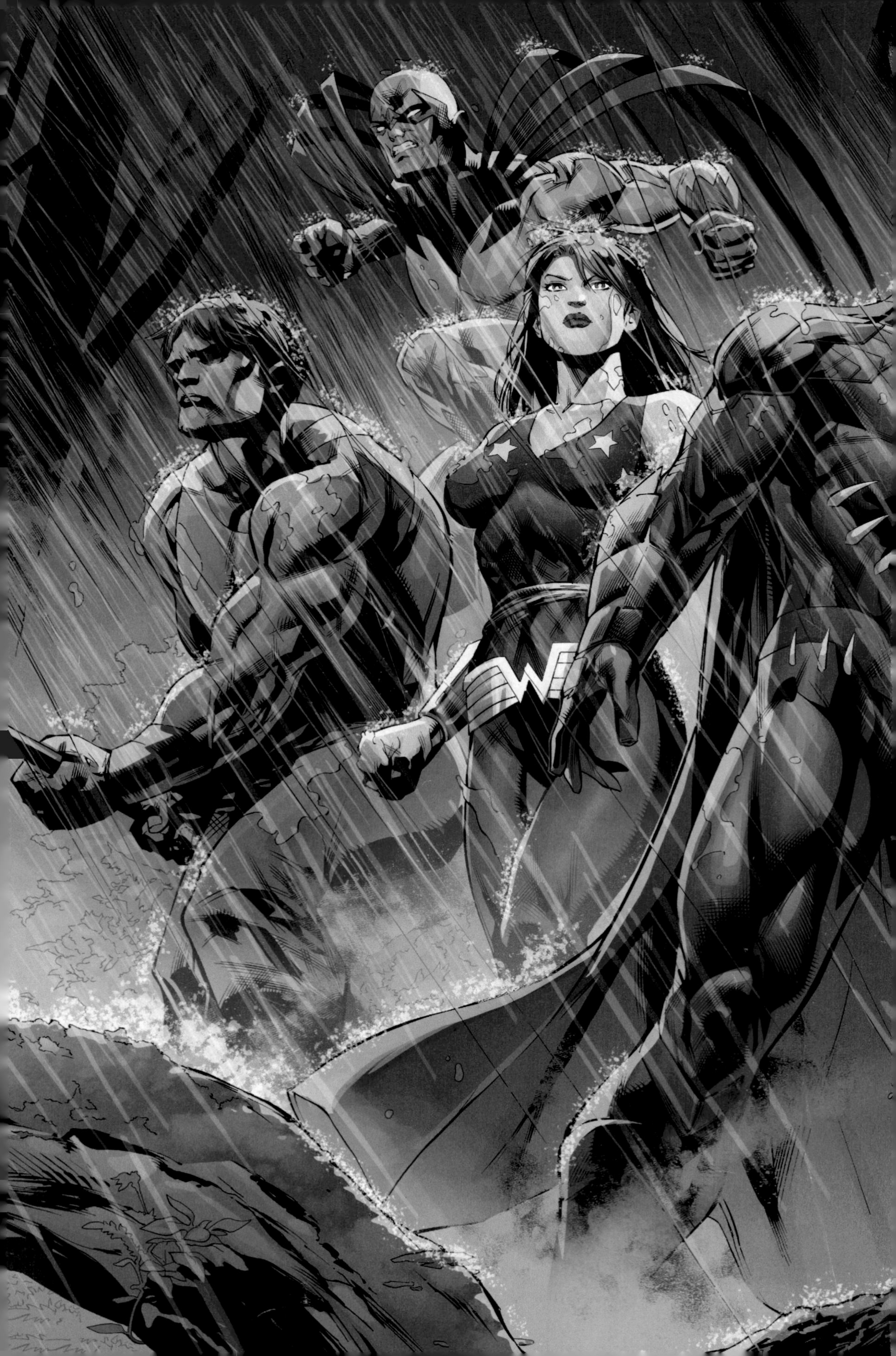

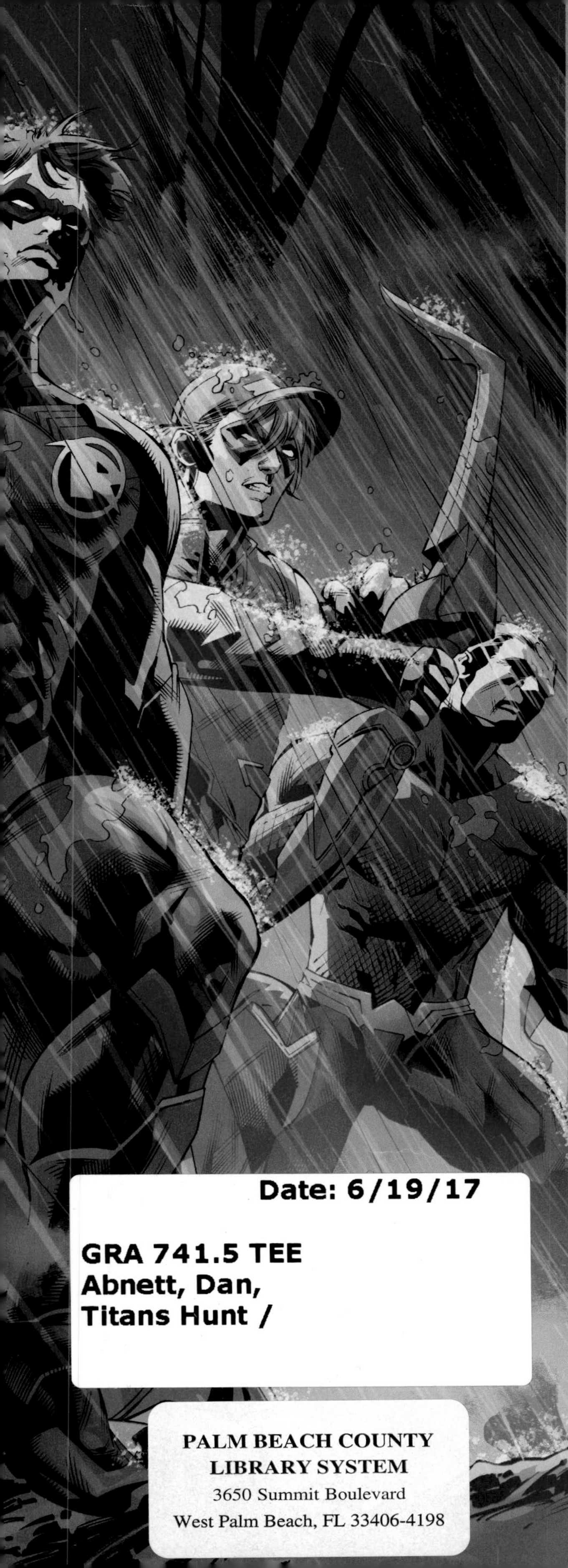

TITANS HUNT

WRITTEN BY
DAN ABNETT

ART BY
PAULO SIQUEIRA
PAUL PELLETIER
BRETT BOOTH
GERALDO BORGES
STEPHEN SEGOVIA
JACKSON HERBERT
ART THIBERT
RAY McCARTHY
WAYNE FAUCHER
SANDRA HOPE
NORM RAPMUND

COLOR BY
HI-FI
ANDREW DALHOUSE
ADRIANO LUCAS

LETTERS BY
CARLOS M. MANGUAL

COLLECTION COVER ART BY
PAULO SIQUEIRA & HI-FI

SUPERMAN CREATED BY
JERRY SIEGEL
AND **JOE SHUSTER**
BY SPECIAL ARRANGEMENT WITH
THE JERRY SIEGEL FAMILY.

TITANS HUNT

Published by DC Comics. Compilation and all new material Copyright © 2016 DC Comics. All Rights Reserved.

Originally published in single magazine form in TITANS HUNT 1-8, TITANS REBIRTH 1, JUSTICE LEAGUE 51.
Copyright © 2015, 2016 DC Comics. All Rights Reserved. All characters, their distinctive likenesses and related
elements featured in this publication are trademarks of DC Comics.
The stories, characters and incidents featured in this publication are entirely fictional.
DC Comics does not read or accept unsolicited submissions of ideas, stories or artwork.

DC Comics, 2900 West Alameda Ave., Burbank, CA 91505
Printed by RR Donnelley, Salem, VA, USA. 8/12/16. First Printing.
ISBN: 978-1-4012-6555-7

Library of Congress Cataloging-in-Publication Data

Names: Abnett, Dan, author. | Siqueira, Paulo, 1982- illustrator. | Segovia,
    Stephen, illustrator.
Title: Titans hunt / Dan Abnett, Paulo Siqueira, Stephen Segovia.
Description: Burbank, CA : DC Comics, [2016]
Identifiers: LCCN 2016017876 | ISBN 9781401265557 (paperback)
Subjects: LCSH: Comic books, strips, etc. | BISAC: COMICS & GRAPHIC NOVELS /
    Superheroes.
Classification: LCC PN6728.T656 A65 2016 | DDC 741.5/973—dc23
LC record available at https://lccn.loc.gov/2016017876

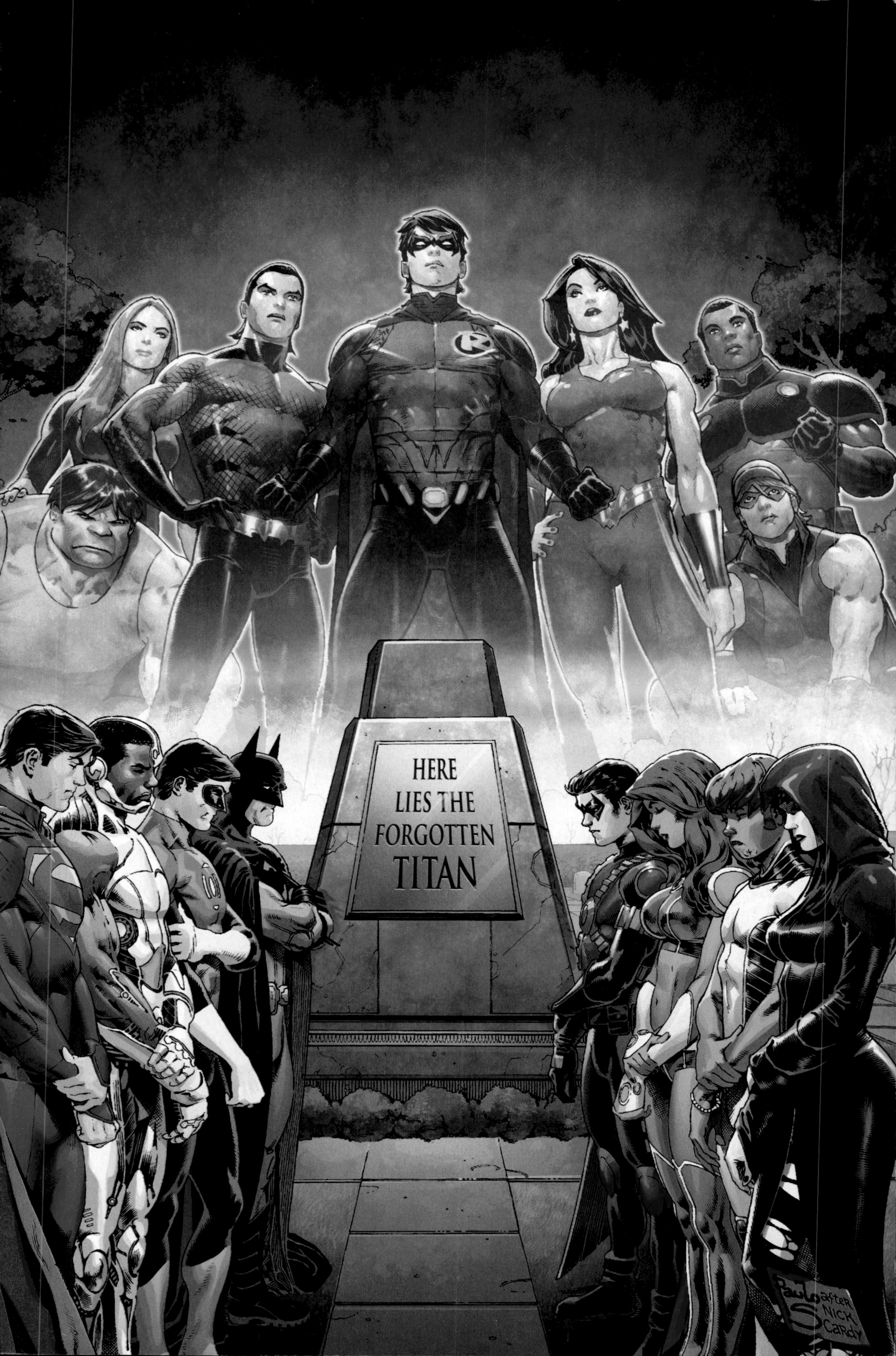
HERE
LIES THE
FORGOTTEN
TITAN
Paulo S after NICK CARDY

CHAPTER ONE: THE BRAVE AND THE BOLD

DAN ABNETT writer PAULO SIQUEIRA & GERALDO BORGES artists HI-FI colorist cover art by PAULO SIQUEIRA & HI-FI

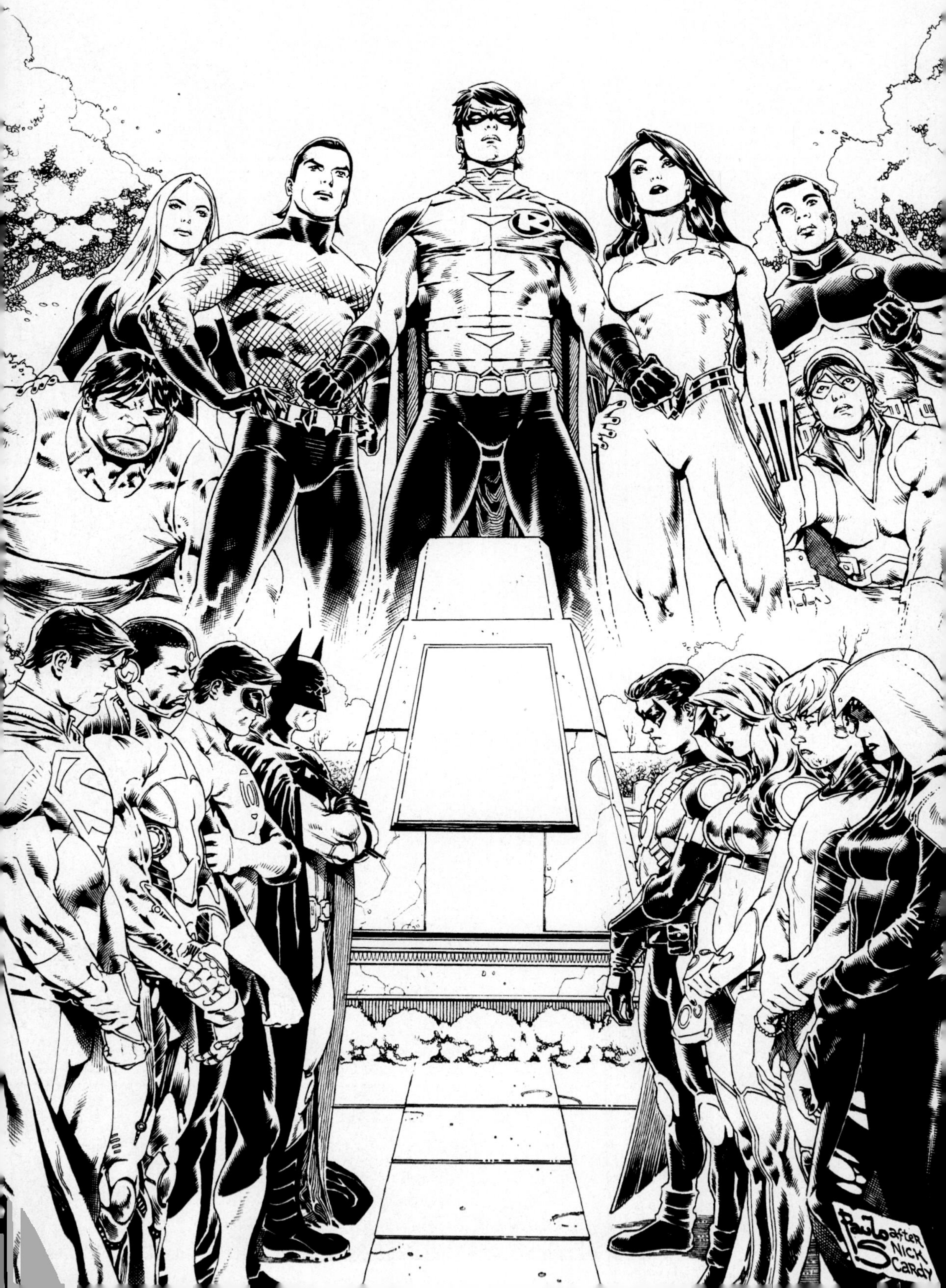
Paulo S after NICK Cardy

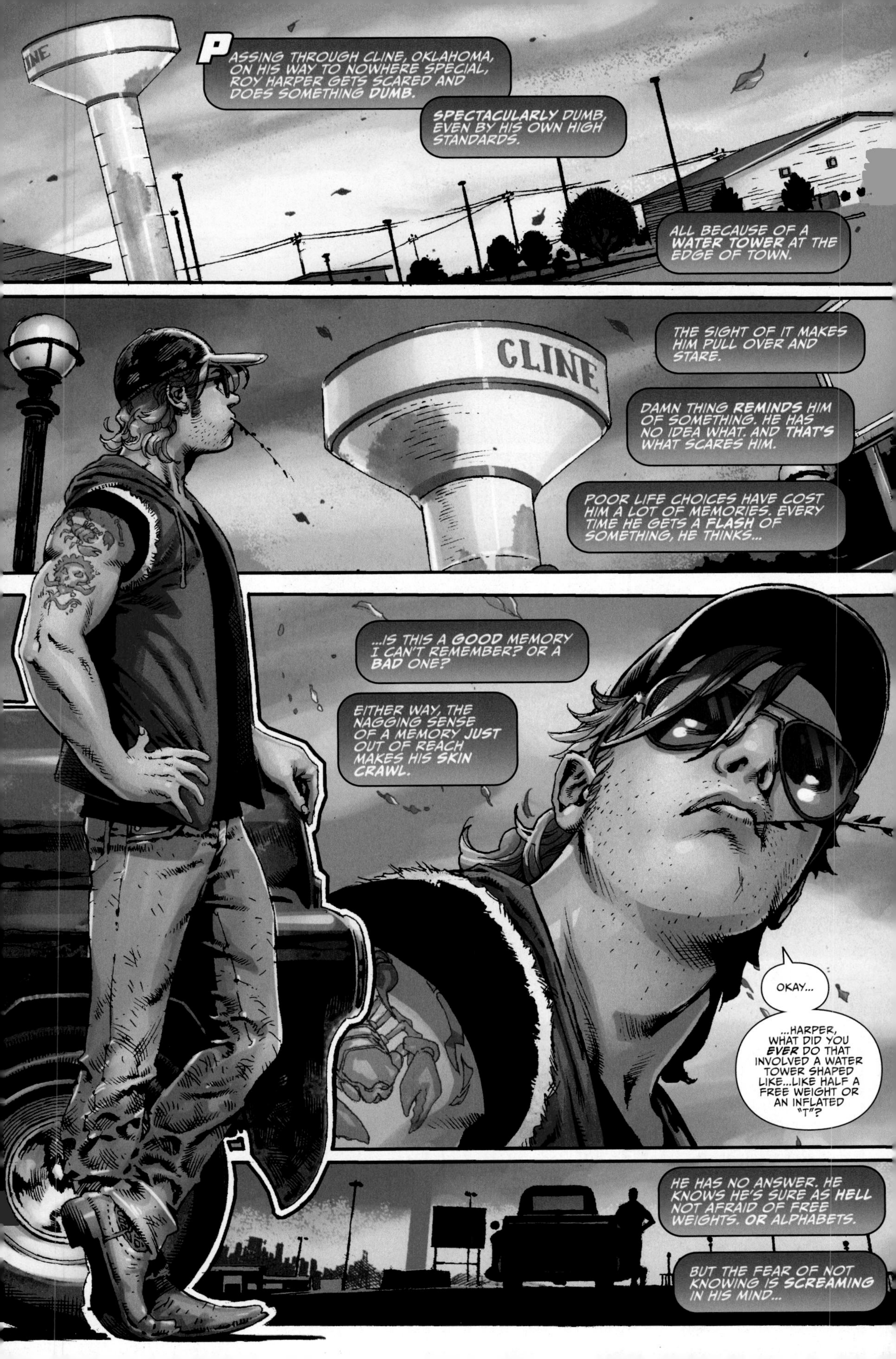
CLINE
PASSING THROUGH CLINE, OKLAHOMA, ON HIS WAY TO NOWHERE SPECIAL, ROY HARPER GETS SCARED AND DOES SOMETHING DUMB.
SPECTACULARLY DUMB, EVEN BY HIS OWN HIGH STANDARDS.
ALL BECAUSE OF A WATER TOWER AT THE EDGE OF TOWN.
CLINE
THE SIGHT OF IT MAKES HIM PULL OVER AND STARE.
DAMN THING REMINDS HIM OF SOMETHING. HE HAS NO IDEA WHAT. AND THAT'S WHAT SCARES HIM.
POOR LIFE CHOICES HAVE COST HIM A LOT OF MEMORIES. EVERY TIME HE GETS A FLASH OF SOMETHING, HE THINKS...
...IS THIS A GOOD MEMORY I CAN'T REMEMBER? OR A BAD ONE?
EITHER WAY, THE NAGGING SENSE OF A MEMORY JUST OUT OF REACH MAKES HIS SKIN CRAWL.
OKAY...
...HARPER, WHAT DID YOU EVER DO THAT INVOLVED A WATER TOWER SHAPED LIKE...LIKE HALF A FREE WEIGHT OR AN INFLATED "T"?
HE HAS NO ANSWER. HE KNOWS HE'S SURE AS HELL NOT AFRAID OF FREE WEIGHTS. OR ALPHABETS.
BUT THE FEAR OF NOT KNOWING IS SCREAMING IN HIS MIND...

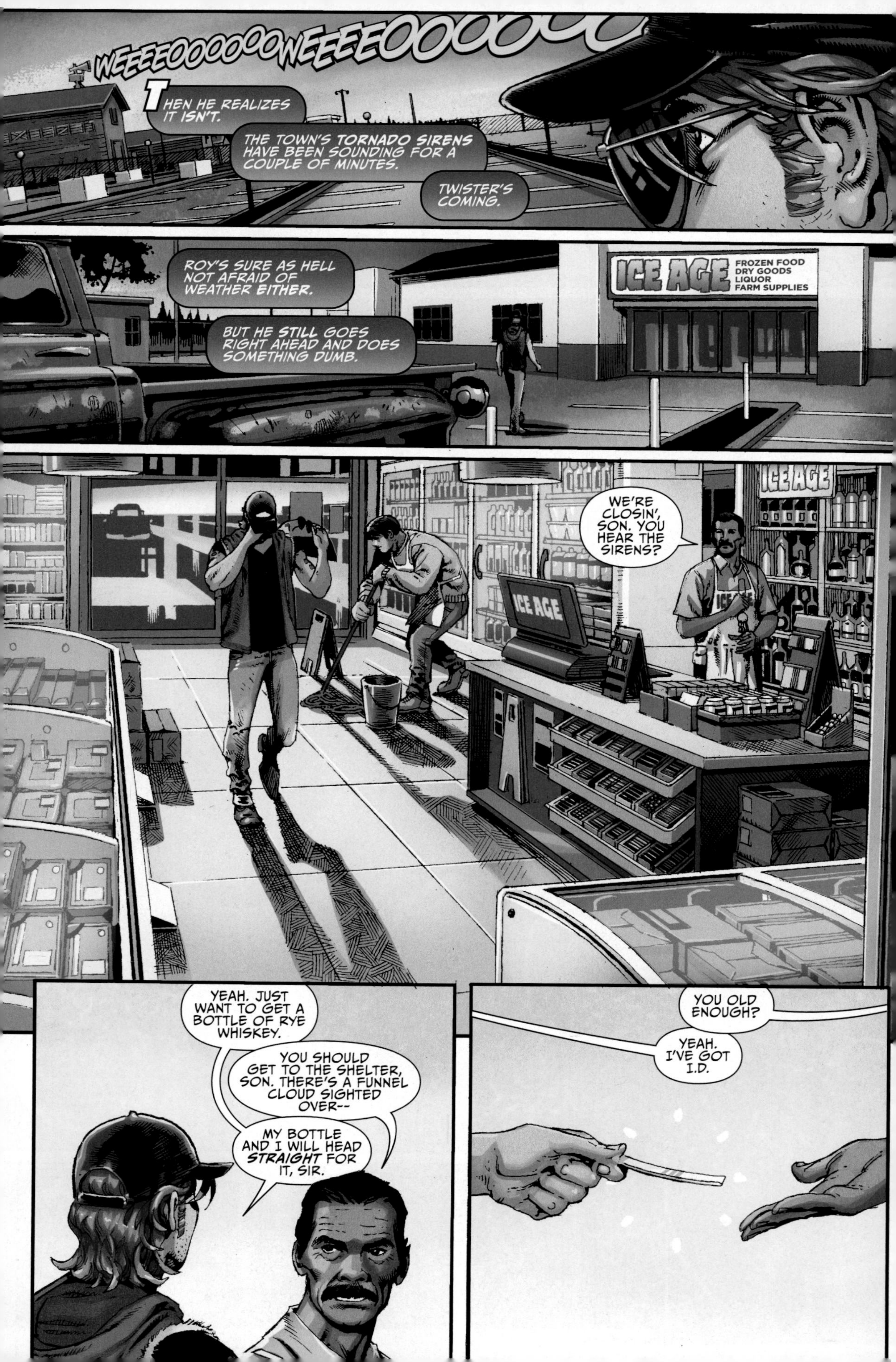
WEEEEOOOOOOWEEEEOOOOOOO
THEN HE REALIZES IT ISN'T.
THE TOWN'S TORNADO SIRENS HAVE BEEN SOUNDING FOR A COUPLE OF MINUTES.
TWISTER'S COMING.
ROY'S SURE AS HELL NOT AFRAID OF WEATHER EITHER.
BUT HE STILL GOES RIGHT AHEAD AND DOES SOMETHING DUMB.
ICE AGE
FROZEN FOOD
DRY GOODS
LIQUOR
FARM SUPPLIES
WE'RE CLOSIN', SON. YOU HEAR THE SIRENS?
ICE AGE
YEAH. JUST WANT TO GET A BOTTLE OF RYE WHISKEY.
YOU SHOULD GET TO THE SHELTER, SON. THERE'S A FUNNEL CLOUD SIGHTED OVER--
MY BOTTLE AND I WILL HEAD STRAIGHT FOR IT, SIR.
YOU OLD ENOUGH?
YEAH. I'VE GOT I.D.

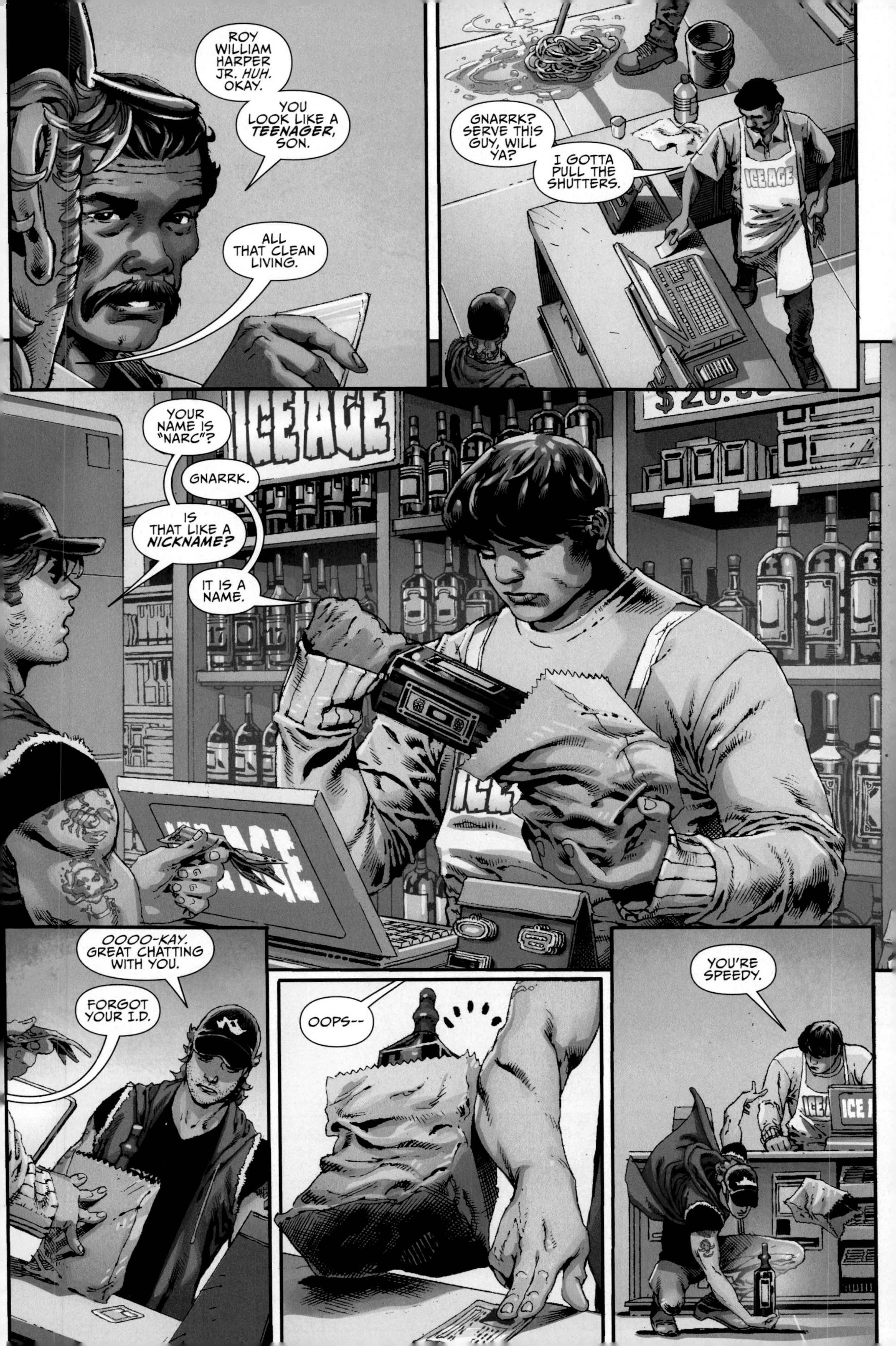
ROY WILLIAM HARPER JR. *HUH.* OKAY.
YOU LOOK LIKE A ***TEENAGER,*** SON.
ALL THAT CLEAN LIVING.
GNARRK? SERVE THIS GUY, WILL YA?
I GOTTA PULL THE SHUTTERS.
ICE AGE
ICE AGE
YOUR NAME IS "NARC"?
GNARRK.
IS THAT LIKE A ***NICKNAME?***
IT IS A NAME.
OOOO-KAY. GREAT CHATTING WITH YOU.
FORGOT YOUR I.D.
OOPS--
YOU'RE SPEEDY.

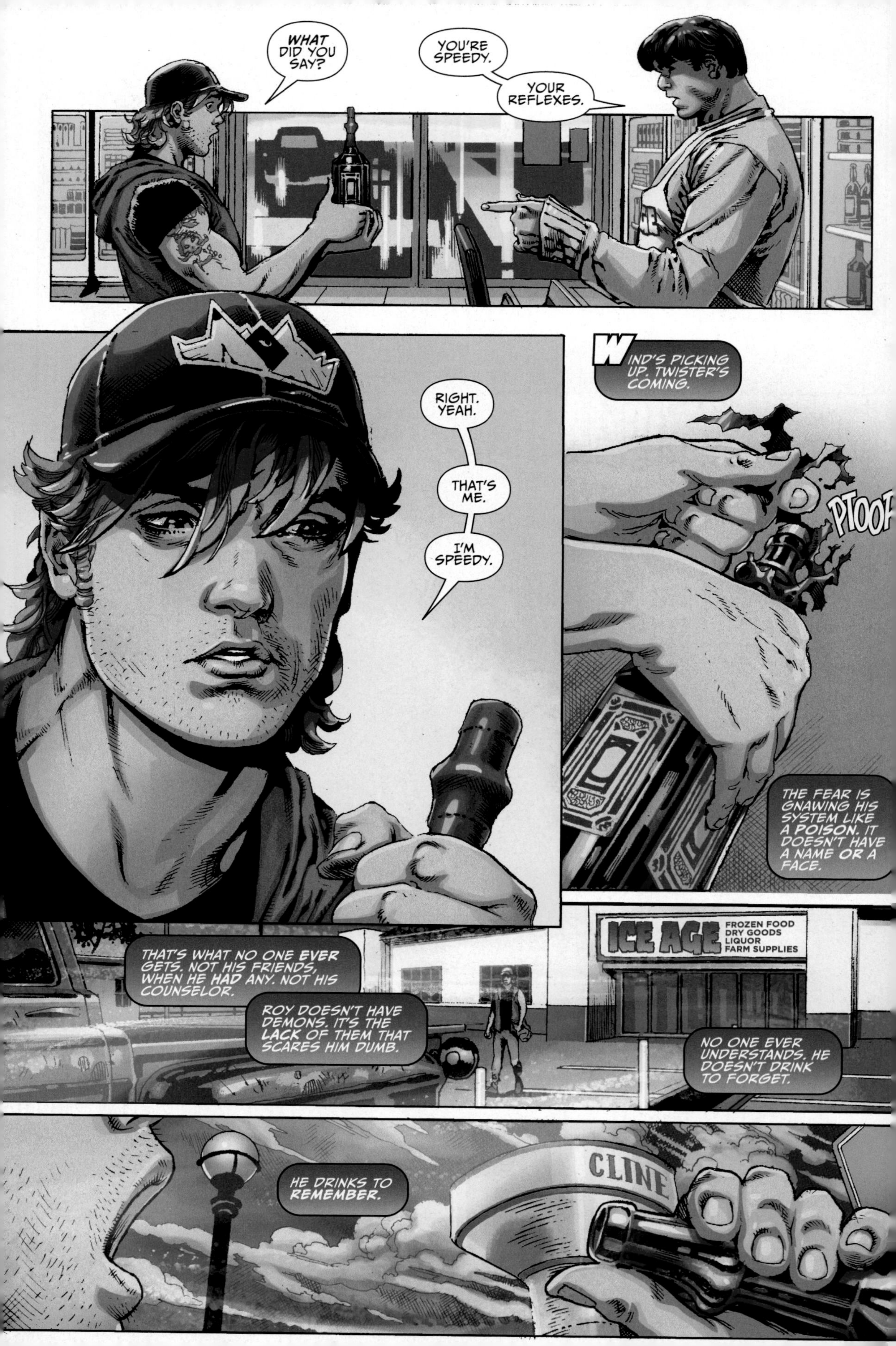
WHAT DID YOU SAY?
YOU'RE SPEEDY.
YOUR REFLEXES.
RIGHT. YEAH.
THAT'S ME.
I'M SPEEDY.
WIND'S PICKING UP. TWISTER'S COMING.
PTOOF
THE FEAR IS GNAWING HIS SYSTEM LIKE A POISON. IT DOESN'T HAVE A NAME OR A FACE.
THAT'S WHAT NO ONE EVER GETS. NOT HIS FRIENDS, WHEN HE HAD ANY. NOT HIS COUNSELOR.
ROY DOESN'T HAVE DEMONS. IT'S THE LACK OF THEM THAT SCARES HIM DUMB.
ICE AGE
FROZEN FOOD
DRY GOODS
LIQUOR
FARM SUPPLIES
NO ONE EVER UNDERSTANDS. HE DOESN'T DRINK TO FORGET.
HE DRINKS TO REMEMBER.
CLINE

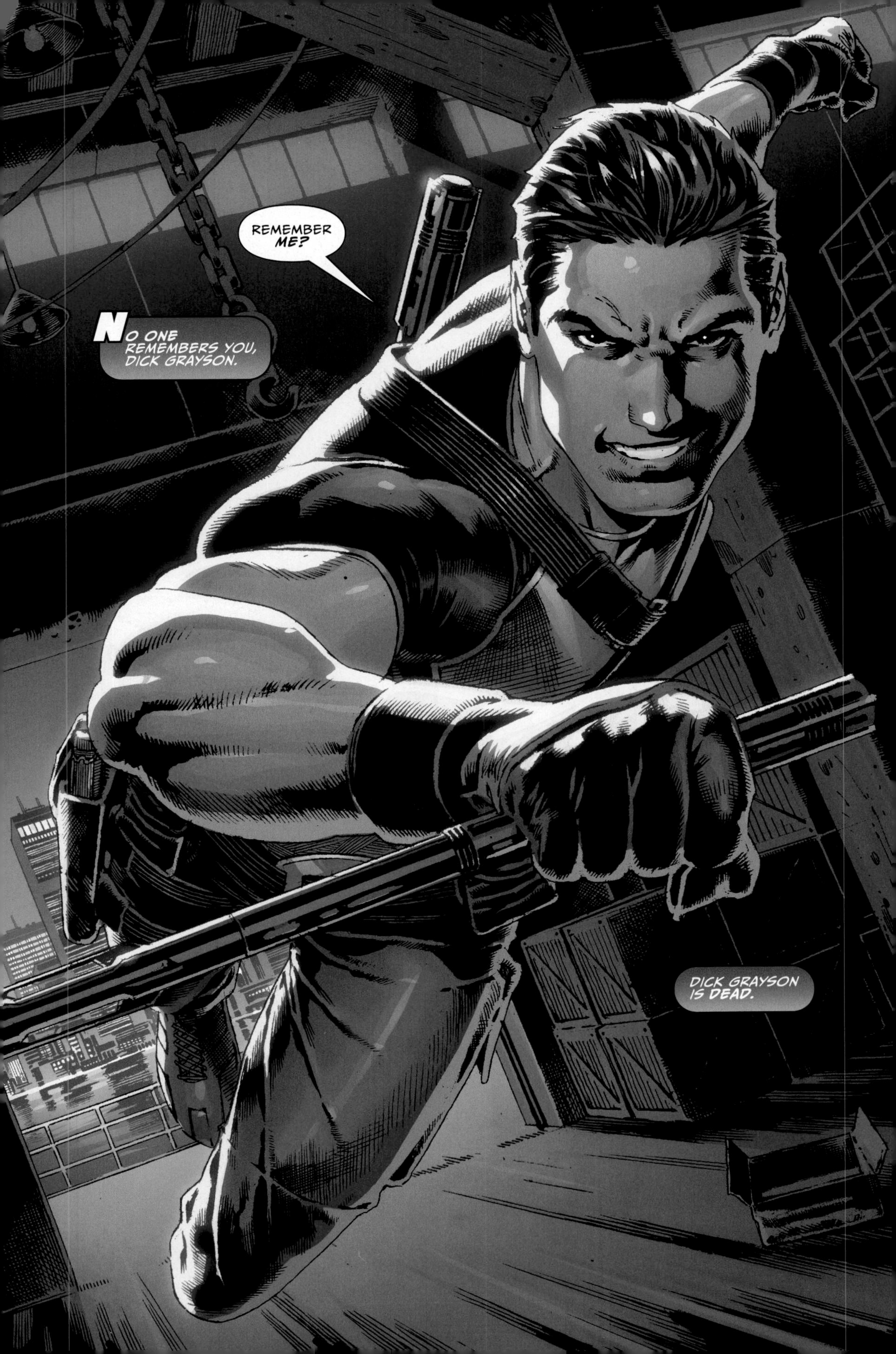

NO ONE REMEMBERS YOU, DICK GRAYSON.
REMEMBER ME?
DICK GRAYSON IS DEAD.

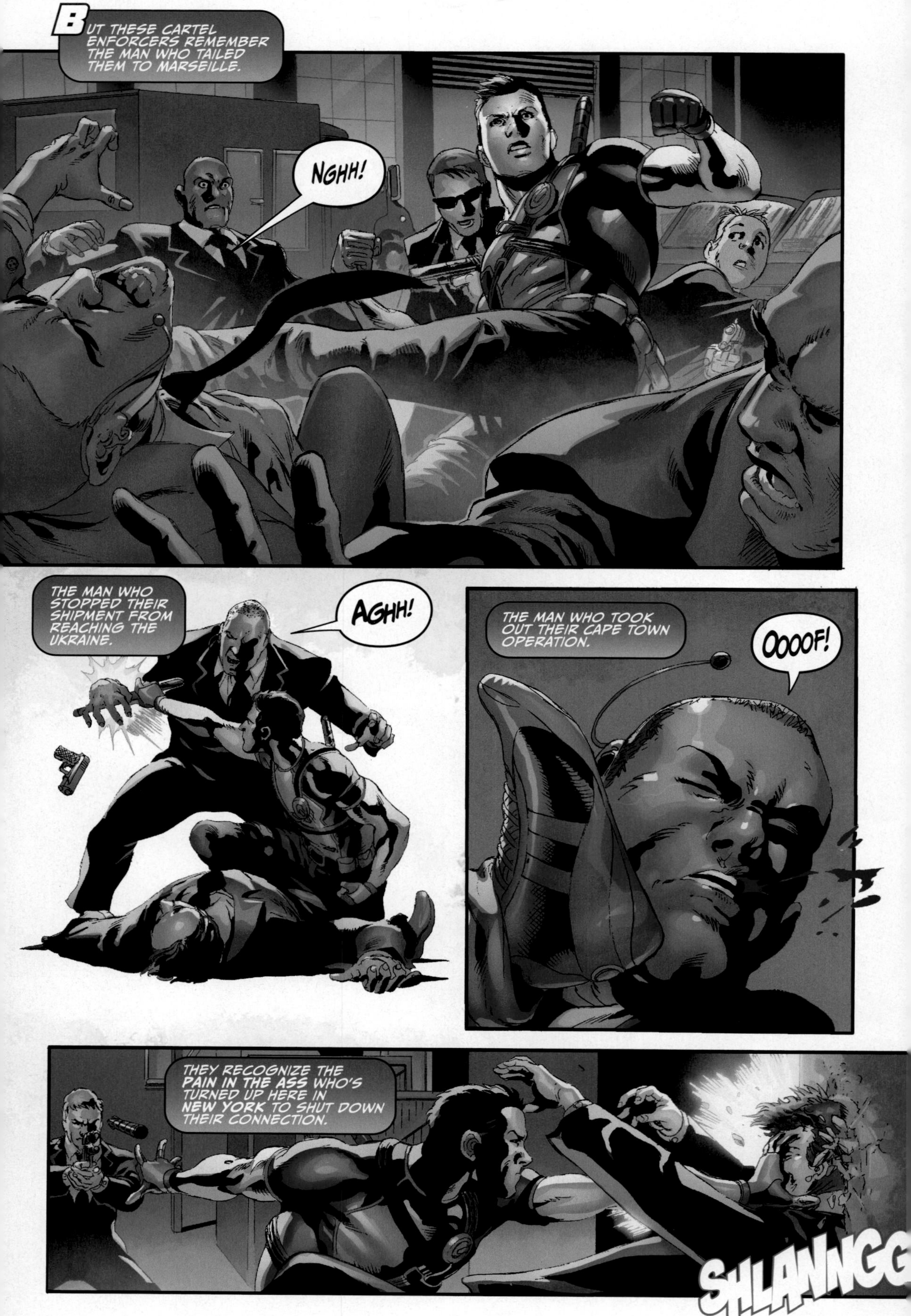
BUT THESE CARTEL ENFORCERS REMEMBER THE MAN WHO TAILED THEM TO MARSEILLE.
NGHH!
THE MAN WHO STOPPED THEIR SHIPMENT FROM REACHING THE UKRAINE.
AGHH!
THE MAN WHO TOOK OUT THEIR CAPE TOWN OPERATION.
OOOOF!
THEY RECOGNIZE THE PAIN IN THE ASS WHO'S TURNED UP HERE IN NEW YORK TO SHUT DOWN THEIR CONNECTION.
SHLANNGG

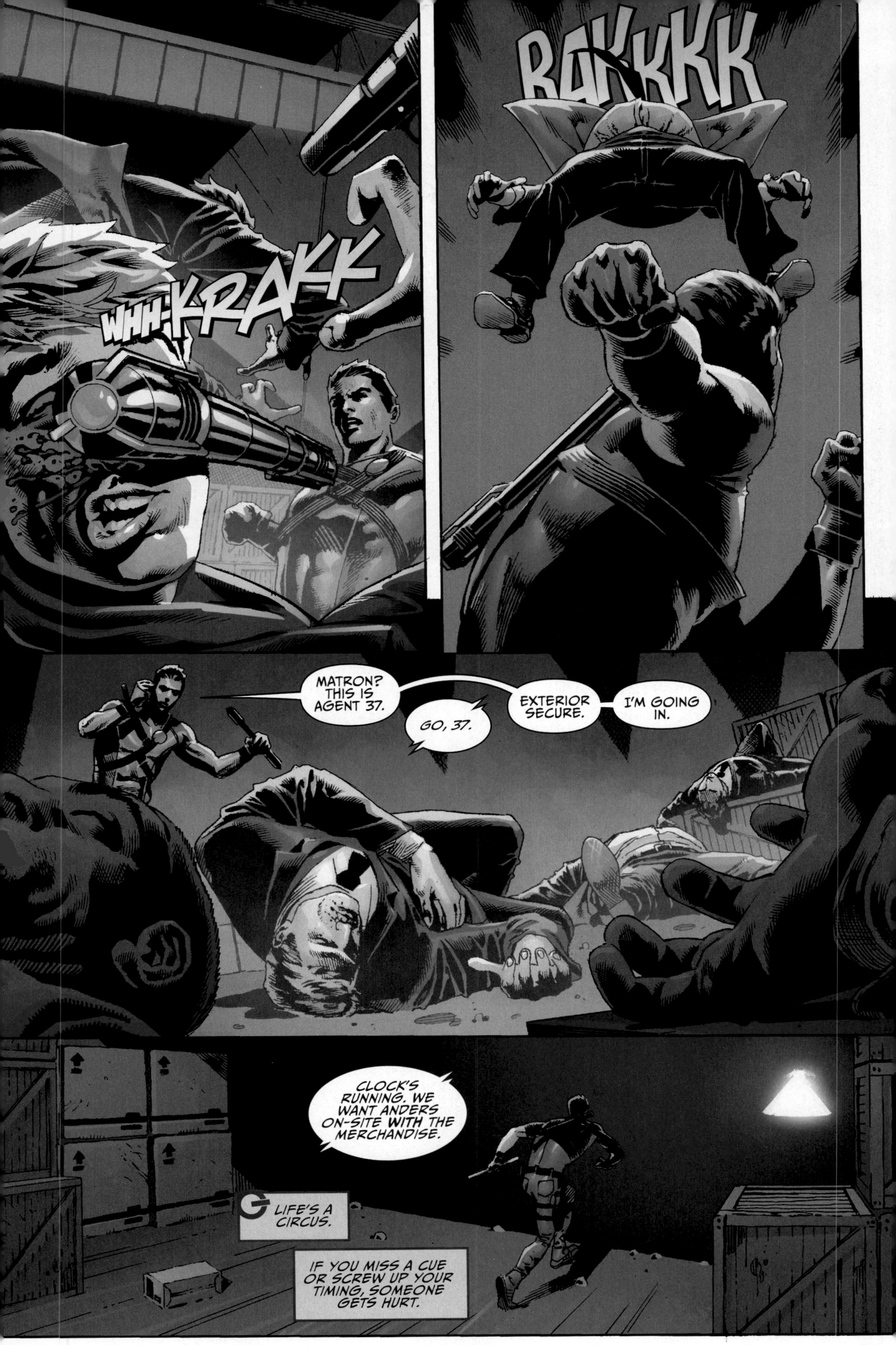
WHH-KRAKK
RAKKKK
MATRON? THIS IS AGENT 37.
GO, 37.
EXTERIOR SECURE.
I'M GOING IN.
CLOCK'S RUNNING. WE WANT ANDERS ON-SITE WITH THE MERCHANDISE.
LIFE'S A CIRCUS.
IF YOU MISS A CUE OR SCREW UP YOUR TIMING, SOMEONE GETS HURT.

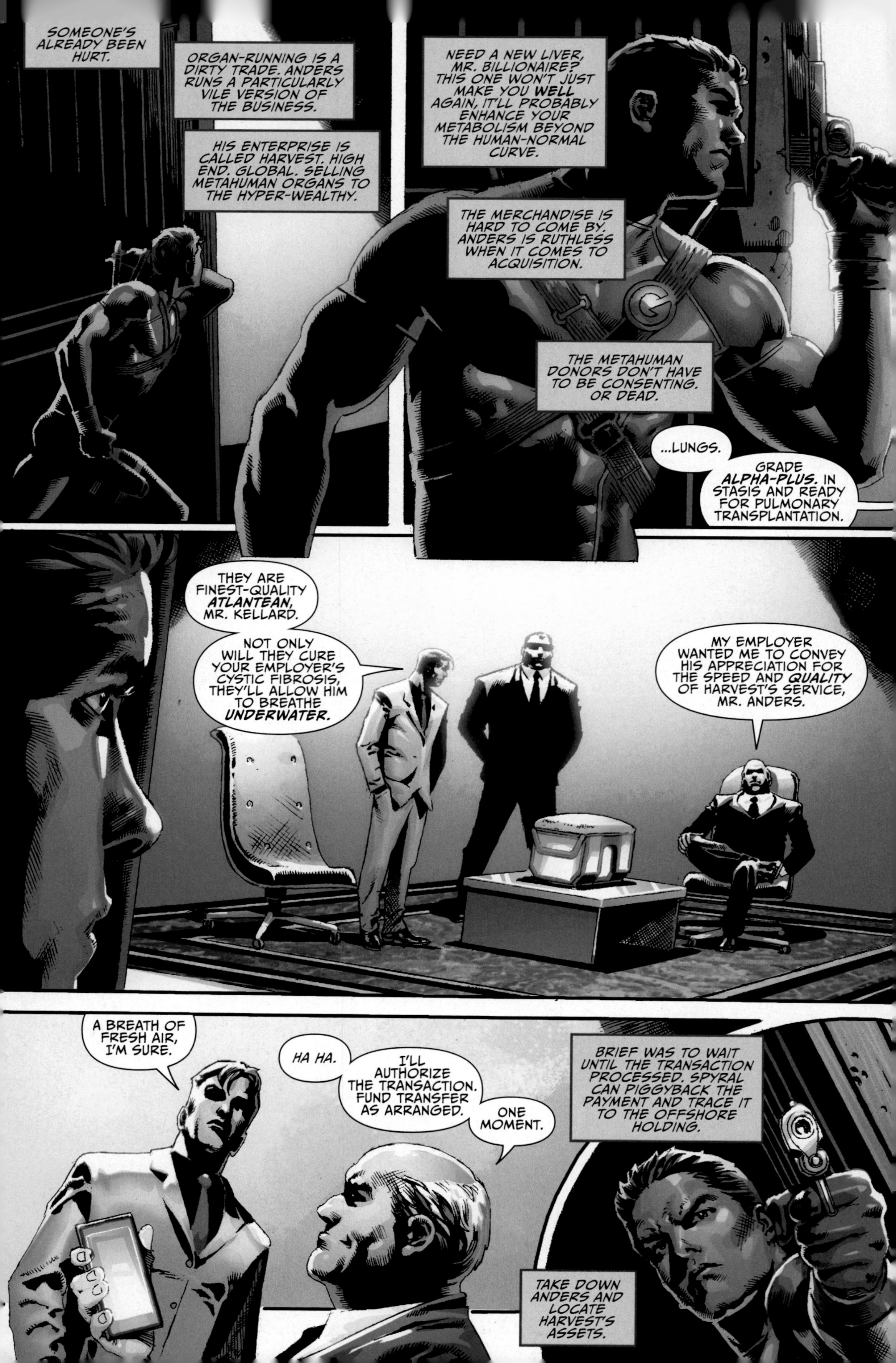
SOMEONE'S ALREADY BEEN HURT.
ORGAN-RUNNING IS A DIRTY TRADE. ANDERS RUNS A PARTICULARLY VILE VERSION OF THE BUSINESS.
HIS ENTERPRISE IS CALLED HARVEST. HIGH END. GLOBAL. SELLING METAHUMAN ORGANS TO THE HYPER-WEALTHY.
NEED A NEW LIVER, MR. BILLIONAIRE? THIS ONE WON'T JUST MAKE YOU WELL AGAIN, IT'LL PROBABLY ENHANCE YOUR METABOLISM BEYOND THE HUMAN-NORMAL CURVE.
THE MERCHANDISE IS HARD TO COME BY. ANDERS IS RUTHLESS WHEN IT COMES TO ACQUISITION.
THE METAHUMAN DONORS DON'T HAVE TO BE CONSENTING. OR DEAD.
...LUNGS.
GRADE ALPHA-PLUS. IN STASIS AND READY FOR PULMONARY TRANSPLANTATION.
THEY ARE FINEST-QUALITY ATLANTEAN, MR. KELLARD.
NOT ONLY WILL THEY CURE YOUR EMPLOYER'S CYSTIC FIBROSIS, THEY'LL ALLOW HIM TO BREATHE UNDERWATER.
MY EMPLOYER WANTED ME TO CONVEY HIS APPRECIATION FOR THE SPEED AND QUALITY OF HARVEST'S SERVICE, MR. ANDERS.
A BREATH OF FRESH AIR, I'M SURE.
HA HA.
I'LL AUTHORIZE THE TRANSACTION. FUND TRANSFER AS ARRANGED.
ONE MOMENT.
BRIEF WAS TO WAIT UNTIL THE TRANSACTION PROCESSED. SPYRAL CAN PIGGYBACK THE PAYMENT AND TRACE IT TO THE OFFSHORE HOLDING.
TAKE DOWN ANDERS AND LOCATE HARVEST'S ASSETS.

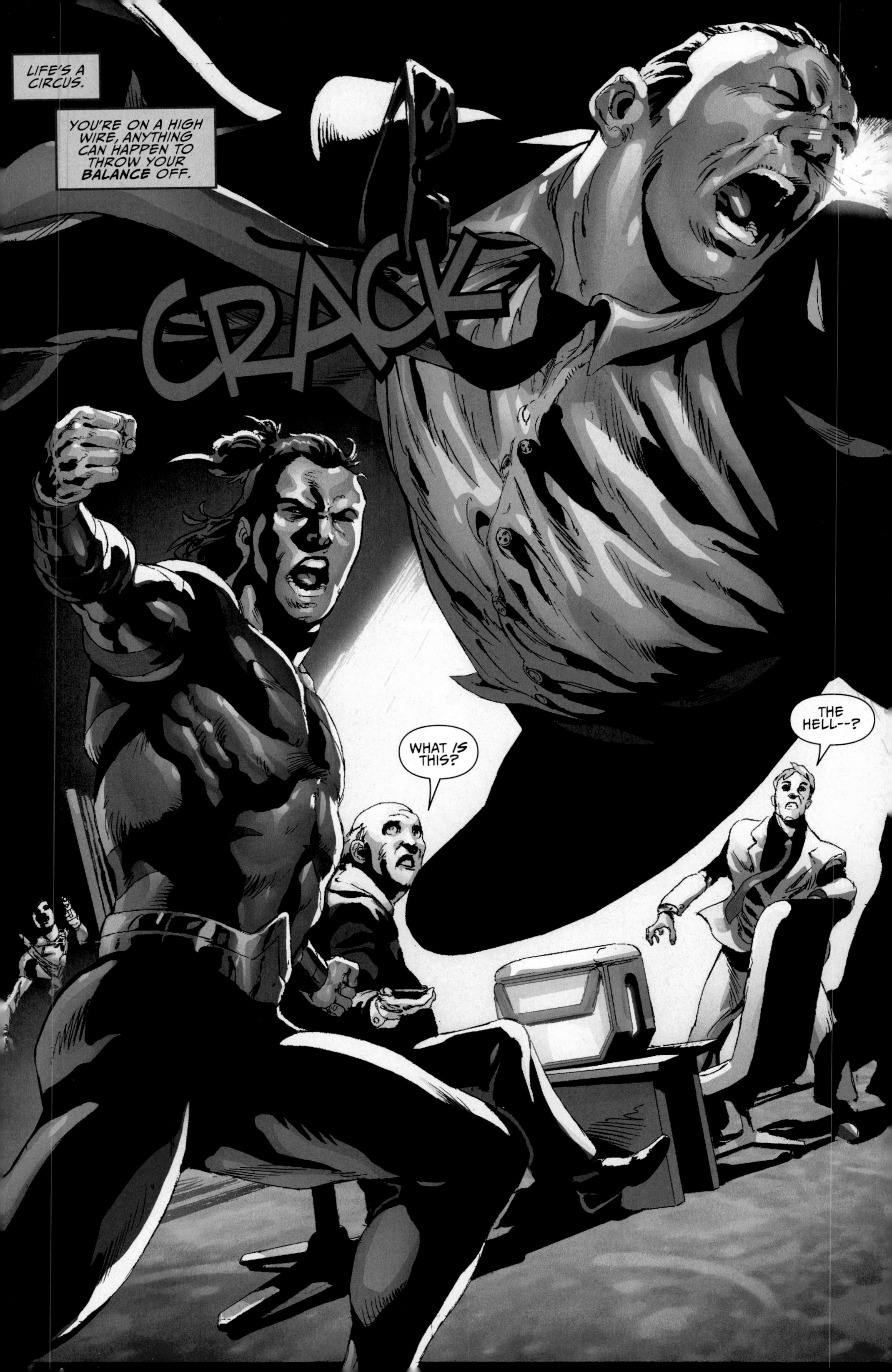
LIFE'S A CIRCUS.
YOU'RE ON A HIGH WIRE, ANYTHING CAN HAPPEN TO THROW YOUR BALANCE OFF.
CRACK
WHAT IS THIS?
THE HELL--?

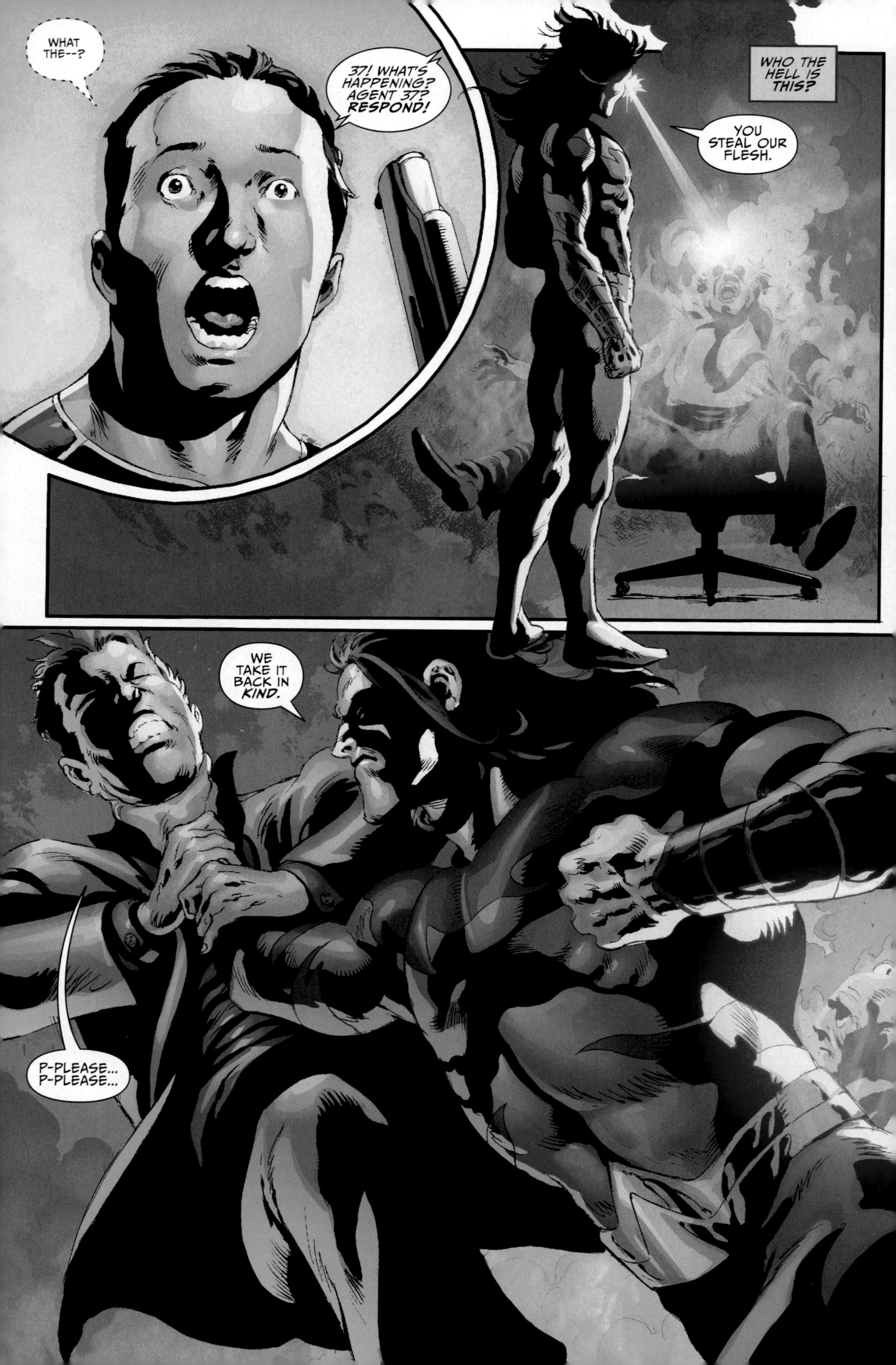
WHAT THE--?
37! WHAT'S HAPPENING? AGENT 37? RESPOND!
WHO THE HELL IS THIS?
YOU STEAL OUR FLESH.
WE TAKE IT BACK IN KIND.
P-PLEASE... P-PLEASE...

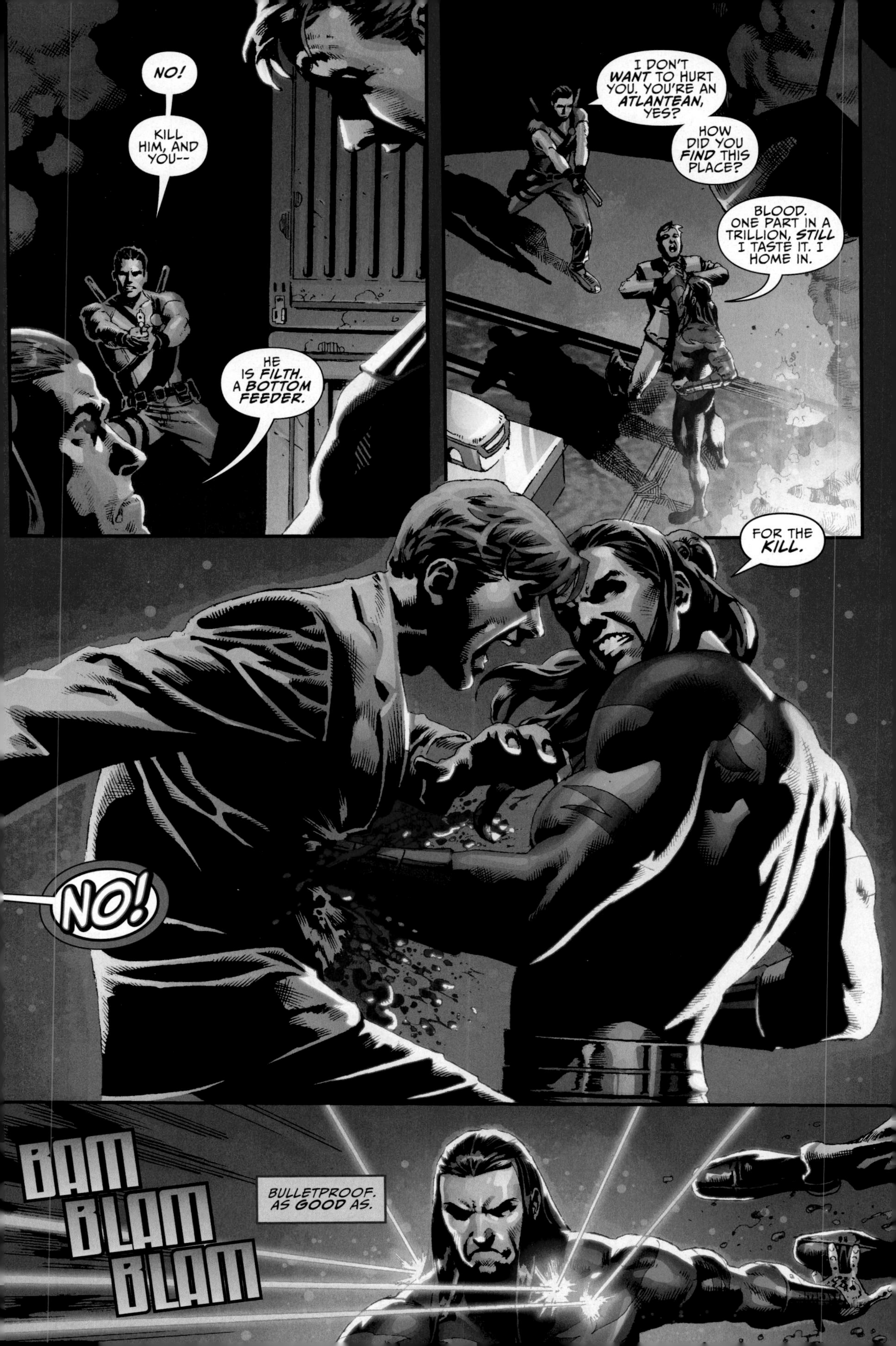
NO!
KILL HIM, AND YOU--
HE IS FILTH. A BOTTOM FEEDER.
I DON'T WANT TO HURT YOU. YOU'RE AN ATLANTEAN, YES?
HOW DID YOU FIND THIS PLACE?
BLOOD. ONE PART IN A TRILLION, STILL I TASTE IT. I HOME IN.
FOR THE KILL.
NO!
BAM BLAM BLAM
BULLETPROOF. AS GOOD AS.

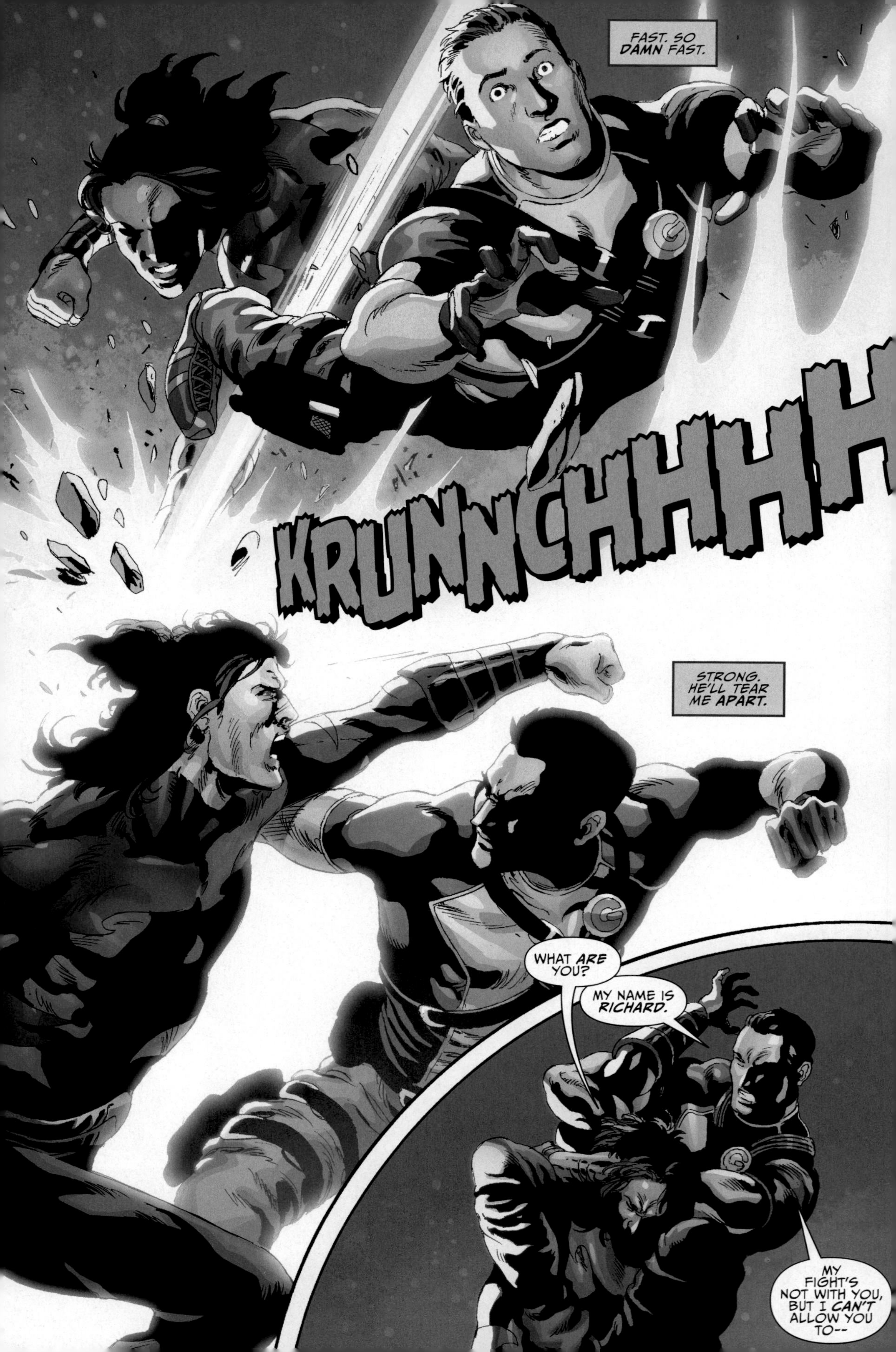
FAST. SO DAMN FAST.
KRUNNCHHHHH
STRONG. HE'LL TEAR ME APART.
WHAT ARE YOU?
MY NAME IS RICHARD.
MY FIGHT'S NOT WITH YOU, BUT I CAN'T ALLOW YOU TO--

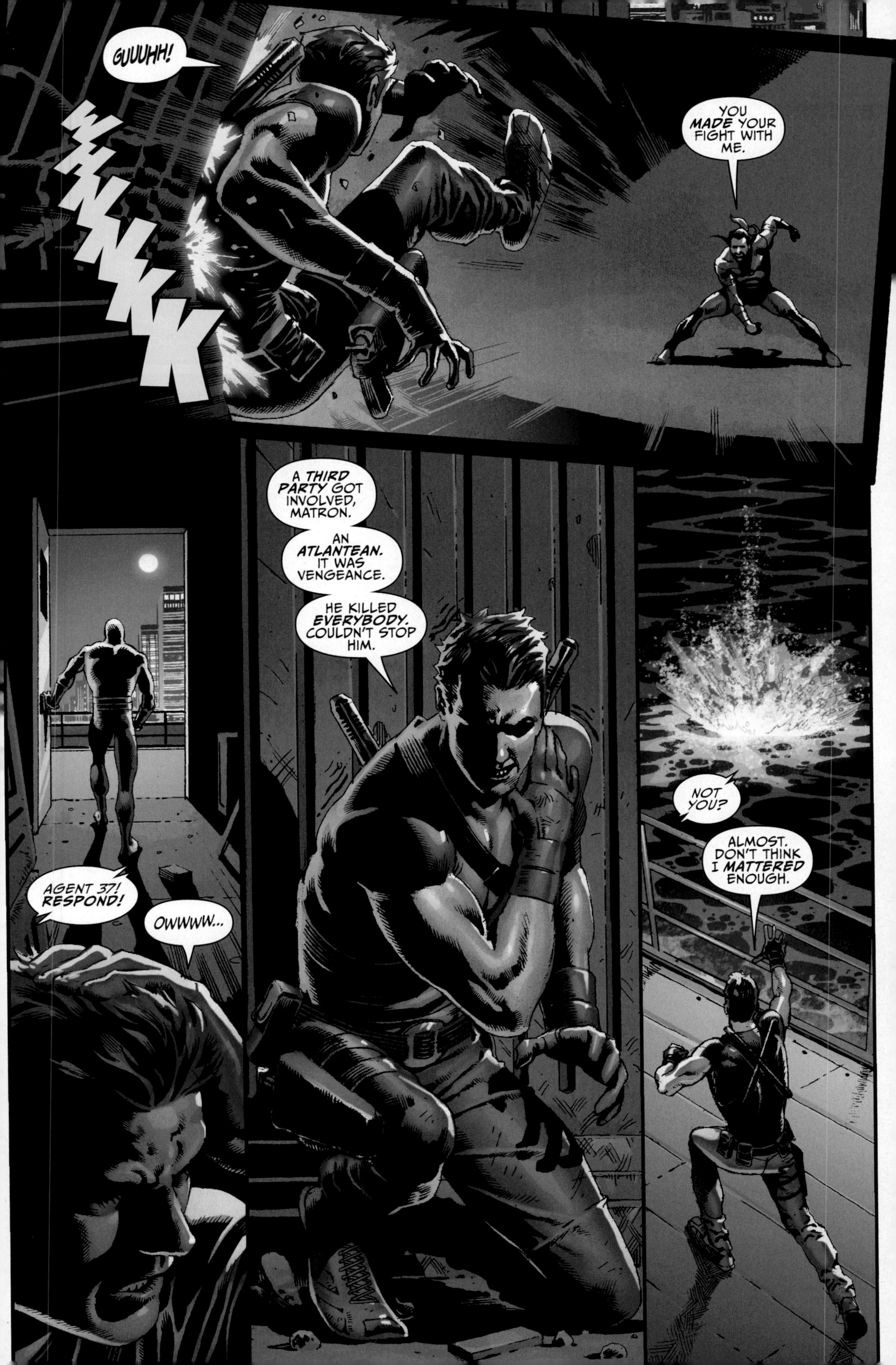

GUUUHH!
WHNKKK
YOU MADE YOUR FIGHT WITH ME.
A THIRD PARTY GOT INVOLVED, MATRON.
AN ATLANTEAN. IT WAS VENGEANCE.
HE KILLED EVERYBODY. COULDN'T STOP HIM.
NOT YOU?
ALMOST. DON'T THINK I MATTERED ENOUGH.
AGENT 37! RESPOND!
OWWWW...

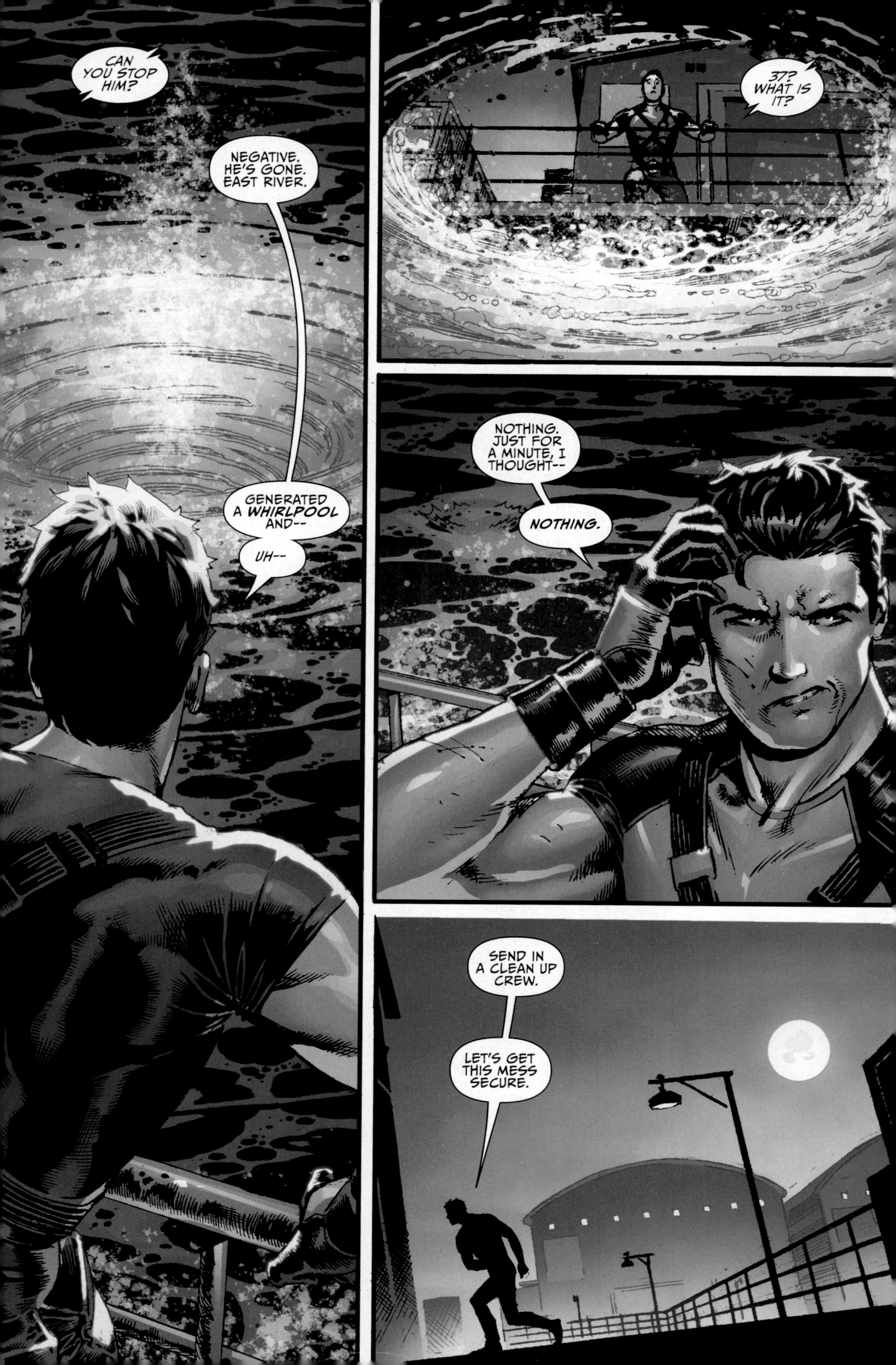
CAN YOU STOP HIM?
NEGATIVE. HE'S GONE. EAST RIVER.
GENERATED A WHIRLPOOL AND--
UH--
37? WHAT IS IT?
NOTHING. JUST FOR A MINUTE, I THOUGHT--
NOTHING.
SEND IN A CLEAN UP CREW.
LET'S GET THIS MESS SECURE.

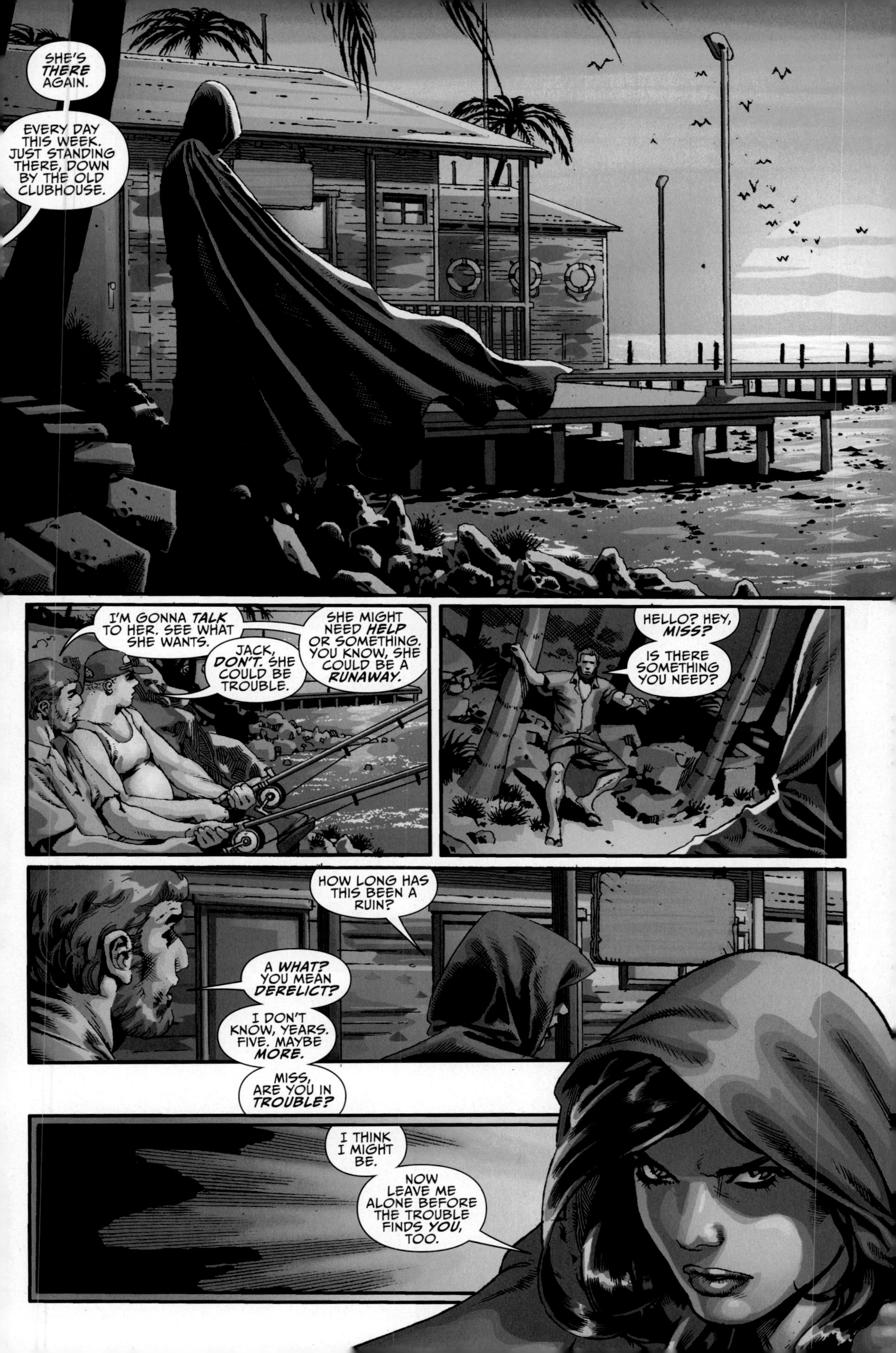

SHE'S THERE AGAIN.
EVERY DAY THIS WEEK. JUST STANDING THERE, DOWN BY THE OLD CLUBHOUSE.
I'M GONNA TALK TO HER. SEE WHAT SHE WANTS.
JACK, DON'T. SHE COULD BE TROUBLE.
SHE MIGHT NEED HELP OR SOMETHING. YOU KNOW, SHE COULD BE A RUNAWAY.
HELLO? HEY, MISS?
IS THERE SOMETHING YOU NEED?
HOW LONG HAS THIS BEEN A RUIN?
A WHAT? YOU MEAN DERELICT?
I DON'T KNOW, YEARS. FIVE. MAYBE MORE.
MISS, ARE YOU IN TROUBLE?
I THINK I MIGHT BE.
NOW LEAVE ME ALONE BEFORE THE TROUBLE FINDS YOU, TOO.

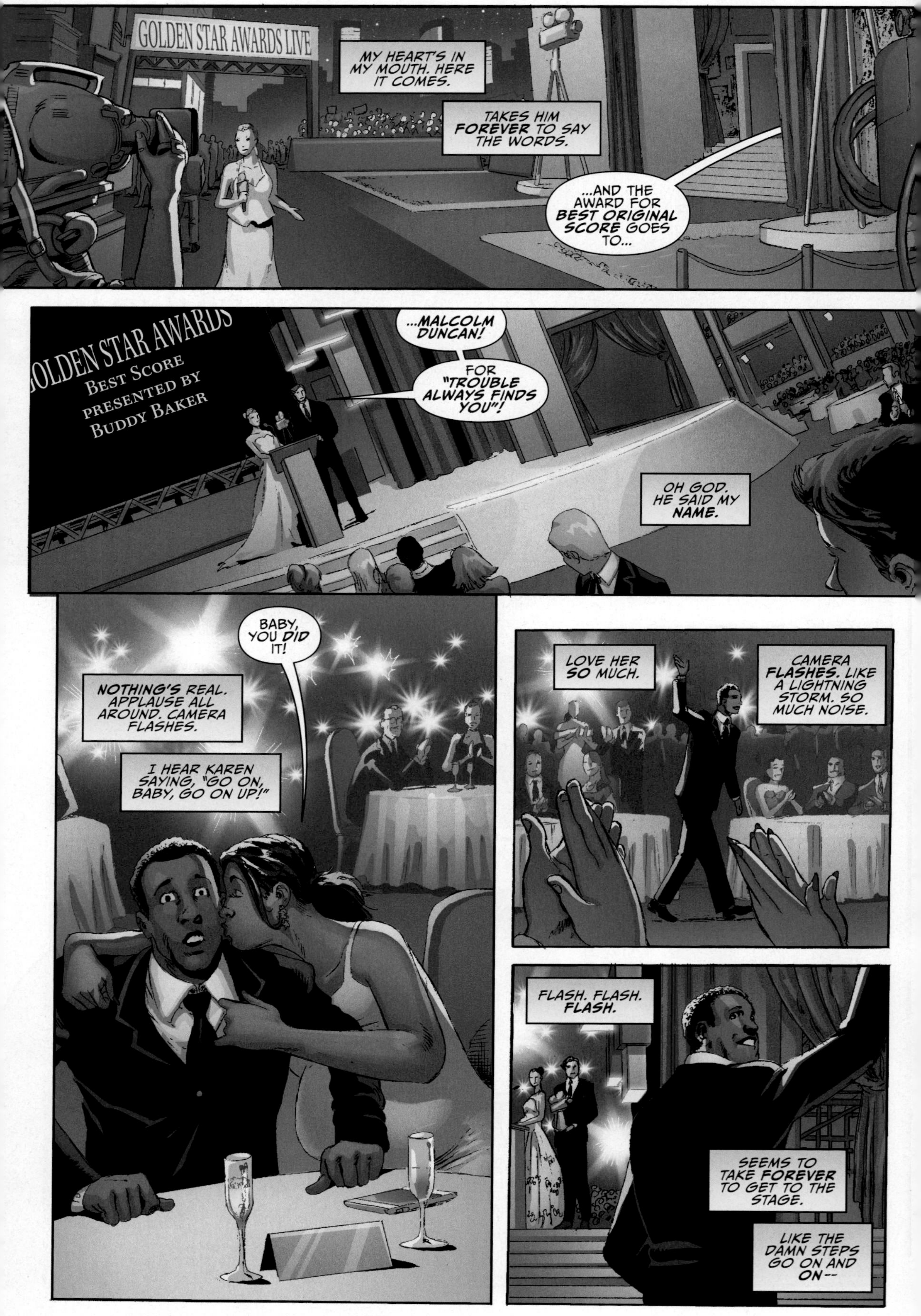
GOLDEN STAR AWARDS LIVE
MY HEART'S IN MY MOUTH. HERE IT COMES.
TAKES HIM FOREVER TO SAY THE WORDS.
...AND THE AWARD FOR BEST ORIGINAL SCORE GOES TO...
GOLDEN STAR AWARDS
Best Score
presented by
Buddy Baker
...MALCOLM DUNCAN!
FOR "TROUBLE ALWAYS FINDS YOU"!
OH GOD. HE SAID MY NAME.
BABY, YOU DID IT!
NOTHING'S REAL. APPLAUSE ALL AROUND. CAMERA FLASHES.
I HEAR KAREN SAYING, "GO ON, BABY, GO ON UP!"
LOVE HER SO MUCH.
CAMERA FLASHES. LIKE A LIGHTNING STORM. SO MUCH NOISE.
FLASH. FLASH. FLASH.
SEEMS TO TAKE FOREVER TO GET TO THE STAGE.
LIKE THE DAMN STEPS GO ON AND ON--

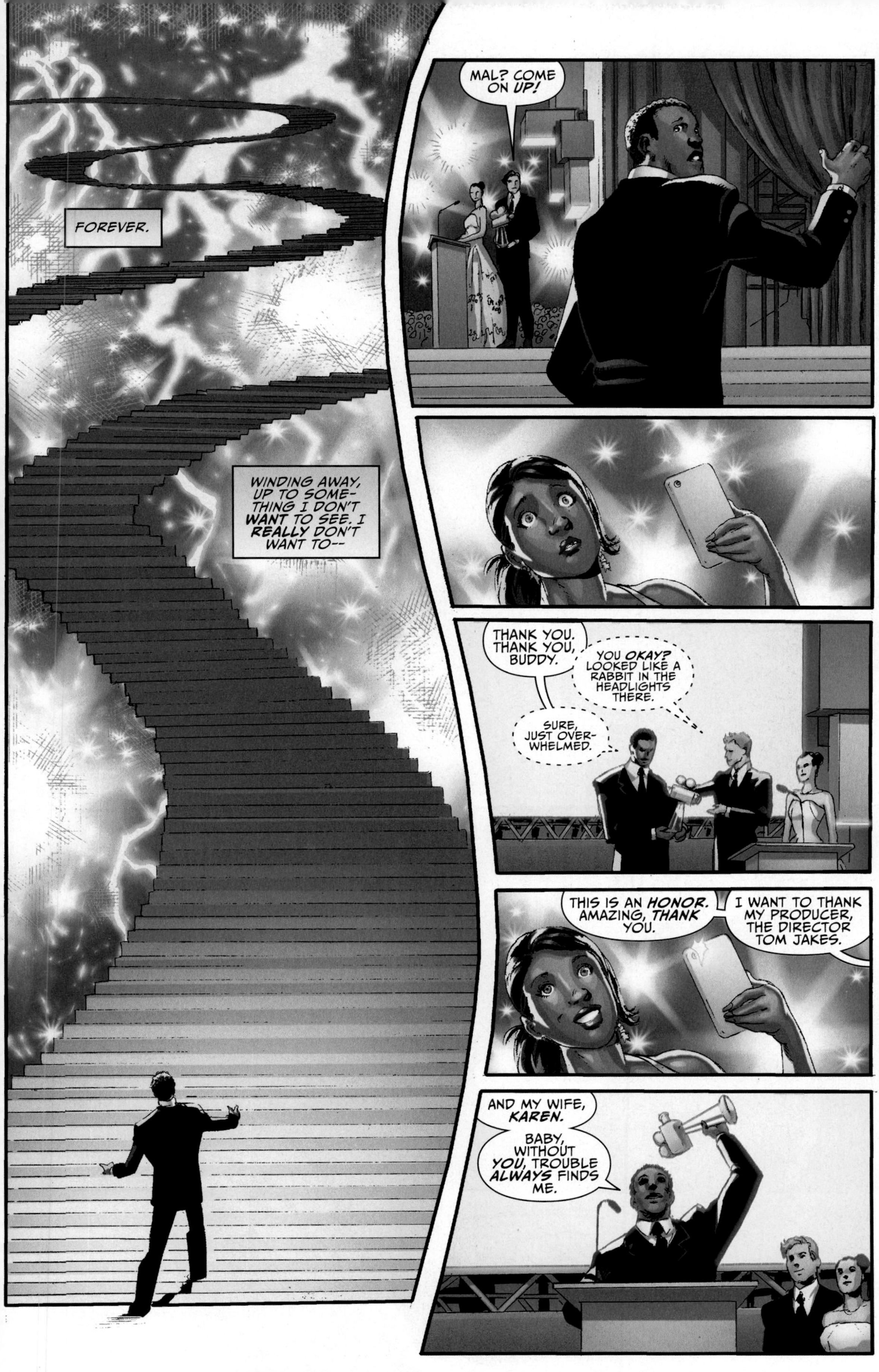
FOREVER.
WINDING AWAY, UP TO SOME-THING I DON'T WANT TO SEE. I REALLY DON'T WANT TO--
MAL? COME ON UP!
THANK YOU. THANK YOU, BUDDY.
YOU OKAY? LOOKED LIKE A RABBIT IN THE HEADLIGHTS THERE.
SURE, JUST OVER-WHELMED.
THIS IS AN HONOR. AMAZING, THANK YOU.
I WANT TO THANK MY PRODUCER, THE DIRECTOR TOM JAKES.
AND MY WIFE, KAREN.
BABY, WITHOUT YOU, TROUBLE ALWAYS FINDS ME.

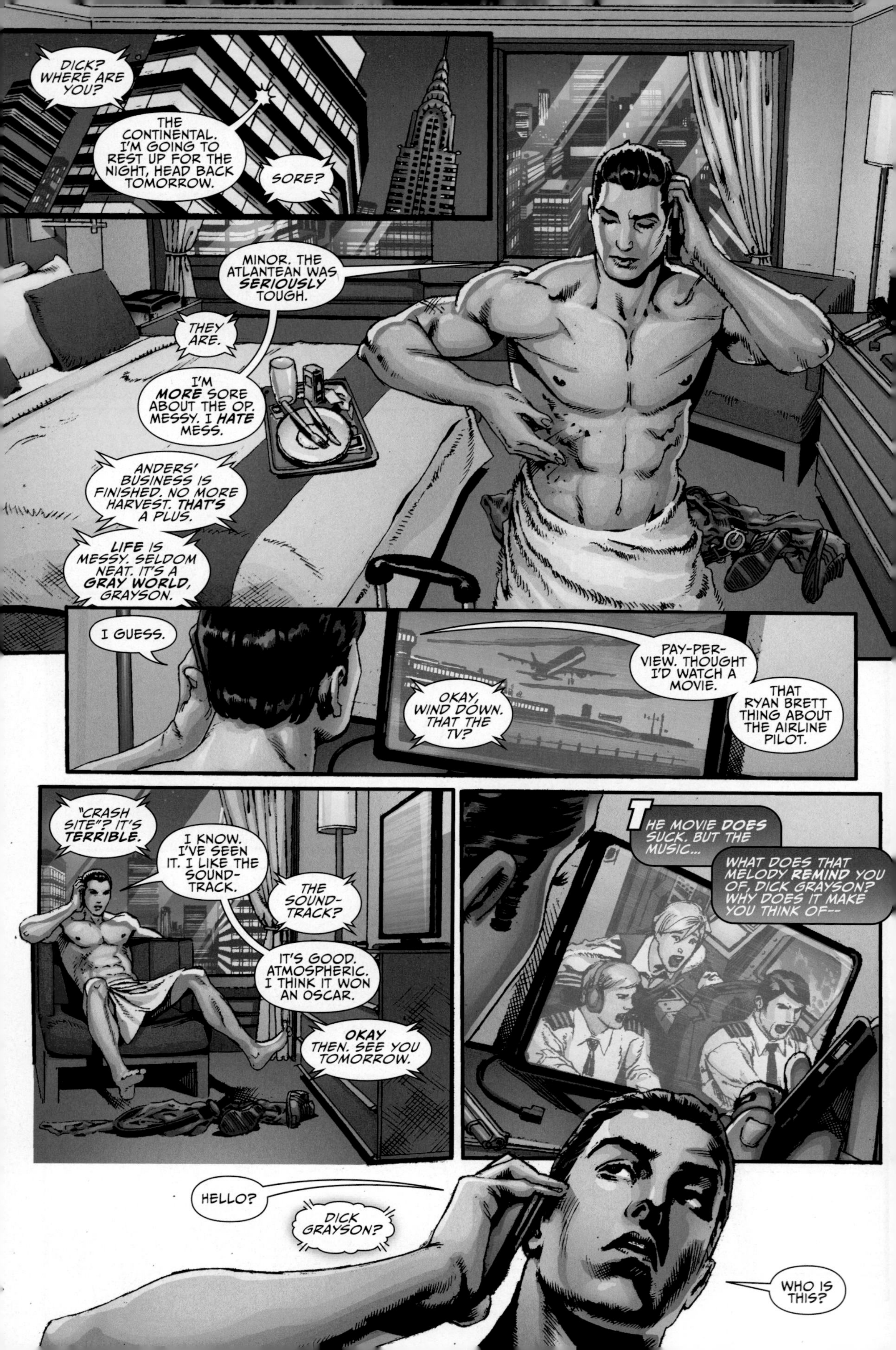
DICK? WHERE ARE YOU?
THE CONTINENTAL. I'M GOING TO REST UP FOR THE NIGHT, HEAD BACK TOMORROW.
SORE?
MINOR. THE ATLANTEAN WAS SERIOUSLY TOUGH.
THEY ARE.
I'M MORE SORE ABOUT THE OP. MESSY. I HATE MESS.
ANDERS' BUSINESS IS FINISHED. NO MORE HARVEST. THAT'S A PLUS.
LIFE IS MESSY. SELDOM NEAT. IT'S A GRAY WORLD, GRAYSON.
I GUESS.
OKAY, WIND DOWN. THAT THE TV?
PAY-PER-VIEW. THOUGHT I'D WATCH A MOVIE.
THAT RYAN BRETT THING ABOUT THE AIRLINE PILOT.
"CRASH SITE"? IT'S TERRIBLE.
I KNOW. I'VE SEEN IT. I LIKE THE SOUND-TRACK.
THE SOUND-TRACK?
IT'S GOOD. ATMOSPHERIC. I THINK IT WON AN OSCAR.
OKAY THEN. SEE YOU TOMORROW.
THE MOVIE DOES SUCK. BUT THE MUSIC...
WHAT DOES THAT MELODY REMIND YOU OF, DICK GRAYSON? WHY DOES IT MAKE YOU THINK OF--
HELLO?
DICK GRAYSON?
WHO IS THIS?

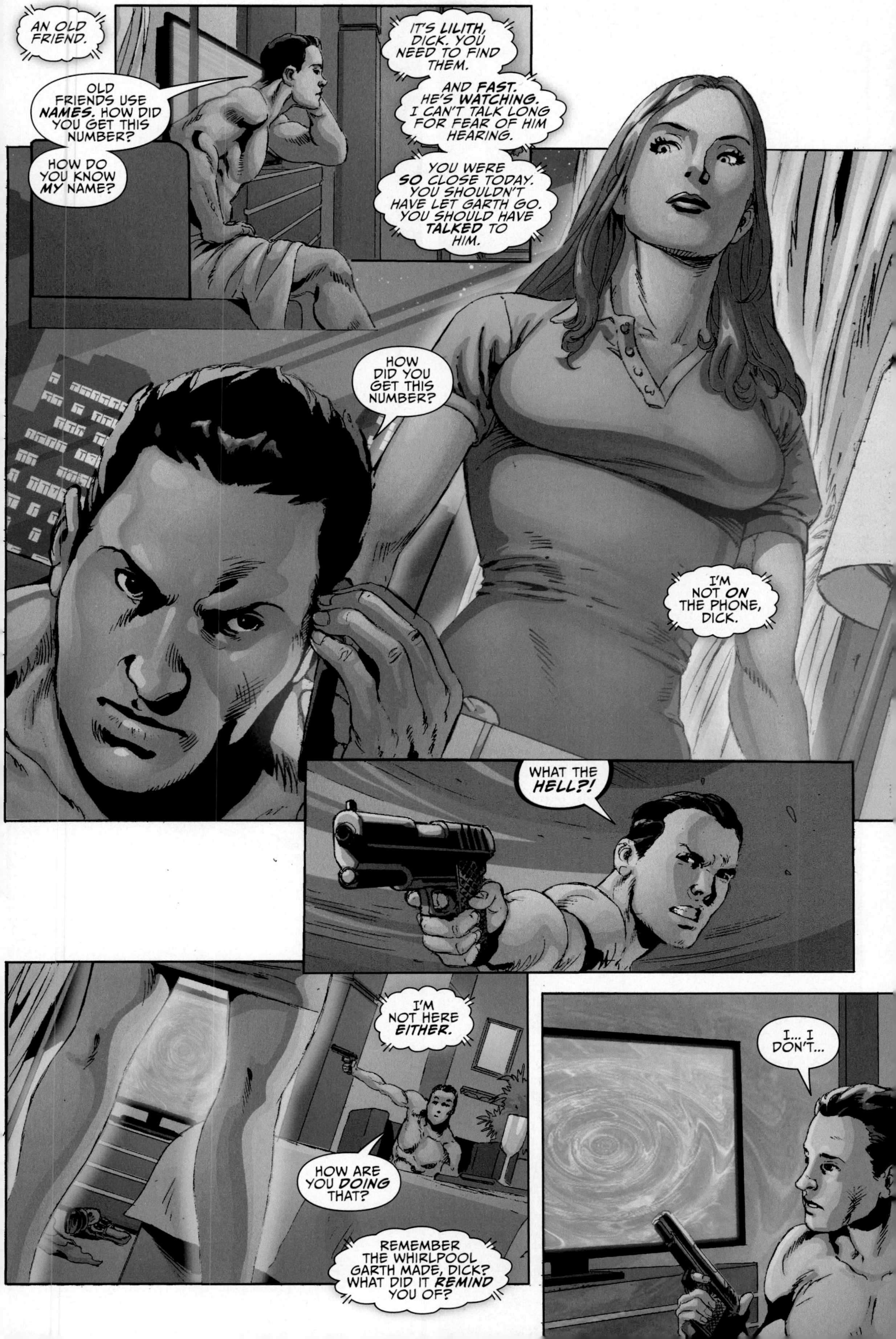
AN OLD FRIEND.
OLD FRIENDS USE NAMES. HOW DID YOU GET THIS NUMBER?
HOW DO YOU KNOW MY NAME?
IT'S LILITH, DICK. YOU NEED TO FIND THEM.
AND FAST. HE'S WATCHING. I CAN'T TALK LONG FOR FEAR OF HIM HEARING.
YOU WERE SO CLOSE TODAY. YOU SHOULDN'T HAVE LET GARTH GO. YOU SHOULD HAVE TALKED TO HIM.
HOW DID YOU GET THIS NUMBER?
I'M NOT ON THE PHONE, DICK.
WHAT THE HELL?!
I'M NOT HERE EITHER.
HOW ARE YOU DOING THAT?
REMEMBER THE WHIRLPOOL GARTH MADE, DICK? WHAT DID IT REMIND YOU OF?
I... I DON'T...

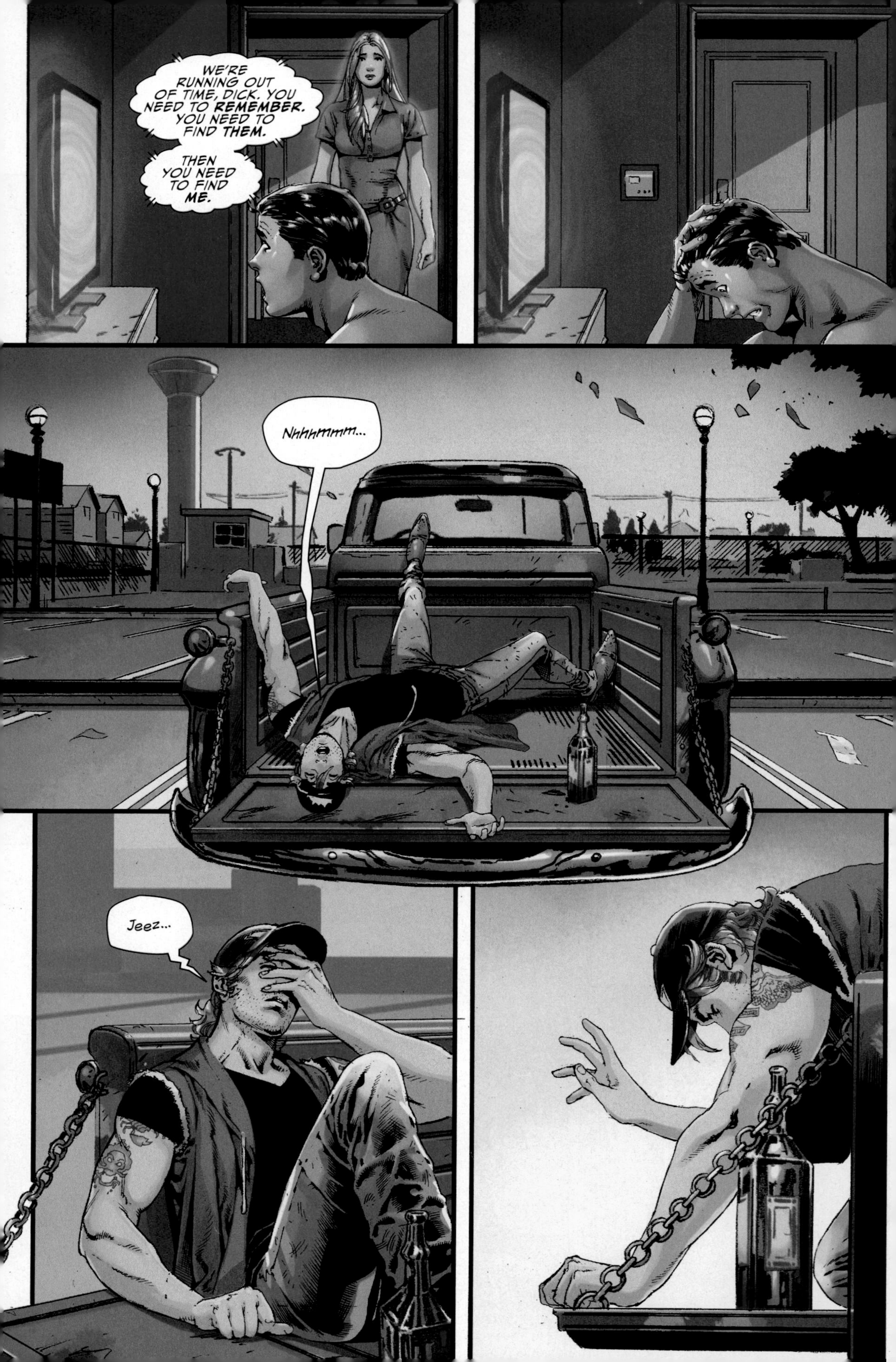
WE'RE RUNNING OUT OF TIME, DICK. YOU NEED TO REMEMBER. YOU NEED TO FIND THEM.
THEN YOU NEED TO FIND ME.
Nhhhmmm...
Jeez...

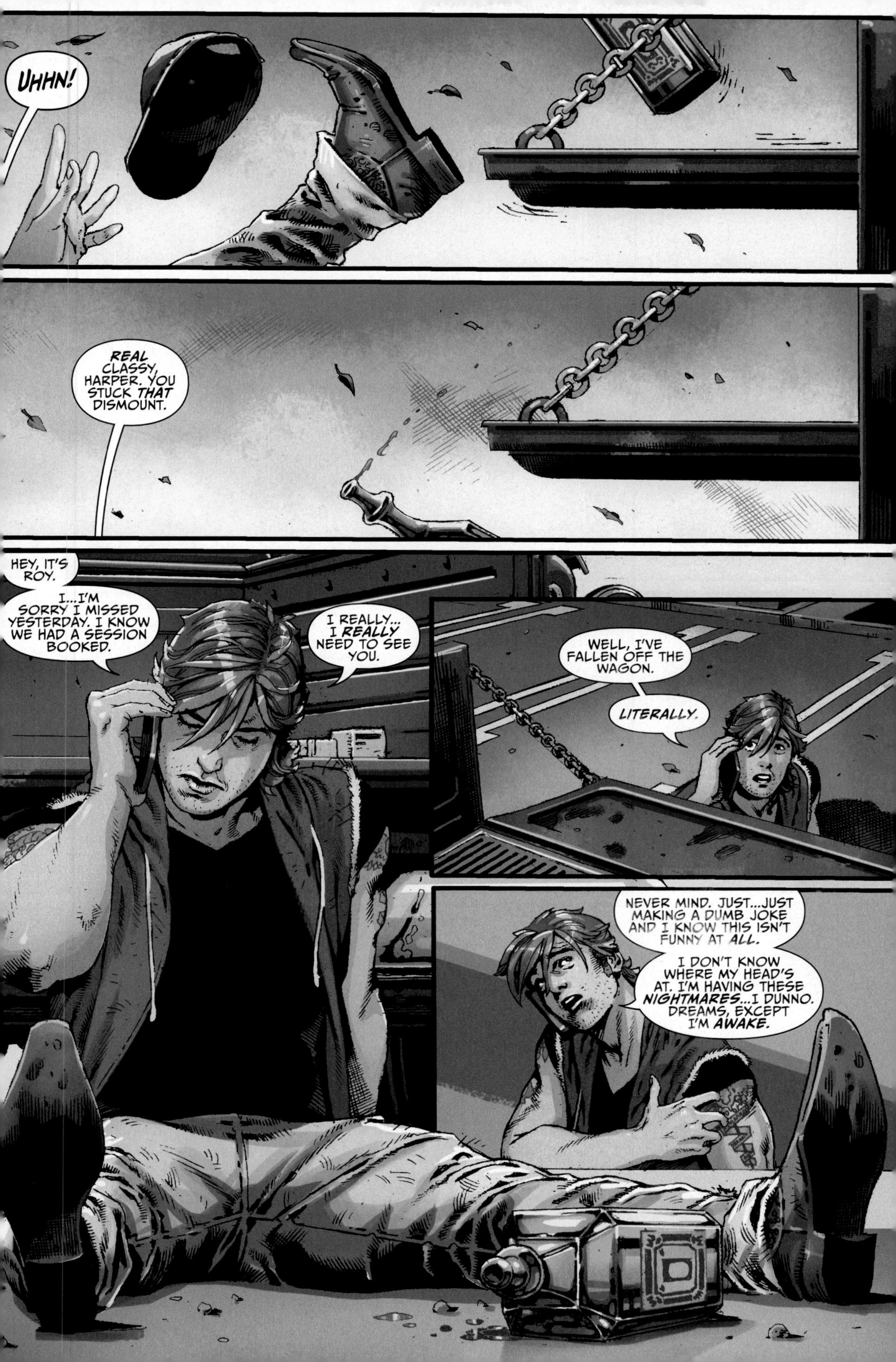
UHHN!
REAL CLASSY, HARPER. YOU STUCK THAT DISMOUNT.
HEY, IT'S ROY.
I...I'M SORRY I MISSED YESTERDAY. I KNOW WE HAD A SESSION BOOKED.
I REALLY... I REALLY NEED TO SEE YOU.
WELL, I'VE FALLEN OFF THE WAGON.
LITERALLY.
NEVER MIND. JUST...JUST MAKING A DUMB JOKE AND I KNOW THIS ISN'T FUNNY AT ALL.
I DON'T KNOW WHERE MY HEAD'S AT. I'M HAVING THESE NIGHTMARES...I DUNNO. DREAMS, EXCEPT I'M AWAKE.

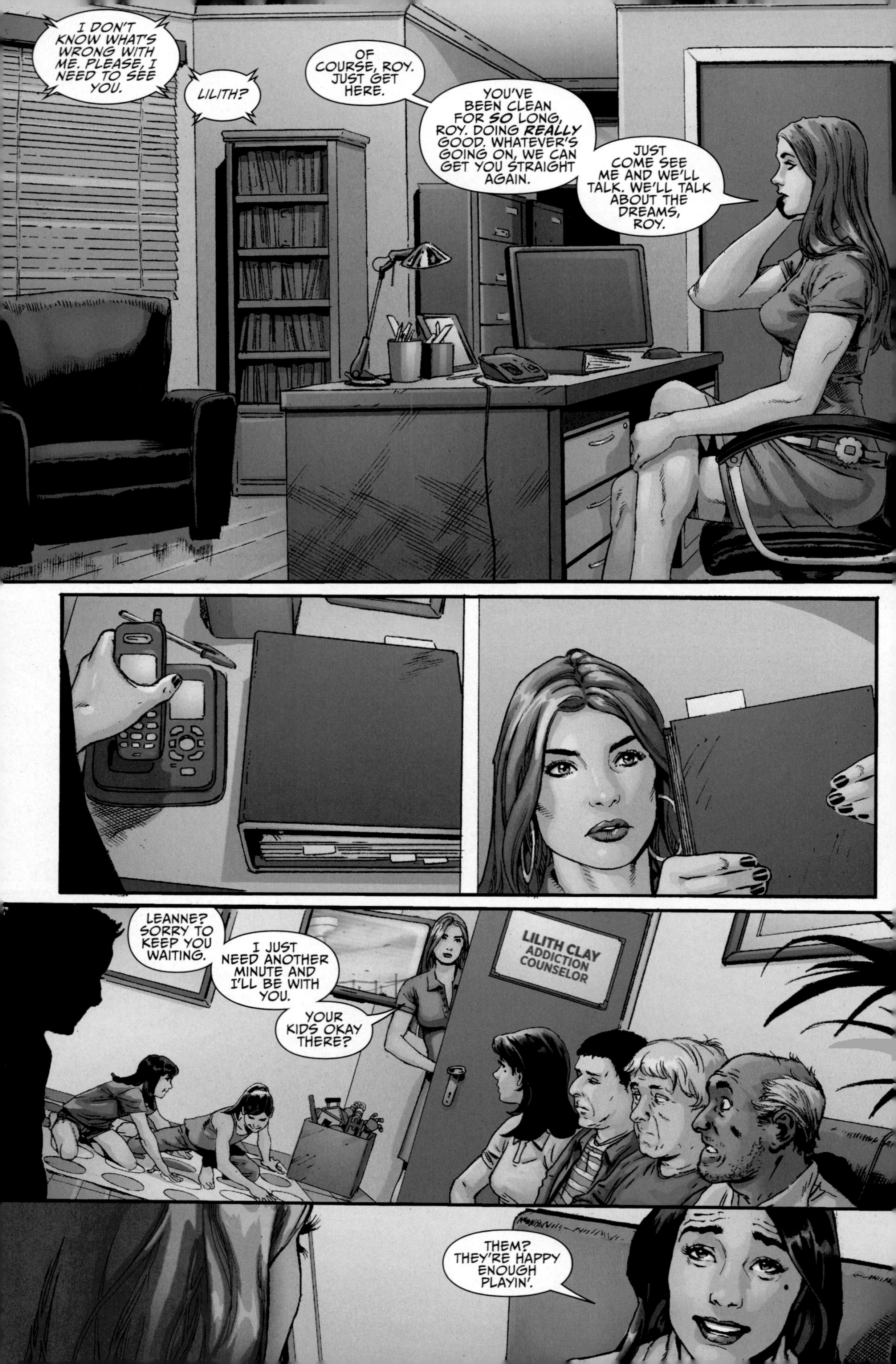

I DON'T KNOW WHAT'S WRONG WITH ME. PLEASE, I NEED TO SEE YOU.
LILITH?
OF COURSE, ROY. JUST GET HERE.
YOU'VE BEEN CLEAN FOR SO LONG, ROY. DOING REALLY GOOD. WHATEVER'S GOING ON, WE CAN GET YOU STRAIGHT AGAIN.
JUST COME SEE ME AND WE'LL TALK. WE'LL TALK ABOUT THE DREAMS, ROY.
LEANNE? SORRY TO KEEP YOU WAITING.
I JUST NEED ANOTHER MINUTE AND I'LL BE WITH YOU.
YOUR KIDS OKAY THERE?
LILITH CLAY
ADDICTION COUNSELOR
THEM? THEY'RE HAPPY ENOUGH PLAYIN'.

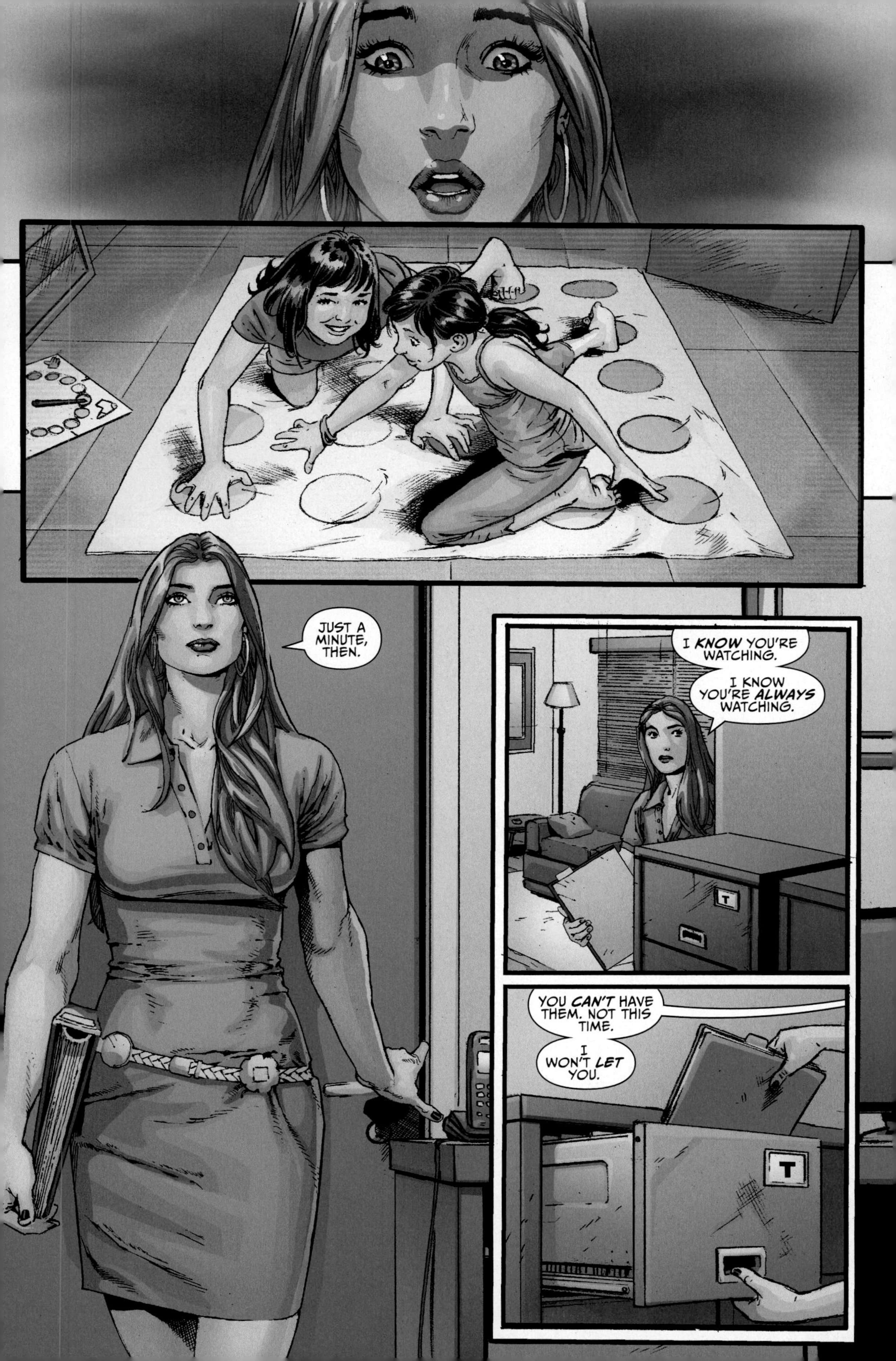
JUST A MINUTE, THEN.
I KNOW YOU'RE WATCHING.
I KNOW YOU'RE ALWAYS WATCHING.
YOU CAN'T HAVE THEM. NOT THIS TIME.
I WON'T LET YOU.

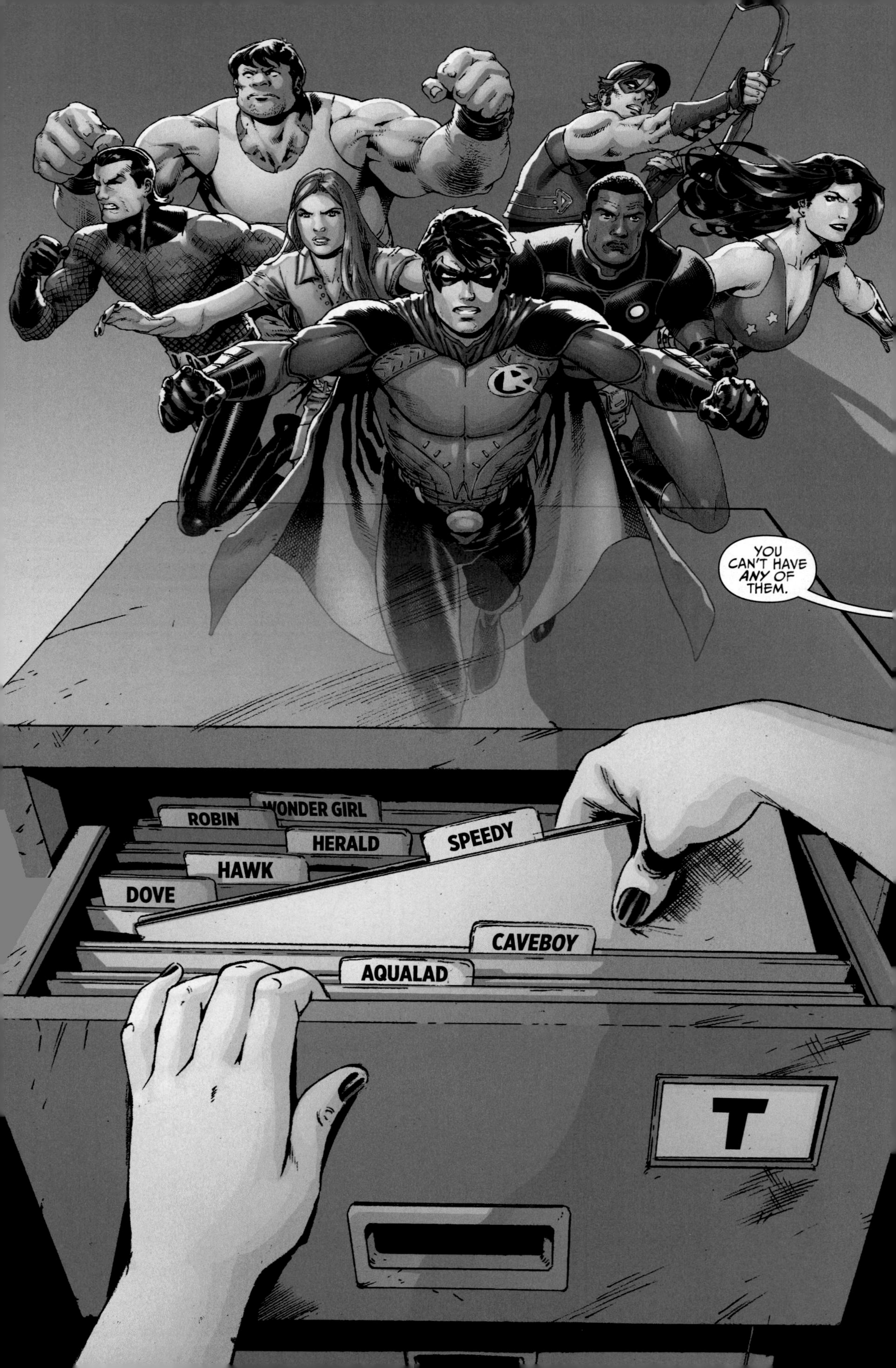
YOU CAN'T HAVE ANY OF THEM.
WONDER GIRL
ROBIN
HERALD
SPEEDY
HAWK
DOVE
CAVEBOY
AQUALAD
T

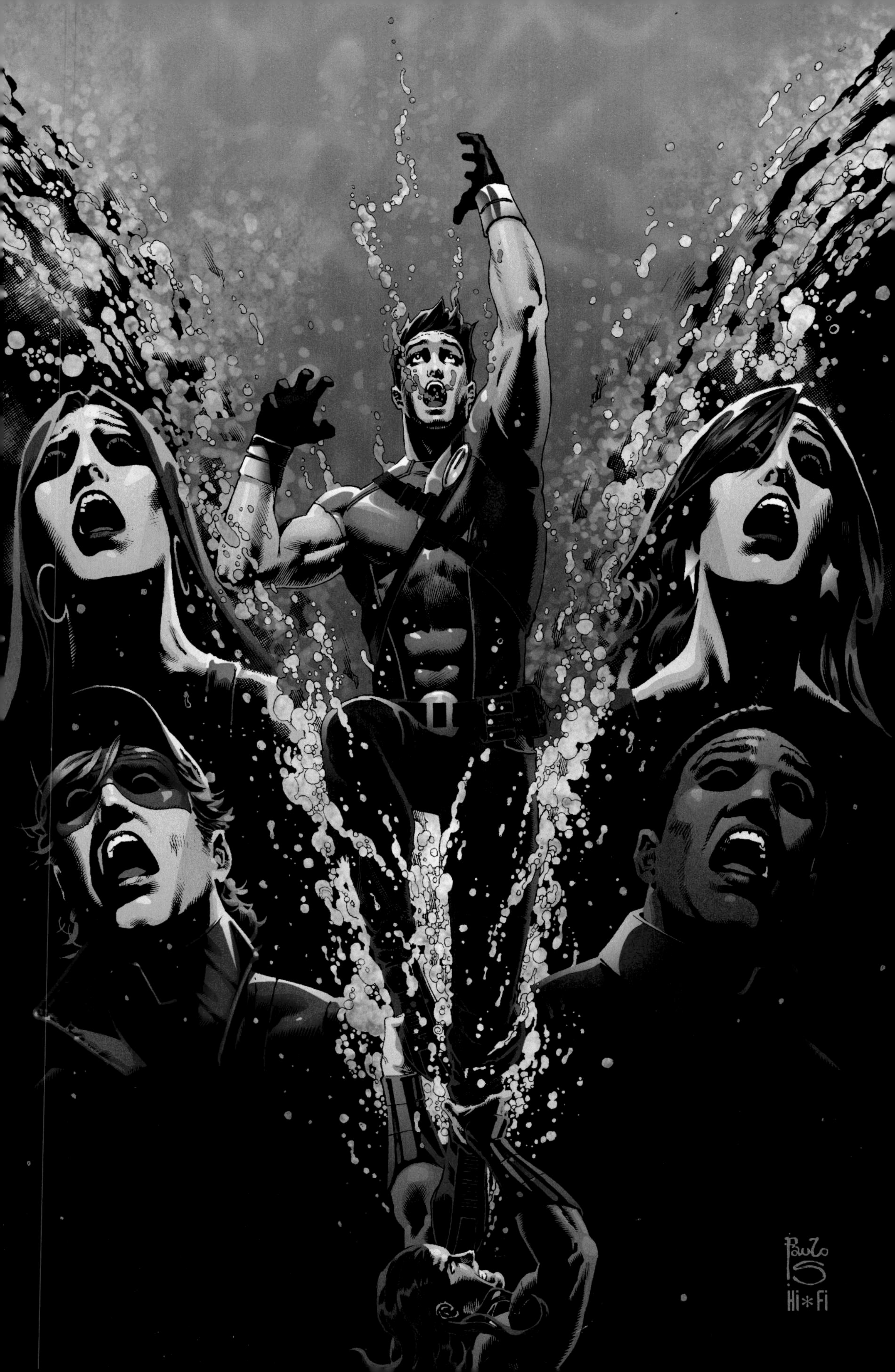
Hi*Fi

CHAPTER TWO: TROUBLE ALWAYS FINDS ME

DAN ABNETT writer STEPHEN SEGOVIA artist HI-FI colorist cover art by PAULO SIQUEIRA & HI-FI

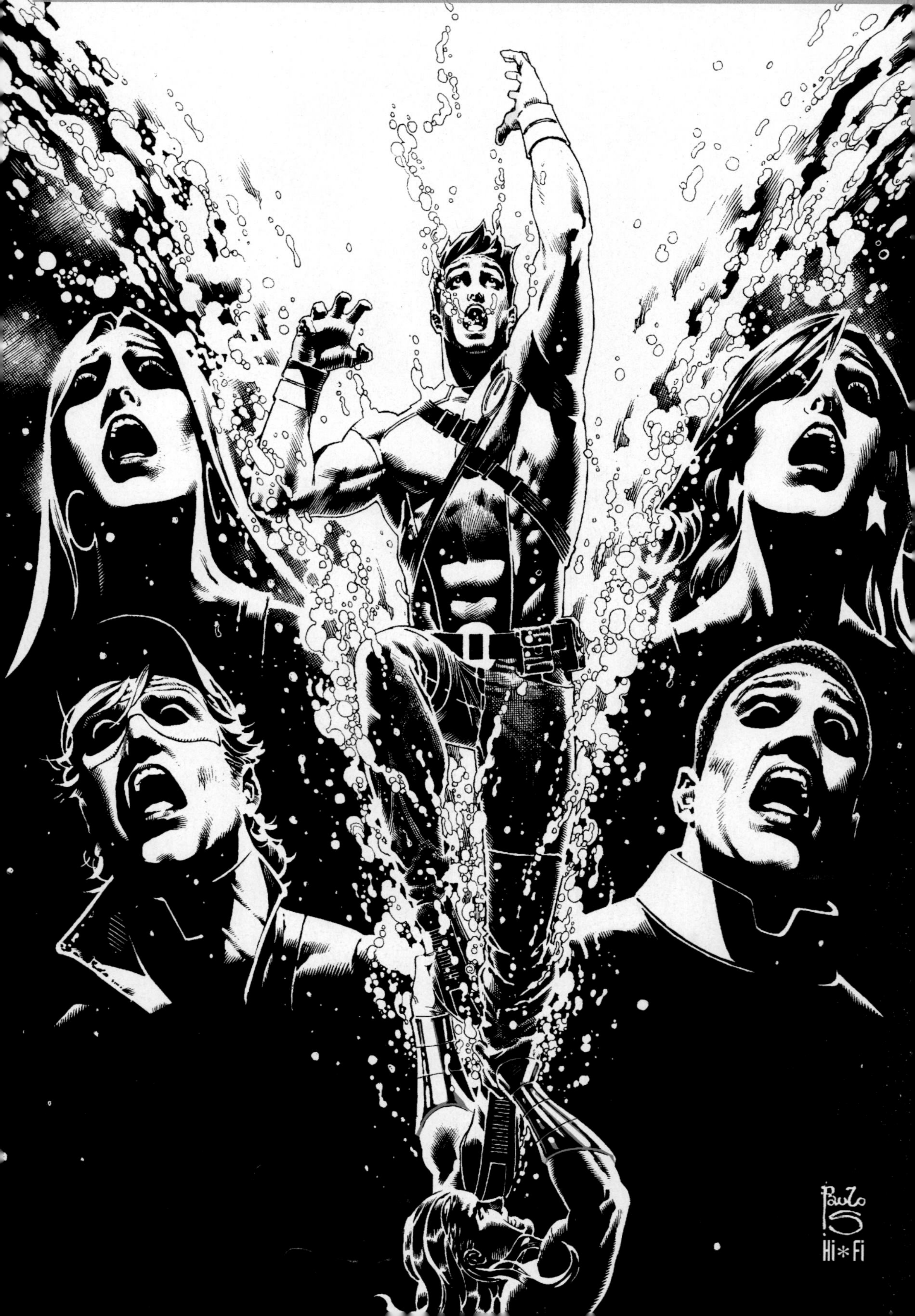

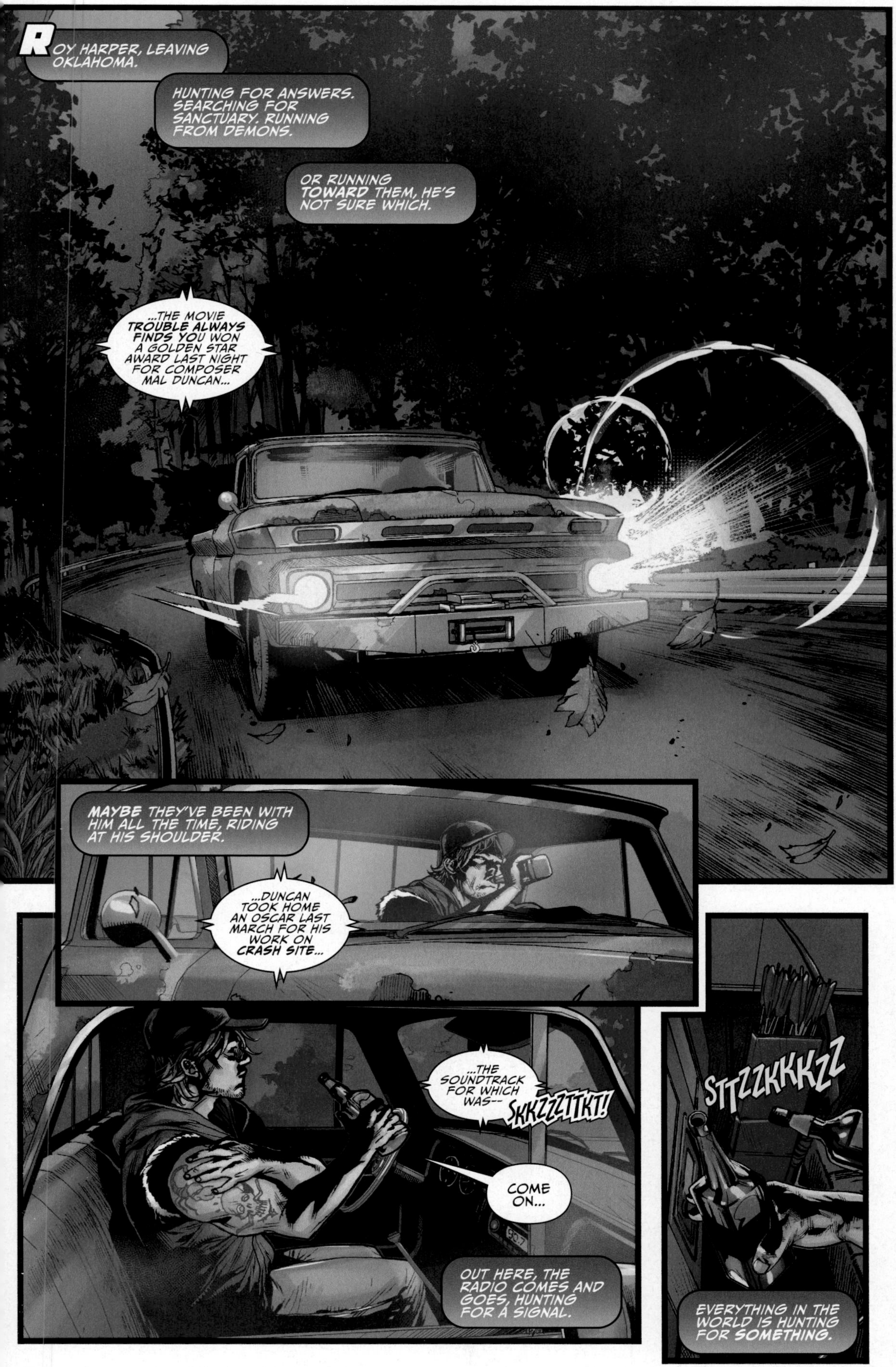
ROY HARPER, LEAVING OKLAHOMA.
HUNTING FOR ANSWERS. SEARCHING FOR SANCTUARY. RUNNING FROM DEMONS.
OR RUNNING TOWARD THEM, HE'S NOT SURE WHICH.
...THE MOVIE TROUBLE ALWAYS FINDS YOU WON A GOLDEN STAR AWARD LAST NIGHT FOR COMPOSER MAL DUNCAN...
MAYBE THEY'VE BEEN WITH HIM ALL THE TIME, RIDING AT HIS SHOULDER.
...DUNCAN TOOK HOME AN OSCAR LAST MARCH FOR HIS WORK ON CRASH SITE...
...THE SOUNDTRACK FOR WHICH WAS--
SKKZZZTTKT!
COME ON...
OUT HERE, THE RADIO COMES AND GOES, HUNTING FOR A SIGNAL.
STTZZKKKZZ
EVERYTHING IN THE WORLD IS HUNTING FOR SOMETHING.

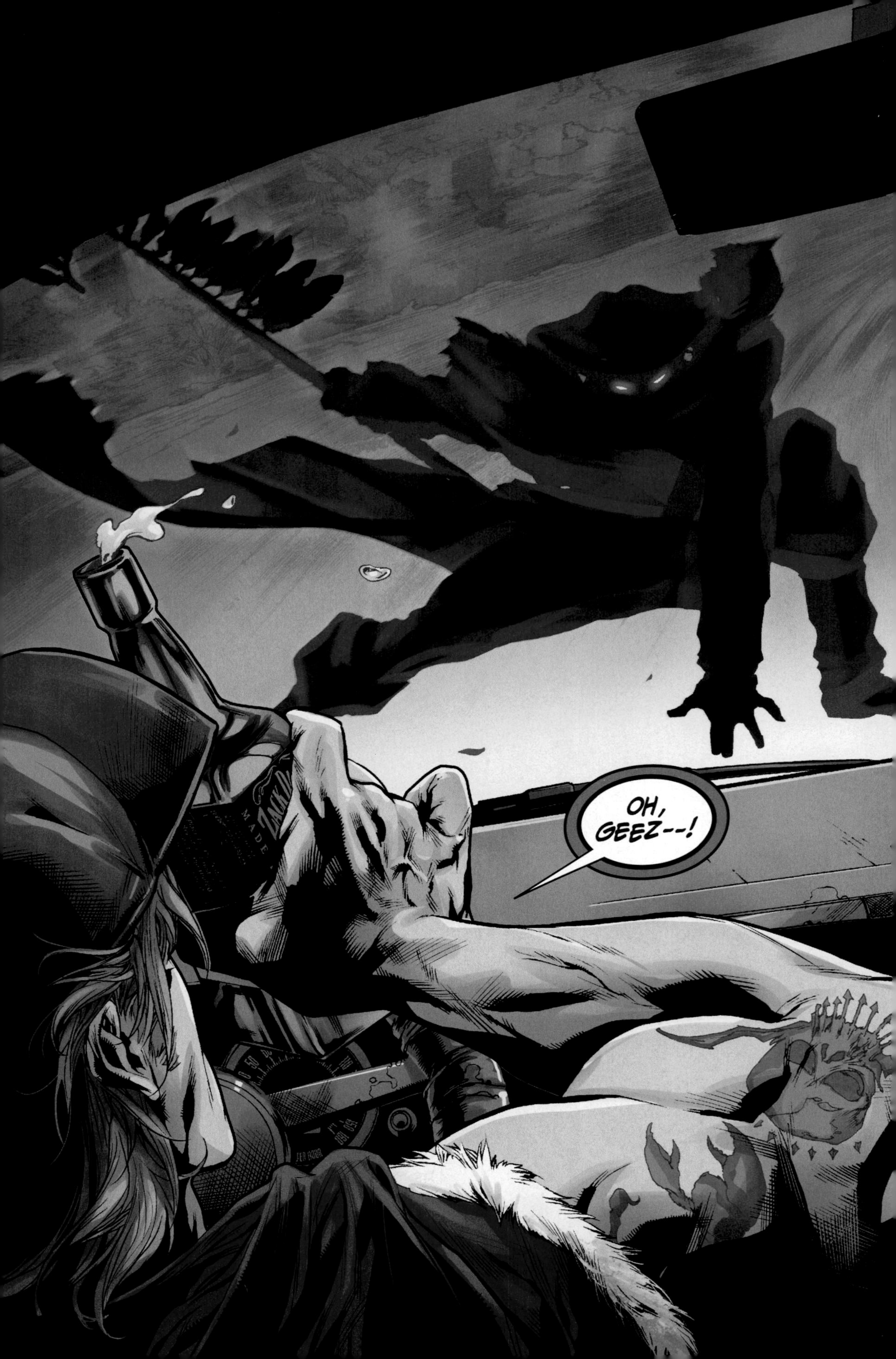
OH, GEEZ--!

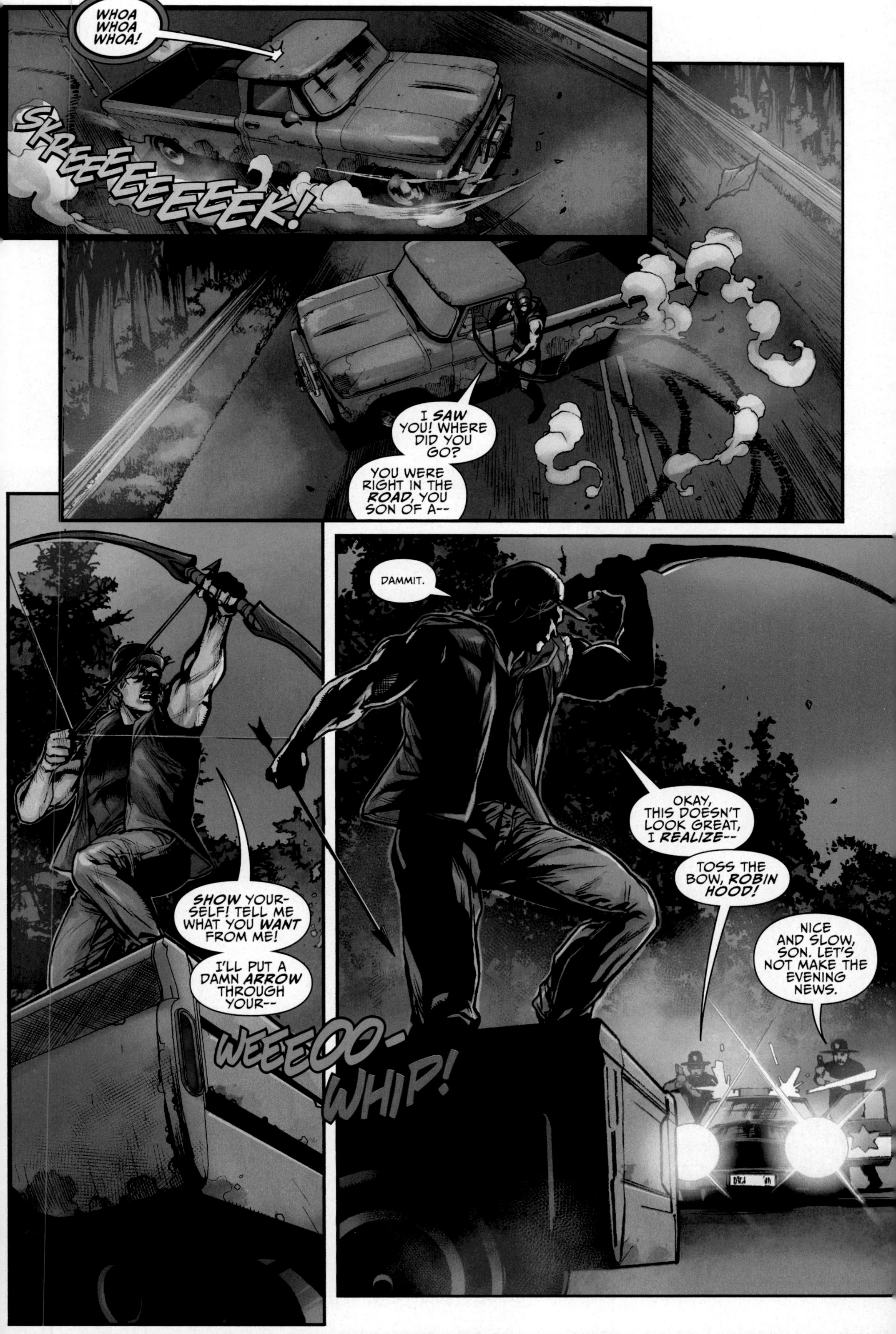
WHOA WHOA WHOA!
SKREEEEEEEEEK!
I SAW YOU! WHERE DID YOU GO?
YOU WERE RIGHT IN THE ROAD, YOU SON OF A--
SHOW YOURSELF! TELL ME WHAT YOU WANT FROM ME!
I'LL PUT A DAMN ARROW THROUGH YOUR--
WEEEOO-WHIP!
DAMMIT.
OKAY, THIS DOESN'T LOOK GREAT, I REALIZE--
TOSS THE BOW, ROBIN HOOD!
NICE AND SLOW, SON. LET'S NOT MAKE THE EVENING NEWS.

FOR KEYWORD AND DATA SEARCH, ENTER YOUR AUTHORIZATION:

R KEYWORD AND DATA SEARCH, ENTER YOUR AUTHORIZATION:

RICHARD GRAYS

HUNTING FOR SOMETHING?

TAPTAPTAPTAPTAP

I SHOULD'VE GUESSED THERE WAS *ZERO* CHANCE I COULD STOP BY WITHOUT YOU KNOWING I WAS HERE.

YOU'RE *ALWAYS* WELCOME, MASTER RICHARD.

FOR KEYWORD AND DA ENTER YOUR AUTHORI

RICHARD GRA

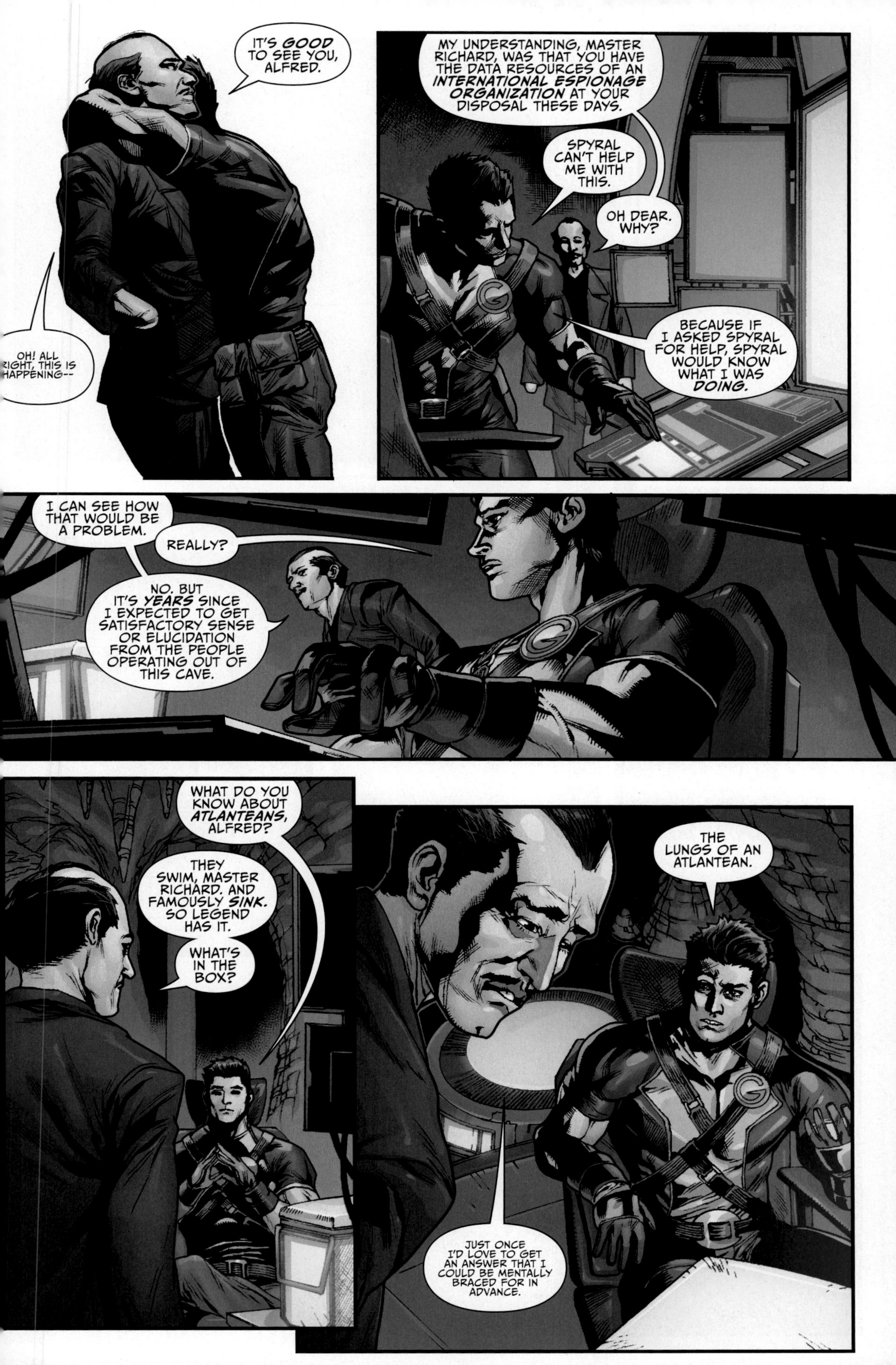
IT'S GOOD TO SEE YOU, ALFRED.
OH! ALL RIGHT, THIS IS HAPPENING--
MY UNDERSTANDING, MASTER RICHARD, WAS THAT YOU HAVE THE DATA RESOURCES OF AN INTERNATIONAL ESPIONAGE ORGANIZATION AT YOUR DISPOSAL THESE DAYS.
SPYRAL CAN'T HELP ME WITH THIS.
OH DEAR. WHY?
BECAUSE IF I ASKED SPYRAL FOR HELP, SPYRAL WOULD KNOW WHAT I WAS DOING.
I CAN SEE HOW THAT WOULD BE A PROBLEM.
REALLY?
NO. BUT IT'S YEARS SINCE I EXPECTED TO GET SATISFACTORY SENSE OR ELUCIDATION FROM THE PEOPLE OPERATING OUT OF THIS CAVE.
WHAT DO YOU KNOW ABOUT ATLANTEANS, ALFRED?
THEY SWIM, MASTER RICHARD. AND FAMOUSLY SINK. SO LEGEND HAS IT.
WHAT'S IN THE BOX?
THE LUNGS OF AN ATLANTEAN.
JUST ONCE I'D LOVE TO GET AN ANSWER THAT I COULD BE MENTALLY BRACED FOR IN ADVANCE.

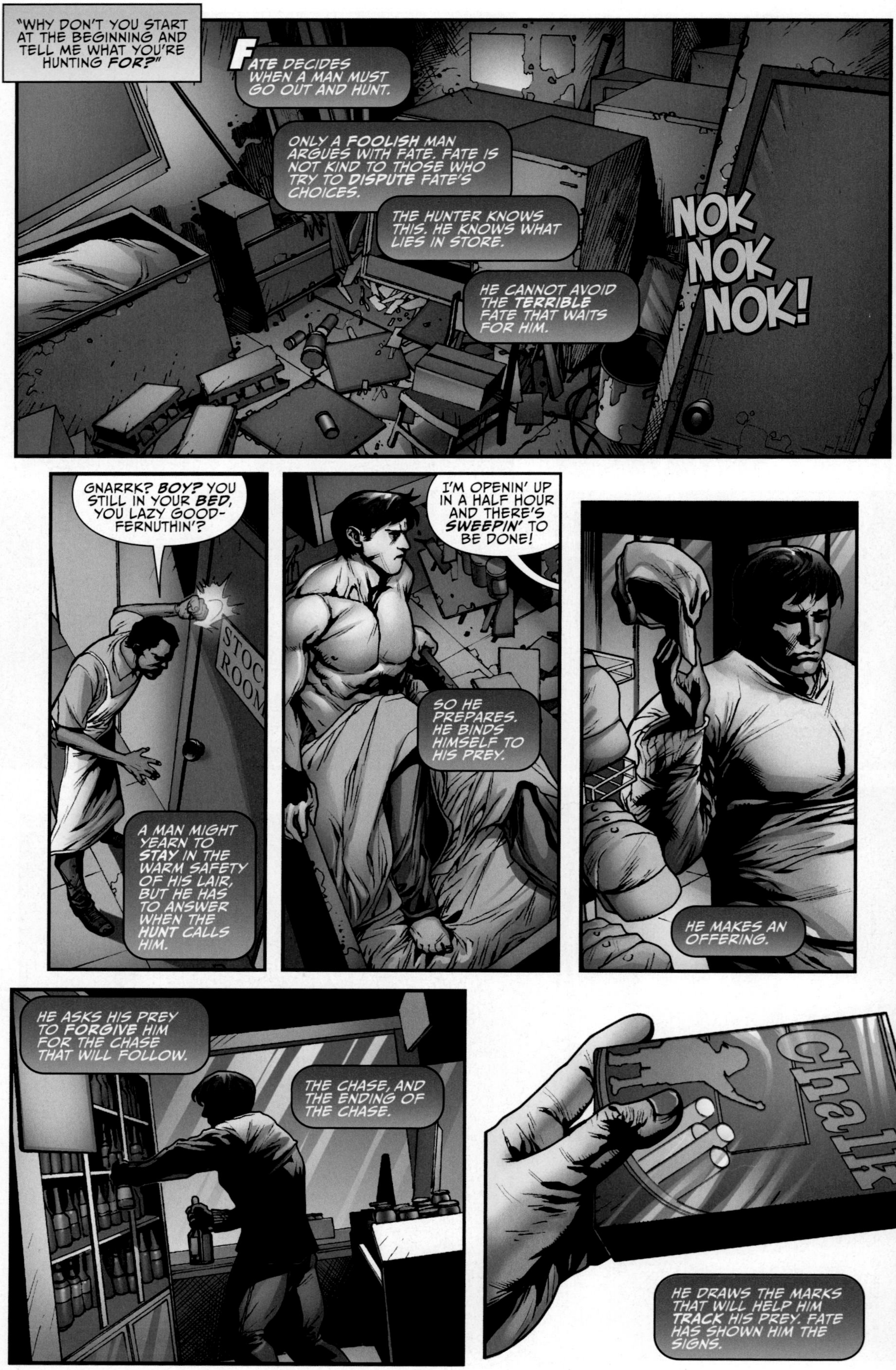
"WHY DON'T YOU START AT THE BEGINNING AND TELL ME WHAT YOU'RE HUNTING FOR?"
FATE DECIDES WHEN A MAN MUST GO OUT AND HUNT.
ONLY A FOOLISH MAN ARGUES WITH FATE. FATE IS NOT KIND TO THOSE WHO TRY TO DISPUTE FATE'S CHOICES.
THE HUNTER KNOWS THIS. HE KNOWS WHAT LIES IN STORE.
HE CANNOT AVOID THE TERRIBLE FATE THAT WAITS FOR HIM.
NOK NOK NOK!
GNARRK? BOY? YOU STILL IN YOUR BED, YOU LAZY GOOD-FERNUTHIN'?
STOCK ROOM
A MAN MIGHT YEARN TO STAY IN THE WARM SAFETY OF HIS LAIR, BUT HE HAS TO ANSWER WHEN THE HUNT CALLS HIM.
I'M OPENIN' UP IN A HALF HOUR AND THERE'S SWEEPIN' TO BE DONE!
SO HE PREPARES. HE BINDS HIMSELF TO HIS PREY.
HE MAKES AN OFFERING.
HE ASKS HIS PREY TO FORGIVE HIM FOR THE CHASE THAT WILL FOLLOW.
THE CHASE, AND THE ENDING OF THE CHASE.
Chalk
HE DRAWS THE MARKS THAT WILL HELP HIM TRACK HIS PREY. FATE HAS SHOWN HIM THE SIGNS.

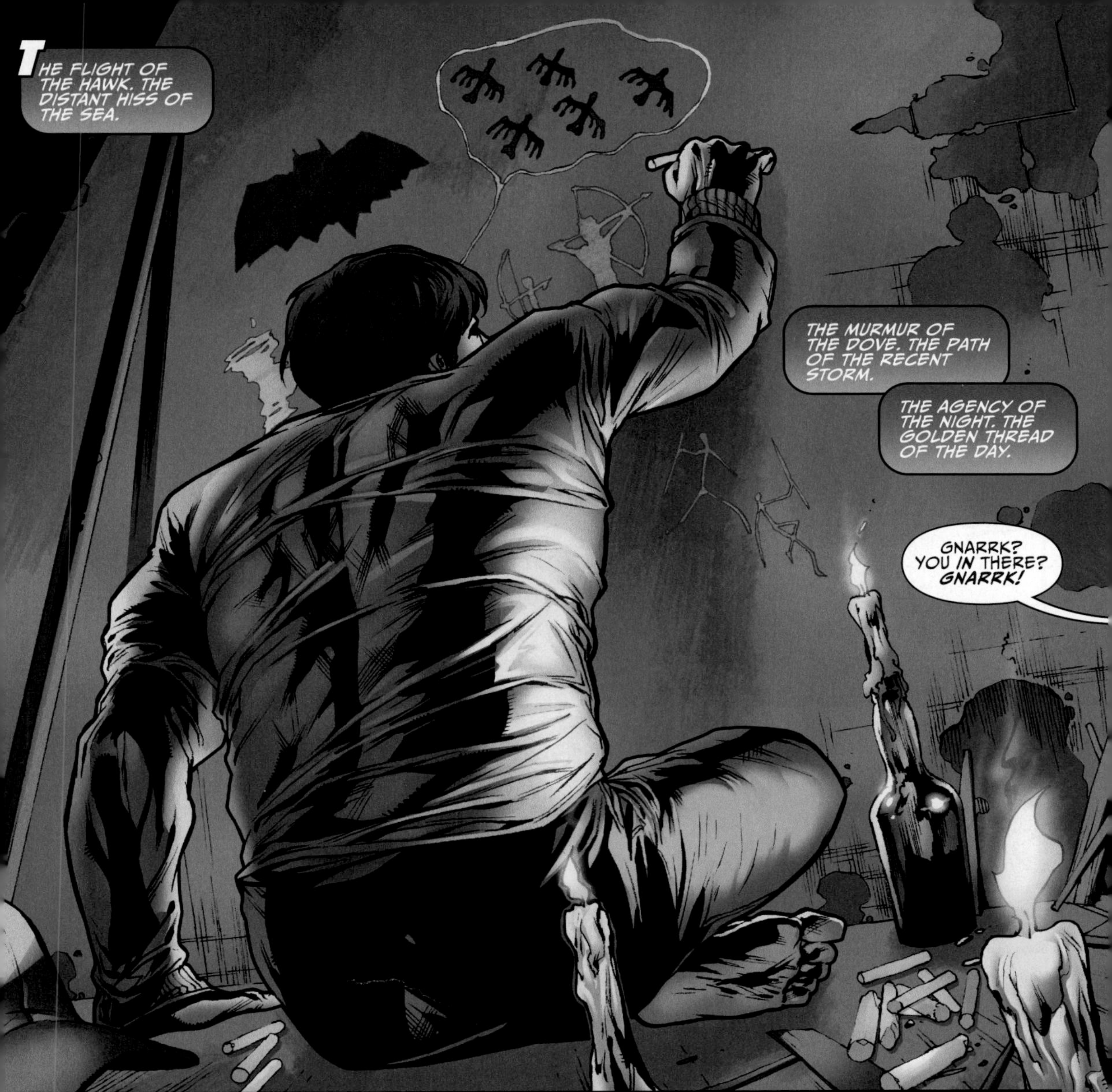
THE FLIGHT OF THE HAWK. THE DISTANT HISS OF THE SEA.
THE MURMUR OF THE DOVE. THE PATH OF THE RECENT STORM.
THE AGENCY OF THE NIGHT. THE GOLDEN THREAD OF THE DAY.
GNARRK? YOU *IN* THERE? ***GNARRK!***

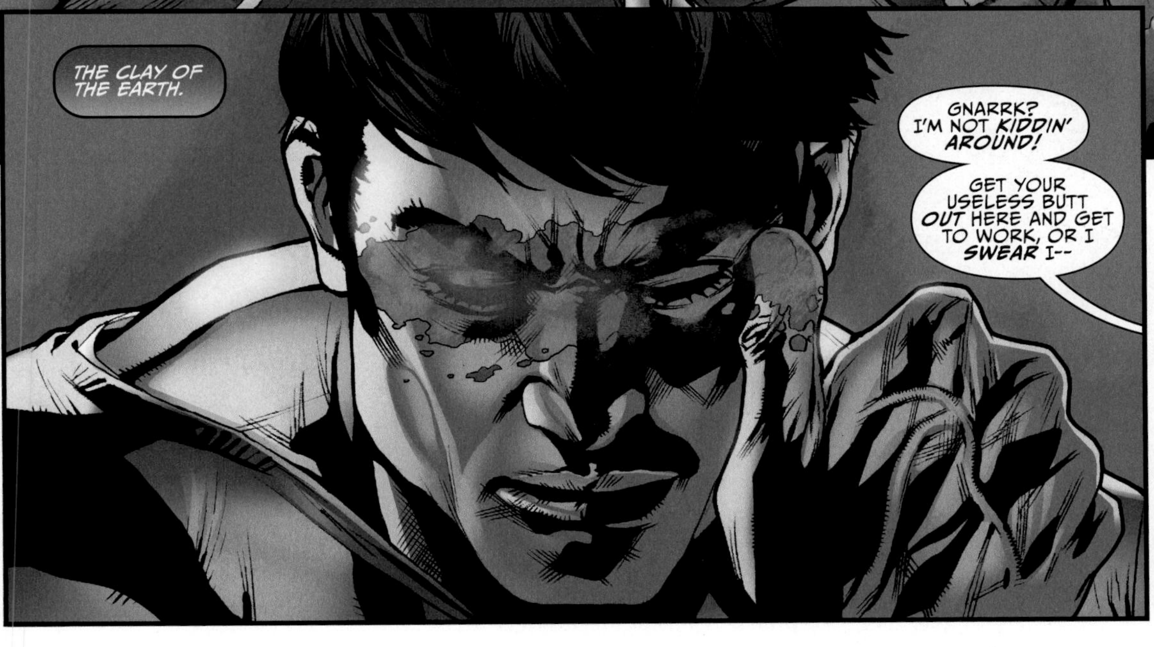
THE CLAY OF THE EARTH.
GNARRK? I'M NOT ***KIDDIN' AROUND!***
GET YOUR USELESS BUTT ***OUT*** HERE AND GET TO WORK, OR I ***SWEAR*** I--

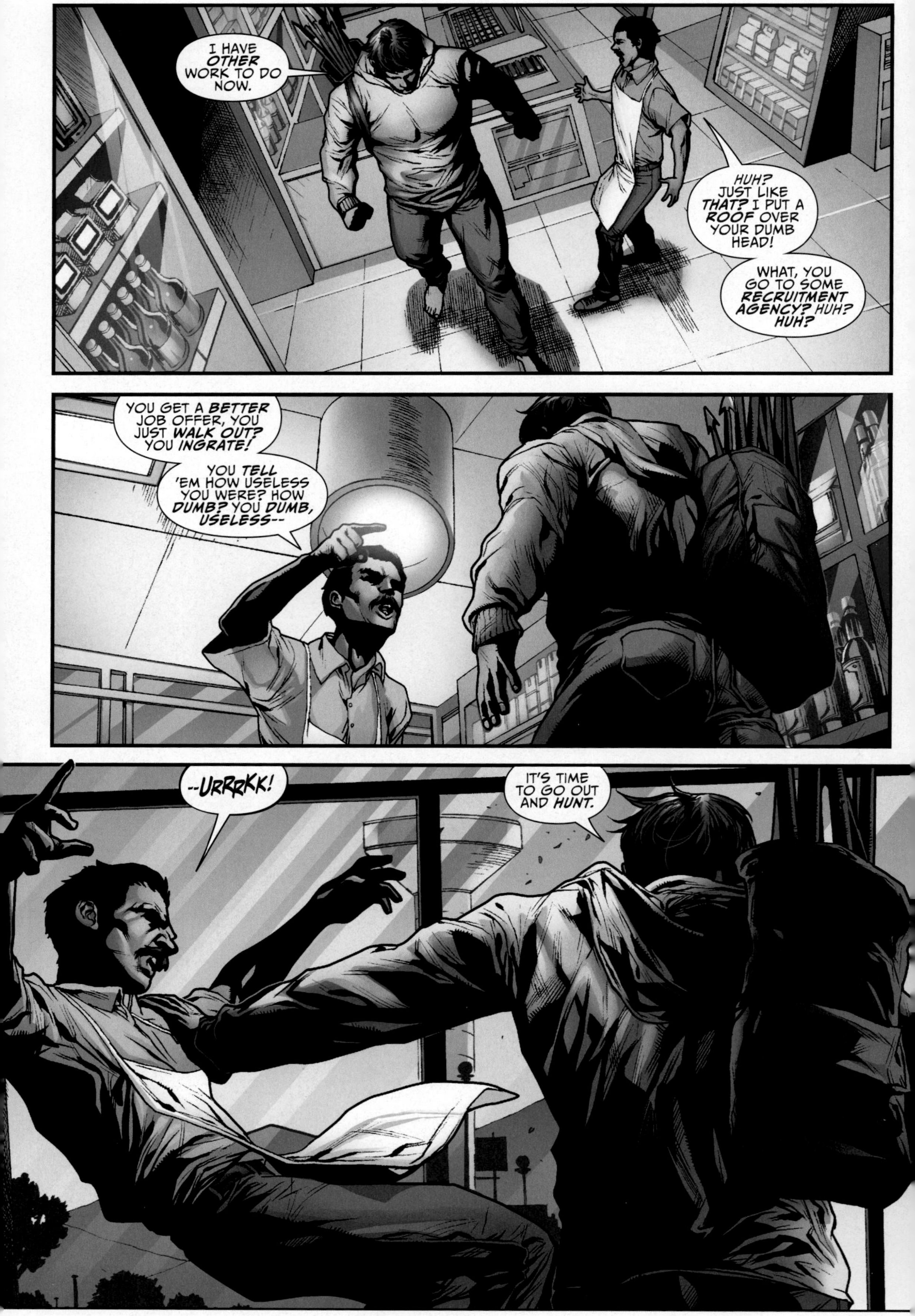
I HAVE OTHER WORK TO DO NOW.
HUH? JUST LIKE THAT? I PUT A ROOF OVER YOUR DUMB HEAD!
WHAT, YOU GO TO SOME RECRUITMENT AGENCY? HUH? HUH?
YOU GET A BETTER JOB OFFER, YOU JUST WALK OUT? YOU INGRATE!
YOU TELL 'EM HOW USELESS YOU WERE? HOW DUMB? YOU DUMB, USELESS--
--URRRKK!
IT'S TIME TO GO OUT AND HUNT.

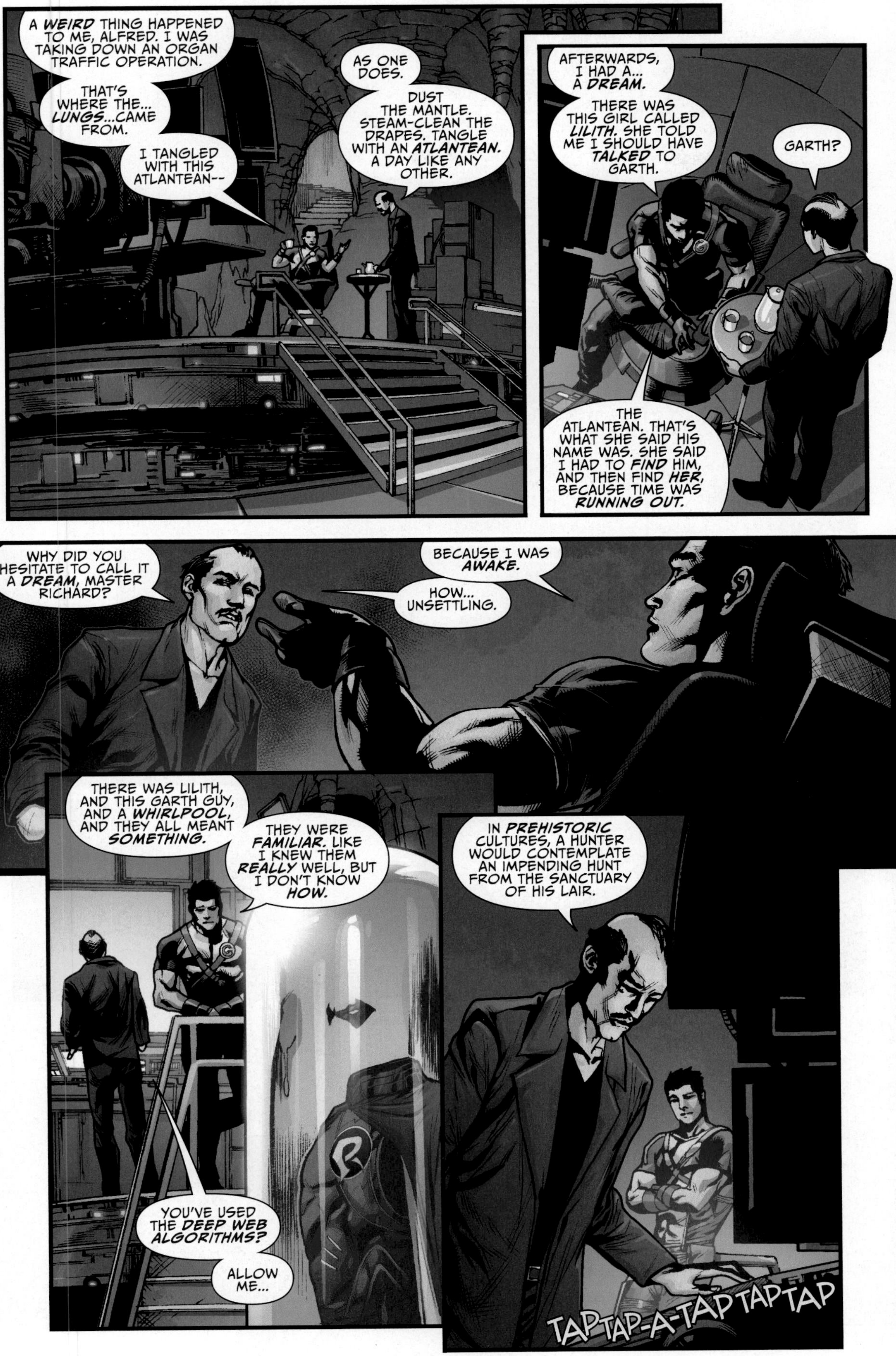
A WEIRD THING HAPPENED TO ME, ALFRED. I WAS TAKING DOWN AN ORGAN TRAFFIC OPERATION.
THAT'S WHERE THE... LUNGS...CAME FROM.
I TANGLED WITH THIS ATLANTEAN--
AS ONE DOES.
DUST THE MANTLE. STEAM-CLEAN THE DRAPES. TANGLE WITH AN ATLANTEAN. A DAY LIKE ANY OTHER.
AFTERWARDS, I HAD A... A DREAM.
THERE WAS THIS GIRL CALLED LILITH. SHE TOLD ME I SHOULD HAVE TALKED TO GARTH.
GARTH?
THE ATLANTEAN. THAT'S WHAT SHE SAID HIS NAME WAS. SHE SAID I HAD TO FIND HIM, AND THEN FIND HER, BECAUSE TIME WAS RUNNING OUT.
WHY DID YOU HESITATE TO CALL IT A DREAM, MASTER RICHARD?
BECAUSE I WAS AWAKE.
HOW... UNSETTLING.
THERE WAS LILITH, AND THIS GARTH GUY, AND A WHIRLPOOL, AND THEY ALL MEANT SOMETHING.
THEY WERE FAMILIAR. LIKE I KNEW THEM REALLY WELL, BUT I DON'T KNOW HOW.
YOU'VE USED THE DEEP WEB ALGORITHMS?
ALLOW ME...
IN PREHISTORIC CULTURES, A HUNTER WOULD CONTEMPLATE AN IMPENDING HUNT FROM THE SANCTUARY OF HIS LAIR.
TAP TAP-A-TAP TAP TAP

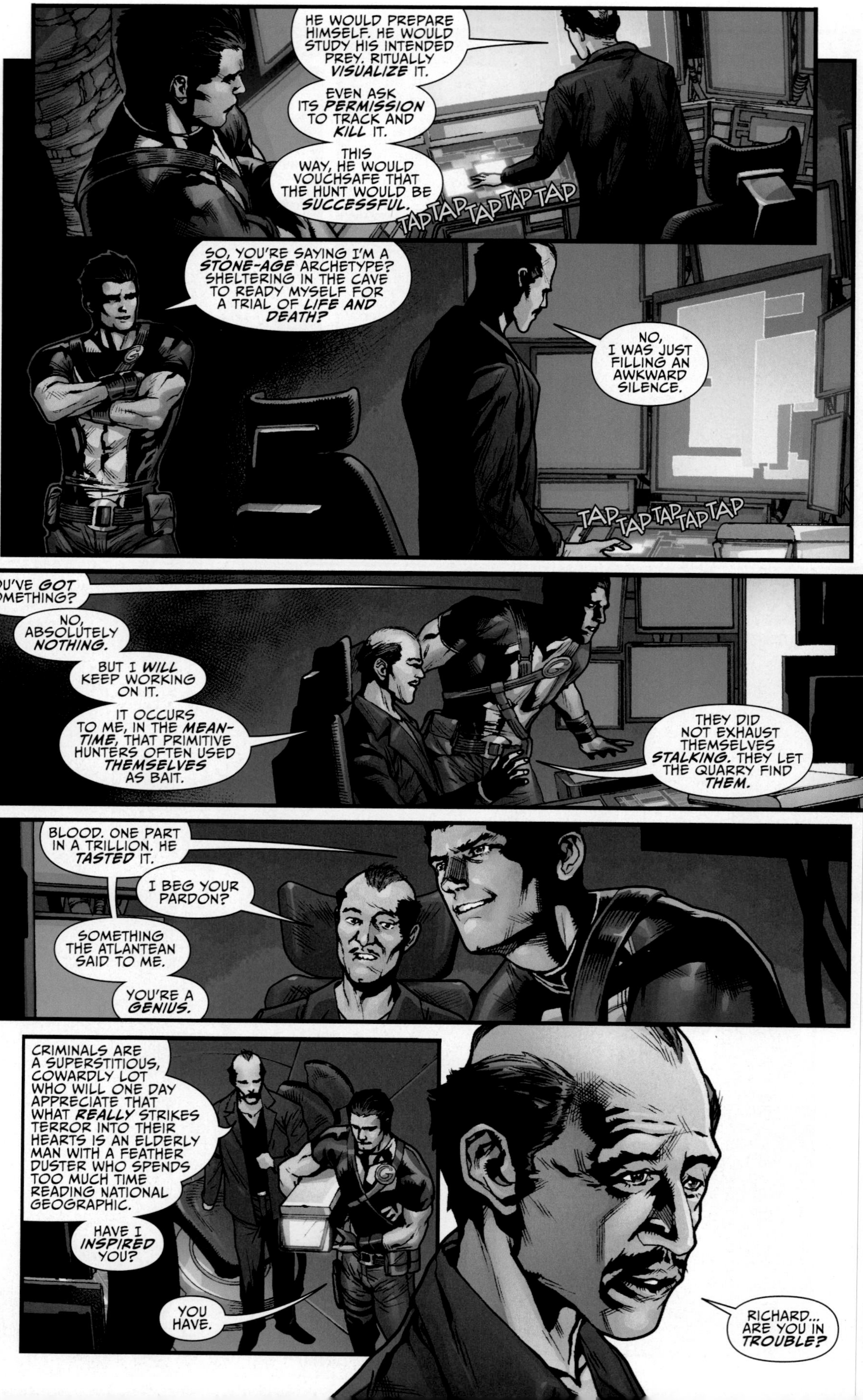
HE WOULD PREPARE HIMSELF. HE WOULD STUDY HIS INTENDED PREY. RITUALLY VISUALIZE IT.
EVEN ASK ITS PERMISSION TO TRACK AND KILL IT.
THIS WAY, HE WOULD VOUCHSAFE THAT THE HUNT WOULD BE SUCCESSFUL.
TAPTAPTAPTAPTAP
SO, YOU'RE SAYING I'M A STONE-AGE ARCHETYPE? SHELTERING IN THE CAVE TO READY MYSELF FOR A TRIAL OF LIFE AND DEATH?
NO, I WAS JUST FILLING AN AWKWARD SILENCE.
TAPTAPTAPTAPTAP
YOU'VE GOT SOMETHING?
NO, ABSOLUTELY NOTHING.
BUT I WILL KEEP WORKING ON IT.
IT OCCURS TO ME, IN THE MEAN-TIME, THAT PRIMITIVE HUNTERS OFTEN USED THEMSELVES AS BAIT.
THEY DID NOT EXHAUST THEMSELVES STALKING. THEY LET THE QUARRY FIND THEM.
BLOOD. ONE PART IN A TRILLION. HE TASTED IT.
I BEG YOUR PARDON?
SOMETHING THE ATLANTEAN SAID TO ME.
YOU'RE A GENIUS.
CRIMINALS ARE A SUPERSTITIOUS, COWARDLY LOT WHO WILL ONE DAY APPRECIATE THAT WHAT REALLY STRIKES TERROR INTO THEIR HEARTS IS AN ELDERLY MAN WITH A FEATHER DUSTER WHO SPENDS TOO MUCH TIME READING NATIONAL GEOGRAPHIC.
HAVE I INSPIRED YOU?
YOU HAVE.
RICHARD... ARE YOU IN TROUBLE?

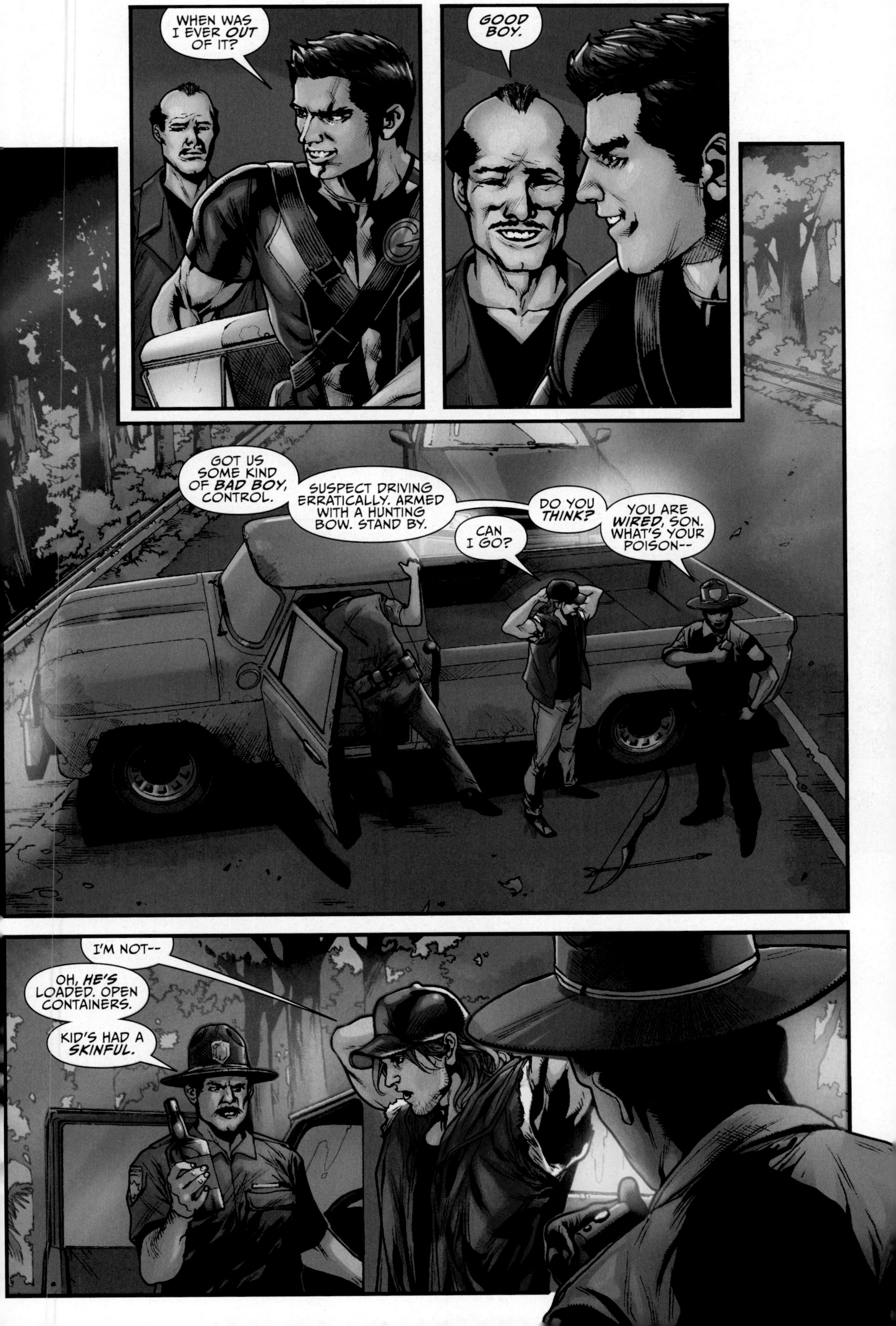
WHEN WAS I EVER OUT OF IT?
GOOD BOY.
GOT US SOME KIND OF BAD BOY, CONTROL.
SUSPECT DRIVING ERRATICALLY. ARMED WITH A HUNTING BOW. STAND BY.
DO YOU THINK?
CAN I GO?
YOU ARE WIRED, SON. WHAT'S YOUR POISON--
I'M NOT--
OH, HE'S LOADED. OPEN CONTAINERS.
KID'S HAD A SKINFUL.

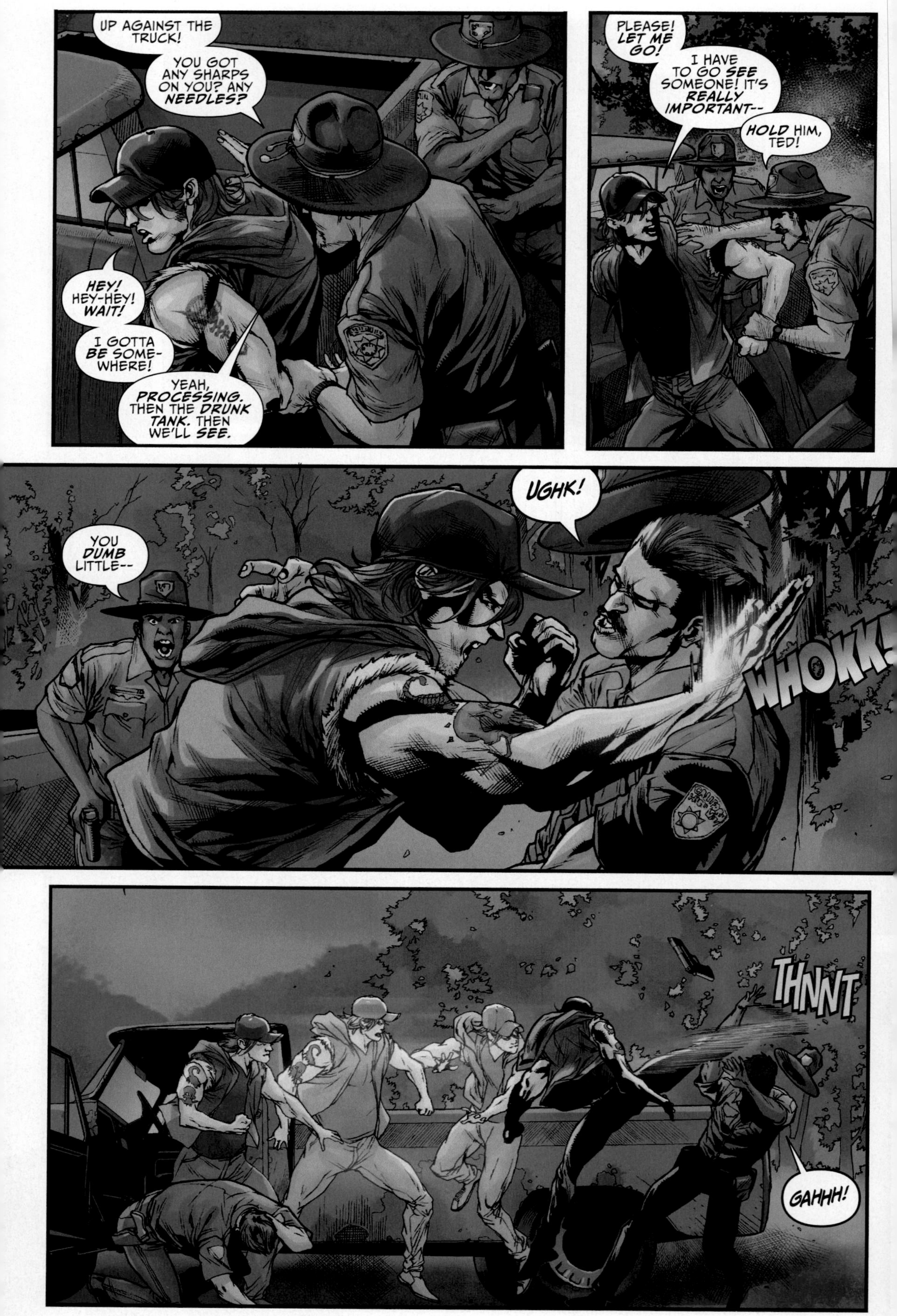
UP AGAINST THE TRUCK!
YOU GOT ANY SHARPS ON YOU? ANY NEEDLES?
HEY! HEY-HEY! WAIT!
I GOTTA BE SOME-WHERE!
YEAH, PROCESSING. THEN THE DRUNK TANK. THEN WE'LL SEE.
PLEASE! LET ME GO!
I HAVE TO GO SEE SOMEONE! IT'S REALLY IMPORTANT--
HOLD HIM, TED!
YOU DUMB LITTLE--
UGHK!
WHOKK!
THNNT
GAHHH!

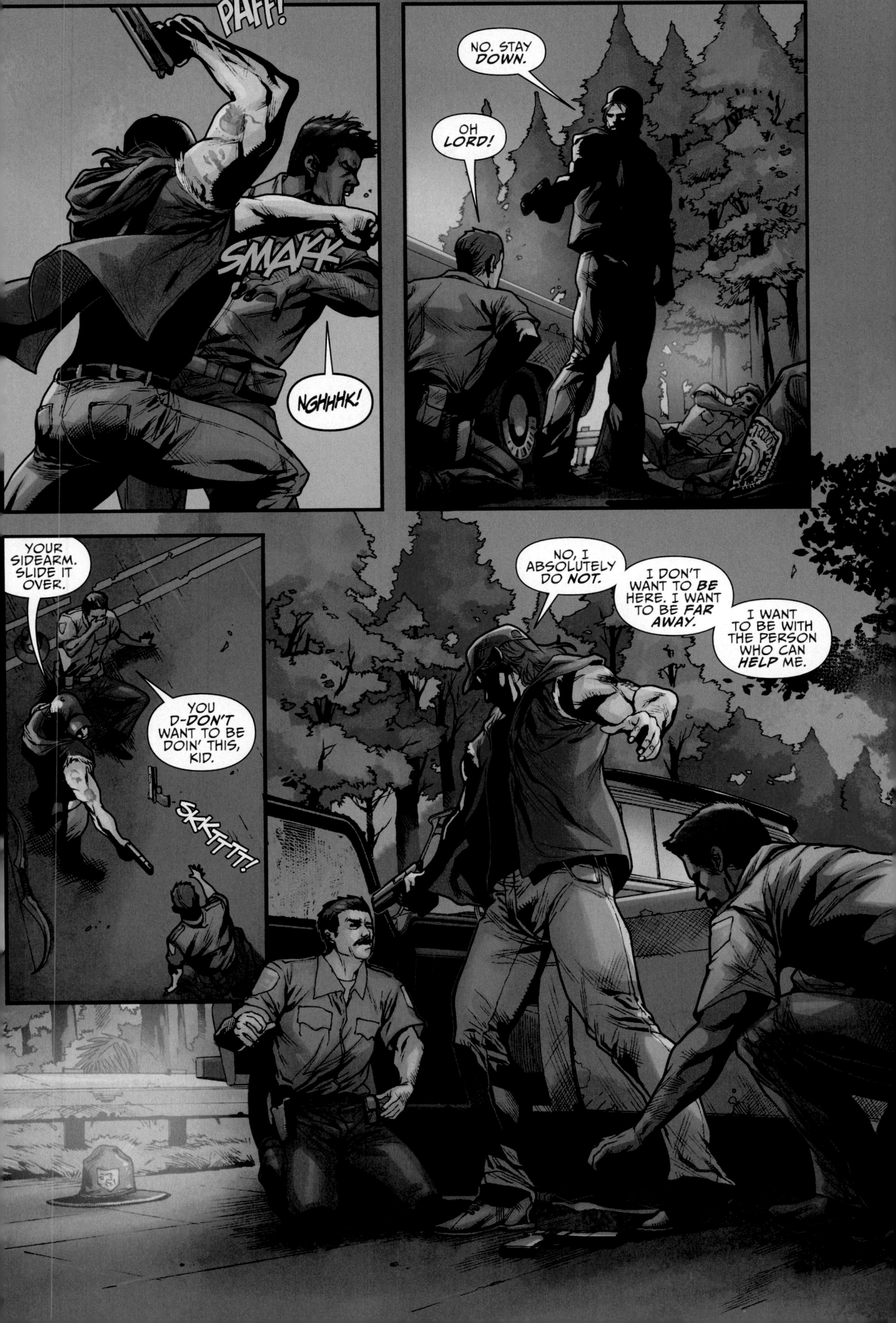
PAFF!
SMAKK
NGHHHK!
NO. STAY DOWN.
OH LORD!
YOUR SIDEARM. SLIDE IT OVER.
YOU D-DON'T WANT TO BE DOIN' THIS, KID.
SKKTTTT!
NO, I ABSOLUTELY DO NOT.
I DON'T WANT TO BE HERE. I WANT TO BE FAR AWAY.
I WANT TO BE WITH THE PERSON WHO CAN HELP ME.

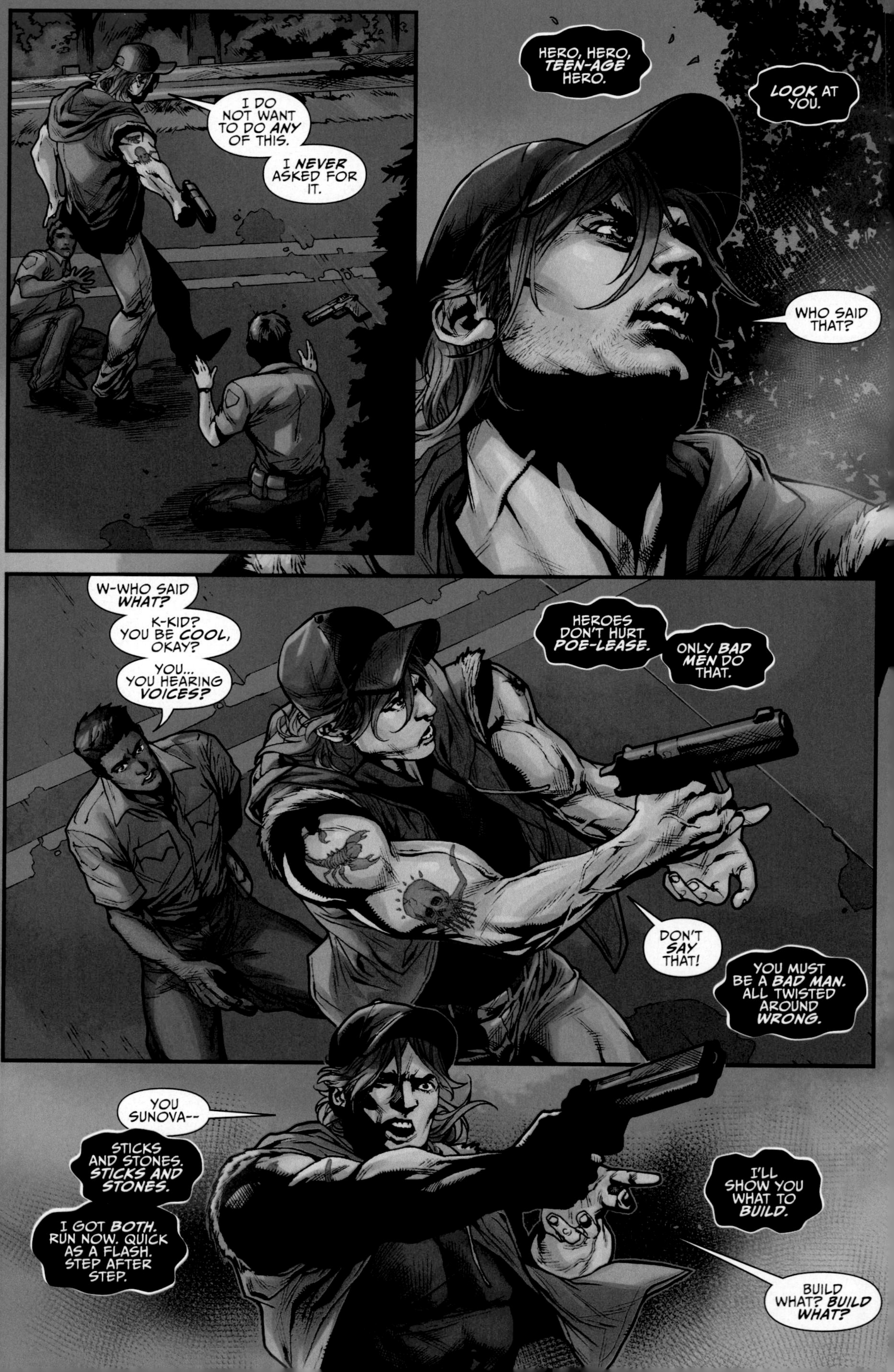
I DO NOT WANT TO DO ANY OF THIS.
I NEVER ASKED FOR IT.
HERO, HERO, TEEN-AGE HERO.
LOOK AT YOU.
WHO SAID THAT?
W-WHO SAID WHAT?
K-KID? YOU BE COOL, OKAY?
YOU... YOU HEARING VOICES?
HEROES DON'T HURT POE-LEASE.
ONLY BAD MEN DO THAT.
DON'T SAY THAT!
YOU MUST BE A BAD MAN. ALL TWISTED AROUND WRONG.
YOU SUNOVA--
STICKS AND STONES. STICKS AND STONES.
I GOT BOTH. RUN NOW. QUICK AS A FLASH. STEP AFTER STEP.
I'LL SHOW YOU WHAT TO BUILD.
BUILD WHAT? BUILD WHAT?

FZXXKKTKKT!

GYAAAAGGHKK!

"IT MUST HAVE BEEN A SHOCK..."

...WINNING ANOTHER MAJOR AWARD.

IT REALLY HASN'T SUNK IN YET.

OH, I'LL BET. MALCOLM, THANKS FOR AGREEING TO THIS INTERVIEW. THE FEATURE'S GOING TO RUN IN OUR SEPTEMBER ISSUE.

IT'S MAL. MAL IS FINE. WHAT CAN I TELL YOU, ALANA?

BIG YEAR FOR YOU. THE OSCAR FOR CRASH SITE, THEN THE GOLDEN STAR THIS WEEK FOR TROUBLE ALWAYS FINDS ME. YOU ARE THE GO-TO GUY FOR SOUNDTRACKS IN HOLLYWOOD RIGHT NOW.

I DON'T KNOW ABOUT THAT...

YOU MET YOUR WIFE KAREN WHILE YOU WERE WORKING ON CRASH SITE?

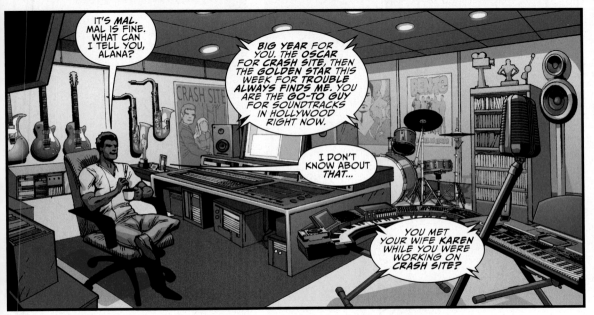

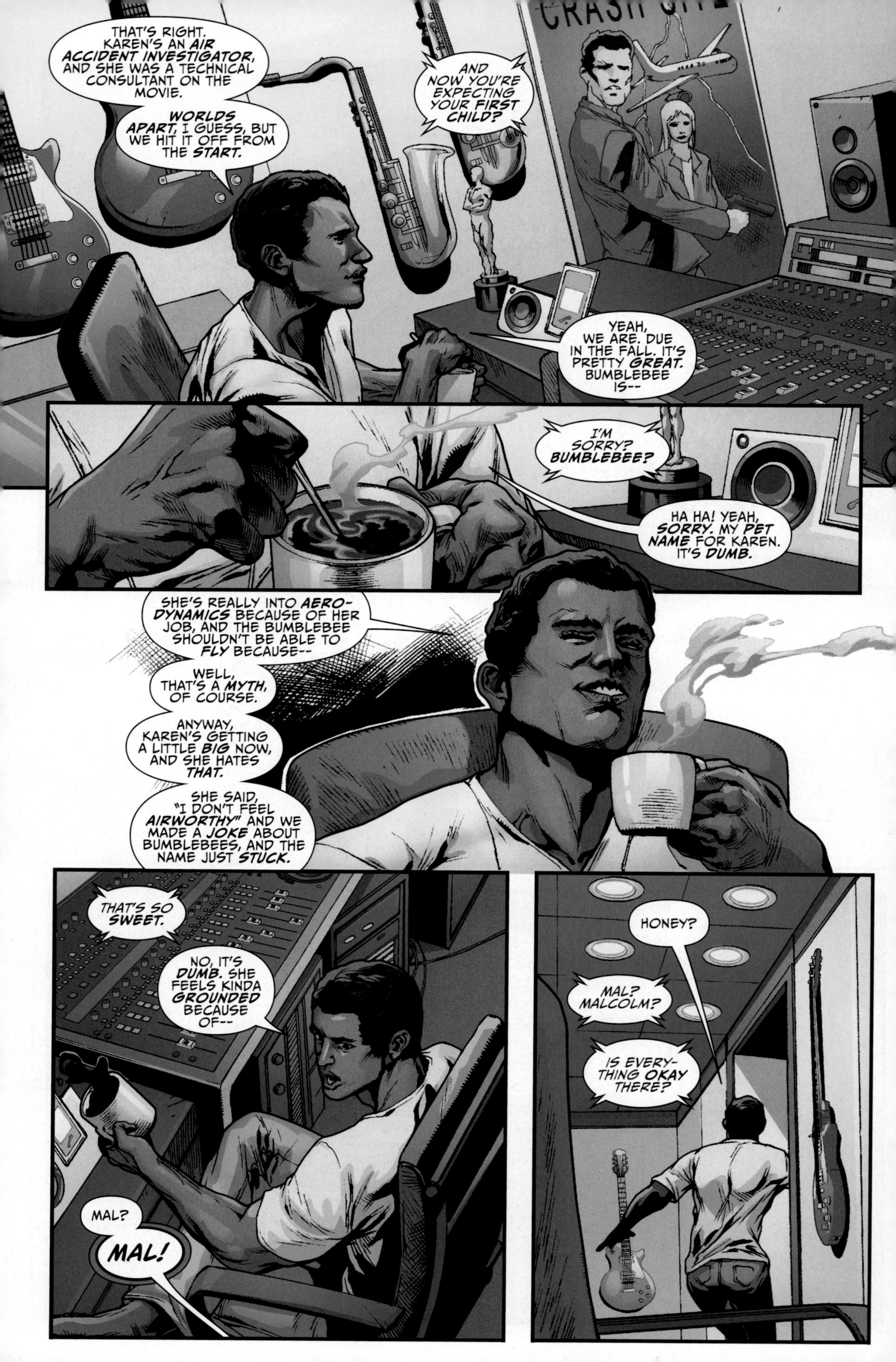
CRASH SITE
THAT'S RIGHT. KAREN'S AN AIR ACCIDENT INVESTIGATOR, AND SHE WAS A TECHNICAL CONSULTANT ON THE MOVIE.
WORLDS APART, I GUESS, BUT WE HIT IT OFF FROM THE START.
AND NOW YOU'RE EXPECTING YOUR FIRST CHILD?
YEAH, WE ARE. DUE IN THE FALL. IT'S PRETTY GREAT. BUMBLEBEE IS--
I'M SORRY? BUMBLEBEE?
HA HA! YEAH, SORRY. MY PET NAME FOR KAREN. IT'S DUMB.
SHE'S REALLY INTO AERO-DYNAMICS BECAUSE OF HER JOB, AND THE BUMBLEBEE SHOULDN'T BE ABLE TO FLY BECAUSE--
WELL, THAT'S A MYTH, OF COURSE.
ANYWAY, KAREN'S GETTING A LITTLE BIG NOW, AND SHE HATES THAT.
SHE SAID, "I DON'T FEEL AIRWORTHY" AND WE MADE A JOKE ABOUT BUMBLEBEES, AND THE NAME JUST STUCK.
THAT'S SO SWEET.
NO, IT'S DUMB. SHE FEELS KINDA GROUNDED BECAUSE OF--
MAL?
MAL!
HONEY?
MAL? MALCOLM?
IS EVERY-THING OKAY THERE?

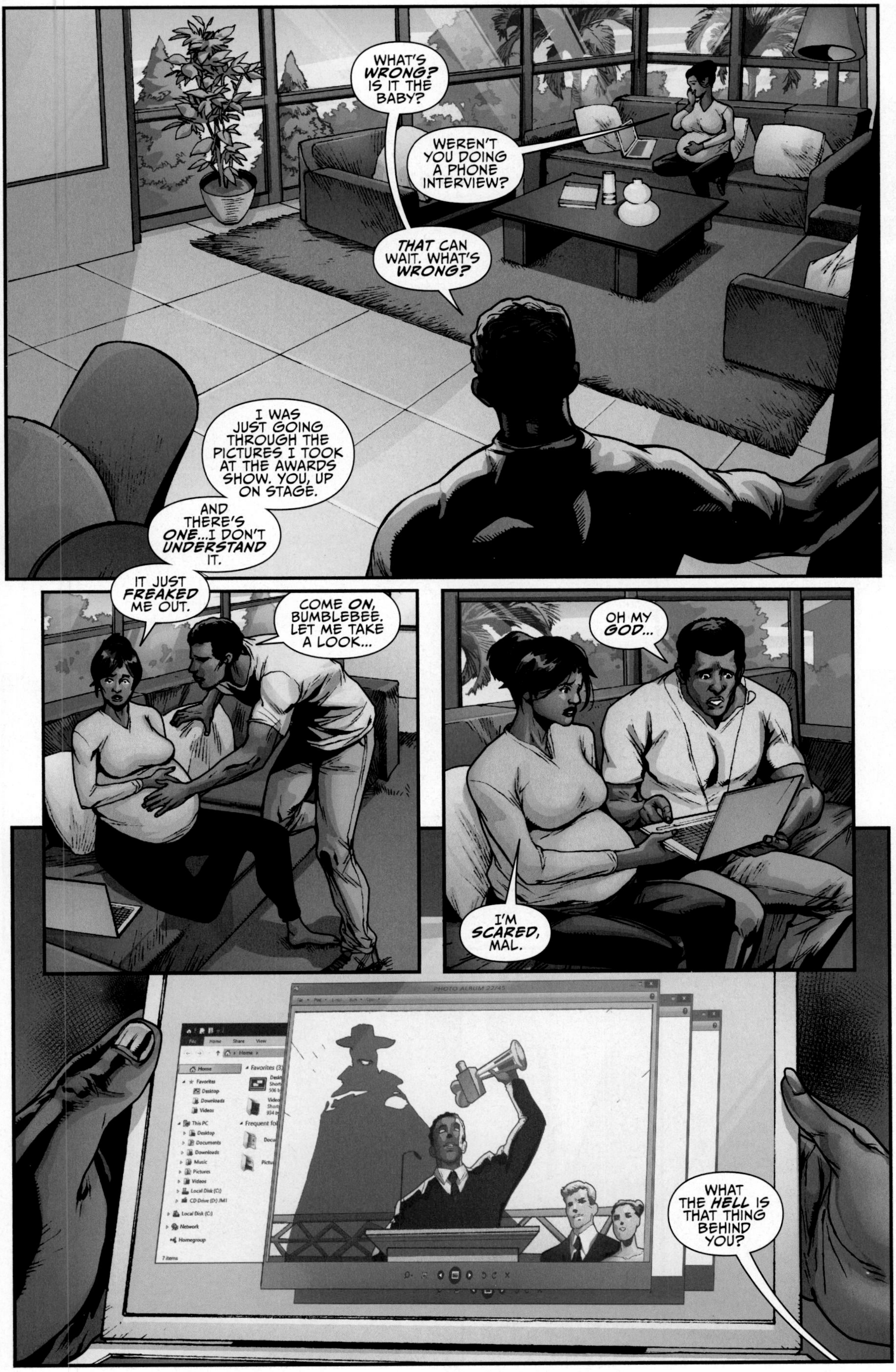
WHAT'S WRONG? IS IT THE BABY?
WEREN'T YOU DOING A PHONE INTERVIEW?
THAT CAN WAIT. WHAT'S WRONG?
I WAS JUST GOING THROUGH THE PICTURES I TOOK AT THE AWARDS SHOW. YOU, UP ON STAGE.
AND THERE'S ONE...I DON'T UNDERSTAND IT.
IT JUST FREAKED ME OUT.
COME ON, BUMBLEBEE. LET ME TAKE A LOOK...
OH MY GOD...
I'M SCARED, MAL.
WHAT THE HELL IS THAT THING BEHIND YOU?

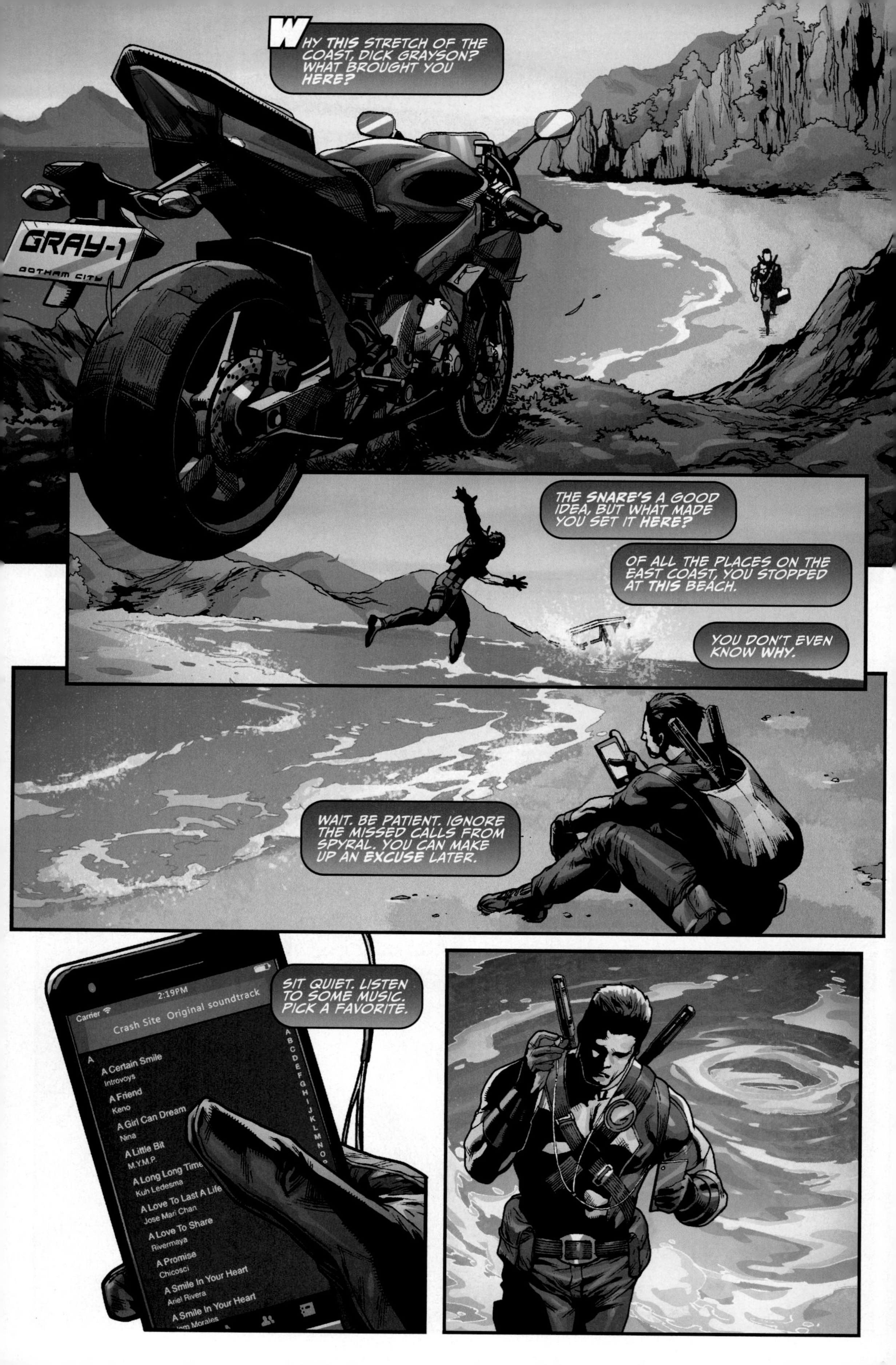
WHY THIS STRETCH OF THE COAST, DICK GRAYSON? WHAT BROUGHT YOU HERE?
GRAY-1
GOTHAM CITY
THE SNARE'S A GOOD IDEA, BUT WHAT MADE YOU SET IT HERE?
OF ALL THE PLACES ON THE EAST COAST, YOU STOPPED AT THIS BEACH.
YOU DON'T EVEN KNOW WHY.
WAIT. BE PATIENT. IGNORE THE MISSED CALLS FROM SPYRAL. YOU CAN MAKE UP AN EXCUSE LATER.
2:19PM
Carrier
Crash Site Original soundtrack
A
A Certain Smile
Introvoys
A Friend
Keno
A Girl Can Dream
Nina
A Little Bit
M.Y.M.P.
A Long Long Time
Kuh Ledesma
A Love To Last A Life
Jose Mari Chan
A Love To Share
Rivermaya
A Promise
Chicosci
A Smile In Your Heart
Ariel Rivera
A Smile In Your Heart
SIT QUIET. LISTEN TO SOME MUSIC. PICK A FAVORITE.

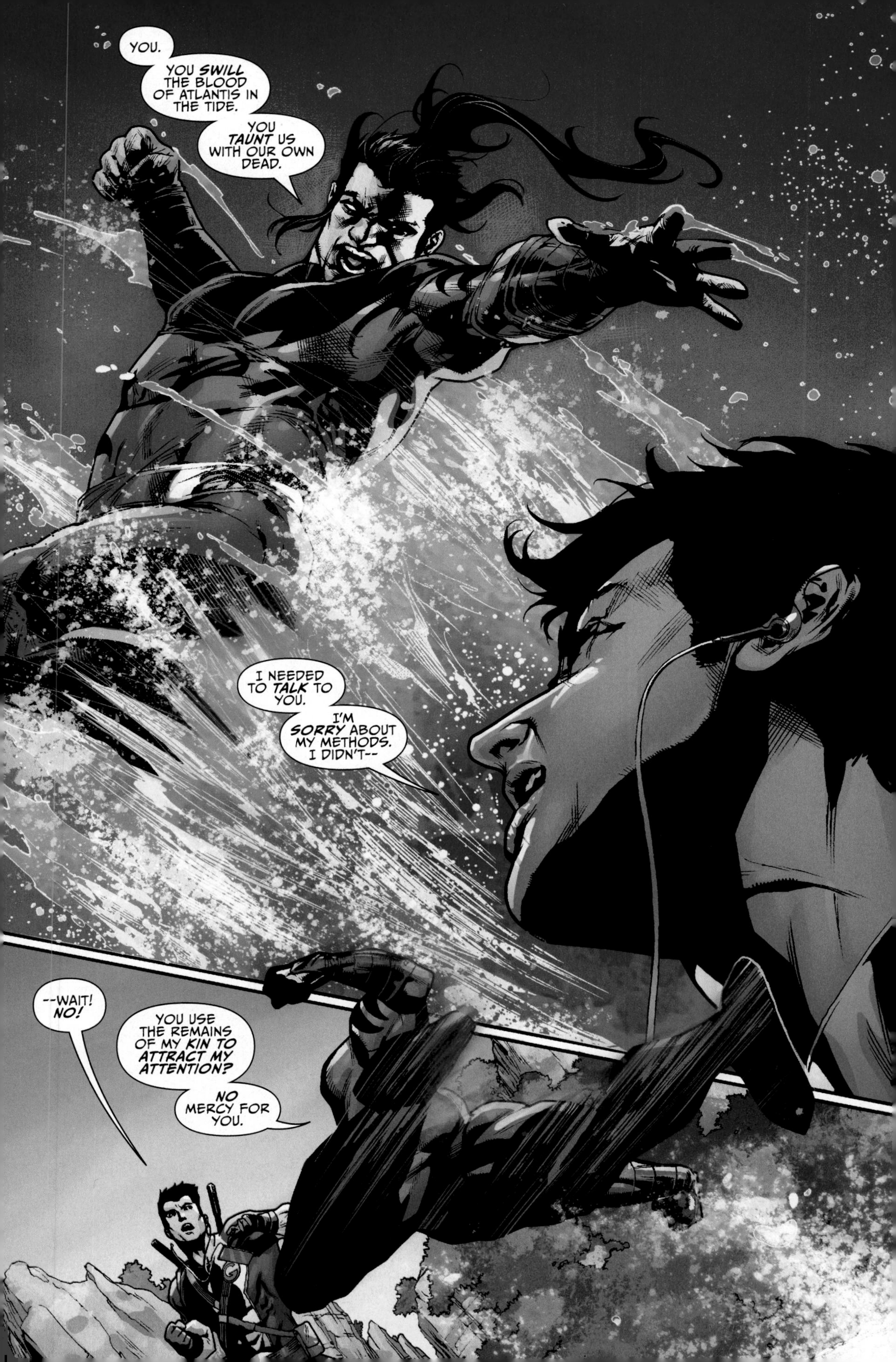
YOU.
YOU SWILL THE BLOOD OF ATLANTIS IN THE TIDE.
YOU TAUNT US WITH OUR OWN DEAD.
I NEEDED TO TALK TO YOU.
I'M SORRY ABOUT MY METHODS. I DIDN'T--
--WAIT! NO!
YOU USE THE REMAINS OF MY KIN TO ATTRACT MY ATTENTION?
NO MERCY FOR YOU.

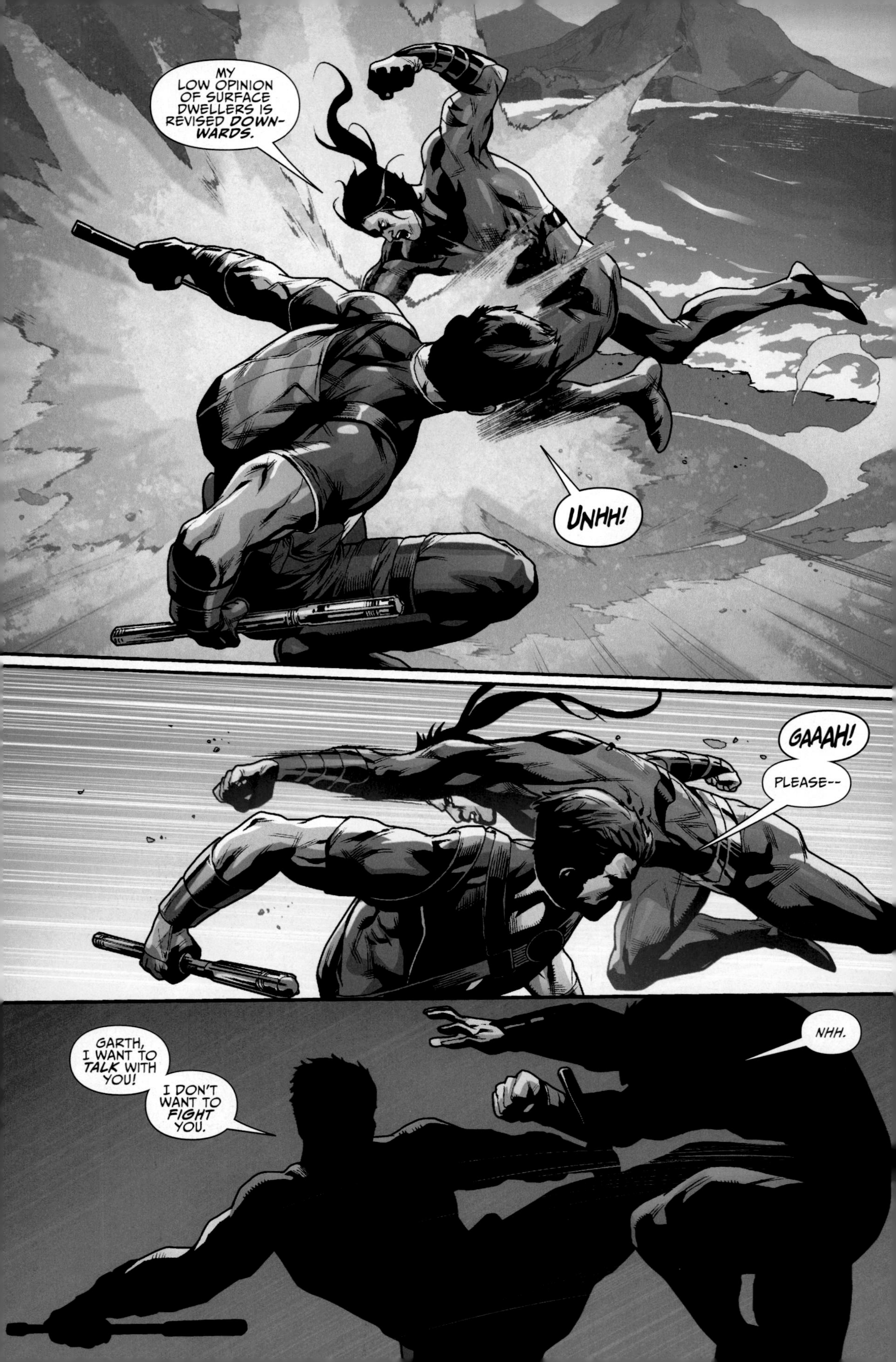
MY LOW OPINION OF SURFACE DWELLERS IS REVISED DOWNWARDS.
UNHH!
GAAAH!
PLEASE--
GARTH, I WANT TO TALK WITH YOU!
I DON'T WANT TO FIGHT YOU.
NHH.

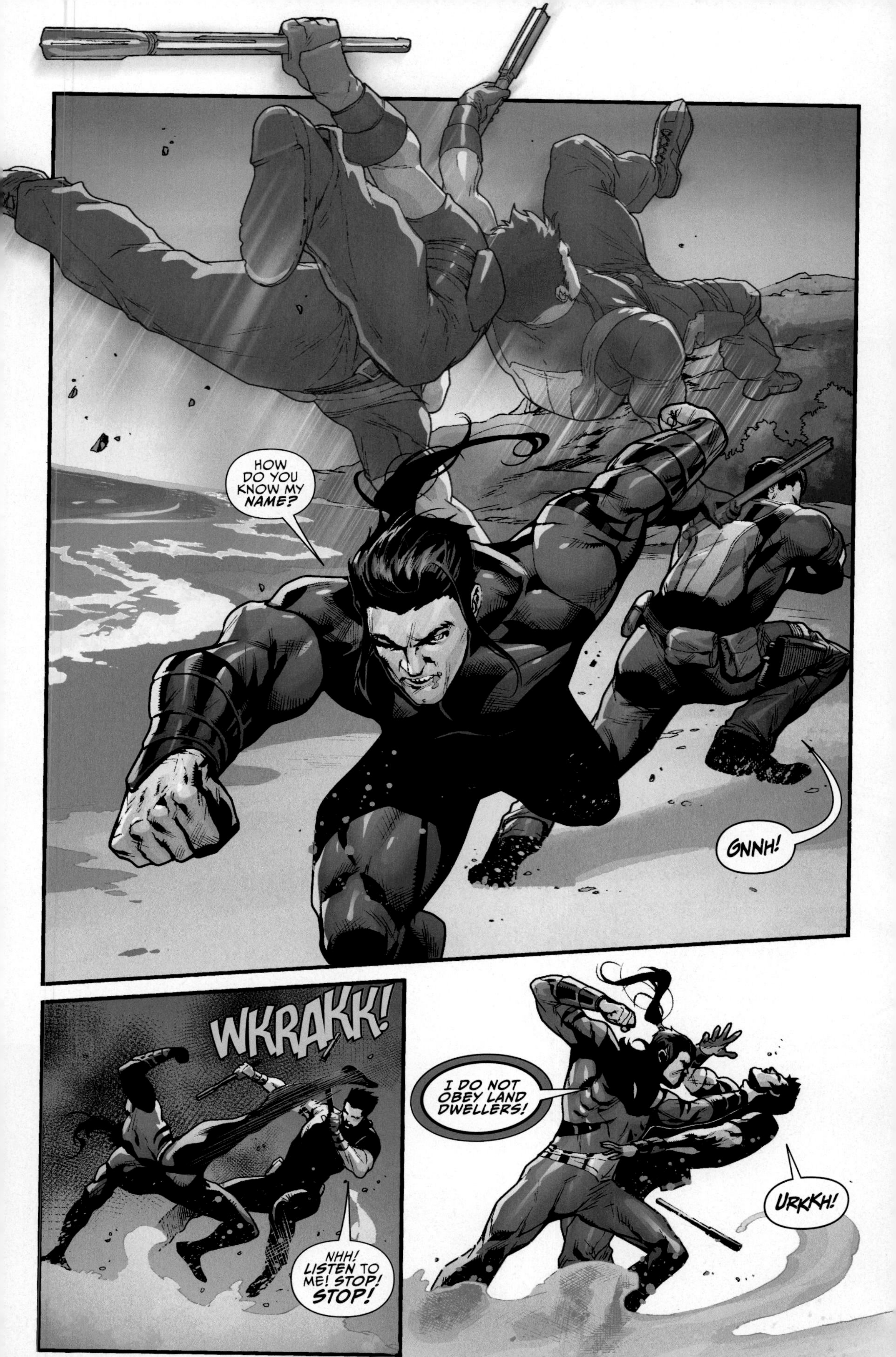

HOW DO YOU KNOW MY NAME?
GNNH!
WKRAKK!
NHH! LISTEN TO ME! STOP! STOP!
I DO NOT OBEY LAND DWELLERS!
URKKH!

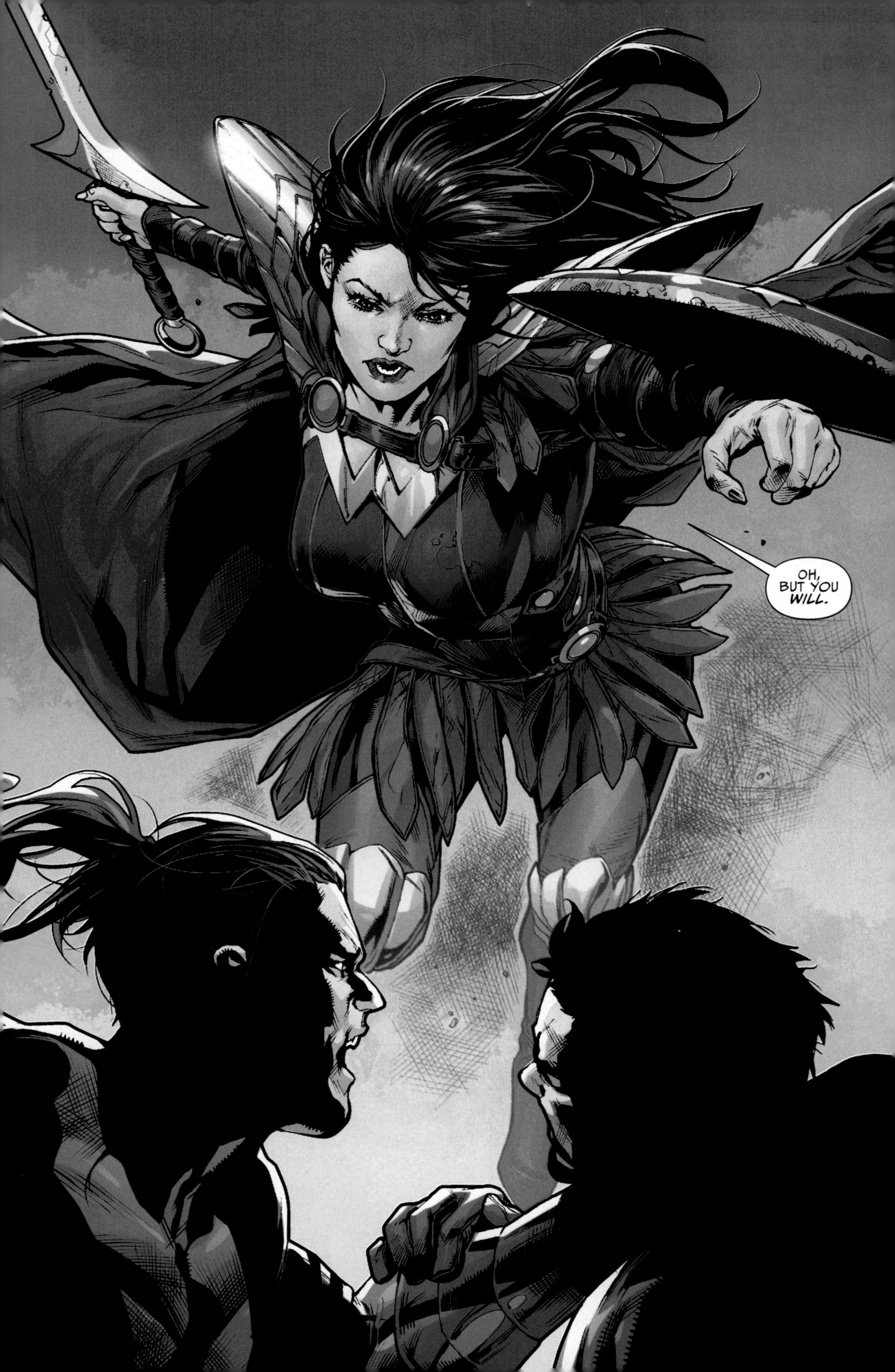
OH, BUT YOU *WILL.*

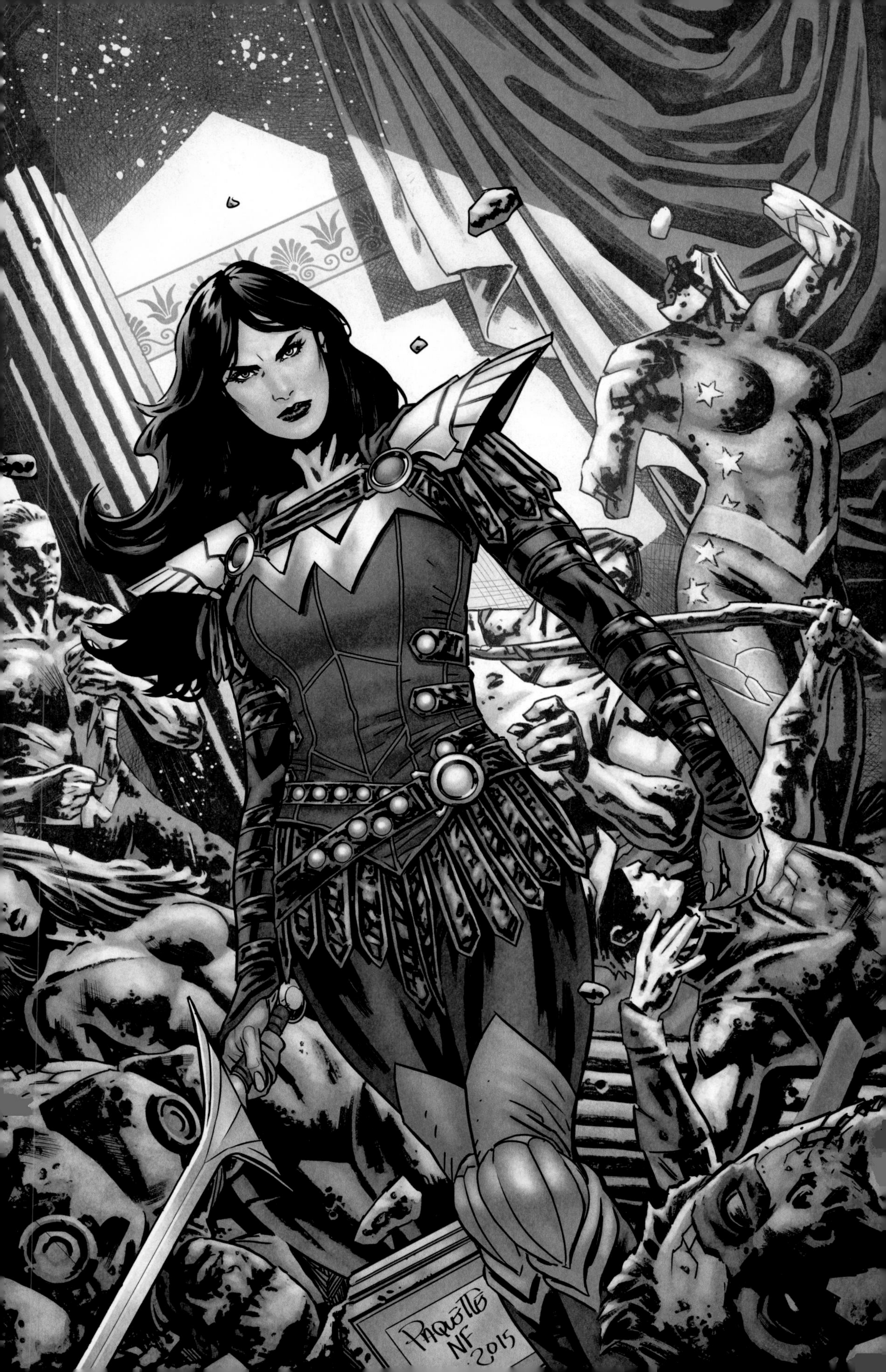

CHAPTER THREE: FRIENDS LIKE THESE

DAN ABNETT writer PAULO SIQUEIRA, GERALDO BORGES & JACKSON HERBERT artists HI-FI colorist cover art by YANICK PAQUETTE & NATHAN FAIRBAIRN

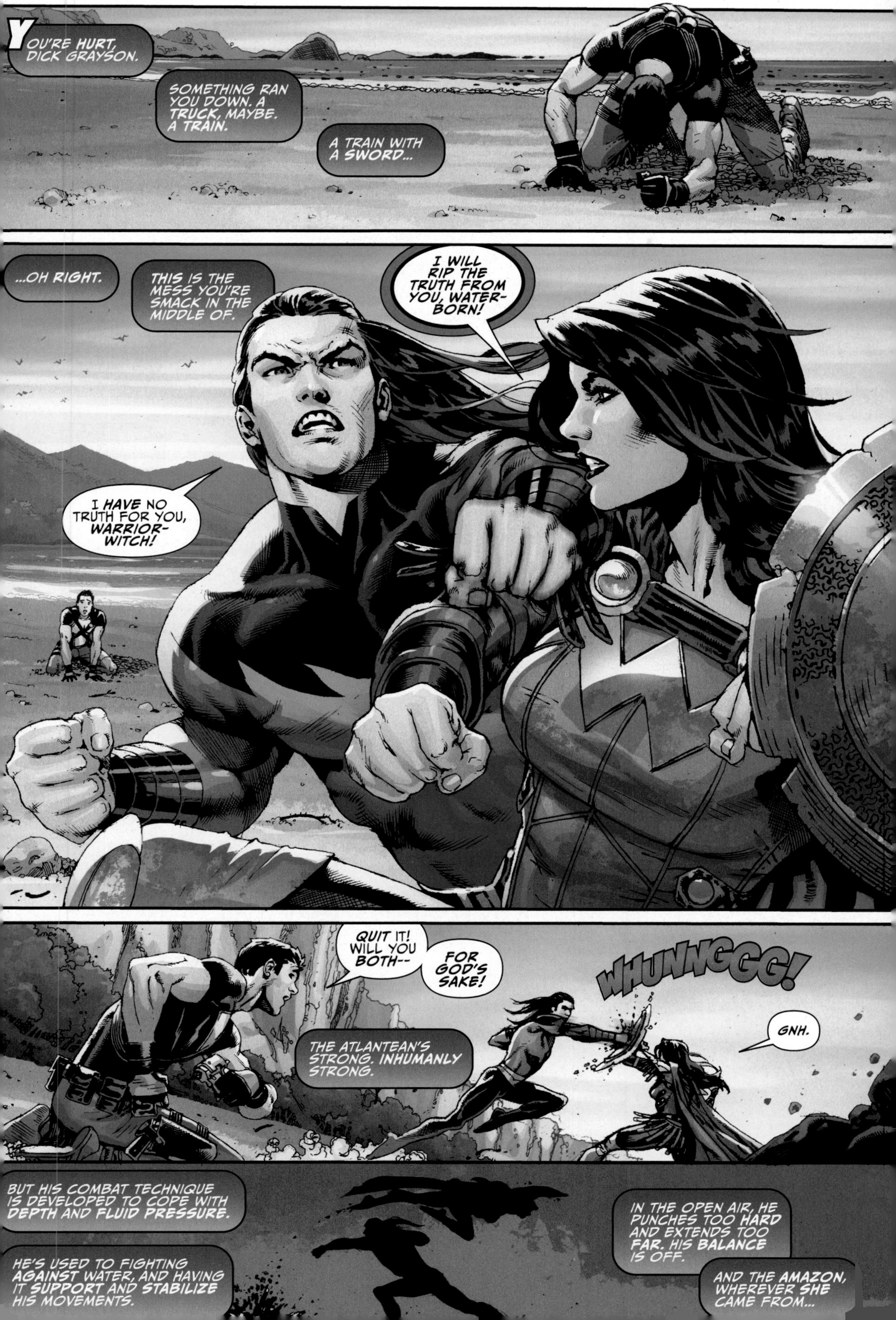
YOU'RE HURT, DICK GRAYSON.
SOMETHING RAN YOU DOWN. A TRUCK, MAYBE. A TRAIN.
A TRAIN WITH A SWORD...
...OH RIGHT.
THIS IS THE MESS YOU'RE SMACK IN THE MIDDLE OF.
I WILL RIP THE TRUTH FROM YOU, WATER-BORN!
I HAVE NO TRUTH FOR YOU, WARRIOR-WITCH!
QUIT IT! WILL YOU BOTH--
FOR GOD'S SAKE!
WHUNNGGG!
GNH.
THE ATLANTEAN'S STRONG. INHUMANLY STRONG.
BUT HIS COMBAT TECHNIQUE IS DEVELOPED TO COPE WITH DEPTH AND FLUID PRESSURE.
HE'S USED TO FIGHTING AGAINST WATER, AND HAVING IT SUPPORT AND STABILIZE HIS MOVEMENTS.
IN THE OPEN AIR, HE PUNCHES TOO HARD AND EXTENDS TOO FAR. HIS BALANCE IS OFF.
AND THE AMAZON, WHEREVER SHE CAME FROM...

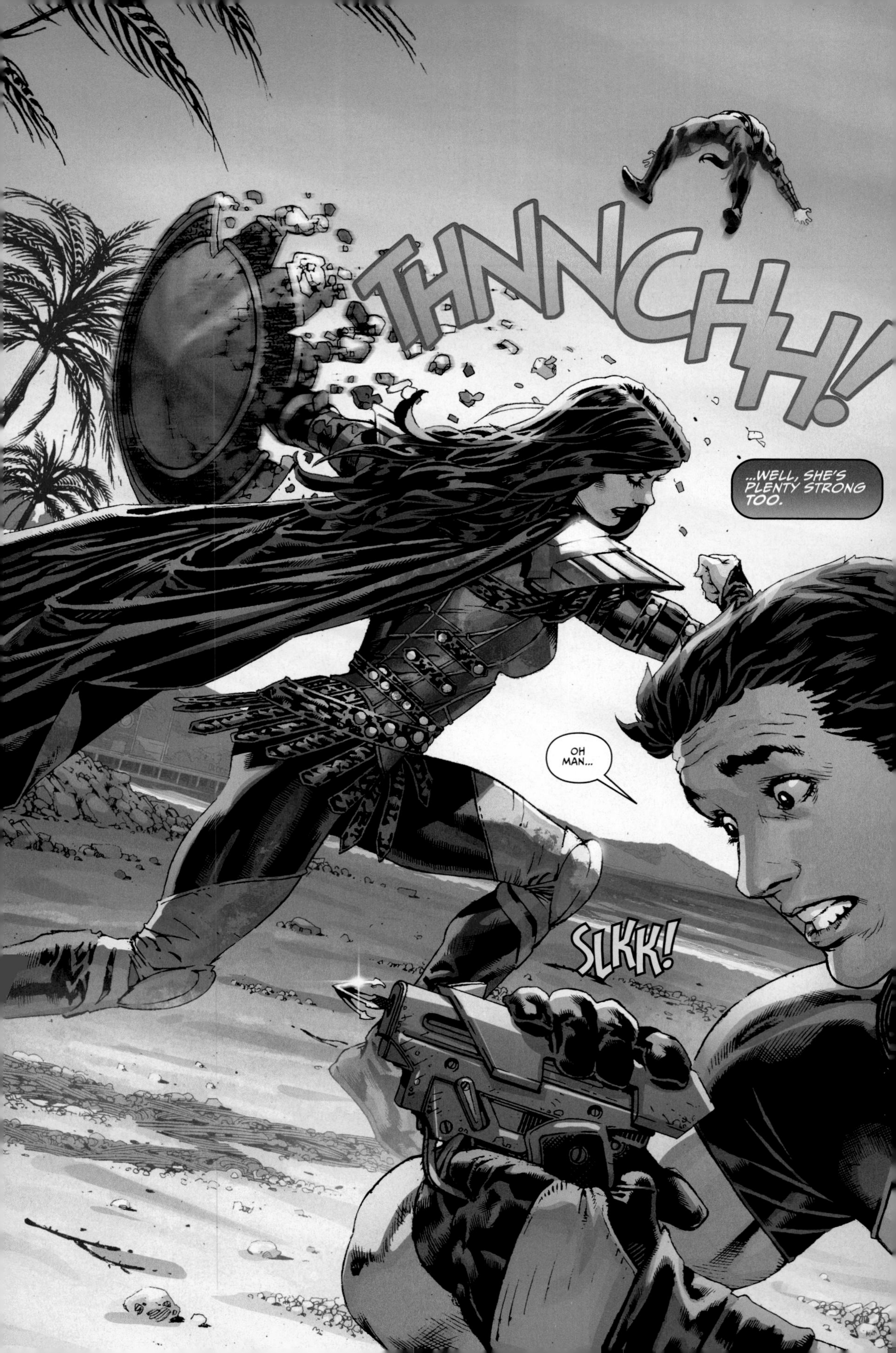
THNNCHH!
...WELL, SHE'S PLENTY STRONG TOO.
OH MAN...
SLKK!

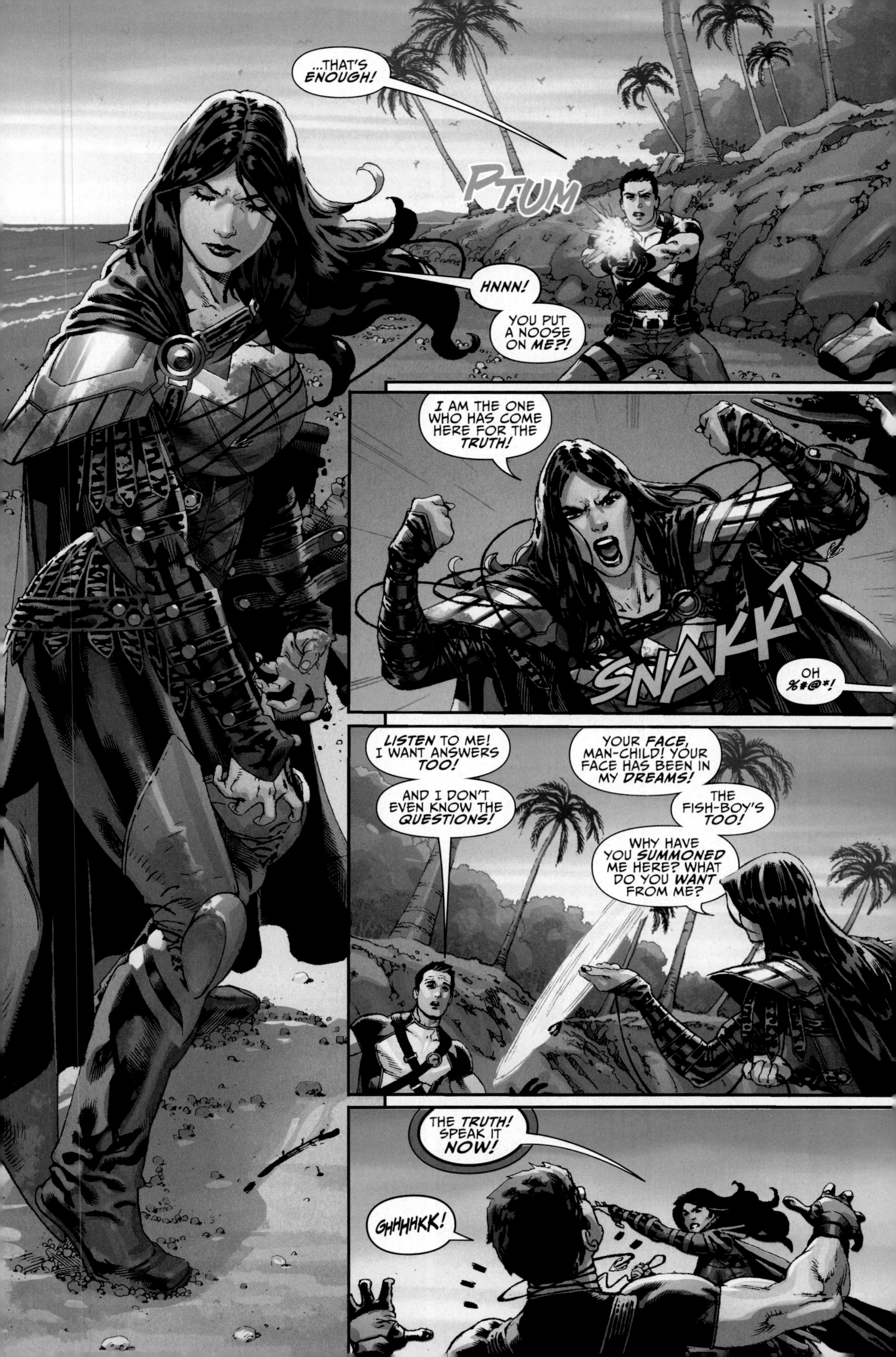
...THAT'S ENOUGH!
PTUM
HNNN!
YOU PUT A NOOSE ON ME?!
I AM THE ONE WHO HAS COME HERE FOR THE TRUTH!
SNAKKT
OH %#@*!
LISTEN TO ME! I WANT ANSWERS TOO!
AND I DON'T EVEN KNOW THE QUESTIONS!
YOUR FACE, MAN-CHILD! YOUR FACE HAS BEEN IN MY DREAMS!
THE FISH-BOY'S TOO!
WHY HAVE YOU SUMMONED ME HERE? WHAT DO YOU WANT FROM ME?
THE TRUTH! SPEAK IT NOW!
GHHHHKK!

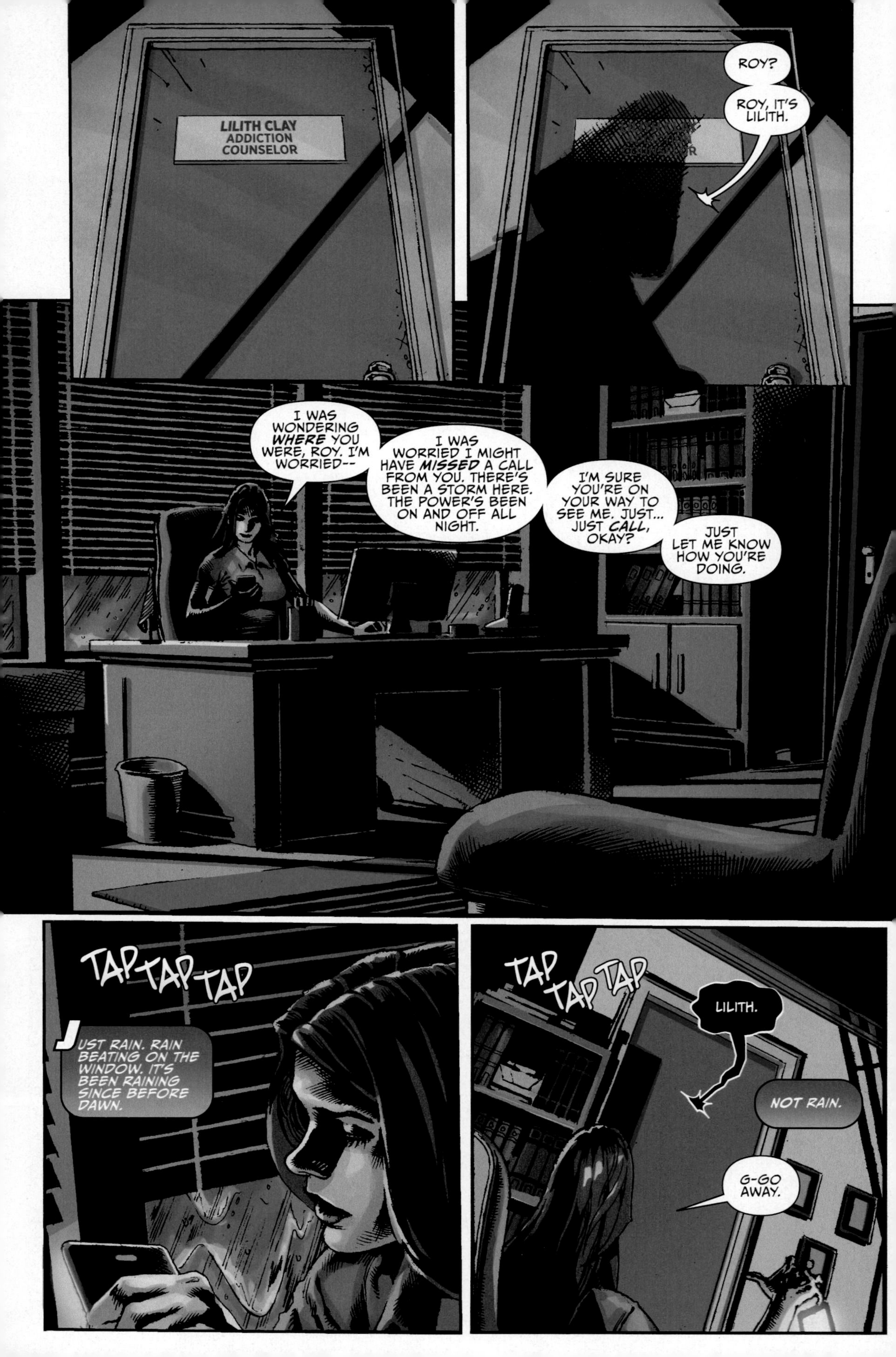
LILITH CLAY
ADDICTION
COUNSELOR
ROY?
ROY, IT'S LILITH.
I WAS WONDERING *WHERE* YOU WERE, ROY. I'M WORRIED--
I WAS WORRIED I MIGHT HAVE *MISSED* A CALL FROM YOU. THERE'S BEEN A STORM HERE. THE POWER'S BEEN ON AND OFF ALL NIGHT.
I'M SURE YOU'RE ON YOUR WAY TO SEE ME. JUST... JUST *CALL*, OKAY?
JUST LET ME KNOW HOW YOU'RE DOING.
TAP-TAP-TAP
JUST RAIN. RAIN BEATING ON THE WINDOW. IT'S BEEN RAINING SINCE BEFORE DAWN.
TAP TAP TAP
LILITH.
NOT RAIN.
G-GO AWAY.

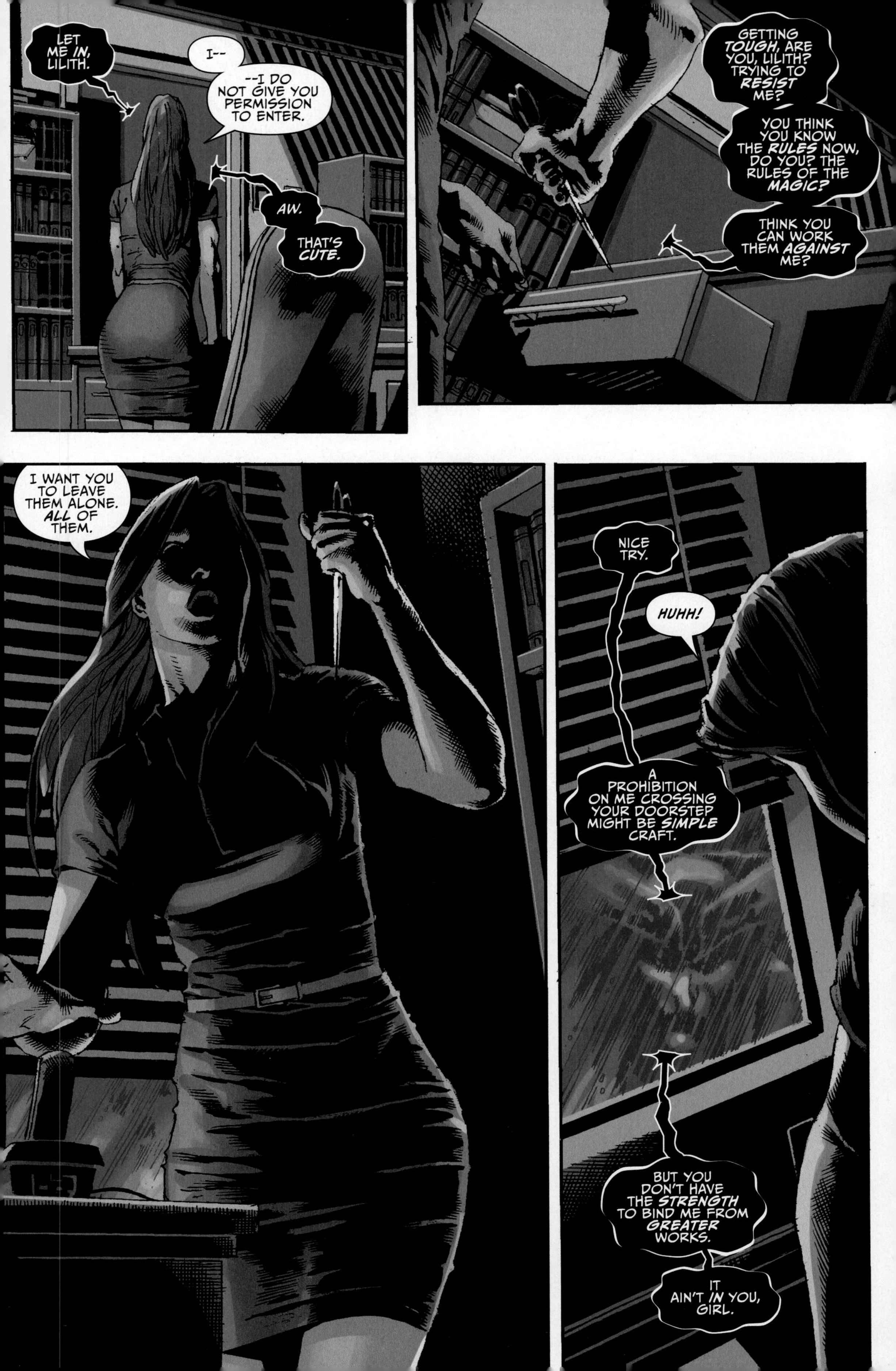
LET ME IN, LILITH.
I--
--I DO NOT GIVE YOU PERMISSION TO ENTER.
AW.
THAT'S CUTE.
GETTING TOUGH, ARE YOU, LILITH? TRYING TO RESIST ME?
YOU THINK YOU KNOW THE RULES NOW, DO YOU? THE RULES OF THE MAGIC?
THINK YOU CAN WORK THEM AGAINST ME?
I WANT YOU TO LEAVE THEM ALONE. ALL OF THEM.
NICE TRY.
HUHH!
A PROHIBITION ON ME CROSSING YOUR DOORSTEP MIGHT BE SIMPLE CRAFT.
BUT YOU DON'T HAVE THE STRENGTH TO BIND ME FROM GREATER WORKS.
IT AIN'T IN YOU, GIRL.

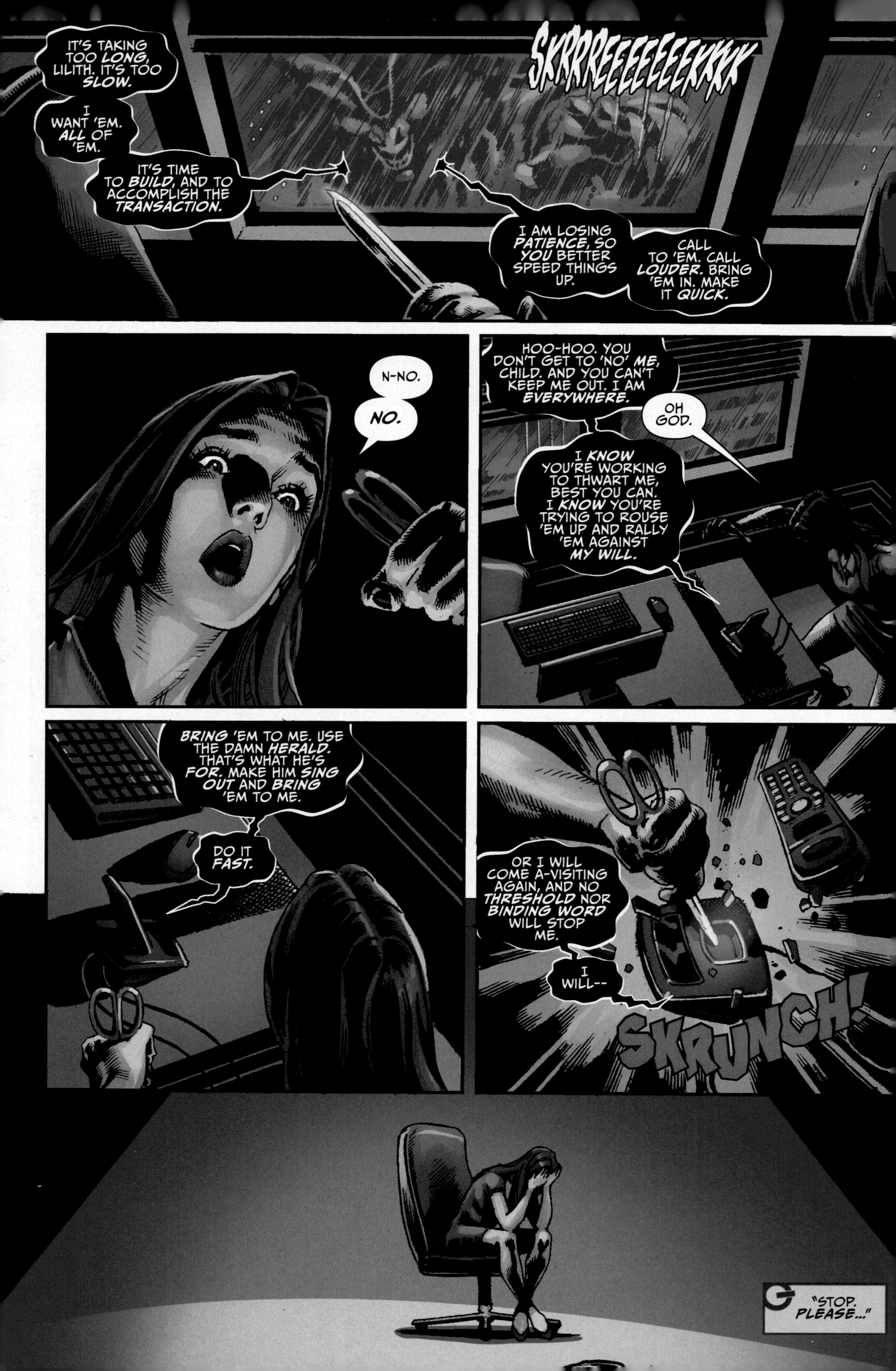

SKRRREEEEEEEKKKK
IT'S TAKING TOO LONG, LILITH. IT'S TOO SLOW.
I WANT 'EM. ALL OF 'EM.
IT'S TIME TO BUILD, AND TO ACCOMPLISH THE TRANSACTION.
I AM LOSING PATIENCE, SO YOU BETTER SPEED THINGS UP.
CALL TO 'EM. CALL LOUDER. BRING 'EM IN. MAKE IT QUICK.
N-NO.
NO.
HOO-HOO. YOU DON'T GET TO 'NO' ME, CHILD. AND YOU CAN'T KEEP ME OUT. I AM EVERYWHERE.
OH GOD.
I KNOW YOU'RE WORKING TO THWART ME, BEST YOU CAN. I KNOW YOU'RE TRYING TO ROUSE 'EM UP AND RALLY 'EM AGAINST MY WILL.
BRING 'EM TO ME. USE THE DAMN HERALD. THAT'S WHAT HE'S FOR. MAKE HIM SING OUT AND BRING 'EM TO ME.
DO IT FAST.
OR I WILL COME A-VISITING AGAIN, AND NO THRESHOLD NOR BINDING WORD WILL STOP ME.
I WILL--
SKRUNCH!
"STOP. PLEASE..."

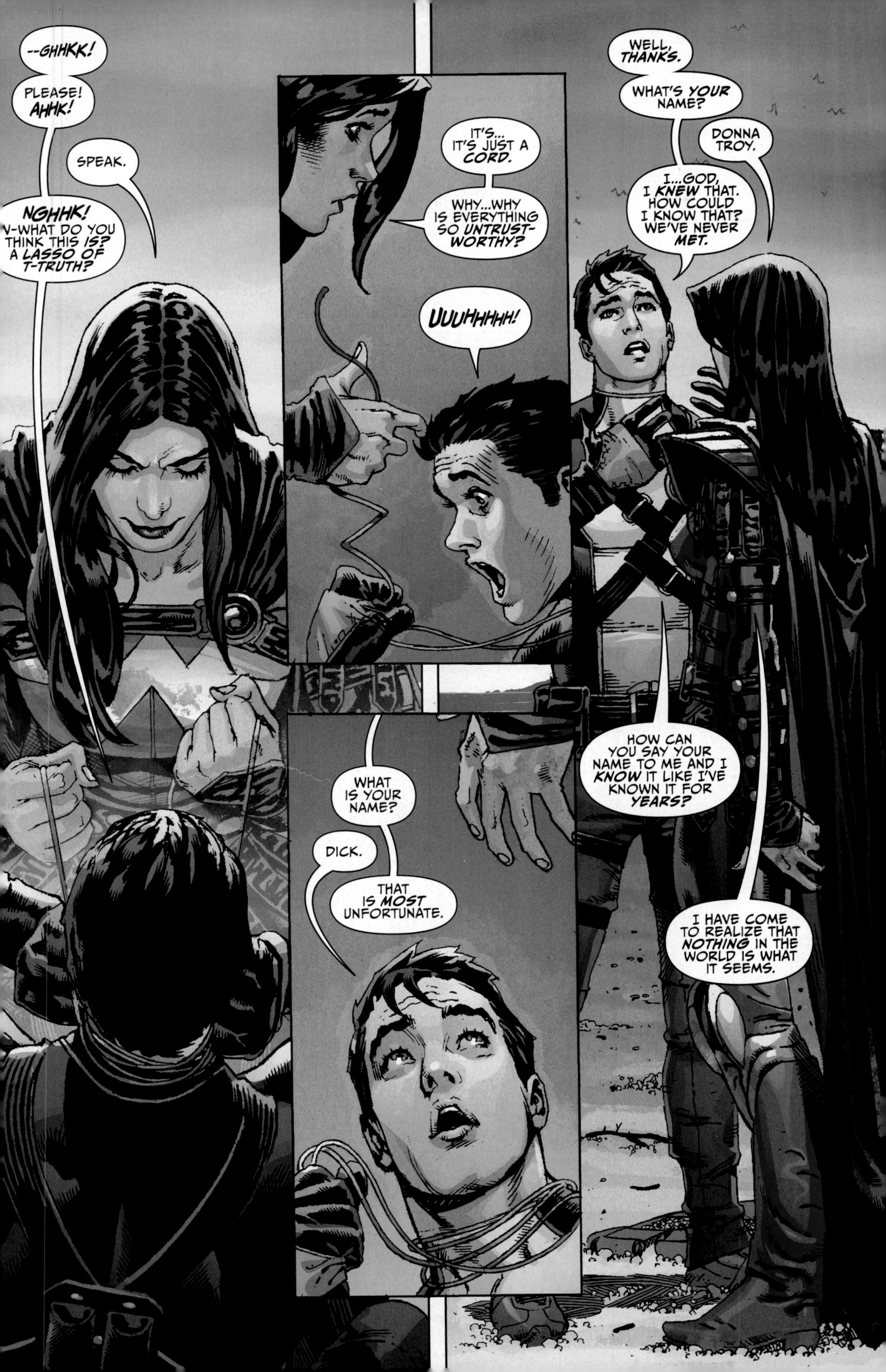
--GHHKK!
PLEASE! AHHK!
SPEAK.
NGHHK! V-WHAT DO YOU THINK THIS IS? A LASSO OF T-TRUTH?
IT'S... IT'S JUST A CORD.
WHY...WHY IS EVERYTHING SO UNTRUST-WORTHY?
UUUHHHHH!
WHAT IS YOUR NAME?
DICK.
THAT IS MOST UNFORTUNATE.
WELL, THANKS.
WHAT'S YOUR NAME?
DONNA TROY.
I...GOD, I KNEW THAT. HOW COULD I KNOW THAT? WE'VE NEVER MET.
HOW CAN YOU SAY YOUR NAME TO ME AND I KNOW IT LIKE I'VE KNOWN IT FOR YEARS?
I HAVE COME TO REALIZE THAT NOTHING IN THE WORLD IS WHAT IT SEEMS.

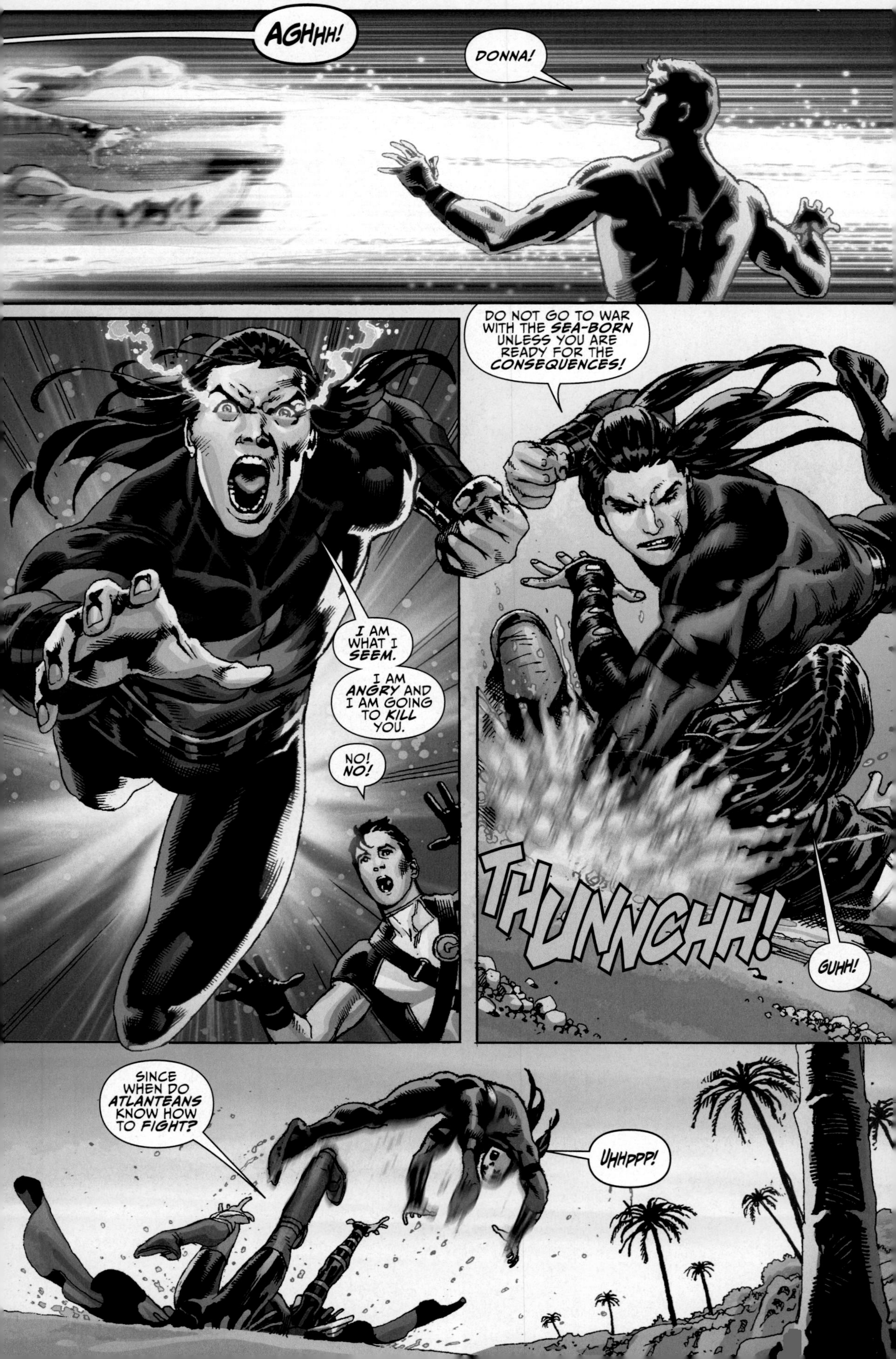
AGHHH!
DONNA!
DO NOT GO TO WAR WITH THE SEA-BORN UNLESS YOU ARE READY FOR THE CONSEQUENCES!
I AM WHAT I SEEM.
I AM ANGRY AND I AM GOING TO KILL YOU.
NO! NO!
THUNNCHH!
GUHH!
SINCE WHEN DO ATLANTEANS KNOW HOW TO FIGHT?
UHHPPP!

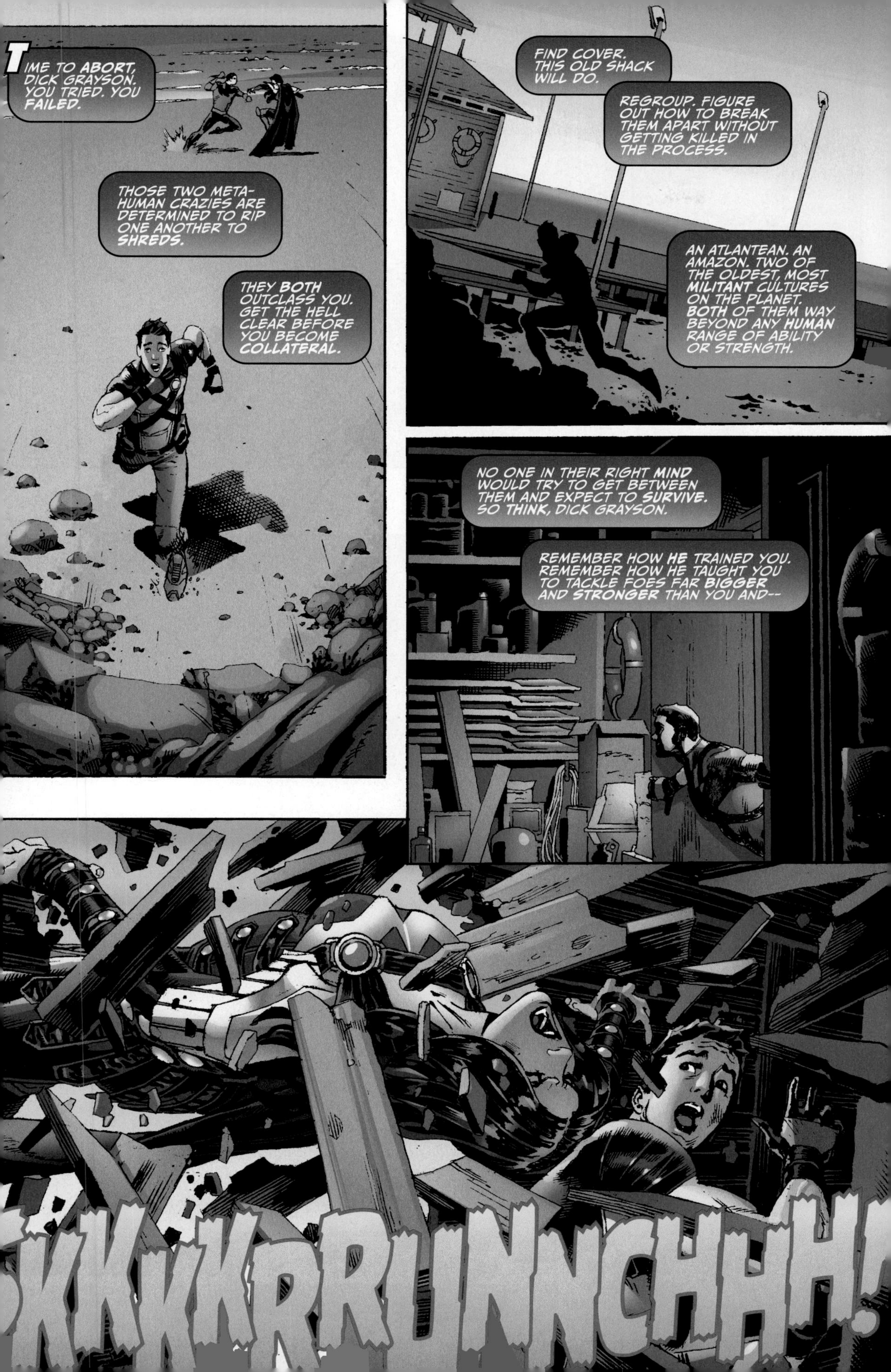
TIME TO ABORT, DICK GRAYSON. YOU TRIED. YOU FAILED.
THOSE TWO META-HUMAN CRAZIES ARE DETERMINED TO RIP ONE ANOTHER TO SHREDS.
THEY BOTH OUTCLASS YOU. GET THE HELL CLEAR BEFORE YOU BECOME COLLATERAL.
FIND COVER. THIS OLD SHACK WILL DO.
REGROUP. FIGURE OUT HOW TO BREAK THEM APART WITHOUT GETTING KILLED IN THE PROCESS.
AN ATLANTEAN. AN AMAZON. TWO OF THE OLDEST, MOST MILITANT CULTURES ON THE PLANET. BOTH OF THEM WAY BEYOND ANY HUMAN RANGE OF ABILITY OR STRENGTH.
NO ONE IN THEIR RIGHT MIND WOULD TRY TO GET BETWEEN THEM AND EXPECT TO SURVIVE. SO THINK, DICK GRAYSON.
REMEMBER HOW HE TRAINED YOU. REMEMBER HOW HE TAUGHT YOU TO TACKLE FOES FAR BIGGER AND STRONGER THAN YOU AND--
SKKKRRUNNCHHH!

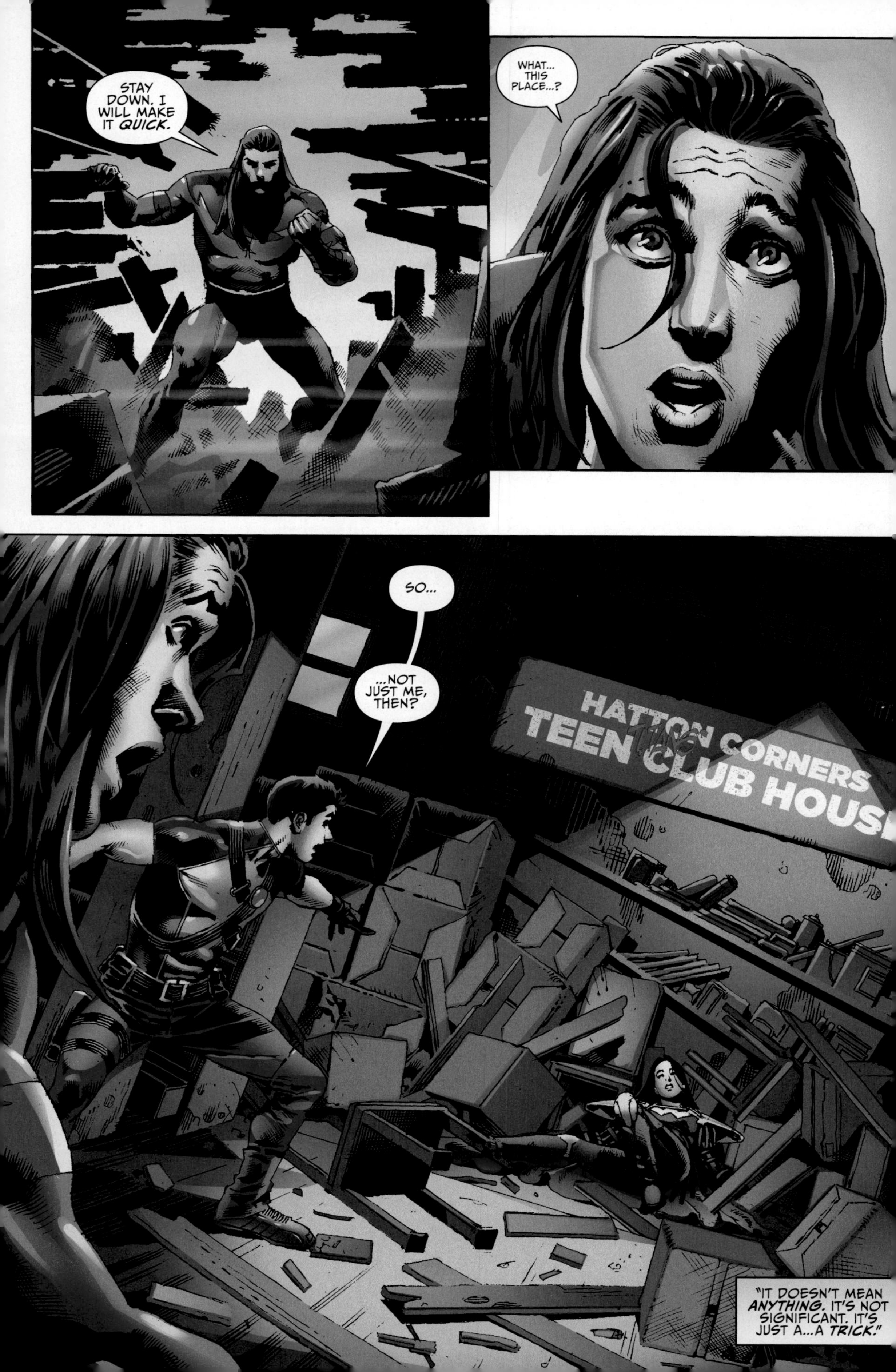
STAY DOWN. I WILL MAKE IT *QUICK.*
WHAT... THIS PLACE...?
SO...
...NOT JUST ME, THEN?
HATTON CORNERS
TEEN TITANS CLUB HOUSE
"IT DOESN'T MEAN *ANYTHING.* IT'S NOT SIGNIFICANT. IT'S JUST A...A *TRICK.*"

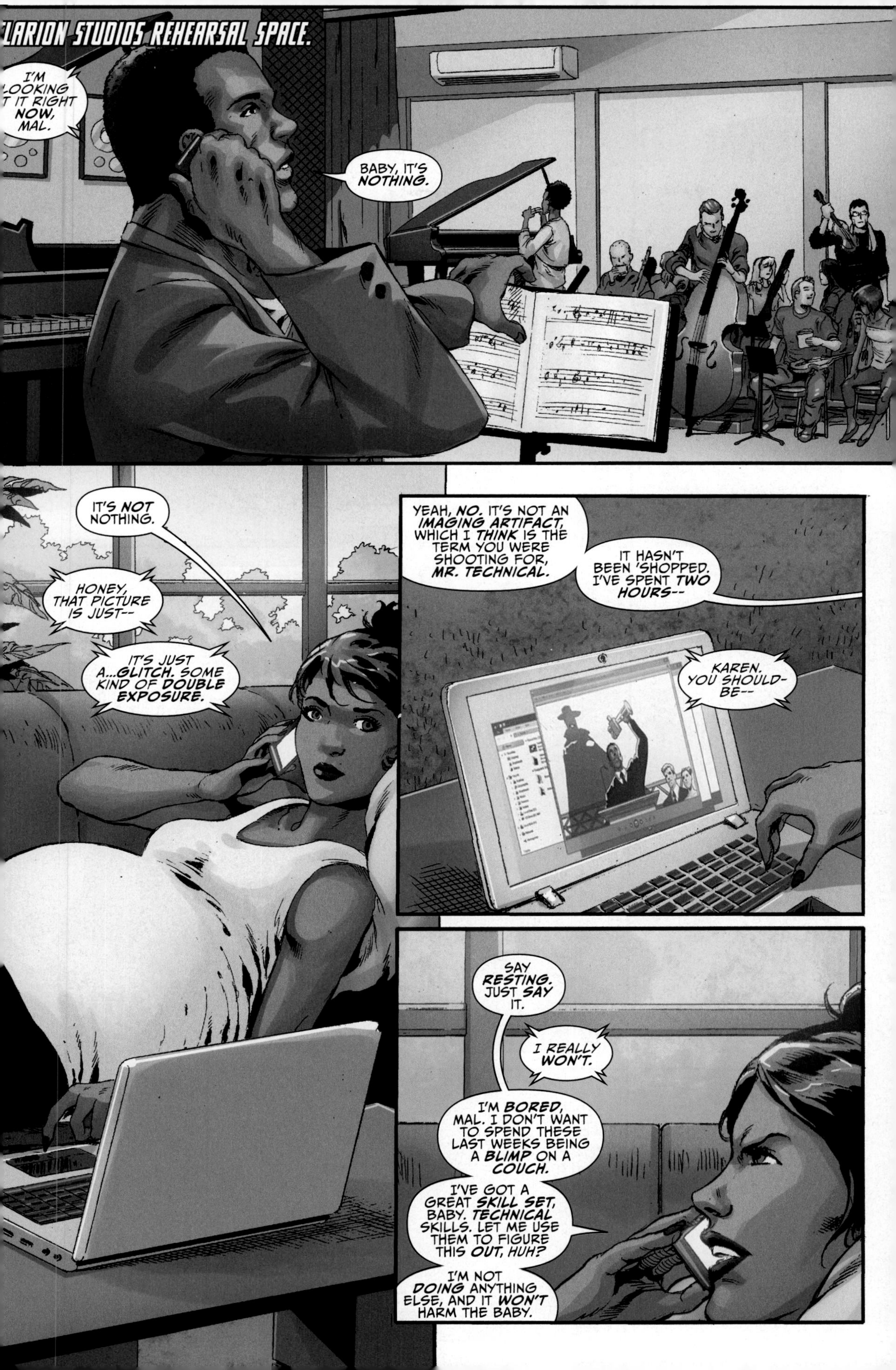
CLARION STUDIOS REHEARSAL SPACE.
I'M LOOKING AT IT RIGHT NOW, MAL.
BABY, IT'S NOTHING.
IT'S NOT NOTHING.
HONEY, THAT PICTURE IS JUST--
IT'S JUST A...GLITCH. SOME KIND OF DOUBLE EXPOSURE.
YEAH, NO. IT'S NOT AN IMAGING ARTIFACT, WHICH I THINK IS THE TERM YOU WERE SHOOTING FOR, MR. TECHNICAL.
IT HASN'T BEEN 'SHOPPED. I'VE SPENT TWO HOURS--
KAREN. YOU SHOULD-BE--
SAY RESTING. JUST SAY IT.
I REALLY WON'T.
I'M BORED, MAL. I DON'T WANT TO SPEND THESE LAST WEEKS BEING A BLIMP ON A COUCH.
I'VE GOT A GREAT SKILL SET, BABY. TECHNICAL SKILLS. LET ME USE THEM TO FIGURE THIS OUT, HUH?
I'M NOT DOING ANYTHING ELSE, AND IT WON'T HARM THE BABY.

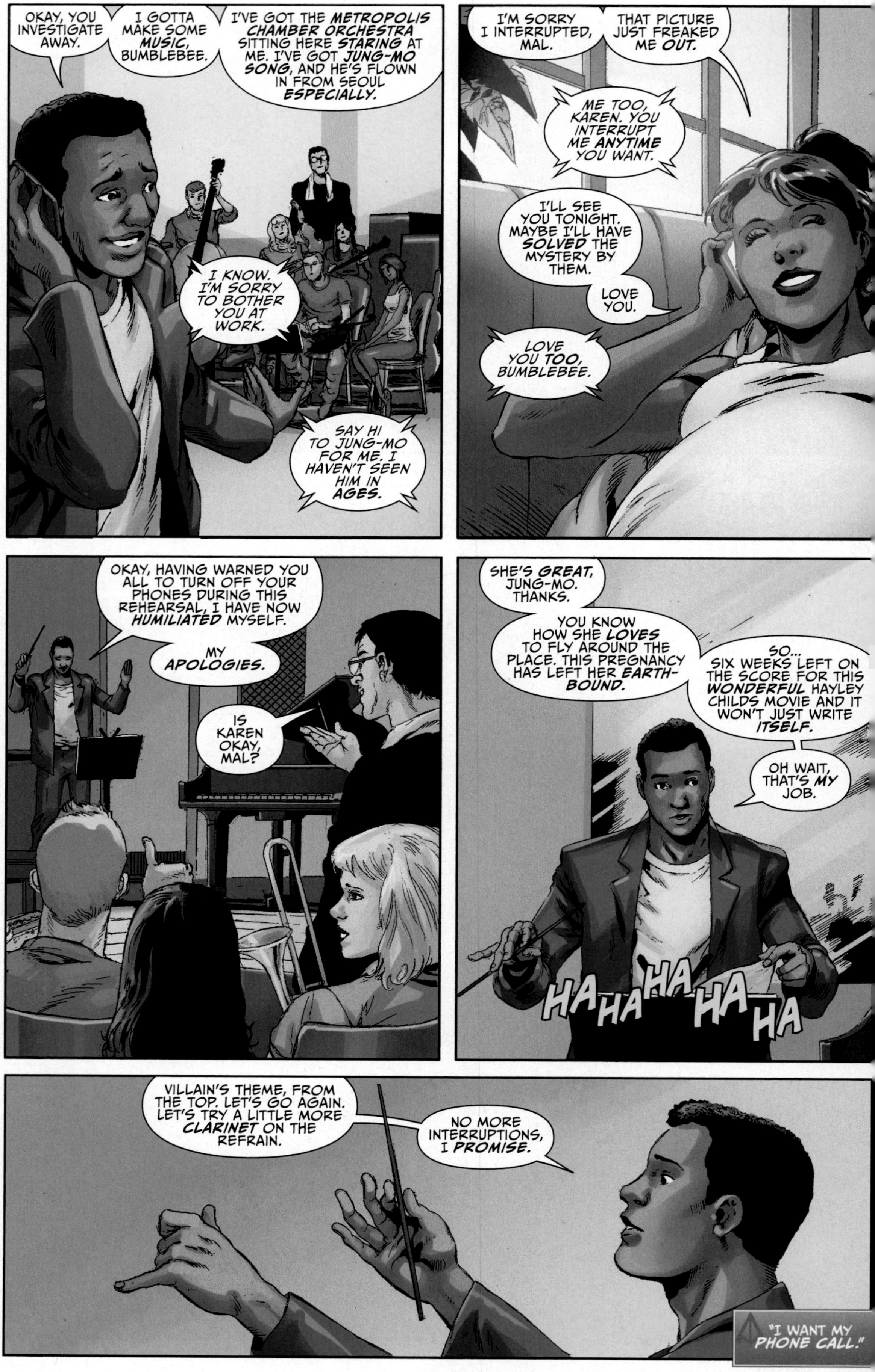

OKAY, YOU INVESTIGATE AWAY.
I GOTTA MAKE SOME MUSIC, BUMBLEBEE.
I'VE GOT THE METROPOLIS CHAMBER ORCHESTRA SITTING HERE STARING AT ME. I'VE GOT JUNG-MO SONG, AND HE'S FLOWN IN FROM SEOUL ESPECIALLY.
I KNOW. I'M SORRY TO BOTHER YOU AT WORK.
SAY HI TO JUNG-MO FOR ME. I HAVEN'T SEEN HIM IN AGES.
I'M SORRY I INTERRUPTED, MAL.
THAT PICTURE JUST FREAKED ME OUT.
ME TOO, KAREN. YOU INTERRUPT ME ANYTIME YOU WANT.
I'LL SEE YOU TONIGHT. MAYBE I'LL HAVE SOLVED THE MYSTERY BY THEM.
LOVE YOU.
LOVE YOU TOO, BUMBLEBEE.
OKAY, HAVING WARNED YOU ALL TO TURN OFF YOUR PHONES DURING THIS REHEARSAL, I HAVE NOW HUMILIATED MYSELF.
MY APOLOGIES.
IS KAREN OKAY, MAL?
SHE'S GREAT, JUNG-MO. THANKS.
YOU KNOW HOW SHE LOVES TO FLY AROUND THE PLACE. THIS PREGNANCY HAS LEFT HER EARTH-BOUND.
SO... SIX WEEKS LEFT ON THE SCORE FOR THIS WONDERFUL HAYLEY CHILDS MOVIE AND IT WON'T JUST WRITE ITSELF.
OH WAIT, THAT'S MY JOB.
HA HA HA HA HA HA HA
VILLAIN'S THEME, FROM THE TOP. LET'S GO AGAIN. LET'S TRY A LITTLE MORE CLARINET ON THE REFRAIN.
NO MORE INTERRUPTIONS, I PROMISE.
"I WANT MY PHONE CALL."

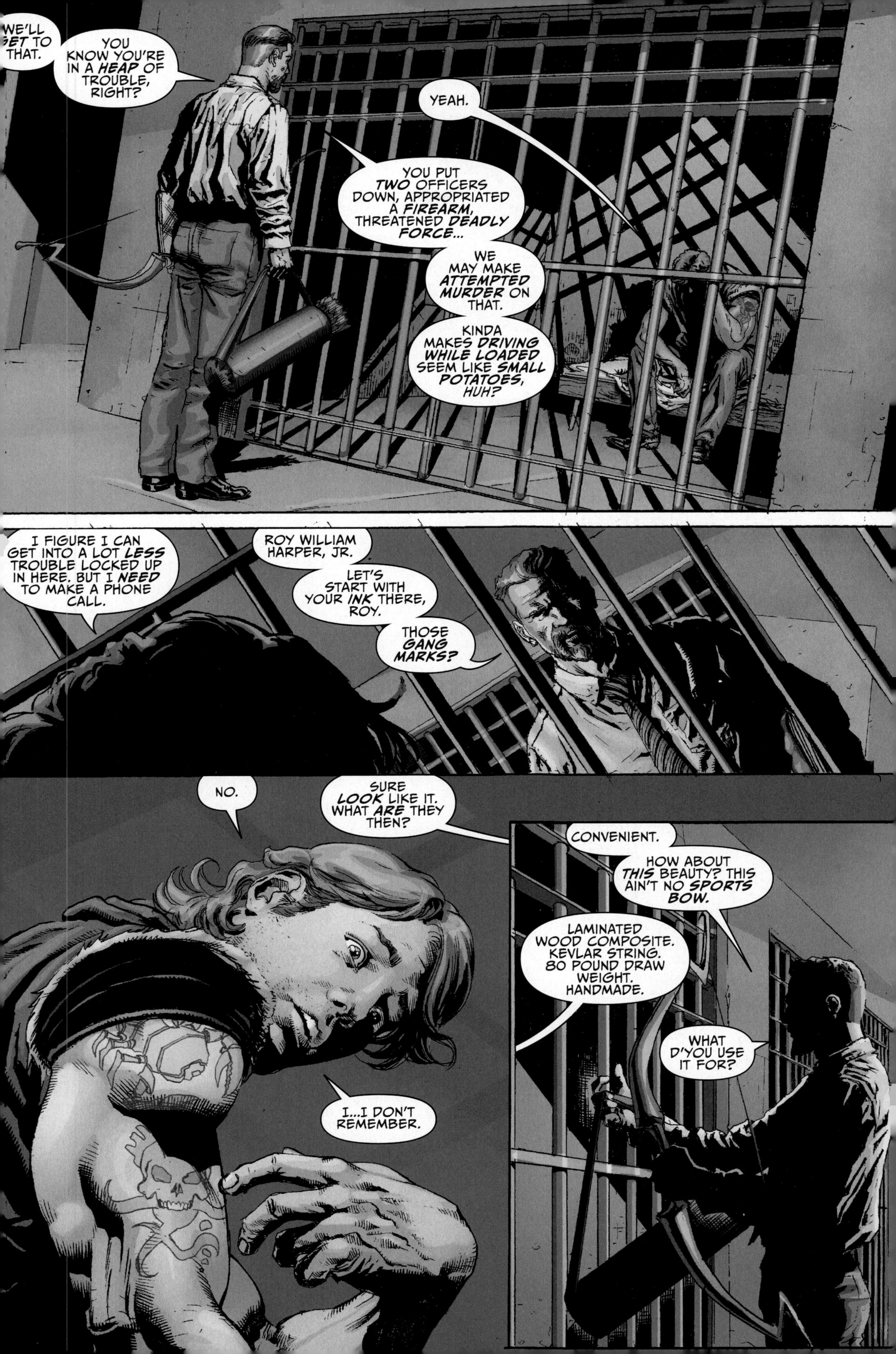
WE'LL GET TO THAT.
YOU KNOW YOU'RE IN A HEAP OF TROUBLE, RIGHT?
YEAH.
YOU PUT TWO OFFICERS DOWN, APPROPRIATED A FIREARM, THREATENED DEADLY FORCE...
WE MAY MAKE ATTEMPTED MURDER ON THAT.
KINDA MAKES DRIVING WHILE LOADED SEEM LIKE SMALL POTATOES, HUH?
I FIGURE I CAN GET INTO A LOT LESS TROUBLE LOCKED UP IN HERE. BUT I NEED TO MAKE A PHONE CALL.
ROY WILLIAM HARPER, JR.
LET'S START WITH YOUR INK THERE, ROY.
THOSE GANG MARKS?
NO.
SURE LOOK LIKE IT. WHAT ARE THEY THEN?
I...I DON'T REMEMBER.
CONVENIENT.
HOW ABOUT THIS BEAUTY? THIS AIN'T NO SPORTS BOW.
LAMINATED WOOD COMPOSITE. KEVLAR STRING. 80 POUND DRAW WEIGHT. HANDMADE.
WHAT D'YOU USE IT FOR?

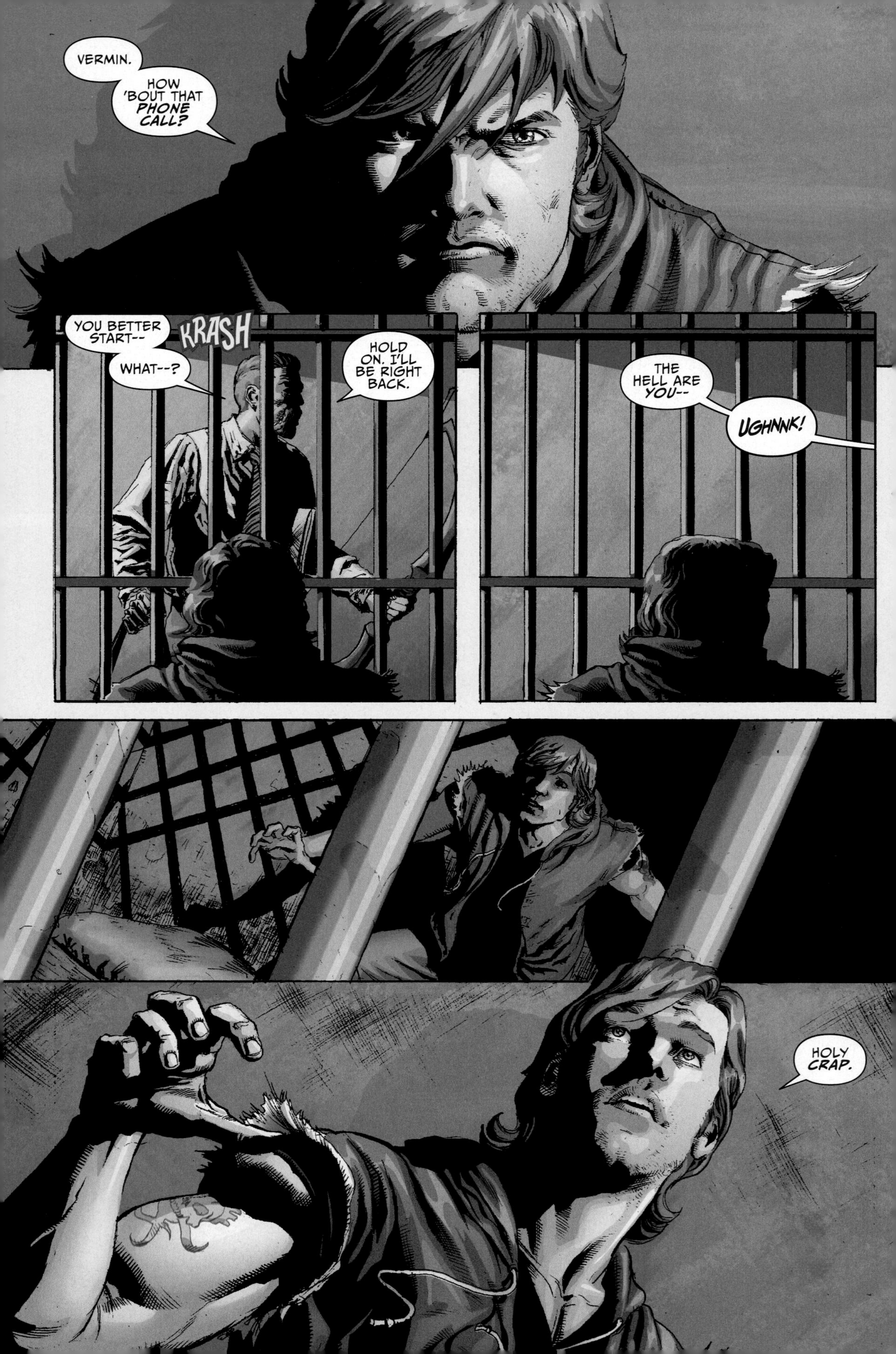
VERMIN.
HOW 'BOUT THAT PHONE CALL?
YOU BETTER START--
KRASH
WHAT--?
HOLD ON. I'LL BE RIGHT BACK.
THE HELL ARE YOU--
UGHNNK!
HOLY CRAP.

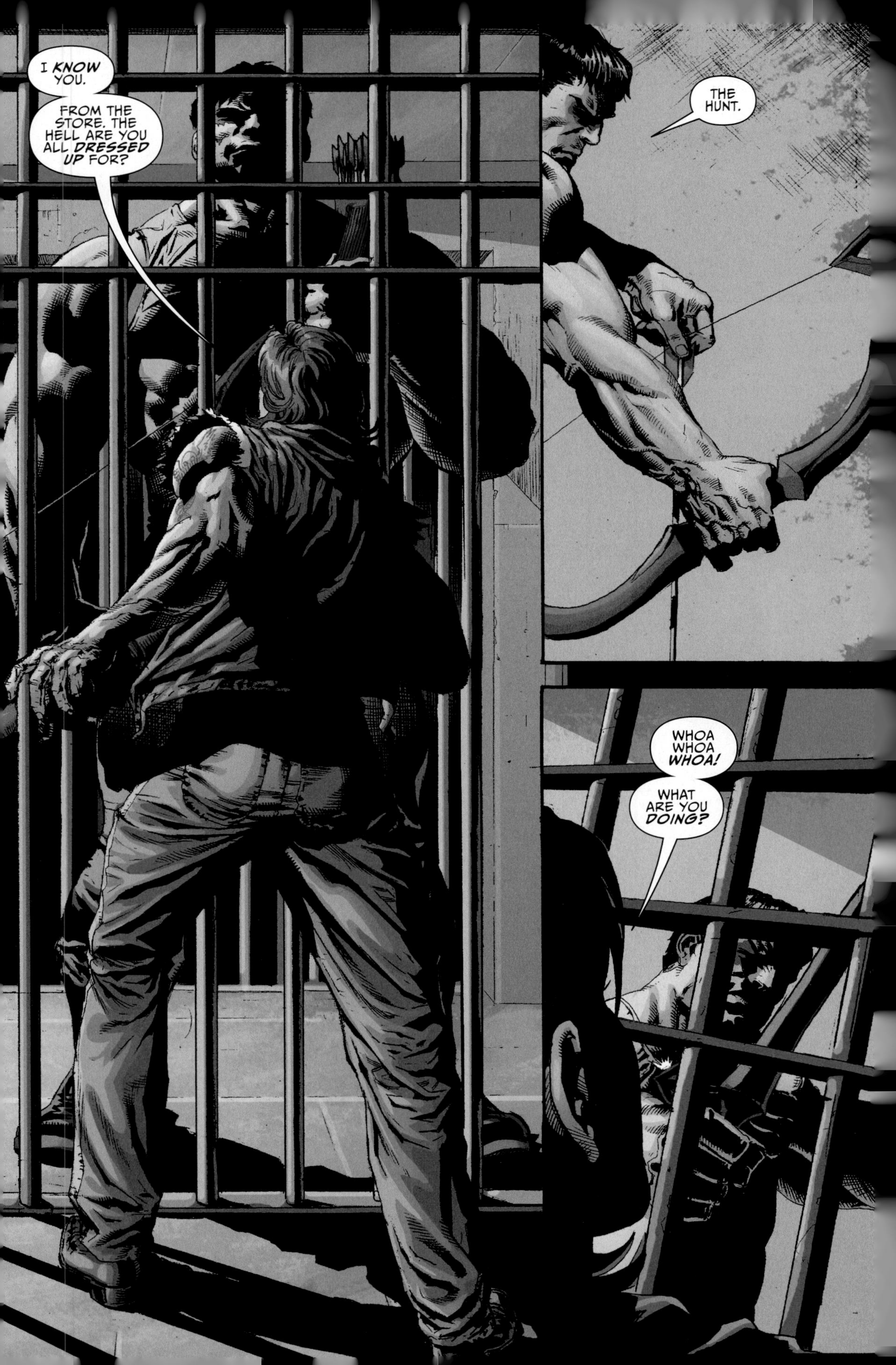
I KNOW YOU.
FROM THE STORE. THE HELL ARE YOU ALL DRESSED UP FOR?
THE HUNT.
WHOA WHOA WHOA!
WHAT ARE YOU DOING?

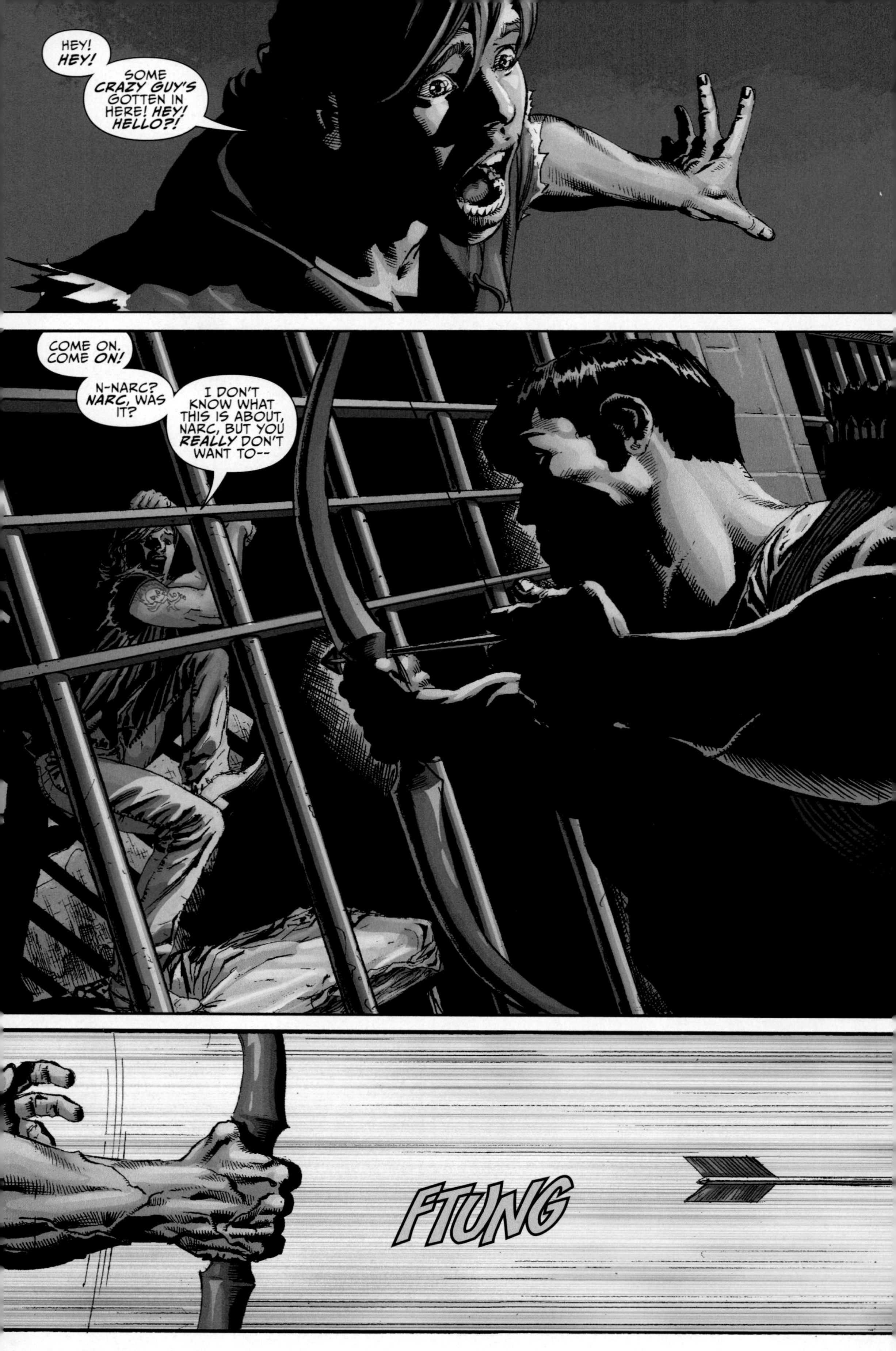
HEY! HEY!
SOME CRAZY GUY'S GOTTEN IN HERE! HEY! HELLO?!
COME ON. COME ON!
N-NARC? NARC, WAS IT?
I DON'T KNOW WHAT THIS IS ABOUT, NARC, BUT YOU REALLY DON'T WANT TO--
FTUNG

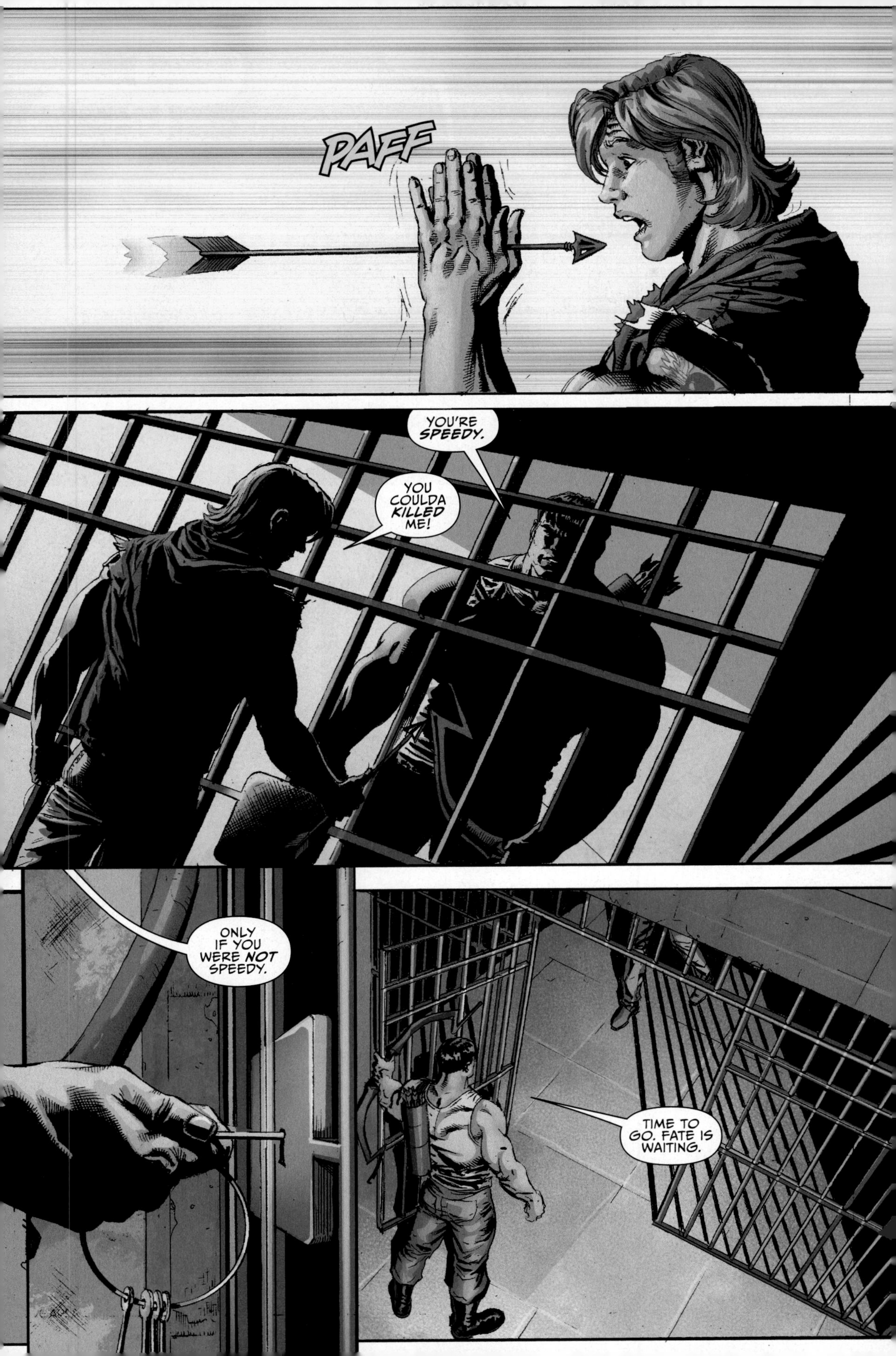
PAFF
YOU'RE SPEEDY.
YOU COULDA KILLED ME!
ONLY IF YOU WERE NOT SPEEDY.
TIME TO GO. FATE IS WAITING.

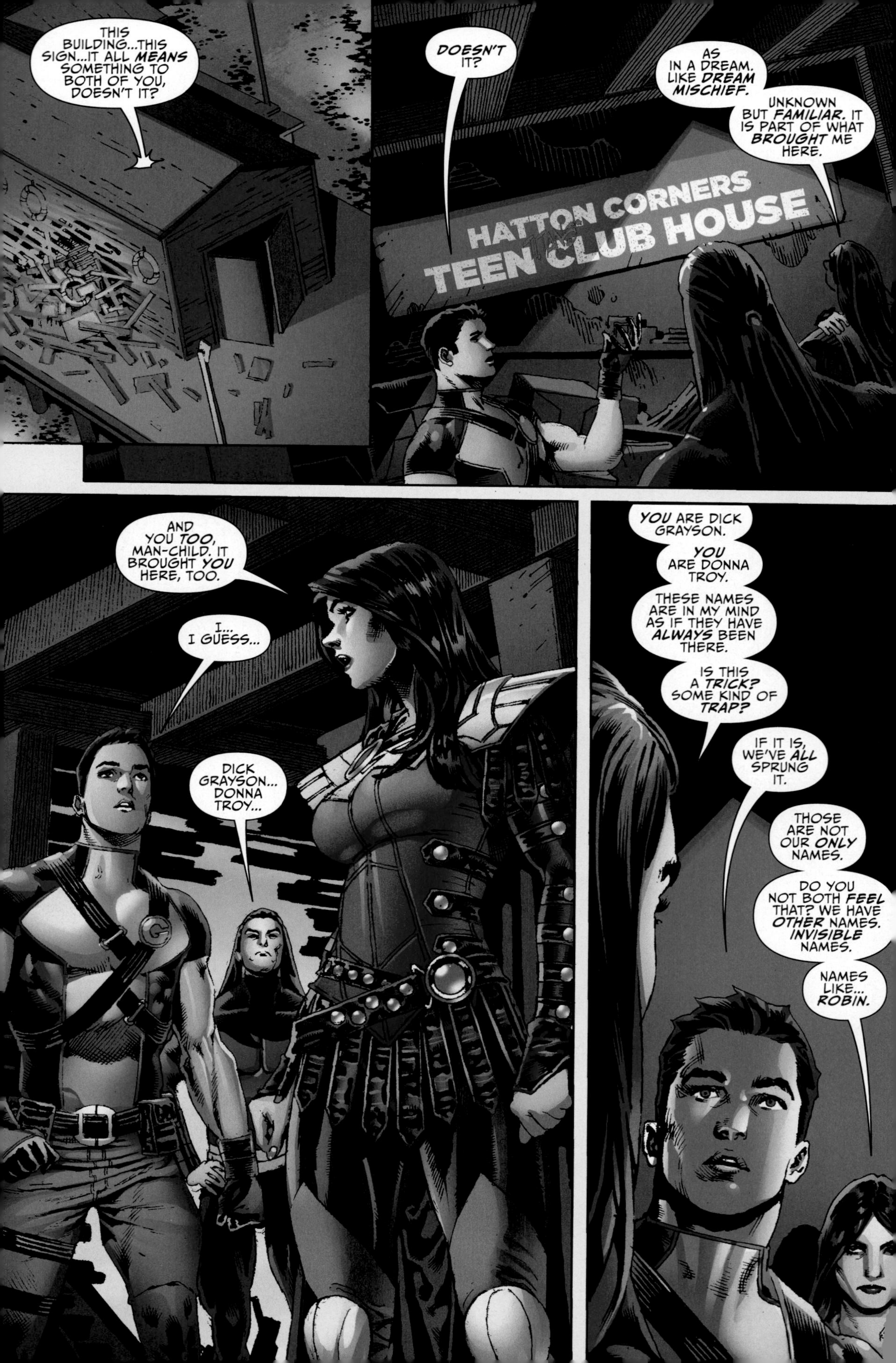
THIS BUILDING...THIS SIGN...IT ALL MEANS SOMETHING TO BOTH OF YOU, DOESN'T IT?
DOESN'T IT?
AS IN A DREAM. LIKE DREAM MISCHIEF.
UNKNOWN BUT FAMILIAR. IT IS PART OF WHAT BROUGHT ME HERE.
HATTON CORNERS
TEEN CLUB HOUSE
AND YOU TOO, MAN-CHILD. IT BROUGHT YOU HERE, TOO.
I... I GUESS...
DICK GRAYSON... DONNA TROY...
YOU ARE DICK GRAYSON.
YOU ARE DONNA TROY.
THESE NAMES ARE IN MY MIND AS IF THEY HAVE ALWAYS BEEN THERE.
IS THIS A TRICK? SOME KIND OF TRAP?
IF IT IS, WE'VE ALL SPRUNG IT.
THOSE ARE NOT OUR ONLY NAMES.
DO YOU NOT BOTH FEEL THAT? WE HAVE OTHER NAMES. INVISIBLE NAMES.
NAMES LIKE... ROBIN.

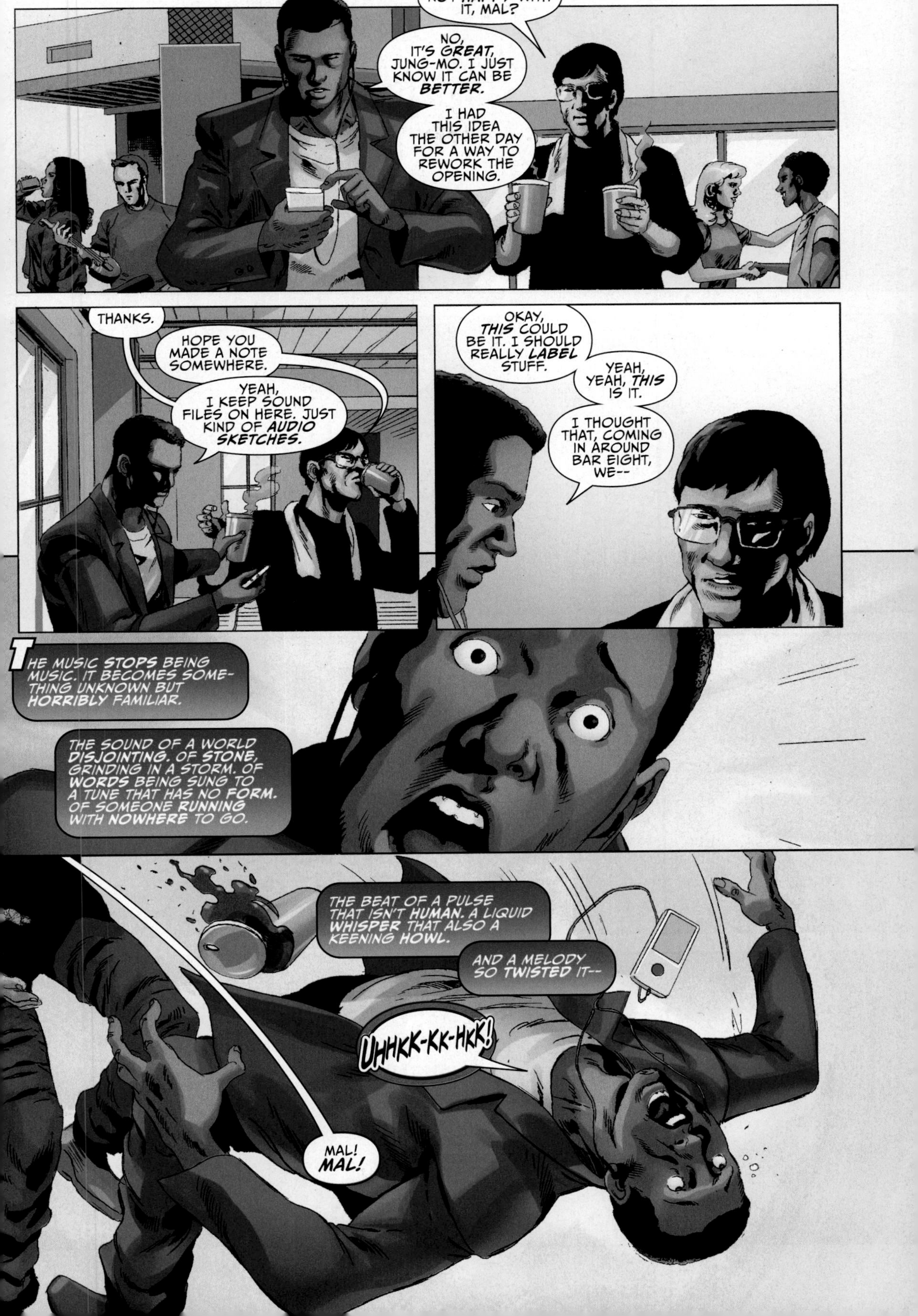
YOU'RE NOT HAPPY WITH IT, MAL?
NO, IT'S GREAT, JUNG-MO. I JUST KNOW IT CAN BE BETTER.
I HAD THIS IDEA THE OTHER DAY FOR A WAY TO REWORK THE OPENING.
THANKS.
HOPE YOU MADE A NOTE SOMEWHERE.
YEAH, I KEEP SOUND FILES ON HERE. JUST KIND OF AUDIO SKETCHES.
OKAY, THIS COULD BE IT. I SHOULD REALLY LABEL STUFF.
YEAH, YEAH, THIS IS IT.
I THOUGHT THAT, COMING IN AROUND BAR EIGHT, WE--
THE MUSIC STOPS BEING MUSIC. IT BECOMES SOMETHING UNKNOWN BUT HORRIBLY FAMILIAR.
THE SOUND OF A WORLD DISJOINTING. OF STONE, GRINDING IN A STORM. OF WORDS BEING SUNG TO A TUNE THAT HAS NO FORM. OF SOMEONE RUNNING WITH NOWHERE TO GO.
THE BEAT OF A PULSE THAT ISN'T HUMAN. A LIQUID WHISPER THAT ALSO A KEENING HOWL.
AND A MELODY SO TWISTED IT--
UHHKK-KK-HKK!
MAL! MAL!

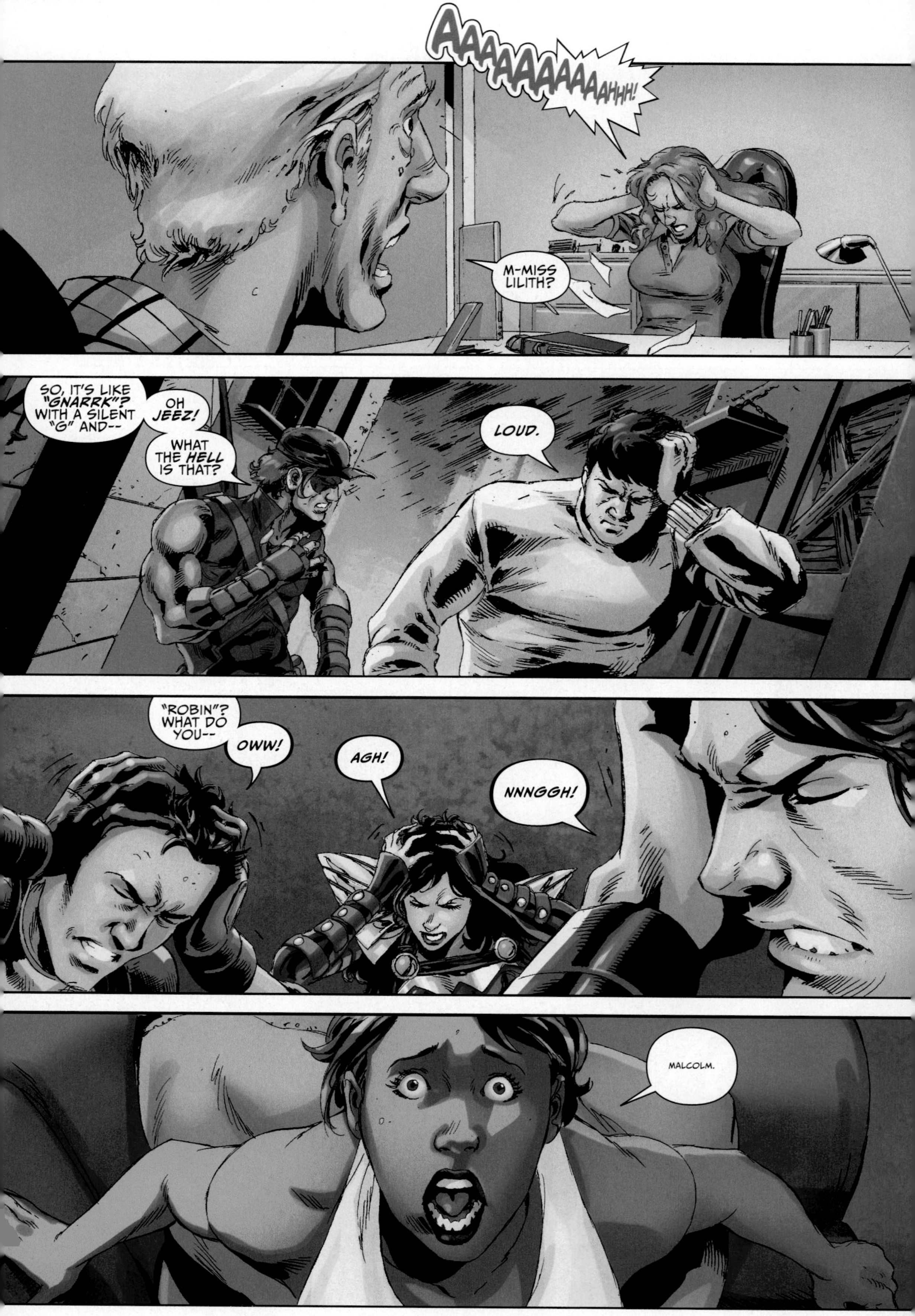
AAAAAAAAAAAAHHH!
M-MISS LILITH?
SO, IT'S LIKE "GNARRK"? WITH A SILENT "G" AND--
OH JEEZ!
WHAT THE HELL IS THAT?
LOUD.
"ROBIN"? WHAT DO YOU--
OWW!
AGH!
NNNGGH!
MALCOLM.

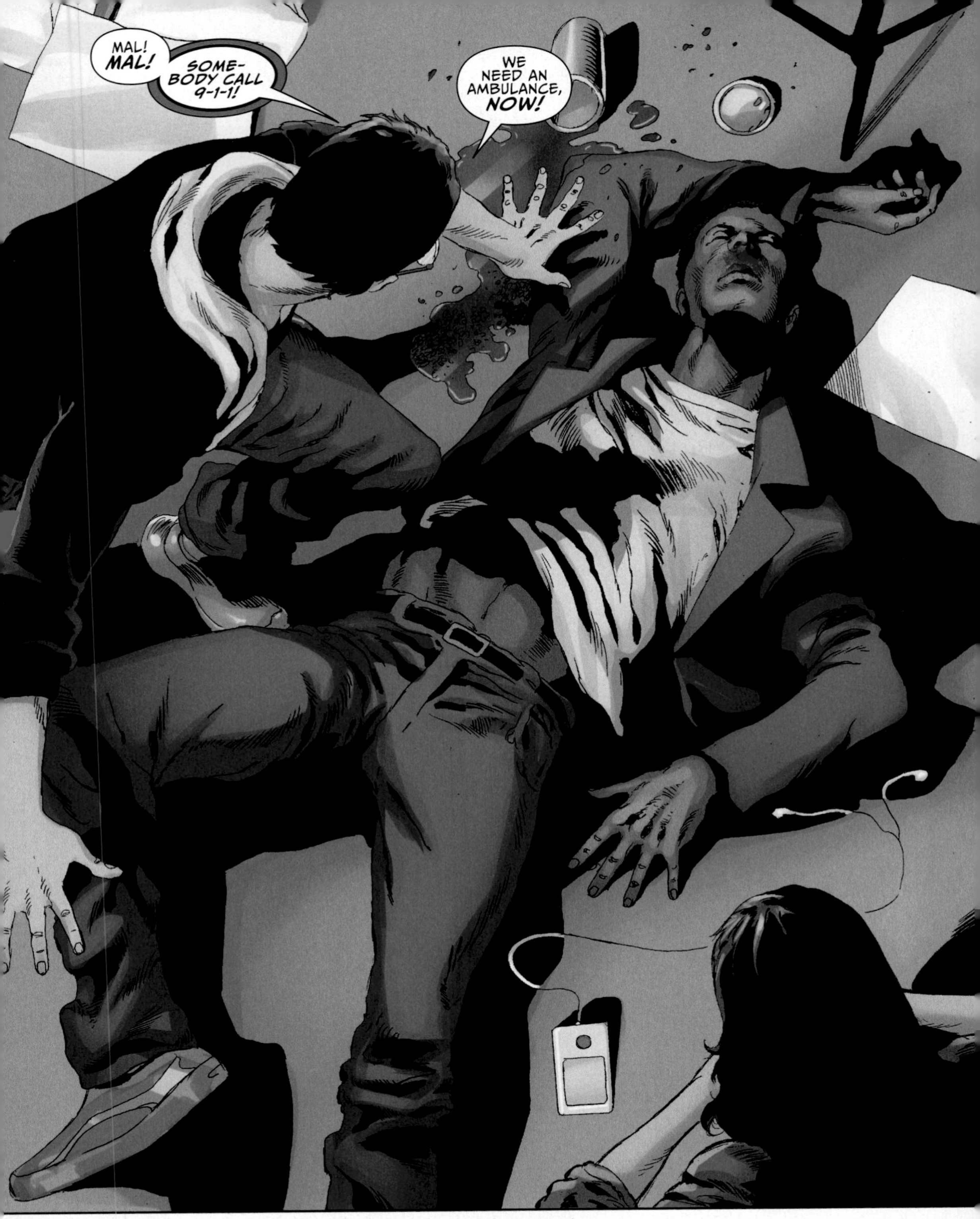
MAL! MAL!
SOME-BODY CALL 9-1-1!
WE NEED AN AMBULANCE, NOW!
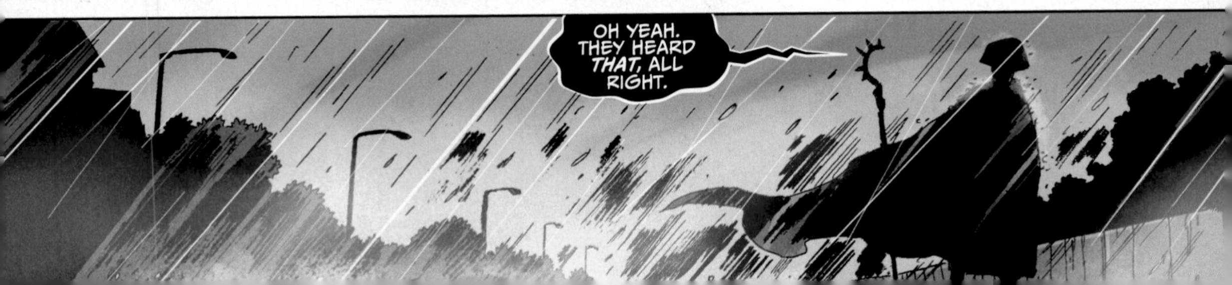
OH YEAH. THEY HEARD THAT, ALL RIGHT.

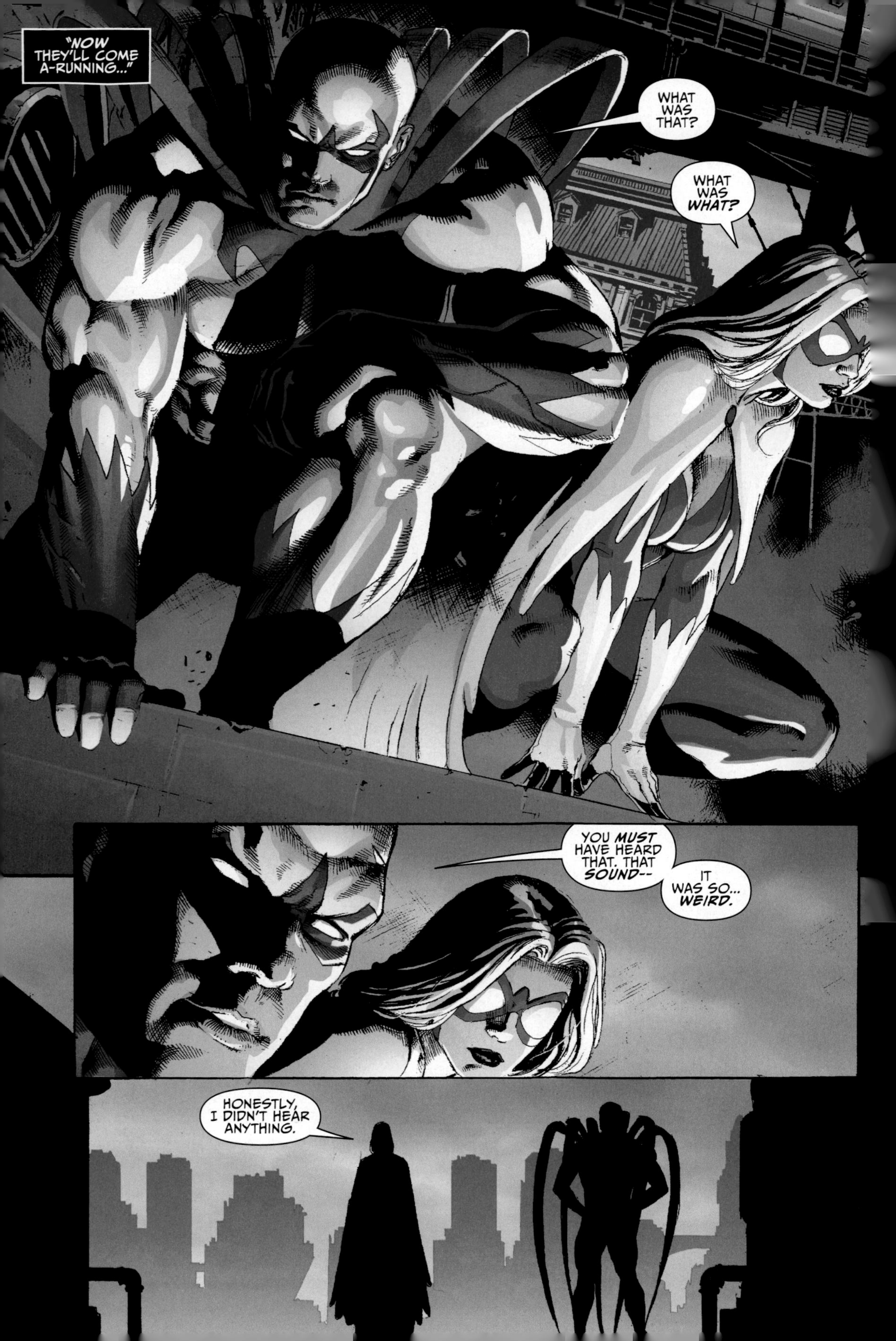
"NOW THEY'LL COME A-RUNNING..."
WHAT WAS THAT?
WHAT WAS *WHAT?*
YOU *MUST* HAVE HEARD THAT. THAT *SOUND*--
IT WAS SO... *WEIRD.*
HONESTLY, I DIDN'T HEAR ANYTHING.

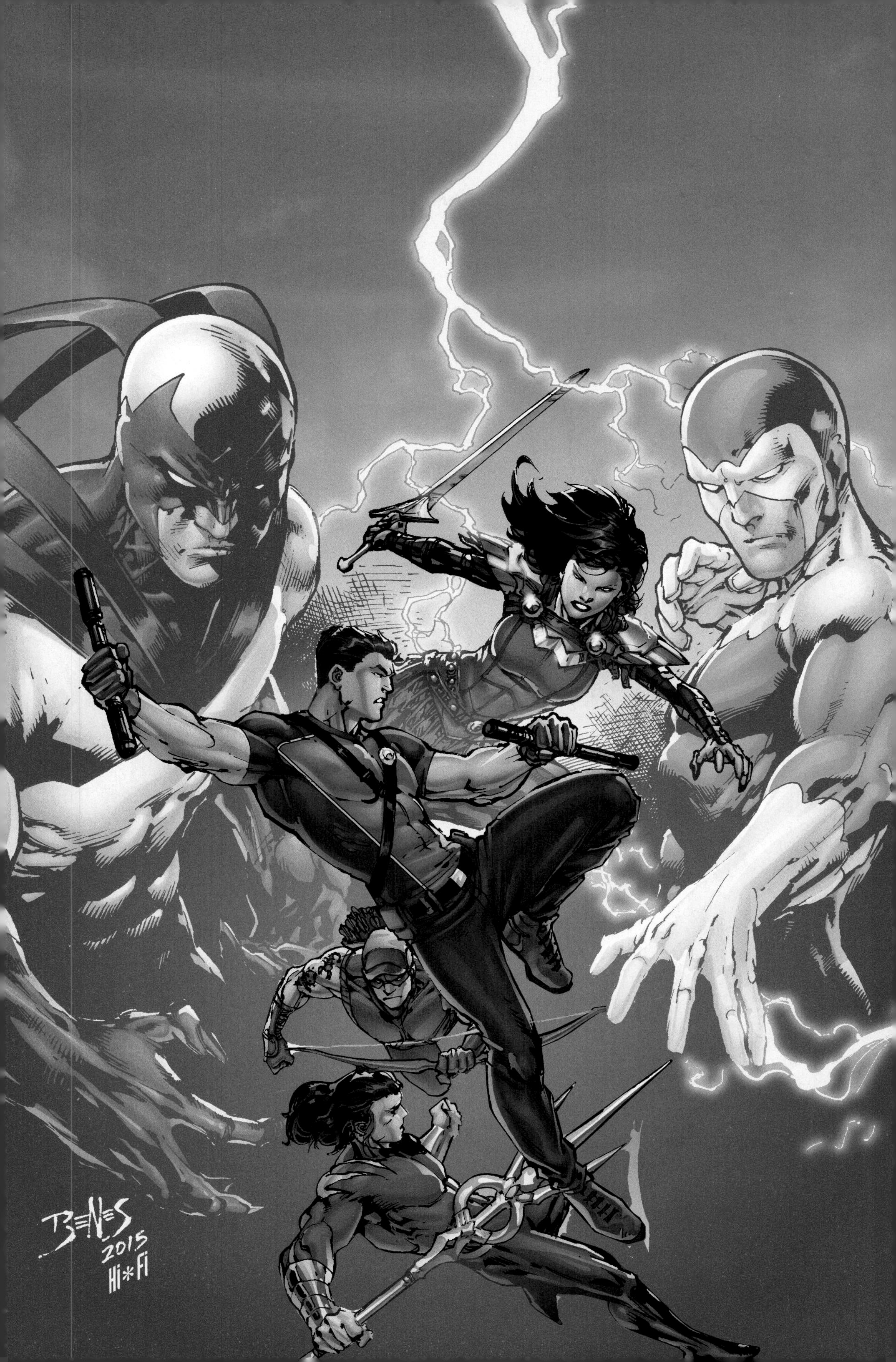
BENES
2015
Hi*Fi

CHAPTER FOUR: MASKS

DAN ABNETT writer STEPHEN SEGOVIA penciller ART THIBERT inker HI-FI colorist cover art by ED BENES & HI-FI

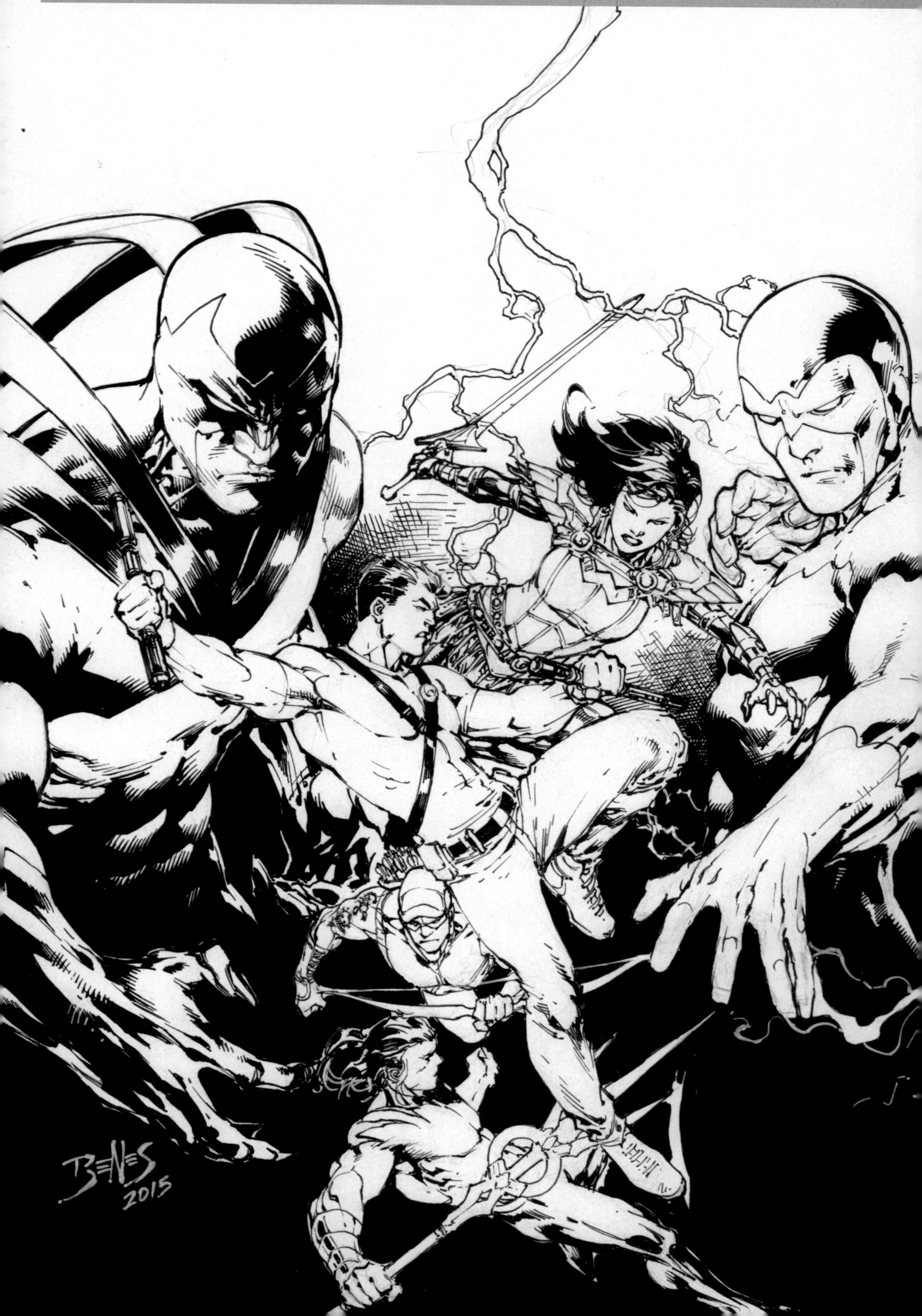
BENES
2015

OH GOD. THAT SCREAM!
WHAT HAPPENED? WHERE'S HERALD?
GONE. THAT...THING CAME OUT OF NOWHERE AND SNATCHED HIM.
IT WAS HUGE...SO FERAL.
DOVE WENT AFTER THEM.
NO!
DAMMIT! I SAID WE STAY TOGETHER!
THIS IS A TEAM! WE HAVE TO--
TEAM? OUR TEAM SUCKS, DUDE. WE'RE FALLING TO PIECES!
YOU OKAY?
JUST WINDED.
IT KNOCKED ME DOWN, AND GRABBED HERALD.
HERALD SCREAMED. I COULD HEAR IT IN MY MIND...
YOU SAID IT WAS FERAL, LILITH.
WORSE THAN BEFORE.

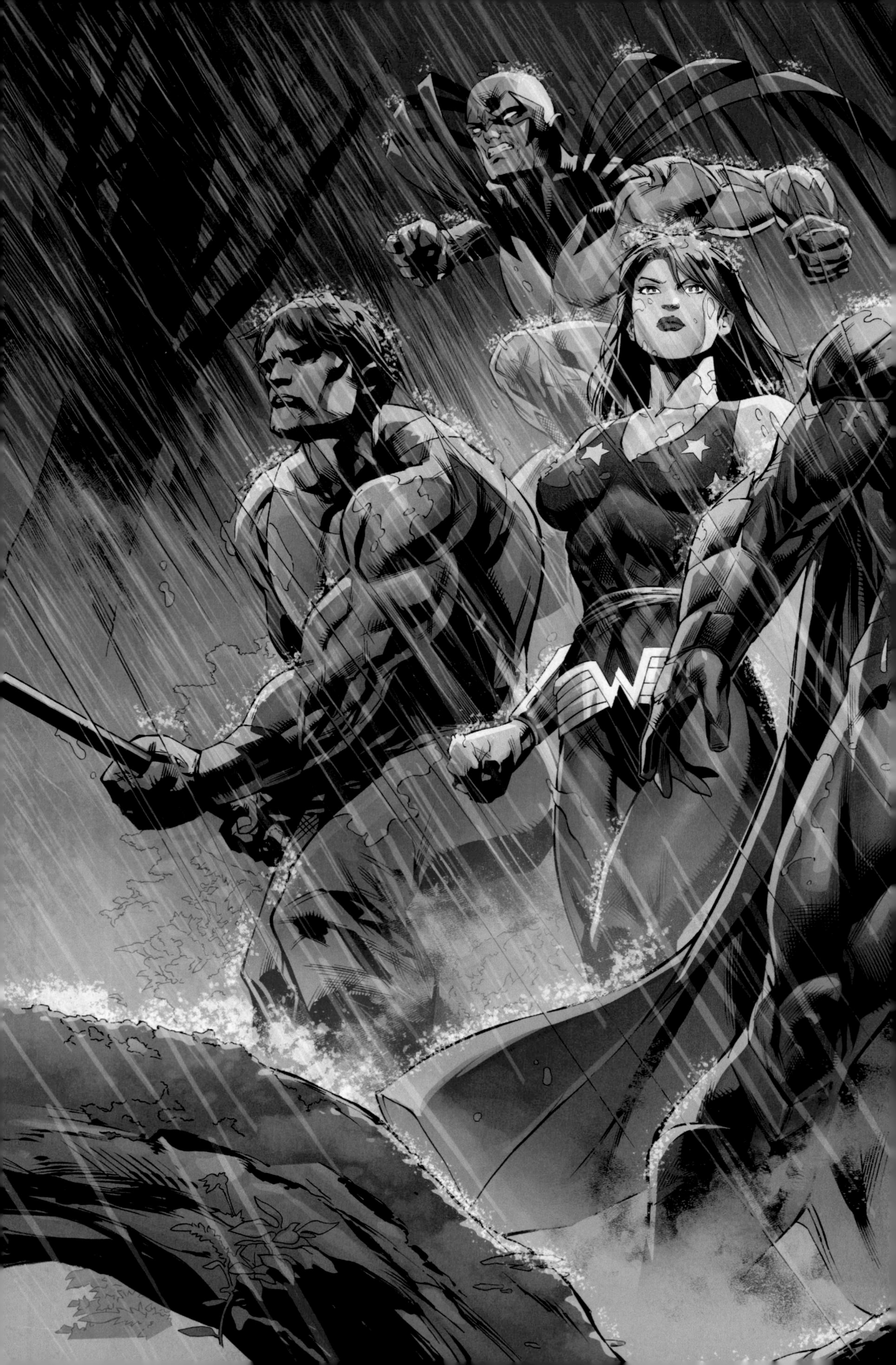

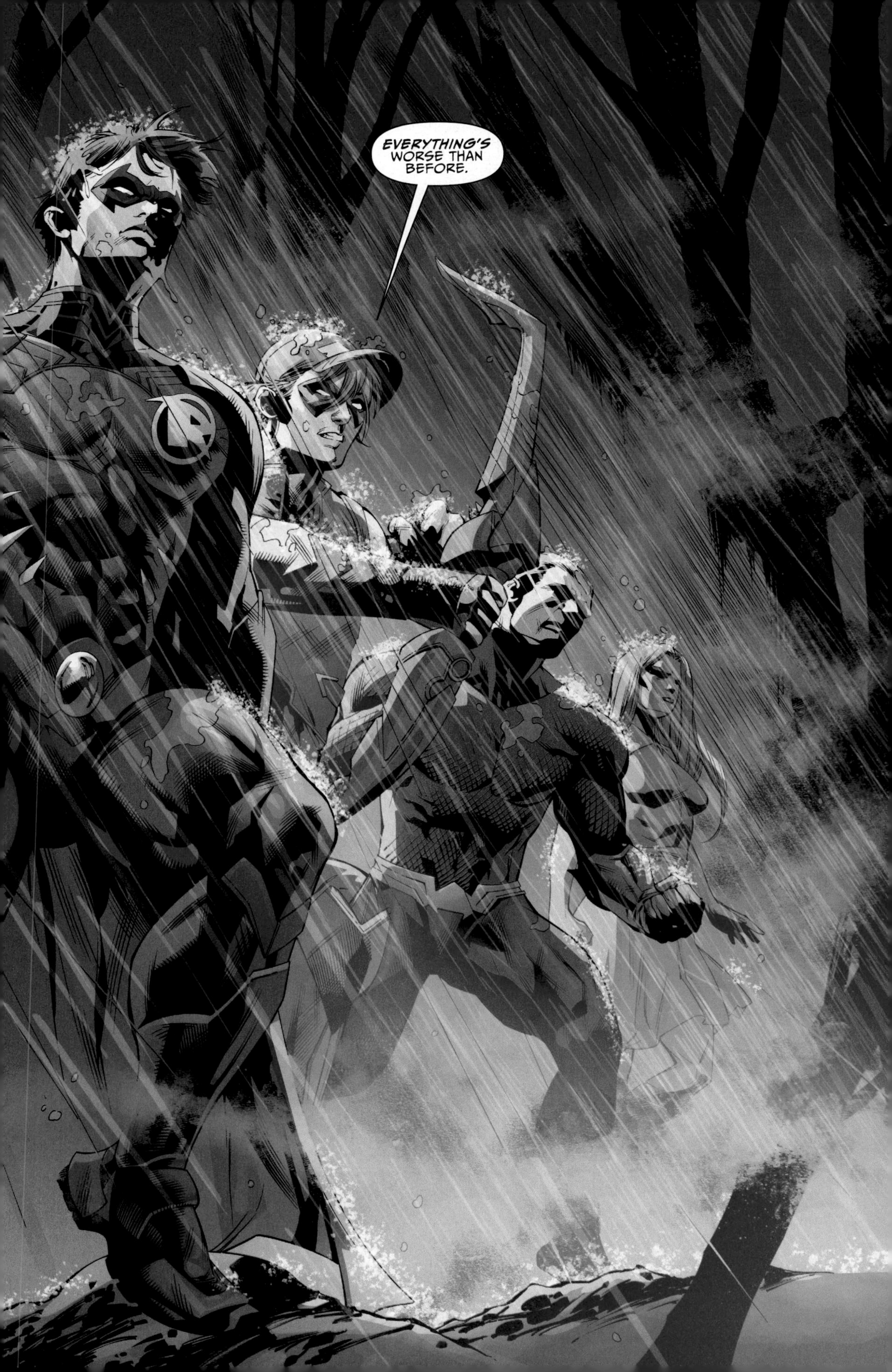
EVERYTHING'S WORSE THAN BEFORE.

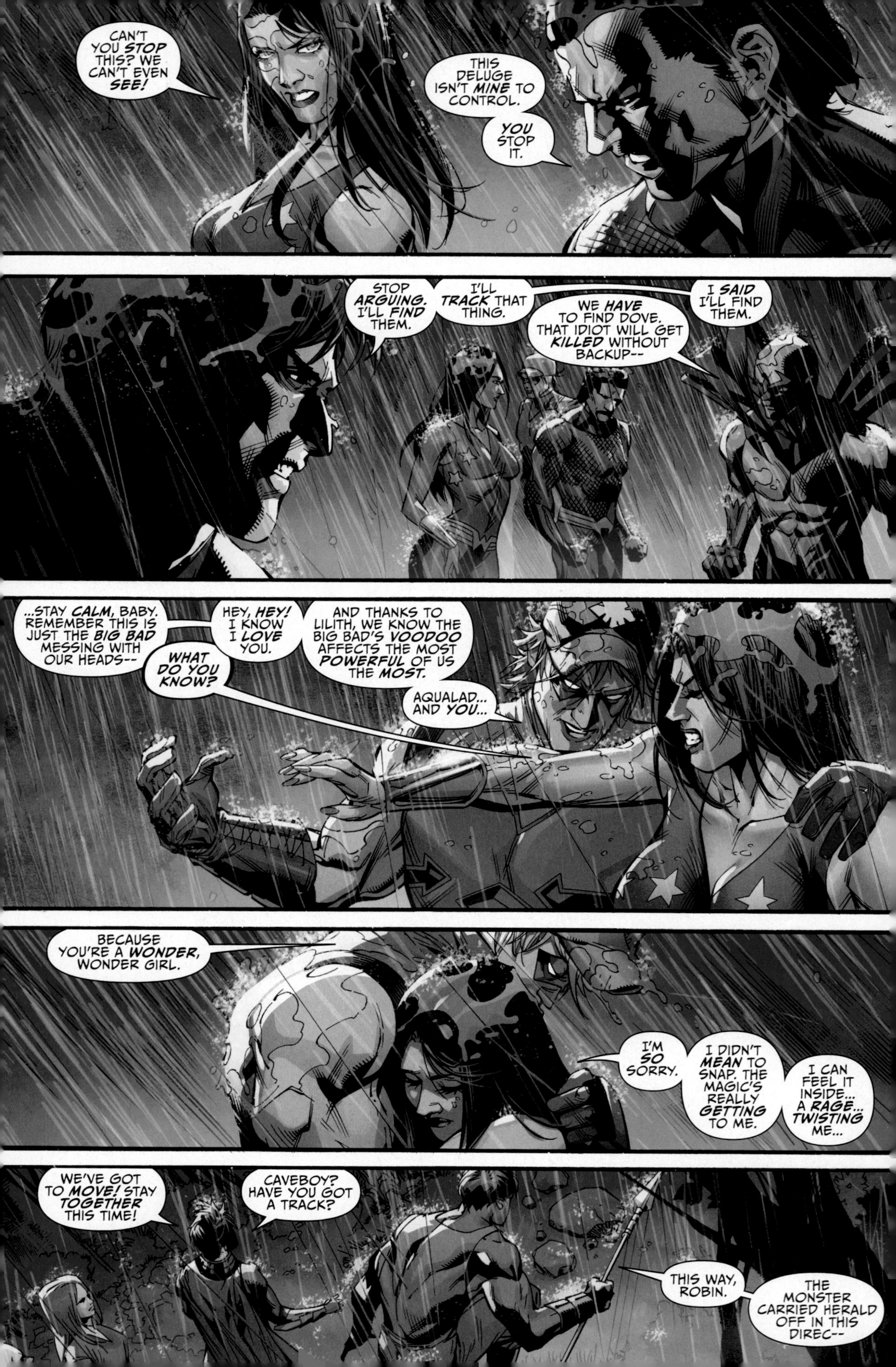
CAN'T YOU STOP THIS? WE CAN'T EVEN SEE!
THIS DELUGE ISN'T MINE TO CONTROL.
YOU STOP IT.
STOP ARGUING. I'LL FIND THEM.
I'LL TRACK THAT THING.
WE HAVE TO FIND DOVE. THAT IDIOT WILL GET KILLED WITHOUT BACKUP--
I SAID I'LL FIND THEM.
...STAY CALM, BABY. REMEMBER THIS IS JUST THE BIG BAD MESSING WITH OUR HEADS--
HEY, HEY! I KNOW I LOVE YOU.
WHAT DO YOU KNOW?
AND THANKS TO LILITH, WE KNOW THE BIG BAD'S VOODOO AFFECTS THE MOST POWERFUL OF US THE MOST.
AQUALAD... AND YOU...
BECAUSE YOU'RE A WONDER, WONDER GIRL.
I'M SO SORRY.
I DIDN'T MEAN TO SNAP. THE MAGIC'S REALLY GETTING TO ME.
I CAN FEEL IT INSIDE... A RAGE... TWISTING ME...
WE'VE GOT TO MOVE! STAY TOGETHER THIS TIME!
CAVEBOY? HAVE YOU GOT A TRACK?
THIS WAY, ROBIN.
THE MONSTER CARRIED HERALD OFF IN THIS DIREC--

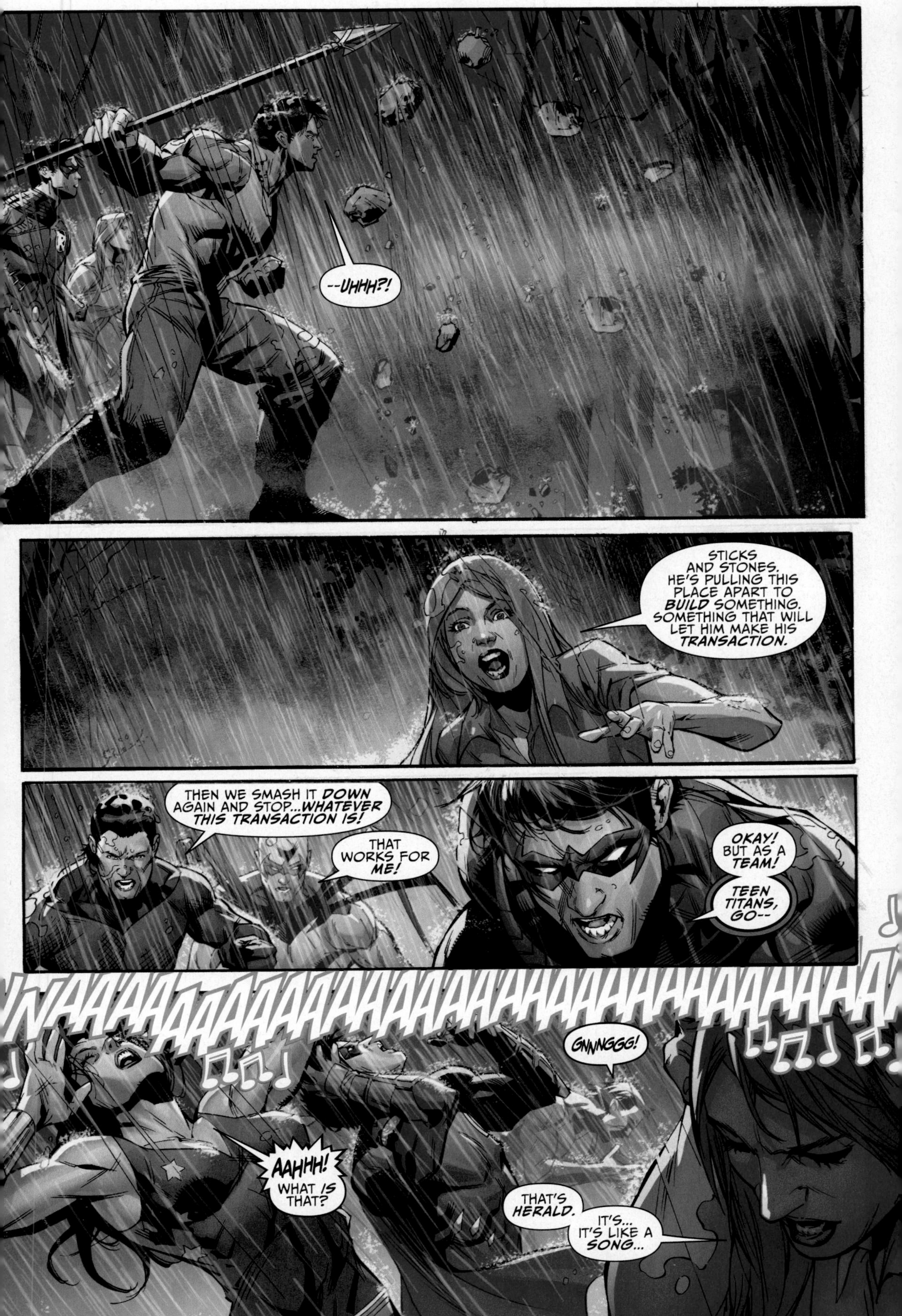
--UHHH?!
STICKS AND STONES. HE'S PULLING THIS PLACE APART TO BUILD SOMETHING. SOMETHING THAT WILL LET HIM MAKE HIS TRANSACTION.
THEN WE SMASH IT DOWN AGAIN AND STOP...WHATEVER THIS TRANSACTION IS!
THAT WORKS FOR ME!
OKAY! BUT AS A TEAM!
TEEN TITANS, GO--
NAAAAAAAAAAAAAAAAAAAAAAAAAAAAAAAAAAAAAA
GNNNGGG!
AAHHH! WHAT IS THAT?
THAT'S HERALD.
IT'S... IT'S LIKE A SONG...

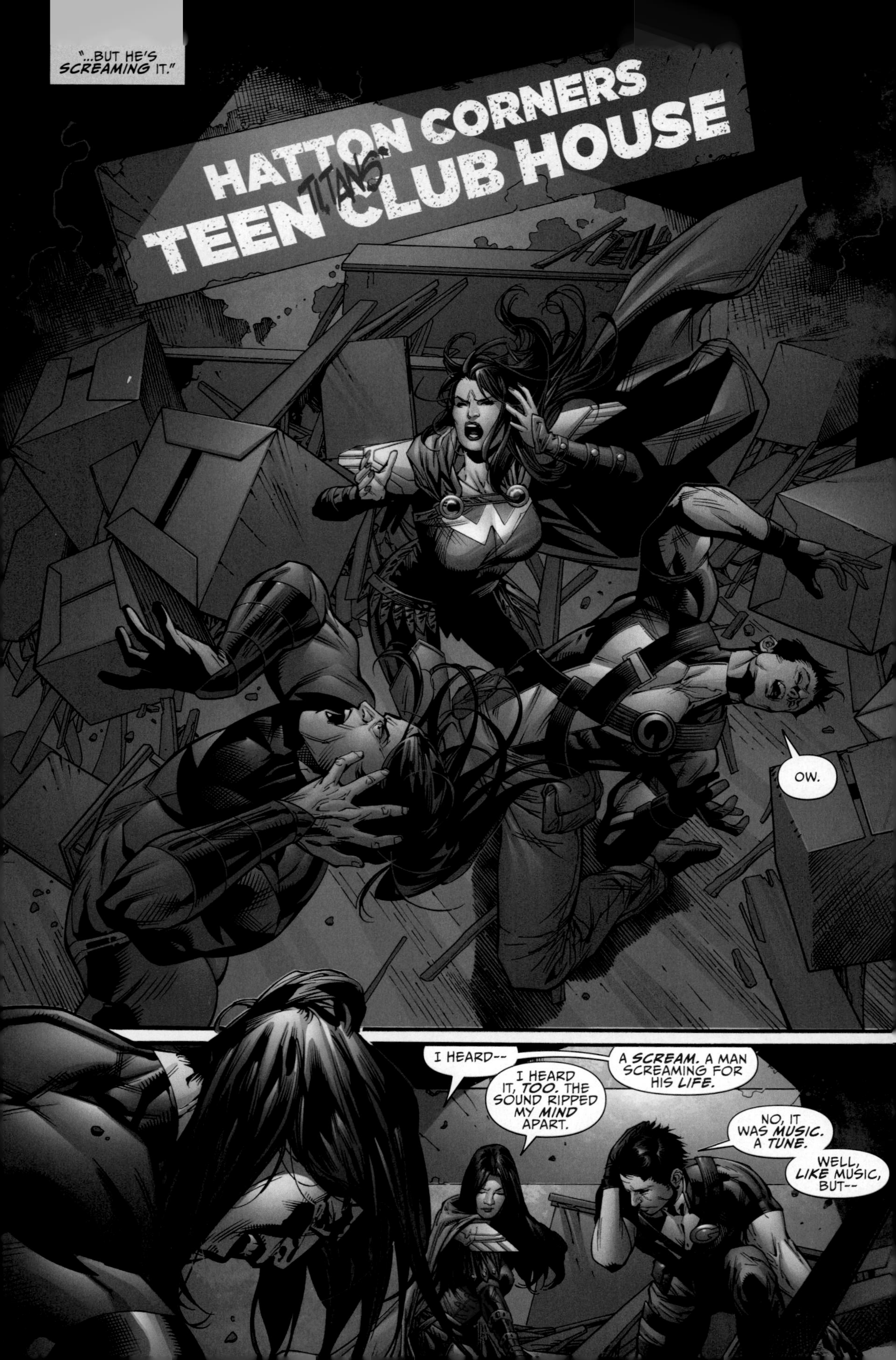
"...BUT HE'S SCREAMING IT."
HATTON CORNERS
TEEN TITANS CLUB HOUSE
OW.
I HEARD--
A SCREAM. A MAN SCREAMING FOR HIS LIFE.
I HEARD IT, TOO. THE SOUND RIPPED MY MIND APART.
NO, IT WAS MUSIC. A TUNE.
WELL, LIKE MUSIC, BUT--

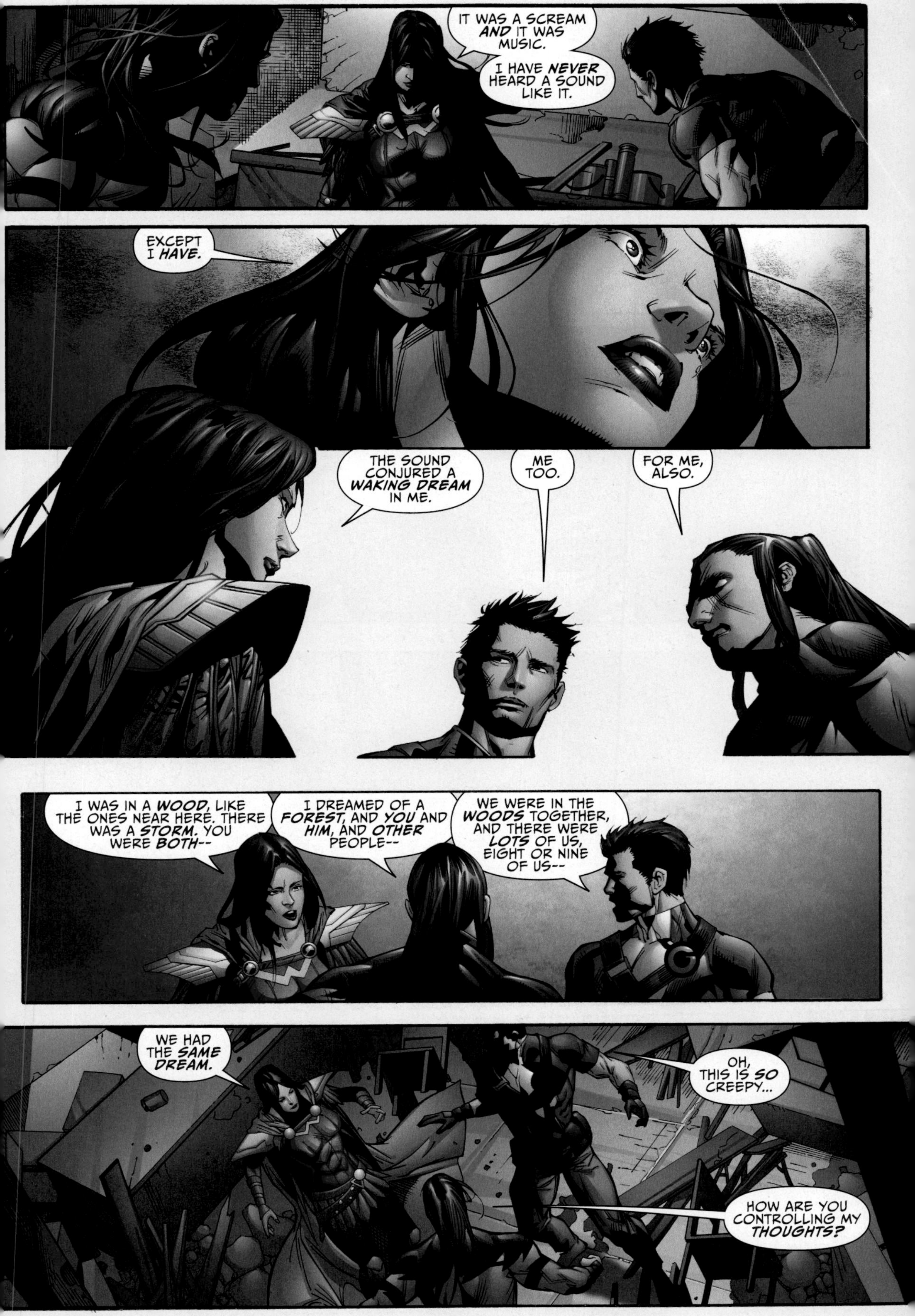
IT WAS A SCREAM AND IT WAS MUSIC.
I HAVE NEVER HEARD A SOUND LIKE IT.
EXCEPT I HAVE.
THE SOUND CONJURED A WAKING DREAM IN ME.
ME TOO.
FOR ME, ALSO.
I WAS IN A WOOD, LIKE THE ONES NEAR HERE. THERE WAS A STORM. YOU WERE BOTH--
I DREAMED OF A FOREST, AND YOU AND HIM, AND OTHER PEOPLE--
WE WERE IN THE WOODS TOGETHER, AND THERE WERE LOTS OF US, EIGHT OR NINE OF US--
WE HAD THE SAME DREAM.
OH, THIS IS SO CREEPY...
HOW ARE YOU CONTROLLING MY THOUGHTS?

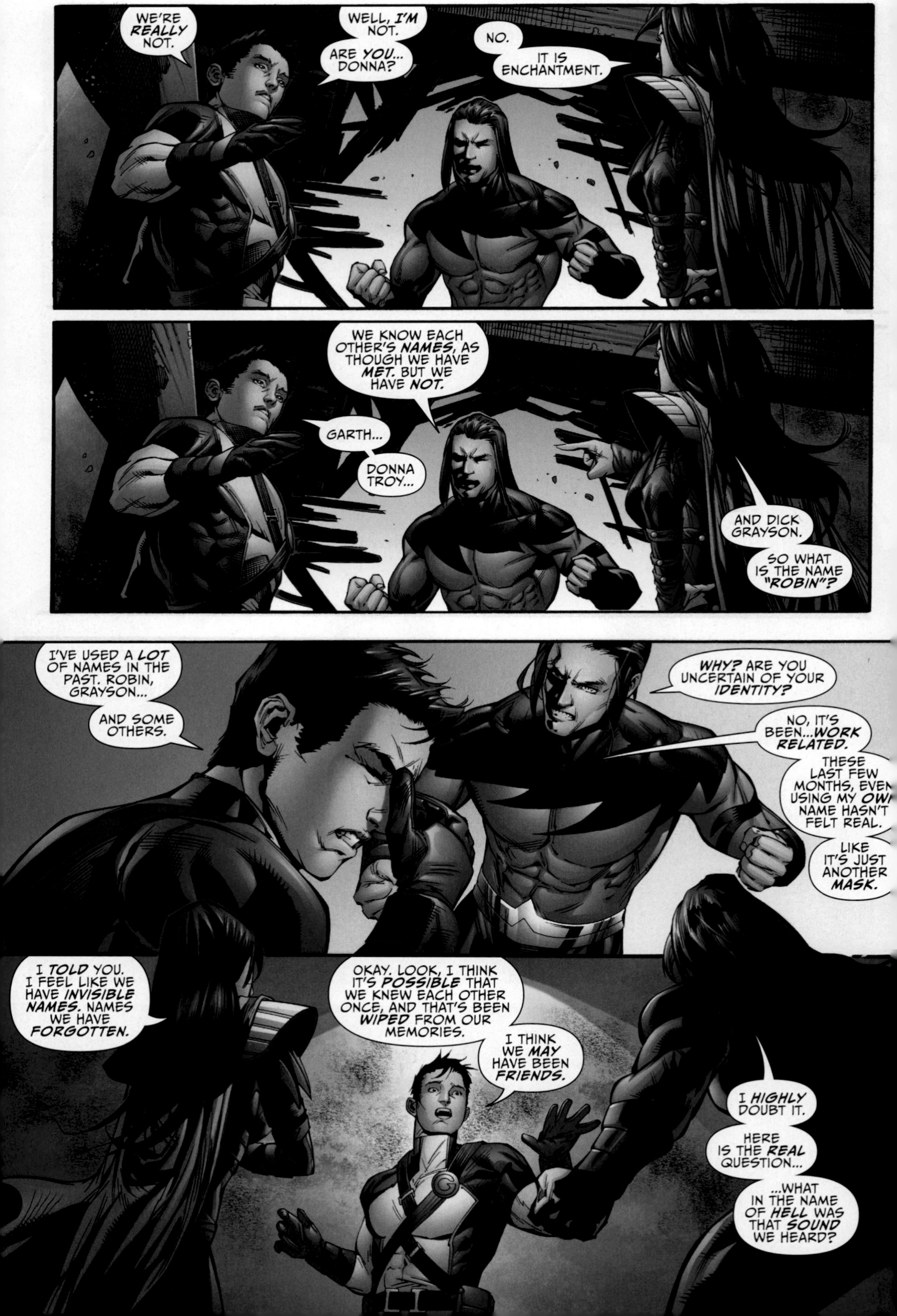
WE'RE REALLY NOT.
WELL, I'M NOT.
ARE YOU... DONNA?
NO.
IT IS ENCHANTMENT.
WE KNOW EACH OTHER'S NAMES, AS THOUGH WE HAVE MET. BUT WE HAVE NOT.
GARTH...
DONNA TROY...
AND DICK GRAYSON.
SO WHAT IS THE NAME "ROBIN"?
I'VE USED A LOT OF NAMES IN THE PAST. ROBIN, GRAYSON...
AND SOME OTHERS.
WHY? ARE YOU UNCERTAIN OF YOUR IDENTITY?
NO, IT'S BEEN...WORK RELATED.
THESE LAST FEW MONTHS, EVEN USING MY OWN NAME HASN'T FELT REAL.
LIKE IT'S JUST ANOTHER MASK.
I TOLD YOU. I FEEL LIKE WE HAVE INVISIBLE NAMES. NAMES WE HAVE FORGOTTEN.
OKAY. LOOK, I THINK IT'S POSSIBLE THAT WE KNEW EACH OTHER ONCE, AND THAT'S BEEN WIPED FROM OUR MEMORIES.
I THINK WE MAY HAVE BEEN FRIENDS.
I HIGHLY DOUBT IT.
HERE IS THE REAL QUESTION...
...WHAT IN THE NAME OF HELL WAS THAT SOUND WE HEARD?

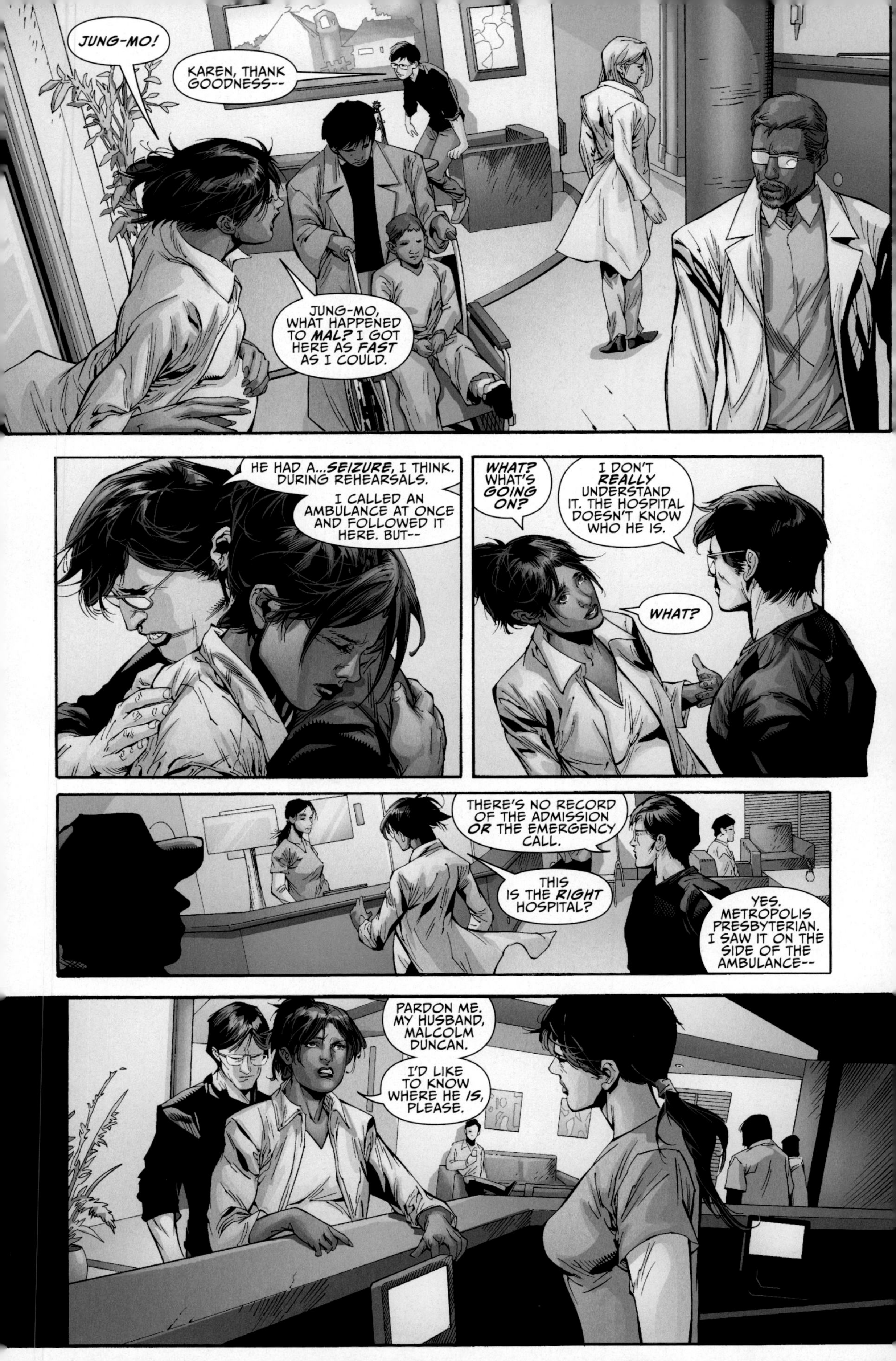

JUNG-MO!
KAREN, THANK GOODNESS--
JUNG-MO, WHAT HAPPENED TO MAL? I GOT HERE AS FAST AS I COULD.
HE HAD A...SEIZURE, I THINK. DURING REHEARSALS.
I CALLED AN AMBULANCE AT ONCE AND FOLLOWED IT HERE. BUT--
WHAT? WHAT'S GOING ON?
I DON'T REALLY UNDERSTAND IT. THE HOSPITAL DOESN'T KNOW WHO HE IS.
WHAT?
THERE'S NO RECORD OF THE ADMISSION OR THE EMERGENCY CALL.
THIS IS THE RIGHT HOSPITAL?
YES. METROPOLIS PRESBYTERIAN. I SAW IT ON THE SIDE OF THE AMBULANCE--
PARDON ME. MY HUSBAND, MALCOLM DUNCAN.
I'D LIKE TO KNOW WHERE HE IS, PLEASE.

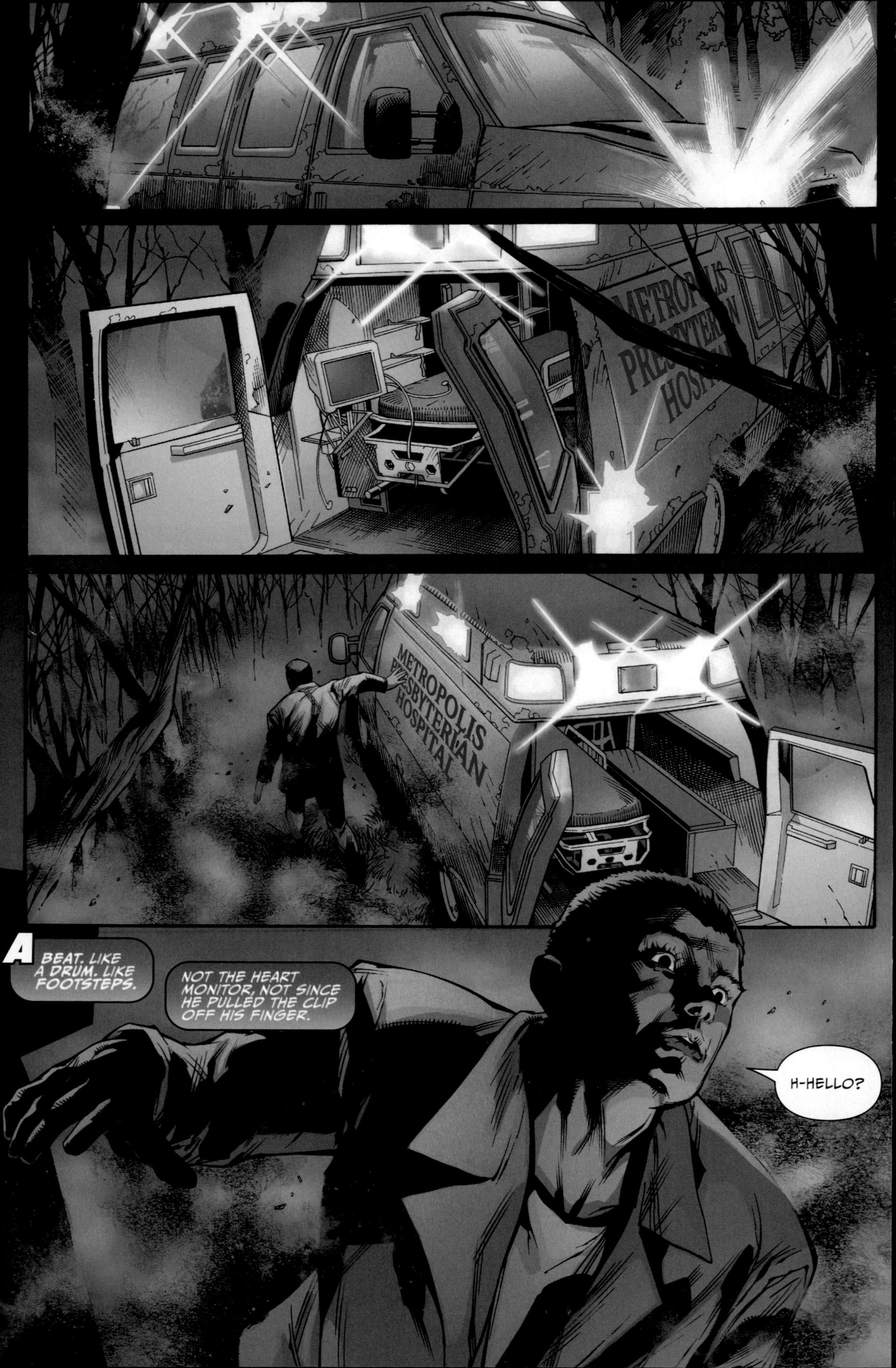
METROPOLIS PRESBYTERIAN HOSPITAL
METROPOLIS PRESBYTERIAN HOSPITAL
A BEAT. LIKE A DRUM. LIKE FOOTSTEPS.
NOT THE HEART MONITOR, NOT SINCE HE PULLED THE CLIP OFF HIS FINGER.
H-HELLO?

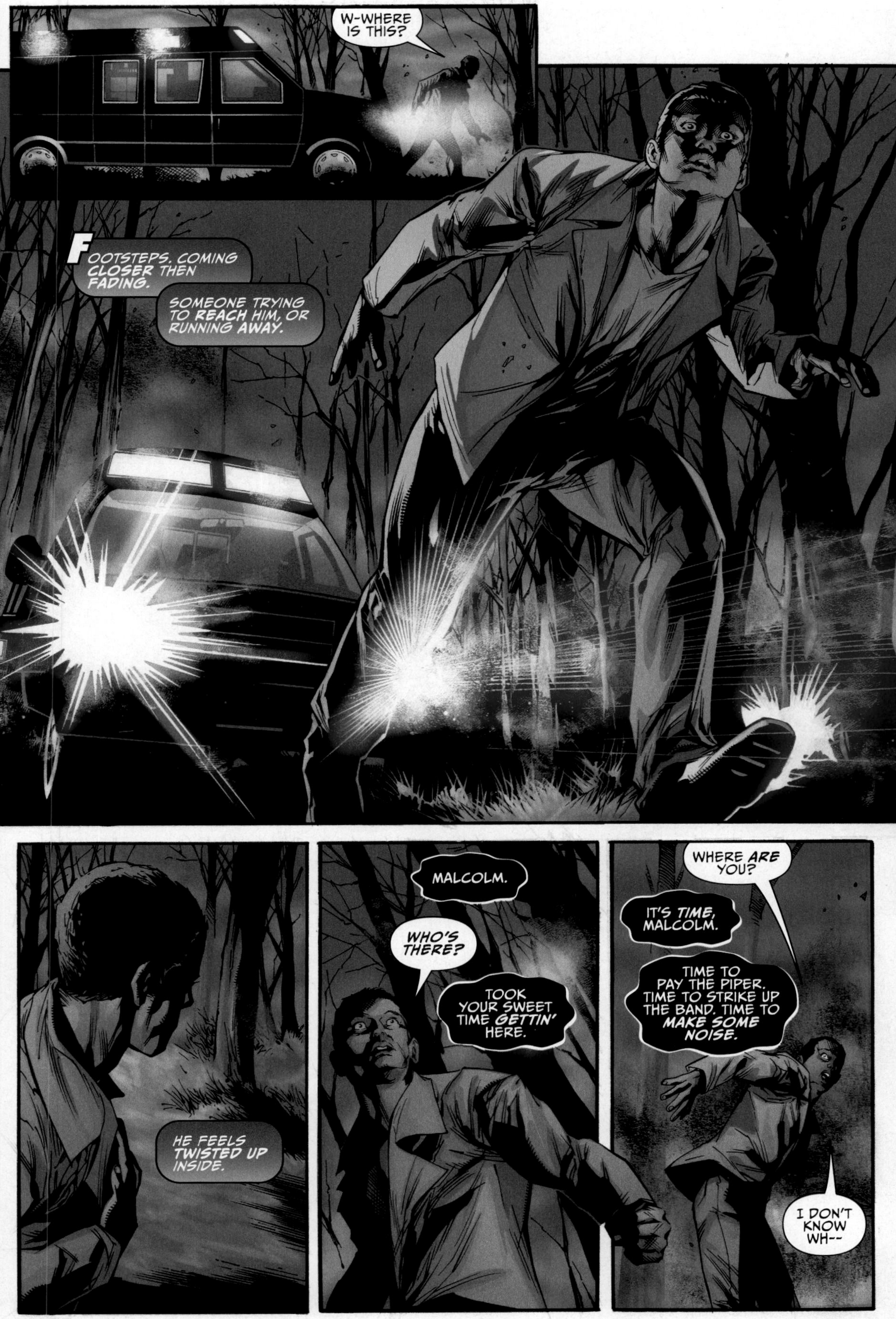
W-WHERE IS THIS?
FOOTSTEPS. COMING CLOSER THEN FADING.
SOMEONE TRYING TO REACH HIM, OR RUNNING AWAY.
HE FEELS TWISTED UP INSIDE.
MALCOLM.
WHO'S THERE?
TOOK YOUR SWEET TIME GETTIN' HERE.
WHERE ARE YOU?
IT'S TIME, MALCOLM.
TIME TO PAY THE PIPER. TIME TO STRIKE UP THE BAND. TIME TO MAKE SOME NOISE.
I DON'T KNOW WH--

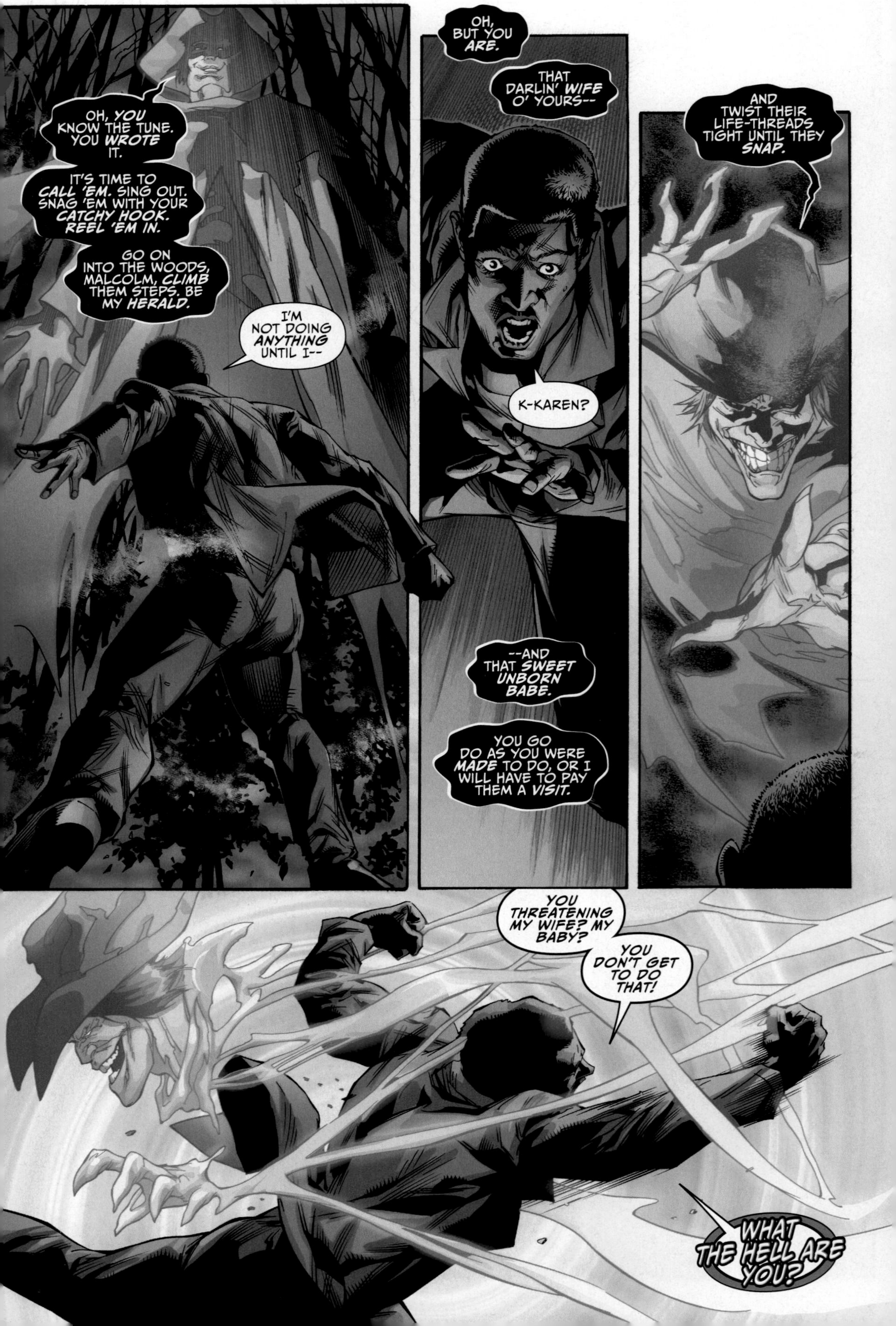
OH, YOU KNOW THE TUNE. YOU WROTE IT.
IT'S TIME TO CALL 'EM. SING OUT. SNAG 'EM WITH YOUR CATCHY HOOK. REEL 'EM IN.
GO ON INTO THE WOODS, MALCOLM, CLIMB THEM STEPS. BE MY HERALD.
I'M NOT DOING ANYTHING UNTIL I--
OH, BUT YOU ARE.
THAT DARLIN' WIFE O' YOURS--
K-KAREN?
--AND THAT SWEET UNBORN BABE.
YOU GO DO AS YOU WERE MADE TO DO, OR I WILL HAVE TO PAY THEM A VISIT.
AND TWIST THEIR LIFE-THREADS TIGHT UNTIL THEY SNAP.
YOU THREATENING MY WIFE? MY BABY?
YOU DON'T GET TO DO THAT!
WHAT THE HELL ARE YOU?

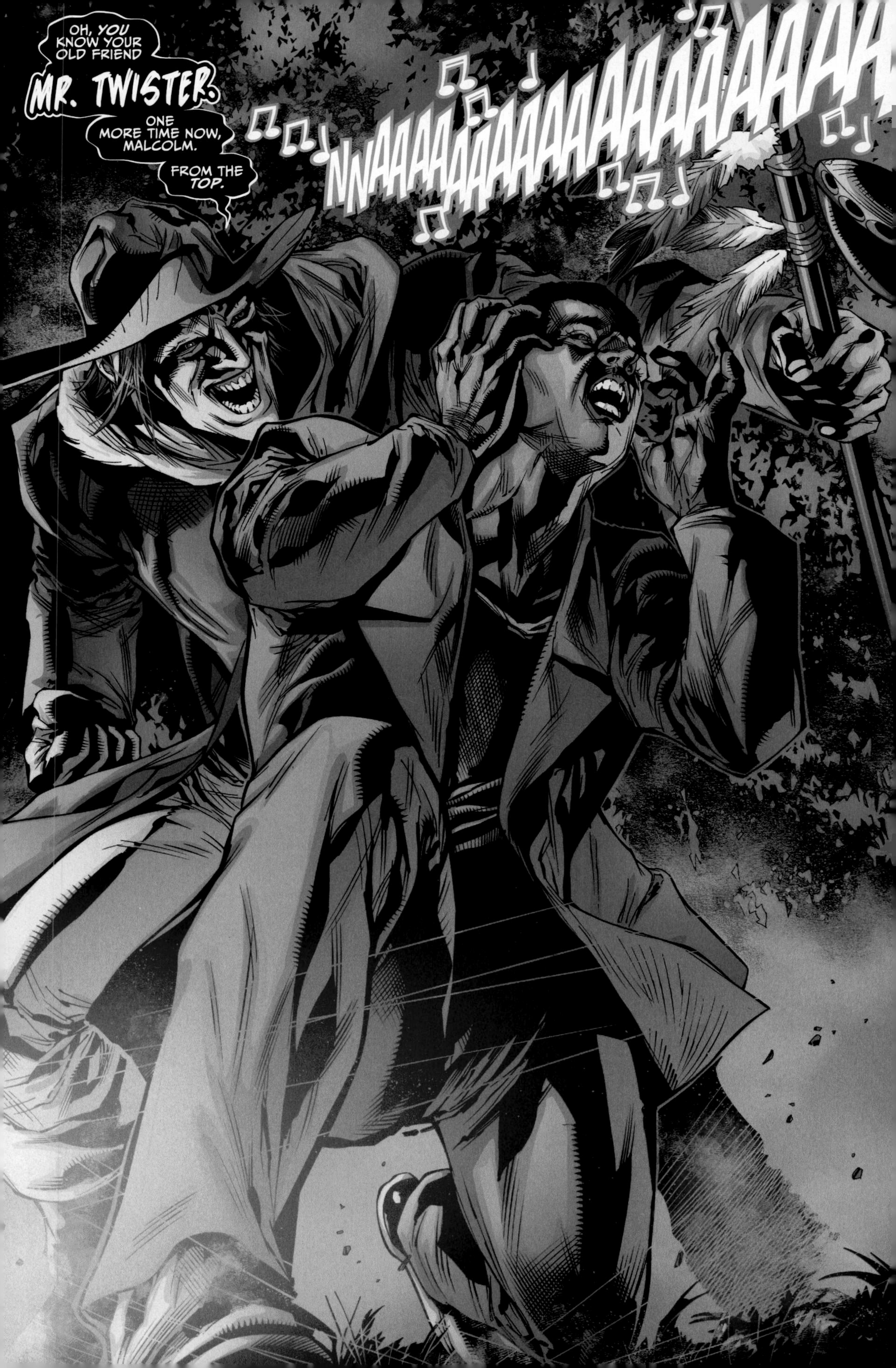
OH, YOU KNOW YOUR OLD FRIEND
MR. TWISTER.
ONE MORE TIME NOW, MALCOLM.
FROM THE TOP.
NNAAAAAAAAAAAAAAAAAAAA

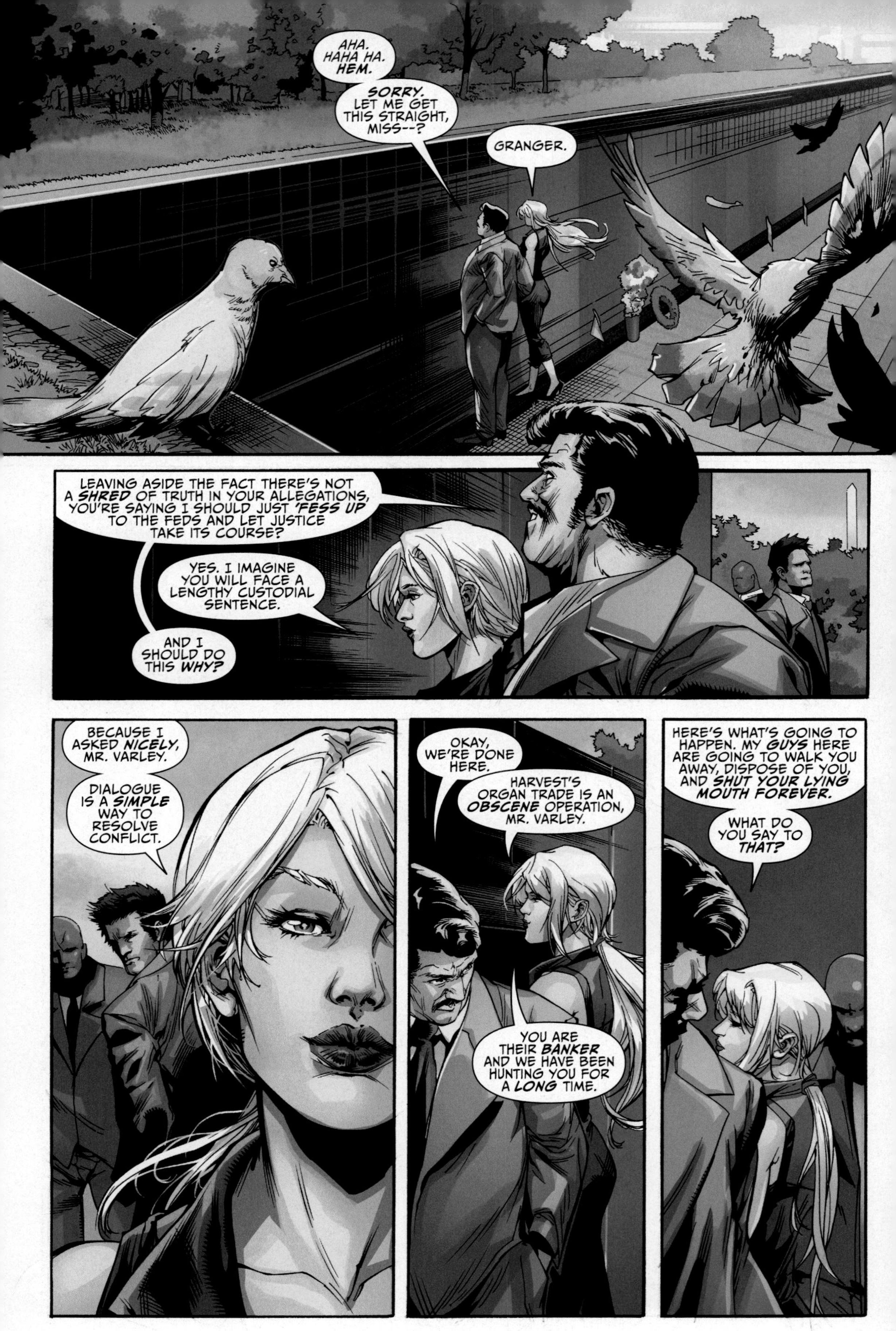
AHA. HAHA HA. HEM.
SORRY. LET ME GET THIS STRAIGHT, MISS--?
GRANGER.
LEAVING ASIDE THE FACT THERE'S NOT A SHRED OF TRUTH IN YOUR ALLEGATIONS, YOU'RE SAYING I SHOULD JUST 'FESS UP TO THE FEDS AND LET JUSTICE TAKE ITS COURSE?
YES. I IMAGINE YOU WILL FACE A LENGTHY CUSTODIAL SENTENCE.
AND I SHOULD DO THIS WHY?
BECAUSE I ASKED NICELY, MR. VARLEY.
DIALOGUE IS A SIMPLE WAY TO RESOLVE CONFLICT.
OKAY, WE'RE DONE HERE.
HARVEST'S ORGAN TRADE IS AN OBSCENE OPERATION, MR. VARLEY.
YOU ARE THEIR BANKER AND WE HAVE BEEN HUNTING YOU FOR A LONG TIME.
HERE'S WHAT'S GOING TO HAPPEN. MY GUYS HERE ARE GOING TO WALK YOU AWAY, DISPOSE OF YOU, AND SHUT YOUR LYING MOUTH FOREVER.
WHAT DO YOU SAY TO THAT?

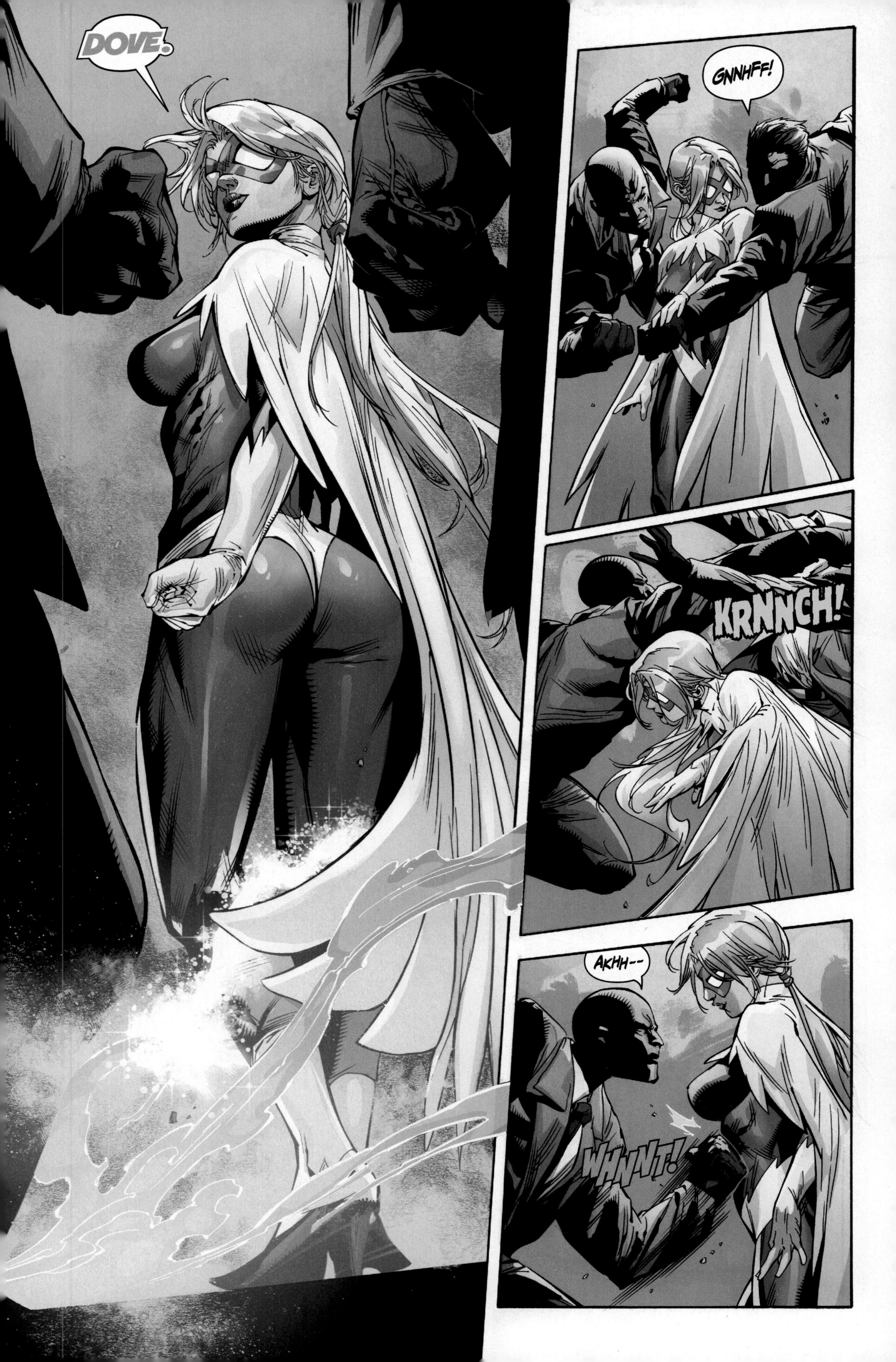
DOVE.
GNNHFF!
KRNNCH!
AKHH--
WHNNT!

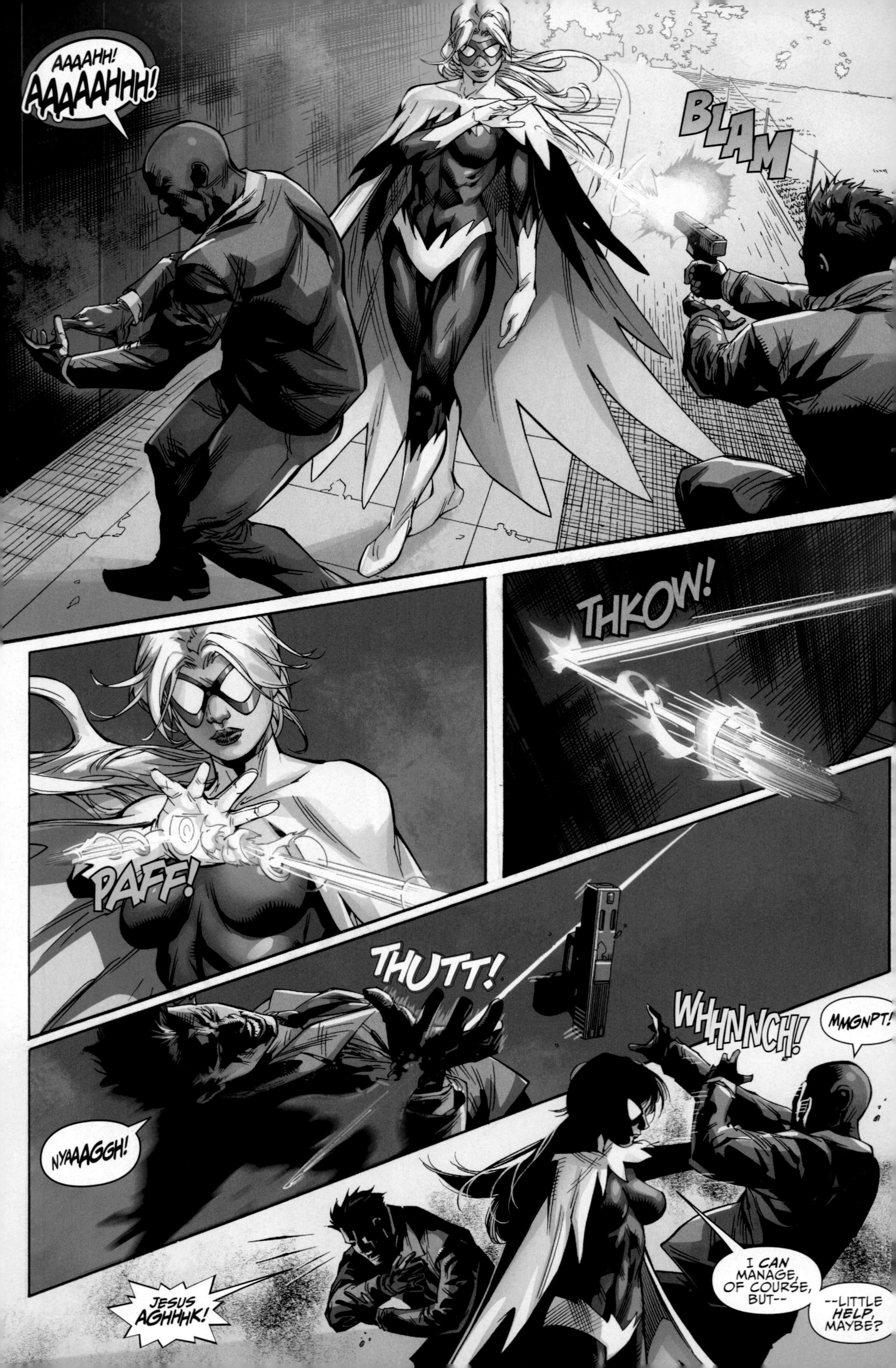
AAAAHH!
AAAAAHHH!
BLAM
THKOW!
PAFF!
THUTT!
WHHNNCH!
MMGNPT!
NYAAAGGH!
JESUS AGHHHK!
I CAN MANAGE, OF COURSE, BUT--
--LITTLE HELP, MAYBE?

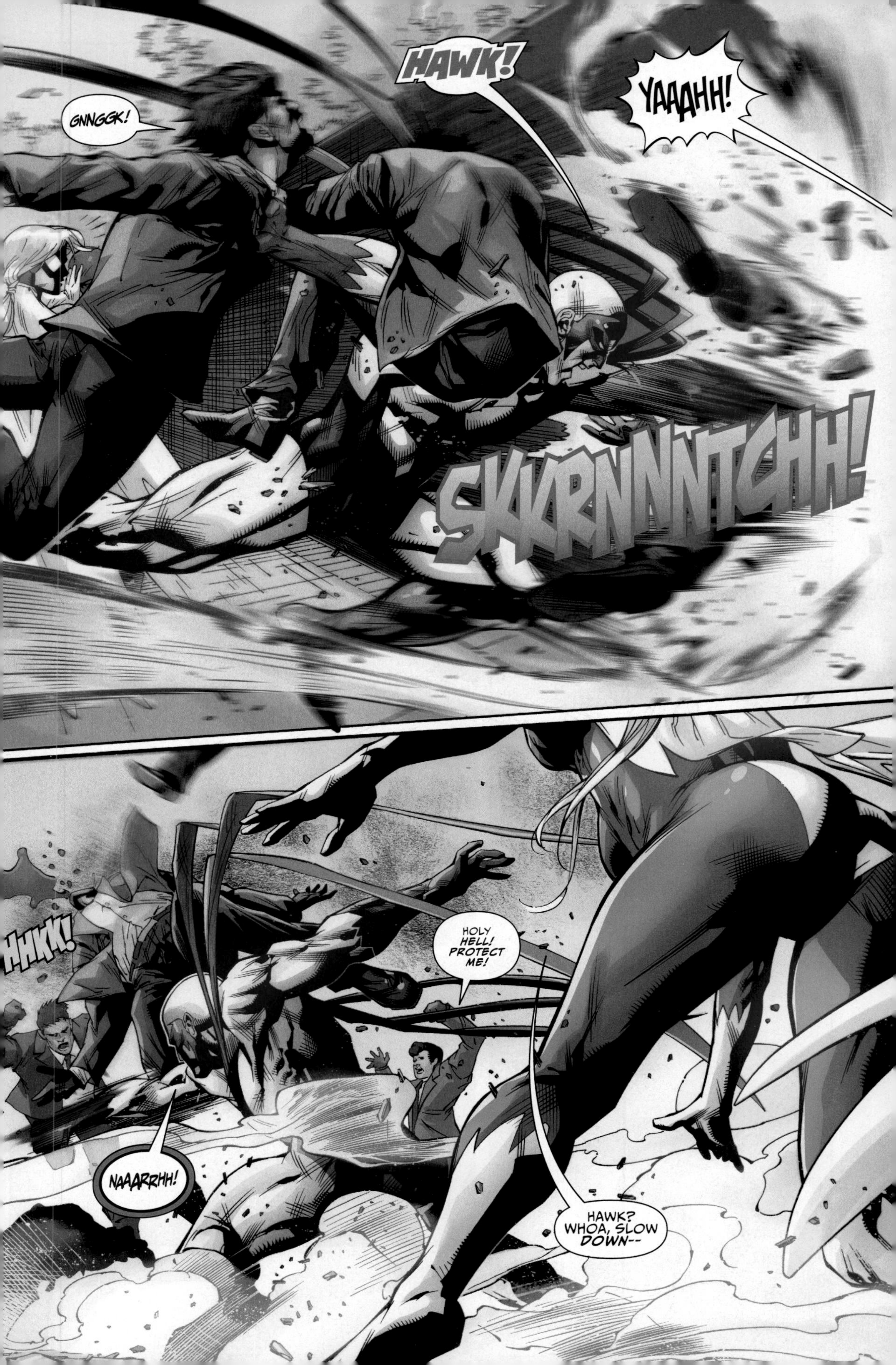
GNNGGK!
HAWK!
YAAAHH!
SKKRNNNTCHH!
HHKK!
HOLY HELL! PROTECT ME!
NAAARRHH!
HAWK? WHOA, SLOW DOWN--

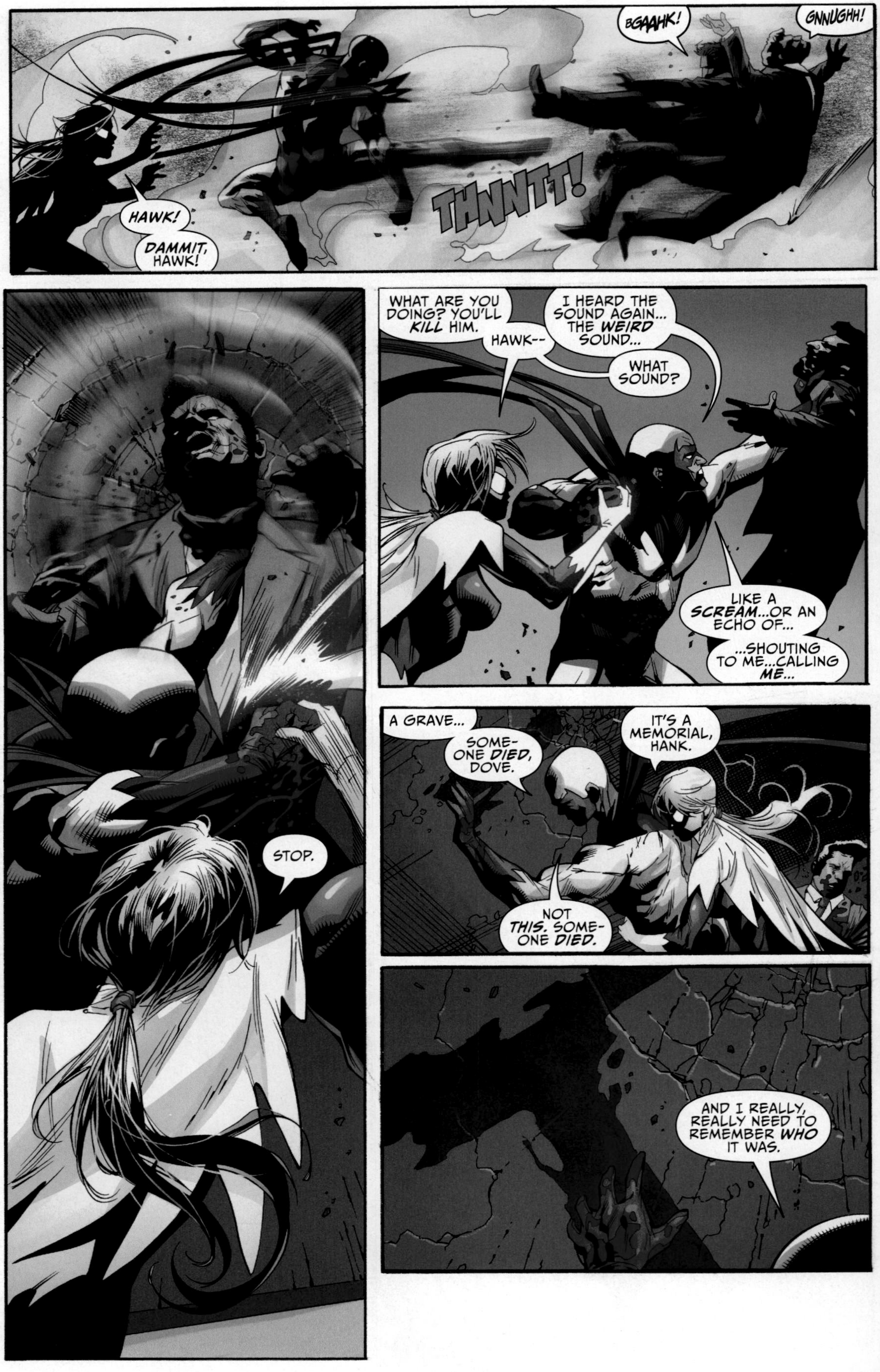
BGAAAHK!
GNNUGHH!
THNNTT!
HAWK!
DAMMIT, HAWK!
WHAT ARE YOU DOING? YOU'LL KILL HIM.
HAWK--
I HEARD THE SOUND AGAIN... THE WEIRD SOUND...
WHAT SOUND?
LIKE A SCREAM...OR AN ECHO OF...
...SHOUTING TO ME...CALLING ME...
STOP.
A GRAVE...
SOME-ONE DIED, DOVE.
IT'S A MEMORIAL, HANK.
NOT THIS. SOME-ONE DIED.
AND I REALLY, REALLY NEED TO REMEMBER WHO IT WAS.

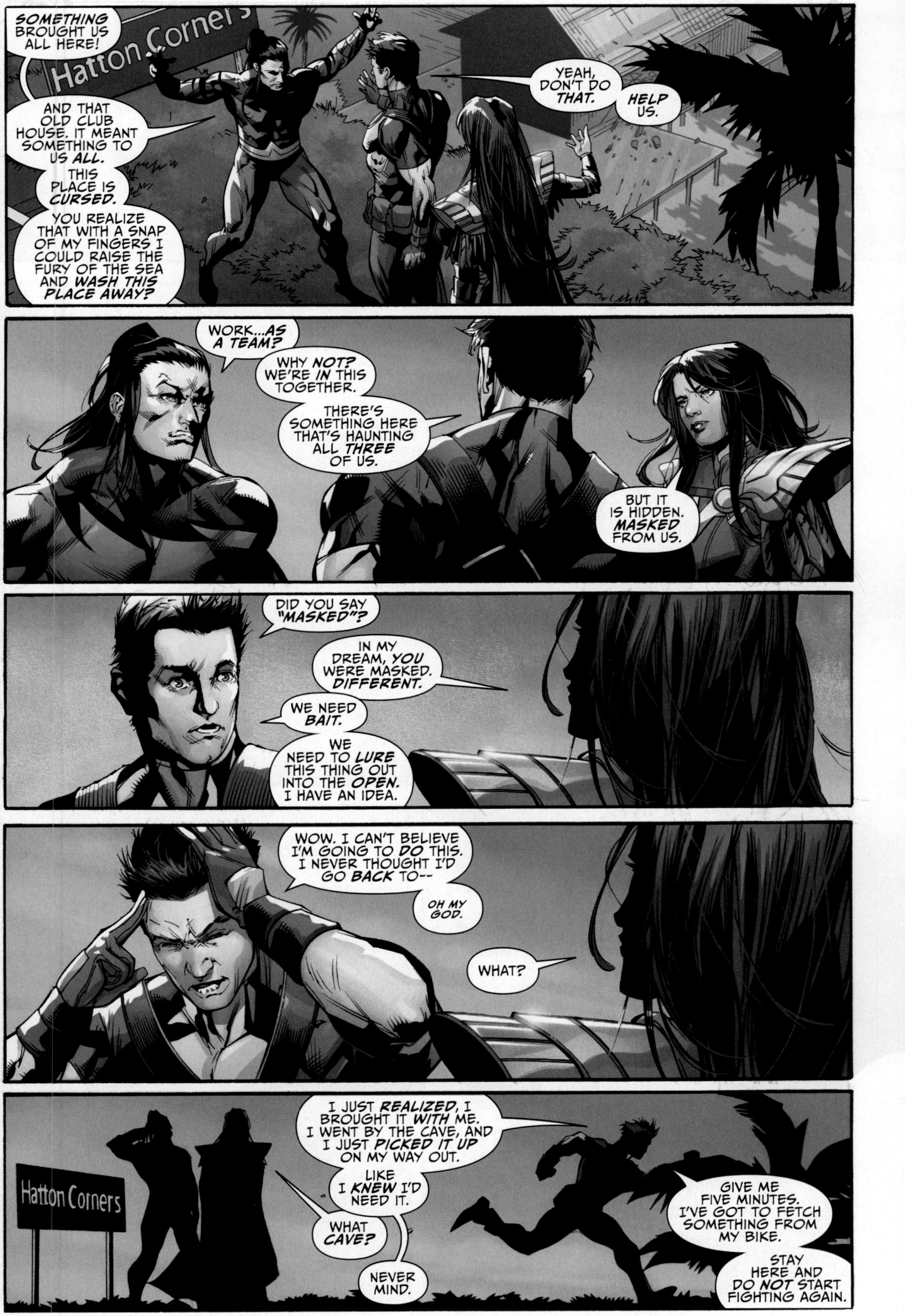

Hatton Corners
SOMETHING BROUGHT US ALL HERE!
AND THAT OLD CLUB HOUSE. IT MEANT SOMETHING TO US ALL.
THIS PLACE IS CURSED.
YOU REALIZE THAT WITH A SNAP OF MY FINGERS I COULD RAISE THE FURY OF THE SEA AND WASH THIS PLACE AWAY?
YEAH, DON'T DO THAT.
HELP US.
WORK...AS A TEAM?
WHY NOT? WE'RE IN THIS TOGETHER.
THERE'S SOMETHING HERE THAT'S HAUNTING ALL THREE OF US.
BUT IT IS HIDDEN. MASKED FROM US.
DID YOU SAY "MASKED"?
IN MY DREAM, YOU WERE MASKED. DIFFERENT.
WE NEED BAIT.
WE NEED TO LURE THIS THING OUT INTO THE OPEN. I HAVE AN IDEA.
WOW. I CAN'T BELIEVE I'M GOING TO DO THIS. I NEVER THOUGHT I'D GO BACK TO--
OH MY GOD.
WHAT?
I JUST REALIZED, I BROUGHT IT WITH ME. I WENT BY THE CAVE, AND I JUST PICKED IT UP ON MY WAY OUT.
LIKE I KNEW I'D NEED IT.
WHAT CAVE?
NEVER MIND.
Hatton Corners
GIVE ME FIVE MINUTES. I'VE GOT TO FETCH SOMETHING FROM MY BIKE.
STAY HERE AND DO NOT START FIGHTING AGAIN.

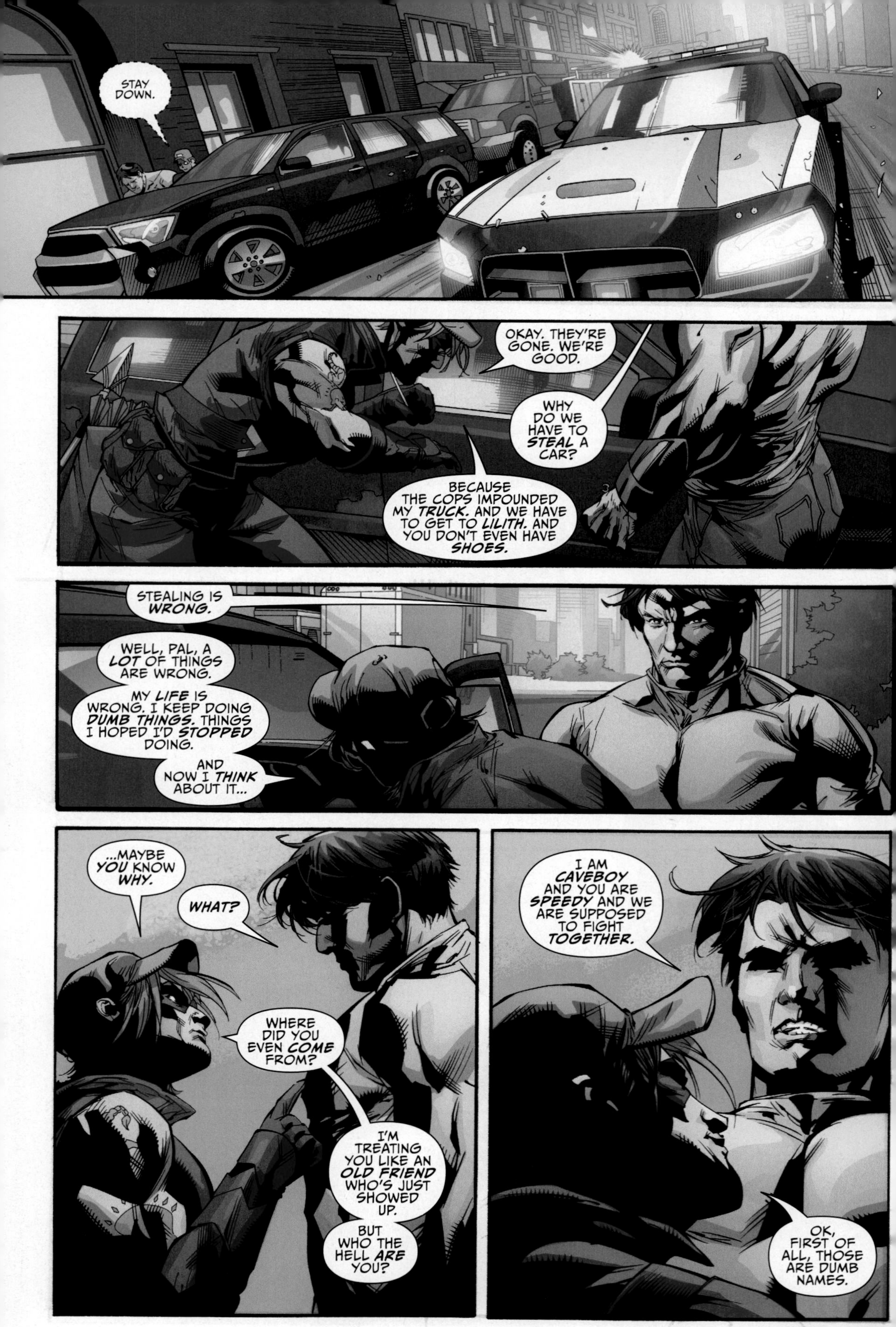
STAY DOWN.
OKAY. THEY'RE GONE. WE'RE GOOD.
WHY DO WE HAVE TO STEAL A CAR?
BECAUSE THE COPS IMPOUNDED MY TRUCK. AND WE HAVE TO GET TO LILITH. AND YOU DON'T EVEN HAVE SHOES.
STEALING IS WRONG.
WELL, PAL, A LOT OF THINGS ARE WRONG.
MY LIFE IS WRONG. I KEEP DOING DUMB THINGS. THINGS I HOPED I'D STOPPED DOING.
AND NOW I THINK ABOUT IT...
...MAYBE YOU KNOW WHY.
WHAT?
WHERE DID YOU EVEN COME FROM?
I'M TREATING YOU LIKE AN OLD FRIEND WHO'S JUST SHOWED UP.
BUT WHO THE HELL ARE YOU?
I AM CAVEBOY AND YOU ARE SPEEDY AND WE ARE SUPPOSED TO FIGHT TOGETHER.
OK, FIRST OF ALL, THOSE ARE DUMB NAMES.

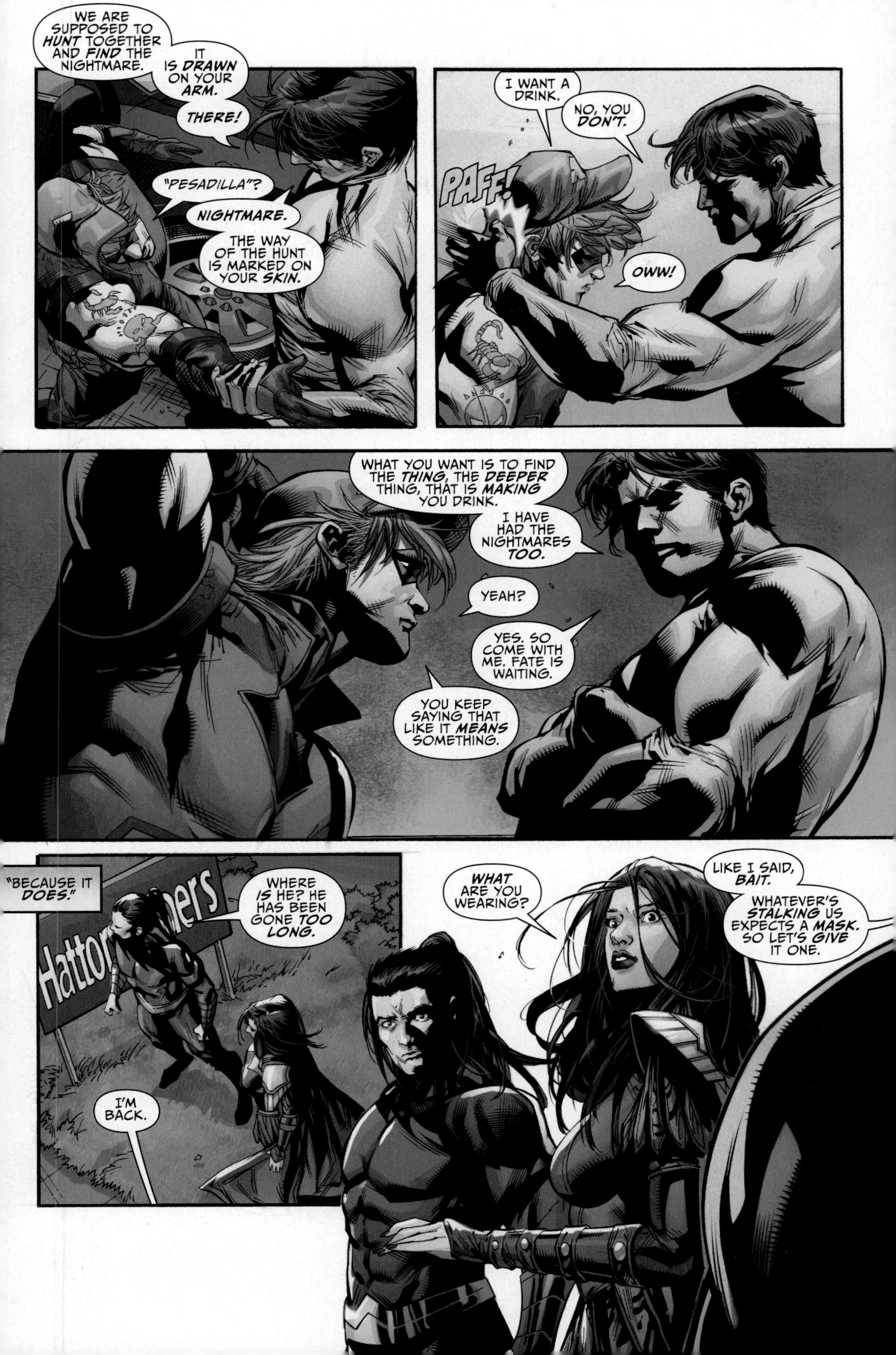

WE ARE SUPPOSED TO HUNT TOGETHER AND FIND THE NIGHTMARE.
IT IS DRAWN ON YOUR ARM.
THERE!
"PESADILLA"?
NIGHTMARE.
THE WAY OF THE HUNT IS MARKED ON YOUR SKIN.
I WANT A DRINK.
NO, YOU DON'T.
PAFF!
OWW!
WHAT YOU WANT IS TO FIND THE THING, THE DEEPER THING, THAT IS MAKING YOU DRINK.
I HAVE HAD THE NIGHTMARES TOO.
YEAH?
YES. SO COME WITH ME. FATE IS WAITING.
YOU KEEP SAYING THAT LIKE IT MEANS SOMETHING.
"BECAUSE IT DOES."
WHERE IS HE? HE HAS BEEN GONE TOO LONG.
I'M BACK.
WHAT ARE YOU WEARING?
LIKE I SAID, BAIT.
WHATEVER'S STALKING US EXPECTS A MASK. SO LET'S GIVE IT ONE.

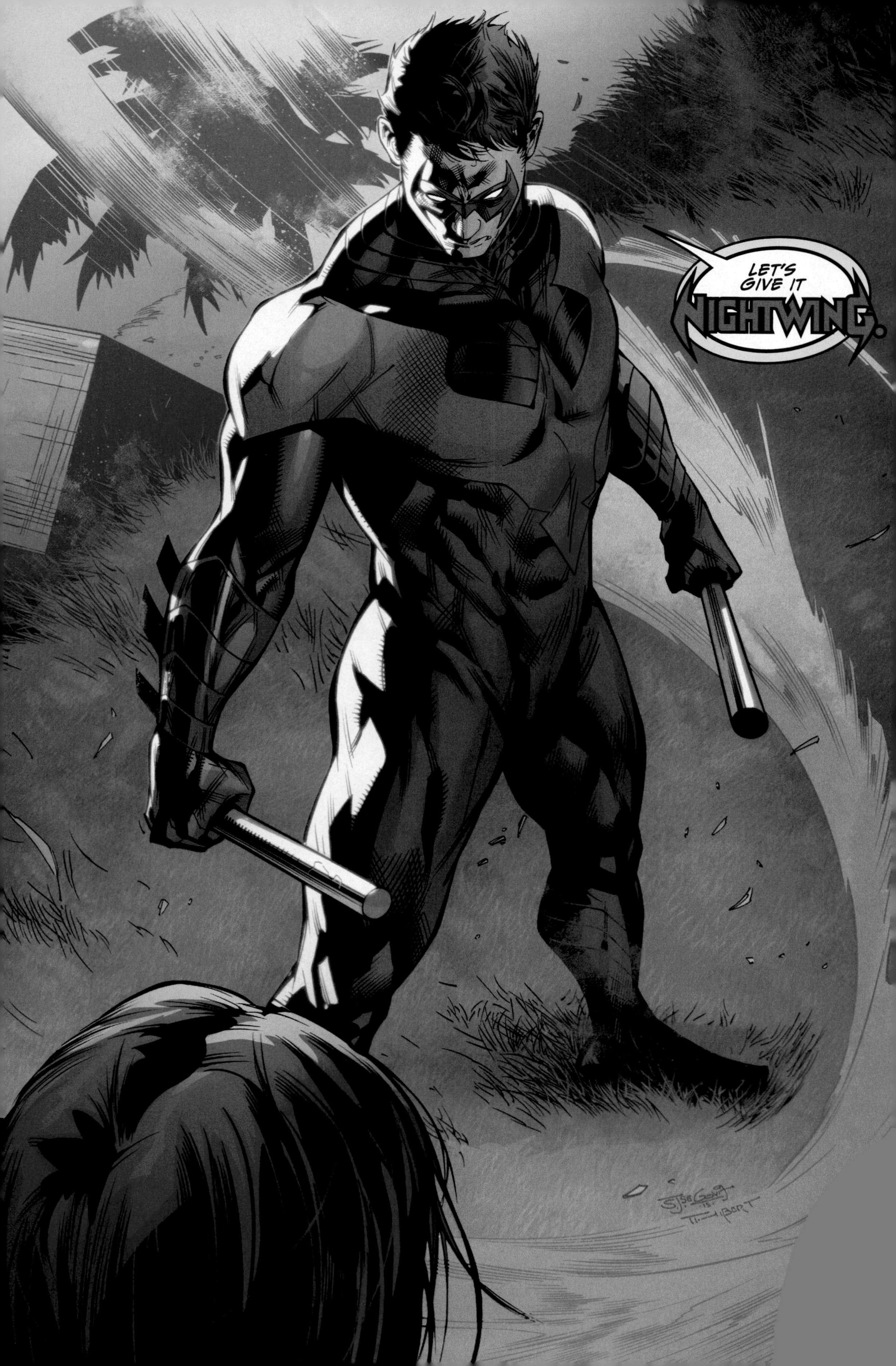
LET'S GIVE IT
NIGHTWING.

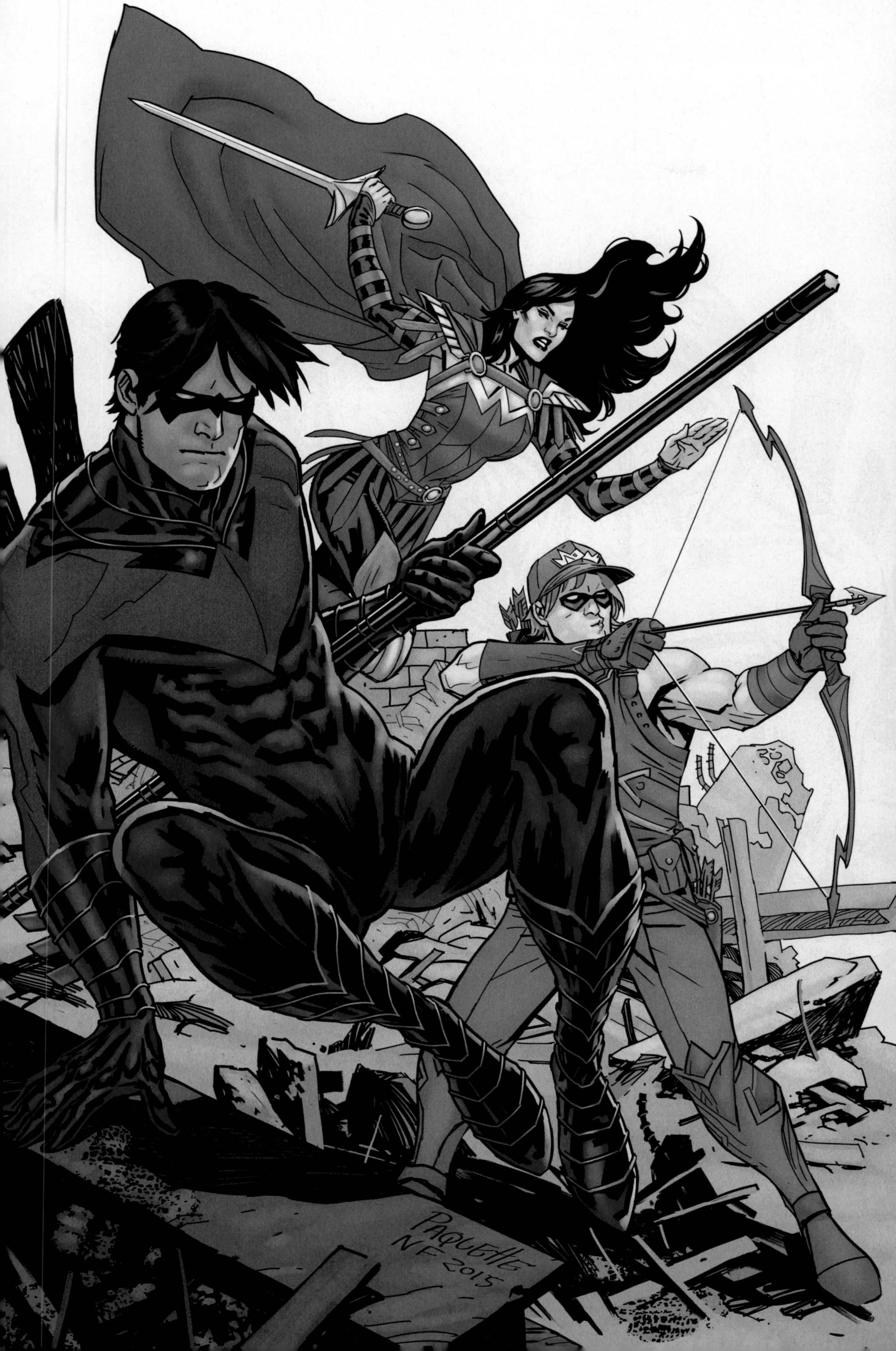
PAQUETTE
NF 2015

CHAPTER FIVE: STICKS AND STONES

DAN ABNETT writer PAULO SIQUEIRA & GERALDO BORGES artists HI-FI colorist cover art by YANICK PAQUETTE & NATHAN FAIRBAIRN

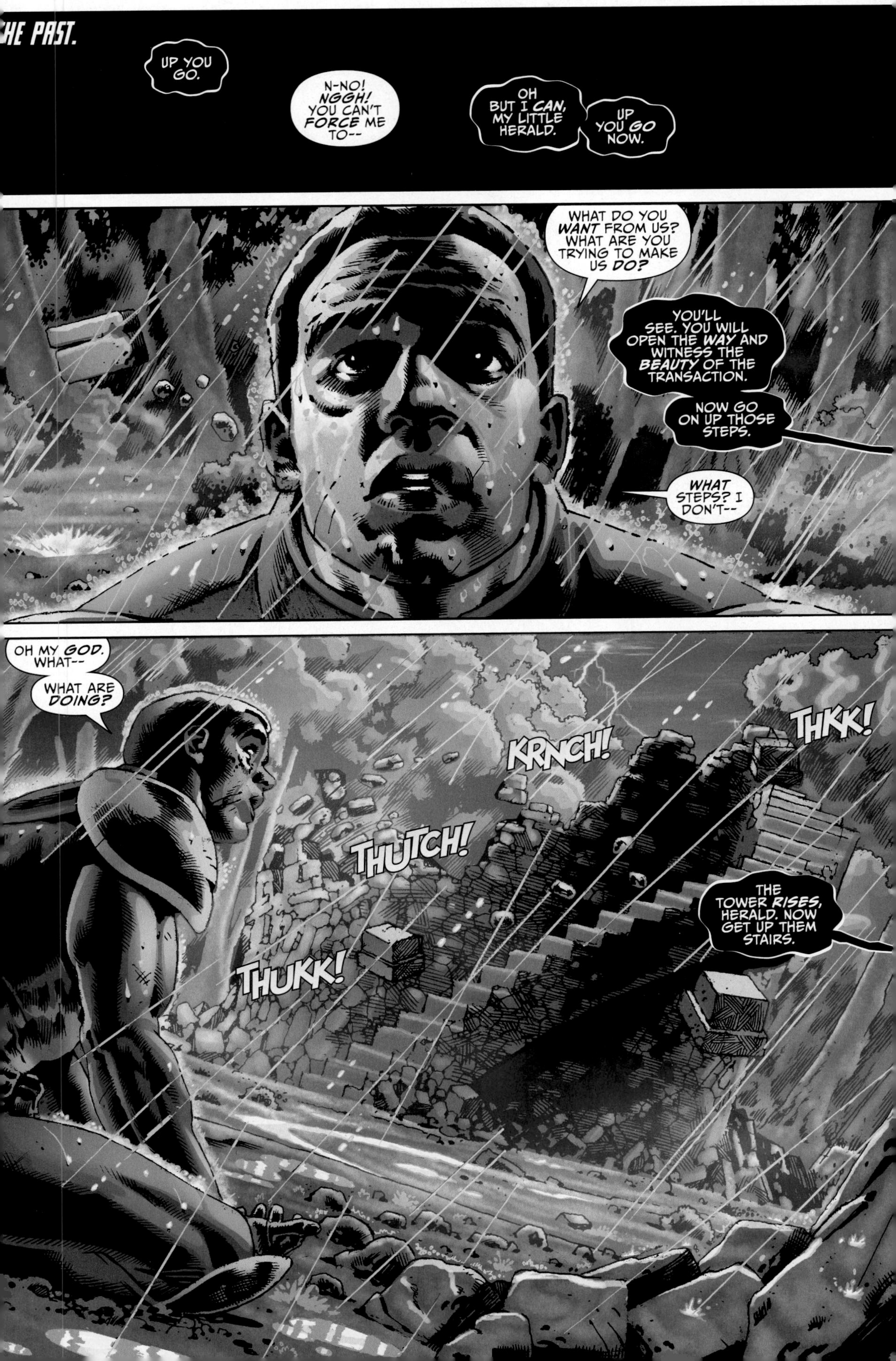
HE PAST.
UP YOU GO.
N-NO! NGGH! YOU CAN'T FORCE ME TO--
OH BUT I CAN, MY LITTLE HERALD.
UP YOU GO NOW.
WHAT DO YOU WANT FROM US? WHAT ARE YOU TRYING TO MAKE US DO?
YOU'LL SEE. YOU WILL OPEN THE WAY AND WITNESS THE BEAUTY OF THE TRANSACTION.
NOW GO ON UP THOSE STEPS.
WHAT STEPS? I DON'T--
OH MY GOD. WHAT--
WHAT ARE DOING?
KRNCH!
THKK!
THUTCH!
THUKK!
THE TOWER RISES, HERALD. NOW GET UP THEM STAIRS.

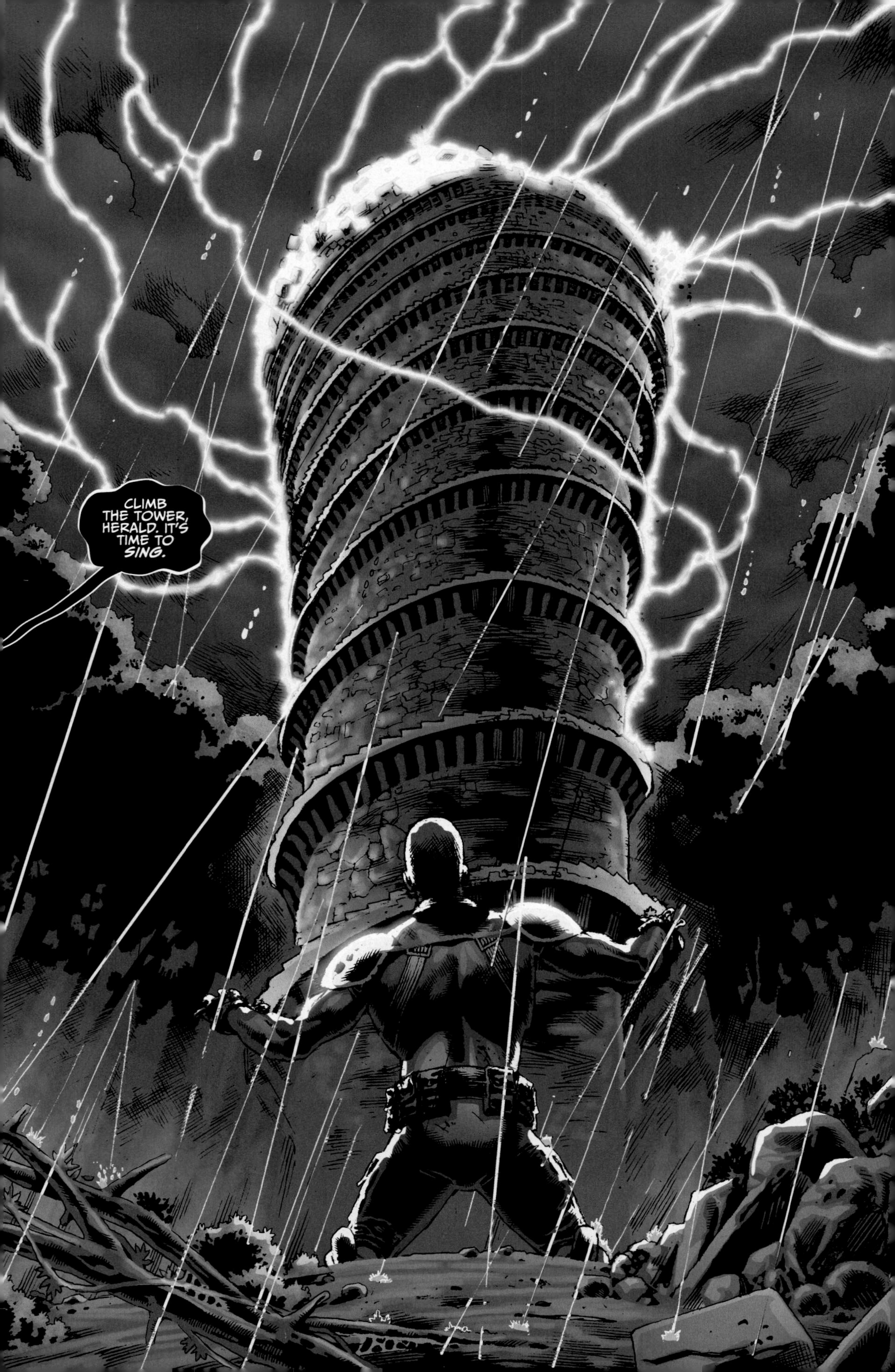
CLIMB THE TOWER, HERALD. IT'S TIME TO *SING.*

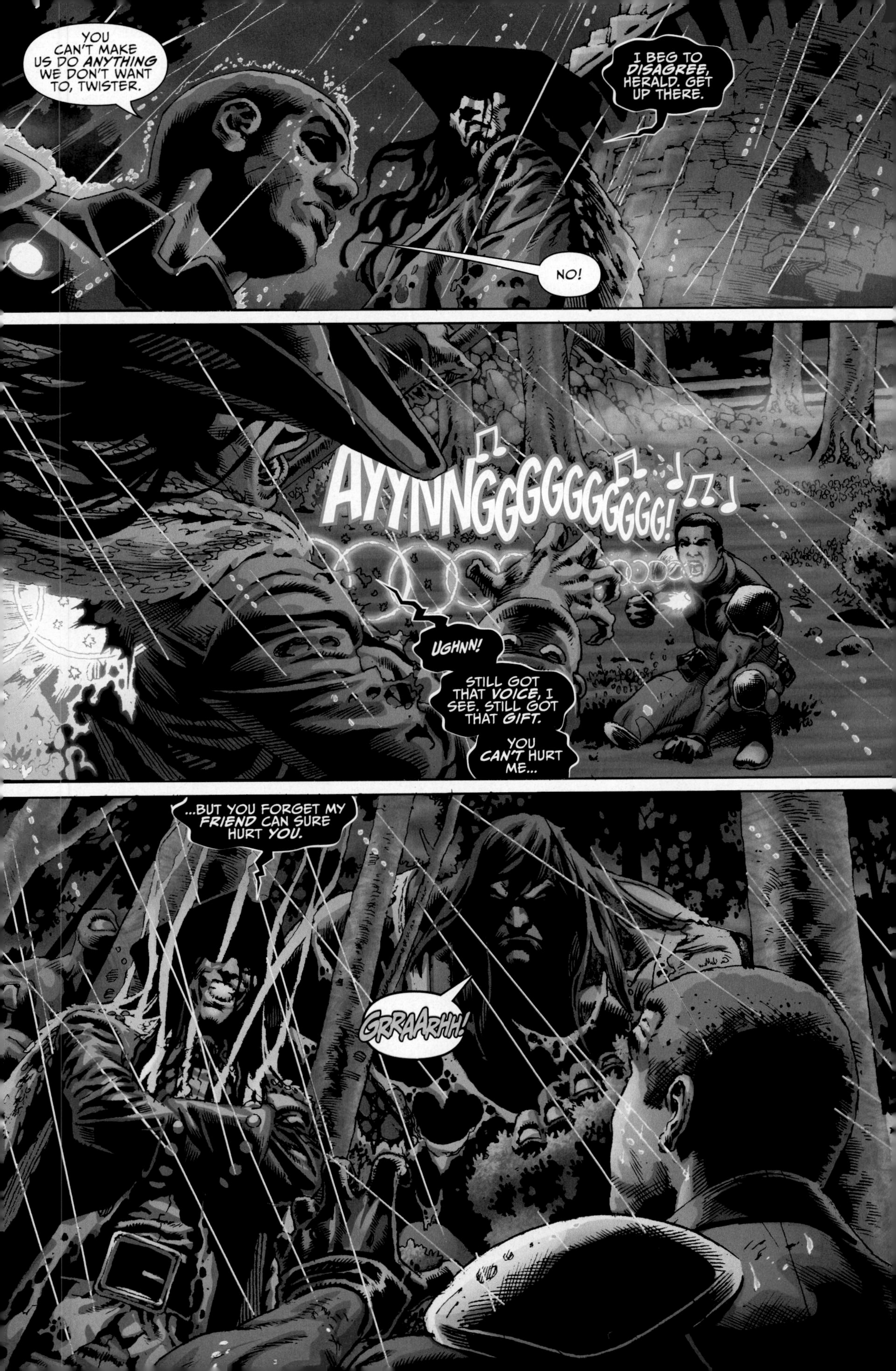
YOU CAN'T MAKE US DO ANYTHING WE DON'T WANT TO, TWISTER.
I BEG TO DISAGREE, HERALD. GET UP THERE.
NO!
AYYNNGGGGGGGGGG!
UGHNN!
STILL GOT THAT VOICE, I SEE. STILL GOT THAT GIFT.
YOU CAN'T HURT ME...
...BUT YOU FORGET MY FRIEND CAN SURE HURT YOU.
GRRAARHH!

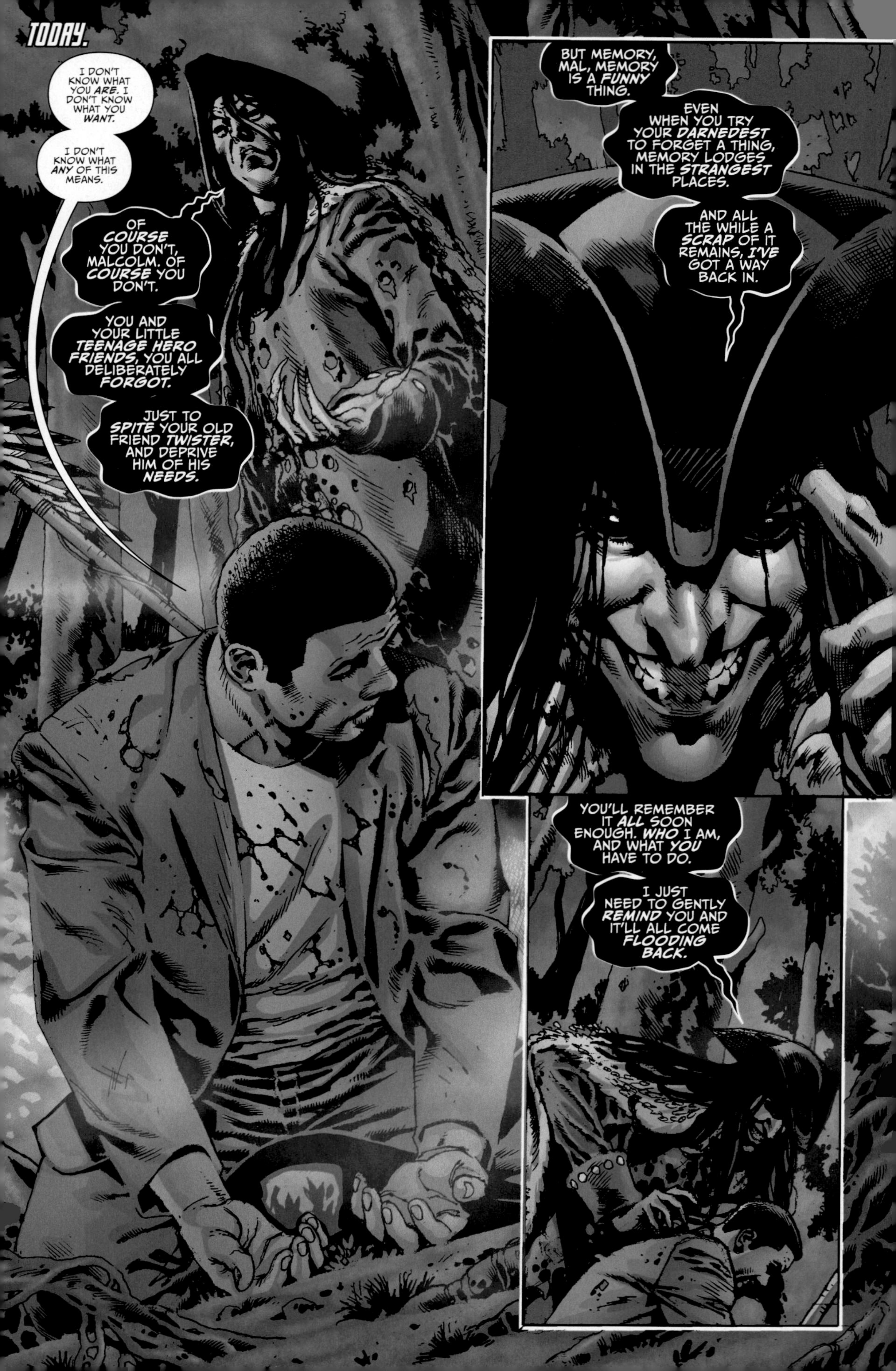
TODAY.
I DON'T KNOW WHAT YOU ARE. I DON'T KNOW WHAT YOU WANT.
I DON'T KNOW WHAT ANY OF THIS MEANS.
OF COURSE YOU DON'T, MALCOLM. OF COURSE YOU DON'T.
YOU AND YOUR LITTLE TEENAGE HERO FRIENDS, YOU ALL DELIBERATELY FORGOT.
JUST TO SPITE YOUR OLD FRIEND TWISTER, AND DEPRIVE HIM OF HIS NEEDS.
BUT MEMORY, MAL, MEMORY IS A FUNNY THING.
EVEN WHEN YOU TRY YOUR DARNEDEST TO FORGET A THING, MEMORY LODGES IN THE STRANGEST PLACES.
AND ALL THE WHILE A SCRAP OF IT REMAINS, I'VE GOT A WAY BACK IN.
YOU'LL REMEMBER IT ALL SOON ENOUGH. WHO I AM, AND WHAT YOU HAVE TO DO.
I JUST NEED TO GENTLY REMIND YOU AND IT'LL ALL COME FLOODING BACK.

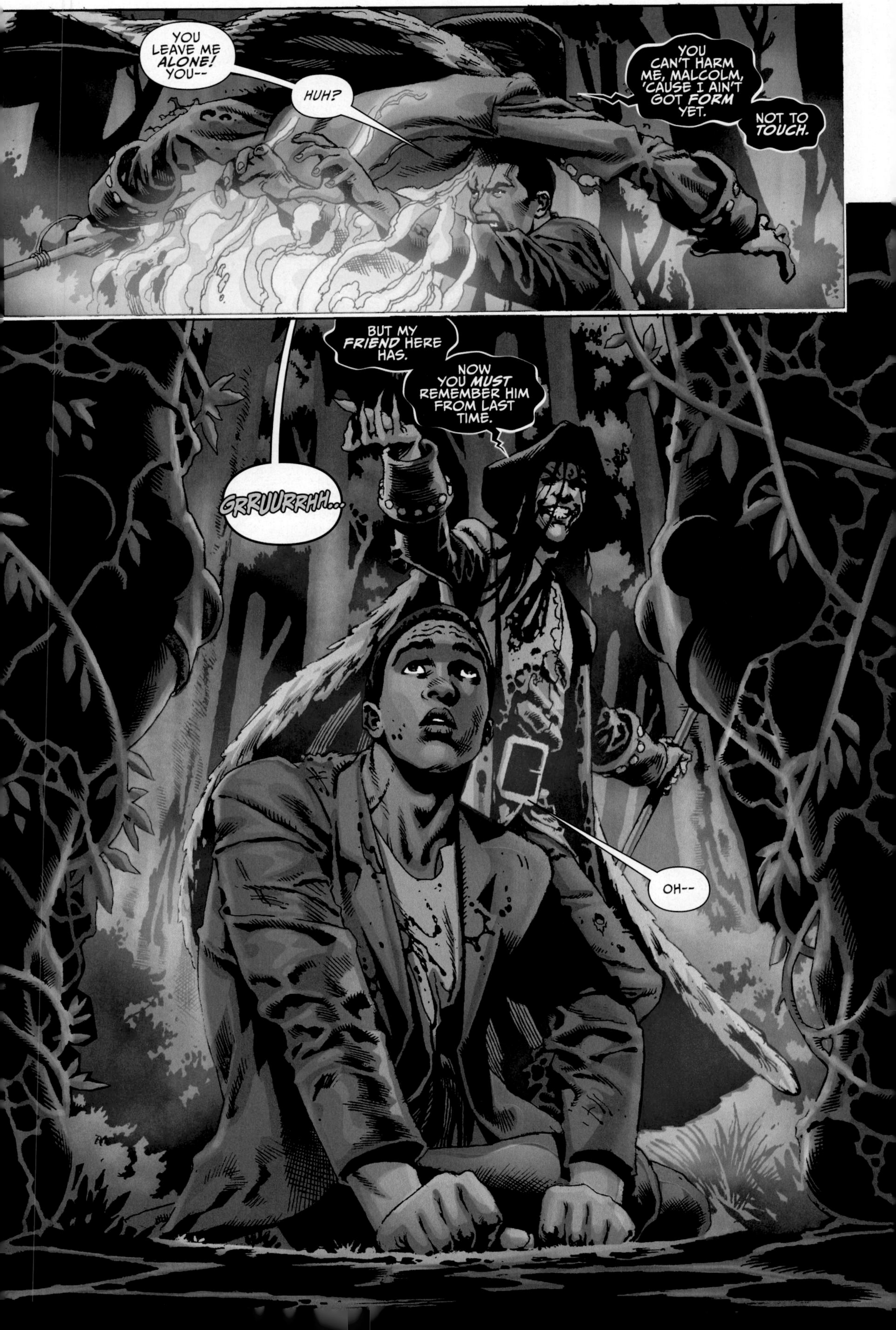
YOU LEAVE ME ALONE! YOU--
HUH?
YOU CAN'T HARM ME, MALCOLM, 'CAUSE I AIN'T GOT FORM YET.
NOT TO TOUCH.
BUT MY FRIEND HERE HAS.
NOW YOU MUST REMEMBER HIM FROM LAST TIME.
GRRUURRHH...
OH--

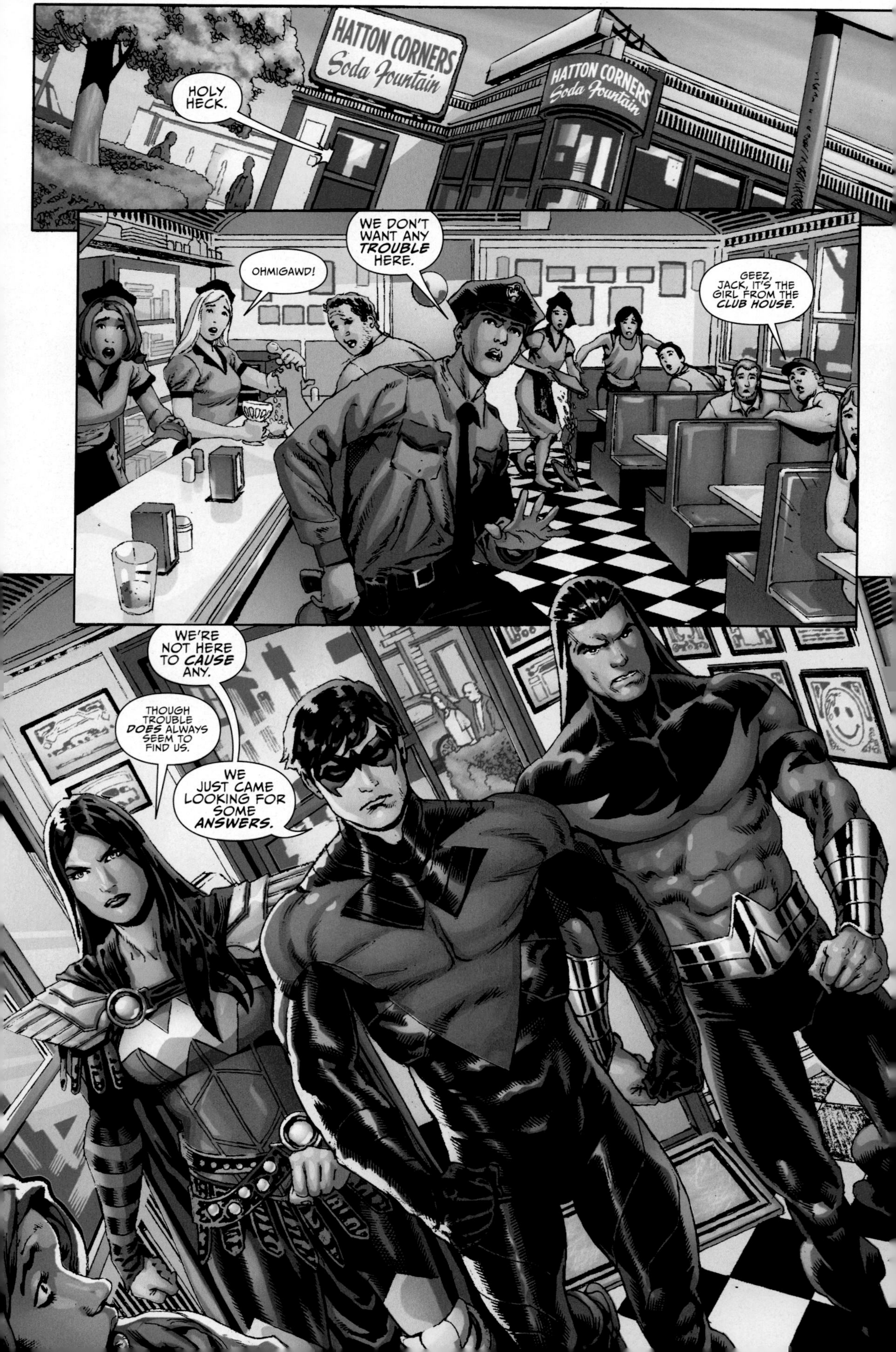
HATTON CORNERS
Soda Fountain
HATTON CORNERS
Soda Fountain
HOLY HECK.
OHMIGAWD!
WE DON'T WANT ANY *TROUBLE* HERE.
GEEZ, JACK, IT'S THE GIRL FROM THE *CLUB HOUSE.*
WE'RE NOT HERE TO *CAUSE* ANY.
THOUGH TROUBLE *DOES* ALWAYS SEEM TO FIND US.
WE JUST CAME LOOKING FOR SOME *ANSWERS.*

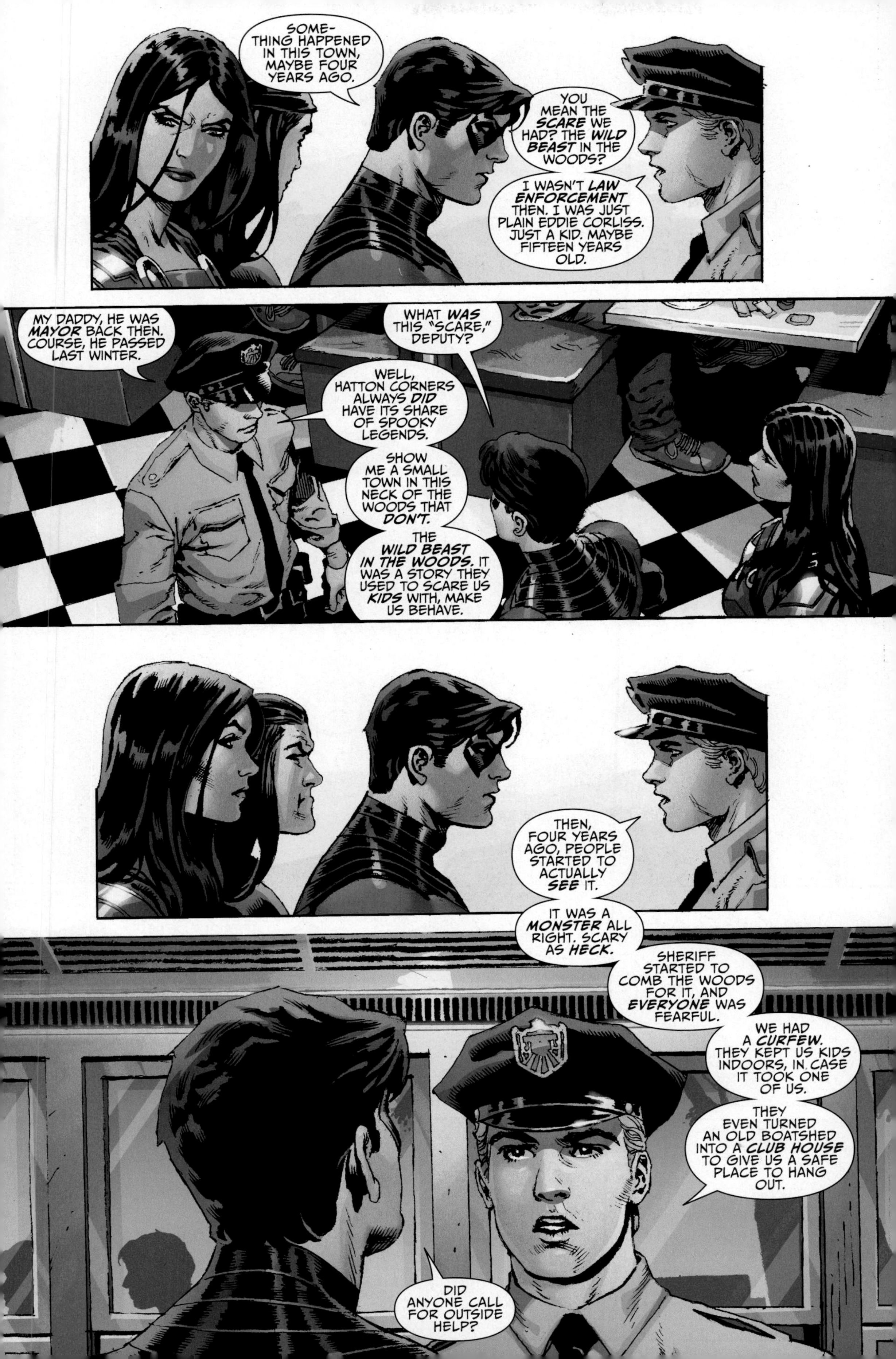
SOMETHING HAPPENED IN THIS TOWN, MAYBE FOUR YEARS AGO.
YOU MEAN THE SCARE WE HAD? THE WILD BEAST IN THE WOODS?
I WASN'T LAW ENFORCEMENT THEN. I WAS JUST PLAIN EDDIE CORLISS. JUST A KID. MAYBE FIFTEEN YEARS OLD.
MY DADDY, HE WAS MAYOR BACK THEN. COURSE, HE PASSED LAST WINTER.
WHAT WAS THIS "SCARE," DEPUTY?
WELL, HATTON CORNERS ALWAYS DID HAVE ITS SHARE OF SPOOKY LEGENDS.
SHOW ME A SMALL TOWN IN THIS NECK OF THE WOODS THAT DON'T.
THE WILD BEAST IN THE WOODS. IT WAS A STORY THEY USED TO SCARE US KIDS WITH, MAKE US BEHAVE.
THEN, FOUR YEARS AGO, PEOPLE STARTED TO ACTUALLY SEE IT.
IT WAS A MONSTER ALL RIGHT. SCARY AS HECK.
SHERIFF STARTED TO COMB THE WOODS FOR IT, AND EVERYONE WAS FEARFUL.
WE HAD A CURFEW. THEY KEPT US KIDS INDOORS, IN CASE IT TOOK ONE OF US.
THEY EVEN TURNED AN OLD BOATSHED INTO A CLUB HOUSE TO GIVE US A SAFE PLACE TO HANG OUT.
DID ANYONE CALL FOR OUTSIDE HELP?

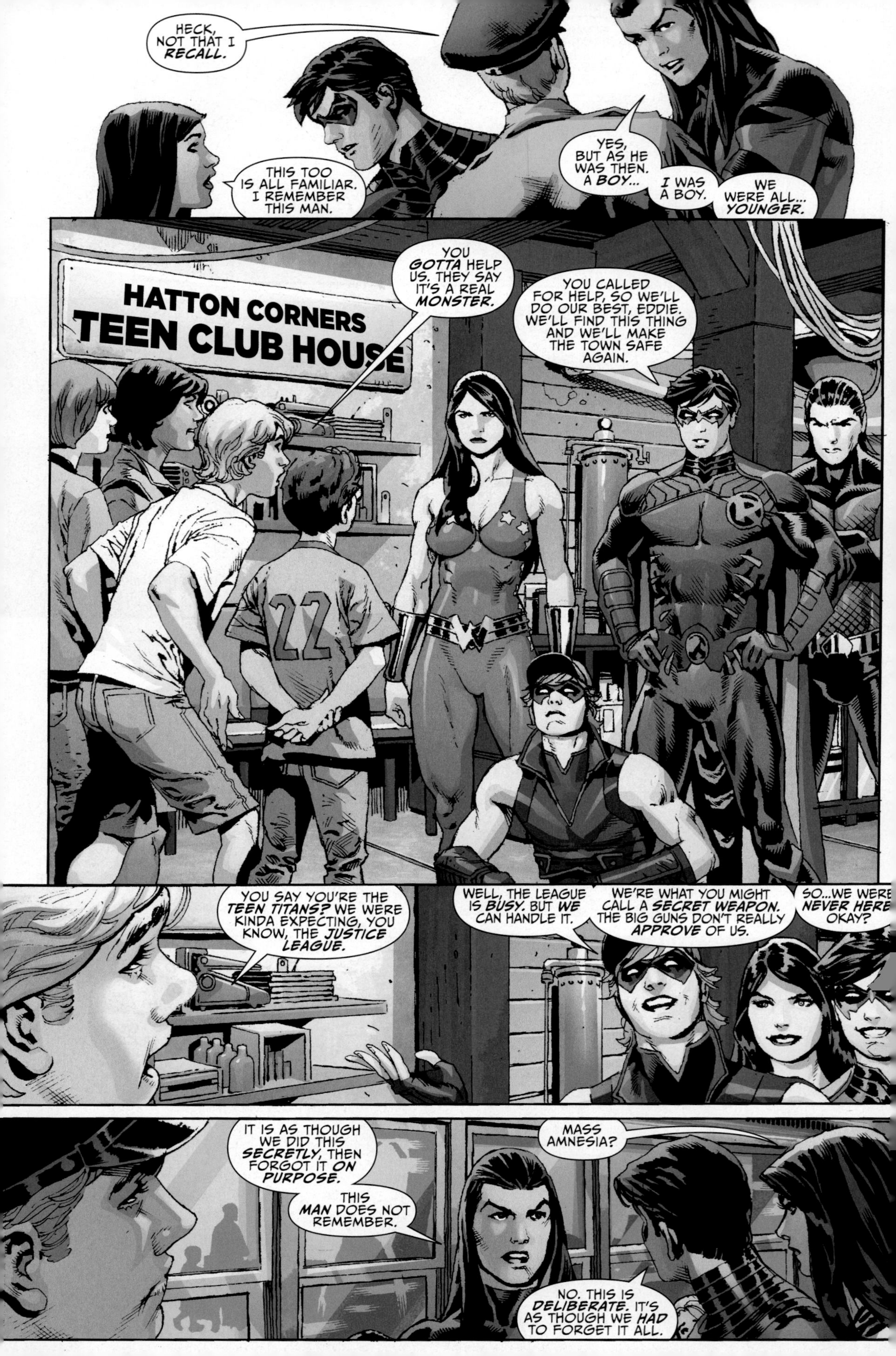
HECK, NOT THAT I RECALL.
THIS TOO IS ALL FAMILIAR. I REMEMBER THIS MAN.
YES, BUT AS HE WAS THEN. A BOY...
I WAS A BOY.
WE WERE ALL... YOUNGER.
HATTON CORNERS TEEN CLUB HOUSE
YOU GOTTA HELP US. THEY SAY IT'S A REAL MONSTER.
YOU CALLED FOR HELP, SO WE'LL DO OUR BEST, EDDIE. WE'LL FIND THIS THING AND WE'LL MAKE THE TOWN SAFE AGAIN.
22
YOU SAY YOU'RE THE TEEN TITANS? WE WERE KINDA EXPECTING, YOU KNOW, THE JUSTICE LEAGUE.
WELL, THE LEAGUE IS BUSY. BUT WE CAN HANDLE IT.
WE'RE WHAT YOU MIGHT CALL A SECRET WEAPON. THE BIG GUNS DON'T REALLY APPROVE OF US.
SO...WE WERE NEVER HERE OKAY?
IT IS AS THOUGH WE DID THIS SECRETLY, THEN FORGOT IT ON PURPOSE.
THIS MAN DOES NOT REMEMBER.
MASS AMNESIA?
NO. THIS IS DELIBERATE. IT'S AS THOUGH WE HAD TO FORGET IT ALL.

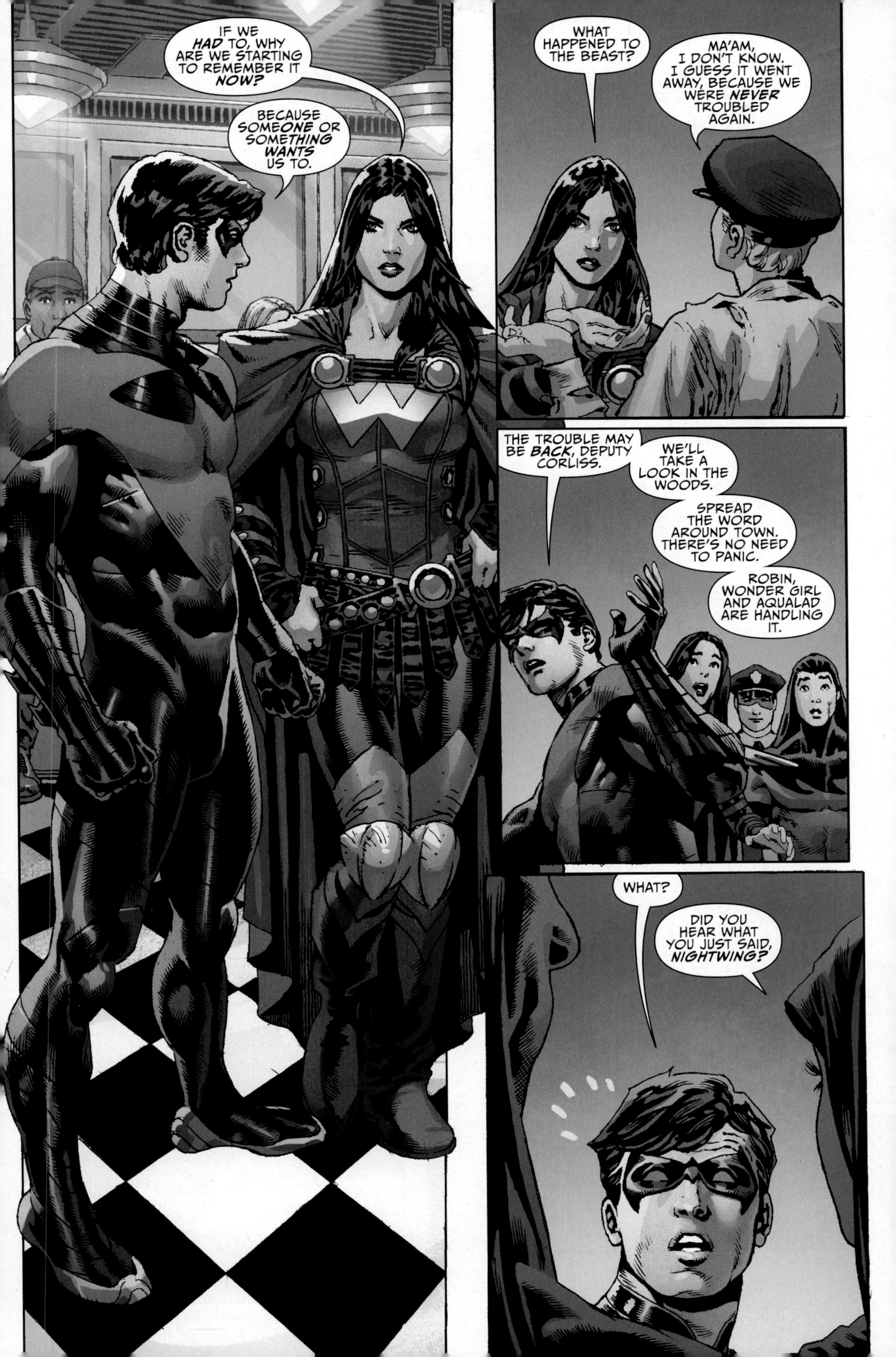
IF WE HAD TO, WHY ARE WE STARTING TO REMEMBER IT NOW?
BECAUSE SOMEONE OR SOMETHING WANTS US TO.
WHAT HAPPENED TO THE BEAST?
MA'AM, I DON'T KNOW. I GUESS IT WENT AWAY, BECAUSE WE WERE NEVER TROUBLED AGAIN.
THE TROUBLE MAY BE BACK, DEPUTY CORLISS.
WE'LL TAKE A LOOK IN THE WOODS.
SPREAD THE WORD AROUND TOWN. THERE'S NO NEED TO PANIC.
ROBIN, WONDER GIRL AND AQUALAD ARE HANDLING IT.
WHAT?
DID YOU HEAR WHAT YOU JUST SAID, NIGHTWING?

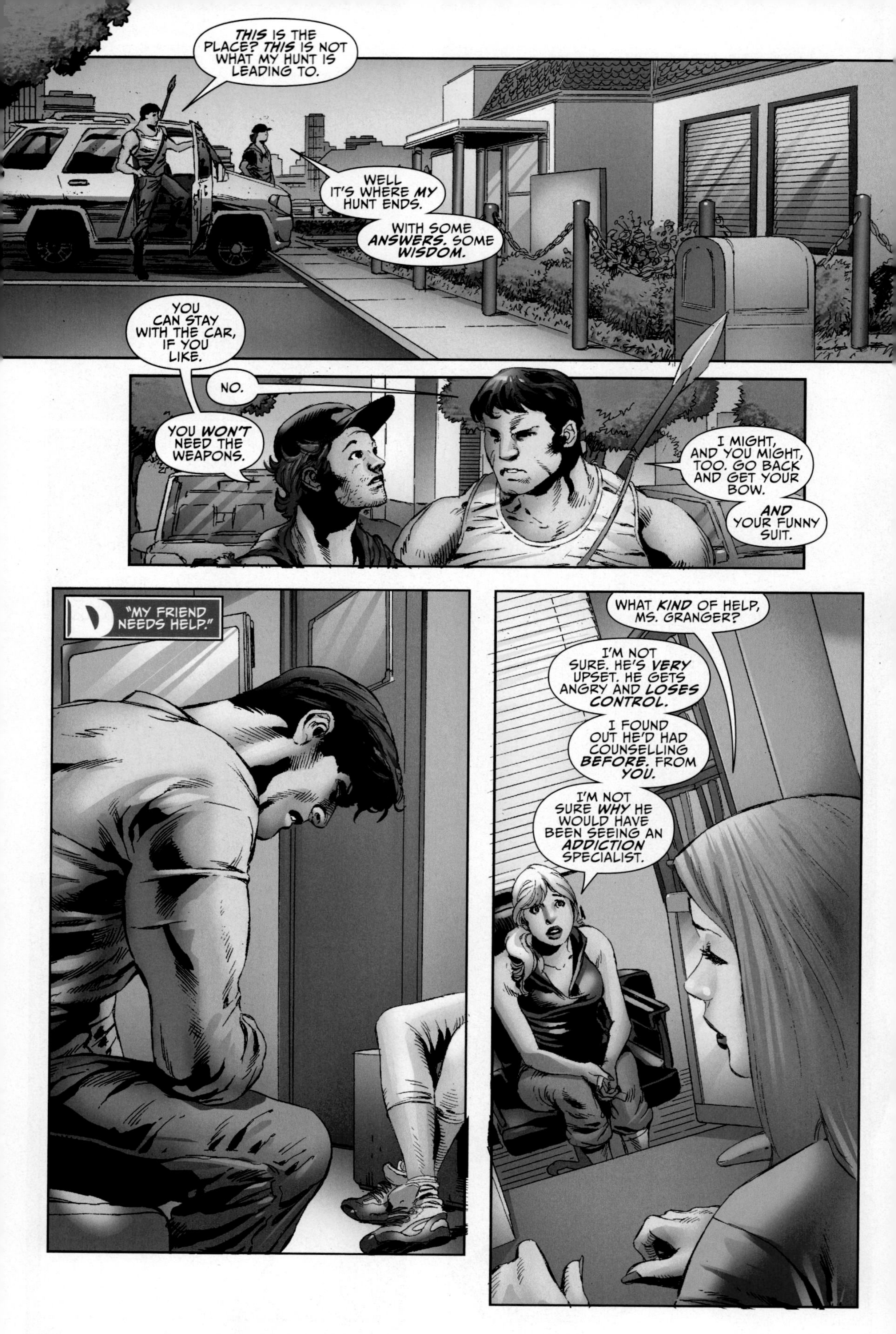
THIS IS THE PLACE? THIS IS NOT WHAT MY HUNT IS LEADING TO.
WELL IT'S WHERE MY HUNT ENDS.
WITH SOME ANSWERS. SOME WISDOM.
YOU CAN STAY WITH THE CAR, IF YOU LIKE.
NO.
YOU WON'T NEED THE WEAPONS.
I MIGHT, AND YOU MIGHT, TOO. GO BACK AND GET YOUR BOW.
AND YOUR FUNNY SUIT.
"MY FRIEND NEEDS HELP."
WHAT KIND OF HELP, MS. GRANGER?
I'M NOT SURE. HE'S VERY UPSET. HE GETS ANGRY AND LOSES CONTROL.
I FOUND OUT HE'D HAD COUNSELLING BEFORE. FROM YOU.
I'M NOT SURE WHY HE WOULD HAVE BEEN SEEING AN ADDICTION SPECIALIST.

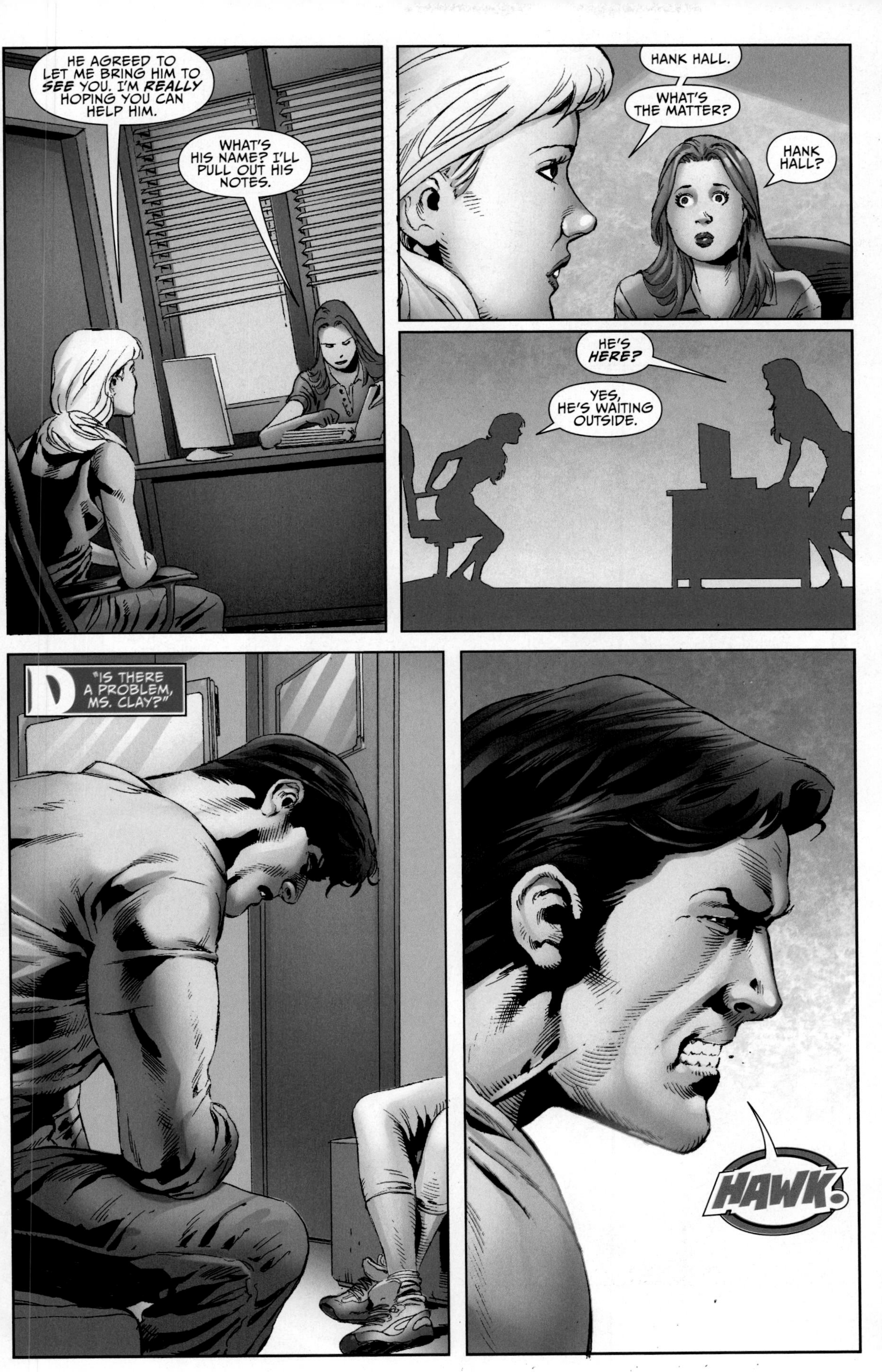
HE AGREED TO LET ME BRING HIM TO SEE YOU. I'M REALLY HOPING YOU CAN HELP HIM.
WHAT'S HIS NAME? I'LL PULL OUT HIS NOTES.
HANK HALL.
WHAT'S THE MATTER?
HANK HALL?
HE'S HERE?
YES, HE'S WAITING OUTSIDE.
"IS THERE A PROBLEM, MS. CLAY?"
HAWK.

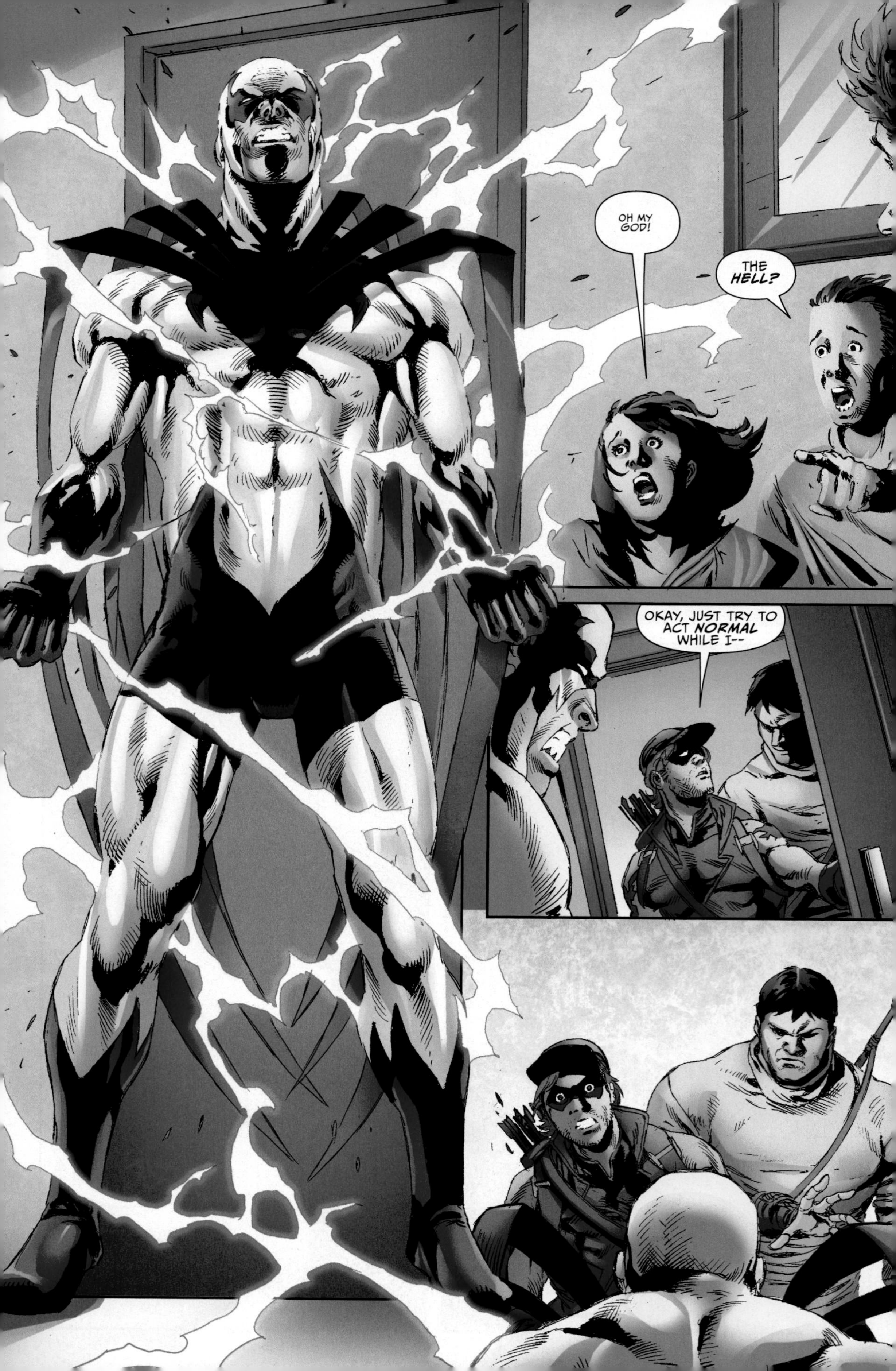
OH MY GOD!
THE HELL?
OKAY, JUST TRY TO ACT NORMAL WHILE I--

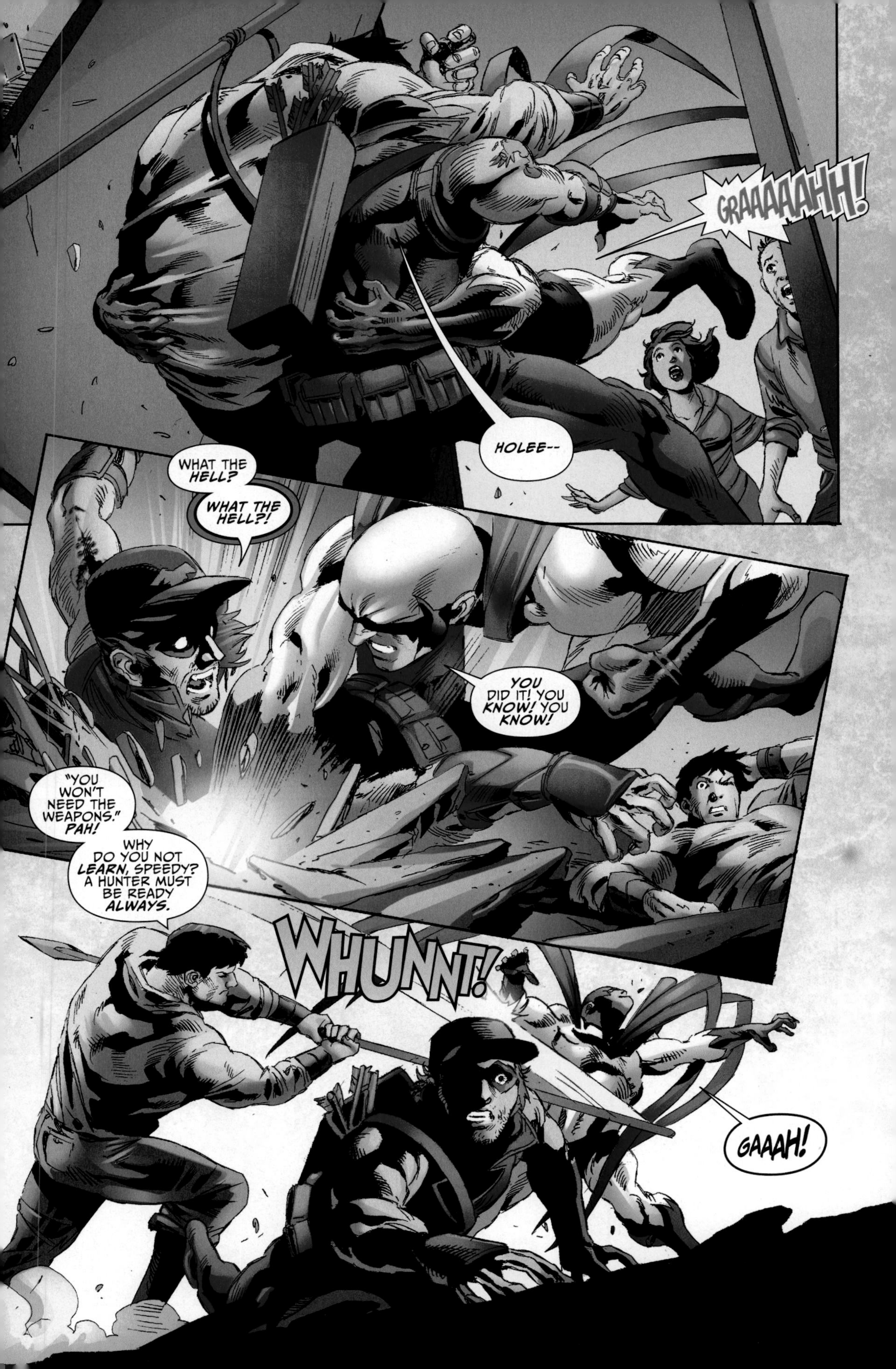
GRAAAAAHH!
HOLEE--
WHAT THE HELL?
WHAT THE HELL?!
YOU DID IT! YOU KNOW! YOU KNOW!
"YOU WON'T NEED THE WEAPONS." PAH!
WHY DO YOU NOT LEARN, SPEEDY? A HUNTER MUST BE READY ALWAYS.
WHUNNT!
GAAAH!

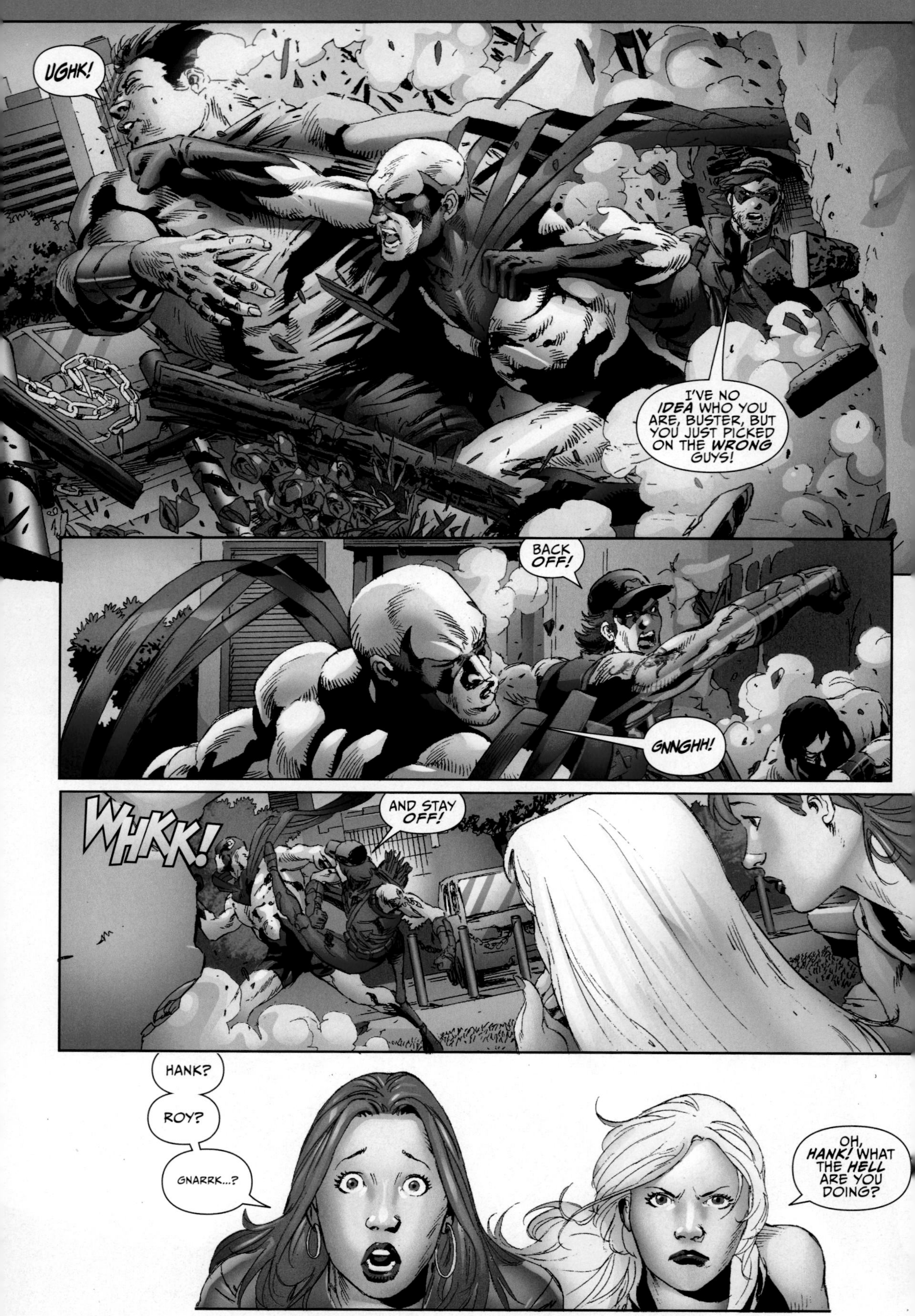
UGHK!
I'VE NO IDEA WHO YOU ARE, BUSTER, BUT YOU JUST PICKED ON THE WRONG GUYS!
BACK OFF!
GNNGHH!
WHKK!
AND STAY OFF!
HANK?
ROY?
GNARRK...?
OH, HANK! WHAT THE HELL ARE YOU DOING?

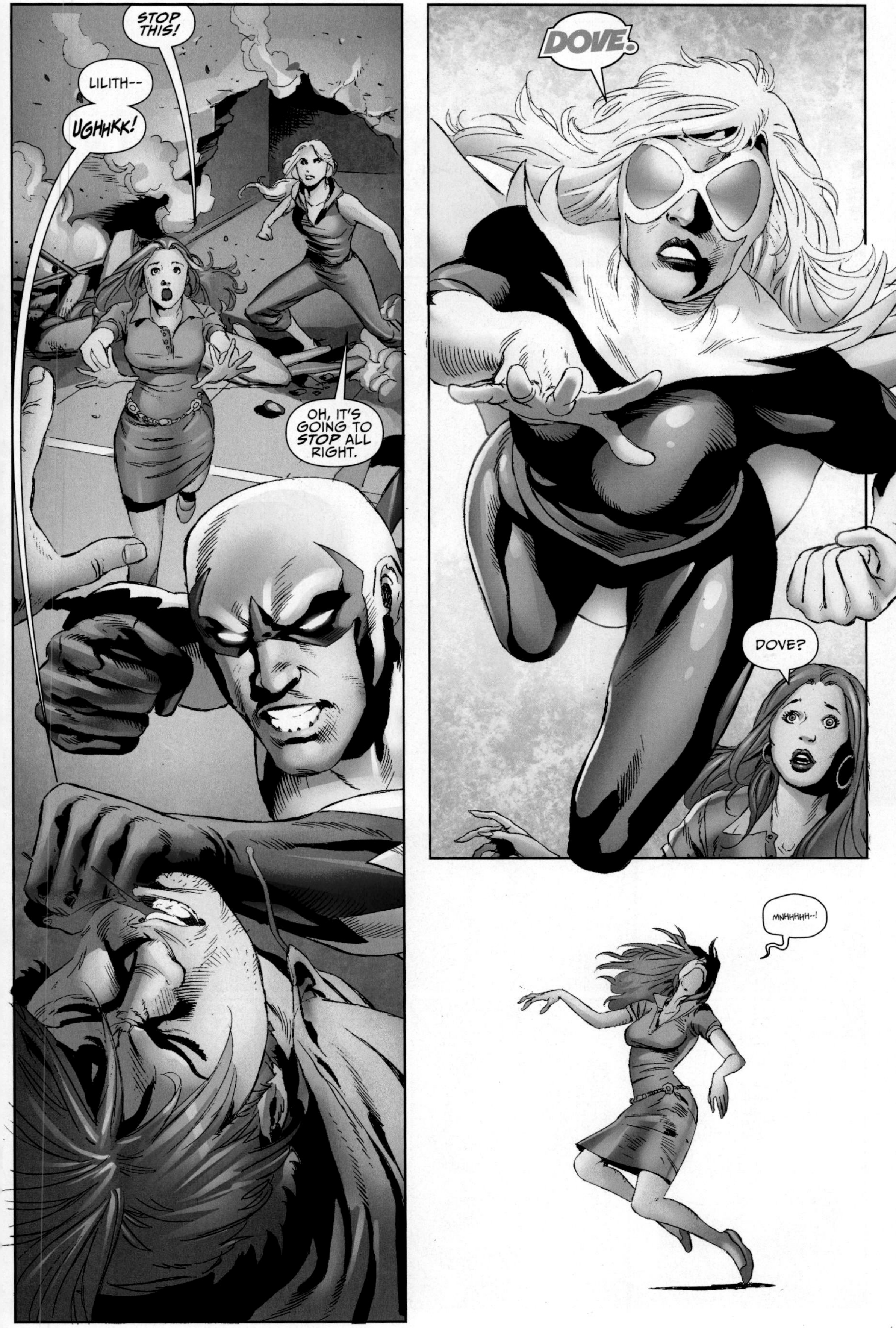
STOP THIS!
LILITH--
UGHHKK!
OH, IT'S GOING TO STOP ALL RIGHT.
DOVE.
DOVE?
MNHHHHH--!

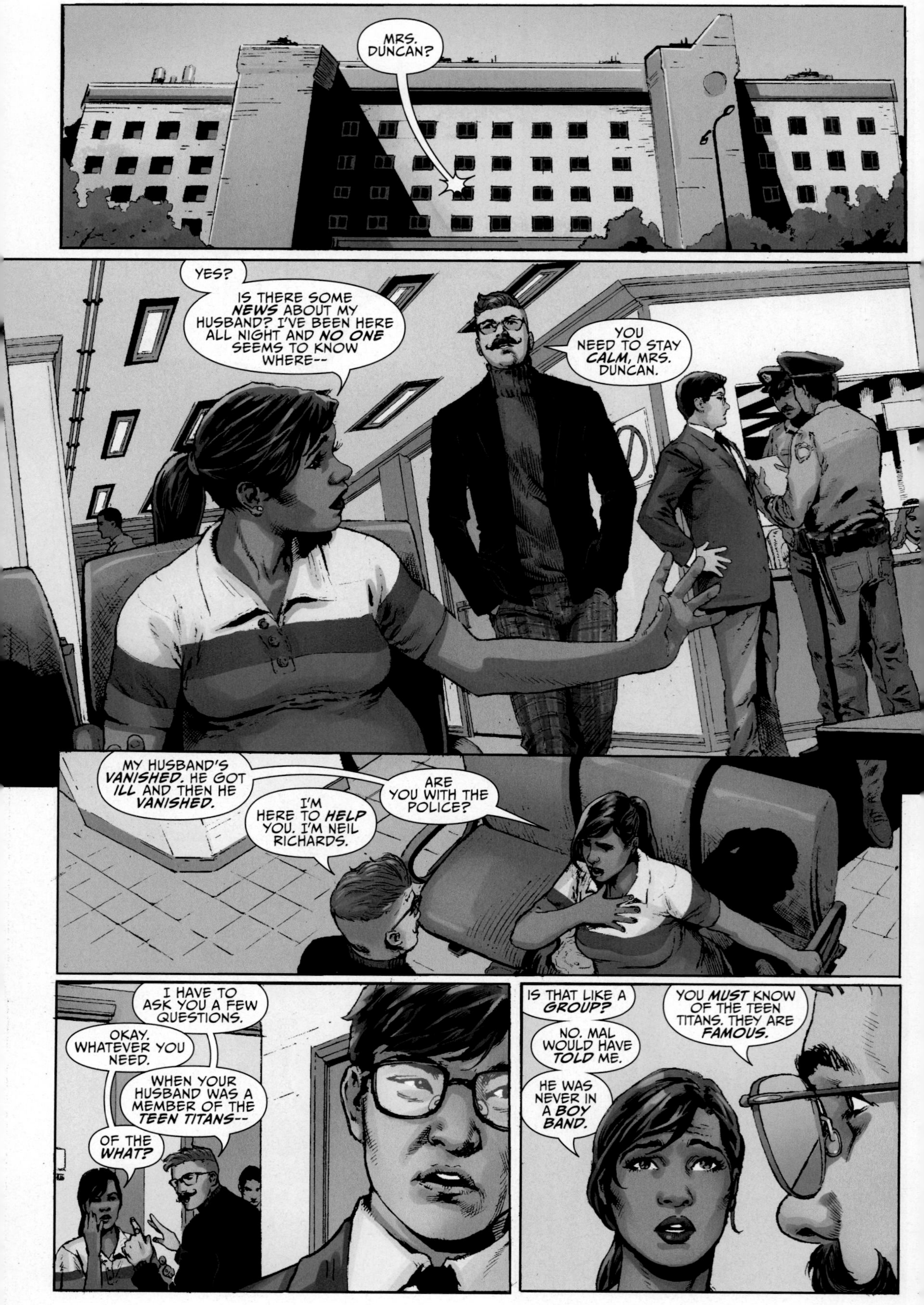

MRS. DUNCAN?
YES?
IS THERE SOME NEWS ABOUT MY HUSBAND? I'VE BEEN HERE ALL NIGHT AND NO ONE SEEMS TO KNOW WHERE--
YOU NEED TO STAY CALM, MRS. DUNCAN.
MY HUSBAND'S VANISHED. HE GOT ILL AND THEN HE VANISHED.
I'M HERE TO HELP YOU. I'M NEIL RICHARDS.
ARE YOU WITH THE POLICE?
I HAVE TO ASK YOU A FEW QUESTIONS.
OKAY. WHATEVER YOU NEED.
WHEN YOUR HUSBAND WAS A MEMBER OF THE TEEN TITANS--
OF THE WHAT?
YOU MUST KNOW OF THE TEEN TITANS. THEY ARE FAMOUS.
IS THAT LIKE A GROUP?
NO. MAL WOULD HAVE TOLD ME.
HE WAS NEVER IN A BOY BAND.

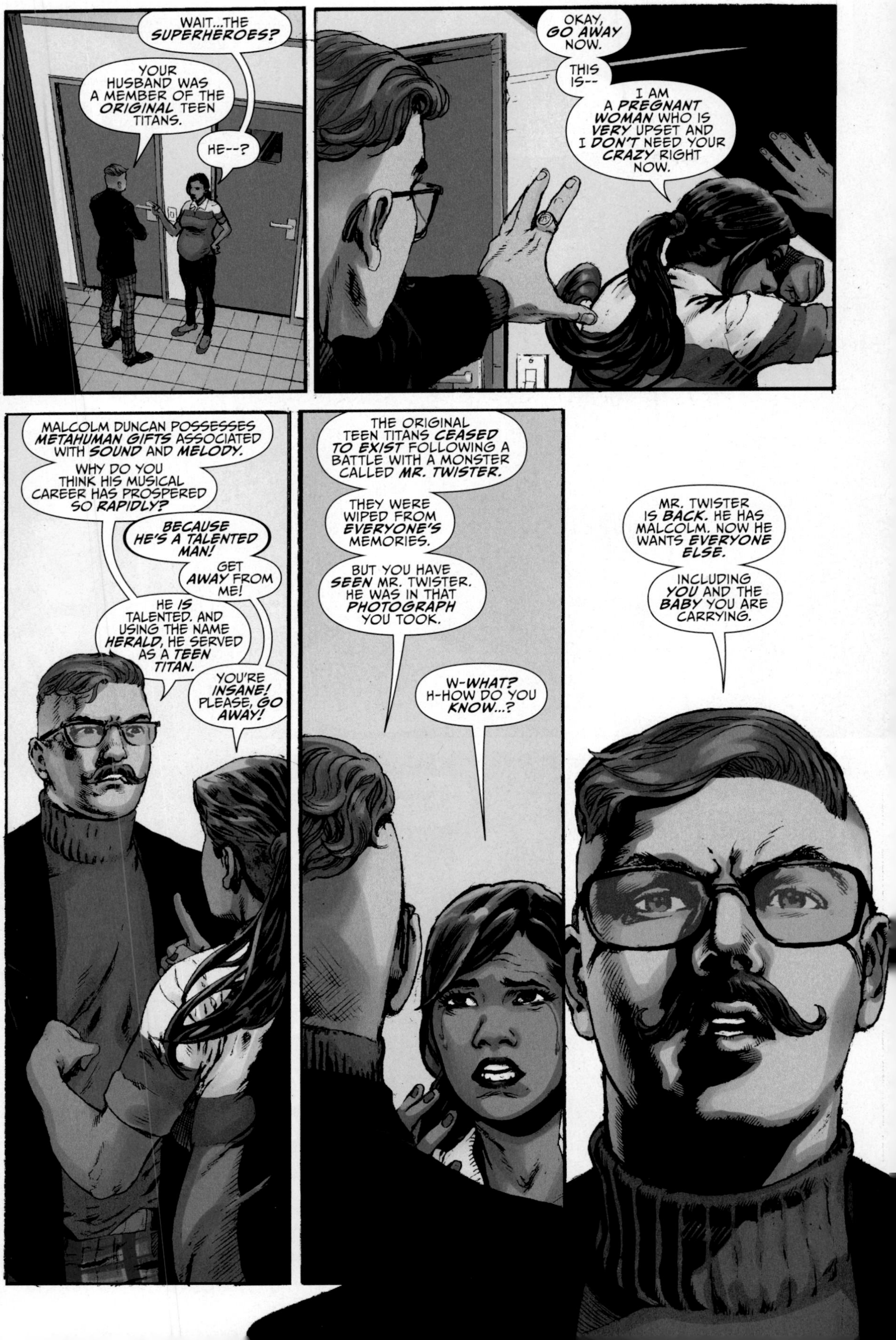
WAIT...THE SUPERHEROES?
YOUR HUSBAND WAS A MEMBER OF THE ORIGINAL TEEN TITANS.
HE--?
OKAY, GO AWAY NOW.
THIS IS--
I AM A PREGNANT WOMAN WHO IS VERY UPSET AND I DON'T NEED YOUR CRAZY RIGHT NOW.
MALCOLM DUNCAN POSSESSES METAHUMAN GIFTS ASSOCIATED WITH SOUND AND MELODY.
WHY DO YOU THINK HIS MUSICAL CAREER HAS PROSPERED SO RAPIDLY?
BECAUSE HE'S A TALENTED MAN!
GET AWAY FROM ME!
HE IS TALENTED. AND USING THE NAME HERALD, HE SERVED AS A TEEN TITAN.
YOU'RE INSANE! PLEASE, GO AWAY!
THE ORIGINAL TEEN TITANS CEASED TO EXIST FOLLOWING A BATTLE WITH A MONSTER CALLED MR. TWISTER.
THEY WERE WIPED FROM EVERYONE'S MEMORIES.
BUT YOU HAVE SEEN MR. TWISTER. HE WAS IN THAT PHOTOGRAPH YOU TOOK.
W-WHAT? H-HOW DO YOU KNOW...?
MR. TWISTER IS BACK. HE HAS MALCOLM. NOW HE WANTS EVERYONE ELSE.
INCLUDING YOU AND THE BABY YOU ARE CARRYING.

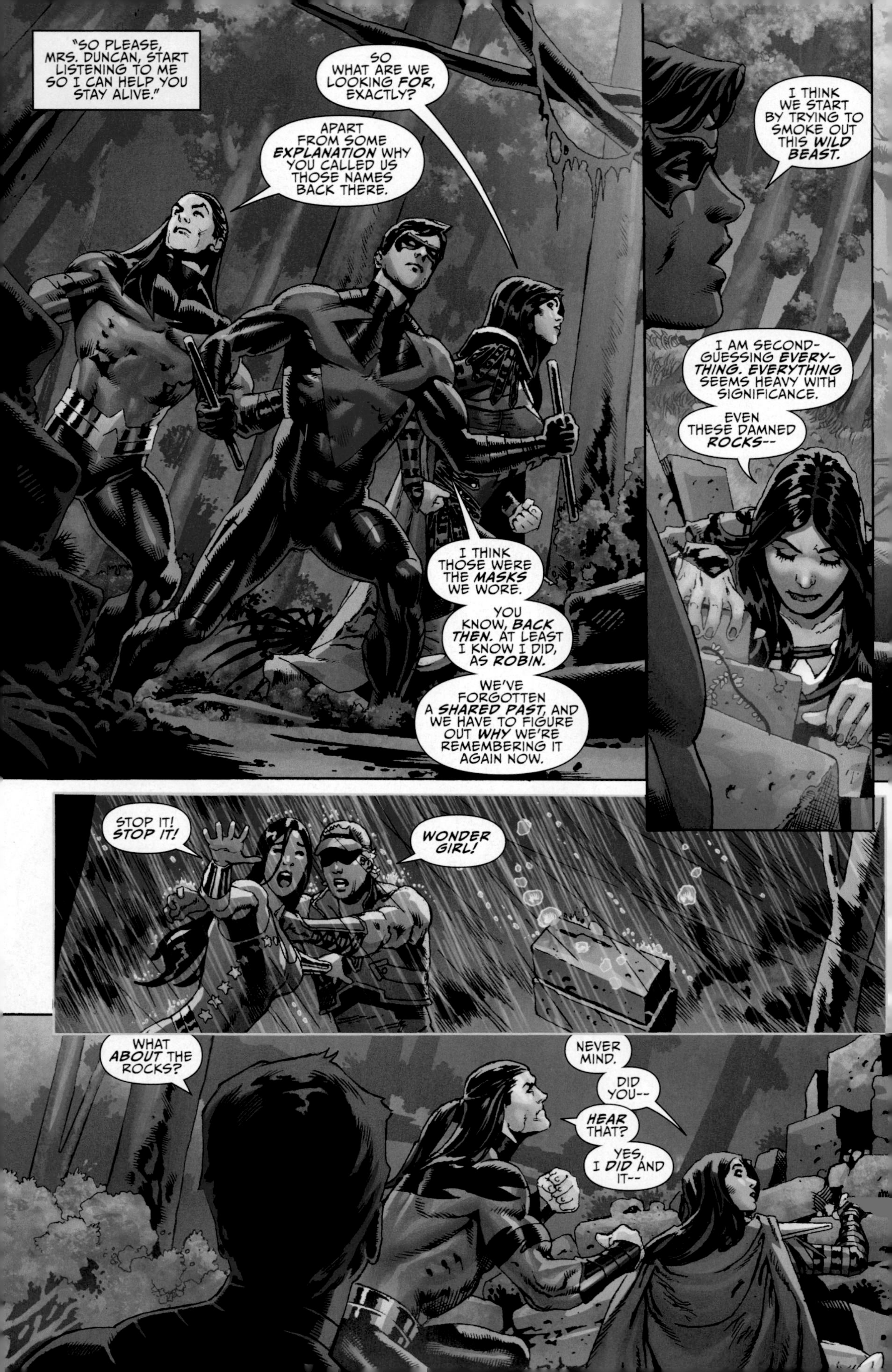

"SO PLEASE, MRS. DUNCAN, START LISTENING TO ME SO I CAN HELP YOU STAY ALIVE."
SO WHAT ARE WE LOOKING FOR, EXACTLY?
APART FROM SOME EXPLANATION WHY YOU CALLED US THOSE NAMES BACK THERE.
I THINK THOSE WERE THE MASKS WE WORE.
YOU KNOW, BACK THEN. AT LEAST I KNOW I DID, AS ROBIN.
WE'VE FORGOTTEN A SHARED PAST, AND WE HAVE TO FIGURE OUT WHY WE'RE REMEMBERING IT AGAIN NOW.
I THINK WE START BY TRYING TO SMOKE OUT THIS WILD BEAST.
I AM SECOND-GUESSING EVERY-THING. EVERYTHING SEEMS HEAVY WITH SIGNIFICANCE.
EVEN THESE DAMNED ROCKS--
STOP IT! STOP IT!
WONDER GIRL!
WHAT ABOUT THE ROCKS?
NEVER MIND.
DID YOU--
HEAR THAT?
YES, I DID AND IT--

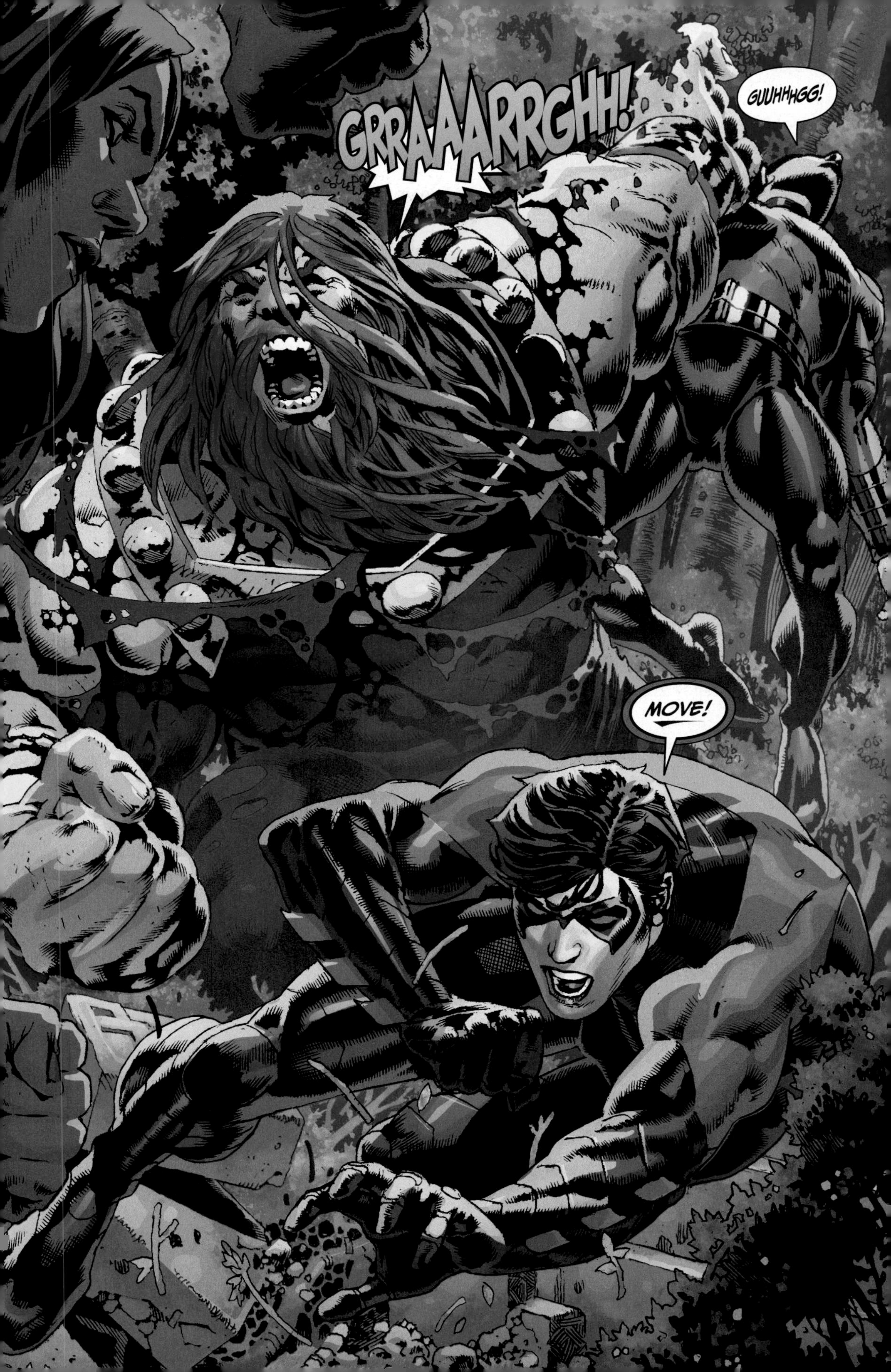
GRRAAARRGHH!
GUUHHHGG!
MOVE!

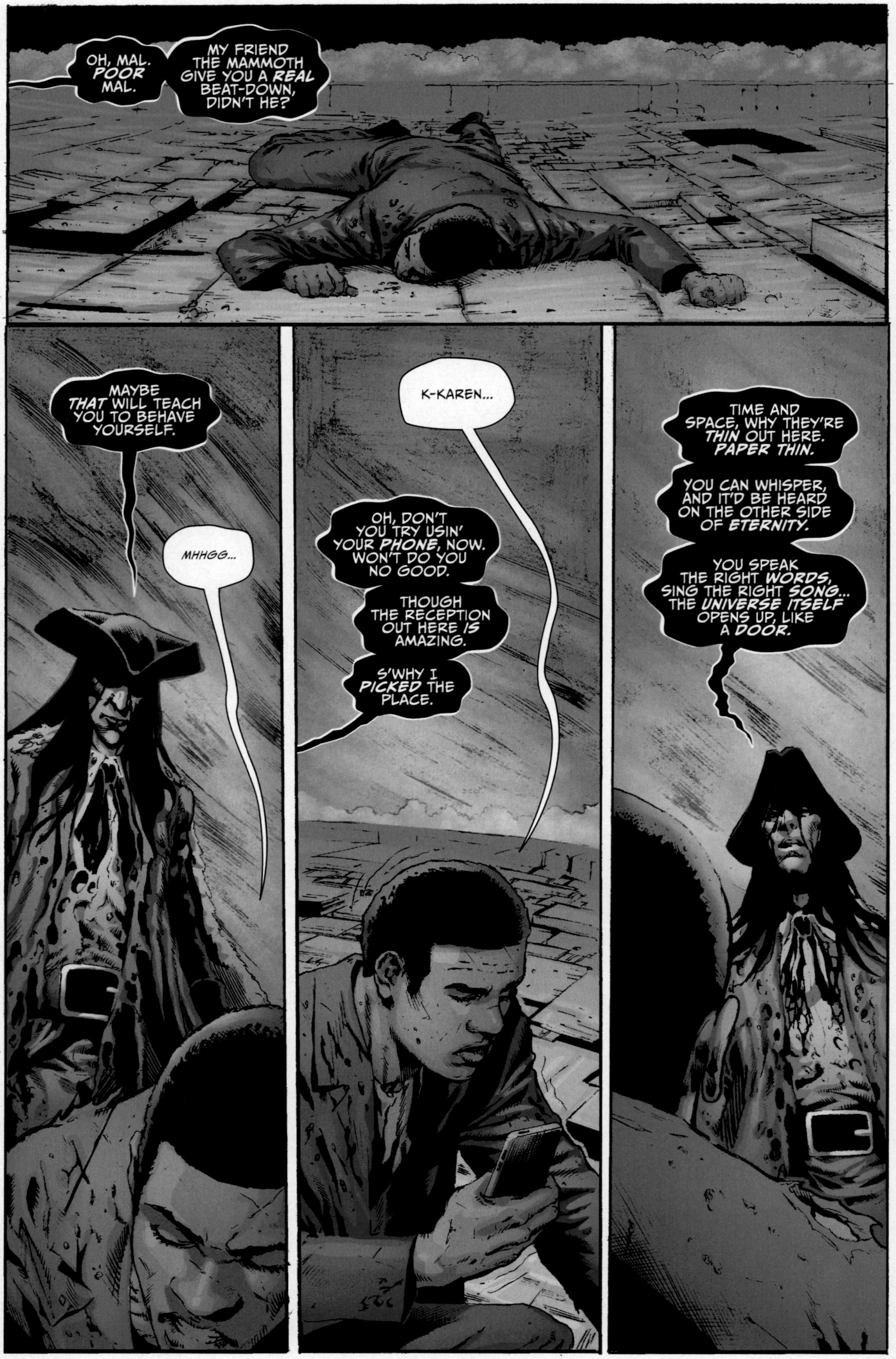
OH, MAL. POOR MAL.
MY FRIEND THE MAMMOTH GIVE YOU A REAL BEAT-DOWN, DIDN'T HE?
MAYBE THAT WILL TEACH YOU TO BEHAVE YOURSELF.
MHHGG...
K-KAREN...
OH, DON'T YOU TRY USIN' YOUR PHONE, NOW. WON'T DO YOU NO GOOD.
THOUGH THE RECEPTION OUT HERE IS AMAZING.
S'WHY I PICKED THE PLACE.
TIME AND SPACE, WHY THEY'RE THIN OUT HERE. PAPER THIN.
YOU CAN WHISPER, AND IT'D BE HEARD ON THE OTHER SIDE OF ETERNITY.
YOU SPEAK THE RIGHT WORDS, SING THE RIGHT SONG... THE UNIVERSE ITSELF OPENS UP, LIKE A DOOR.

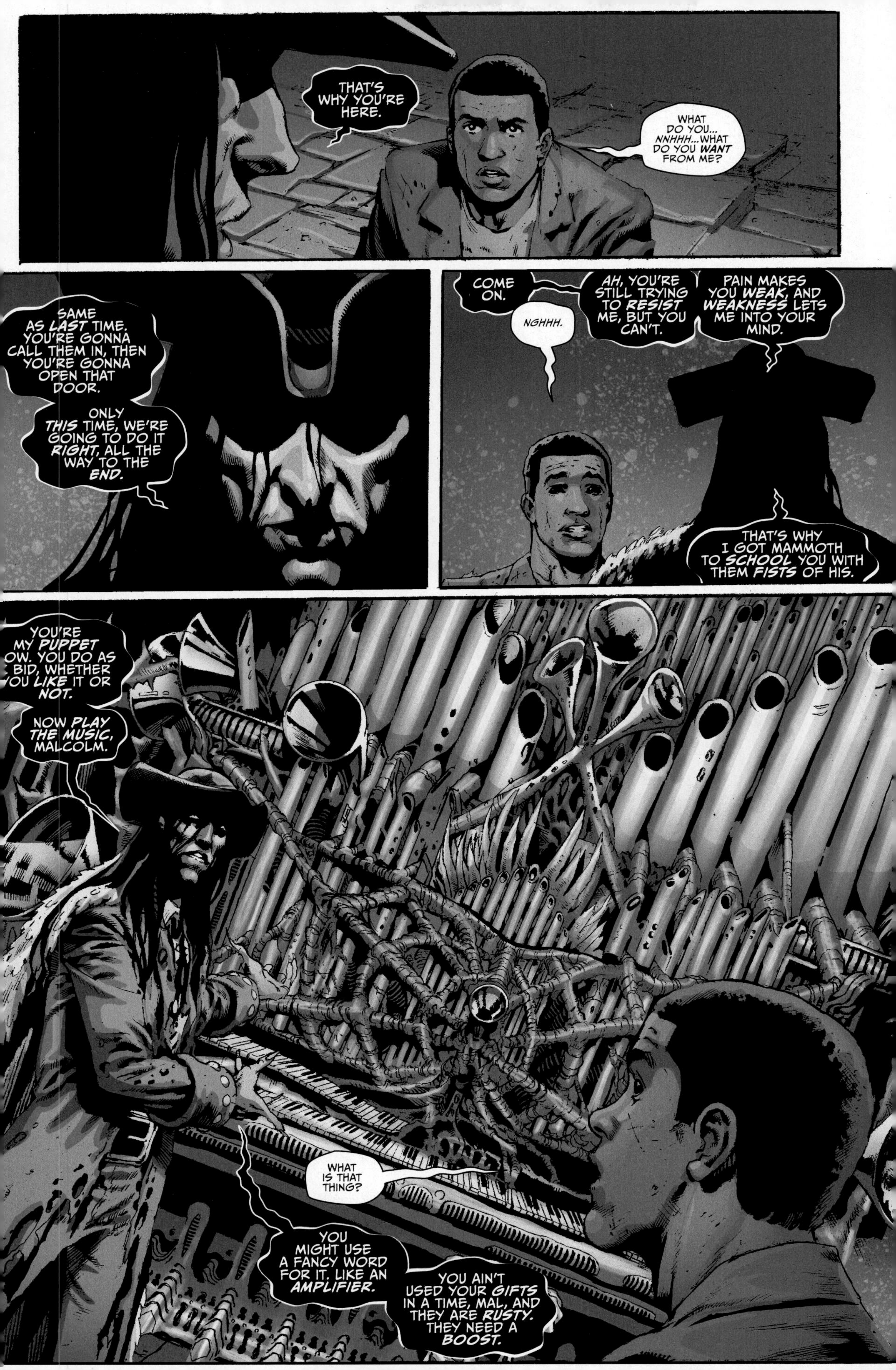
THAT'S WHY YOU'RE HERE.
WHAT DO YOU... NNHHH...WHAT DO YOU WANT FROM ME?
SAME AS LAST TIME. YOU'RE GONNA CALL THEM IN, THEN YOU'RE GONNA OPEN THAT DOOR.
ONLY THIS TIME, WE'RE GOING TO DO IT RIGHT, ALL THE WAY TO THE END.
COME ON.
NGHHH.
AH, YOU'RE STILL TRYING TO RESIST ME, BUT YOU CAN'T.
PAIN MAKES YOU WEAK, AND WEAKNESS LETS ME INTO YOUR MIND.
THAT'S WHY I GOT MAMMOTH TO SCHOOL YOU WITH THEM FISTS OF HIS.
YOU'RE MY PUPPET OW. YOU DO AS BID, WHETHER YOU LIKE IT OR NOT.
NOW PLAY THE MUSIC, MALCOLM.
WHAT IS THAT THING?
YOU MIGHT USE A FANCY WORD FOR IT. LIKE AN AMPLIFIER.
YOU AIN'T USED YOUR GIFTS IN A TIME, MAL, AND THEY ARE RUSTY. THEY NEED A BOOST.

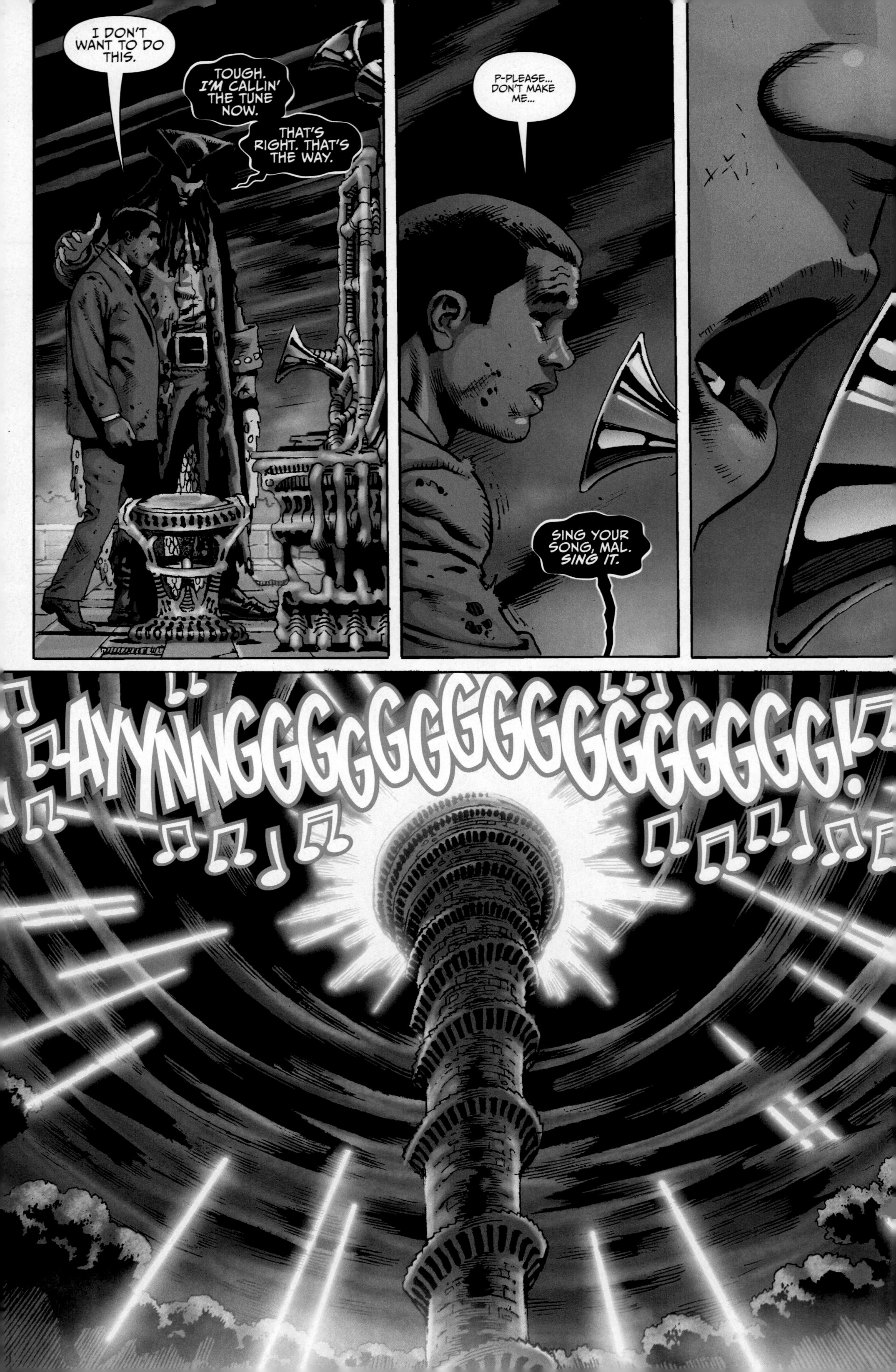
I DON'T WANT TO DO THIS.
TOUGH. I'M CALLIN' THE TUNE NOW.
THAT'S RIGHT. THAT'S THE WAY.
P-PLEASE... DON'T MAKE ME...
SING YOUR SONG, MAL. SING IT.
AYYNNGGGGGGGGGGGGGGG!

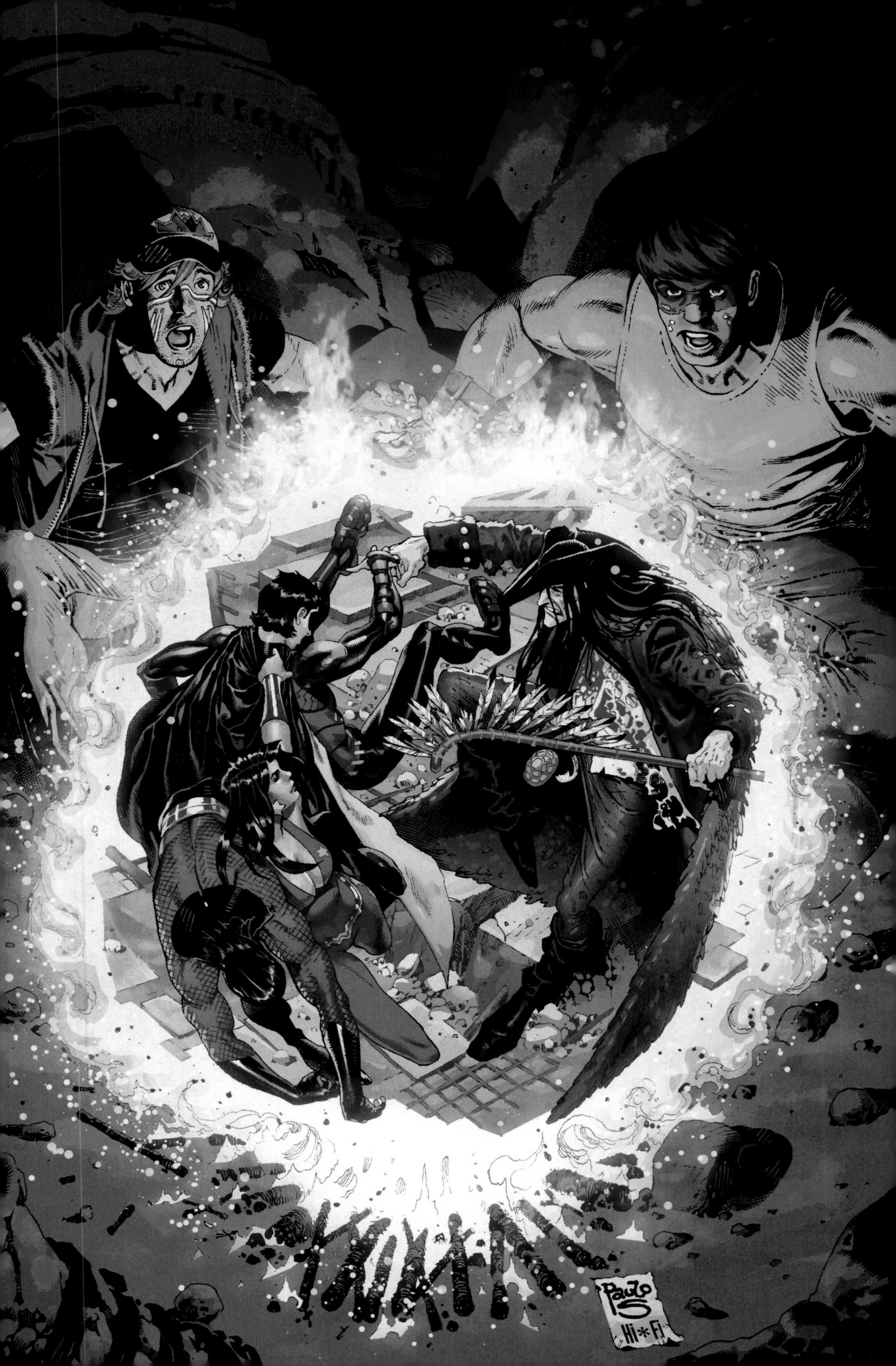

CHAPTER SIX: DIABOLIC

DAN ABNETT writer STEPHEN SEGOVIA penciller ART THIBERT inker HI-FI colorist cover art by PAULO SIQUEIRA & HI-FI

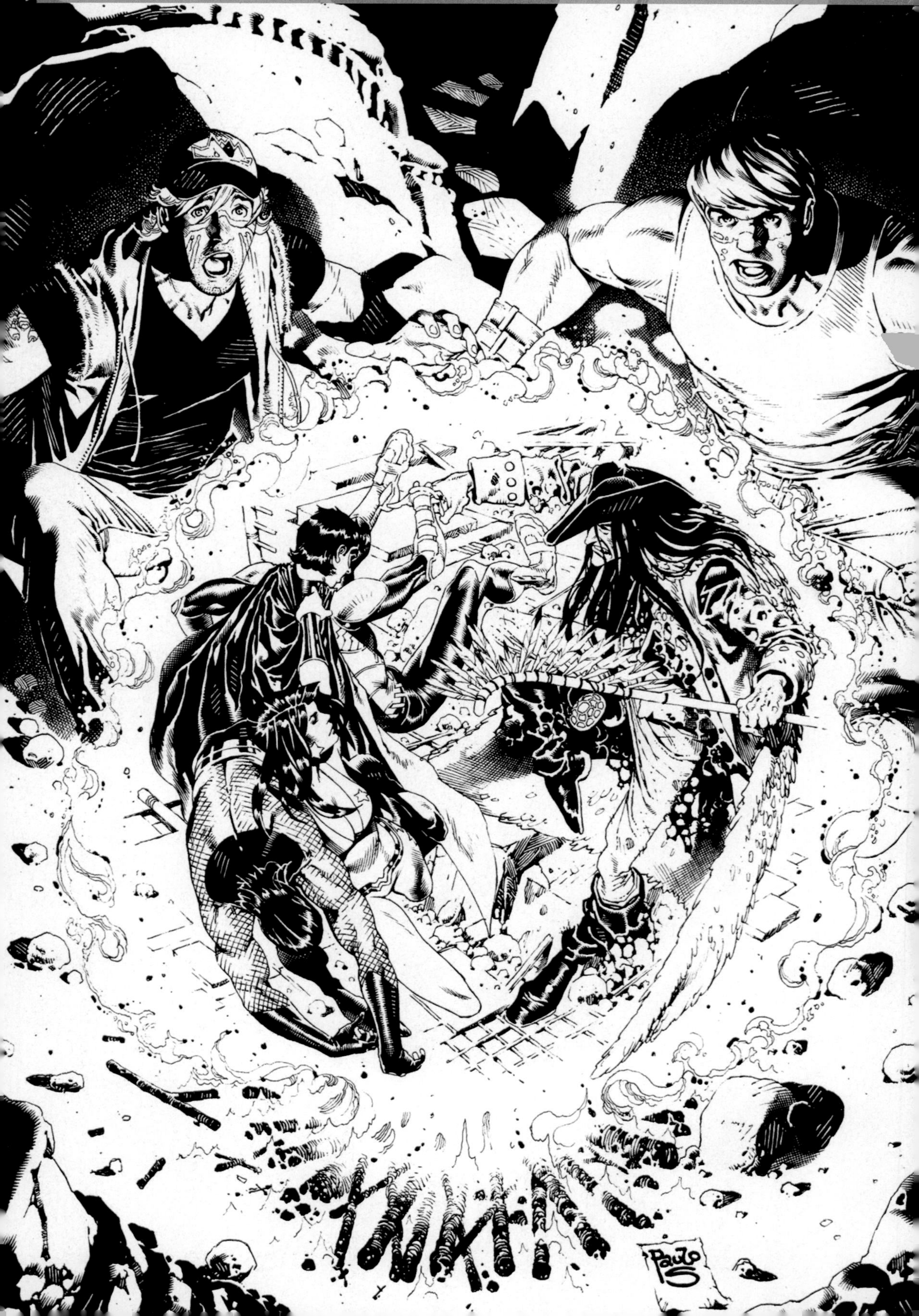

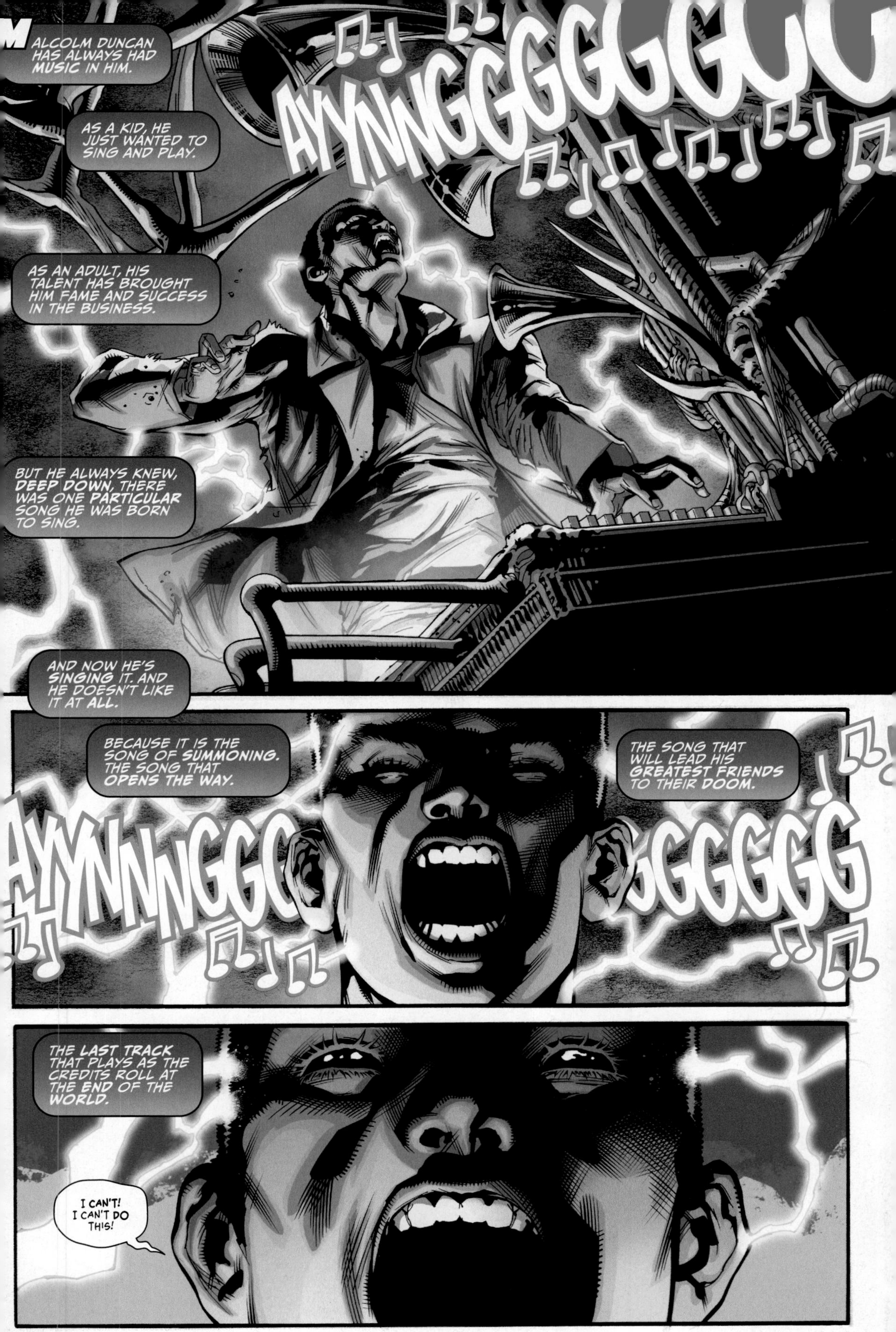
MALCOLM DUNCAN HAS ALWAYS HAD MUSIC IN HIM.
AYYNNGGGGGGGG
AS A KID, HE JUST WANTED TO SING AND PLAY.
AS AN ADULT, HIS TALENT HAS BROUGHT HIM FAME AND SUCCESS IN THE BUSINESS.
BUT HE ALWAYS KNEW, DEEP DOWN, THERE WAS ONE PARTICULAR SONG HE WAS BORN TO SING.
AND NOW HE'S SINGING IT. AND HE DOESN'T LIKE IT AT ALL.
BECAUSE IT IS THE SONG OF SUMMONING. THE SONG THAT OPENS THE WAY.
THE SONG THAT WILL LEAD HIS GREATEST FRIENDS TO THEIR DOOM.
AYYNNNGGGGGGGG
THE LAST TRACK THAT PLAYS AS THE CREDITS ROLL AT THE END OF THE WORLD.
I CAN'T! I CAN'T DO THIS!

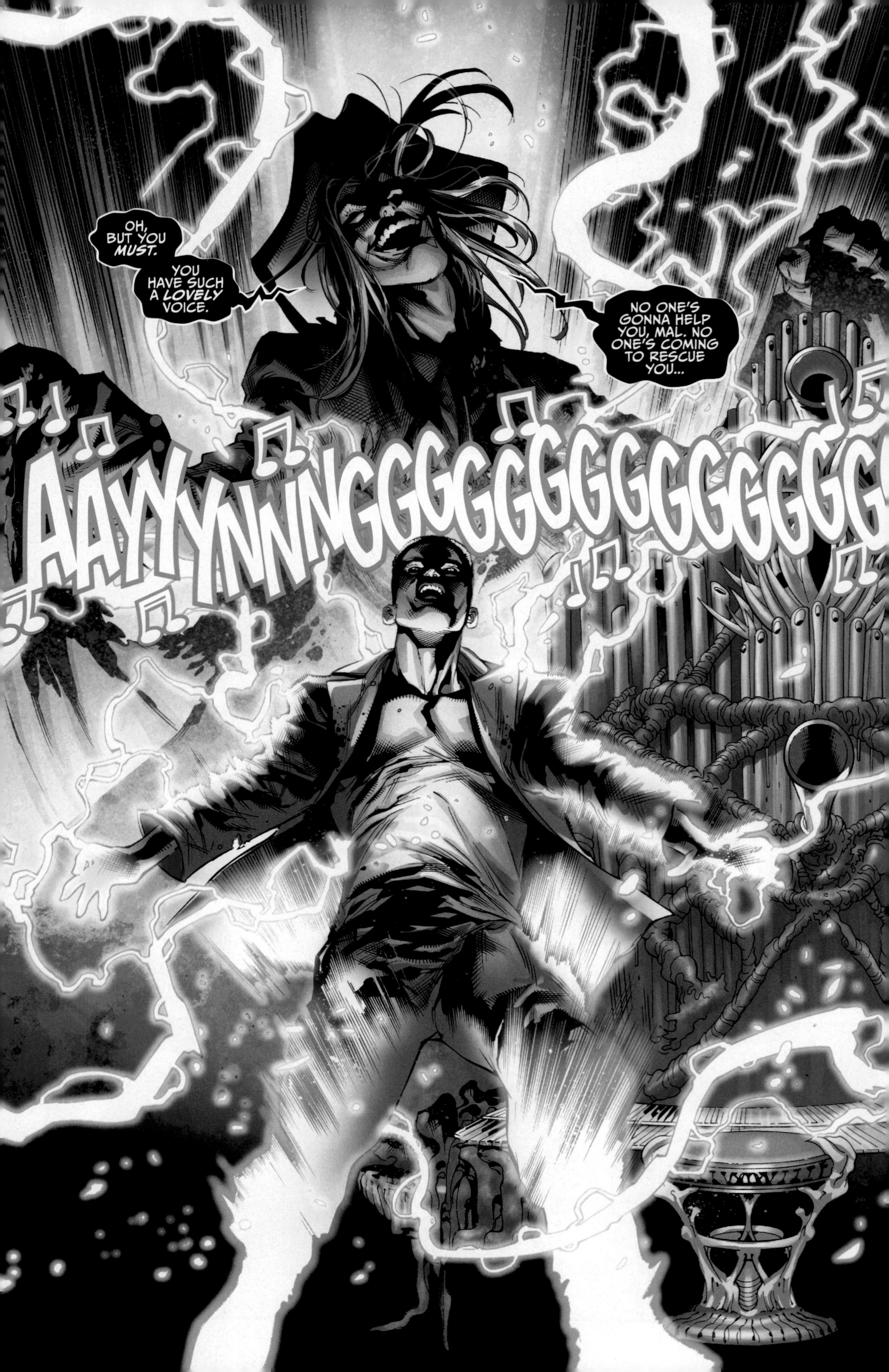
OH, BUT YOU MUST.
YOU HAVE SUCH A LOVELY VOICE.
NO ONE'S GONNA HELP YOU, MAL. NO ONE'S COMING TO RESCUE YOU...
AAYYYNNNGGGGGGGGGGGGGG

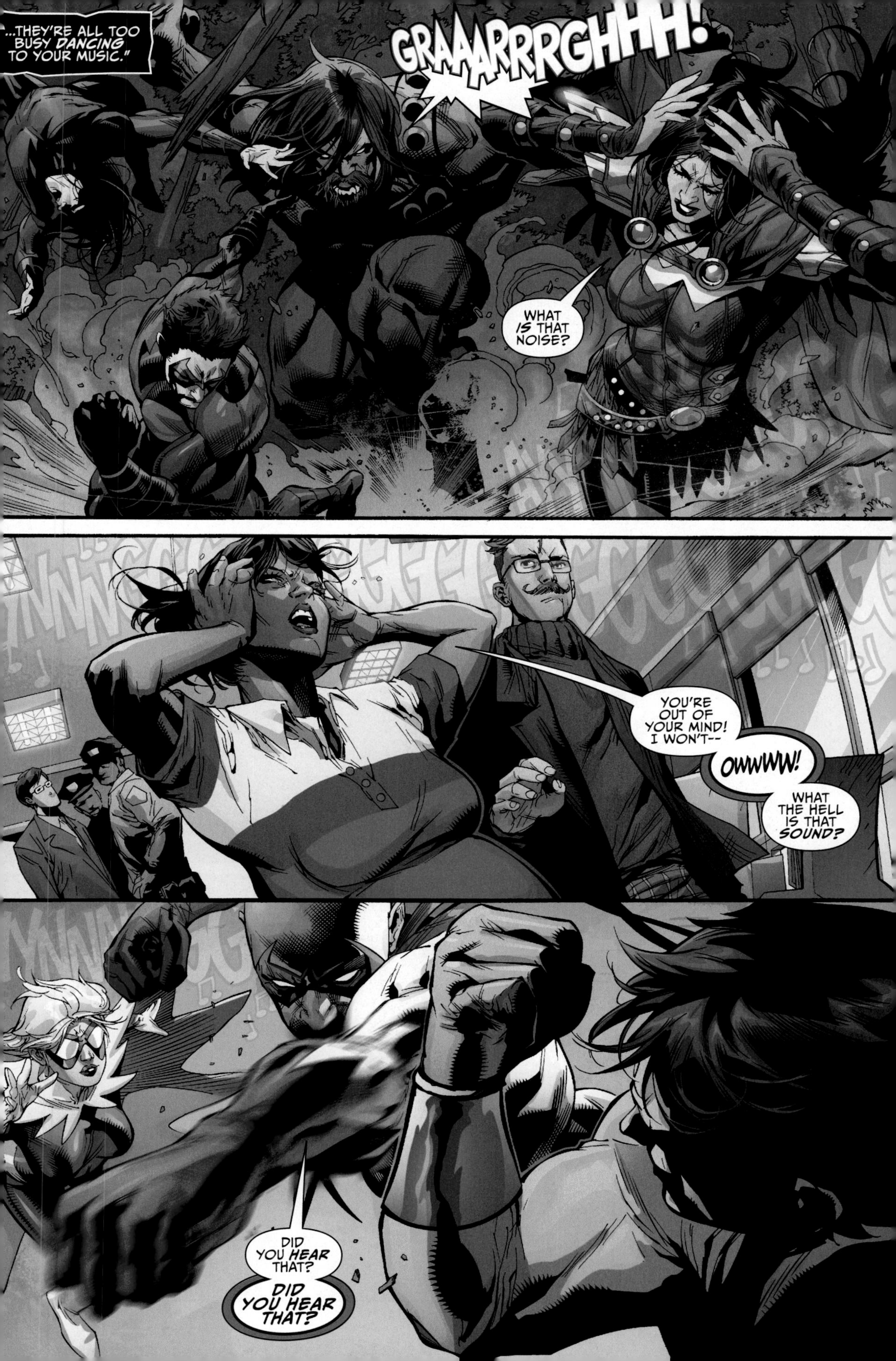

"...THEY'RE ALL TOO BUSY *DANCING* TO YOUR MUSIC."
GRAAARRRGHHH!
WHAT *IS* THAT NOISE?
YOU'RE OUT OF YOUR MIND! I WON'T--
OWWWW!
WHAT THE HELL IS THAT *SOUND?*
DID YOU *HEAR* THAT?
DID YOU HEAR THAT?

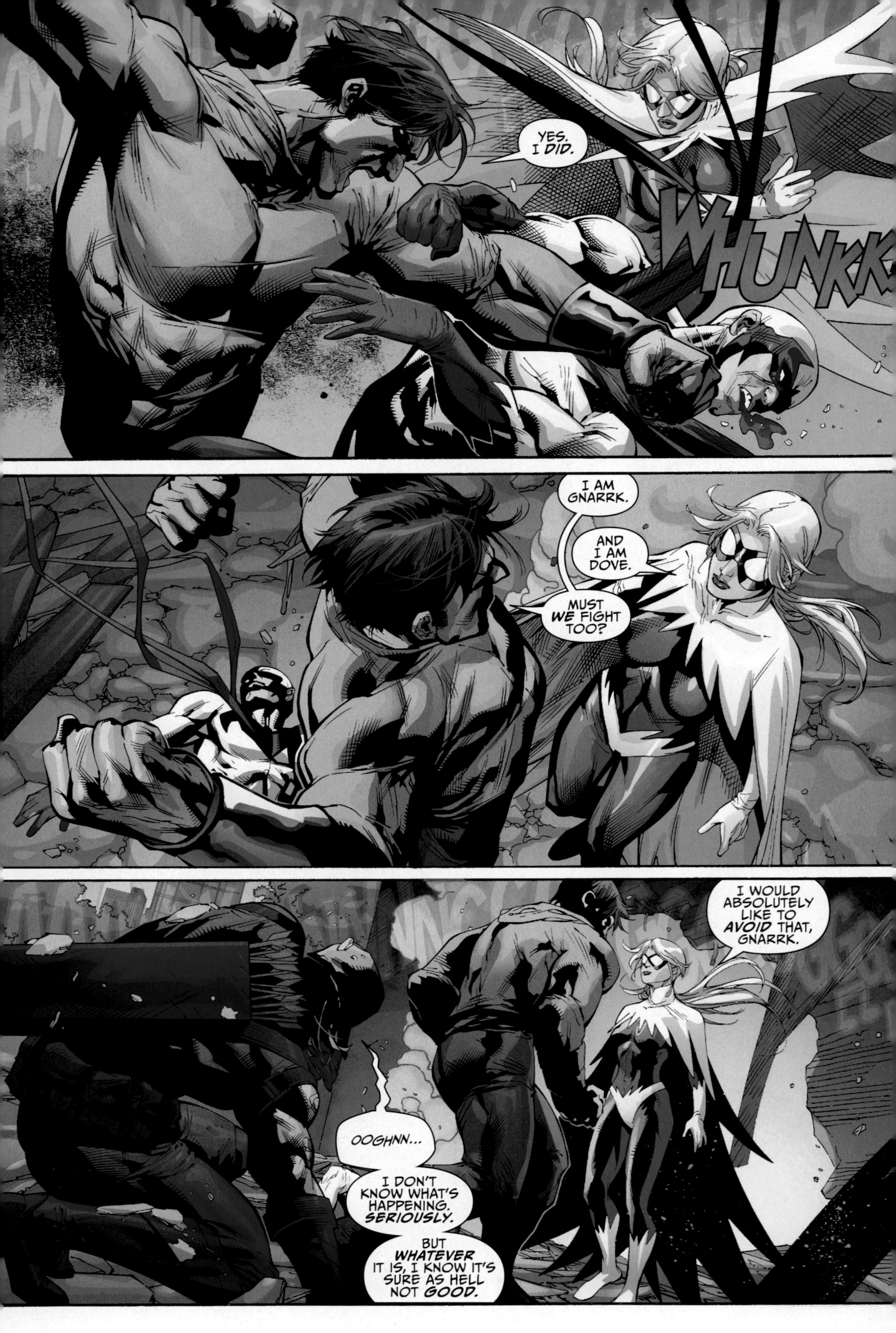
YES. I DID.
WHUNKK
I AM GNARRK.
AND I AM DOVE.
MUST WE FIGHT TOO?
I WOULD ABSOLUTELY LIKE TO AVOID THAT, GNARRK.
OOGHNN...
I DON'T KNOW WHAT'S HAPPENING. SERIOUSLY.
BUT WHATEVER IT IS, I KNOW IT'S SURE AS HELL NOT GOOD.

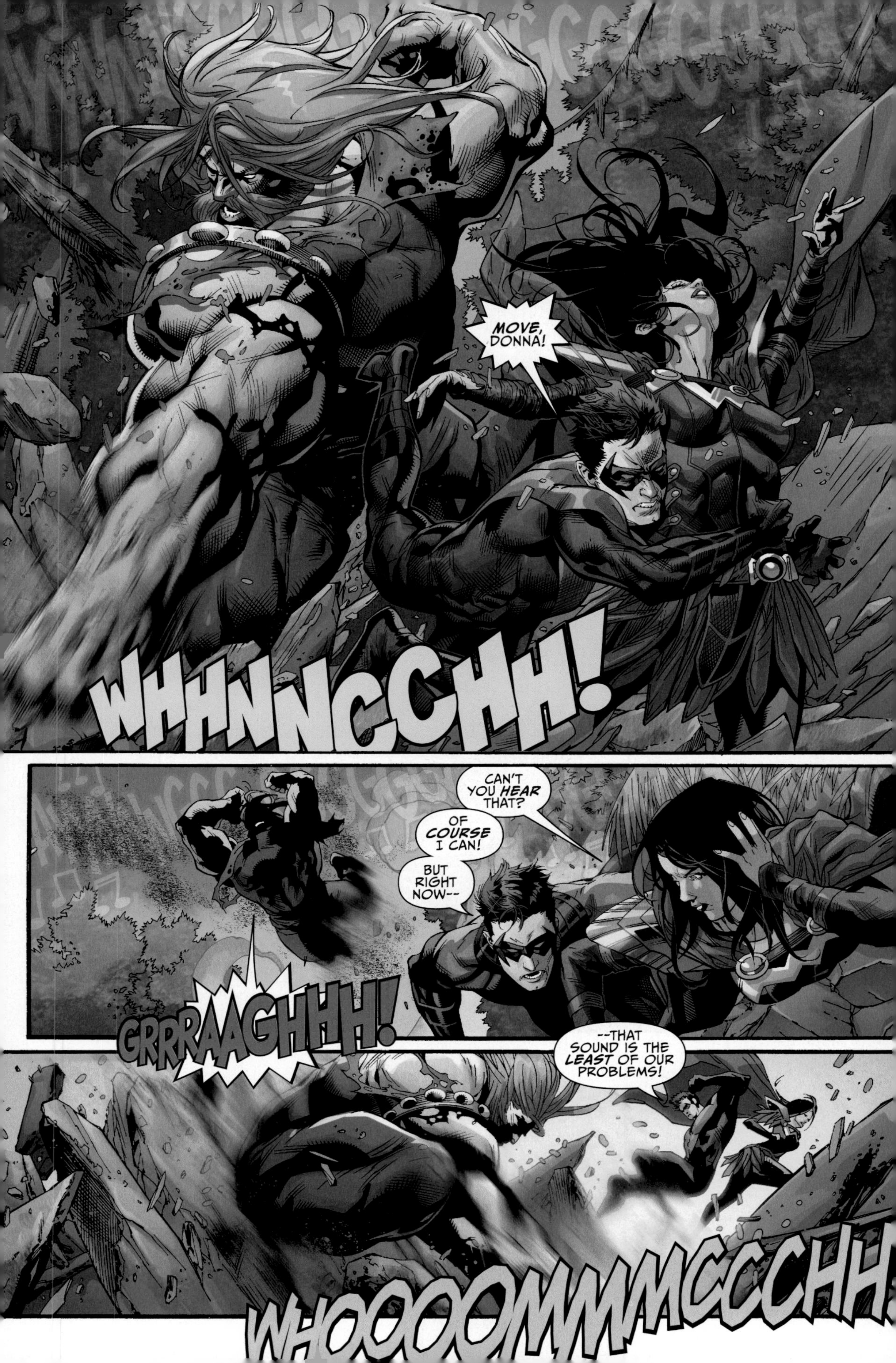
MOVE, DONNA!
WHHNNCCHH!
CAN'T YOU HEAR THAT?
OF COURSE I CAN!
BUT RIGHT NOW--
GRRRAAGHHH!
--THAT SOUND IS THE LEAST OF OUR PROBLEMS!
WHOOOOMMMMCCCHH

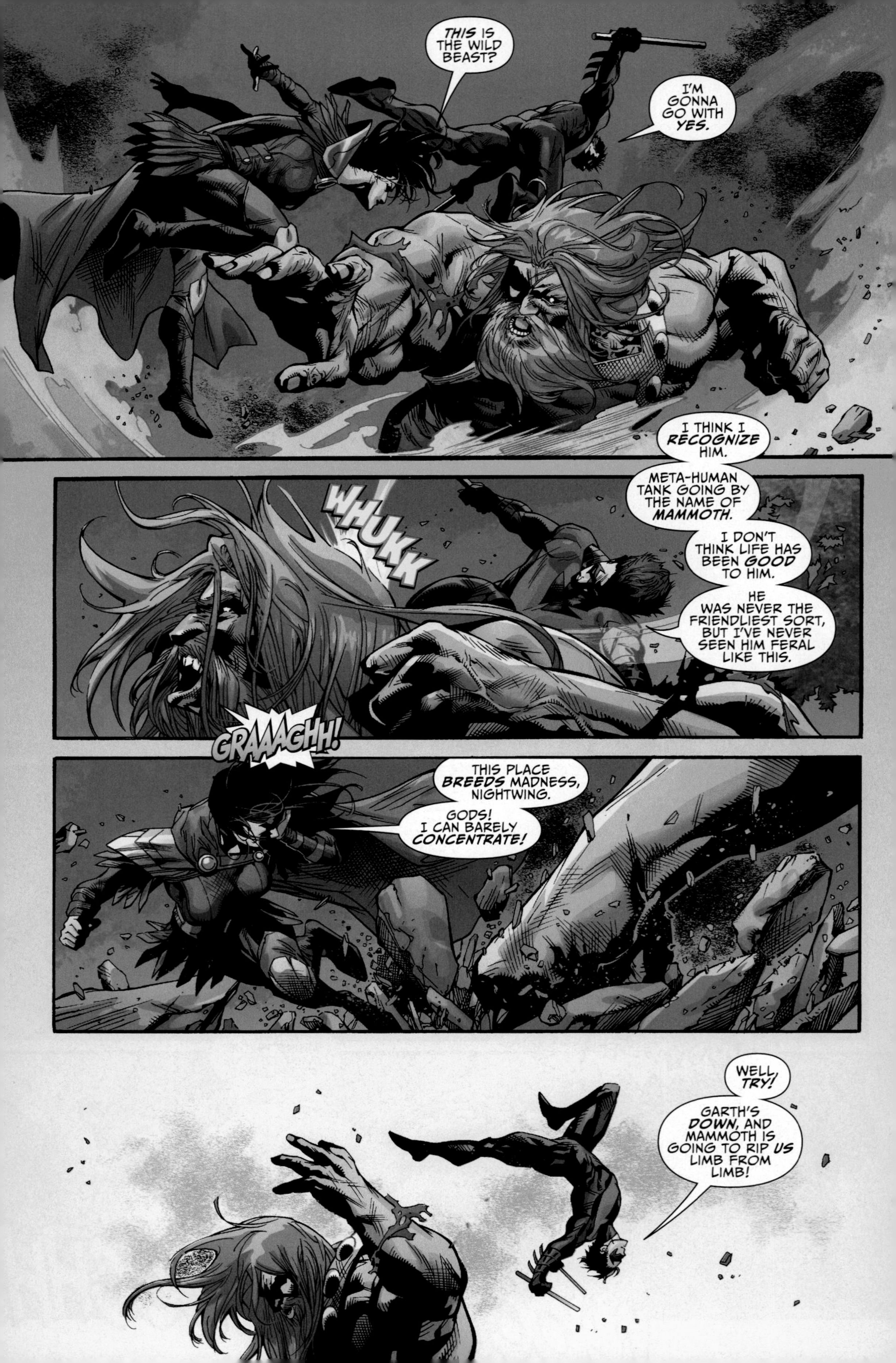
THIS IS THE WILD BEAST?
I'M GONNA GO WITH YES.
I THINK I RECOGNIZE HIM.
META-HUMAN TANK GOING BY THE NAME OF MAMMOTH.
WHUKK
I DON'T THINK LIFE HAS BEEN GOOD TO HIM.
HE WAS NEVER THE FRIENDLIEST SORT, BUT I'VE NEVER SEEN HIM FERAL LIKE THIS.
GRAAAGHH!
THIS PLACE BREEDS MADNESS, NIGHTWING.
GODS! I CAN BARELY CONCENTRATE!
WELL, TRY!
GARTH'S DOWN, AND MAMMOTH IS GOING TO RIP US LIMB FROM LIMB!

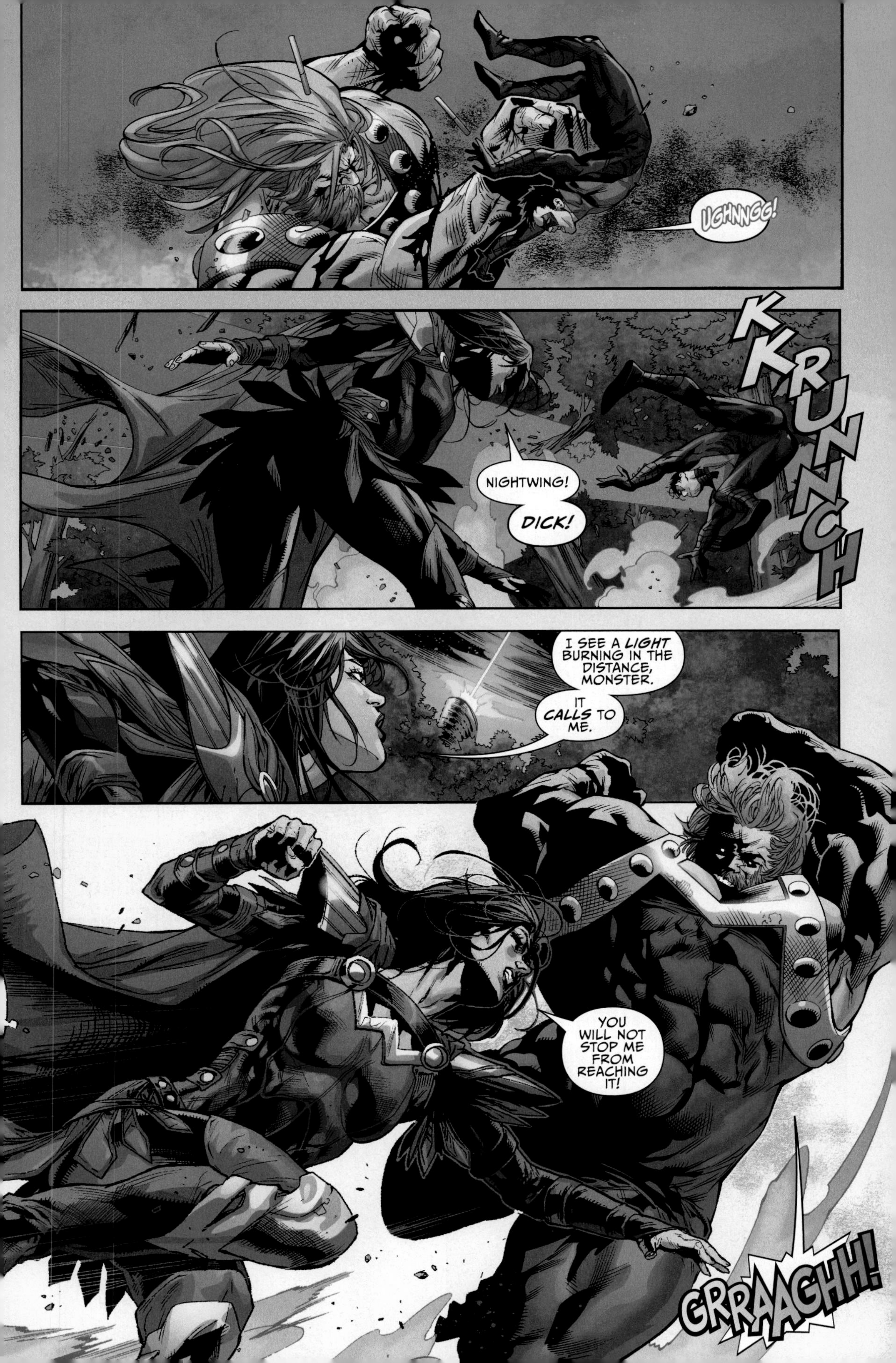
UGHNNGG!
KKRUNCH
NIGHTWING!
DICK!
I SEE A LIGHT BURNING IN THE DISTANCE, MONSTER.
IT CALLS TO ME.
YOU WILL NOT STOP ME FROM REACHING IT!
GRRAAGHH!

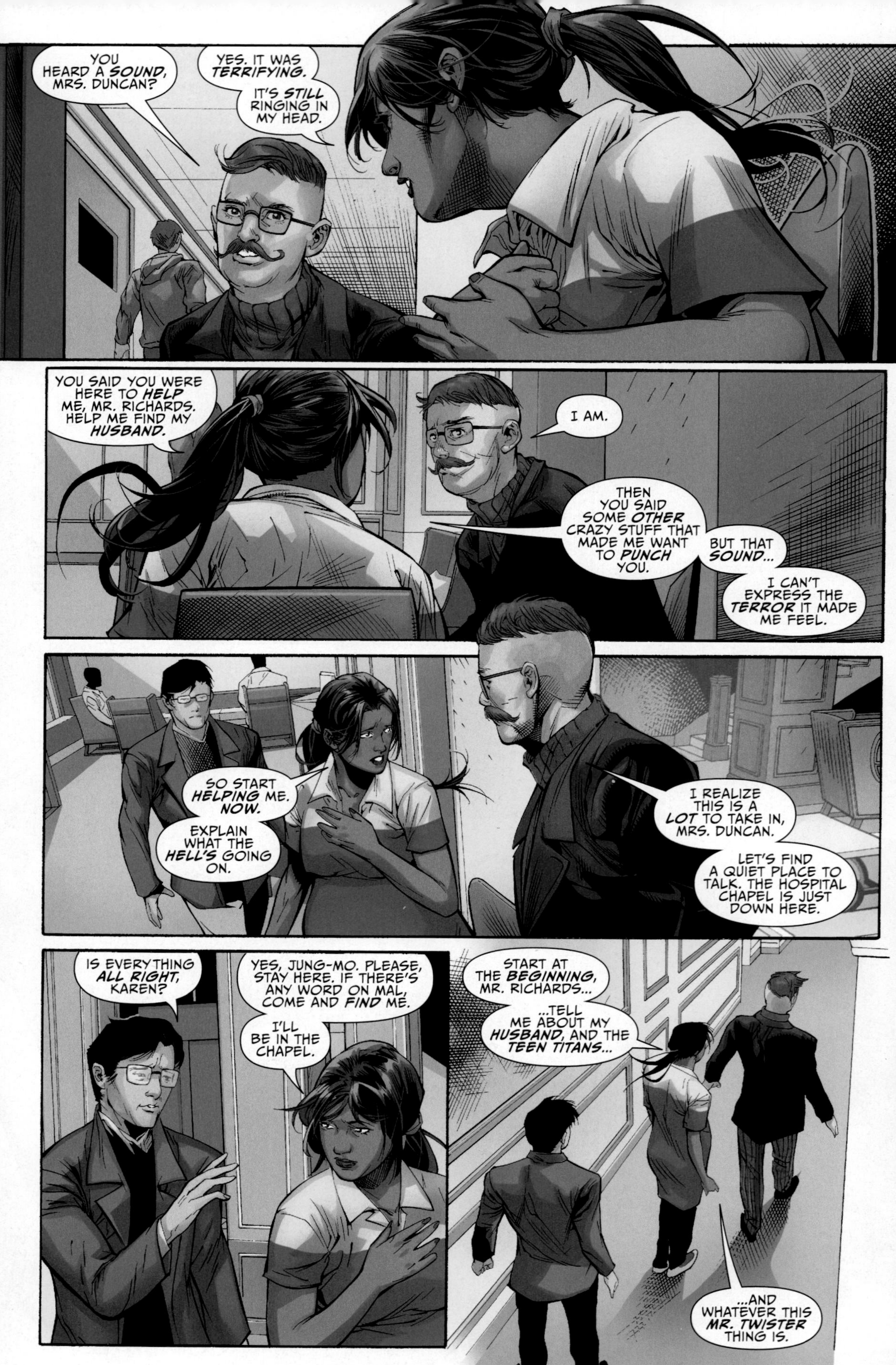
YOU HEARD A SOUND, MRS. DUNCAN?
YES. IT WAS TERRIFYING.
IT'S STILL RINGING IN MY HEAD.
YOU SAID YOU WERE HERE TO HELP ME, MR. RICHARDS. HELP ME FIND MY HUSBAND.
I AM.
THEN YOU SAID SOME OTHER CRAZY STUFF THAT MADE ME WANT TO PUNCH YOU.
BUT THAT SOUND...
I CAN'T EXPRESS THE TERROR IT MADE ME FEEL.
SO START HELPING ME. NOW.
EXPLAIN WHAT THE HELL'S GOING ON.
I REALIZE THIS IS A LOT TO TAKE IN, MRS. DUNCAN.
LET'S FIND A QUIET PLACE TO TALK. THE HOSPITAL CHAPEL IS JUST DOWN HERE.
IS EVERYTHING ALL RIGHT, KAREN?
YES, JUNG-MO. PLEASE, STAY HERE. IF THERE'S ANY WORD ON MAL, COME AND FIND ME.
I'LL BE IN THE CHAPEL.
START AT THE BEGINNING, MR. RICHARDS...
...TELL ME ABOUT MY HUSBAND, AND THE TEEN TITANS...
...AND WHATEVER THIS MR. TWISTER THING IS.

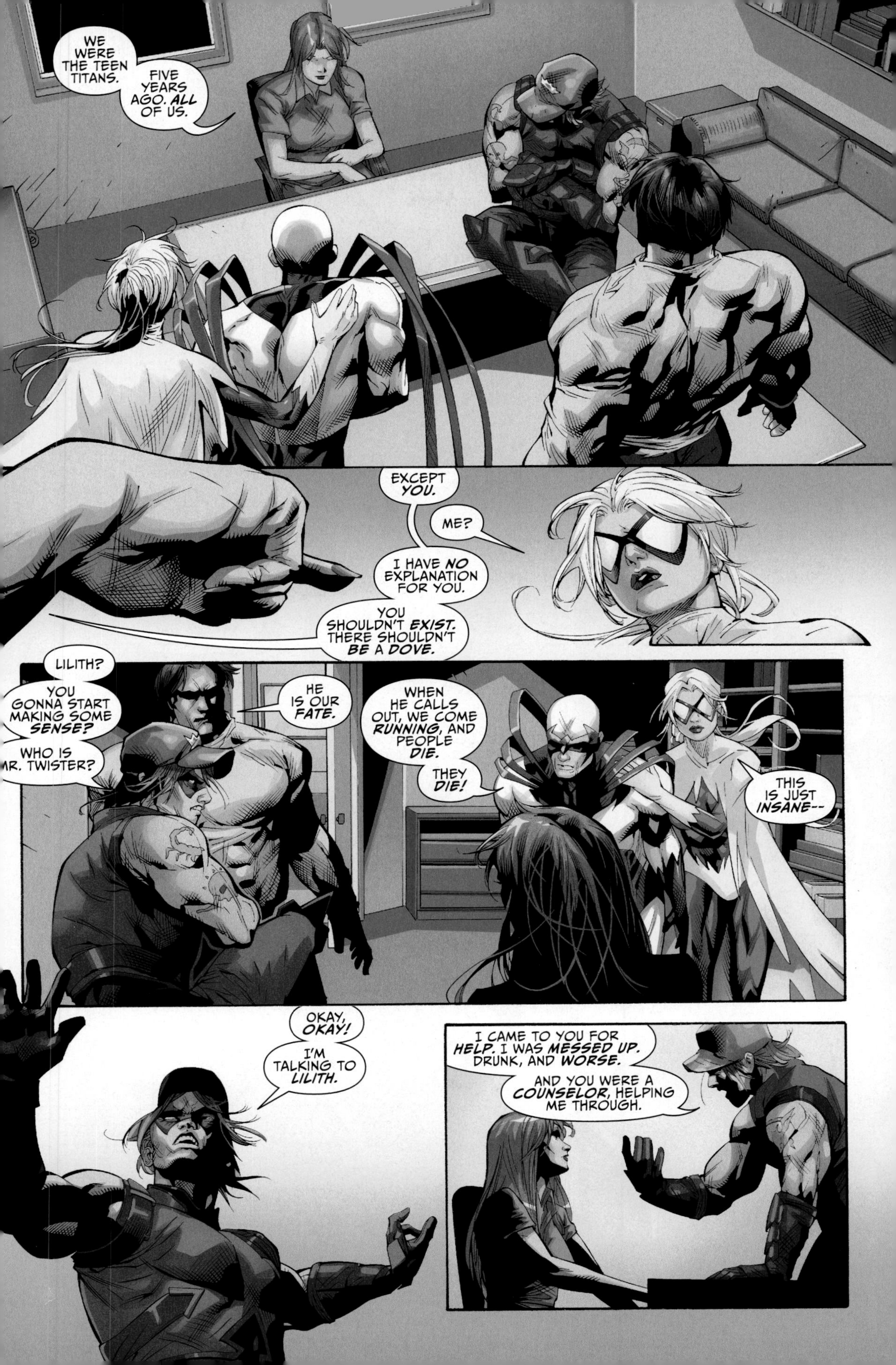
WE WERE THE TEEN TITANS.
FIVE YEARS AGO. ALL OF US.
EXCEPT YOU.
ME?
I HAVE NO EXPLANATION FOR YOU.
YOU SHOULDN'T EXIST. THERE SHOULDN'T BE A DOVE.
LILITH?
YOU GONNA START MAKING SOME SENSE?
WHO IS MR. TWISTER?
HE IS OUR FATE.
WHEN HE CALLS OUT, WE COME RUNNING, AND PEOPLE DIE.
THEY DIE!
THIS IS JUST INSANE--
OKAY, OKAY!
I'M TALKING TO LILITH.
I CAME TO YOU FOR HELP. I WAS MESSED UP. DRUNK, AND WORSE.
AND YOU WERE A COUNSELOR, HELPING ME THROUGH.

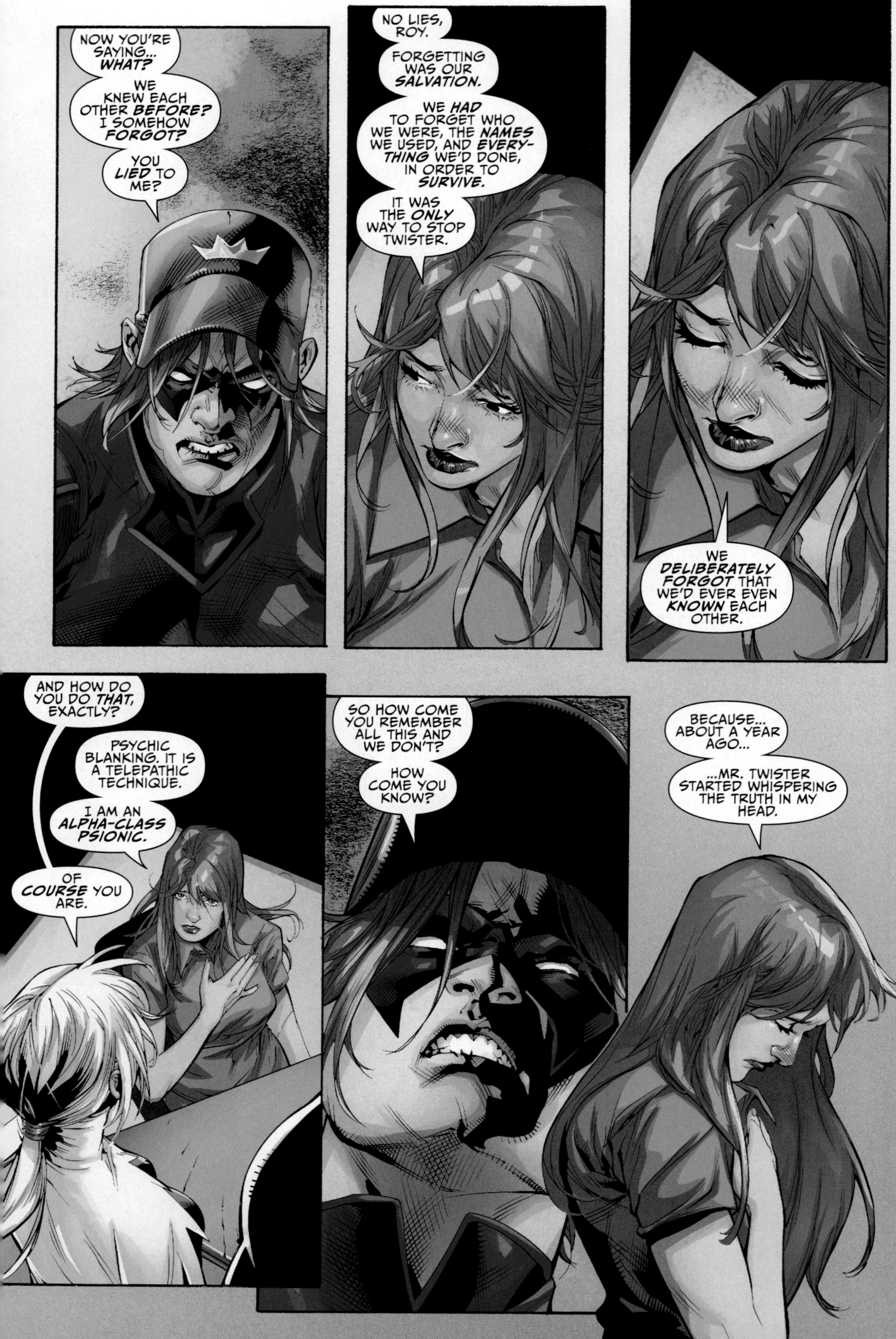

NOW YOU'RE SAYING... WHAT?
WE KNEW EACH OTHER BEFORE? I SOMEHOW FORGOT?
YOU LIED TO ME?
NO LIES, ROY.
FORGETTING WAS OUR SALVATION.
WE HAD TO FORGET WHO WE WERE, THE NAMES WE USED, AND EVERY-THING WE'D DONE, IN ORDER TO SURVIVE.
IT WAS THE ONLY WAY TO STOP TWISTER.
WE DELIBERATELY FORGOT THAT WE'D EVER EVEN KNOWN EACH OTHER.
AND HOW DO YOU DO THAT, EXACTLY?
PSYCHIC BLANKING. IT IS A TELEPATHIC TECHNIQUE.
I AM AN ALPHA-CLASS PSIONIC.
OF COURSE YOU ARE.
SO HOW COME YOU REMEMBER ALL THIS AND WE DON'T?
HOW COME YOU KNOW?
BECAUSE... ABOUT A YEAR AGO...
...MR. TWISTER STARTED WHISPERING THE TRUTH IN MY HEAD.

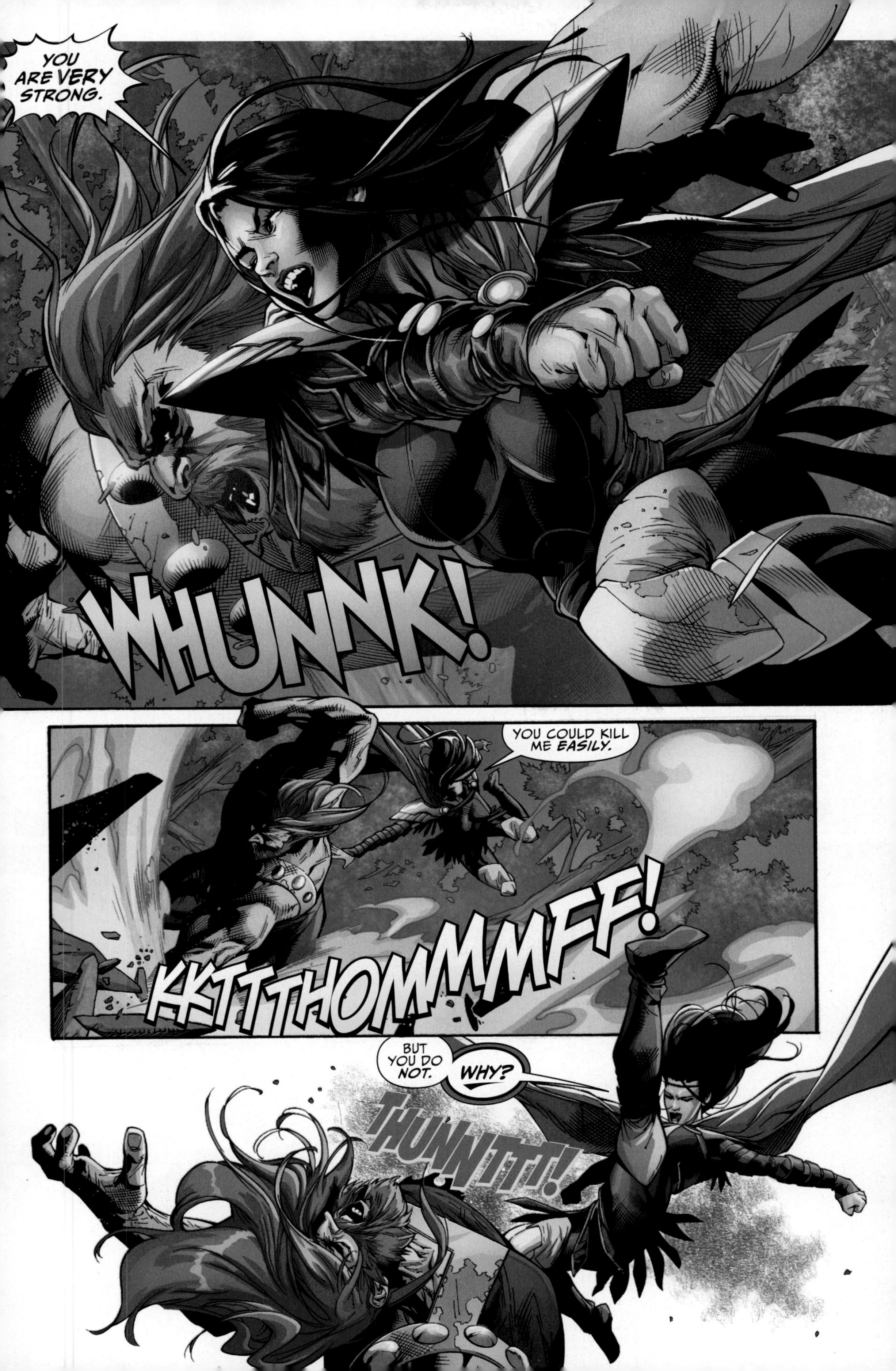
YOU ARE VERY STRONG.
WHUNNK!
YOU COULD KILL ME EASILY.
KKTTTHOMMMMFF!
BUT YOU DO NOT.
WHY?
THUNNTTT!

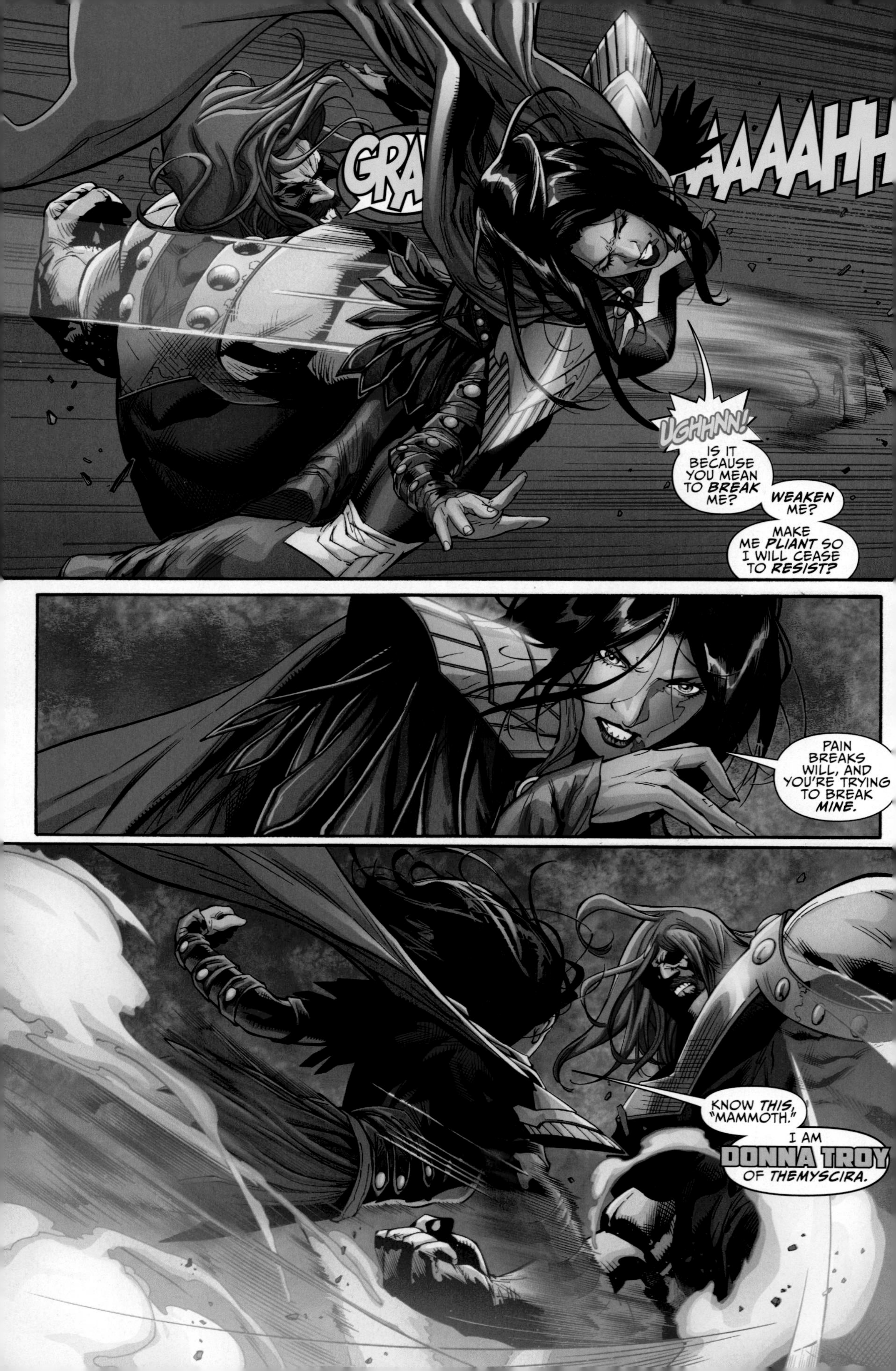
GRAAAAAHH
UGHHNN!
IS IT BECAUSE YOU MEAN TO BREAK ME?
WEAKEN ME?
MAKE ME PLIANT SO I WILL CEASE TO RESIST?
PAIN BREAKS WILL, AND YOU'RE TRYING TO BREAK MINE.
KNOW THIS, "MAMMOTH."
I AM DONNA TROY OF THEMYSCIRA.

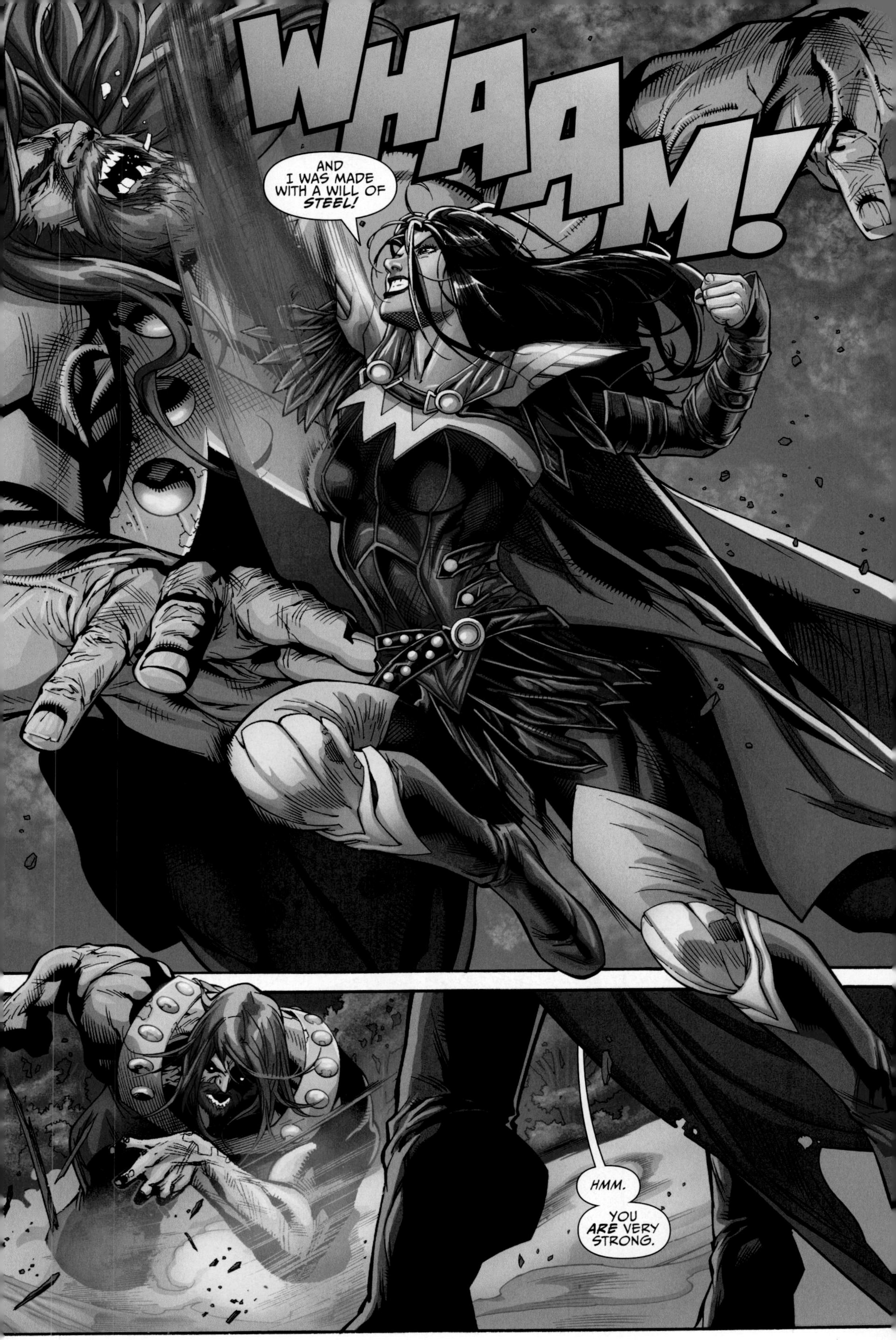
WHAAAM!
AND I WAS MADE WITH A WILL OF STEEL!
HMM.
YOU ARE VERY STRONG.

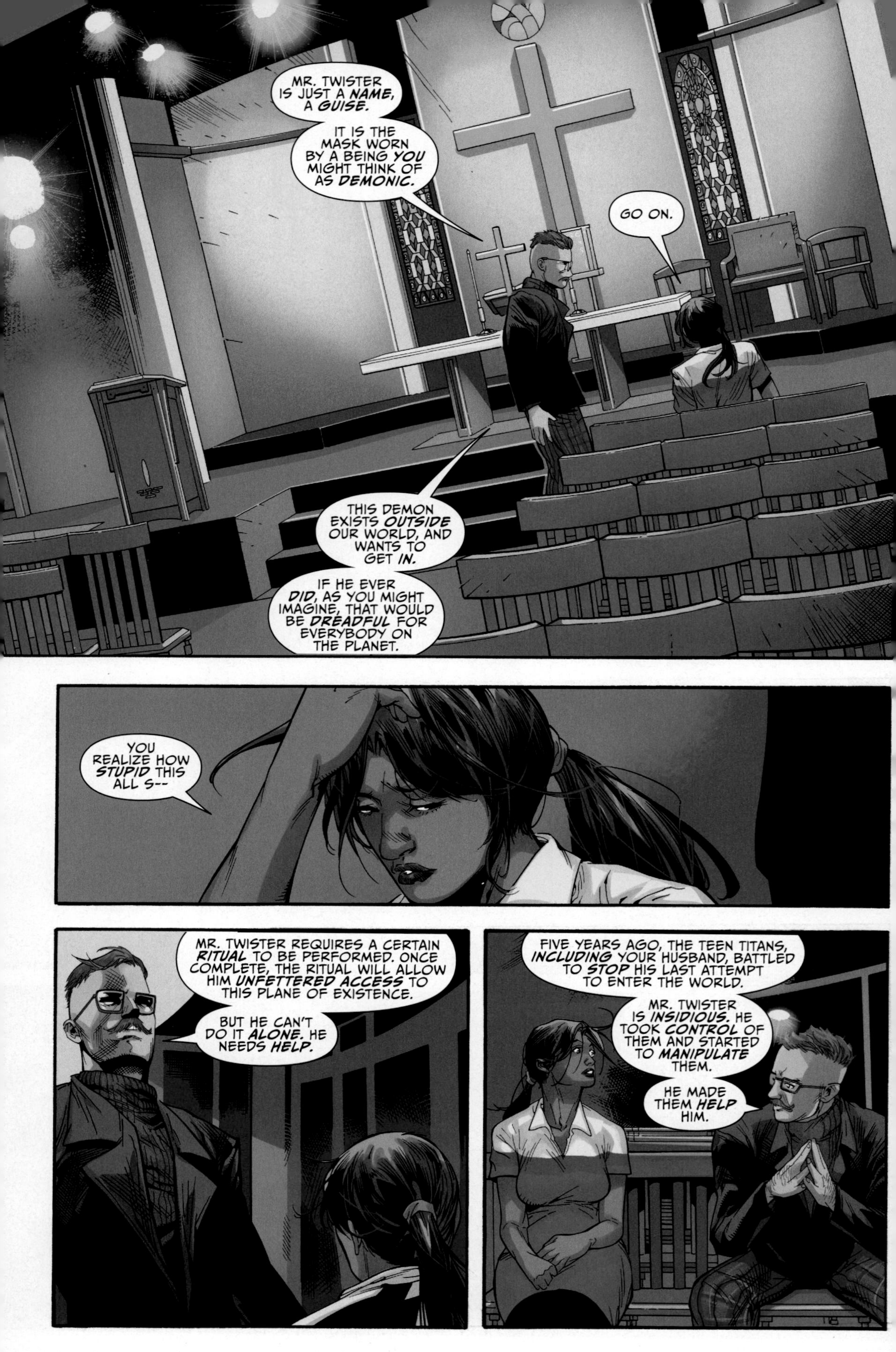
MR. TWISTER IS JUST A NAME, A GUISE.
IT IS THE MASK WORN BY A BEING YOU MIGHT THINK OF AS DEMONIC.
GO ON.
THIS DEMON EXISTS OUTSIDE OUR WORLD, AND WANTS TO GET IN.
IF HE EVER DID, AS YOU MIGHT IMAGINE, THAT WOULD BE DREADFUL FOR EVERYBODY ON THE PLANET.
YOU REALIZE HOW STUPID THIS ALL S--
MR. TWISTER REQUIRES A CERTAIN RITUAL TO BE PERFORMED. ONCE COMPLETE, THE RITUAL WILL ALLOW HIM UNFETTERED ACCESS TO THIS PLANE OF EXISTENCE.
BUT HE CAN'T DO IT ALONE. HE NEEDS HELP.
FIVE YEARS AGO, THE TEEN TITANS, INCLUDING YOUR HUSBAND, BATTLED TO STOP HIS LAST ATTEMPT TO ENTER THE WORLD.
MR. TWISTER IS INSIDIOUS. HE TOOK CONTROL OF THEM AND STARTED TO MANIPULATE THEM.
HE MADE THEM HELP HIM.

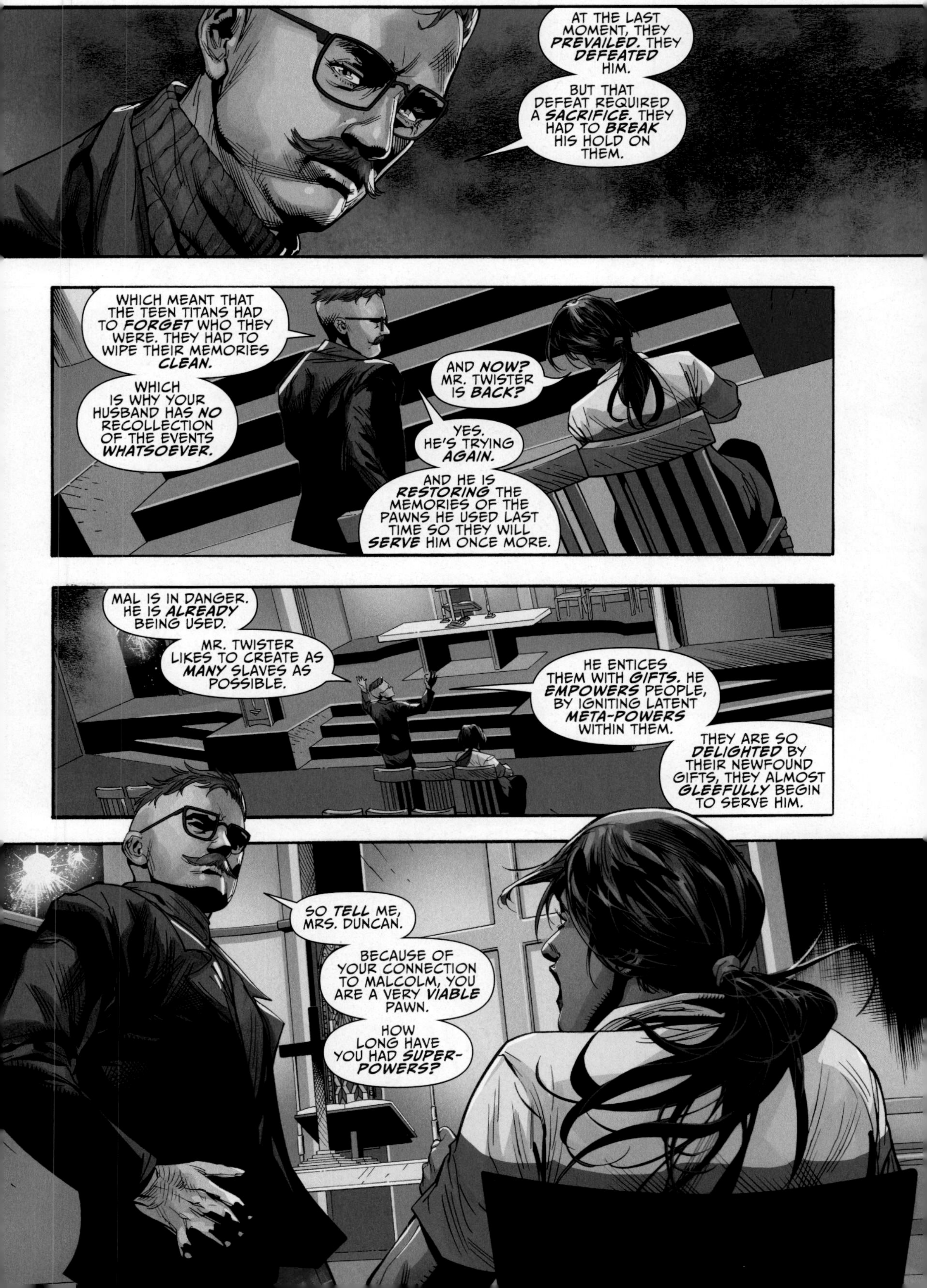
AT THE LAST MOMENT, THEY PREVAILED. THEY DEFEATED HIM.
BUT THAT DEFEAT REQUIRED A SACRIFICE. THEY HAD TO BREAK HIS HOLD ON THEM.
WHICH MEANT THAT THE TEEN TITANS HAD TO FORGET WHO THEY WERE. THEY HAD TO WIPE THEIR MEMORIES CLEAN.
WHICH IS WHY YOUR HUSBAND HAS NO RECOLLECTION OF THE EVENTS WHATSOEVER.
AND NOW? MR. TWISTER IS BACK?
YES. HE'S TRYING AGAIN.
AND HE IS RESTORING THE MEMORIES OF THE PAWNS HE USED LAST TIME SO THEY WILL SERVE HIM ONCE MORE.
MAL IS IN DANGER. HE IS ALREADY BEING USED.
MR. TWISTER LIKES TO CREATE AS MANY SLAVES AS POSSIBLE.
HE ENTICES THEM WITH GIFTS. HE EMPOWERS PEOPLE, BY IGNITING LATENT META-POWERS WITHIN THEM.
THEY ARE SO DELIGHTED BY THEIR NEWFOUND GIFTS, THEY ALMOST GLEEFULLY BEGIN TO SERVE HIM.
SO TELL ME, MRS. DUNCAN.
BECAUSE OF YOUR CONNECTION TO MALCOLM, YOU ARE A VERY VIABLE PAWN.
HOW LONG HAVE YOU HAD SUPER-POWERS?

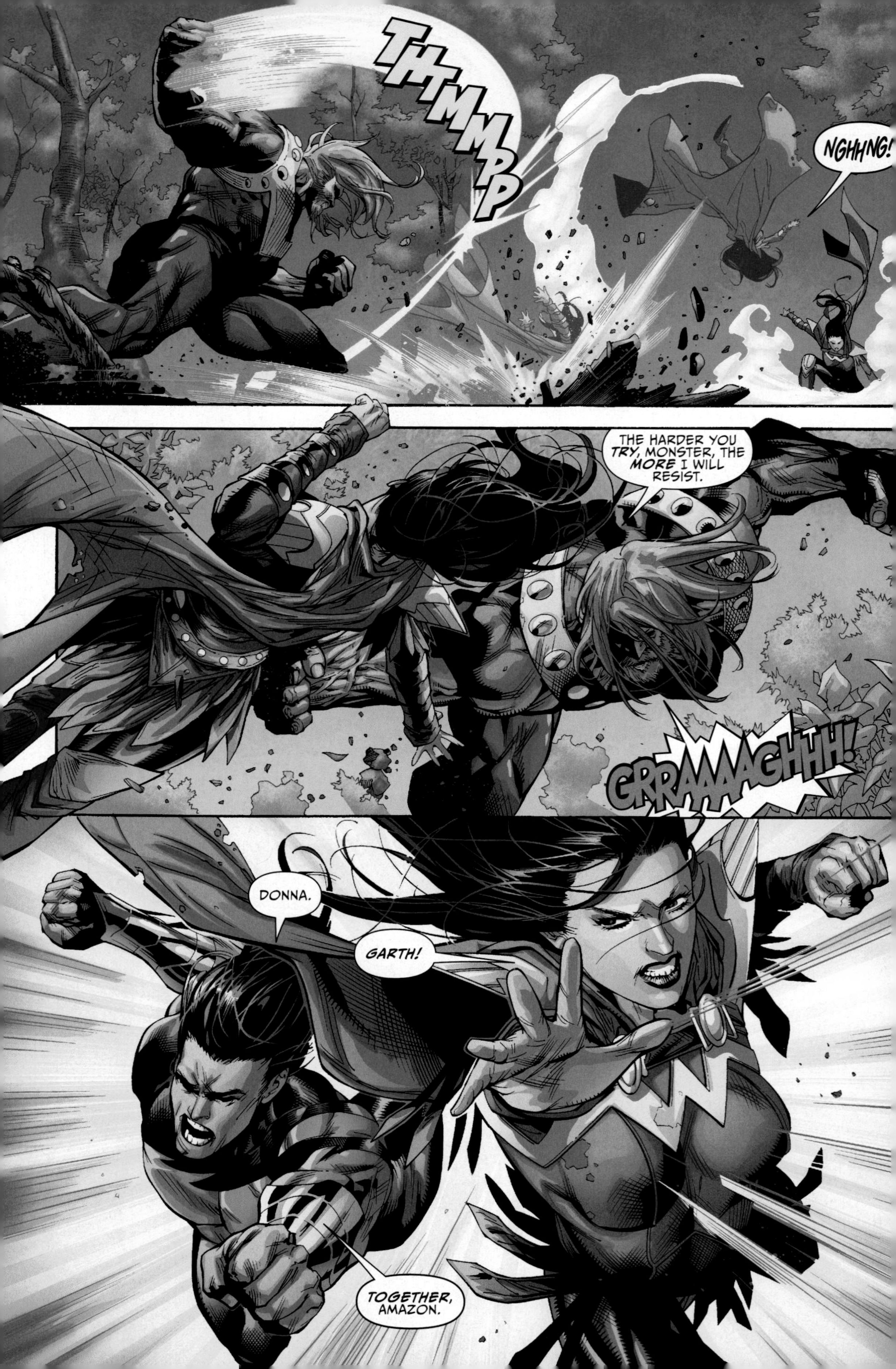
THHMMPP
NGHHNG!
THE HARDER YOU TRY, MONSTER, THE MORE I WILL RESIST.
GRRAAAAGHHH!
DONNA.
GARTH!
TOGETHER, AMAZON.

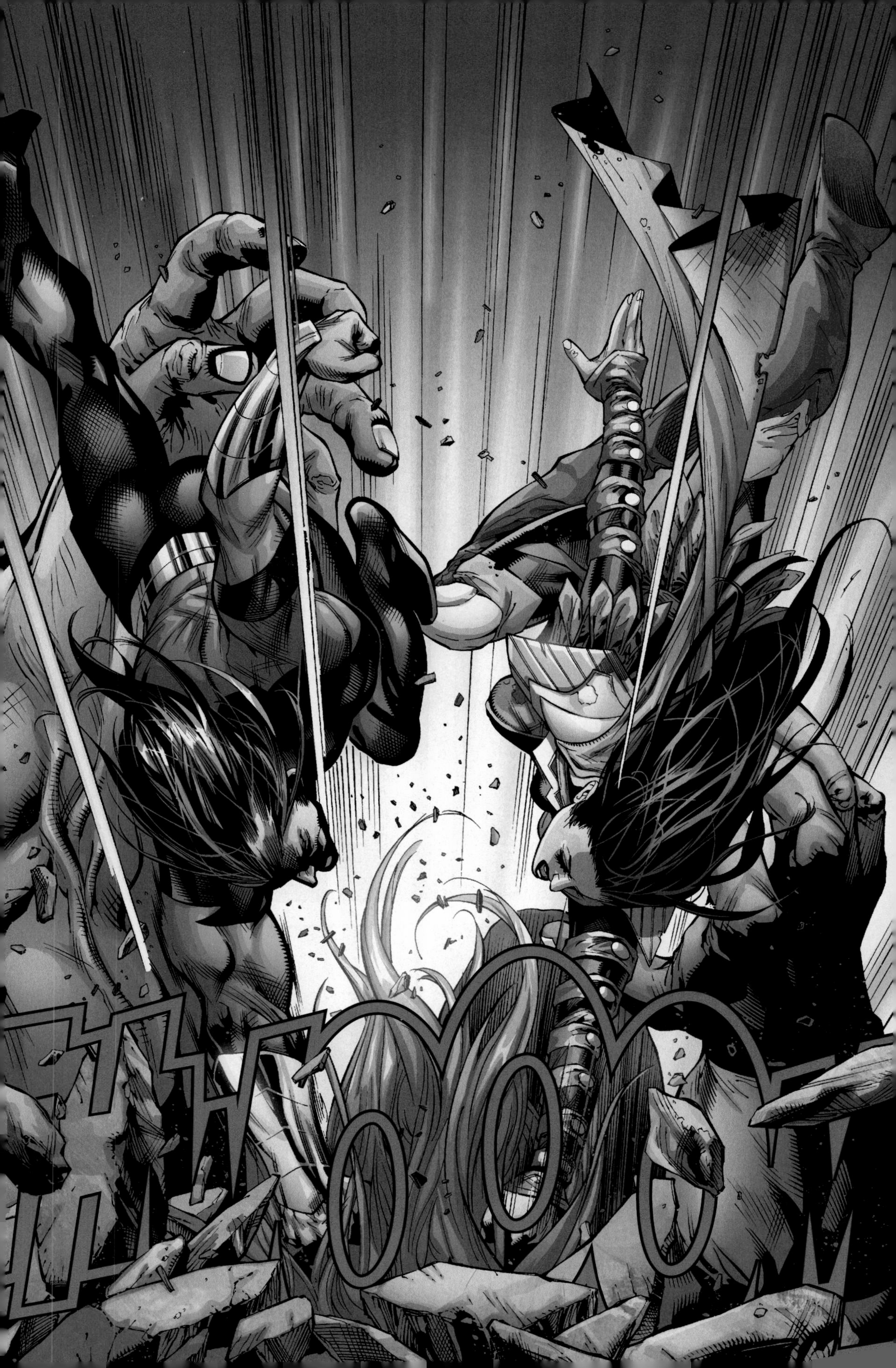
THOOOOOOM

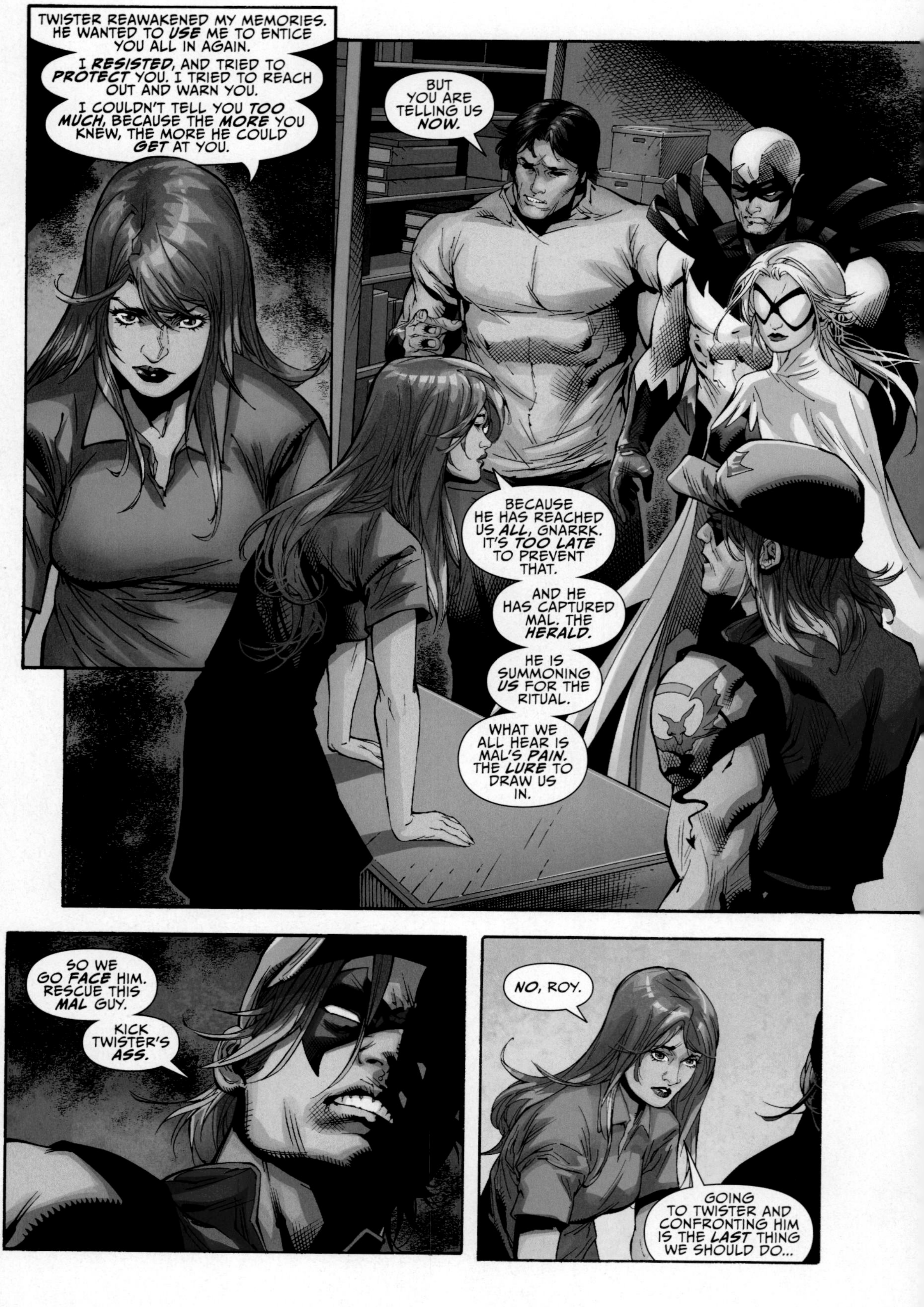
TWISTER REAWAKENED MY MEMORIES. HE WANTED TO USE ME TO ENTICE YOU ALL IN AGAIN.
I RESISTED, AND TRIED TO PROTECT YOU. I TRIED TO REACH OUT AND WARN YOU.
I COULDN'T TELL YOU TOO MUCH, BECAUSE THE MORE YOU KNEW, THE MORE HE COULD GET AT YOU.
BUT YOU ARE TELLING US NOW.
BECAUSE HE HAS REACHED US ALL, GNARRK. IT'S TOO LATE TO PREVENT THAT.
AND HE HAS CAPTURED MAL. THE HERALD.
HE IS SUMMONING US FOR THE RITUAL.
WHAT WE ALL HEAR IS MAL'S PAIN. THE LURE TO DRAW US IN.
SO WE GO FACE HIM. RESCUE THIS MAL GUY.
KICK TWISTER'S ASS.
NO, ROY.
GOING TO TWISTER AND CONFRONTING HIM IS THE LAST THING WE SHOULD DO...

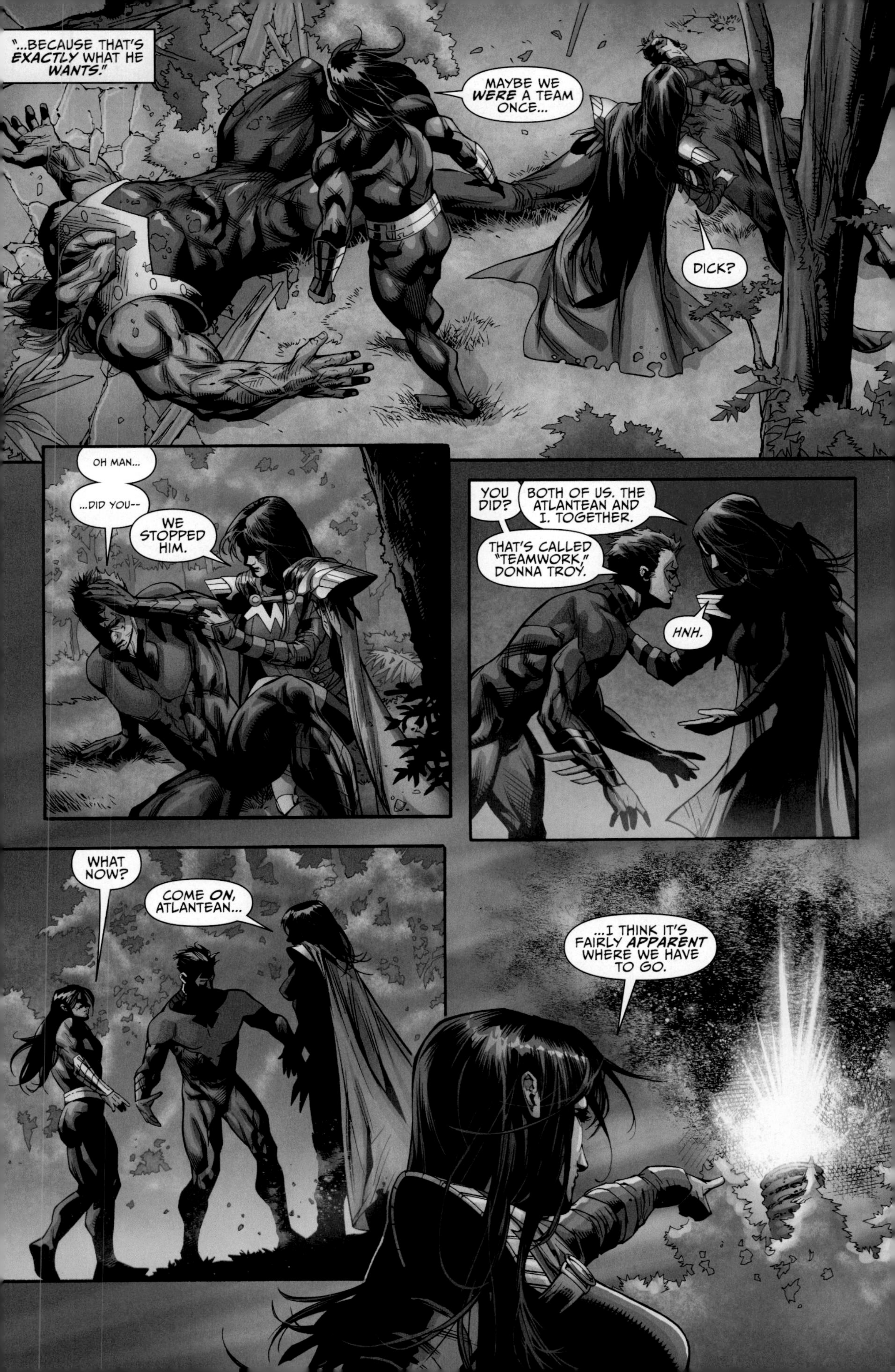
"...BECAUSE THAT'S *EXACTLY* WHAT HE *WANTS*."
MAYBE WE *WERE* A TEAM ONCE...
DICK?
OH MAN...
...DID YOU--
WE STOPPED HIM.
YOU DID?
BOTH OF US. THE ATLANTEAN AND I. TOGETHER.
THAT'S CALLED "TEAMWORK," DONNA TROY.
HNH.
WHAT NOW?
COME *ON*, ATLANTEAN...
...I THINK IT'S FAIRLY *APPARENT* WHERE WE HAVE TO GO.

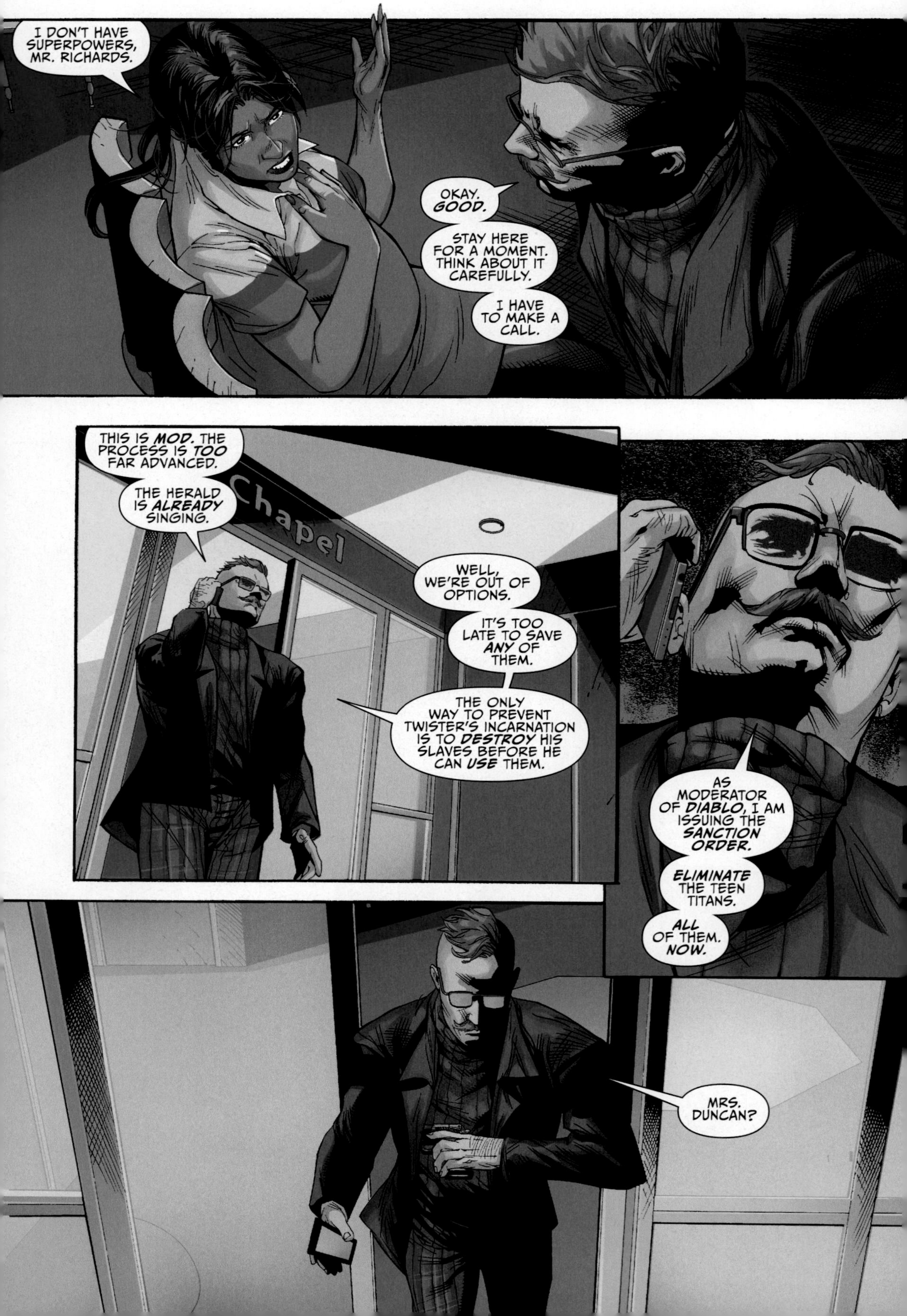
I DON'T HAVE SUPERPOWERS, MR. RICHARDS.
OKAY. GOOD.
STAY HERE FOR A MOMENT. THINK ABOUT IT CAREFULLY.
I HAVE TO MAKE A CALL.
THIS IS MOD. THE PROCESS IS TOO FAR ADVANCED.
THE HERALD IS ALREADY SINGING.
Chapel
WELL, WE'RE OUT OF OPTIONS.
IT'S TOO LATE TO SAVE ANY OF THEM.
THE ONLY WAY TO PREVENT TWISTER'S INCARNATION IS TO DESTROY HIS SLAVES BEFORE HE CAN USE THEM.
AS MODERATOR OF DIABLO, I AM ISSUING THE SANCTION ORDER.
ELIMINATE THE TEEN TITANS.
ALL OF THEM. NOW.
MRS. DUNCAN?

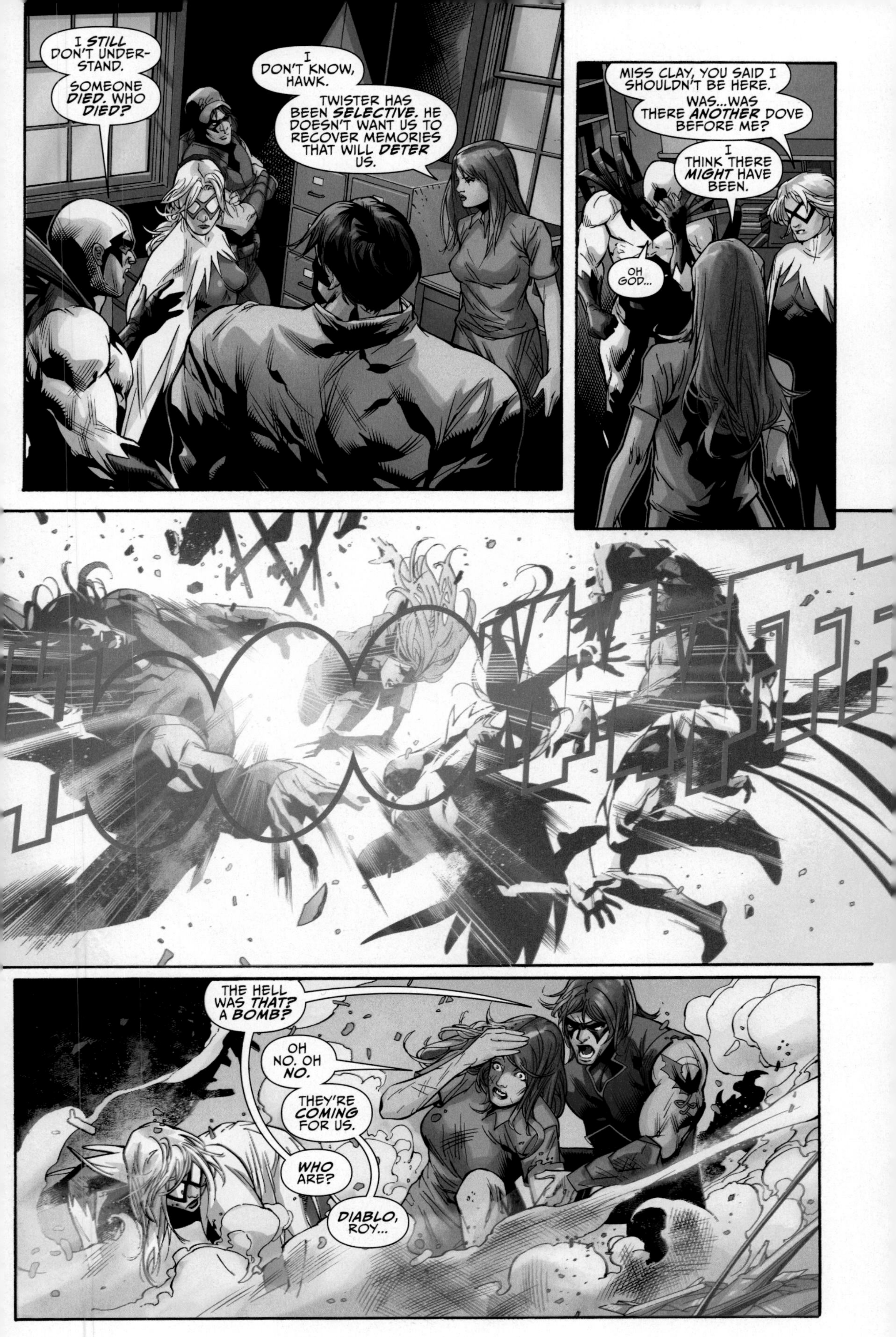
I STILL DON'T UNDERSTAND.
SOMEONE DIED. WHO DIED?
I DON'T KNOW, HAWK.
TWISTER HAS BEEN SELECTIVE. HE DOESN'T WANT US TO RECOVER MEMORIES THAT WILL DETER US.
MISS CLAY, YOU SAID I SHOULDN'T BE HERE.
WAS...WAS THERE ANOTHER DOVE BEFORE ME?
I THINK THERE MIGHT HAVE BEEN.
OH GOD...
THE HELL WAS THAT? A BOMB?
OH NO. OH NO.
THEY'RE COMING FOR US.
WHO ARE?
DIABLO, ROY...

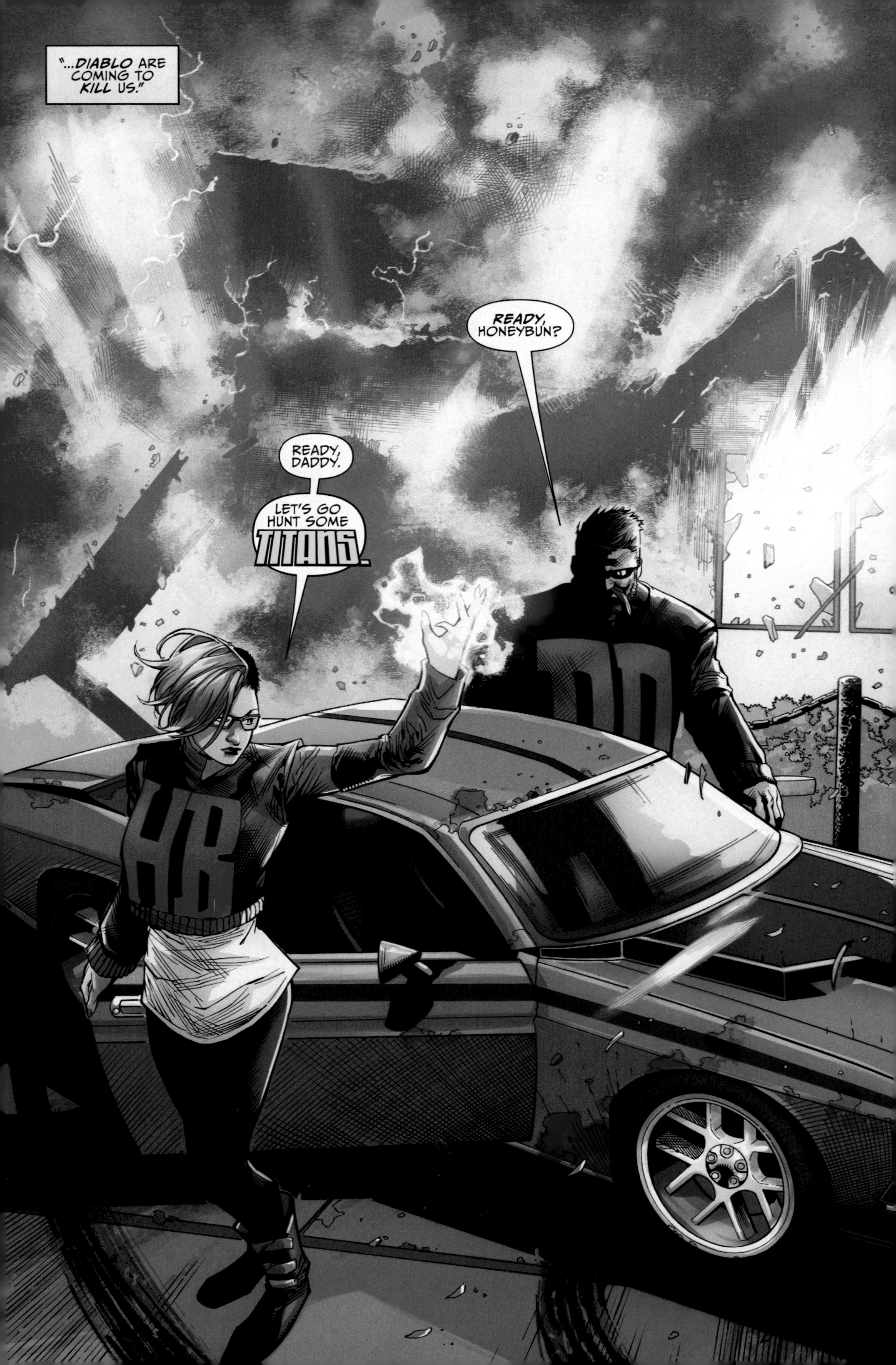
"...DIABLO ARE COMING TO KILL US."
READY, HONEYBUN?
READY, DADDY.
LET'S GO HUNT SOME TITANS.

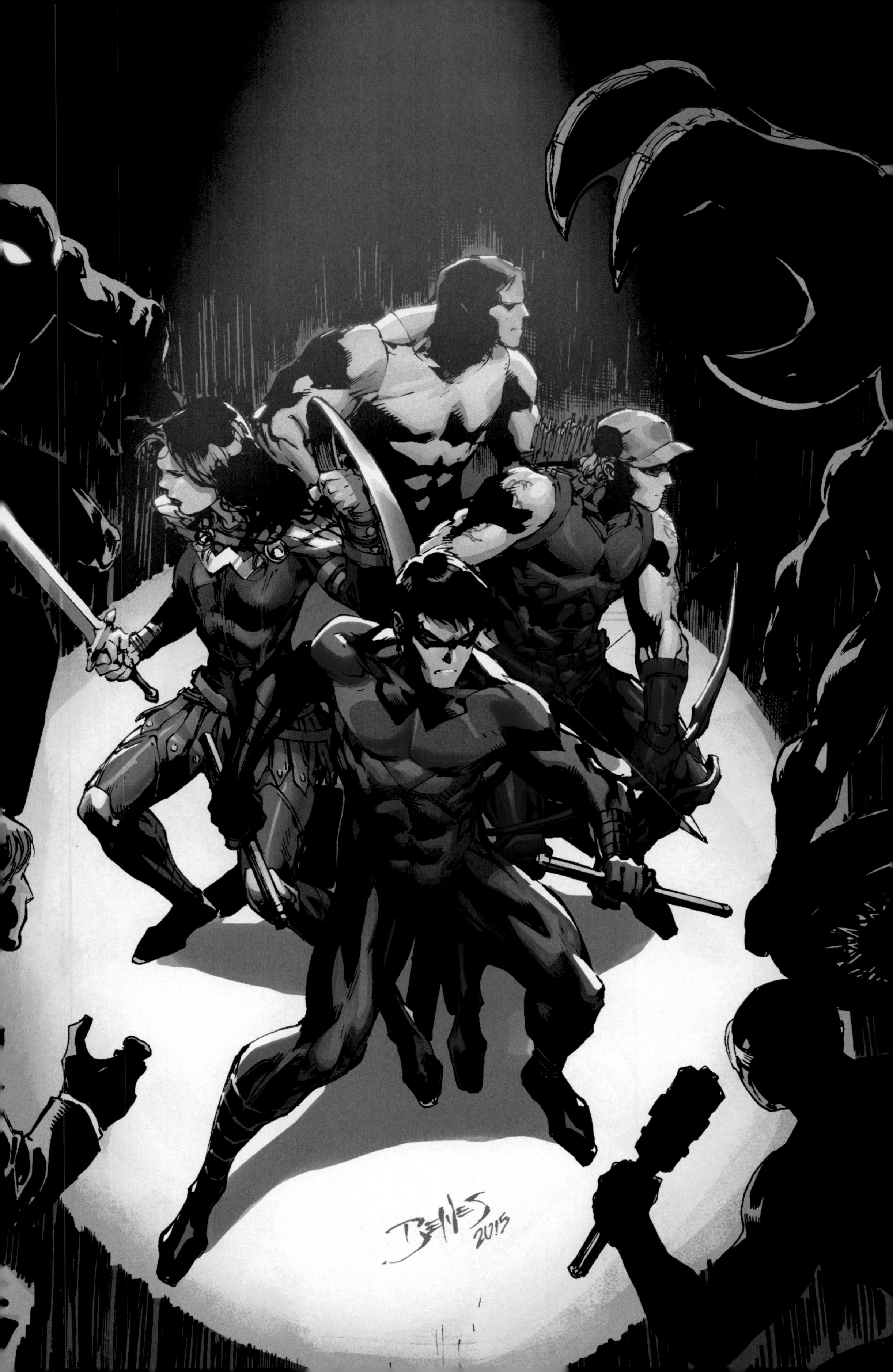
BELLES
2015

CHAPTER SEVEN: SWAN SONG

DAN ABNETT writer PAULO SIQUEIRA artist HI-FI colorist cover art by ED BENES & HI-FI

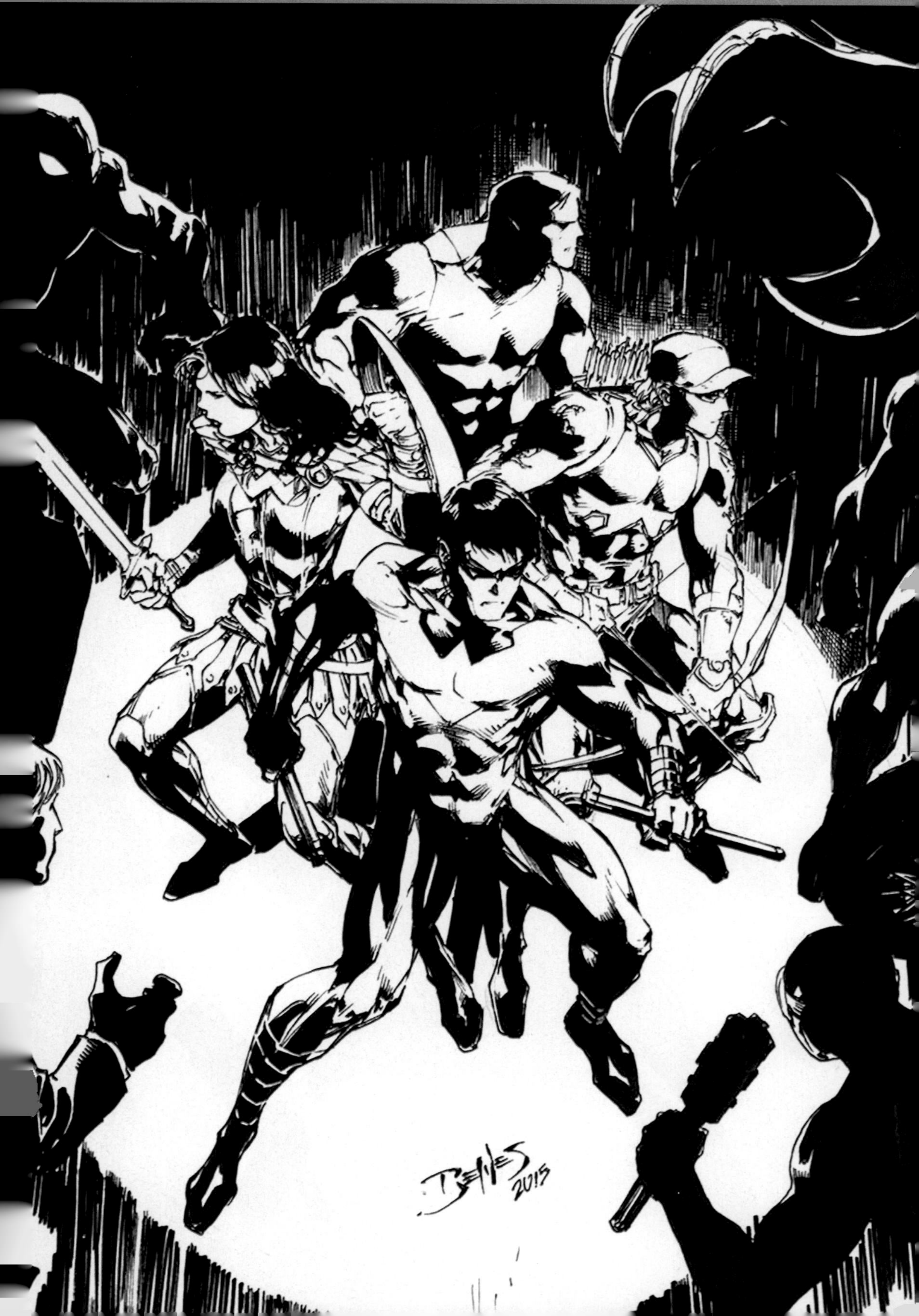

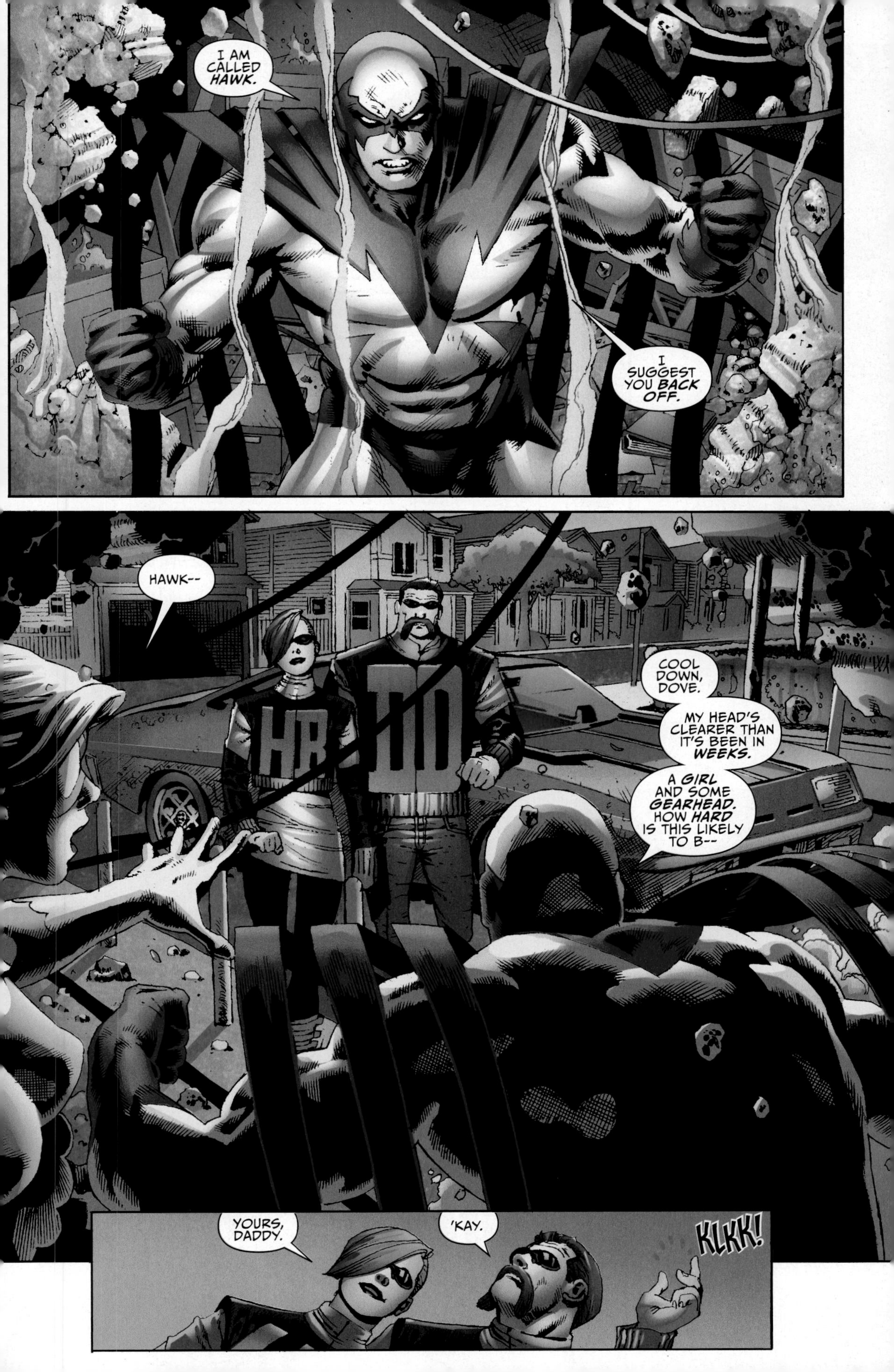
I AM CALLED HAWK.
I SUGGEST YOU BACK OFF.
HAWK--
COOL DOWN, DOVE.
MY HEAD'S CLEARER THAN IT'S BEEN IN WEEKS.
A GIRL AND SOME GEARHEAD. HOW HARD IS THIS LIKELY TO B--
YOURS, DADDY.
'KAY.
KLKK!

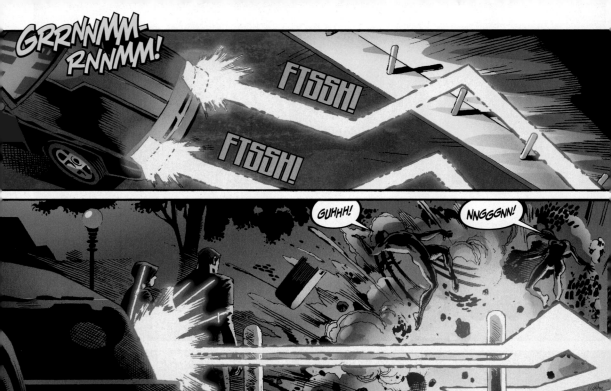

GRRNNMM-
RNNMM!

FTSSH!

FTSSH!

GUHHH!

NNGGGNN!

FLOOOMMCHHH!

BAG UP THE TRASH, D-DADDY.

I'VE GOT THE OTHERS.

ANYTHING FOR MY HONEYBUN.

SHHHLLLRKKKKK

GO DO YOUR DO, BABY...

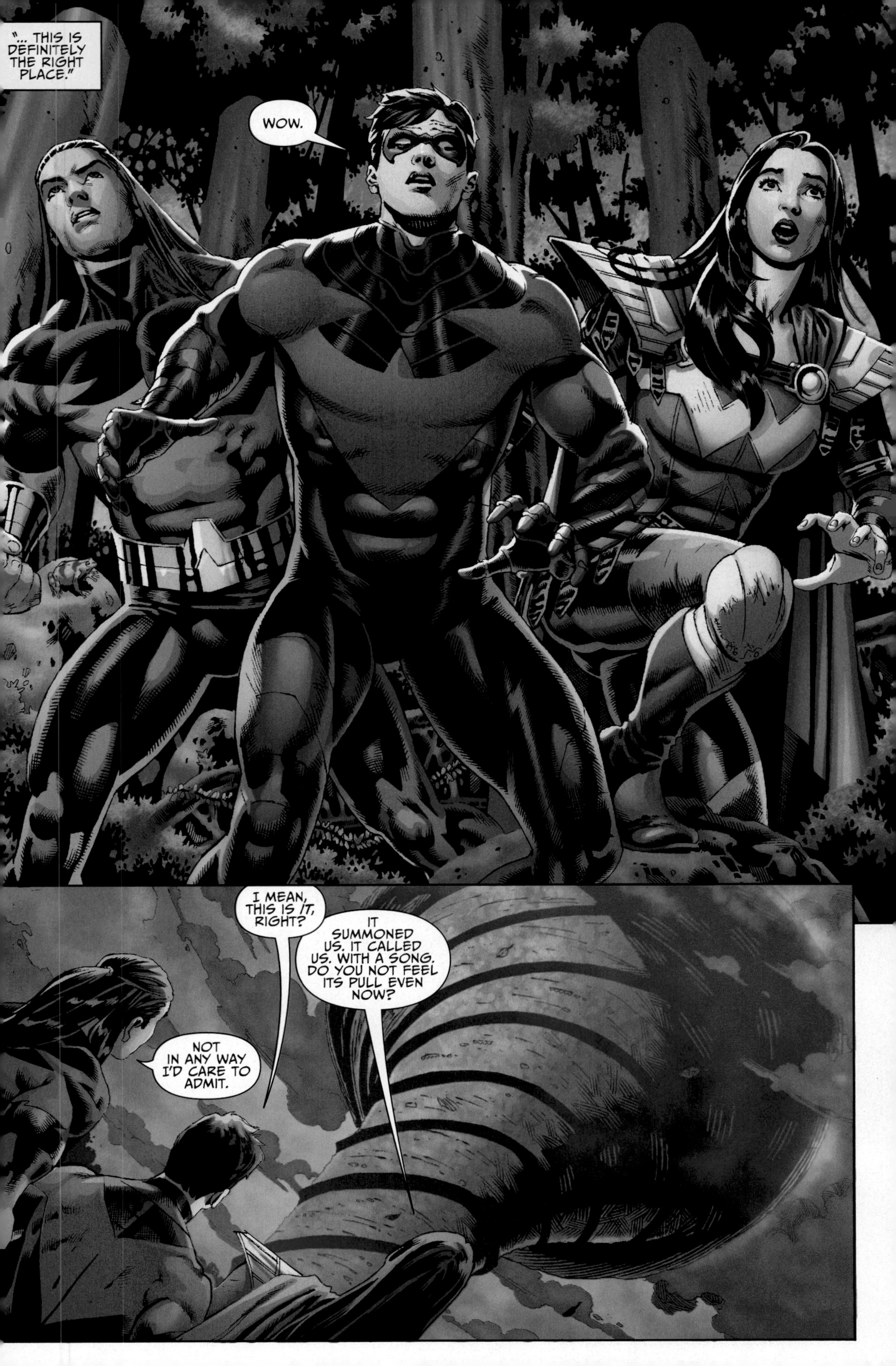
"... THIS IS DEFINITELY THE RIGHT PLACE."
WOW.
I MEAN, THIS IS IT, RIGHT?
IT SUMMONED US. IT CALLED US. WITH A SONG. DO YOU NOT FEEL ITS PULL EVEN NOW?
NOT IN ANY WAY I'D CARE TO ADMIT.

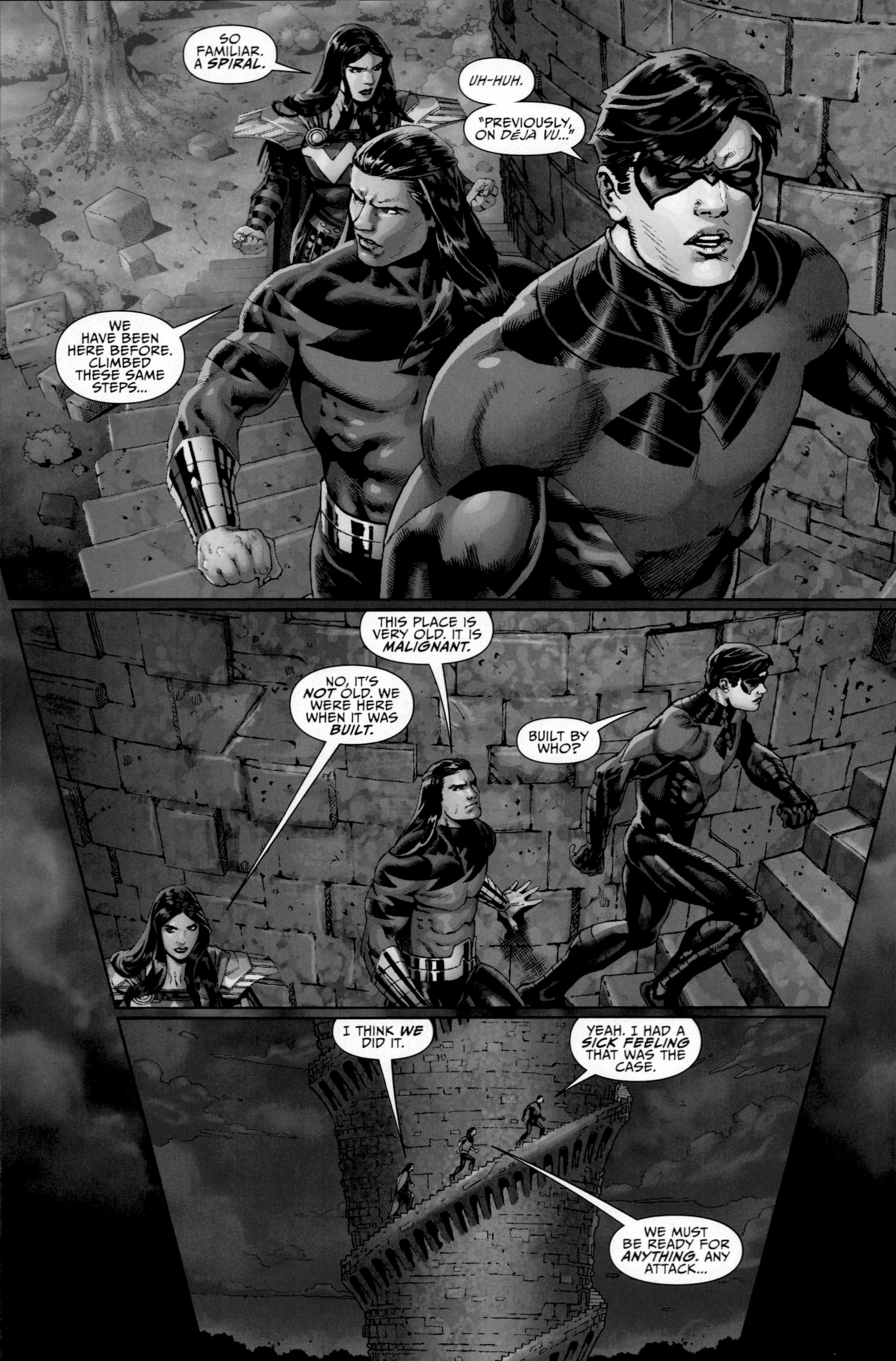
SO FAMILIAR. A *SPIRAL.*
UH-HUH.
"PREVIOUSLY, ON *DÉJÀ VU...*"
WE HAVE BEEN HERE BEFORE. CLIMBED THESE SAME STEPS...
THIS PLACE IS VERY OLD. IT IS *MALIGNANT.*
NO, IT'S *NOT* OLD. WE WERE HERE WHEN IT WAS *BUILT.*
BUILT BY WHO?
I THINK *WE* DID IT.
YEAH. I HAD A *SICK FEELING* THAT WAS THE CASE.
WE MUST BE READY FOR *ANYTHING.* ANY ATTACK...

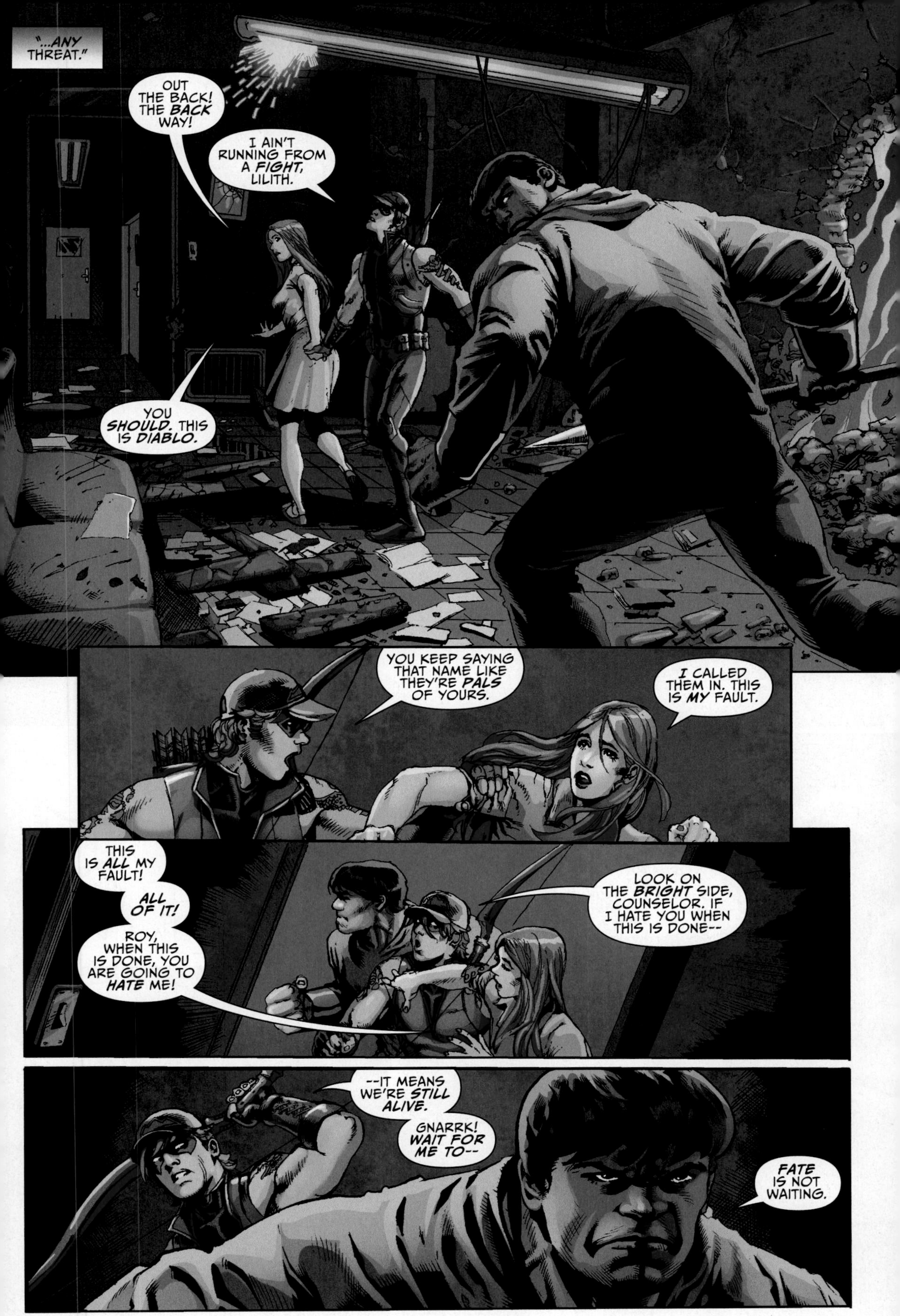
"...ANY THREAT."
OUT THE BACK! THE BACK WAY!
I AIN'T RUNNING FROM A FIGHT, LILITH.
YOU SHOULD. THIS IS DIABLO.
YOU KEEP SAYING THAT NAME LIKE THEY'RE PALS OF YOURS.
I CALLED THEM IN. THIS IS MY FAULT.
THIS IS ALL MY FAULT!
ALL OF IT!
ROY, WHEN THIS IS DONE, YOU ARE GOING TO HATE ME!
LOOK ON THE BRIGHT SIDE, COUNSELOR. IF I HATE YOU WHEN THIS IS DONE--
--IT MEANS WE'RE STILL ALIVE.
GNARRK! WAIT FOR ME TO--
FATE IS NOT WAITING.

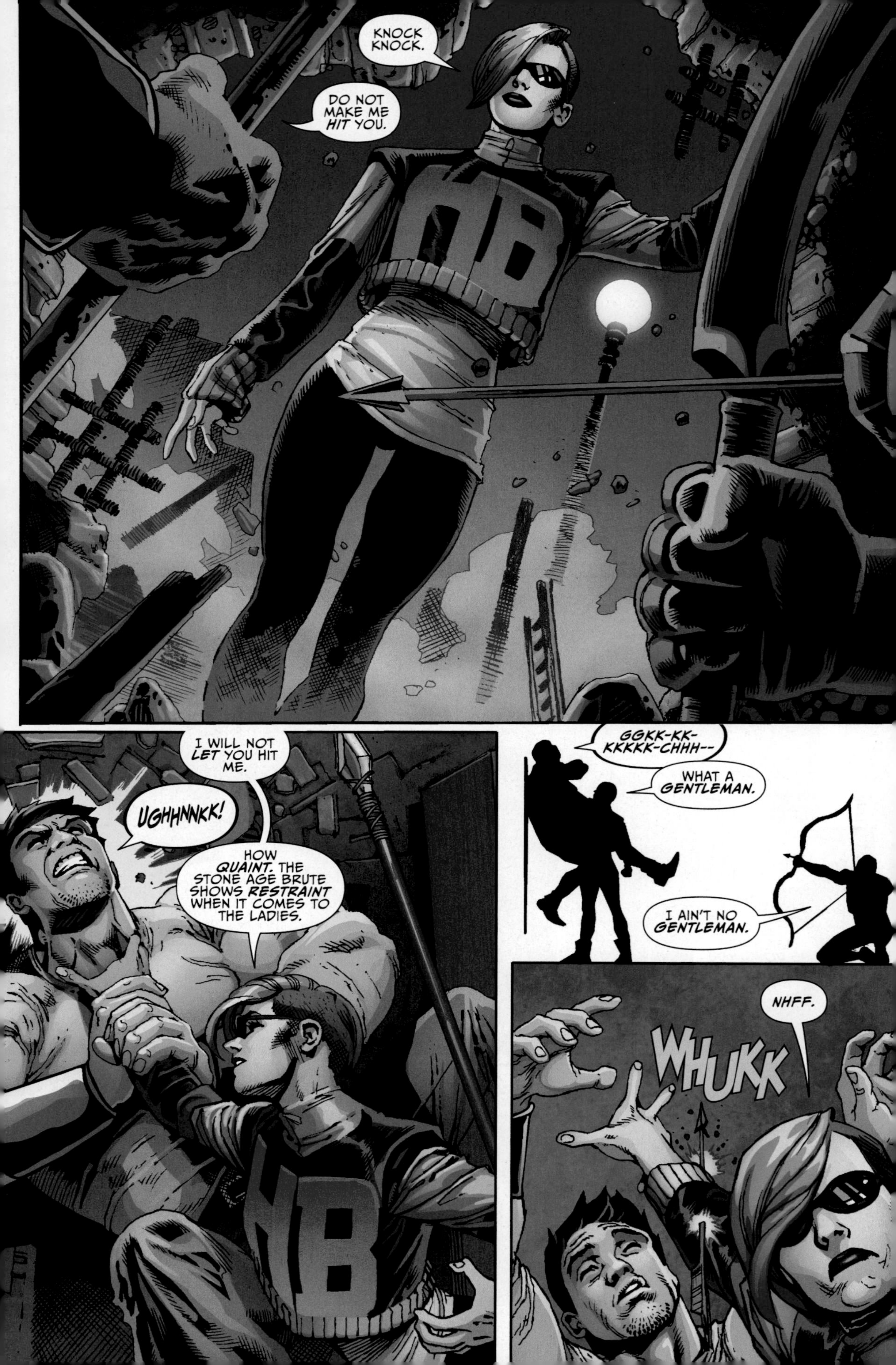
KNOCK KNOCK.
DO NOT MAKE ME HIT YOU.
I WILL NOT LET YOU HIT ME.
UGHHNNKK!
HOW QUAINT. THE STONE AGE BRUTE SHOWS RESTRAINT WHEN IT COMES TO THE LADIES.
GGKK-KK-KKKKK-CHHH--
WHAT A GENTLEMAN.
I AIN'T NO GENTLEMAN.
NHFF.
WHUKK

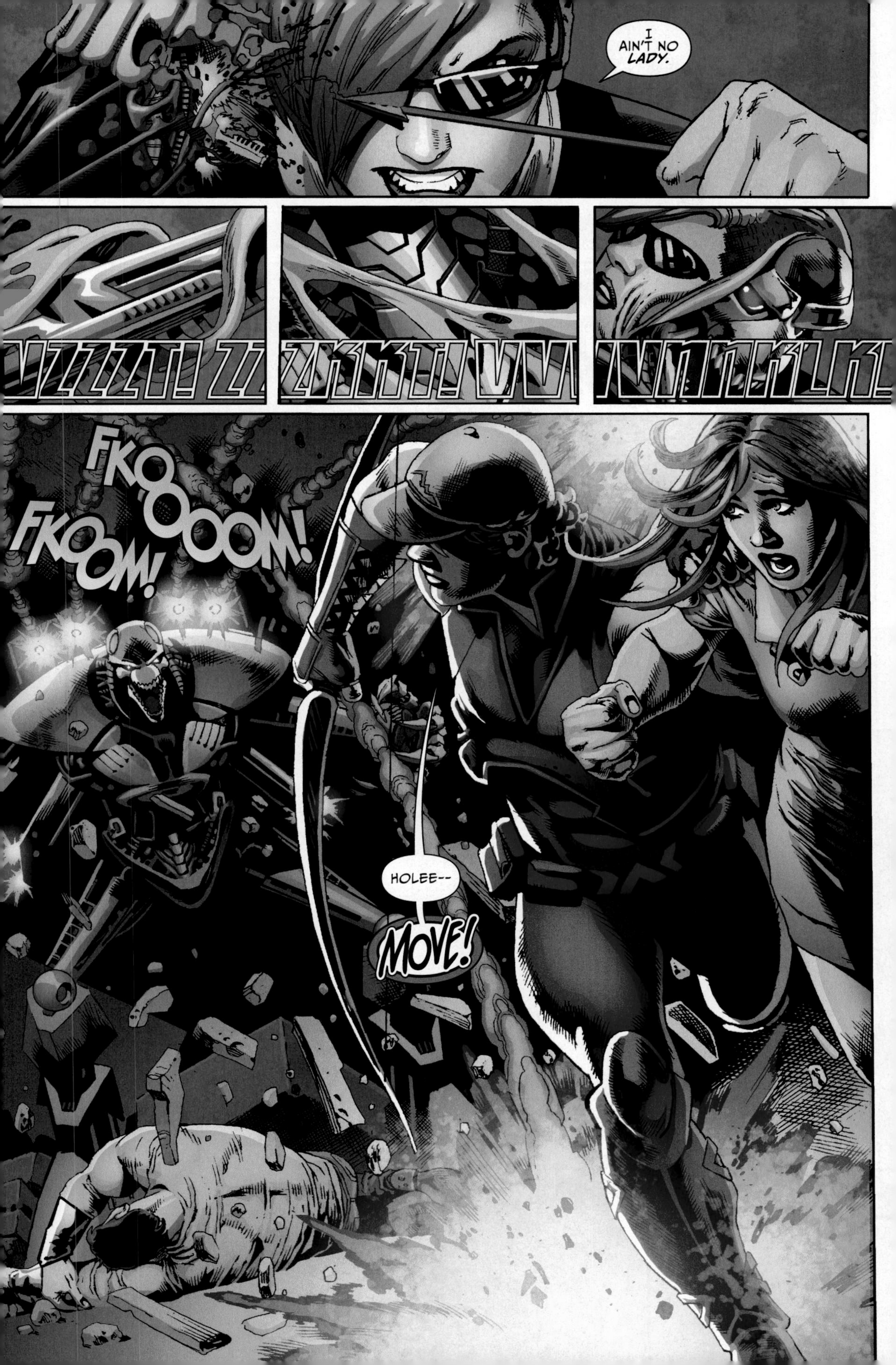
I AIN'T NO LADY.
VZZZZT! ZZKKKT! VVVVNNNKLK!
FKOOOOOM!
FKOOM!
HOLEE--
MOVE!

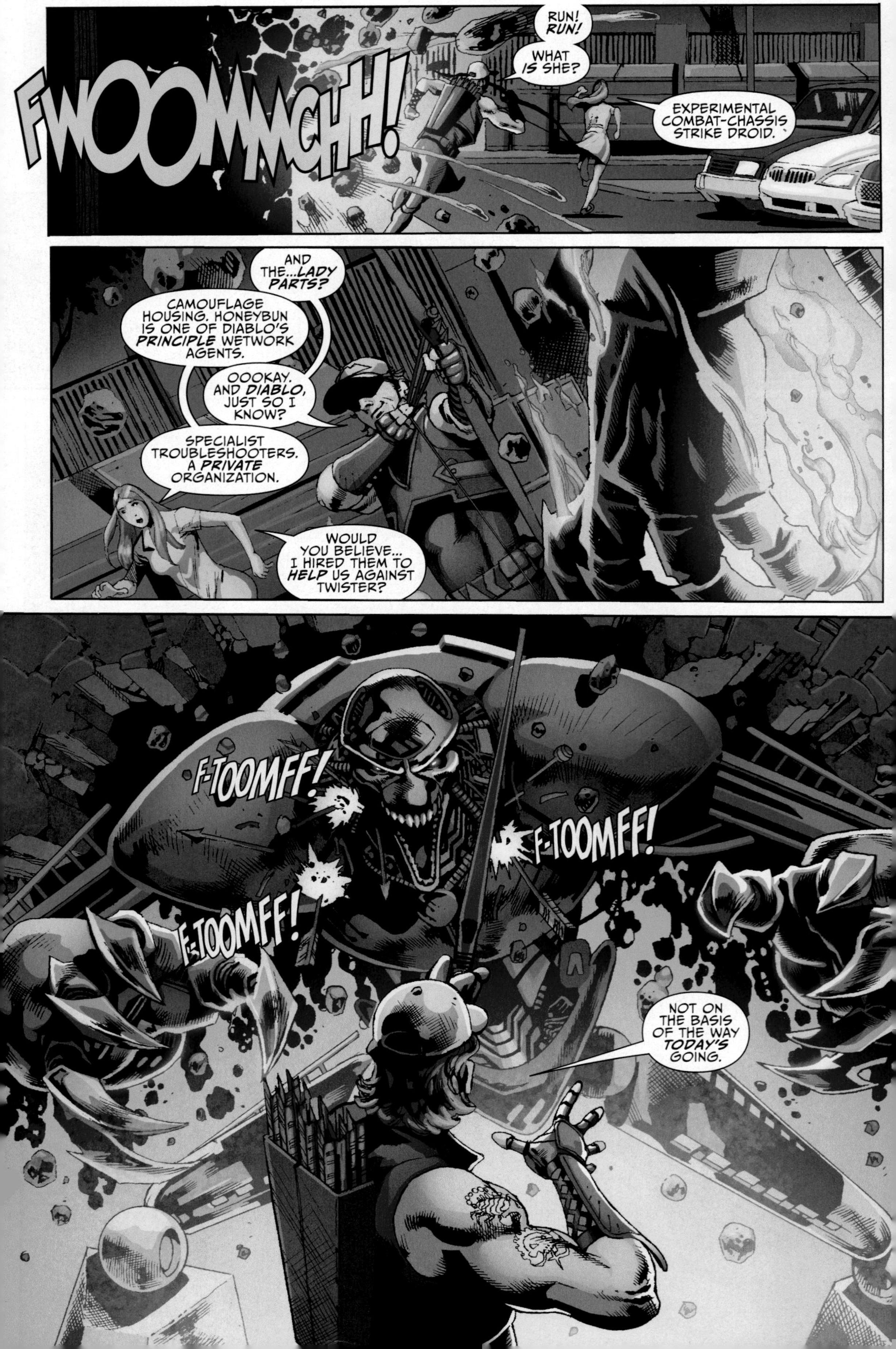
FWOOMMCHH!
RUN! RUN!
WHAT IS SHE?
EXPERIMENTAL COMBAT-CHASSIS STRIKE DROID.
AND THE...LADY PARTS?
CAMOUFLAGE HOUSING. HONEYBUN IS ONE OF DIABLO'S PRINCIPLE WETWORK AGENTS.
OOOKAY. AND DIABLO, JUST SO I KNOW?
SPECIALIST TROUBLESHOOTERS. A PRIVATE ORGANIZATION.
WOULD YOU BELIEVE... I HIRED THEM TO HELP US AGAINST TWISTER?
F-TOOMFF!
F-TOOMFF!
F-TOOMFF!
NOT ON THE BASIS OF THE WAY TODAY'S GOING.

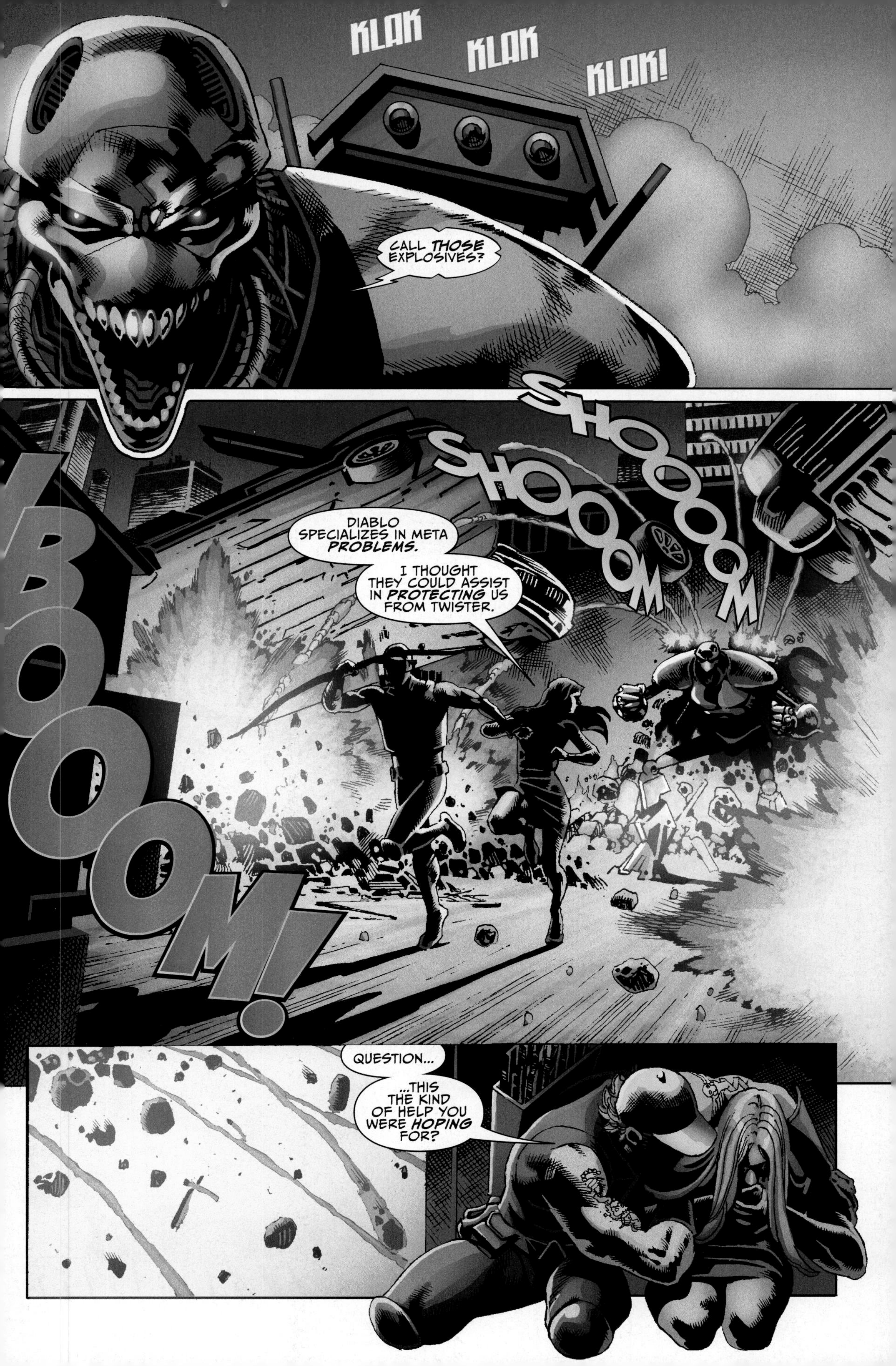
KLAK
KLAK
KLAK!
CALL THOSE EXPLOSIVES?
SHOOOOOOM
SHOOOOOOM
DIABLO SPECIALIZES IN META PROBLEMS.
I THOUGHT THEY COULD ASSIST IN PROTECTING US FROM TWISTER.
BOOOOM!
QUESTION...
...THIS THE KIND OF HELP YOU WERE HOPING FOR?

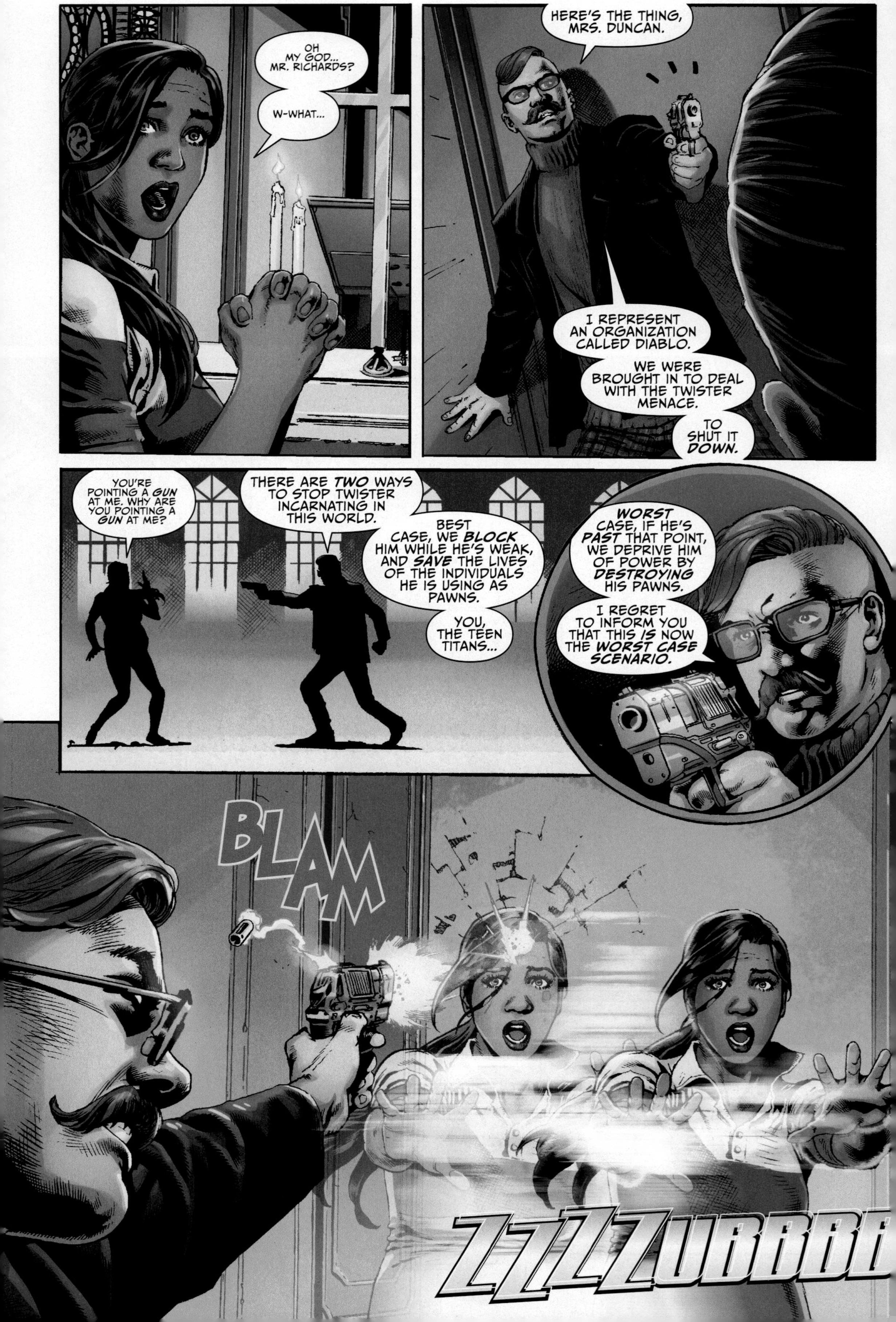
OH MY GOD... MR. RICHARDS?
W-WHAT...
HERE'S THE THING, MRS. DUNCAN.
I REPRESENT AN ORGANIZATION CALLED DIABLO.
WE WERE BROUGHT IN TO DEAL WITH THE TWISTER MENACE.
TO SHUT IT DOWN.
YOU'RE POINTING A GUN AT ME. WHY ARE YOU POINTING A GUN AT ME?
THERE ARE TWO WAYS TO STOP TWISTER INCARNATING IN THIS WORLD.
BEST CASE, WE BLOCK HIM WHILE HE'S WEAK, AND SAVE THE LIVES OF THE INDIVIDUALS HE IS USING AS PAWNS.
YOU, THE TEEN TITANS...
WORST CASE, IF HE'S PAST THAT POINT, WE DEPRIVE HIM OF POWER BY DESTROYING HIS PAWNS.
I REGRET TO INFORM YOU THAT THIS IS NOW THE WORST CASE SCENARIO.
BLAM
ZZZZUBBBB

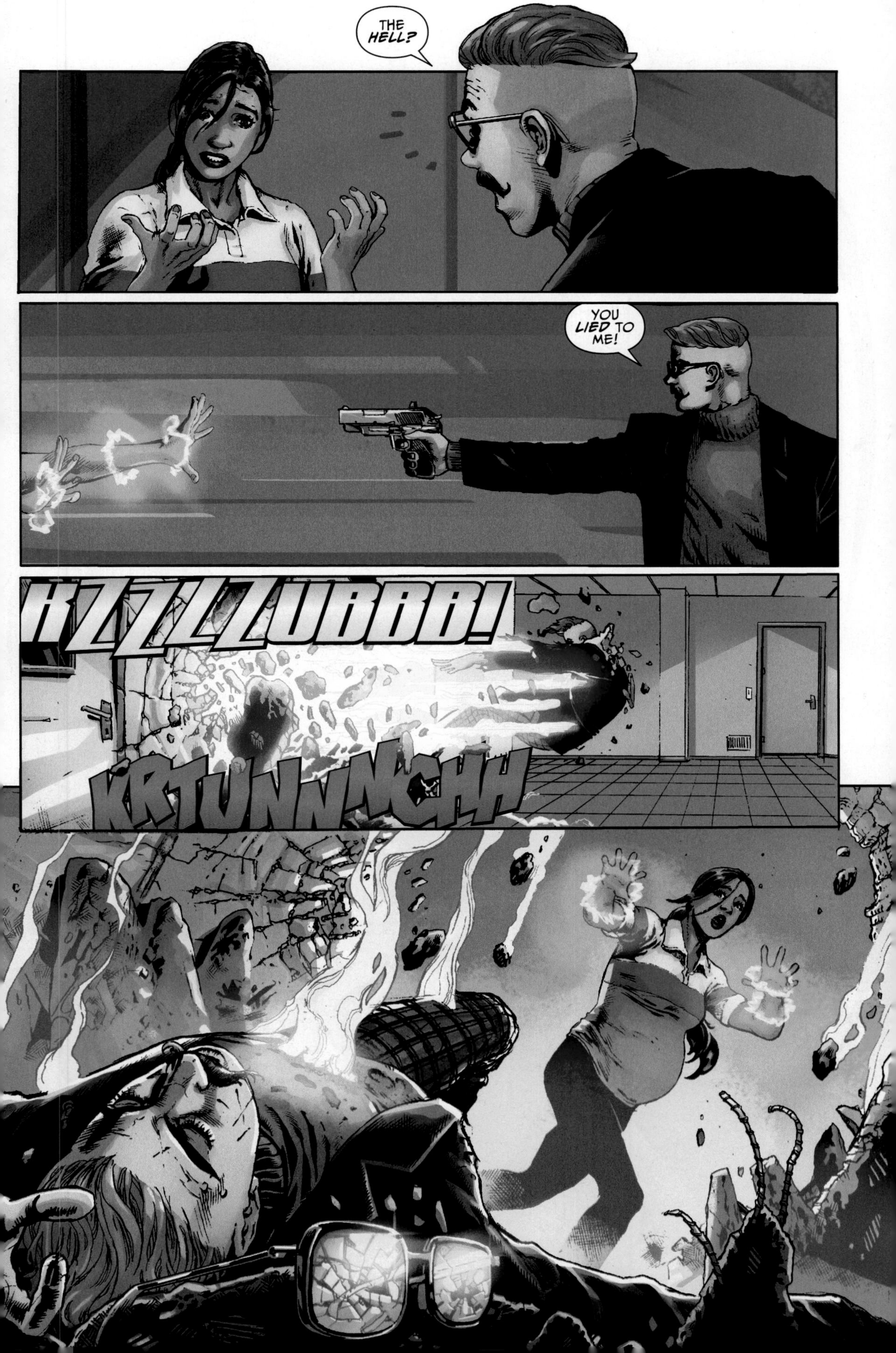
THE HELL?
YOU LIED TO ME!
KZZZZUBBB!
KRTUNNNCHH

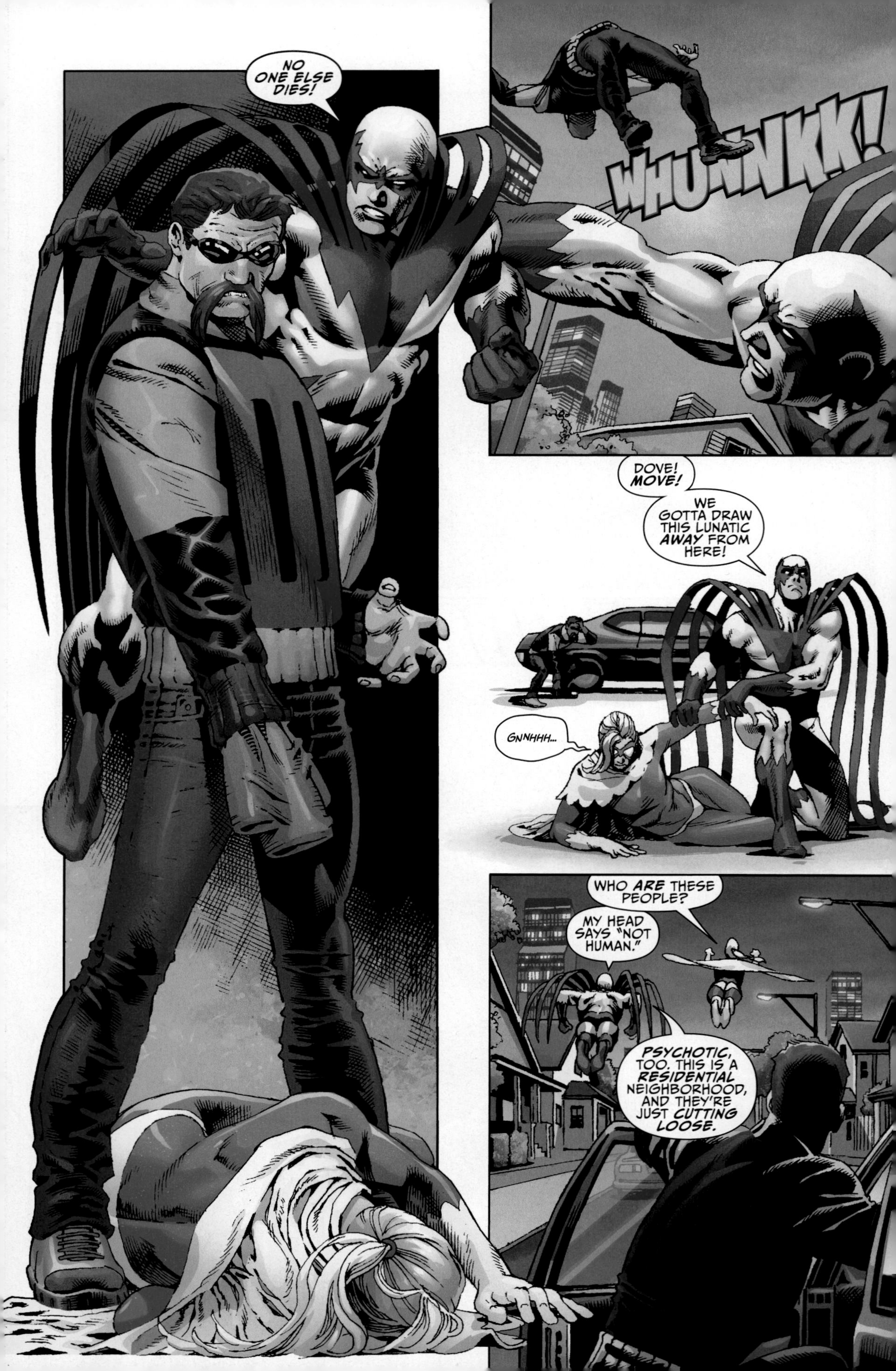
NO ONE ELSE DIES!
WHUNNKK!
DOVE! MOVE!
WE GOTTA DRAW THIS LUNATIC AWAY FROM HERE!
GNHHH...
WHO ARE THESE PEOPLE?
MY HEAD SAYS "NOT HUMAN."
PSYCHOTIC, TOO. THIS IS A RESIDENTIAL NEIGHBORHOOD, AND THEY'RE JUST CUTTING LOOSE.

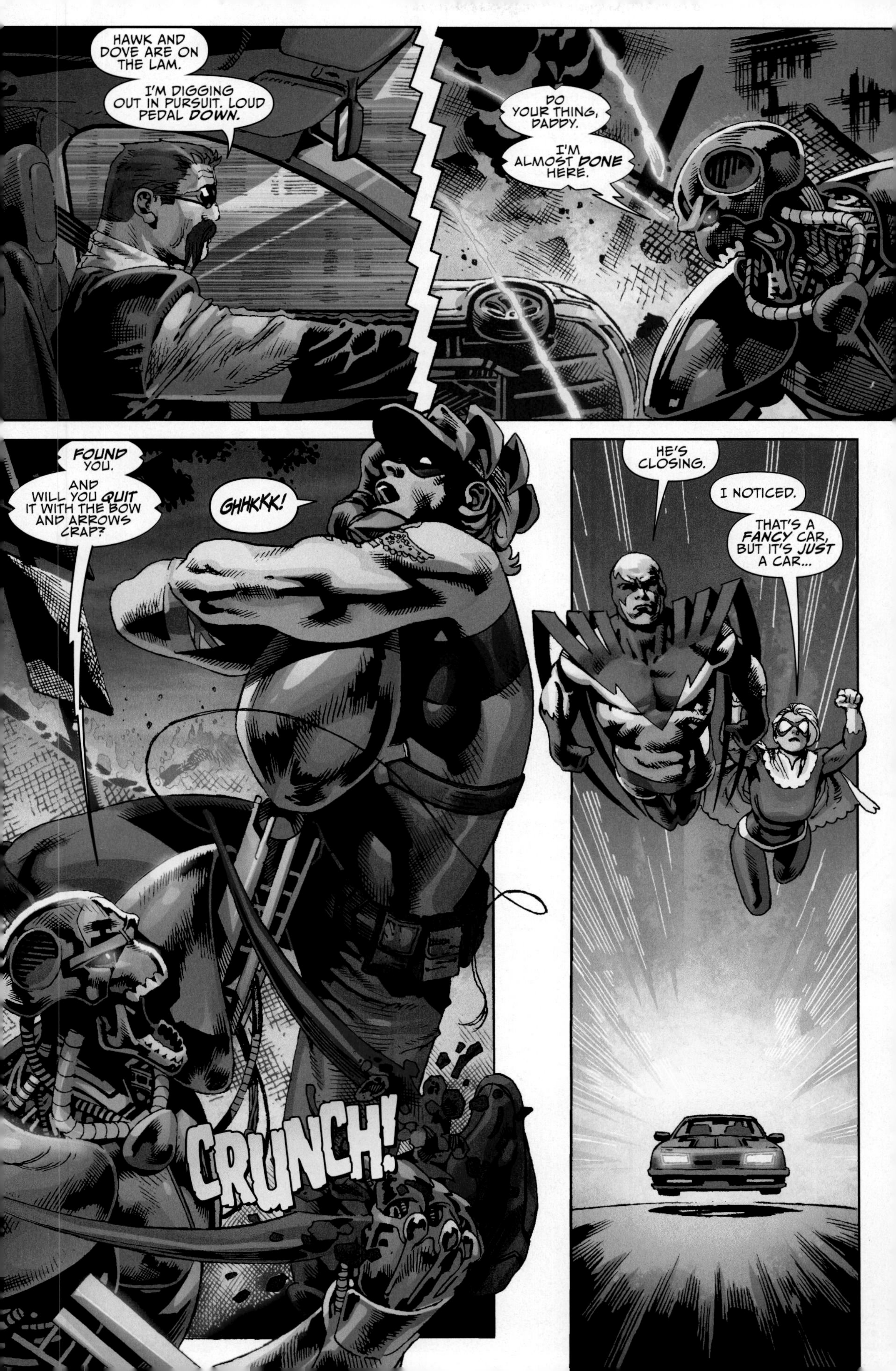
HAWK AND DOVE ARE ON THE LAM.
I'M DIGGING OUT IN PURSUIT. LOUD PEDAL DOWN.
DO YOUR THING, DADDY.
I'M ALMOST DONE HERE.
FOUND YOU.
AND WILL YOU QUIT IT WITH THE BOW AND ARROWS CRAP?
GHHKKK!
CRUNCH!
HE'S CLOSING.
I NOTICED.
THAT'S A FANCY CAR, BUT IT'S JUST A CAR...

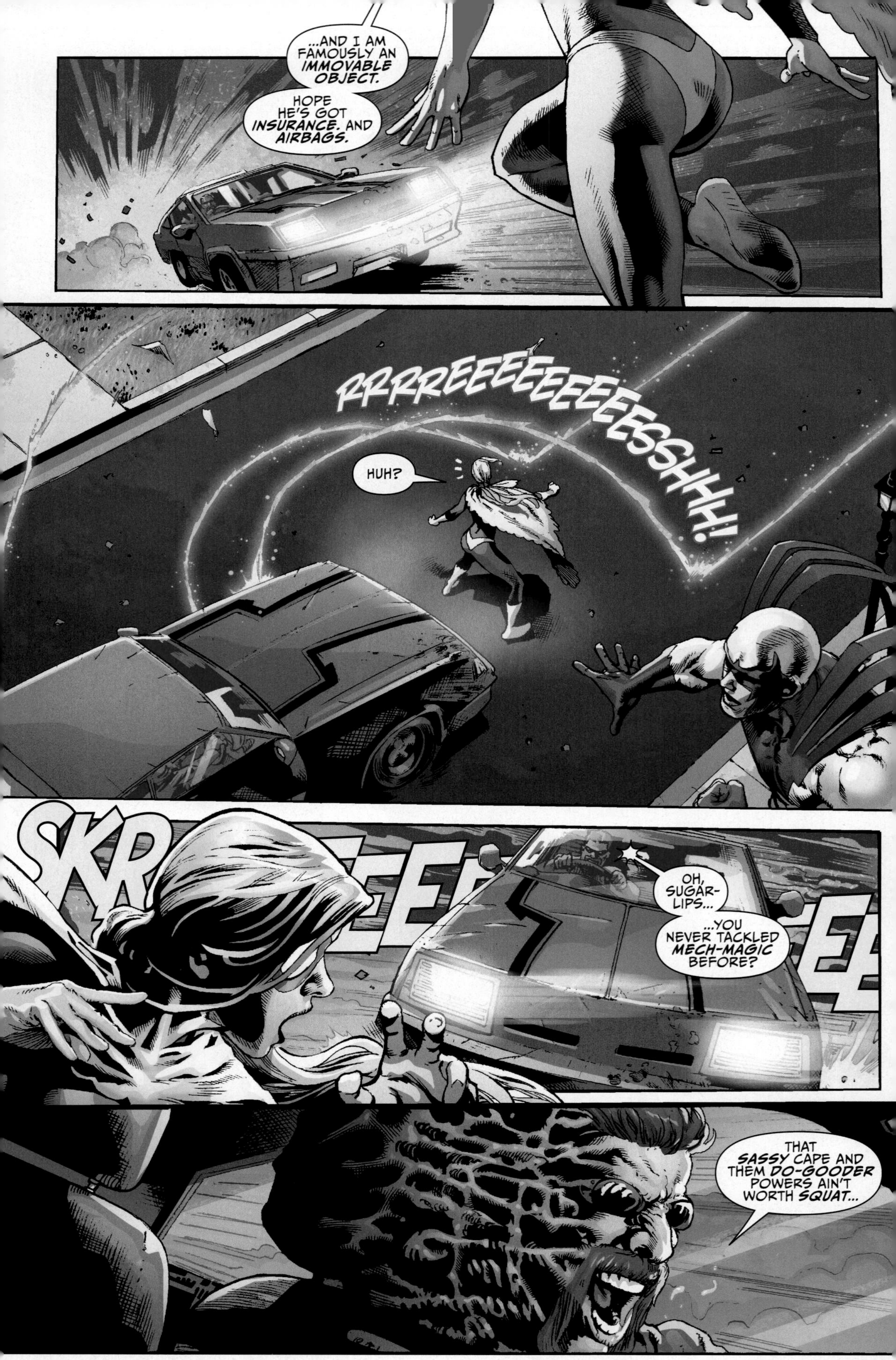
...AND I AM FAMOUSLY AN *IMMOVABLE OBJECT*.
HOPE HE'S GOT *INSURANCE*. AND *AIRBAGS*.
RRRREEEEEEEEEESSHHH!
HUH?
SKREEEEEEE
OH, SUGAR-LIPS...
...YOU NEVER TACKLED *MECH-MAGIC* BEFORE?
THAT *SASSY* CAPE AND THEM *DO-GOODER* POWERS AIN'T WORTH *SQUAT*...

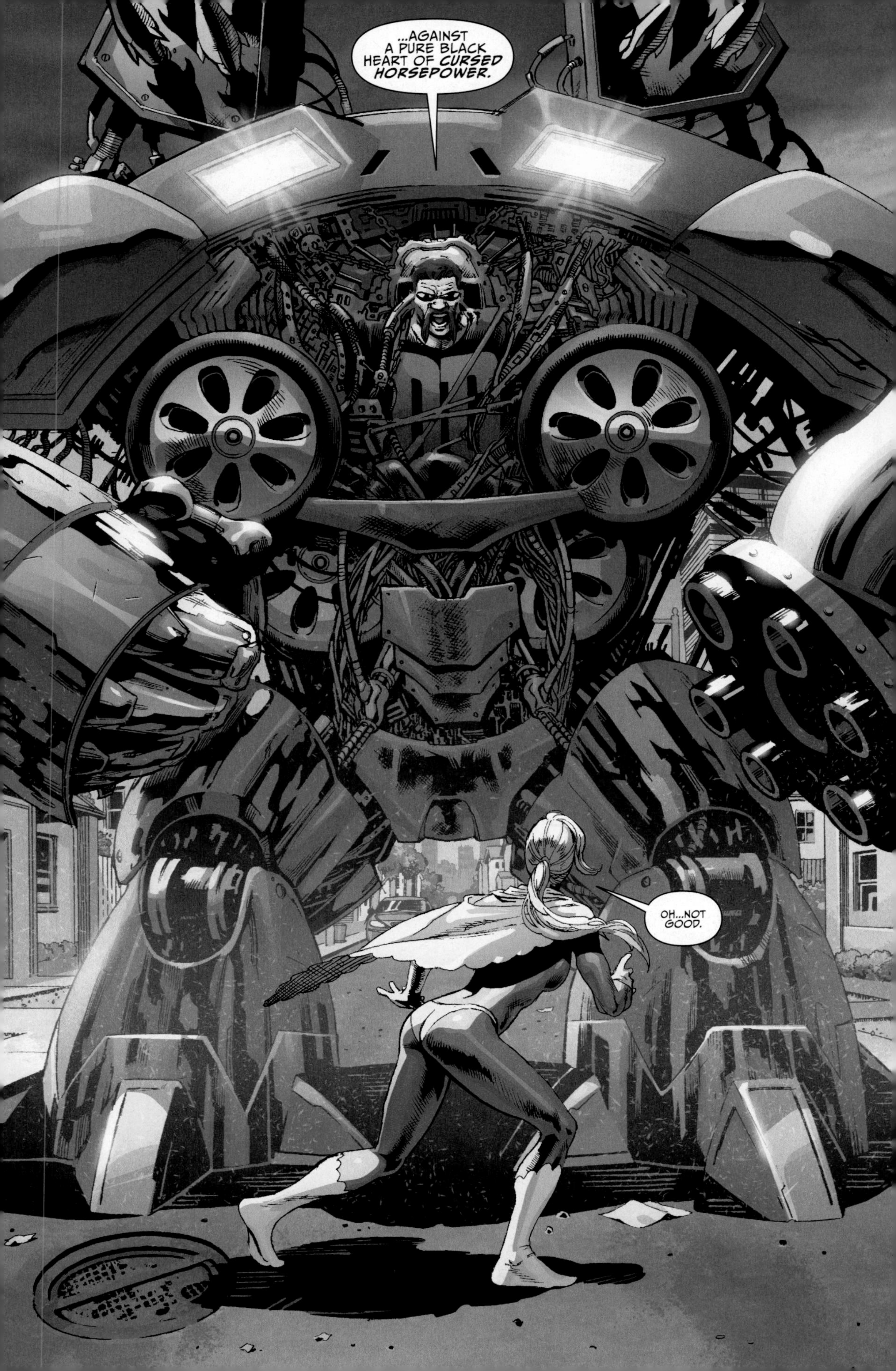
...AGAINST A PURE BLACK HEART OF CURSED HORSEPOWER.
OH...NOT GOOD.

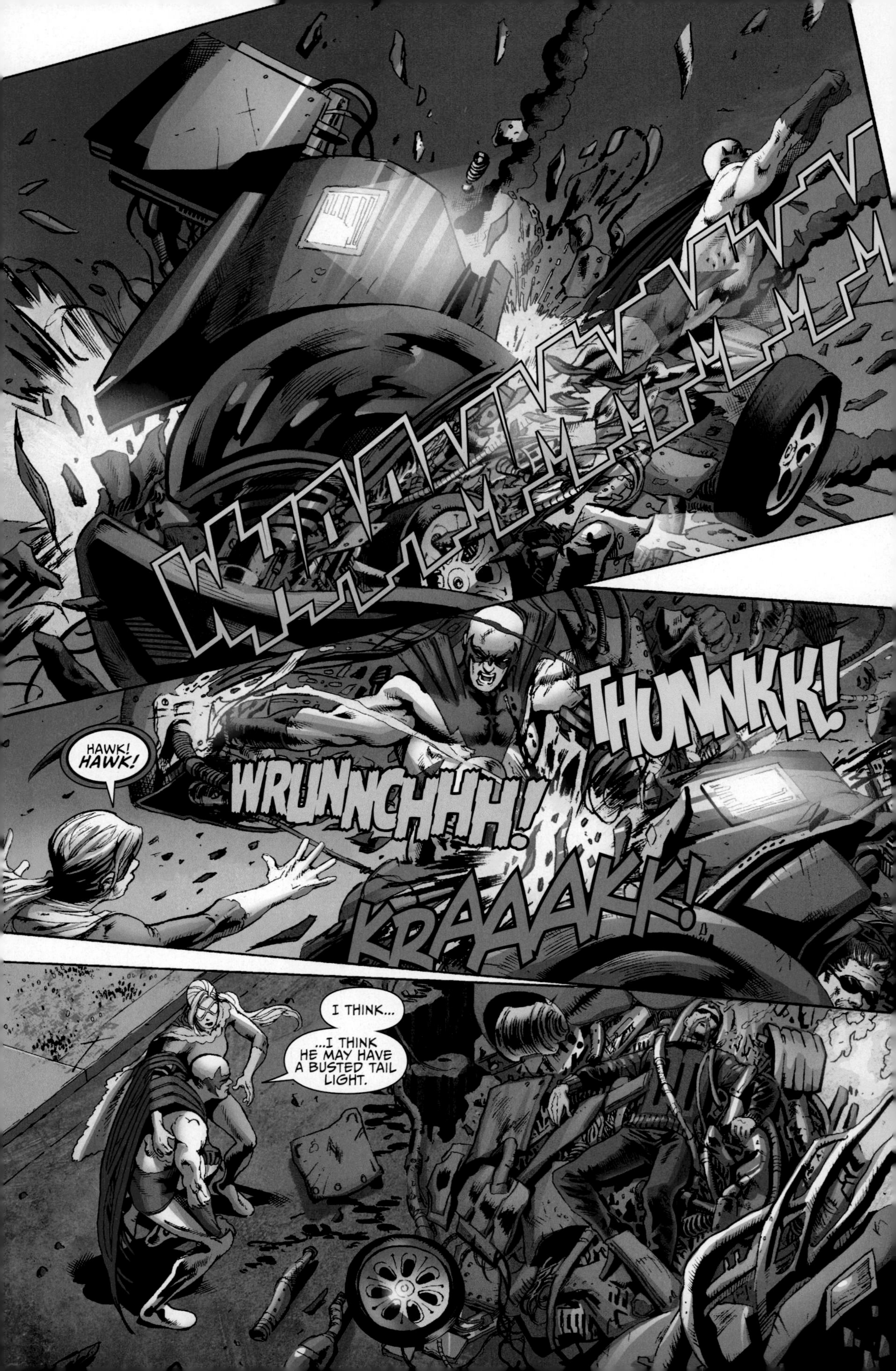
WHHAAMMM
HAWK! HAWK!
THUNNKK!
WRUNNCHHH!
KRAAAKK!
I THINK...
...I THINK HE MAY HAVE A BUSTED TAIL LIGHT.

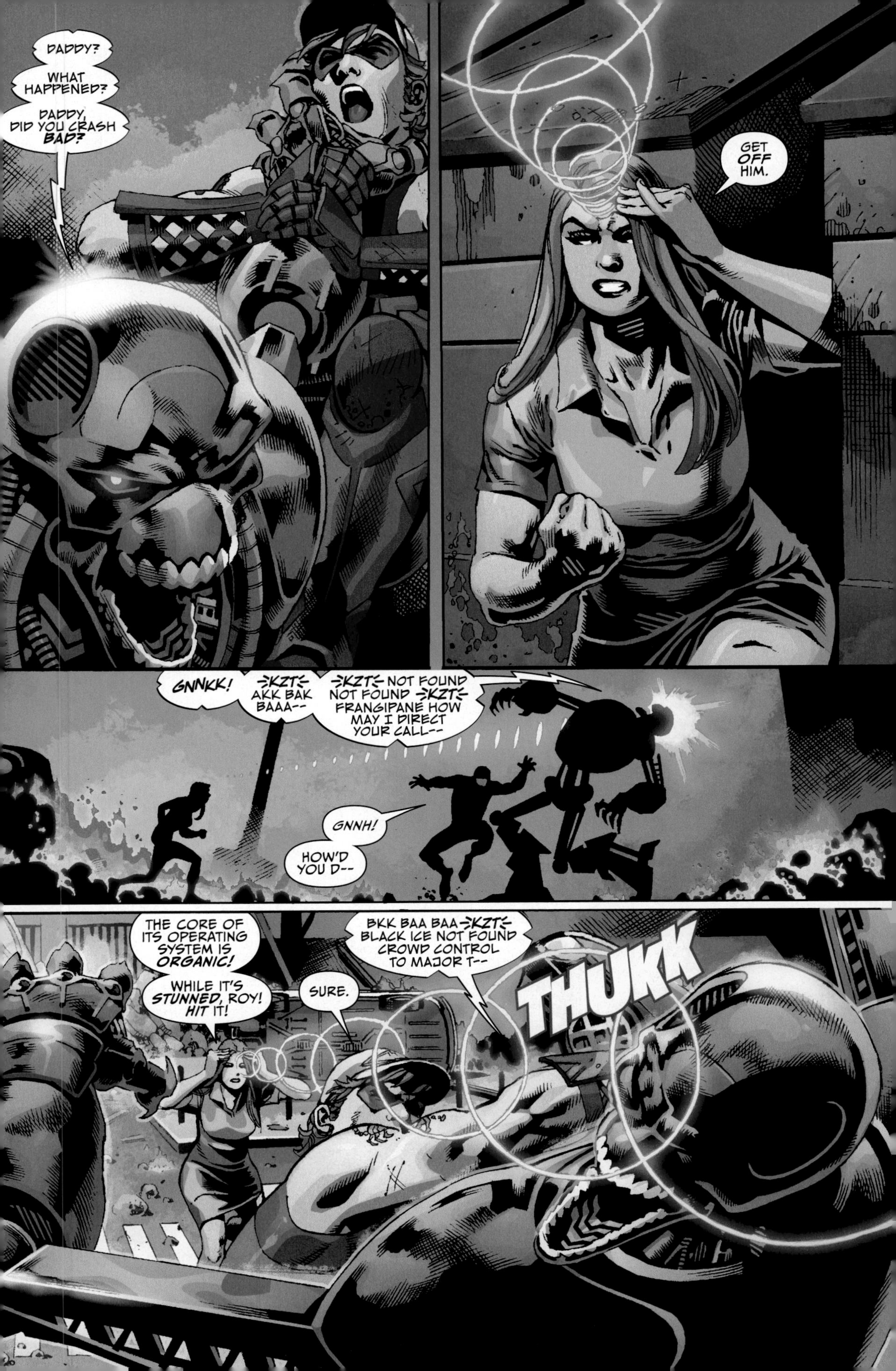
DADDY?
WHAT HAPPENED?
DADDY, DID YOU CRASH BAD?
GET OFF HIM.
GNNKK!
-KZT- AKK BAK BAAA--
-KZT- NOT FOUND NOT FOUND -KZT- FRANGIPANE HOW MAY I DIRECT YOUR CALL--
GNNH!
HOW'D YOU D--
THE CORE OF ITS OPERATING SYSTEM IS ORGANIC!
WHILE IT'S STUNNED, ROY! HIT IT!
SURE.
BKK BAA BAA -KZT- BLACK ICE NOT FOUND CROWD CONTROL TO MAJOR T--
THUKK

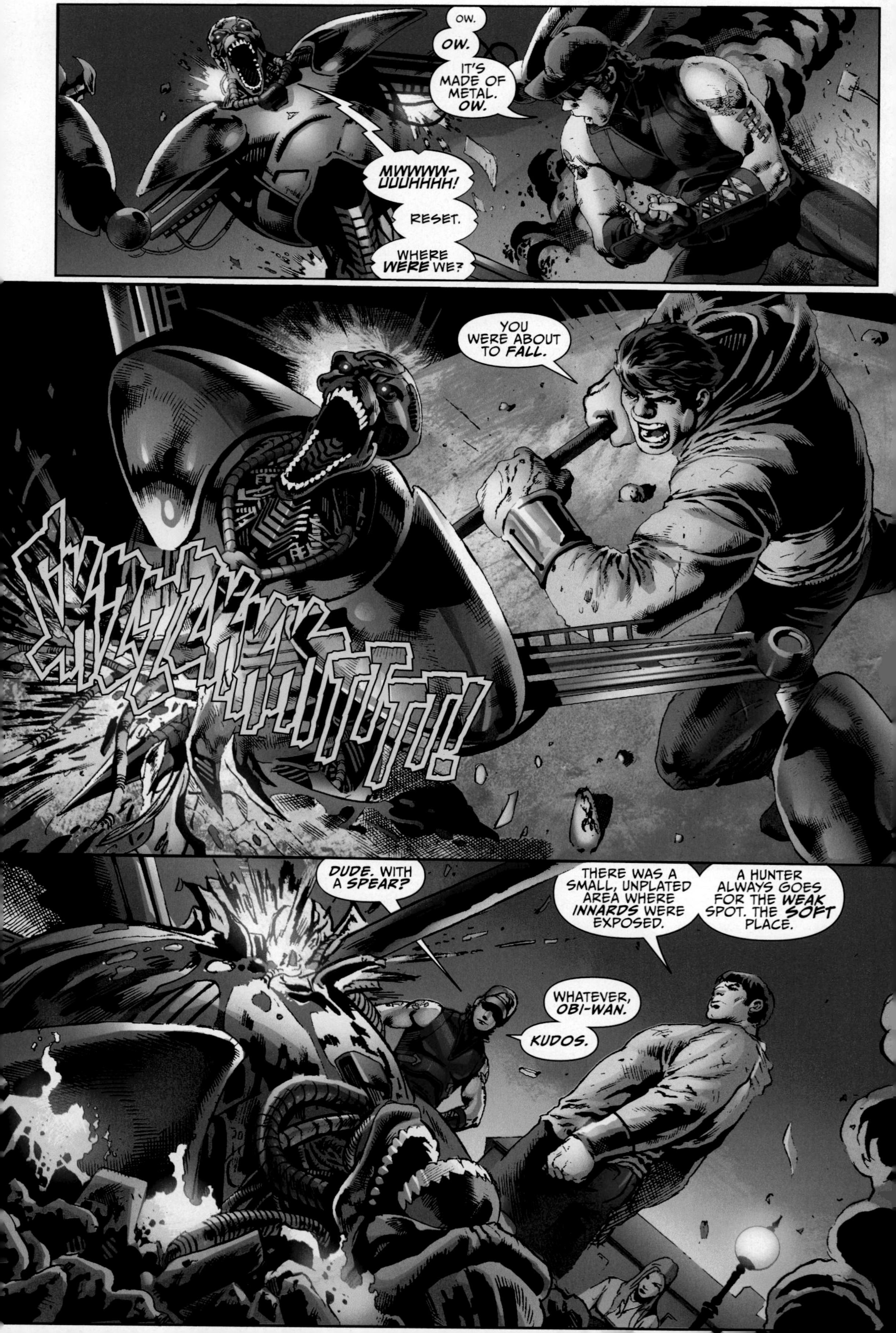
OW.
OW.
IT'S MADE OF METAL. OW.
MWWWW-UUUHHHH!
RESET.
WHERE WERE WE?
YOU WERE ABOUT TO FALL.
DUDE. WITH A SPEAR?
THERE WAS A SMALL, UNPLATED AREA WHERE INNARDS WERE EXPOSED.
A HUNTER ALWAYS GOES FOR THE WEAK SPOT. THE SOFT PLACE.
WHATEVER, OBI-WAN.
KUDOS.

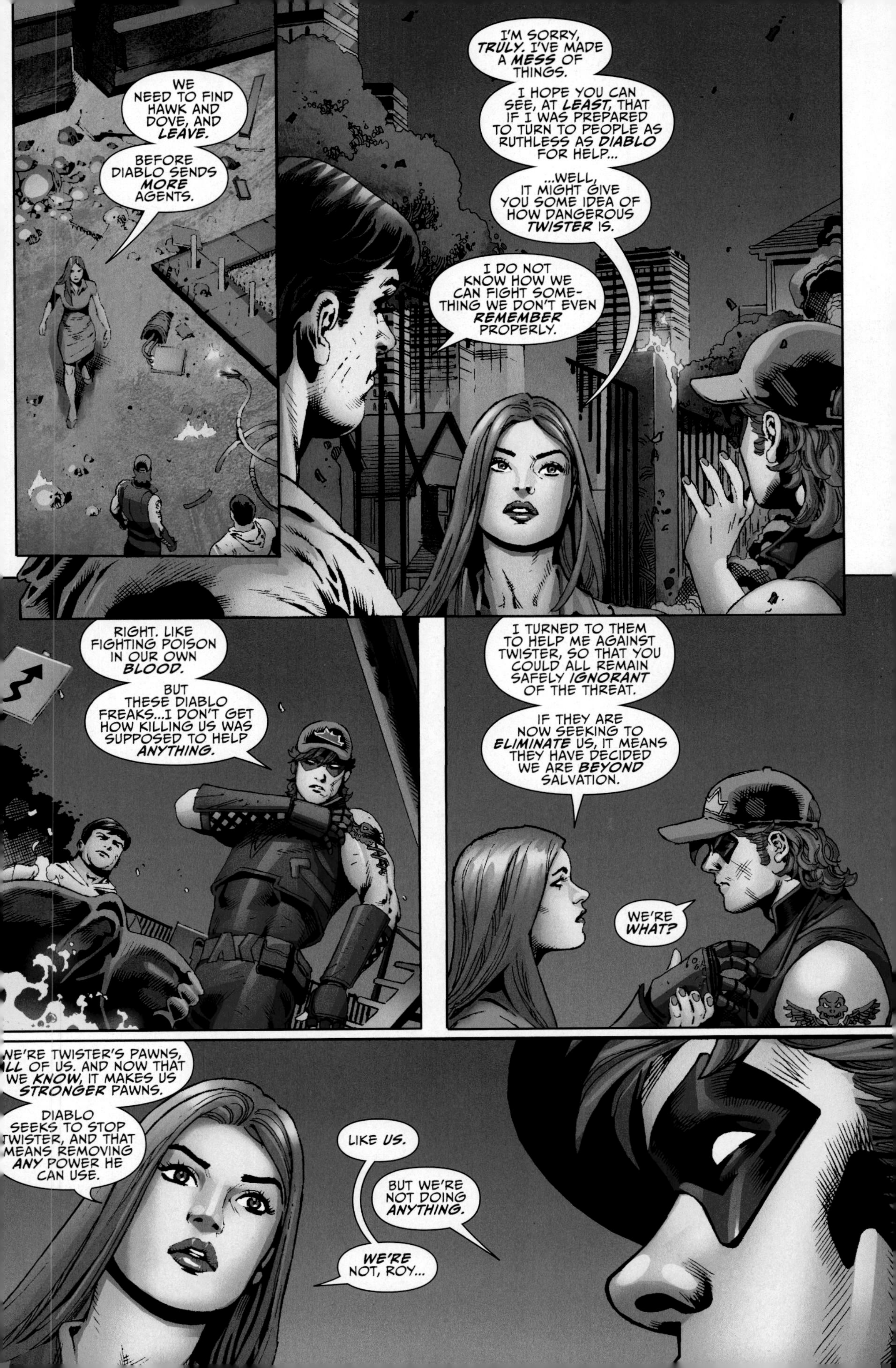
WE NEED TO FIND HAWK AND DOVE, AND LEAVE.
BEFORE DIABLO SENDS MORE AGENTS.
I'M SORRY, TRULY. I'VE MADE A MESS OF THINGS.
I HOPE YOU CAN SEE, AT LEAST, THAT IF I WAS PREPARED TO TURN TO PEOPLE AS RUTHLESS AS DIABLO FOR HELP...
...WELL, IT MIGHT GIVE YOU SOME IDEA OF HOW DANGEROUS TWISTER IS.
I DO NOT KNOW HOW WE CAN FIGHT SOME-THING WE DON'T EVEN REMEMBER PROPERLY.
RIGHT. LIKE FIGHTING POISON IN OUR OWN BLOOD.
BUT THESE DIABLO FREAKS...I DON'T GET HOW KILLING US WAS SUPPOSED TO HELP ANYTHING.
I TURNED TO THEM TO HELP ME AGAINST TWISTER, SO THAT YOU COULD ALL REMAIN SAFELY IGNORANT OF THE THREAT.
IF THEY ARE NOW SEEKING TO ELIMINATE US, IT MEANS THEY HAVE DECIDED WE ARE BEYOND SALVATION.
WE'RE WHAT?
WE'RE TWISTER'S PAWNS, LL OF US. AND NOW THAT WE KNOW, IT MAKES US STRONGER PAWNS.
DIABLO SEEKS TO STOP TWISTER, AND THAT MEANS REMOVING ANY POWER HE CAN USE.
LIKE US.
BUT WE'RE NOT DOING ANYTHING.
WE'RE NOT, ROY...

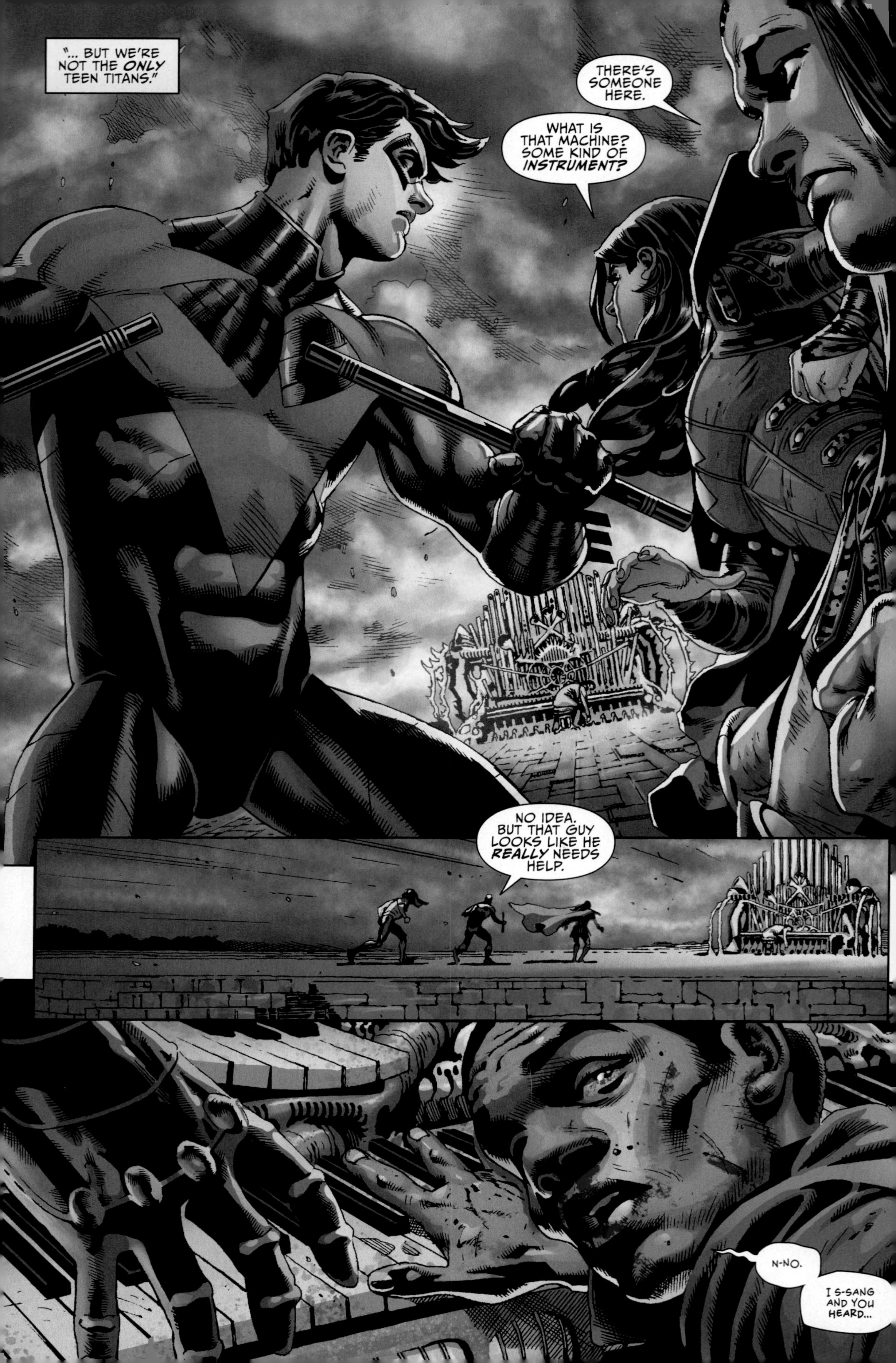
"... BUT WE'RE NOT THE *ONLY* TEEN TITANS."
THERE'S SOMEONE HERE.
WHAT IS THAT MACHINE? SOME KIND OF *INSTRUMENT?*
NO IDEA. BUT THAT GUY LOOKS LIKE HE *REALLY* NEEDS HELP.
N-NO.
I S-SANG AND YOU HEARD...

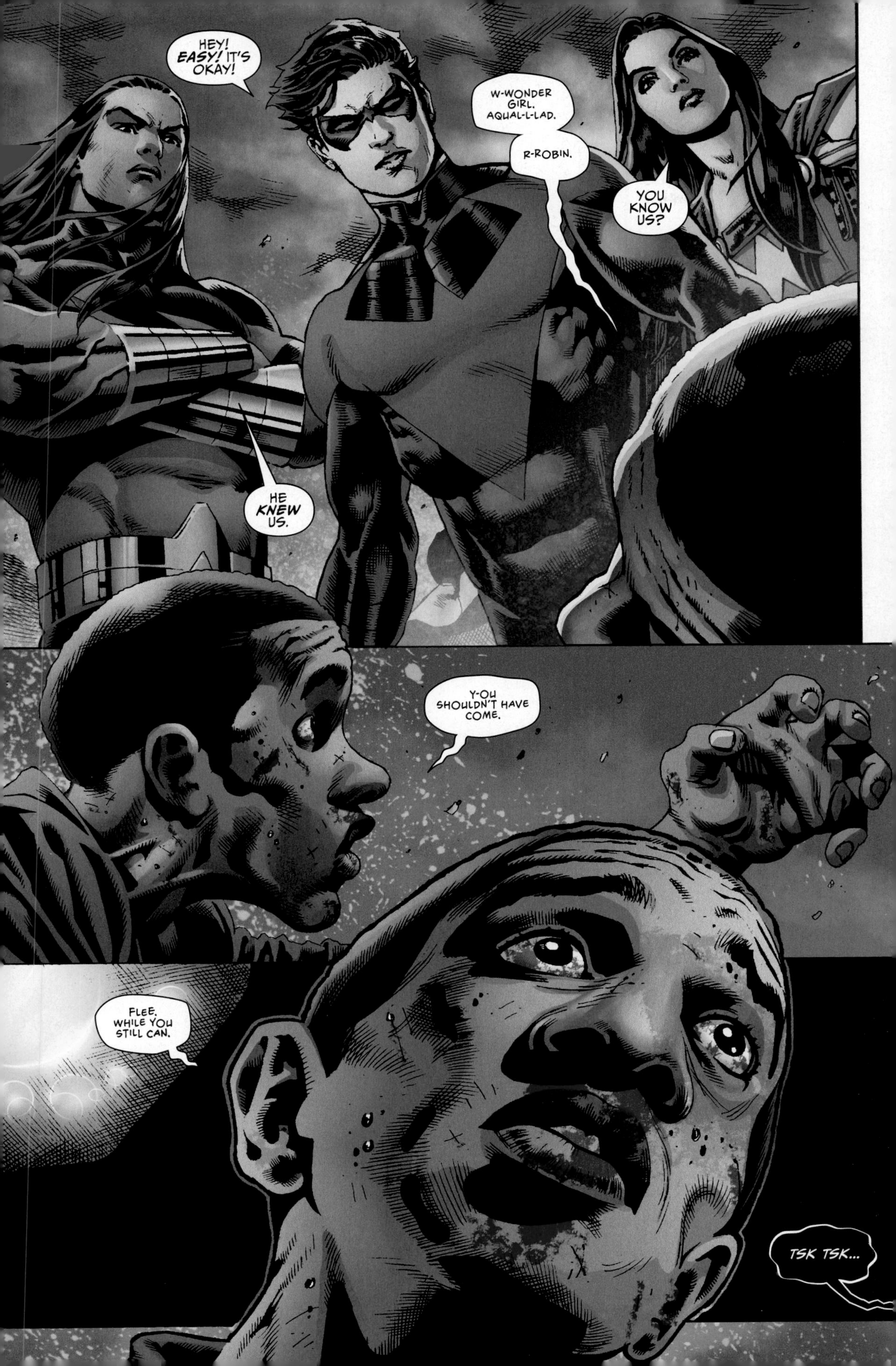

HEY! EASY! IT'S OKAY!
W-WONDER GIRL. AQUAL-L-LAD.
R-ROBIN.
YOU KNOW US?
HE KNEW US.
Y-OU SHOULDN'T HAVE COME.
FLEE. WHILE YOU STILL CAN.
TSK TSK...

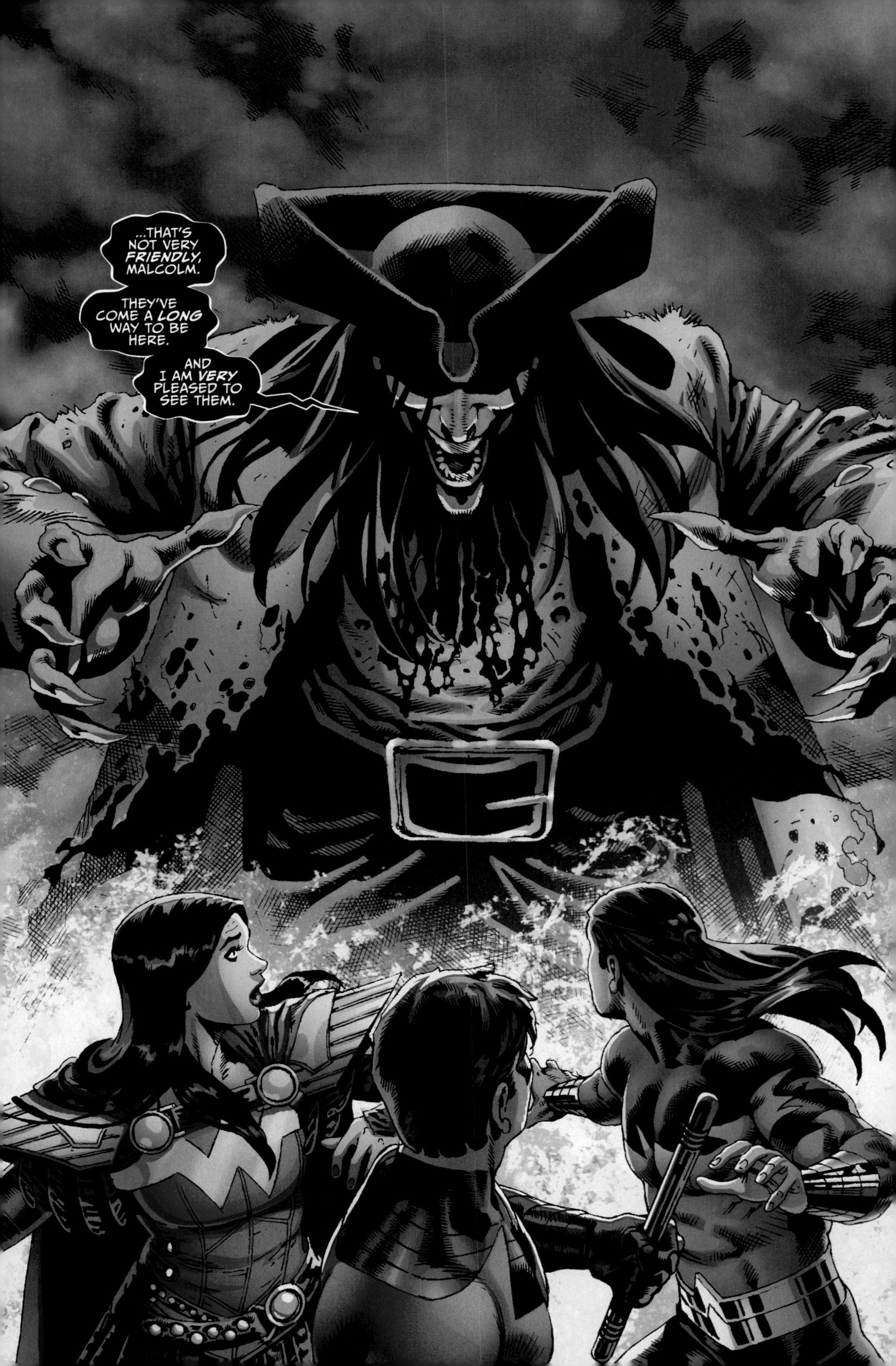
...THAT'S NOT VERY FRIENDLY, MALCOLM.
THEY'VE COME A LONG WAY TO BE HERE.
AND I AM VERY PLEASED TO SEE THEM.

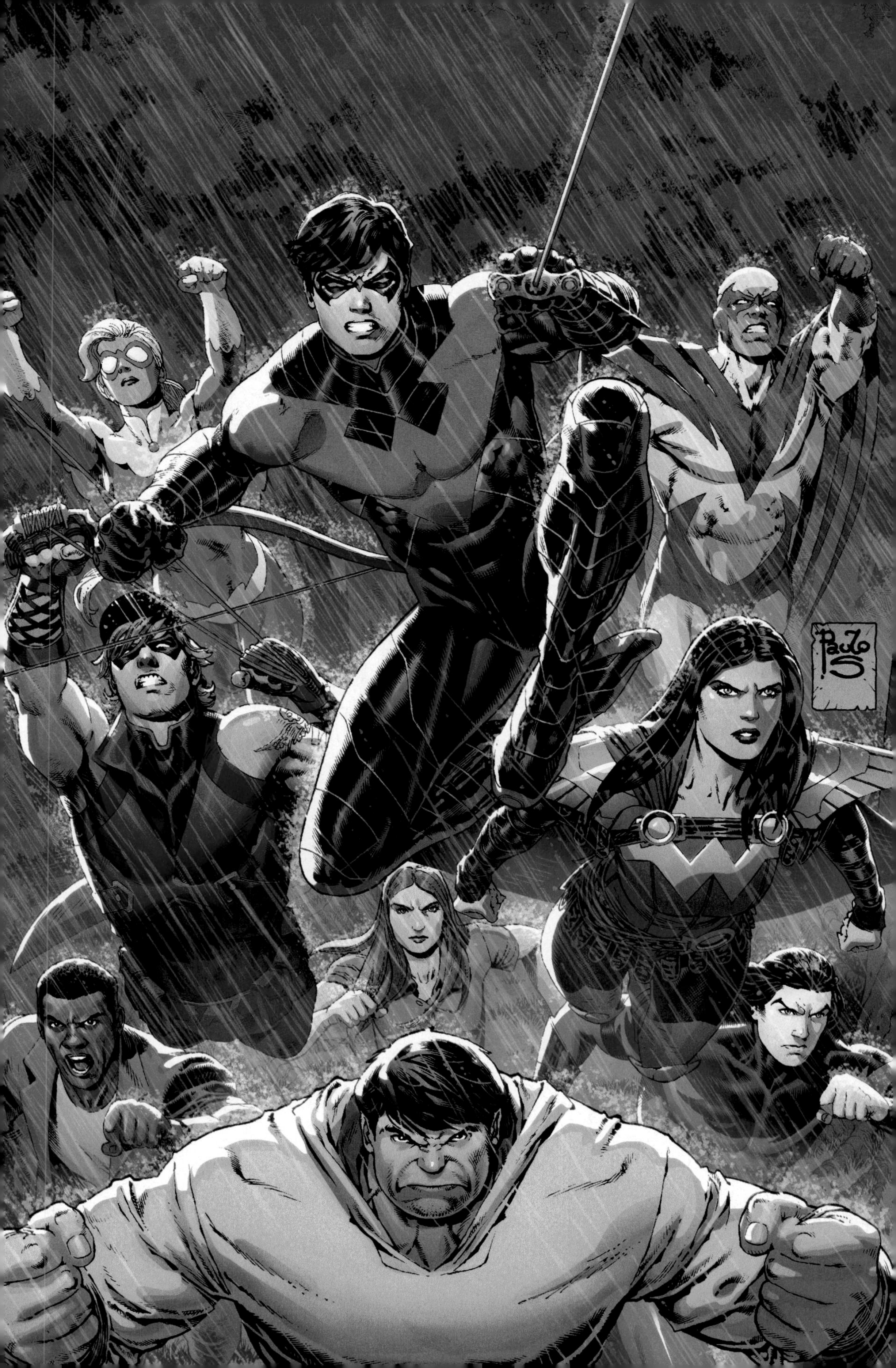

CHAPTER EIGHT: THE OTHER SIDE

DAN ABNETT writer PAUL PELLETIER penciller RAY McCARTHY & WAYNE FAUCHER inkers HI-FI colorist cover art by PAULO SIQUEIRA & HI-FI

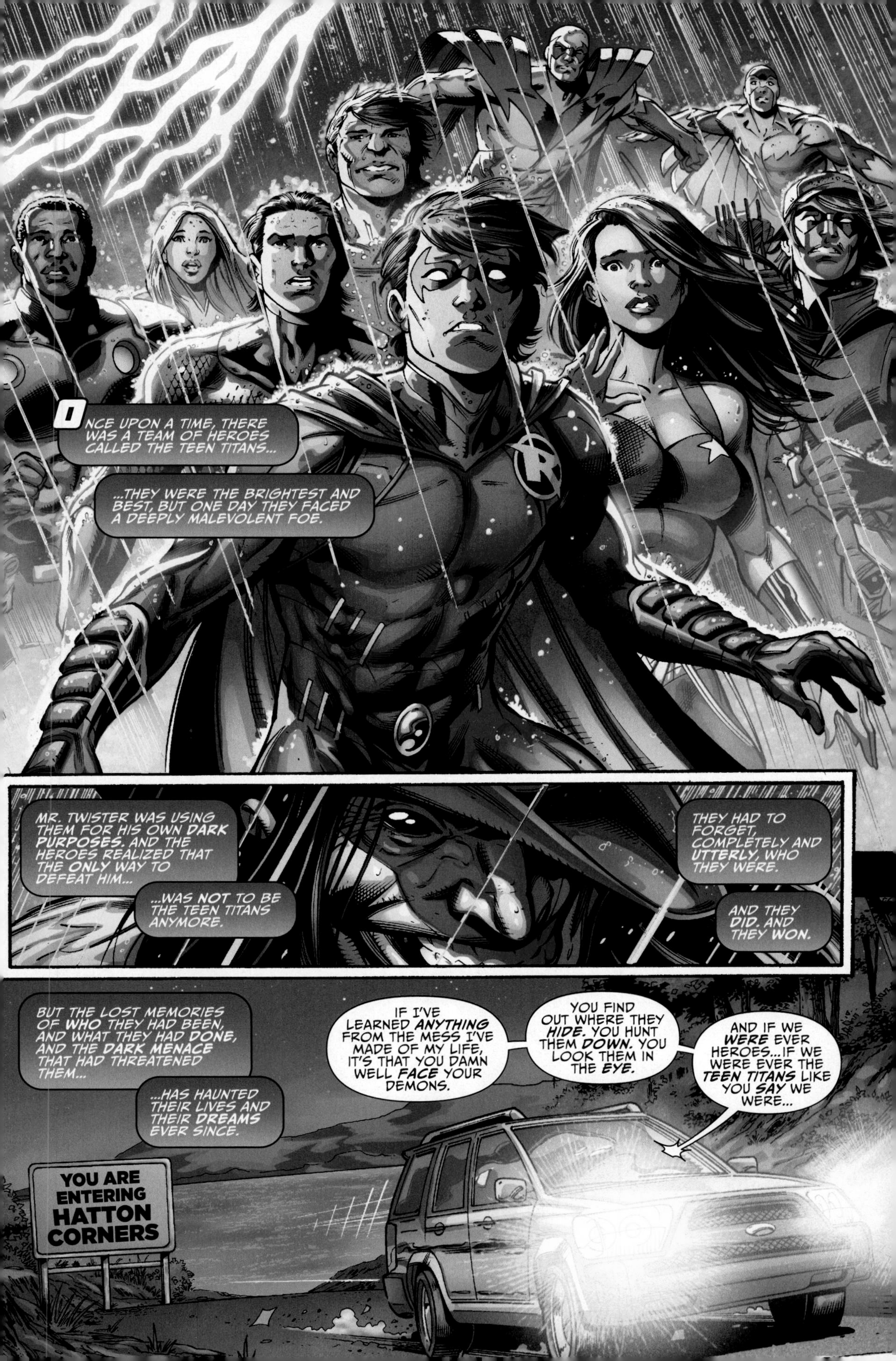
ONCE UPON A TIME, THERE WAS A TEAM OF HEROES CALLED THE TEEN TITANS...
...THEY WERE THE BRIGHTEST AND BEST, BUT ONE DAY THEY FACED A DEEPLY MALEVOLENT FOE.
MR. TWISTER WAS USING THEM FOR HIS OWN DARK PURPOSES. AND THE HEROES REALIZED THAT THE ONLY WAY TO DEFEAT HIM...
...WAS NOT TO BE THE TEEN TITANS ANYMORE.
THEY HAD TO FORGET, COMPLETELY AND UTTERLY, WHO THEY WERE.
AND THEY DID. AND THEY WON.
BUT THE LOST MEMORIES OF WHO THEY HAD BEEN, AND WHAT THEY HAD DONE, AND THE DARK MENACE THAT HAD THREATENED THEM...
...HAS HAUNTED THEIR LIVES AND THEIR DREAMS EVER SINCE.
IF I'VE LEARNED ANYTHING FROM THE MESS I'VE MADE OF MY LIFE, IT'S THAT YOU DAMN WELL FACE YOUR DEMONS.
YOU FIND OUT WHERE THEY HIDE. YOU HUNT THEM DOWN. YOU LOOK THEM IN THE EYE.
AND IF WE WERE EVER HEROES...IF WE WERE EVER THE TEEN TITANS LIKE YOU SAY WE WERE...
YOU ARE ENTERING HATTON CORNERS

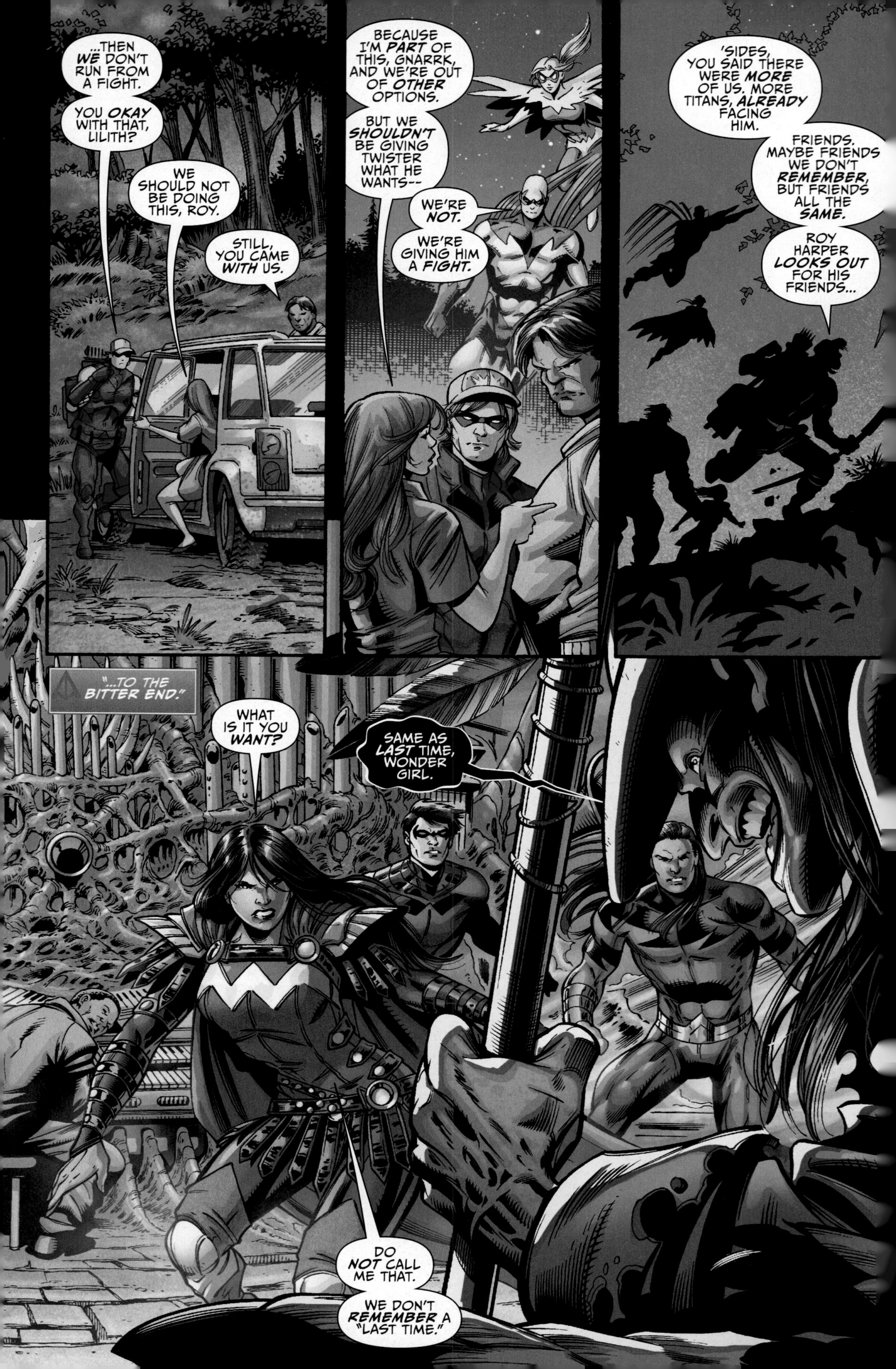
...THEN WE DON'T RUN FROM A FIGHT.
YOU OKAY WITH THAT, LILITH?
WE SHOULD NOT BE DOING THIS, ROY.
STILL, YOU CAME WITH US.
BECAUSE I'M PART OF THIS, GNARRK, AND WE'RE OUT OF OTHER OPTIONS.
BUT WE SHOULDN'T BE GIVING TWISTER WHAT HE WANTS--
WE'RE NOT.
WE'RE GIVING HIM A FIGHT.
'SIDES, YOU SAID THERE WERE MORE OF US. MORE TITANS, ALREADY FACING HIM.
FRIENDS. MAYBE FRIENDS WE DON'T REMEMBER, BUT FRIENDS ALL THE SAME.
ROY HARPER LOOKS OUT FOR HIS FRIENDS...
"...TO THE BITTER END."
WHAT IS IT YOU WANT?
SAME AS LAST TIME, WONDER GIRL.
DO NOT CALL ME THAT.
WE DON'T REMEMBER A "LAST TIME."

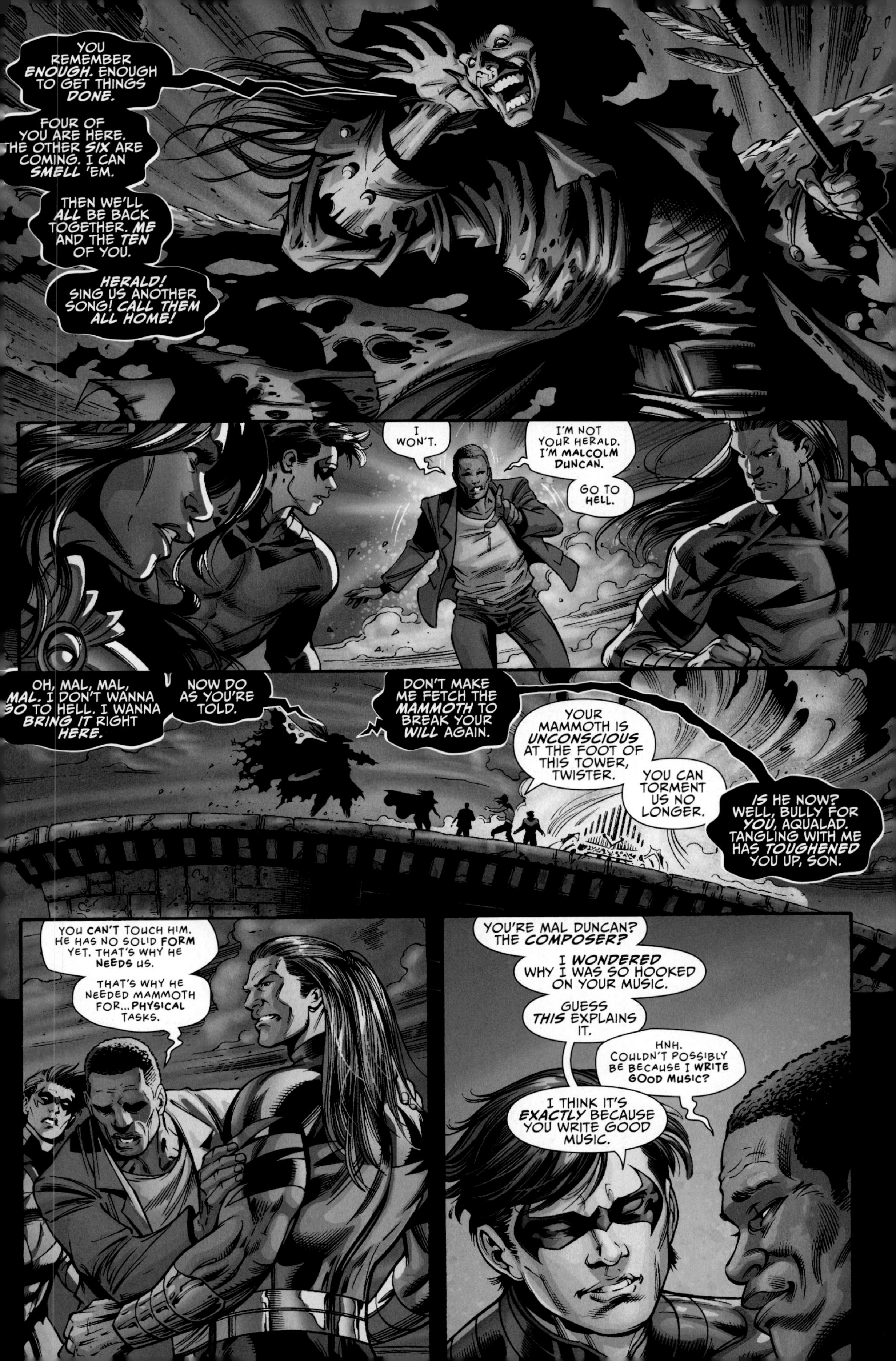
YOU REMEMBER ENOUGH. ENOUGH TO GET THINGS DONE.
FOUR OF YOU ARE HERE. THE OTHER SIX ARE COMING. I CAN SMELL 'EM.
THEN WE'LL ALL BE BACK TOGETHER. ME AND THE TEN OF YOU.
HERALD! SING US ANOTHER SONG! CALL THEM ALL HOME!
I WON'T.
I'M NOT YOUR HERALD. I'M MALCOLM DUNCAN.
GO TO HELL.
OH, MAL, MAL, MAL. I DON'T WANNA GO TO HELL. I WANNA BRING IT RIGHT HERE.
NOW DO AS YOU'RE TOLD.
DON'T MAKE ME FETCH THE MAMMOTH TO BREAK YOUR WILL AGAIN.
YOUR MAMMOTH IS UNCONSCIOUS AT THE FOOT OF THIS TOWER, TWISTER.
YOU CAN TORMENT US NO LONGER.
IS HE NOW? WELL, BULLY FOR YOU, AQUALAD. TANGLING WITH ME HAS TOUGHENED YOU UP, SON.
YOU CAN'T TOUCH HIM. HE HAS NO SOLID FORM YET. THAT'S WHY HE NEEDS US.
THAT'S WHY HE NEEDED MAMMOTH FOR...PHYSICAL TASKS.
YOU'RE MAL DUNCAN? THE COMPOSER?
I WONDERED WHY I WAS SO HOOKED ON YOUR MUSIC.
GUESS THIS EXPLAINS IT.
HNH. COULDN'T POSSIBLY BE BECAUSE I WRITE GOOD MUSIC?
I THINK IT'S EXACTLY BECAUSE YOU WRITE GOOD MUSIC.

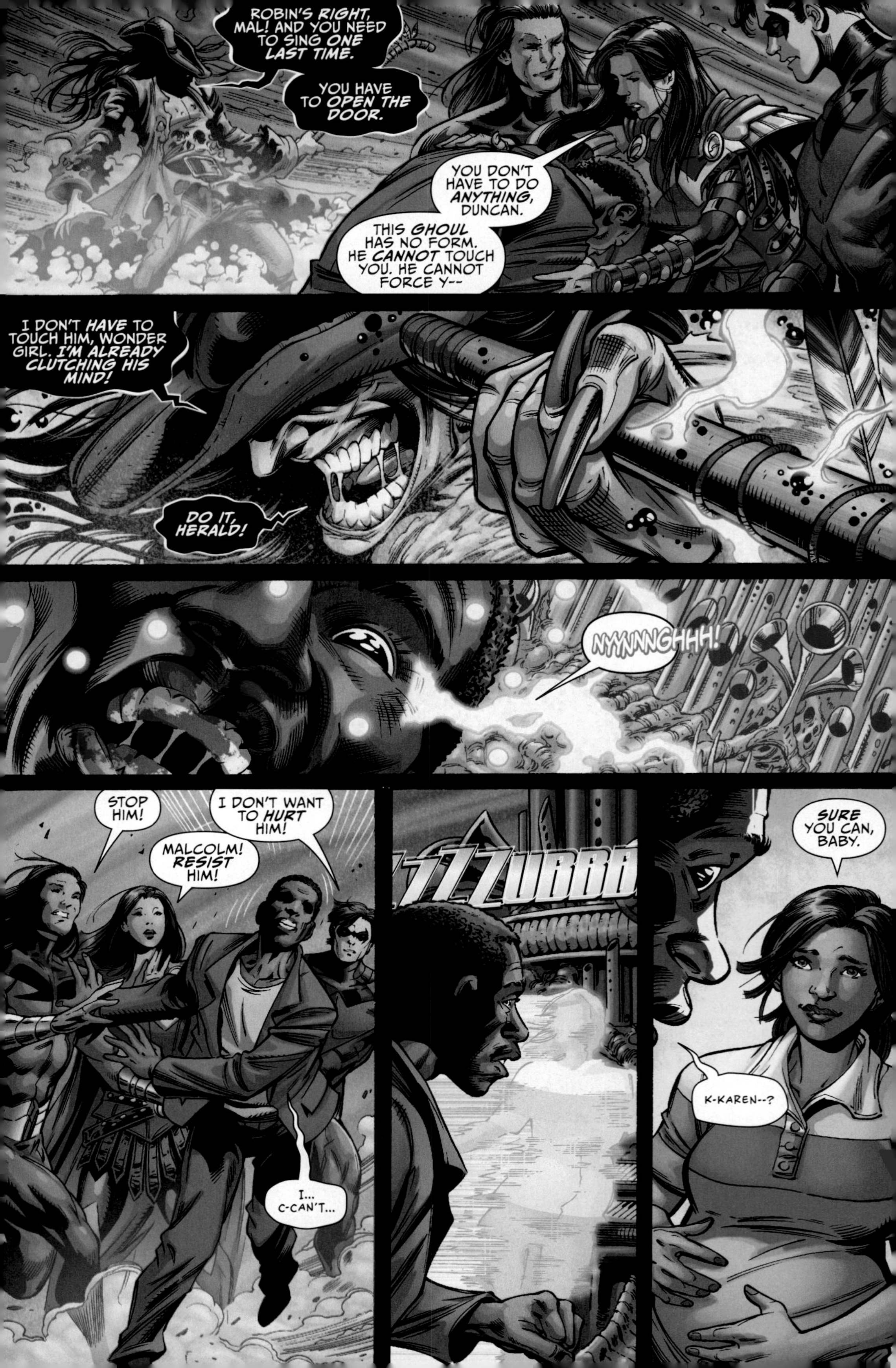
ROBIN'S RIGHT, MAL! AND YOU NEED TO SING ONE LAST TIME.
YOU HAVE TO OPEN THE DOOR.
YOU DON'T HAVE TO DO ANYTHING, DUNCAN.
THIS GHOUL HAS NO FORM. HE CANNOT TOUCH YOU. HE CANNOT FORCE Y--
I DON'T HAVE TO TOUCH HIM, WONDER GIRL. I'M ALREADY CLUTCHING HIS MIND!
DO IT, HERALD!
NYYNNNGHHH!
STOP HIM!
MALCOLM! RESIST HIM!
I DON'T WANT TO HURT HIM!
I... C-CAN'T...
ZZZZUBBB
SURE YOU CAN, BABY.
K-KAREN--?

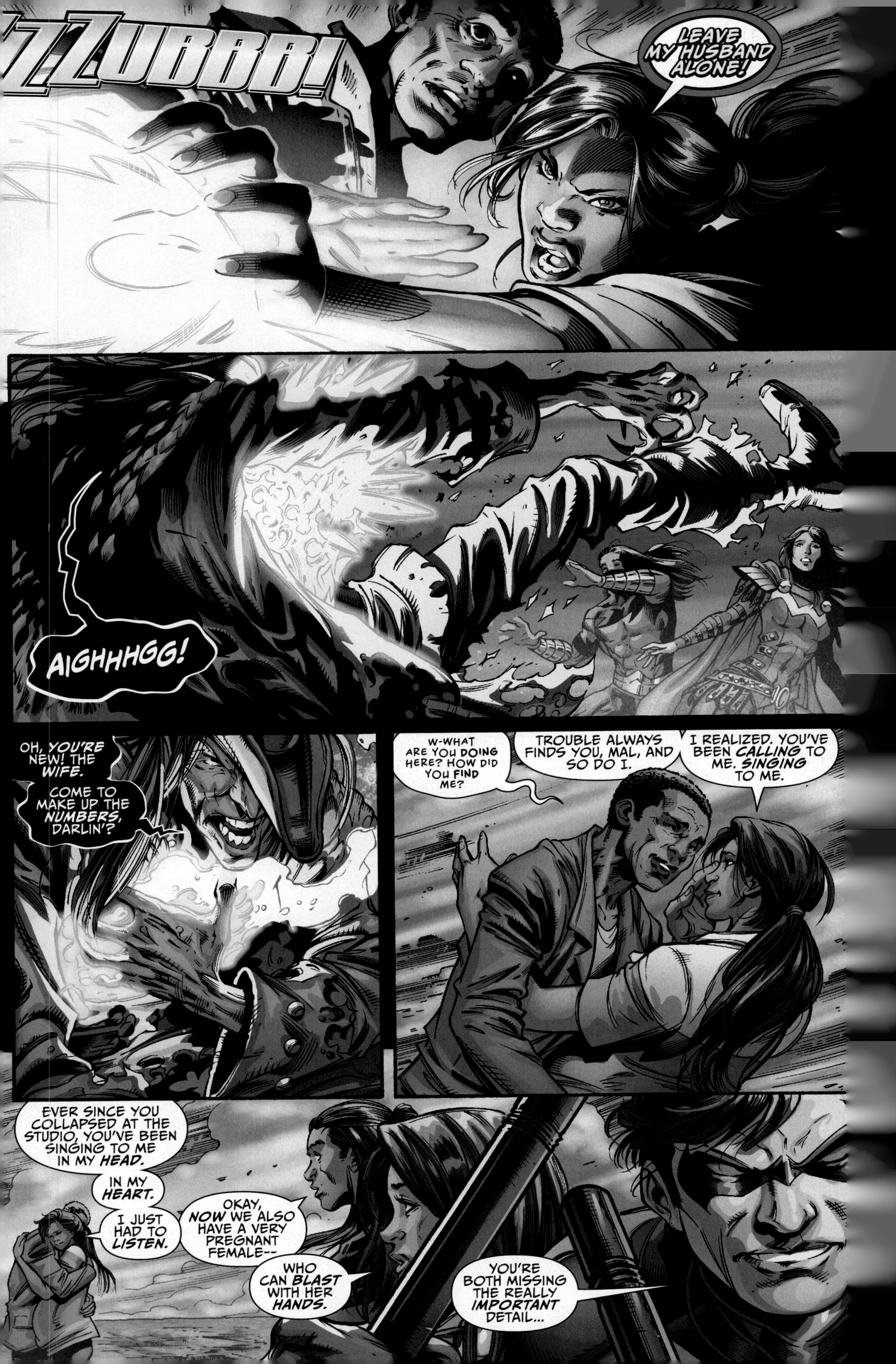
ZZUBBB!
LEAVE MY HUSBAND ALONE!
AIGHHHGG!
OH, YOU'RE NEW! THE WIFE.
COME TO MAKE UP THE NUMBERS, DARLIN'?
W-WHAT ARE YOU DOING HERE? HOW DID YOU FIND ME?
TROUBLE ALWAYS FINDS YOU, MAL, AND SO DO I.
I REALIZED. YOU'VE BEEN CALLING TO ME. SINGING TO ME.
EVER SINCE YOU COLLAPSED AT THE STUDIO, YOU'VE BEEN SINGING TO ME IN MY HEAD.
IN MY HEART.
I JUST HAD TO LISTEN.
OKAY, NOW WE ALSO HAVE A VERY PREGNANT FEMALE--
WHO CAN BLAST WITH HER HANDS.
YOU'RE BOTH MISSING THE REALLY IMPORTANT DETAIL...

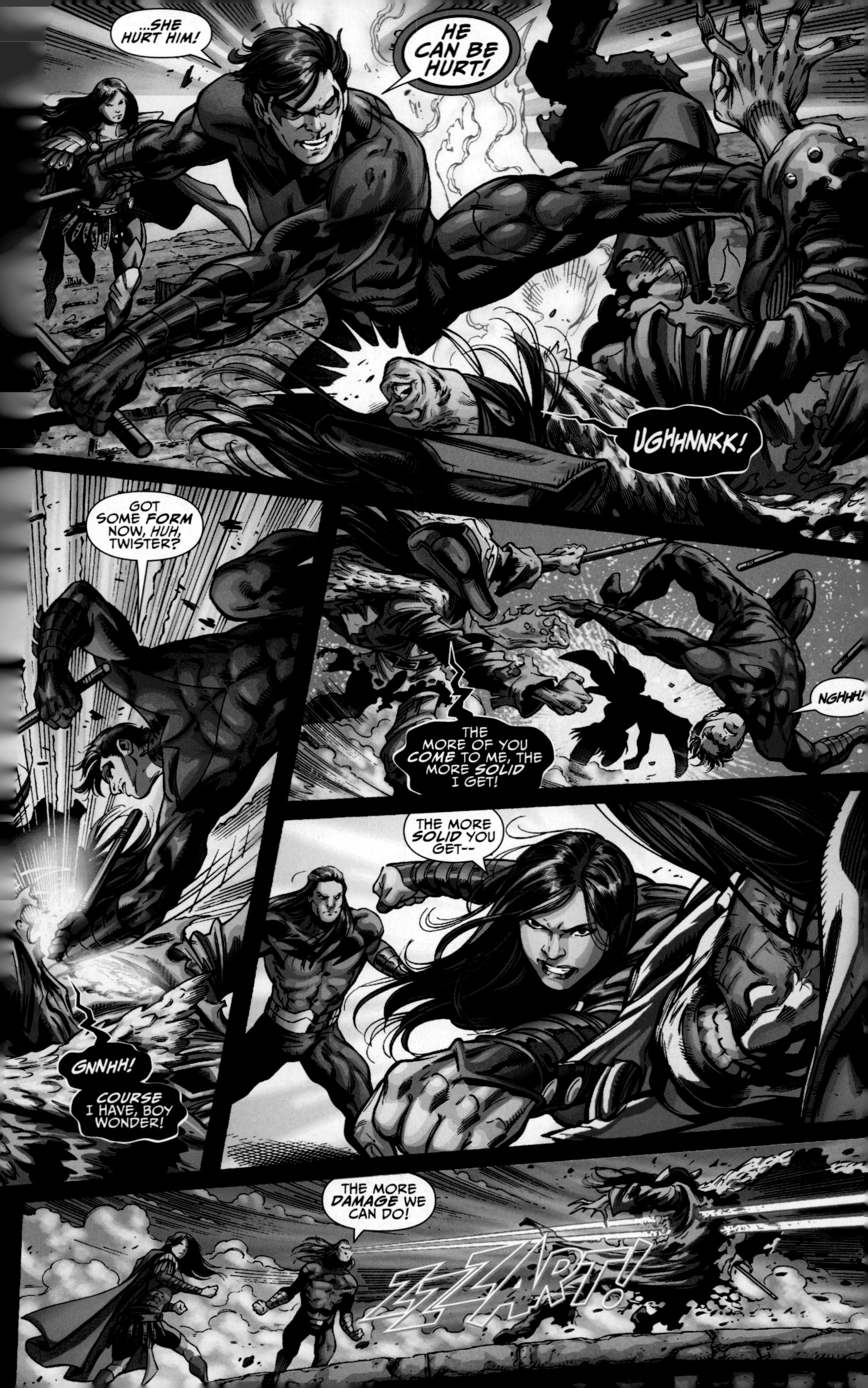
...SHE HURT HIM!
HE CAN BE HURT!
UGHHNNKK!
GOT SOME FORM NOW, HUH, TWISTER?
GNNHH!
COURSE I HAVE, BOY WONDER!
THE MORE OF YOU COME TO ME, THE MORE SOLID I GET!
NGHH!
THE MORE SOLID YOU GET--
THE MORE DAMAGE WE CAN DO!
ZZZART!

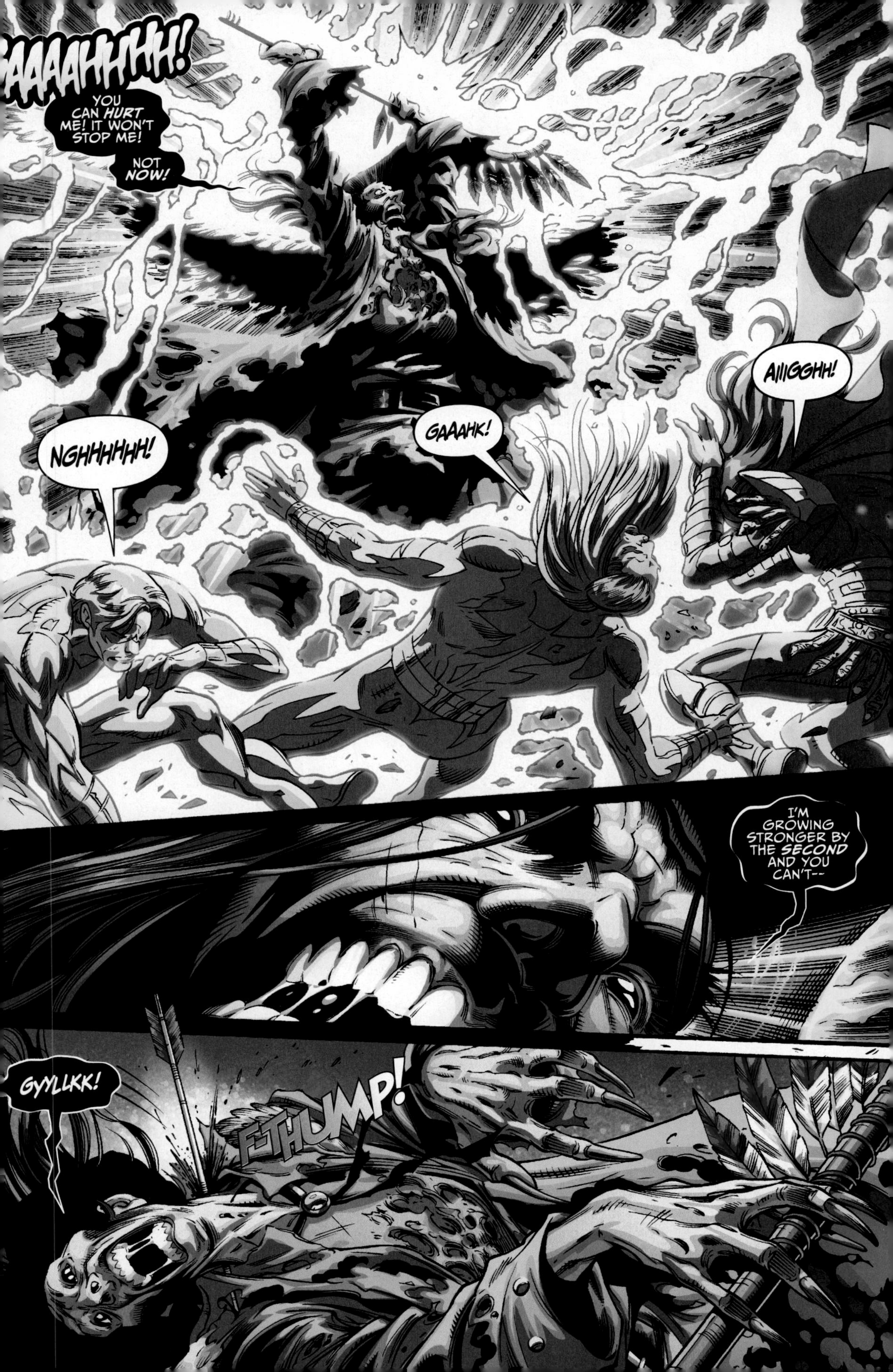
AAAAHHHH!
YOU CAN HURT ME! IT WON'T STOP ME!
NOT NOW!
AIIIGGHH!
GAAAHK!
NGHHHHHH!
I'M GROWING STRONGER BY THE SECOND AND YOU CAN'T--
GYYLLKK!
F-THUMP!

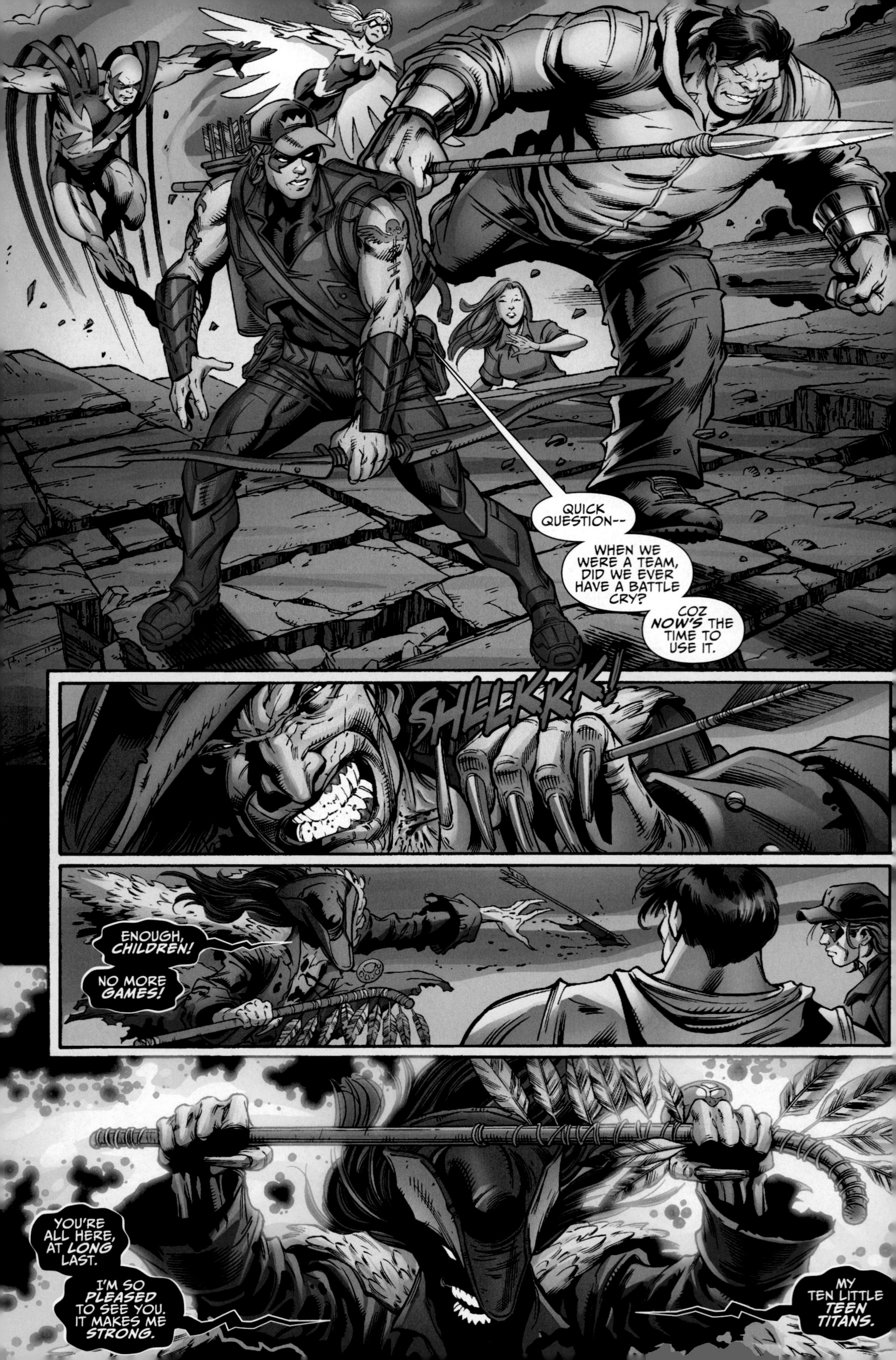

QUICK QUESTION--
WHEN WE WERE A TEAM, DID WE EVER HAVE A BATTLE CRY?
COZ NOW'S THE TIME TO USE IT.
SHLLKKK!
ENOUGH, CHILDREN!
NO MORE GAMES!
YOU'RE ALL HERE, AT LONG LAST.
I'M SO PLEASED TO SEE YOU. IT MAKES ME STRONG.
MY TEN LITTLE TEEN TITANS.

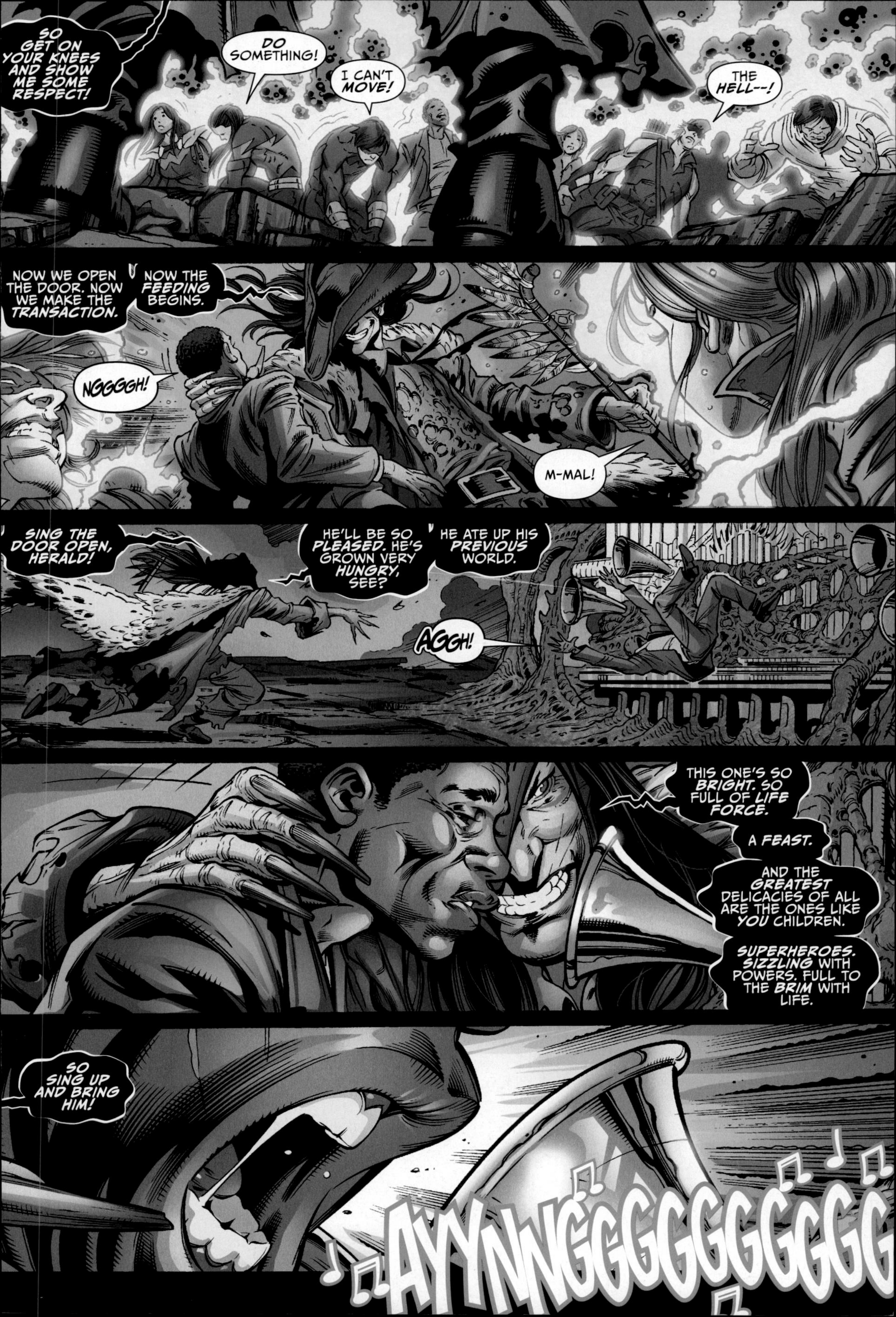
SO GET ON YOUR KNEES AND SHOW ME SOME RESPECT!
DO SOMETHING!
I CAN'T MOVE!
THE HELL--!
NOW WE OPEN THE DOOR. NOW WE MAKE THE TRANSACTION.
NOW THE FEEDING BEGINS.
NGGGGH!
M-MAL!
SING THE DOOR OPEN, HERALD!
HE'LL BE SO PLEASED. HE'S GROWN VERY HUNGRY, SEE?
HE ATE UP HIS PREVIOUS WORLD.
AGGH!
THIS ONE'S SO BRIGHT. SO FULL OF LIFE FORCE.
A FEAST.
AND THE GREATEST DELICACIES OF ALL ARE THE ONES LIKE YOU CHILDREN.
SUPERHEROES. SIZZLING WITH POWERS. FULL TO THE BRIM WITH LIFE.
SO SING UP AND BRING HIM!
AYYNNGGGGGGGGGG

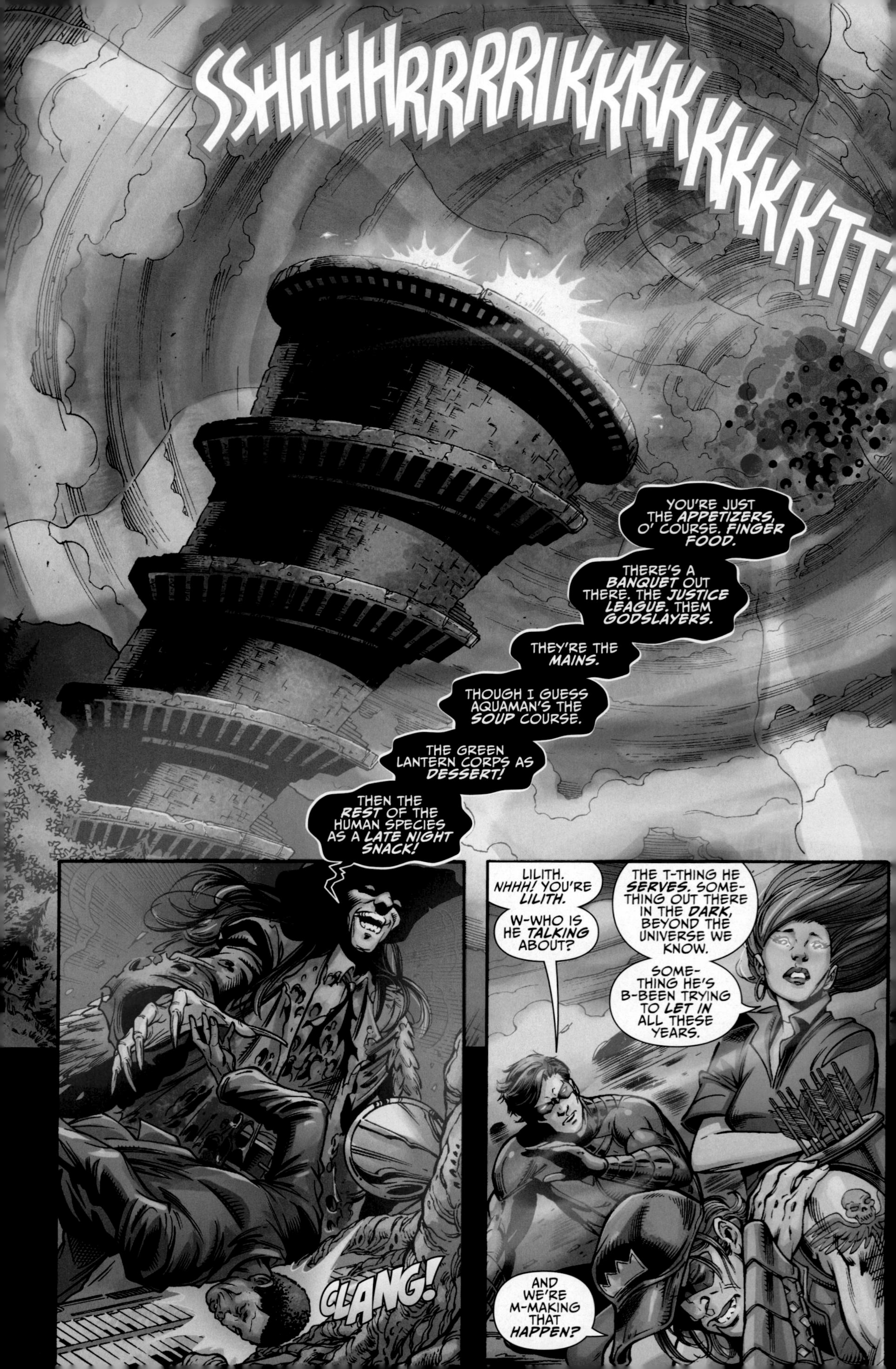
SSHHHHRRRRRIKKKKKKKKKKTTT!
YOU'RE JUST THE APPETIZERS, O' COURSE. FINGER FOOD.
THERE'S A BANQUET OUT THERE. THE JUSTICE LEAGUE. THEM GODSLAYERS.
THEY'RE THE MAINS.
THOUGH I GUESS AQUAMAN'S THE SOUP COURSE.
THE GREEN LANTERN CORPS AS DESSERT!
THEN THE REST OF THE HUMAN SPECIES AS A LATE NIGHT SNACK!
CLANG!
LILITH. NHHH! YOU'RE LILITH.
W-WHO IS HE TALKING ABOUT?
THE T-THING HE SERVES. SOMETHING OUT THERE IN THE DARK, BEYOND THE UNIVERSE WE KNOW.
SOMETHING HE'S B-BEEN TRYING TO LET IN ALL THESE YEARS.
AND WE'RE M-MAKING THAT HAPPEN?

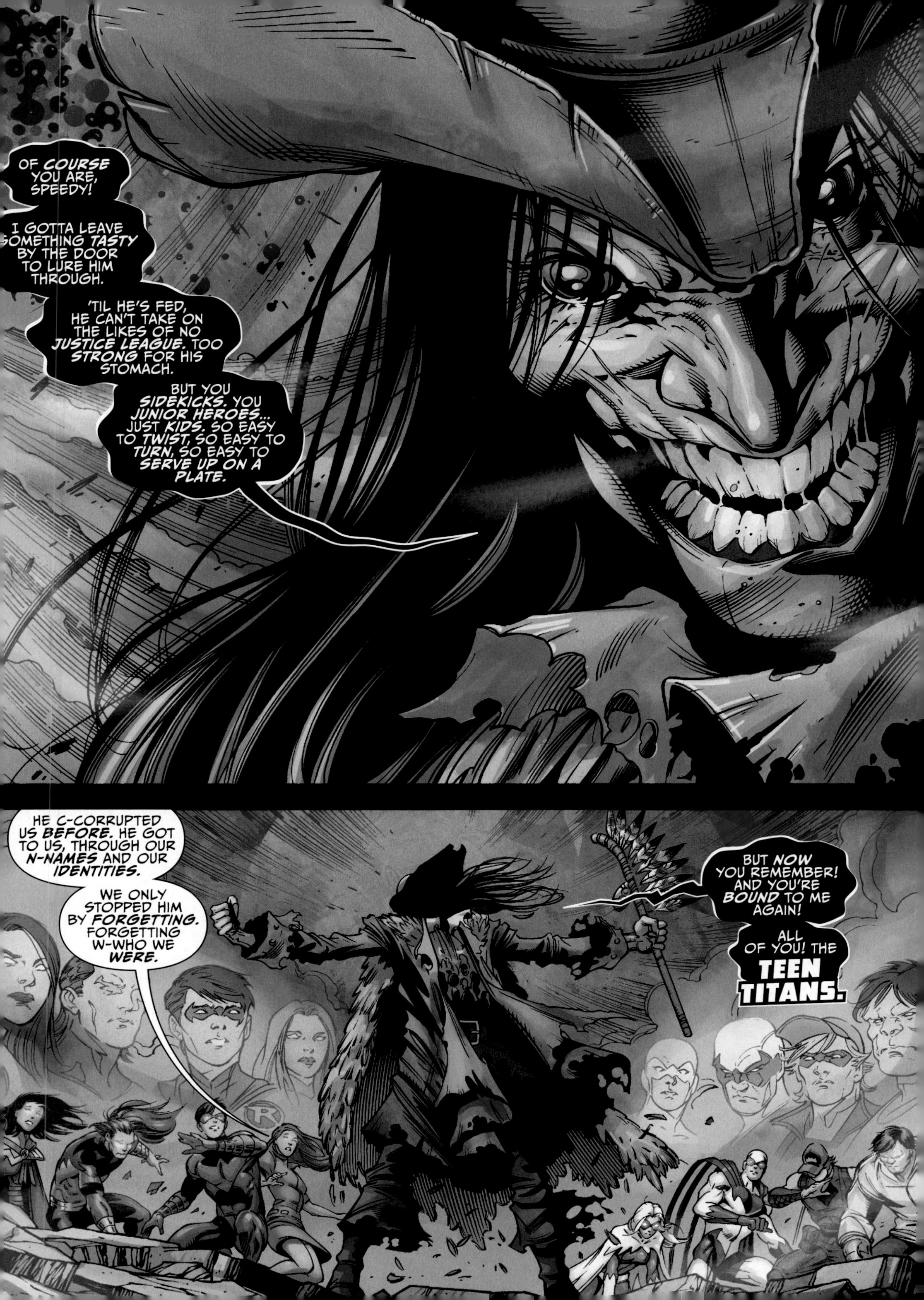
OF COURSE YOU ARE, SPEEDY!
I GOTTA LEAVE SOMETHING TASTY BY THE DOOR TO LURE HIM THROUGH.
'TIL HE'S FED, HE CAN'T TAKE ON THE LIKES OF NO JUSTICE LEAGUE. TOO STRONG FOR HIS STOMACH.
BUT YOU SIDEKICKS. YOU JUNIOR HEROES... JUST KIDS. SO EASY TO TWIST, SO EASY TO TURN, SO EASY TO SERVE UP ON A PLATE.
HE C-CORRUPTED US BEFORE. HE GOT TO US, THROUGH OUR N-NAMES AND OUR IDENTITIES.
WE ONLY STOPPED HIM BY FORGETTING. FORGETTING W-WHO WE WERE.
BUT NOW YOU REMEMBER! AND YOU'RE BOUND TO ME AGAIN!
ALL OF YOU! THE TEEN TITANS.

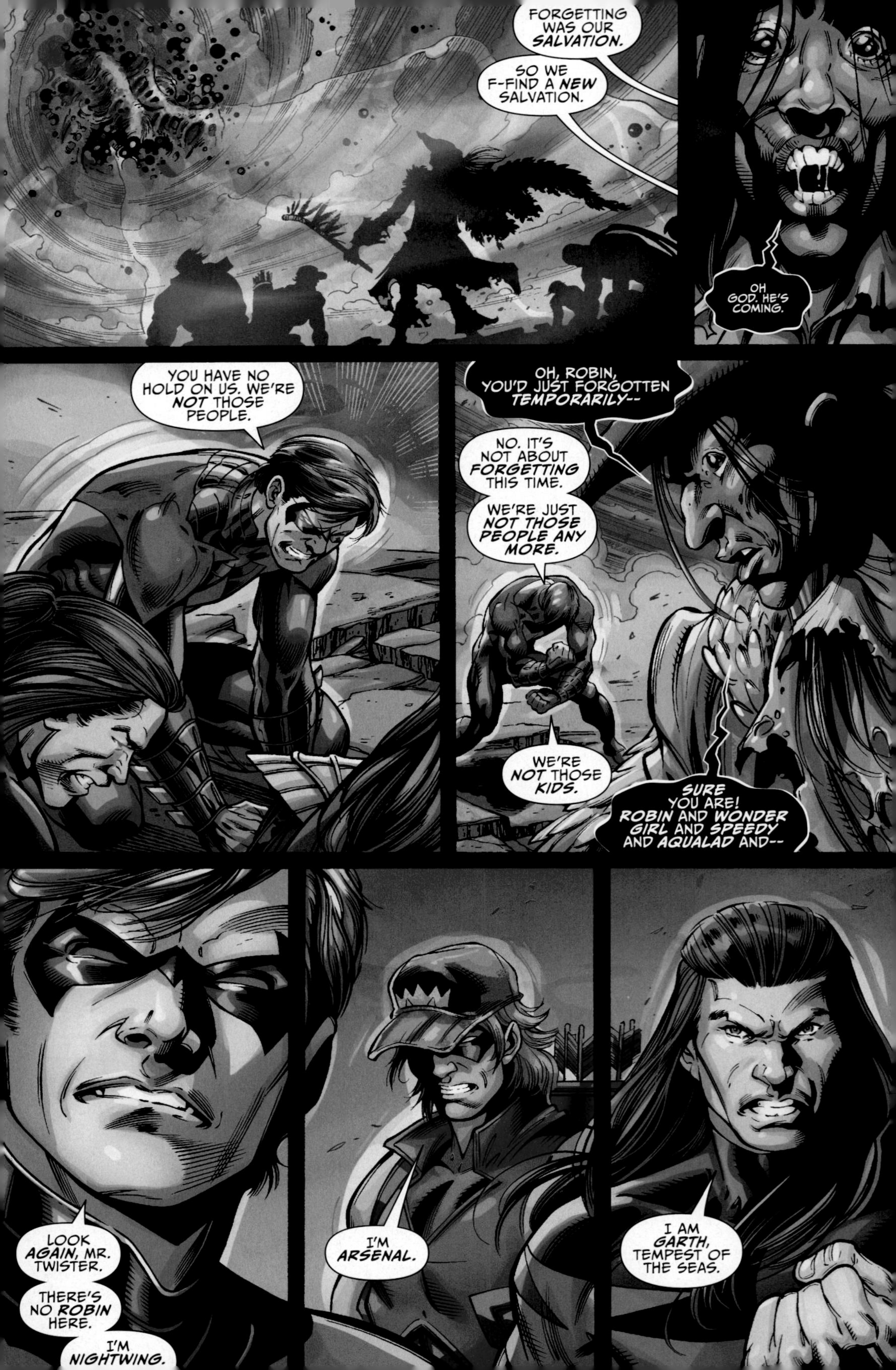
FORGETTING WAS OUR SALVATION.
SO WE F-FIND A NEW SALVATION.
OH GOD. HE'S COMING.
YOU HAVE NO HOLD ON US. WE'RE NOT THOSE PEOPLE.
OH, ROBIN, YOU'D JUST FORGOTTEN TEMPORARILY--
NO. IT'S NOT ABOUT FORGETTING THIS TIME.
WE'RE JUST NOT THOSE PEOPLE ANY MORE.
WE'RE NOT THOSE KIDS.
SURE YOU ARE! ROBIN AND WONDER GIRL AND SPEEDY AND AQUALAD AND--
LOOK AGAIN, MR. TWISTER.
THERE'S NO ROBIN HERE.
I'M NIGHTWING.
I'M ARSENAL.
I AM GARTH, TEMPEST OF THE SEAS.

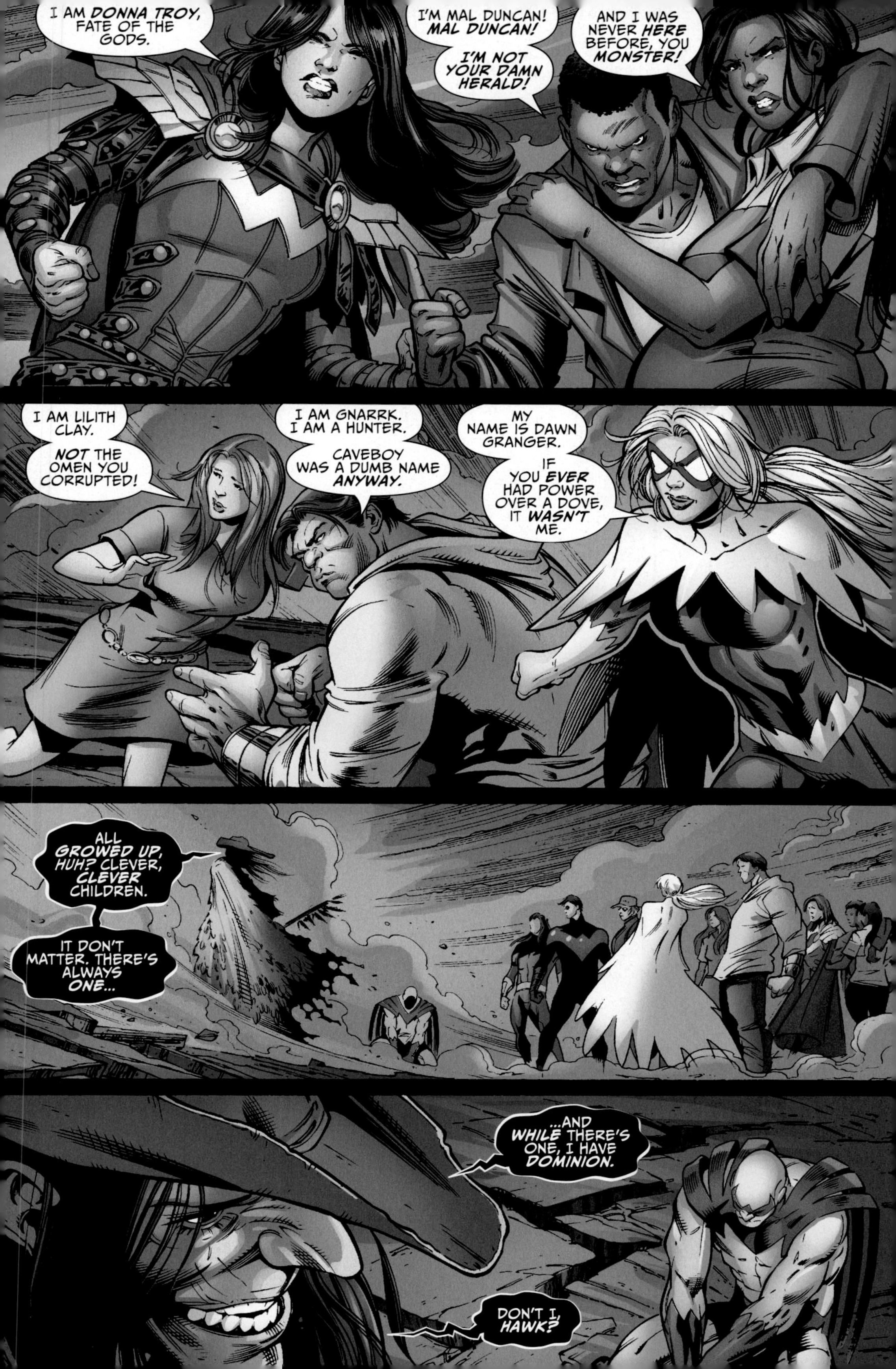
I AM DONNA TROY, FATE OF THE GODS.
I'M MAL DUNCAN! MAL DUNCAN!
I'M NOT YOUR DAMN HERALD!
AND I WAS NEVER HERE BEFORE, YOU MONSTER!
I AM LILITH CLAY.
NOT THE OMEN YOU CORRUPTED!
I AM GNARRK. I AM A HUNTER.
CAVEBOY WAS A DUMB NAME ANYWAY.
MY NAME IS DAWN GRANGER.
IF YOU EVER HAD POWER OVER A DOVE, IT WASN'T ME.
ALL GROWED UP, HUH? CLEVER, CLEVER CHILDREN.
IT DON'T MATTER. THERE'S ALWAYS ONE...
...AND WHILE THERE'S ONE, I HAVE DOMINION.
DON'T I, HAWK?

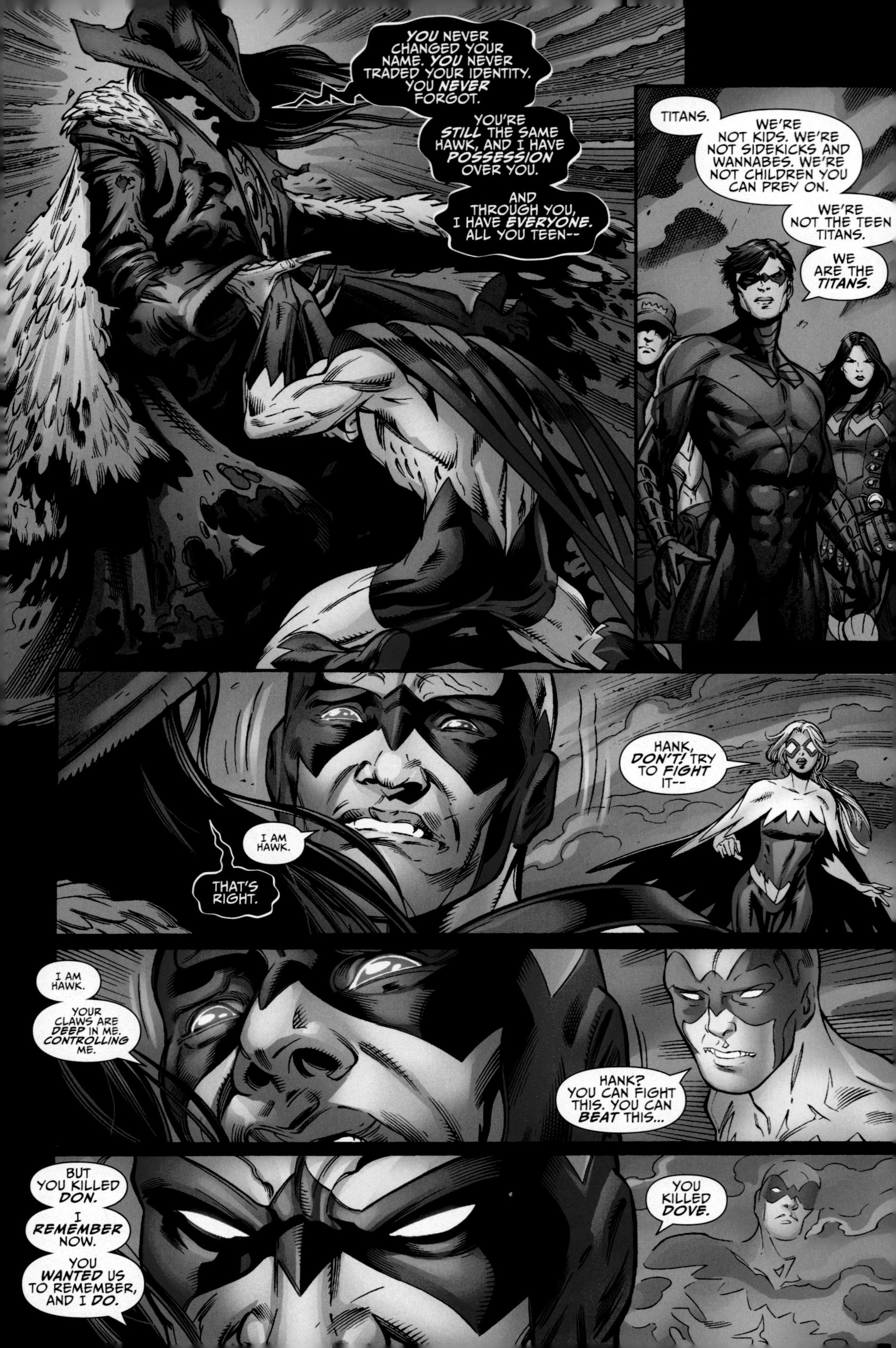
YOU NEVER CHANGED YOUR NAME. YOU NEVER TRADED YOUR IDENTITY. YOU NEVER FORGOT.
YOU'RE STILL THE SAME HAWK, AND I HAVE POSSESSION OVER YOU.
AND THROUGH YOU, I HAVE EVERYONE. ALL YOU TEEN--
TITANS.
WE'RE NOT KIDS. WE'RE NOT SIDEKICKS AND WANNABES. WE'RE NOT CHILDREN YOU CAN PREY ON.
WE'RE NOT THE TEEN TITANS.
WE ARE THE TITANS.
I AM HAWK.
THAT'S RIGHT.
HANK, DON'T! TRY TO FIGHT IT--
I AM HAWK.
YOUR CLAWS ARE DEEP IN ME. CONTROLLING ME.
HANK? YOU CAN FIGHT THIS. YOU CAN BEAT THIS...
BUT YOU KILLED DON.
I REMEMBER NOW.
YOU WANTED US TO REMEMBER, AND I DO.
YOU KILLED DOVE.

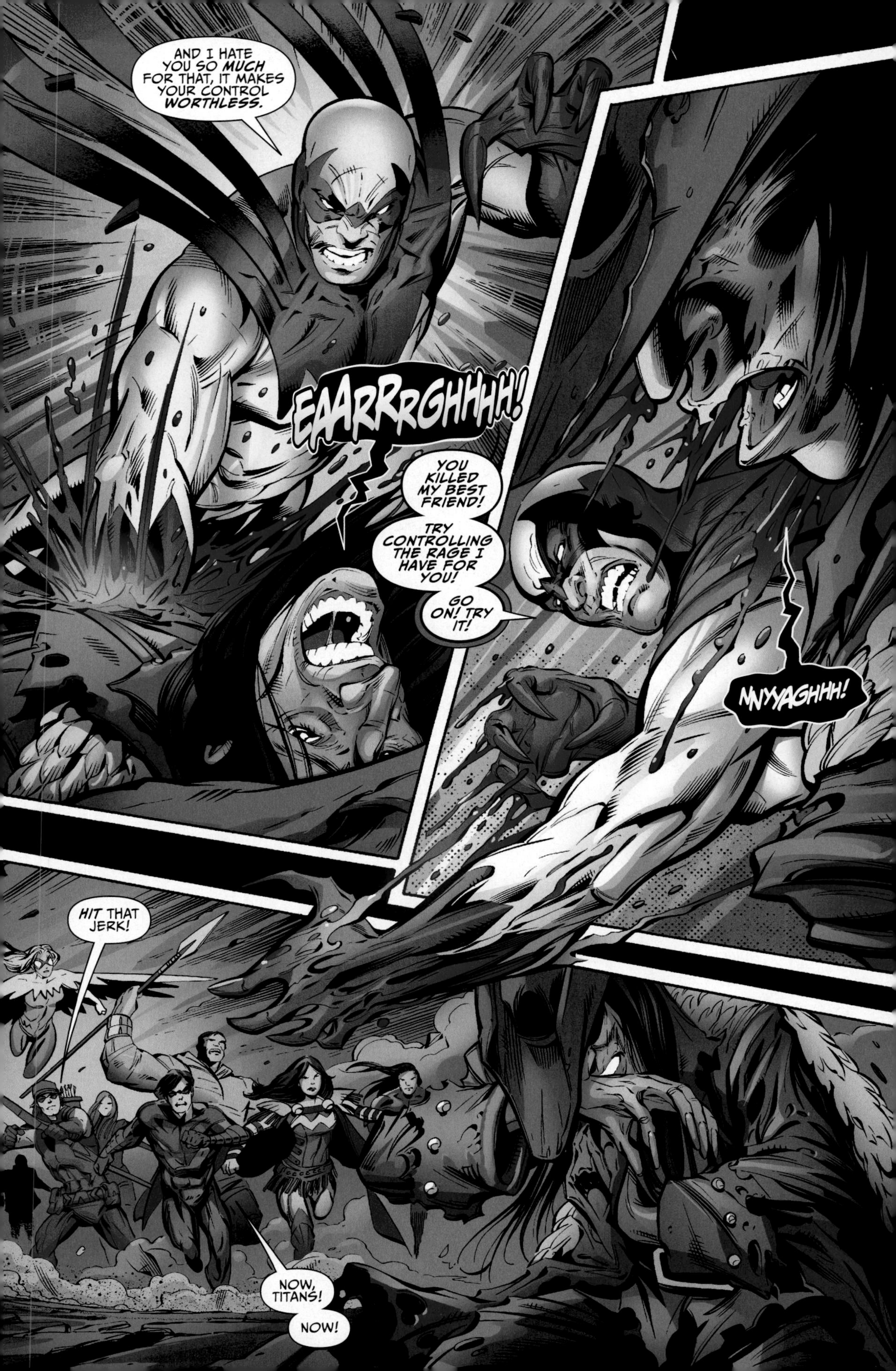
AND I HATE YOU SO MUCH FOR THAT, IT MAKES YOUR CONTROL WORTHLESS.
EAARRRGHHHH!
YOU KILLED MY BEST FRIEND!
TRY CONTROLLING THE RAGE I HAVE FOR YOU!
GO ON! TRY IT!
NNYYAGHHH!
HIT THAT JERK!
NOW, TITANS!
NOW!

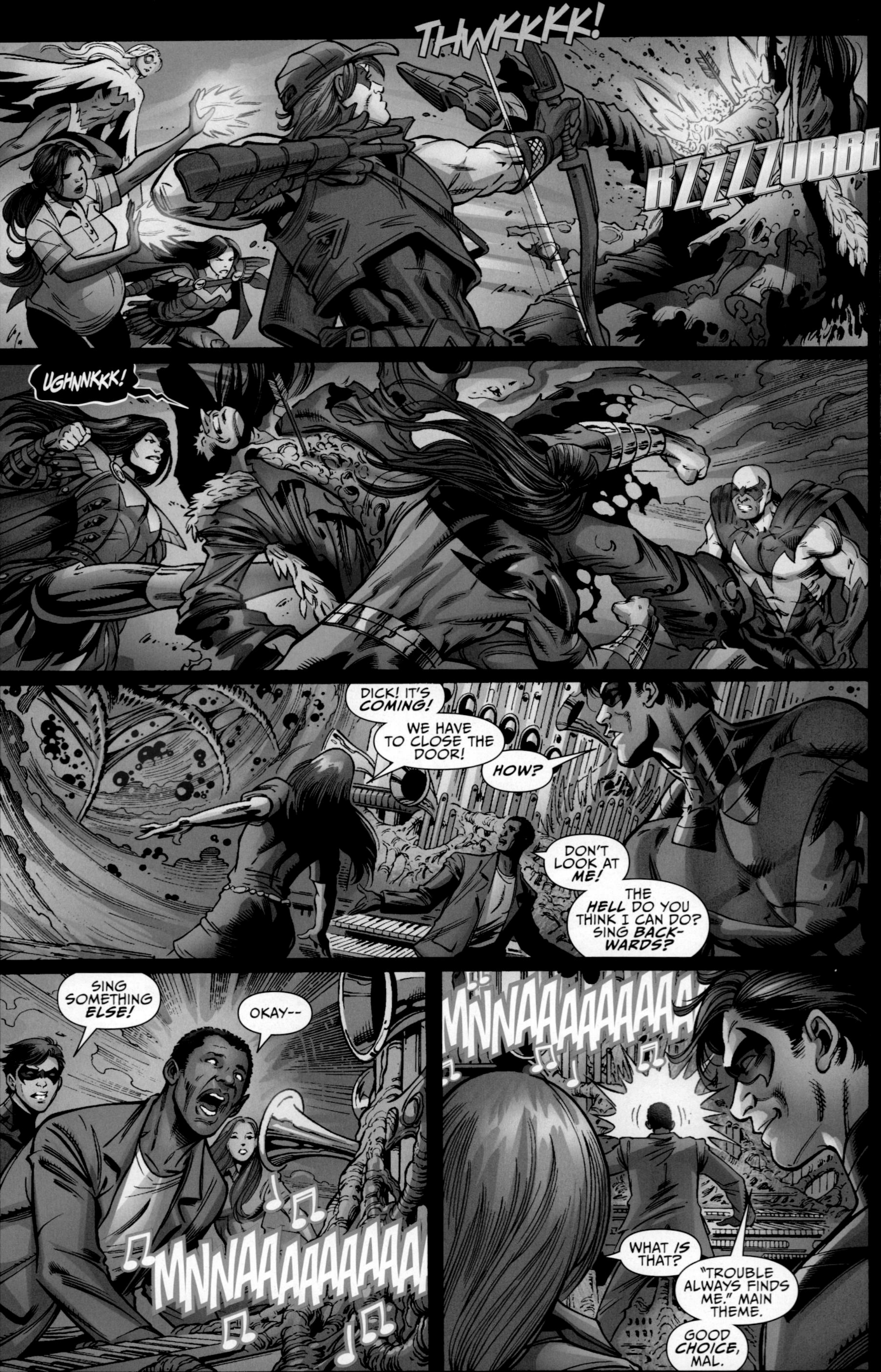
THWKKKK!
KZZZZUBBB
UGHNNKKK!
DICK! IT'S COMING!
WE HAVE TO CLOSE THE DOOR!
HOW?
DON'T LOOK AT ME!
THE HELL DO YOU THINK I CAN DO? SING BACKWARDS?
SING SOMETHING ELSE!
OKAY--
MNNAAAAAAAAA
MNNAAAAAAAAA
WHAT IS THAT?
"TROUBLE ALWAYS FINDS ME." MAIN THEME.
GOOD CHOICE, MAL.

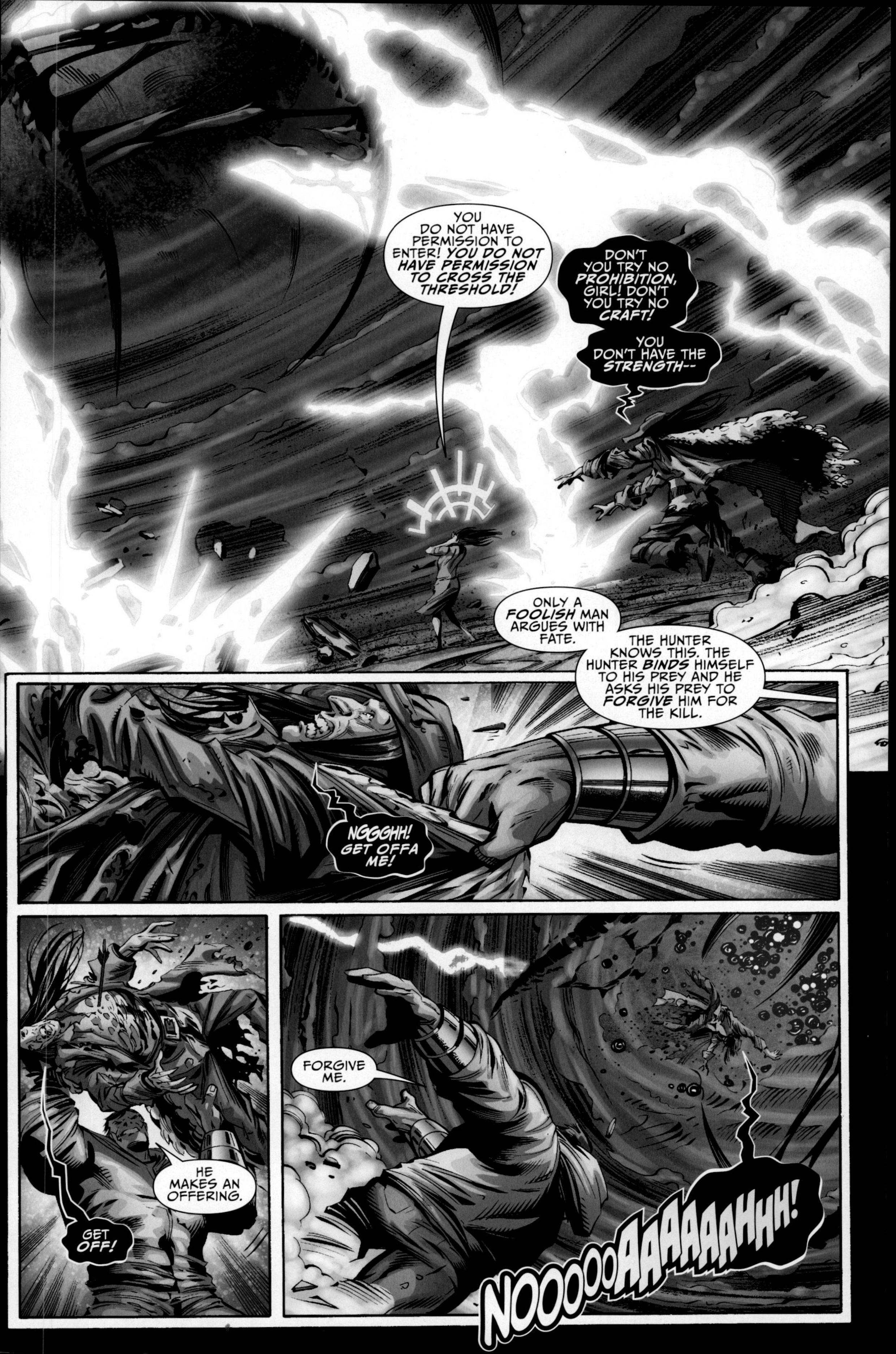

YOU DO NOT HAVE PERMISSION TO ENTER! YOU DO NOT HAVE PERMISSION TO CROSS THE THRESHOLD!
DON'T YOU TRY NO PROHIBITION, GIRL! DON'T YOU TRY NO CRAFT!
YOU DON'T HAVE THE STRENGTH--
ONLY A FOOLISH MAN ARGUES WITH FATE.
THE HUNTER KNOWS THIS. THE HUNTER BINDS HIMSELF TO HIS PREY AND HE ASKS HIS PREY TO FORGIVE HIM FOR THE KILL.
NGGGHH! GET OFFA ME!
HE MAKES AN OFFERING.
GET OFF!
FORGIVE ME.
NOOOOOAAAAAAHHH!

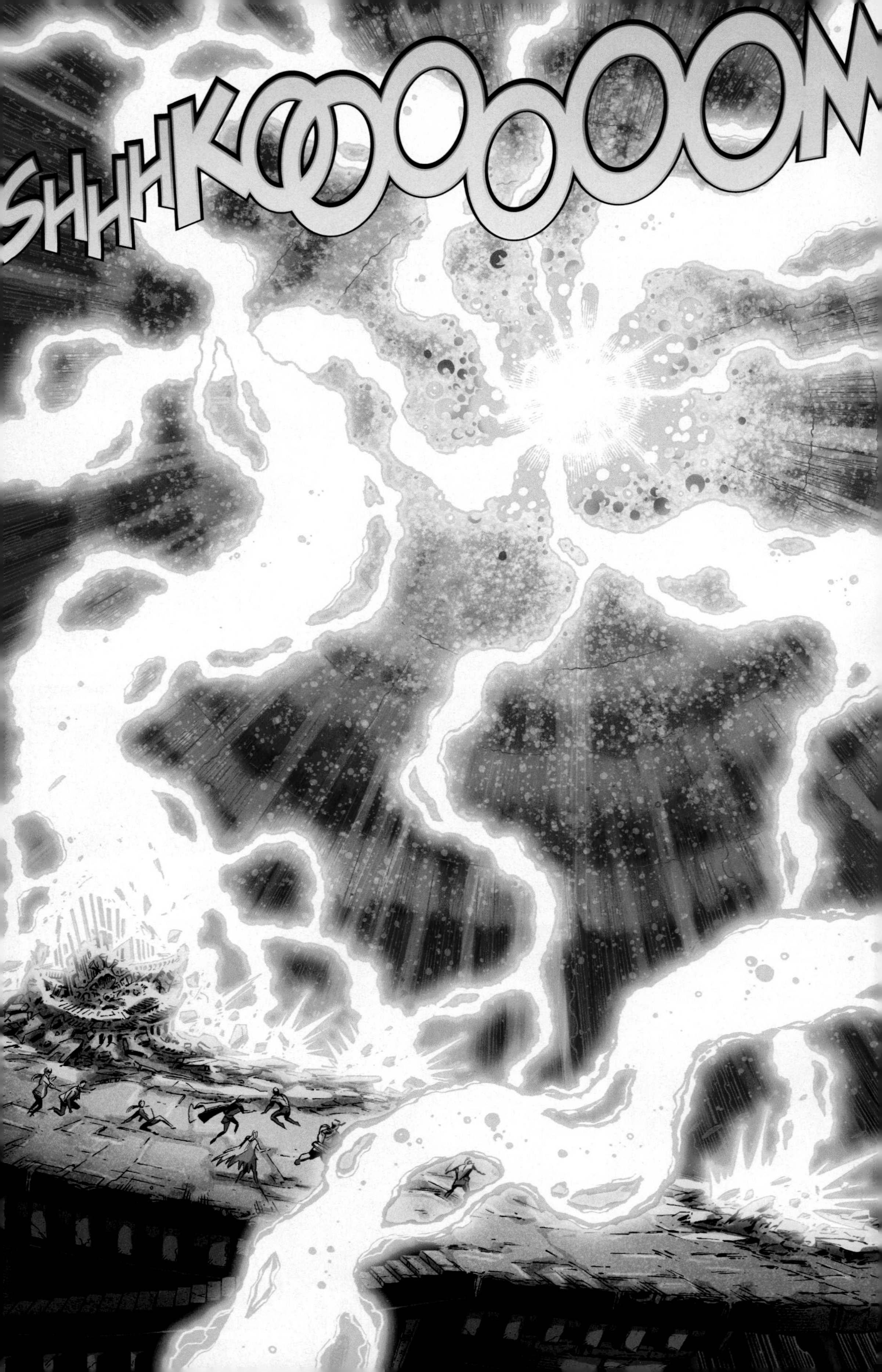
SHHKOOOOOOOM

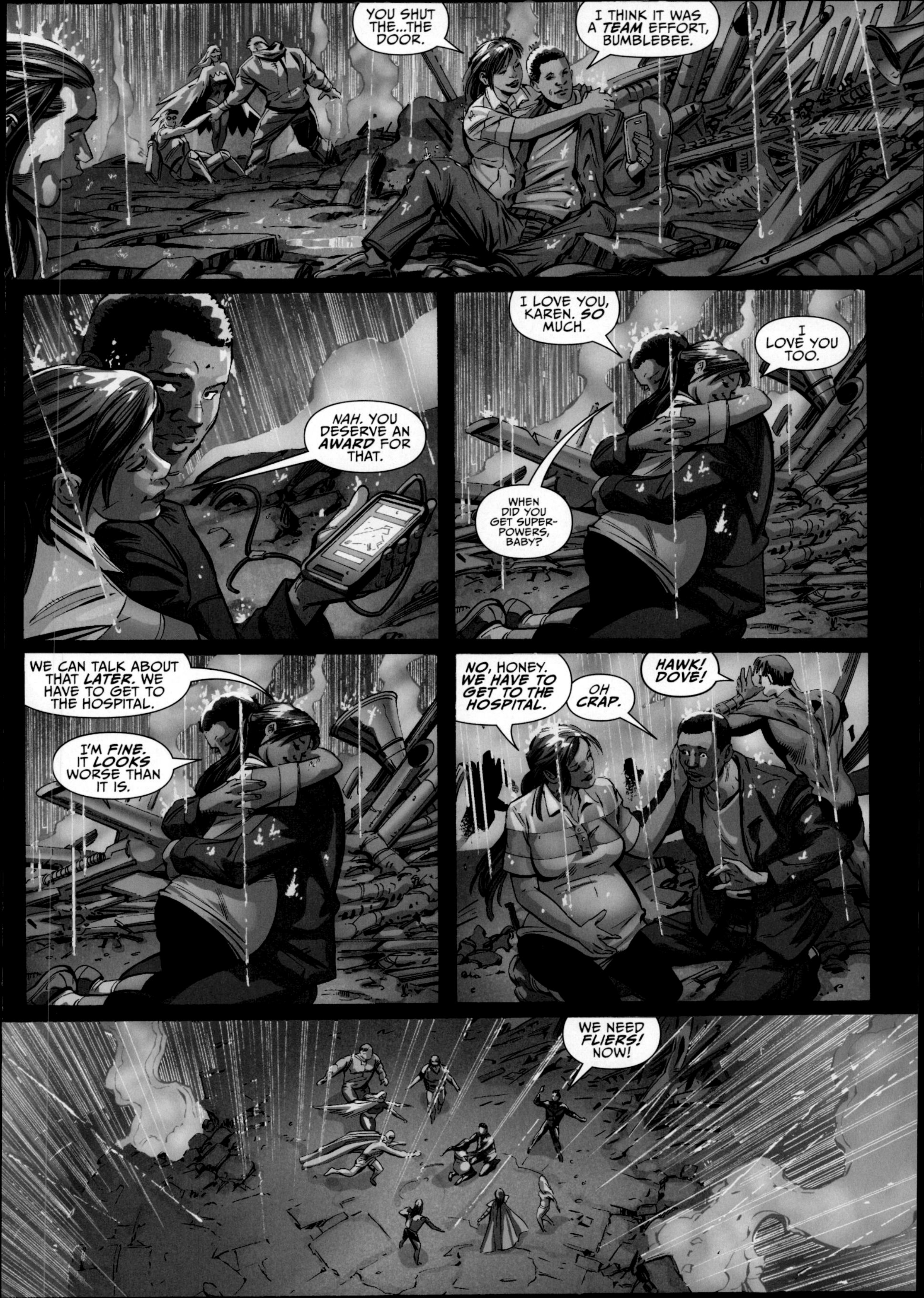
YOU SHUT THE...THE DOOR.
I THINK IT WAS A TEAM EFFORT, BUMBLEBEE.
NAH. YOU DESERVE AN AWARD FOR THAT.
I LOVE YOU, KAREN. SO MUCH.
I LOVE YOU TOO.
WHEN DID YOU GET SUPER-POWERS, BABY?
WE CAN TALK ABOUT THAT LATER. WE HAVE TO GET TO THE HOSPITAL.
I'M FINE. IT LOOKS WORSE THAN IT IS.
NO, HONEY. WE HAVE TO GET TO THE HOSPITAL.
OH CRAP.
HAWK! DOVE!
WE NEED FLIERS! NOW!

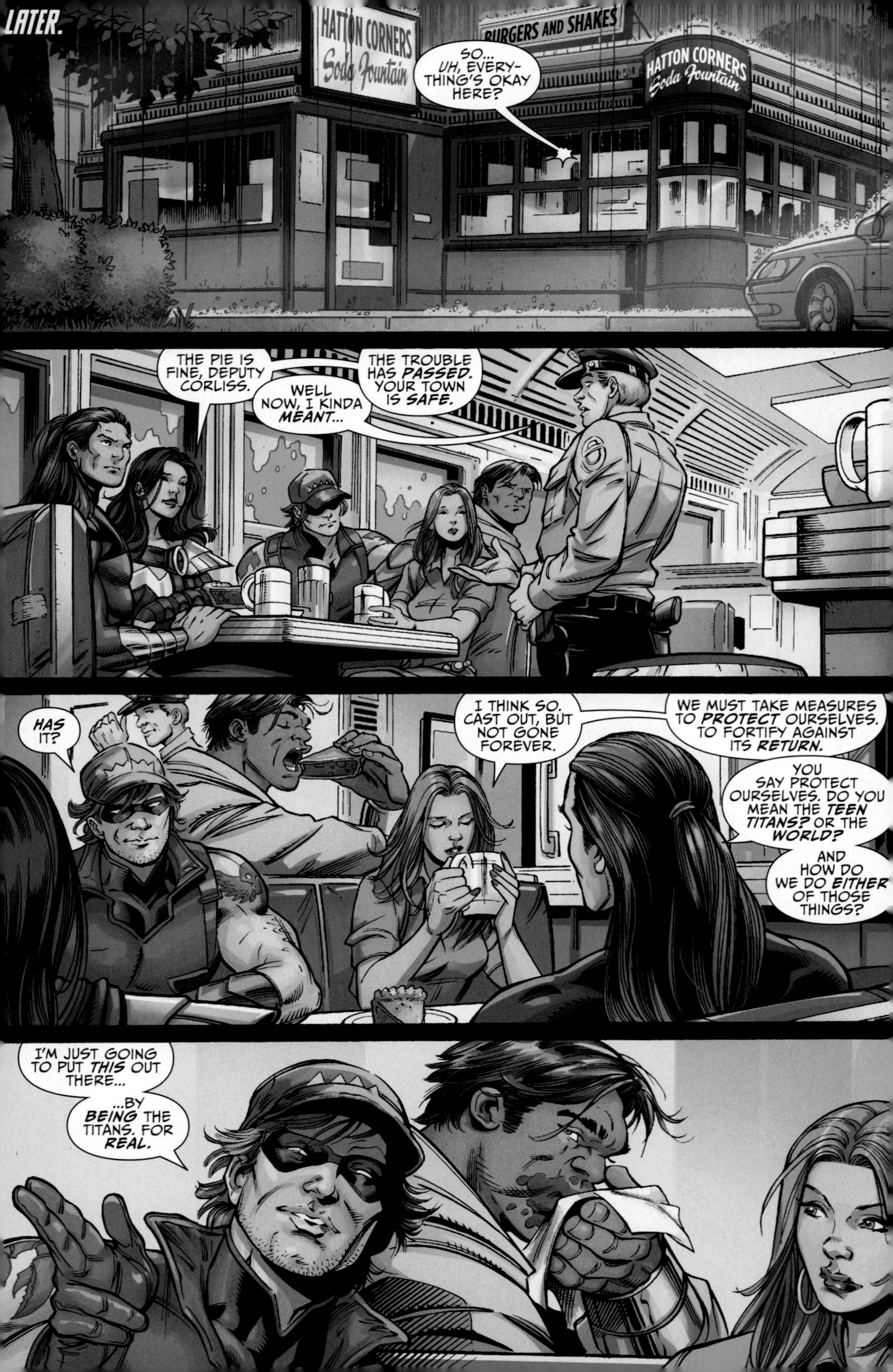
LATER.
HATTON CORNERS Soda Fountain
BURGERS AND SHAKES
HATTON CORNERS Soda Fountain
SO... UH, EVERY-THING'S OKAY HERE?
THE PIE IS FINE, DEPUTY CORLISS.
THE TROUBLE HAS PASSED. YOUR TOWN IS SAFE.
WELL NOW, I KINDA MEANT...
HAS IT?
I THINK SO. CAST OUT, BUT NOT GONE FOREVER.
WE MUST TAKE MEASURES TO PROTECT OURSELVES. TO FORTIFY AGAINST ITS RETURN.
YOU SAY PROTECT OURSELVES. DO YOU MEAN THE TEEN TITANS? OR THE WORLD?
AND HOW DO WE DO EITHER OF THOSE THINGS?
I'M JUST GOING TO PUT THIS OUT THERE...
...BY BEING THE TITANS. FOR REAL.

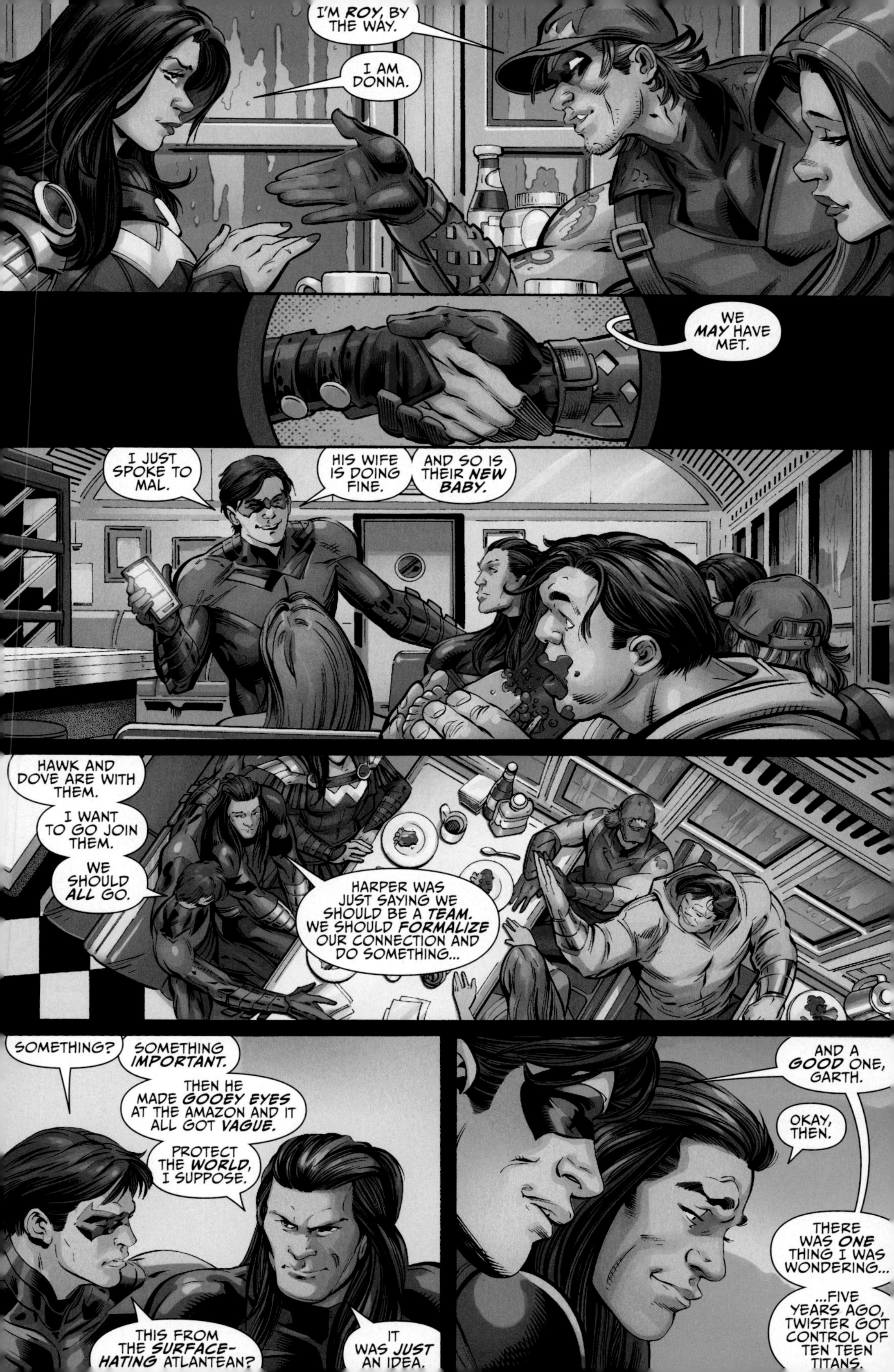
I'M ROY, BY THE WAY.
I AM DONNA.
WE MAY HAVE MET.
I JUST SPOKE TO MAL.
HIS WIFE IS DOING FINE.
AND SO IS THEIR NEW BABY.
HAWK AND DOVE ARE WITH THEM.
I WANT TO GO JOIN THEM.
WE SHOULD ALL GO.
HARPER WAS JUST SAYING WE SHOULD BE A TEAM. WE SHOULD FORMALIZE OUR CONNECTION AND DO SOMETHING...
SOMETHING?
SOMETHING IMPORTANT.
THEN HE MADE GOOEY EYES AT THE AMAZON AND IT ALL GOT VAGUE.
PROTECT THE WORLD, I SUPPOSE.
THIS FROM THE SURFACE-HATING ATLANTEAN?
IT WAS JUST AN IDEA.
AND A GOOD ONE, GARTH.
OKAY, THEN.
THERE WAS ONE THING I WAS WONDERING...
...FIVE YEARS AGO, TWISTER GOT CONTROL OF TEN TEEN TITANS.

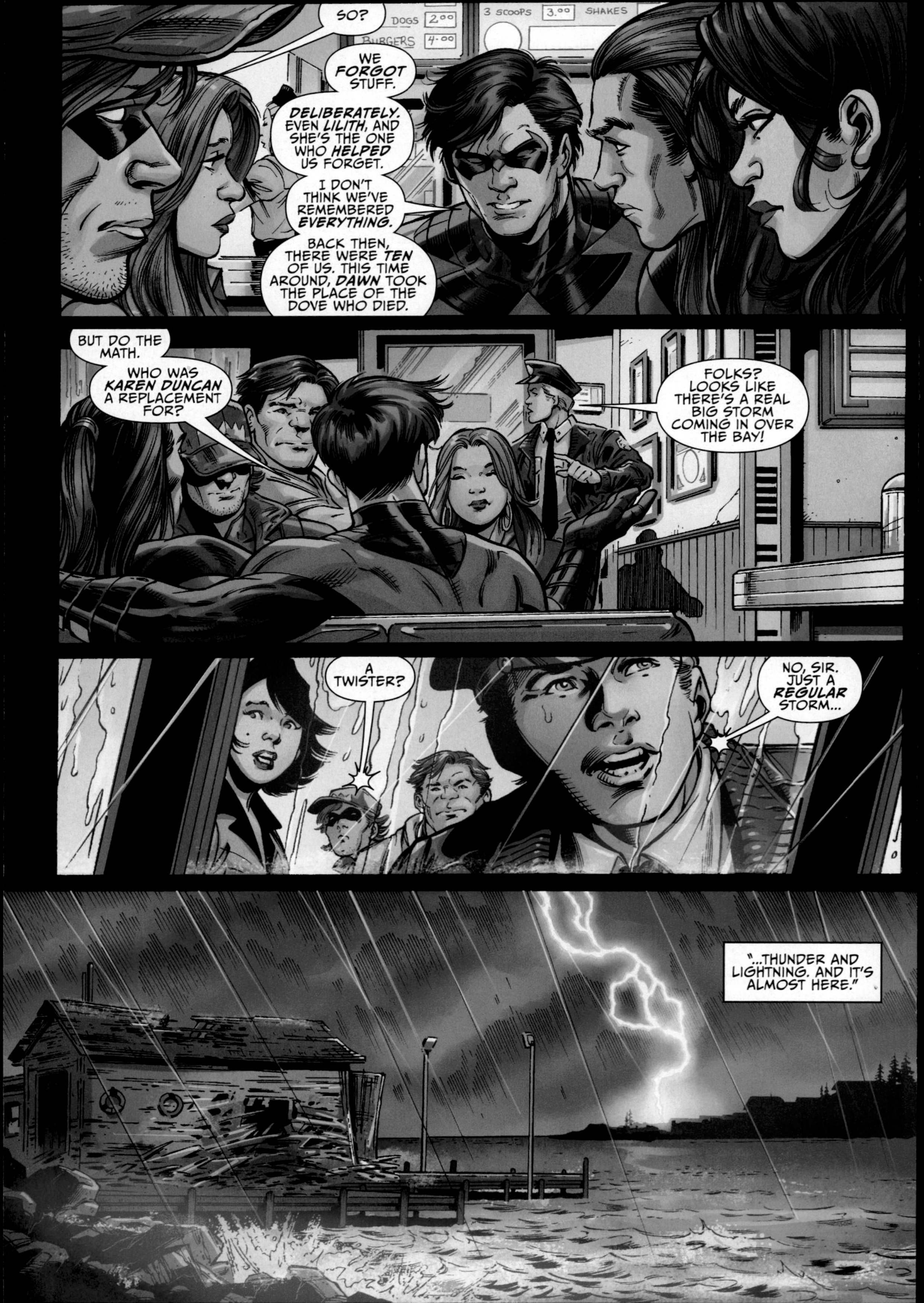
SO?
DOGS 2.00
BURGERS 4.00
3 SCOOPS 3.00
SHAKES
WE FORGOT STUFF.
DELIBERATELY. EVEN LILITH, AND SHE'S THE ONE WHO HELPED US FORGET.
I DON'T THINK WE'VE REMEMBERED EVERYTHING.
BACK THEN, THERE WERE TEN OF US. THIS TIME AROUND, DAWN TOOK THE PLACE OF THE DOVE WHO DIED.
BUT DO THE MATH.
WHO WAS KAREN DUNCAN A REPLACEMENT FOR?
FOLKS? LOOKS LIKE THERE'S A REAL BIG STORM COMING IN OVER THE BAY!
A TWISTER?
NO, SIR. JUST A REGULAR STORM...
"...THUNDER AND LIGHTNING. AND IT'S ALMOST HERE."

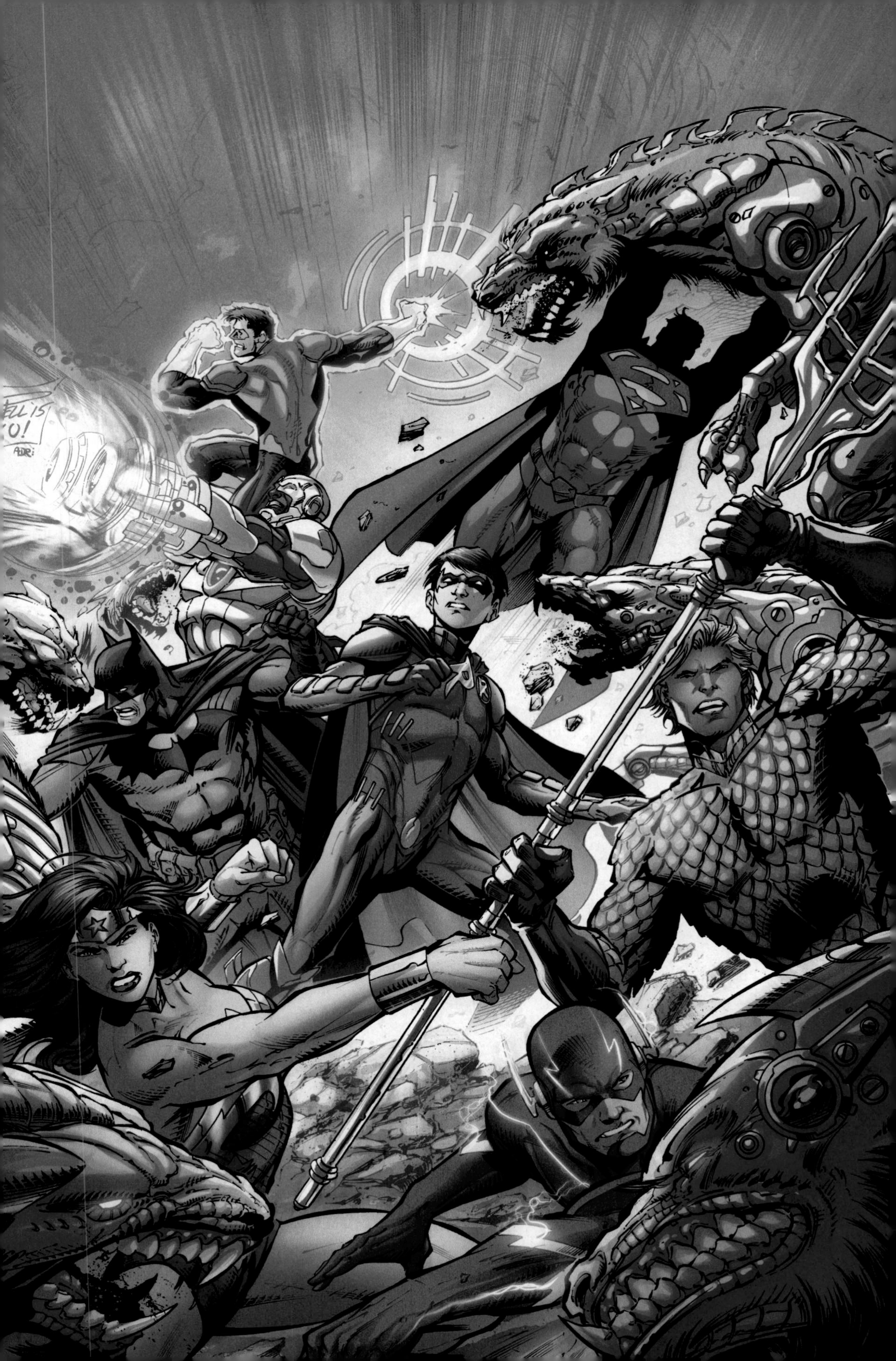

FIRST IMPRESSIONS

DAN ABNETT writer **PAUL PELLETIER** penciller **SANDRA HOPE** inker **ADRIANO LUCAS** colorist cover art by **PAUL PELLETIER, TONY KORDOS & ADRIANO LUCAS**

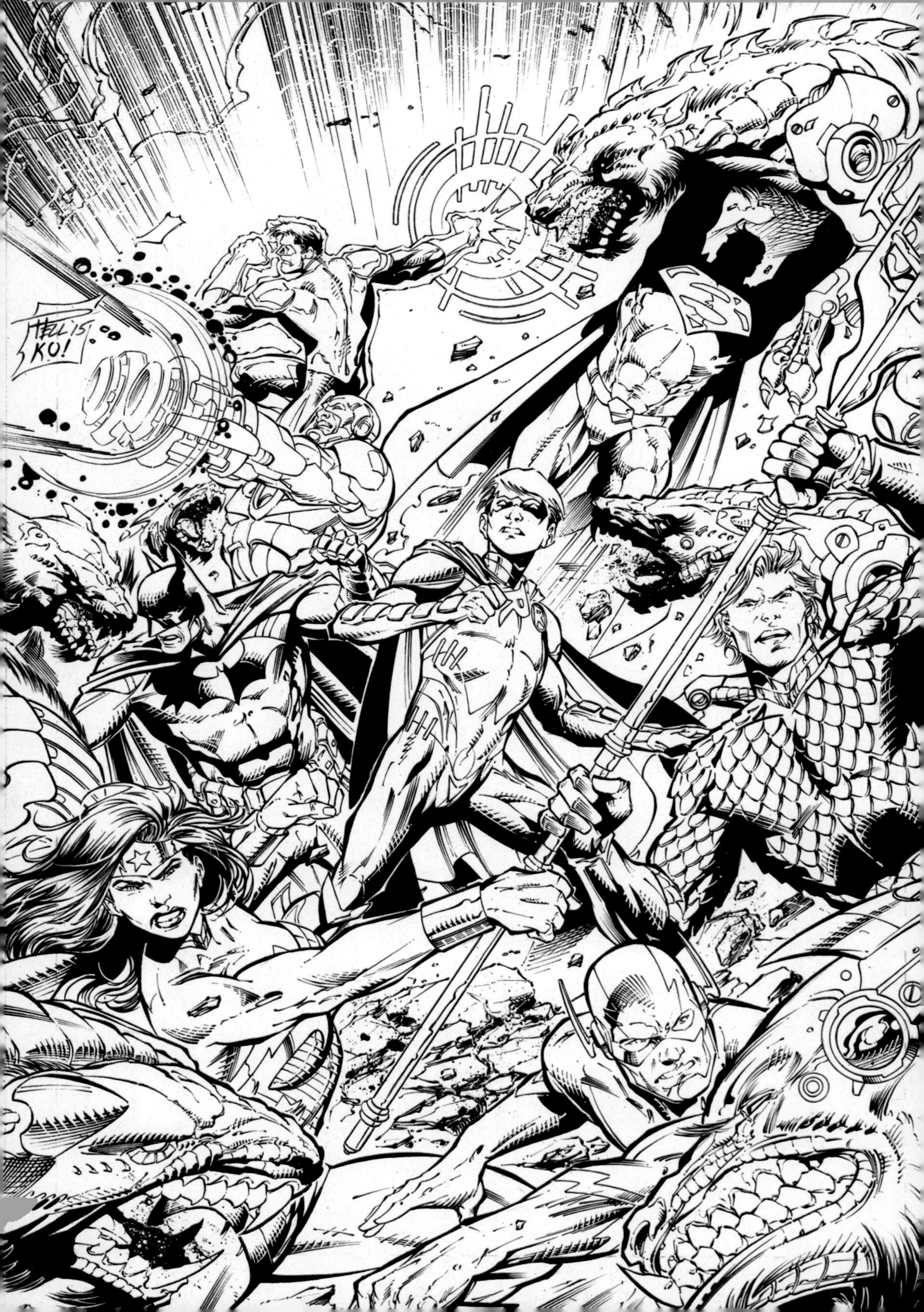

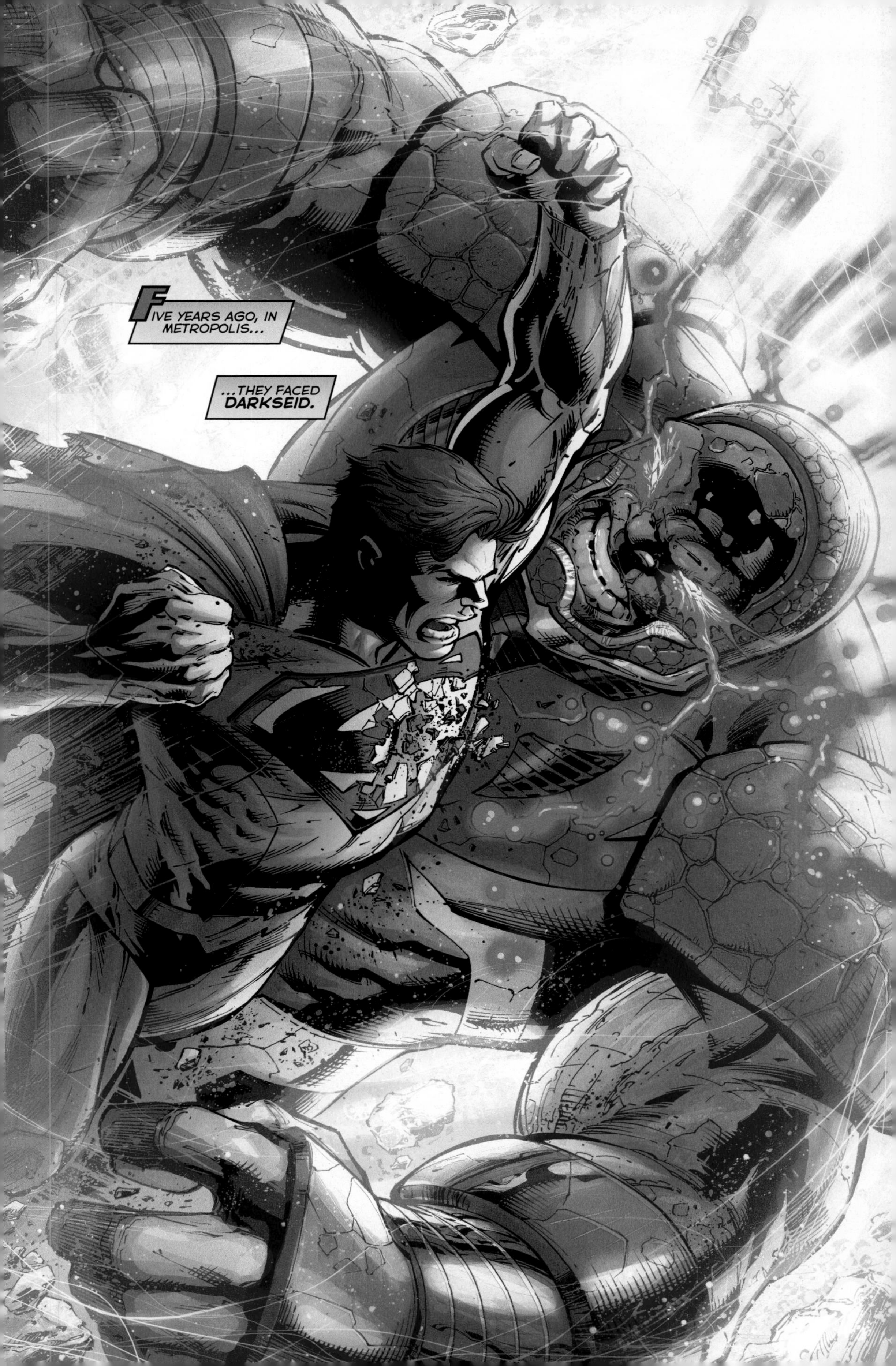
FIVE YEARS AGO, IN METROPOLIS...
...THEY FACED DARKSEID.

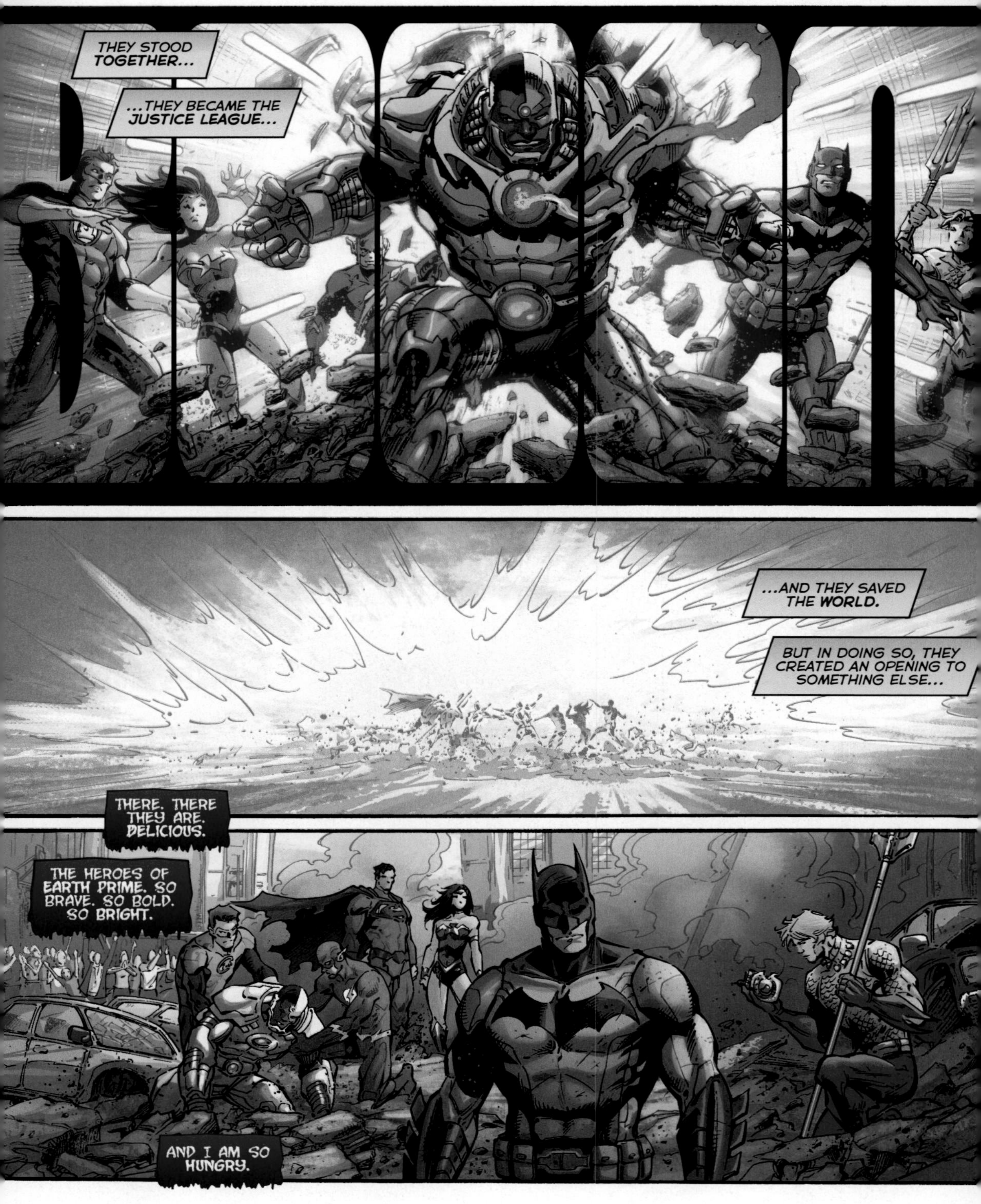
THEY STOOD TOGETHER...
...THEY BECAME THE JUSTICE LEAGUE...
...AND THEY SAVED THE WORLD.
BUT IN DOING SO, THEY CREATED AN OPENING TO SOMETHING ELSE...
THERE. THERE THEY ARE. DELICIOUS.
THE HEROES OF EARTH PRIME. SO BRAVE. SO BOLD. SO BRIGHT.
AND I AM SO HUNGRY.

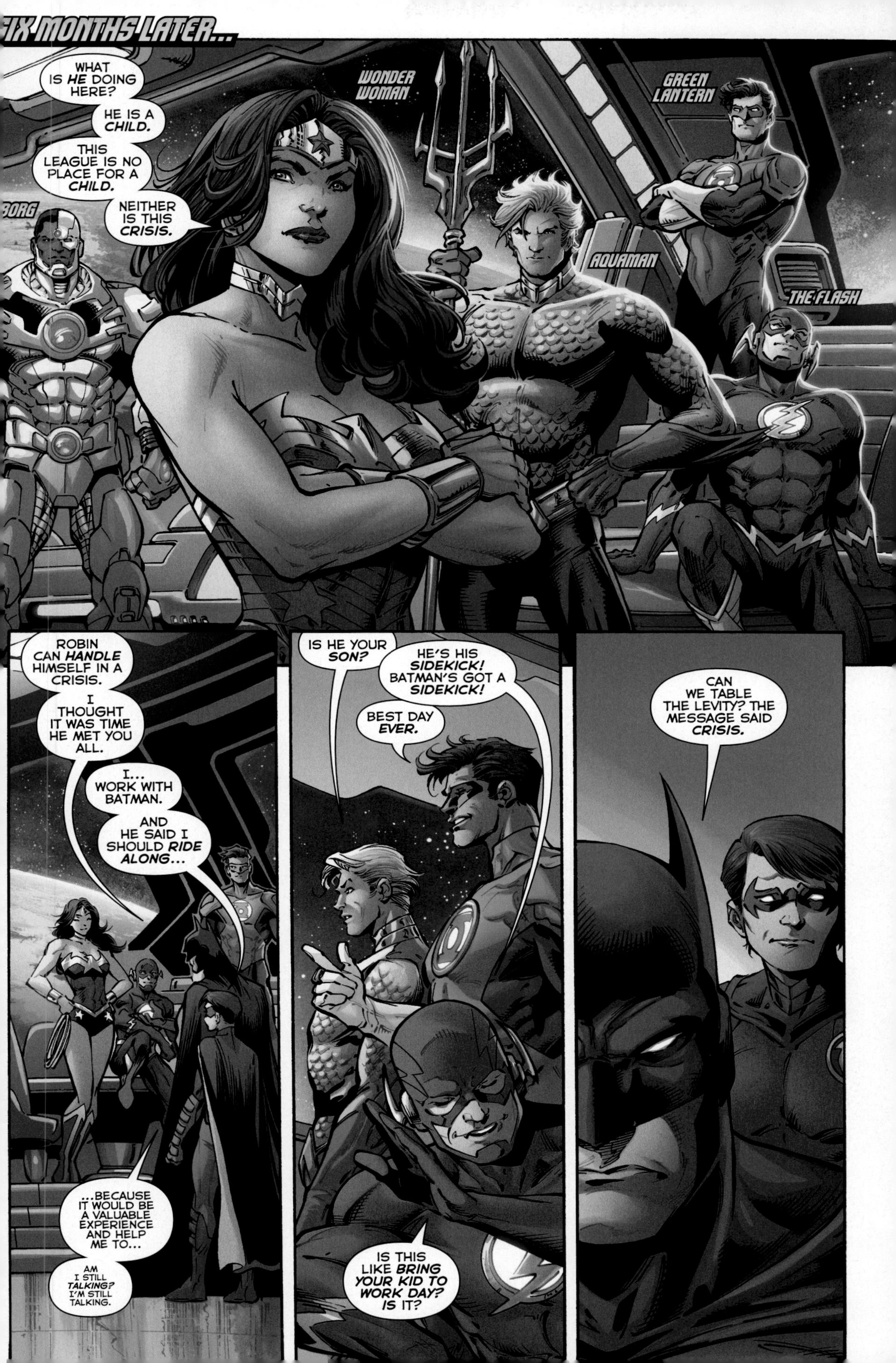
SIX MONTHS LATER...
WHAT IS HE DOING HERE?
HE IS A CHILD.
THIS LEAGUE IS NO PLACE FOR A CHILD.
NEITHER IS THIS CRISIS.
WONDER WOMAN
GREEN LANTERN
AQUAMAN
THE FLASH
ROBIN CAN HANDLE HIMSELF IN A CRISIS.
I THOUGHT IT WAS TIME HE MET YOU ALL.
I... WORK WITH BATMAN.
AND HE SAID I SHOULD RIDE ALONG...
...BECAUSE IT WOULD BE A VALUABLE EXPERIENCE AND HELP ME TO...
AM I STILL TALKING? I'M STILL TALKING.
IS HE YOUR SON?
HE'S HIS SIDEKICK! BATMAN'S GOT A SIDEKICK!
BEST DAY EVER.
IS THIS LIKE BRING YOUR KID TO WORK DAY? IS IT?
CAN WE TABLE THE LEVITY? THE MESSAGE SAID CRISIS.

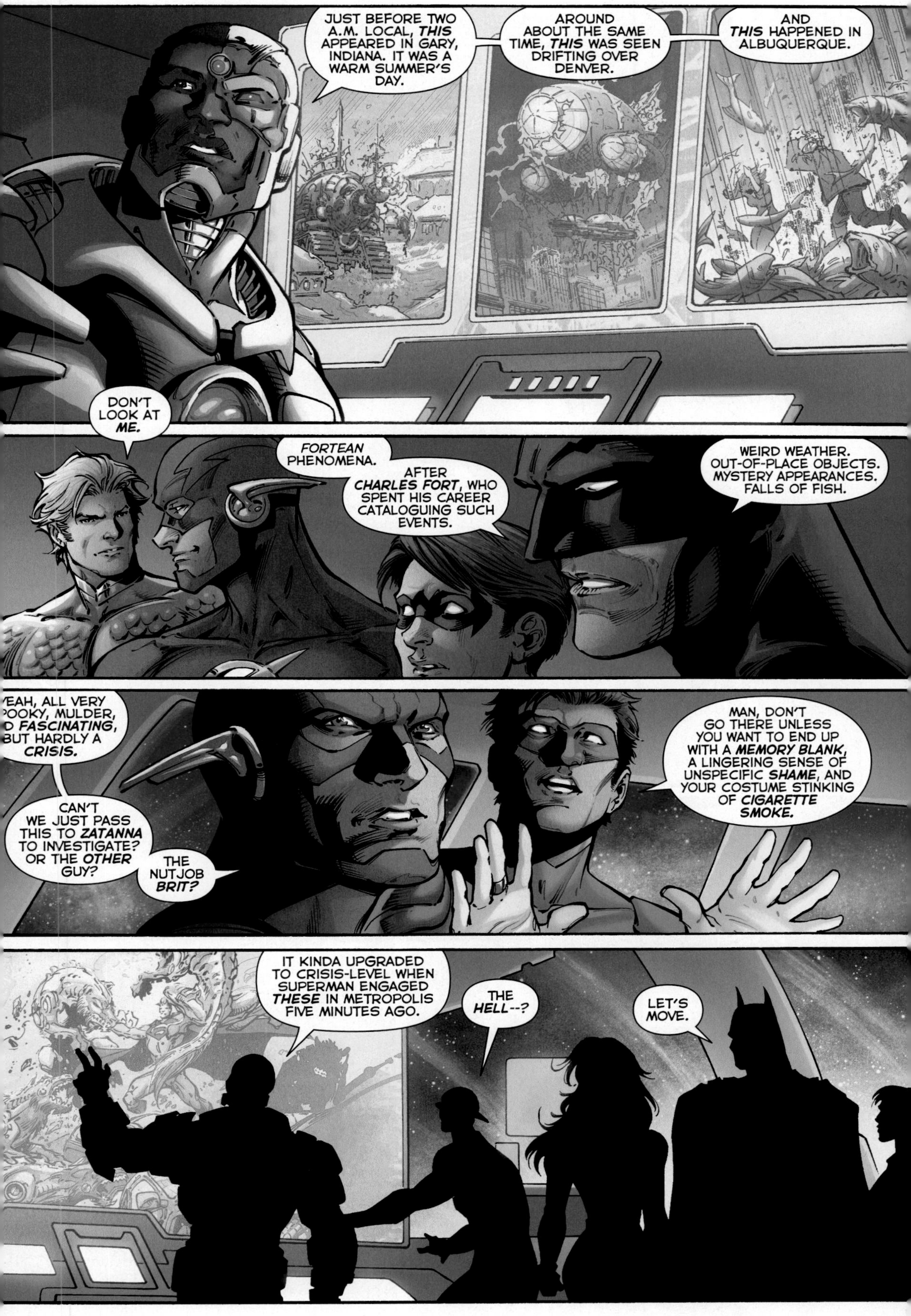
JUST BEFORE TWO A.M. LOCAL, THIS APPEARED IN GARY, INDIANA. IT WAS A WARM SUMMER'S DAY.
AROUND ABOUT THE SAME TIME, THIS WAS SEEN DRIFTING OVER DENVER.
AND THIS HAPPENED IN ALBUQUERQUE.
DON'T LOOK AT ME.
FORTEAN PHENOMENA.
AFTER CHARLES FORT, WHO SPENT HIS CAREER CATALOGUING SUCH EVENTS.
WEIRD WEATHER. OUT-OF-PLACE OBJECTS. MYSTERY APPEARANCES. FALLS OF FISH.
YEAH, ALL VERY SPOOKY, MULDER, AND FASCINATING, BUT HARDLY A CRISIS.
CAN'T WE JUST PASS THIS TO ZATANNA TO INVESTIGATE? OR THE OTHER GUY?
THE NUTJOB BRIT?
MAN, DON'T GO THERE UNLESS YOU WANT TO END UP WITH A MEMORY BLANK, A LINGERING SENSE OF UNSPECIFIC SHAME, AND YOUR COSTUME STINKING OF CIGARETTE SMOKE.
IT KINDA UPGRADED TO CRISIS-LEVEL WHEN SUPERMAN ENGAGED THESE IN METROPOLIS FIVE MINUTES AGO.
THE HELL--?
LET'S MOVE.

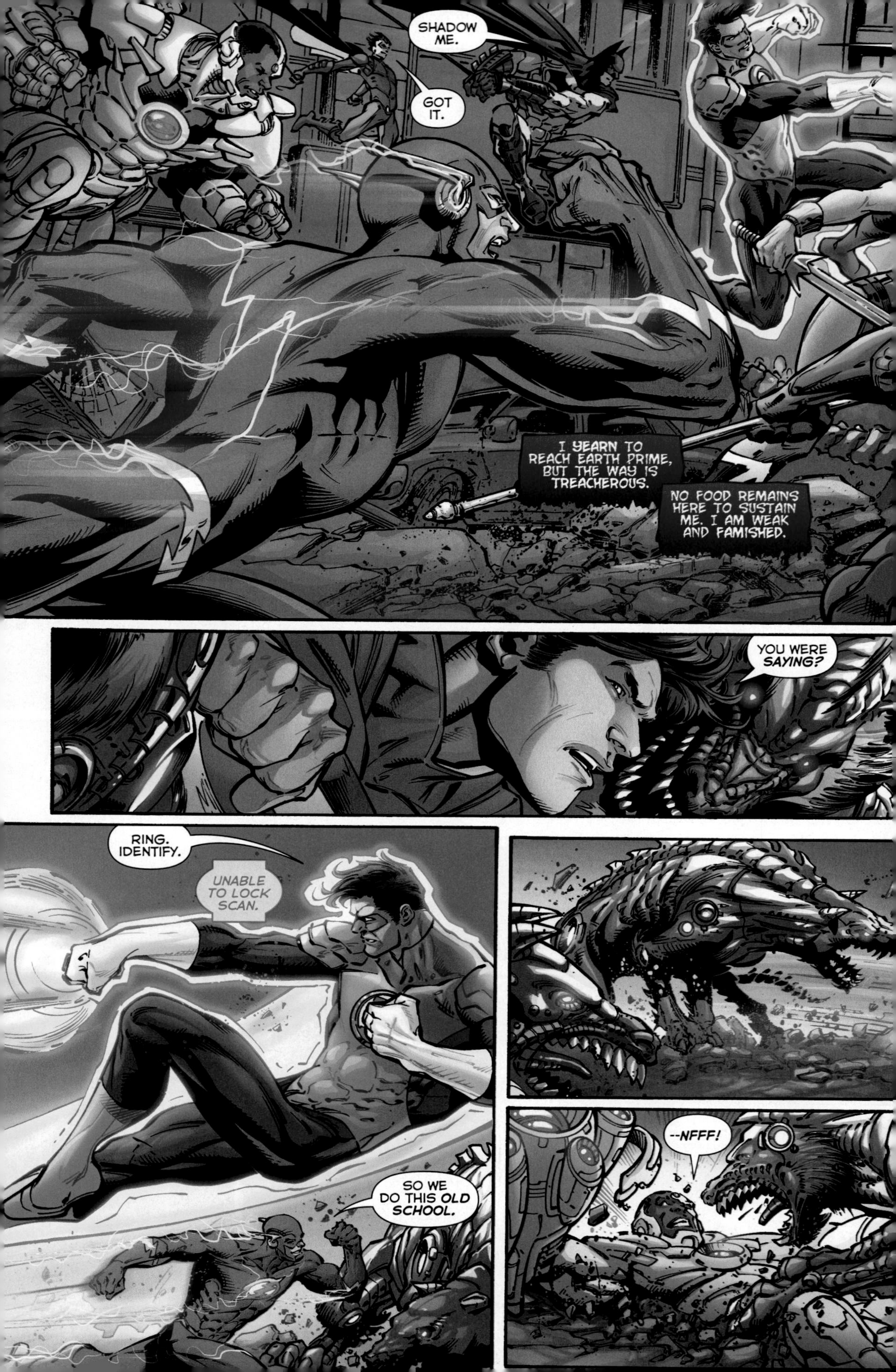
SHADOW ME.
GOT IT.
I YEARN TO REACH EARTH PRIME, BUT THE WAY IS TREACHEROUS.
NO FOOD REMAINS HERE TO SUSTAIN ME. I AM WEAK AND FAMISHED.
YOU WERE SAYING?
RING. IDENTIFY.
UNABLE TO LOCK SCAN.
SO WE DO THIS OLD SCHOOL.
--NFFF!

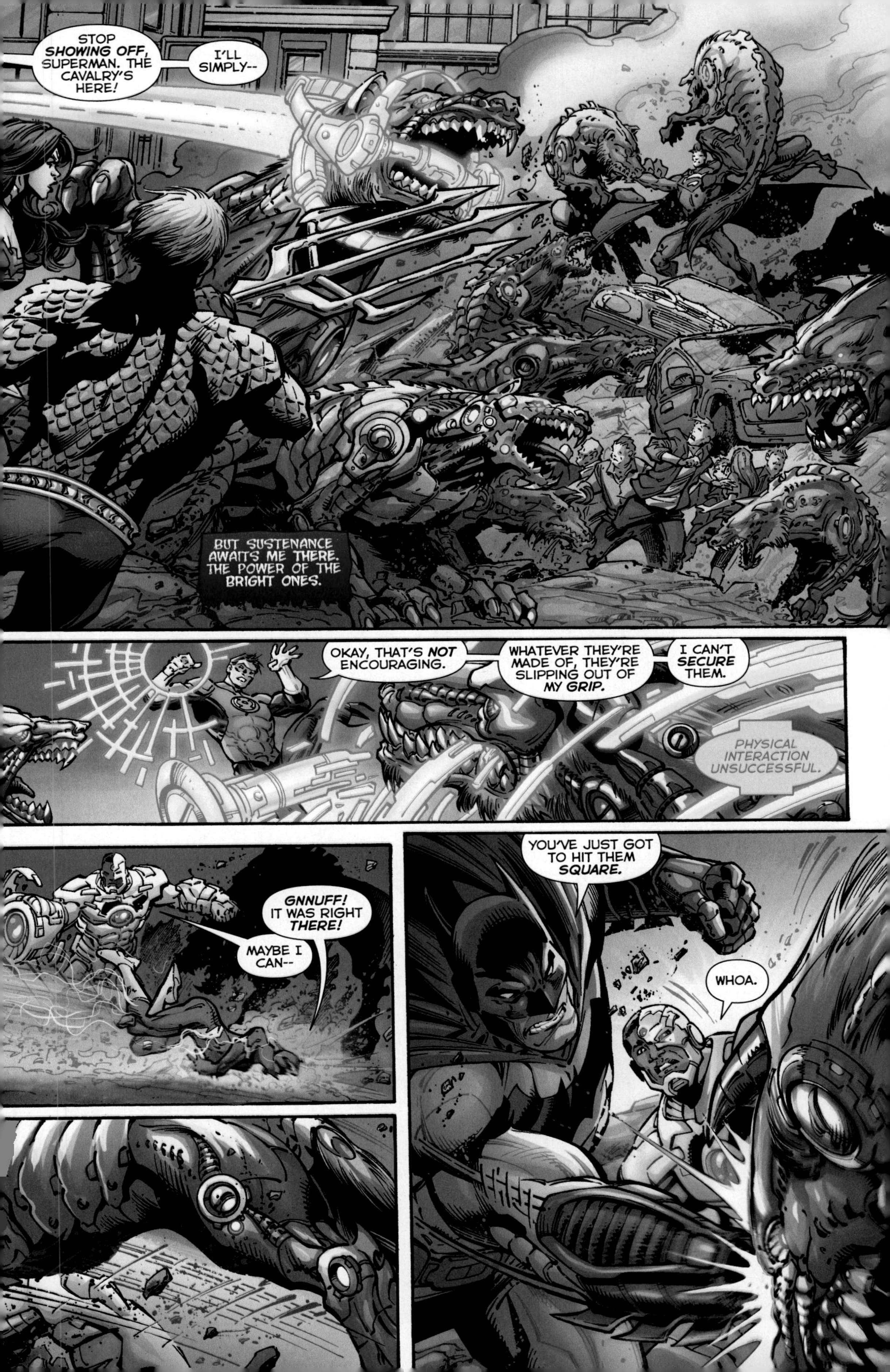
STOP SHOWING OFF, SUPERMAN. THE CAVALRY'S HERE!
I'LL SIMPLY--
BUT SUSTENANCE AWAITS ME THERE. THE POWER OF THE BRIGHT ONES.
OKAY, THAT'S NOT ENCOURAGING.
WHATEVER THEY'RE MADE OF, THEY'RE SLIPPING OUT OF MY GRIP.
I CAN'T SECURE THEM.
PHYSICAL INTERACTION UNSUCCESSFUL.
GNNUFF! IT WAS RIGHT THERE!
MAYBE I CAN--
YOU'VE JUST GOT TO HIT THEM SQUARE.
WHOA.

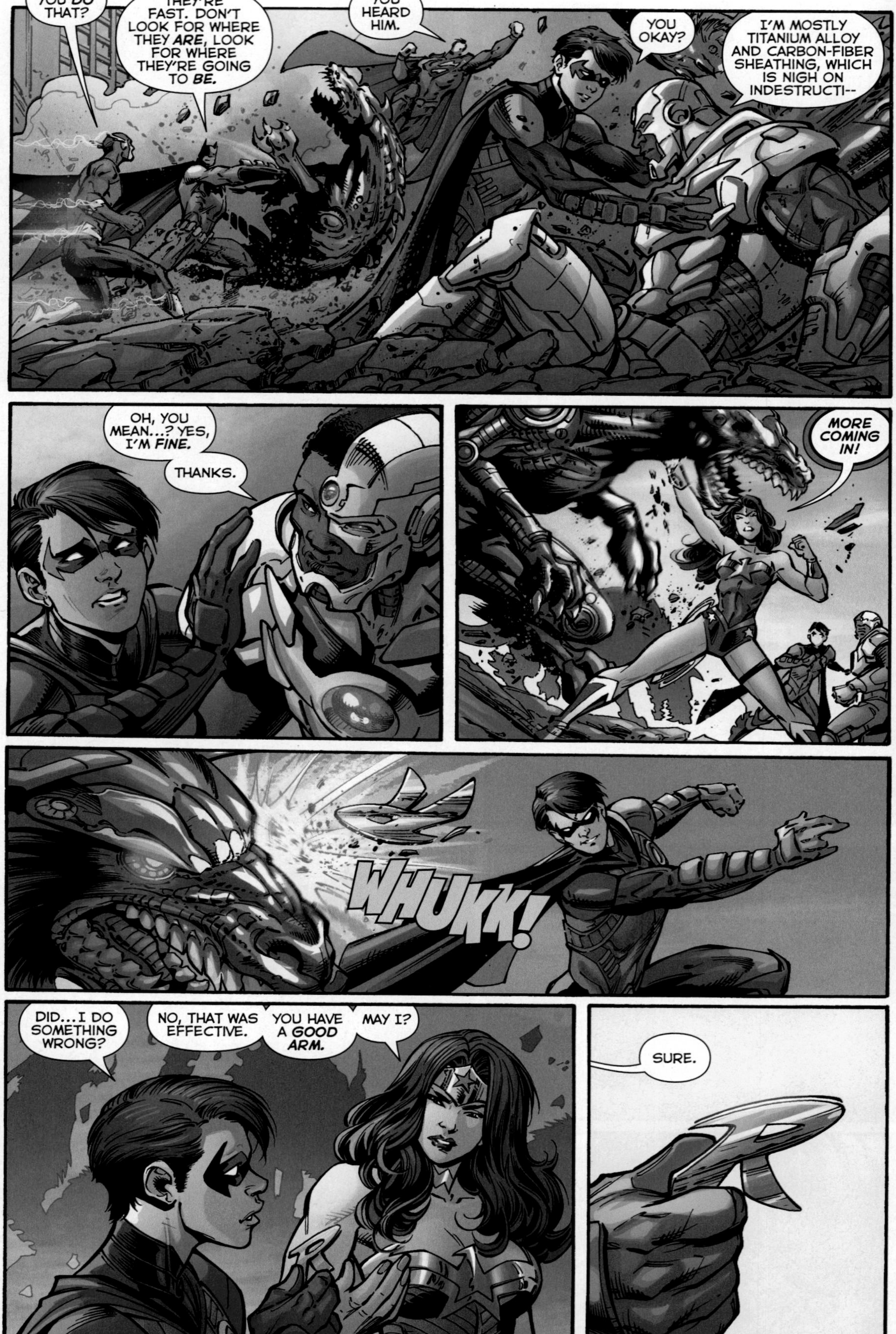
HOW'D YOU *DO* THAT?
THEY'RE FAST. DON'T LOOK FOR WHERE THEY *ARE*, LOOK FOR WHERE THEY'RE GOING TO *BE.*
YOU HEARD HIM.
YOU OKAY?
I'M MOSTLY TITANIUM ALLOY AND CARBON-FIBER SHEATHING, WHICH IS NIGH ON INDESTRUCTI--
OH, YOU MEAN...? YES, I'M *FINE.*
THANKS.
MORE COMING IN!
WHUKK!
DID...I DO SOMETHING WRONG?
NO, THAT WAS EFFECTIVE.
YOU HAVE A *GOOD ARM.*
MAY I?
SURE.

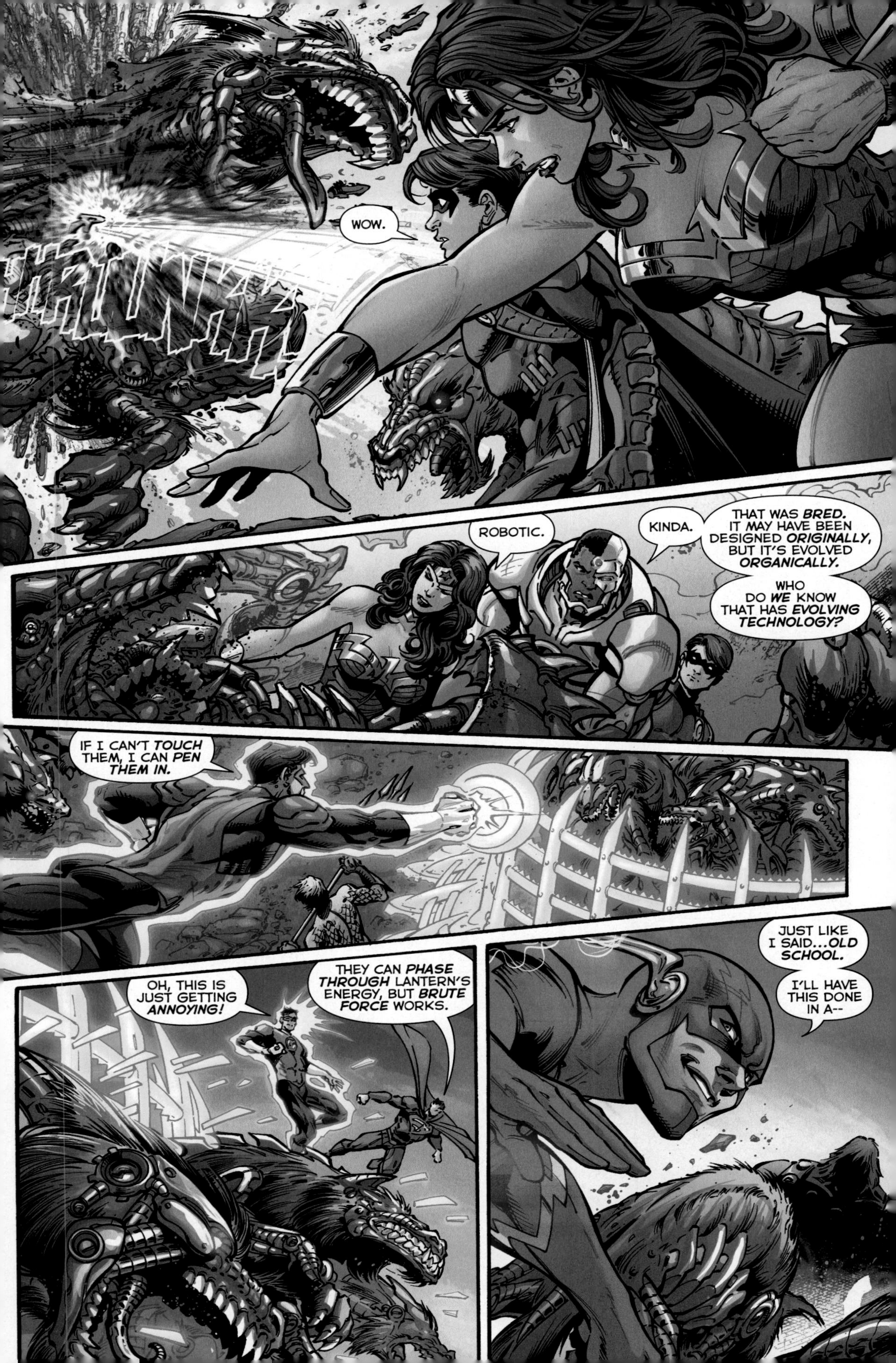
WOW.
ROBOTIC.
KINDA.
THAT WAS *BRED.* IT MAY HAVE BEEN DESIGNED *ORIGINALLY,* BUT IT'S EVOLVED *ORGANICALLY.*
WHO DO *WE* KNOW THAT HAS *EVOLVING TECHNOLOGY?*
IF I CAN'T *TOUCH* THEM, I CAN *PEN THEM IN.*
OH, THIS IS JUST GETTING *ANNOYING!*
THEY CAN *PHASE THROUGH* LANTERN'S ENERGY, BUT *BRUTE FORCE* WORKS.
JUST LIKE I SAID...*OLD SCHOOL.*
I'LL HAVE THIS DONE IN A--

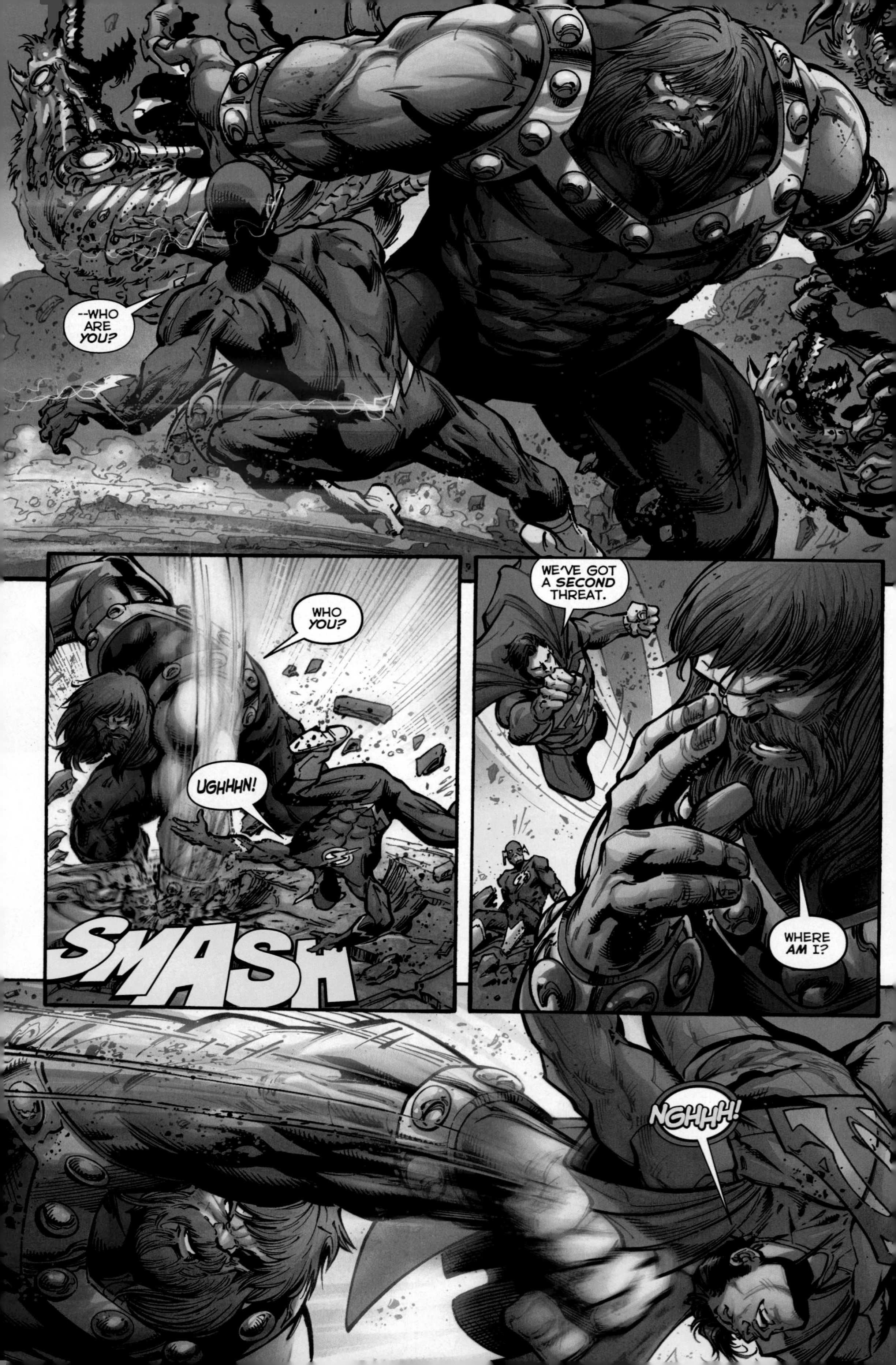
--WHO ARE *YOU*?
WHO *YOU*?
UGHHHN!
SMASH
WE'VE GOT A *SECOND* THREAT.
WHERE *AM* I?
NGHHH!

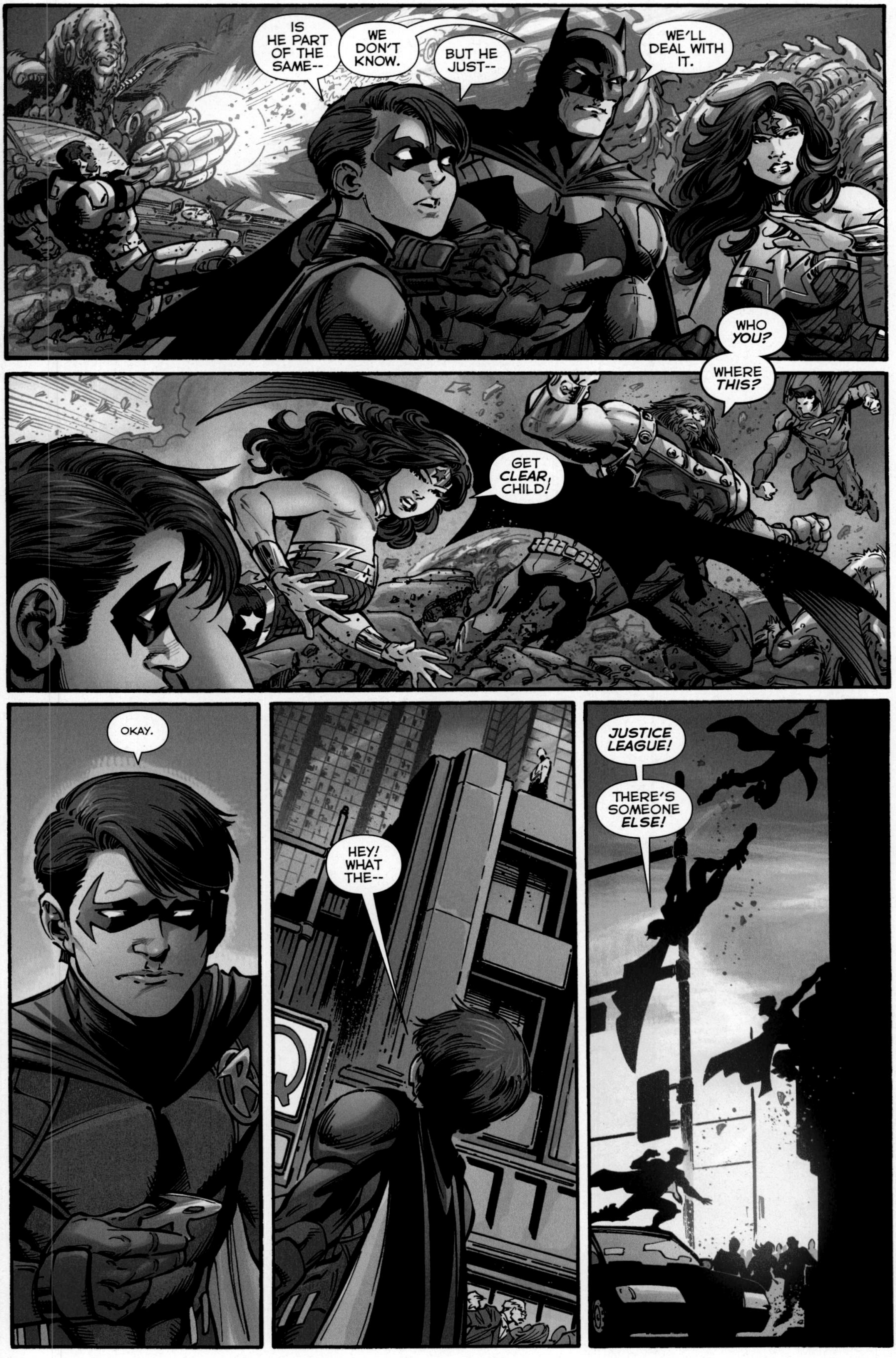
IS HE PART OF THE SAME--
WE DON'T KNOW.
BUT HE JUST--
WE'LL DEAL WITH IT.
WHO YOU?
WHERE THIS?
GET CLEAR, CHILD!
OKAY.
HEY! WHAT THE--
JUSTICE LEAGUE!
THERE'S SOMEONE ELSE!

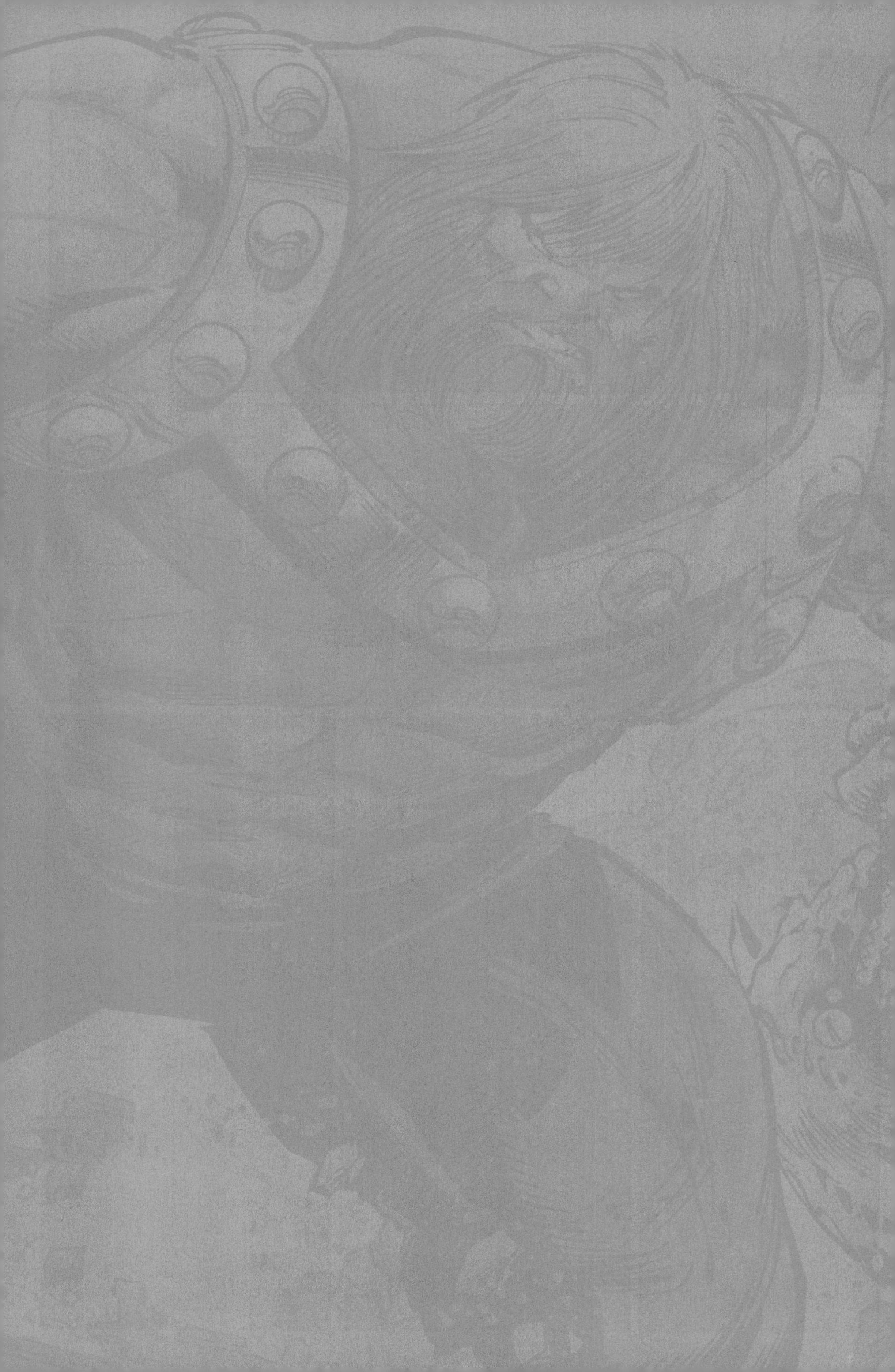

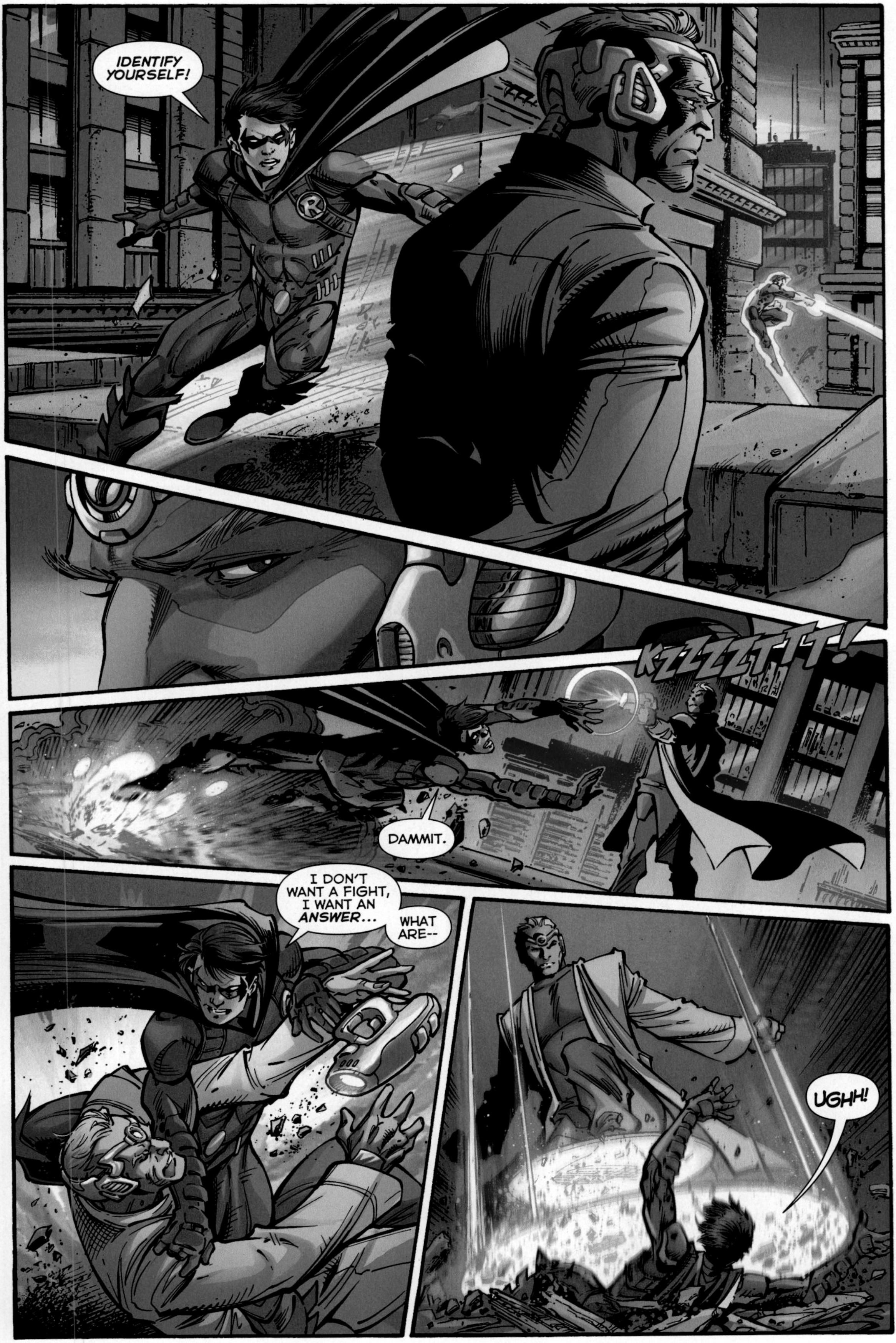
IDENTIFY YOURSELF!
KZZZZTTTT!
DAMMIT.
I DON'T WANT A FIGHT, I WANT AN *ANSWER*...
WHAT ARE--
UGHH!

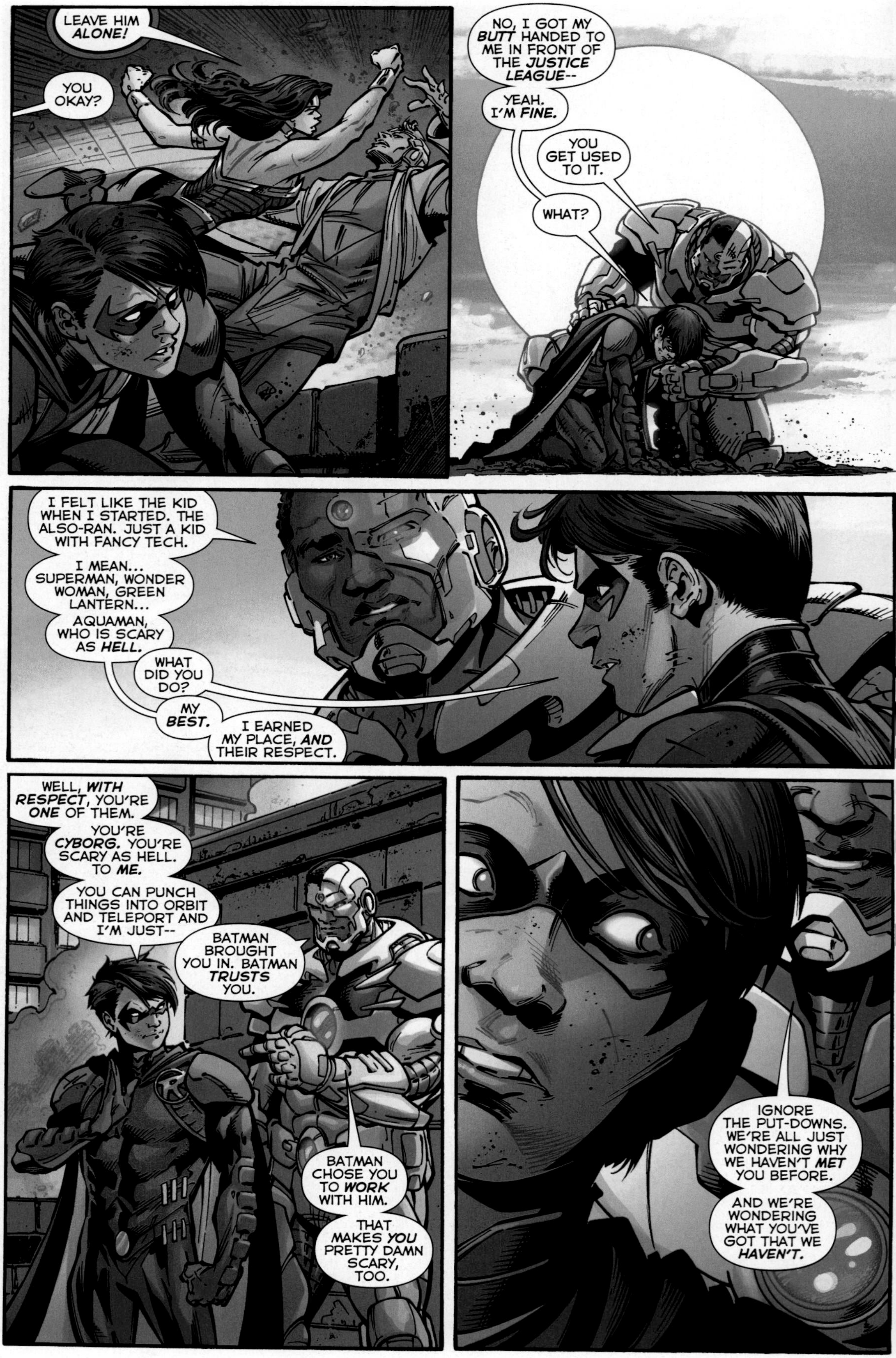
LEAVE HIM ALONE!
YOU OKAY?
NO, I GOT MY BUTT HANDED TO ME IN FRONT OF THE JUSTICE LEAGUE--
YEAH. I'M FINE.
YOU GET USED TO IT.
WHAT?
I FELT LIKE THE KID WHEN I STARTED. THE ALSO-RAN. JUST A KID WITH FANCY TECH.
I MEAN... SUPERMAN, WONDER WOMAN, GREEN LANTERN...
AQUAMAN, WHO IS SCARY AS HELL.
WHAT DID YOU DO?
MY BEST.
I EARNED MY PLACE, AND THEIR RESPECT.
WELL, WITH RESPECT, YOU'RE ONE OF THEM.
YOU'RE CYBORG. YOU'RE SCARY AS HELL. TO ME.
YOU CAN PUNCH THINGS INTO ORBIT AND TELEPORT AND I'M JUST--
BATMAN BROUGHT YOU IN. BATMAN TRUSTS YOU.
BATMAN CHOSE YOU TO WORK WITH HIM.
THAT MAKES YOU PRETTY DAMN SCARY, TOO.
IGNORE THE PUT-DOWNS. WE'RE ALL JUST WONDERING WHY WE HAVEN'T MET YOU BEFORE.
AND WE'RE WONDERING WHAT YOU'VE GOT THAT WE HAVEN'T.

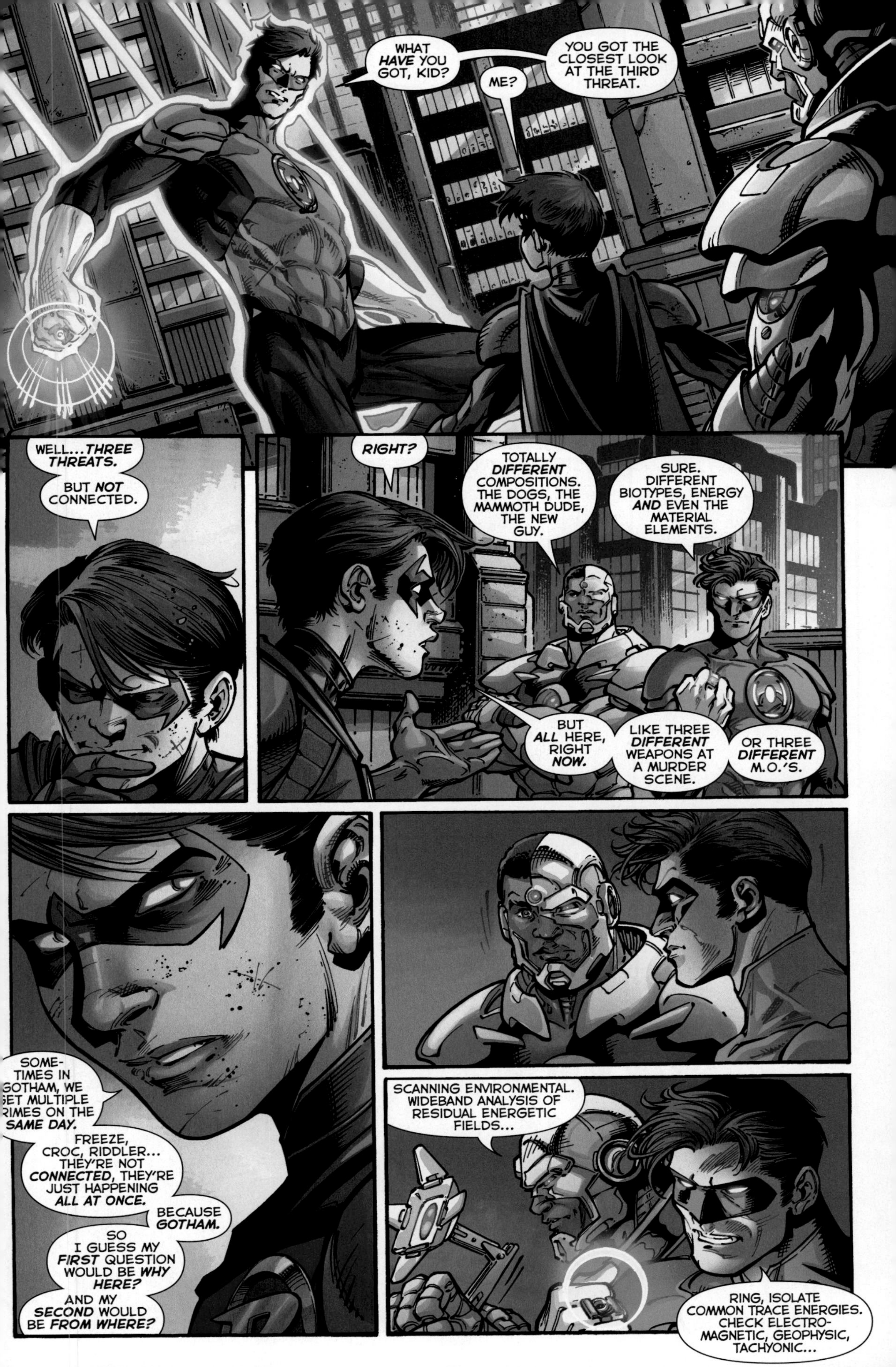
WHAT HAVE YOU GOT, KID?
ME?
YOU GOT THE CLOSEST LOOK AT THE THIRD THREAT.
WELL...THREE THREATS.
BUT NOT CONNECTED.
RIGHT?
TOTALLY DIFFERENT COMPOSITIONS. THE DOGS, THE MAMMOTH DUDE, THE NEW GUY.
SURE. DIFFERENT BIOTYPES, ENERGY AND EVEN THE MATERIAL ELEMENTS.
BUT ALL HERE, RIGHT NOW.
LIKE THREE DIFFERENT WEAPONS AT A MURDER SCENE.
OR THREE DIFFERENT M.O.'S.
SOME-TIMES IN GOTHAM, WE GET MULTIPLE CRIMES ON THE SAME DAY.
FREEZE, CROC, RIDDLER... THEY'RE NOT CONNECTED, THEY'RE JUST HAPPENING ALL AT ONCE.
BECAUSE GOTHAM.
SO I GUESS MY FIRST QUESTION WOULD BE WHY HERE?
AND MY SECOND WOULD BE FROM WHERE?
SCANNING ENVIRONMENTAL. WIDEBAND ANALYSIS OF RESIDUAL ENERGETIC FIELDS...
RING, ISOLATE COMMON TRACE ENERGIES. CHECK ELECTRO-MAGNETIC, GEOPHYSIC, TACHYONIC...

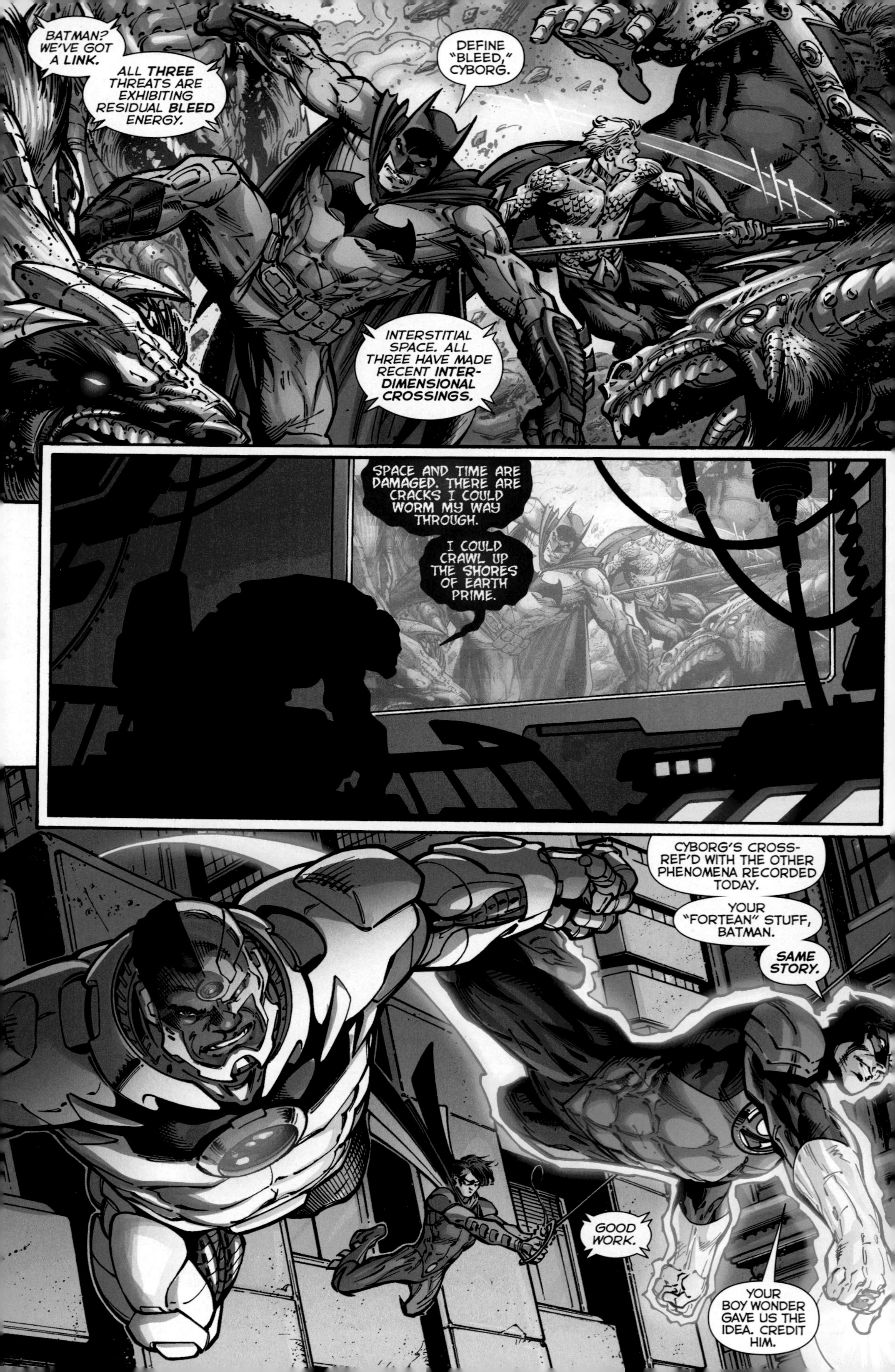
BATMAN? WE'VE GOT A LINK.
ALL THREE THREATS ARE EXHIBITING RESIDUAL BLEED ENERGY.
DEFINE "BLEED," CYBORG.
INTERSTITIAL SPACE. ALL THREE HAVE MADE RECENT INTER-DIMENSIONAL CROSSINGS.
SPACE AND TIME ARE DAMAGED. THERE ARE CRACKS I COULD WORM MY WAY THROUGH.
I COULD CRAWL UP THE SHORES OF EARTH PRIME.
CYBORG'S CROSS-REF'D WITH THE OTHER PHENOMENA RECORDED TODAY.
YOUR "FORTEAN" STUFF, BATMAN.
SAME STORY.
GOOD WORK.
YOUR BOY WONDER GAVE US THE IDEA. CREDIT HIM.

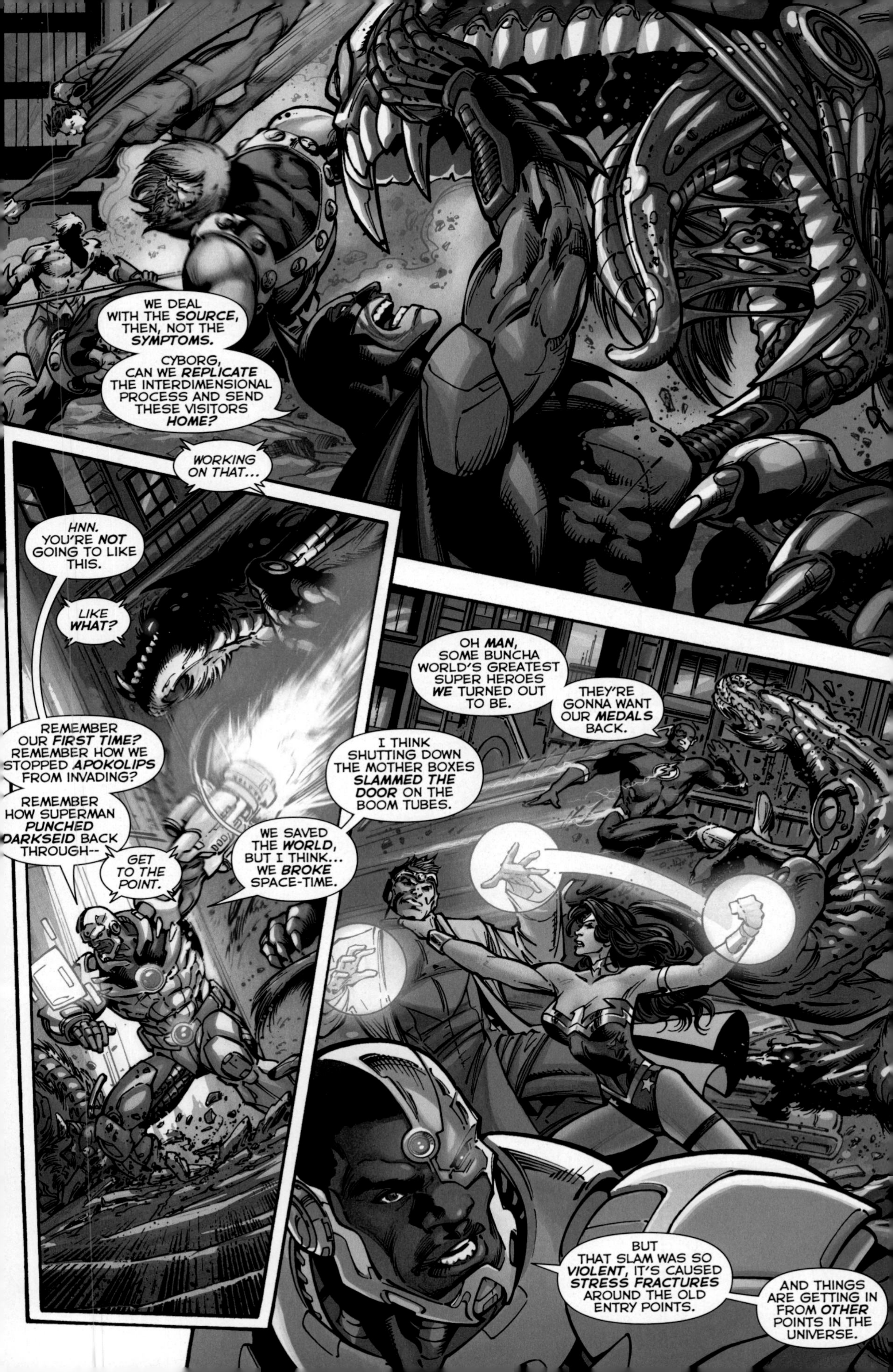
WE DEAL WITH THE SOURCE, THEN, NOT THE SYMPTOMS.
CYBORG, CAN WE REPLICATE THE INTERDIMENSIONAL PROCESS AND SEND THESE VISITORS HOME?
WORKING ON THAT...
HNN. YOU'RE NOT GOING TO LIKE THIS.
LIKE WHAT?
REMEMBER OUR FIRST TIME? REMEMBER HOW WE STOPPED APOKOLIPS FROM INVADING?
REMEMBER HOW SUPERMAN PUNCHED DARKSEID BACK THROUGH--
GET TO THE POINT.
I THINK SHUTTING DOWN THE MOTHER BOXES SLAMMED THE DOOR ON THE BOOM TUBES.
WE SAVED THE WORLD, BUT I THINK... WE BROKE SPACE-TIME.
OH MAN, SOME BUNCHA WORLD'S GREATEST SUPER HEROES WE TURNED OUT TO BE.
THEY'RE GONNA WANT OUR MEDALS BACK.
BUT THAT SLAM WAS SO VIOLENT, IT'S CAUSED STRESS FRACTURES AROUND THE OLD ENTRY POINTS.
AND THINGS ARE GETTING IN FROM OTHER POINTS IN THE UNIVERSE.

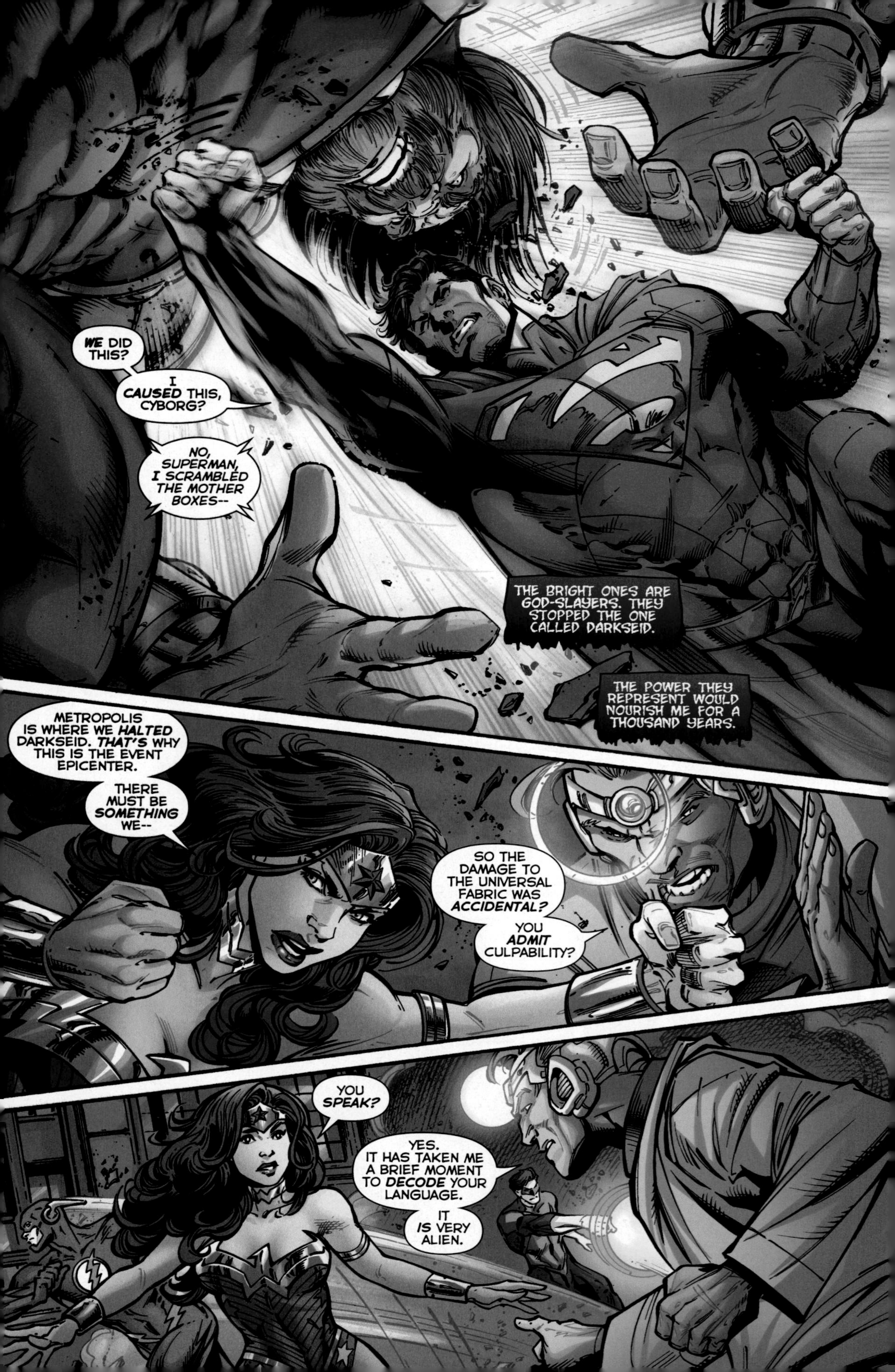
WE DID THIS?
I CAUSED THIS, CYBORG?
NO, SUPERMAN, I SCRAMBLED THE MOTHER BOXES--
THE BRIGHT ONES ARE GOD-SLAYERS. THEY STOPPED THE ONE CALLED DARKSEID.
THE POWER THEY REPRESENT WOULD NOURISH ME FOR A THOUSAND YEARS.
METROPOLIS IS WHERE WE HALTED DARKSEID. THAT'S WHY THIS IS THE EVENT EPICENTER.
THERE MUST BE SOMETHING WE--
SO THE DAMAGE TO THE UNIVERSAL FABRIC WAS ACCIDENTAL?
YOU ADMIT CULPABILITY?
YOU SPEAK?
YES. IT HAS TAKEN ME A BRIEF MOMENT TO DECODE YOUR LANGUAGE.
IT IS VERY ALIEN.

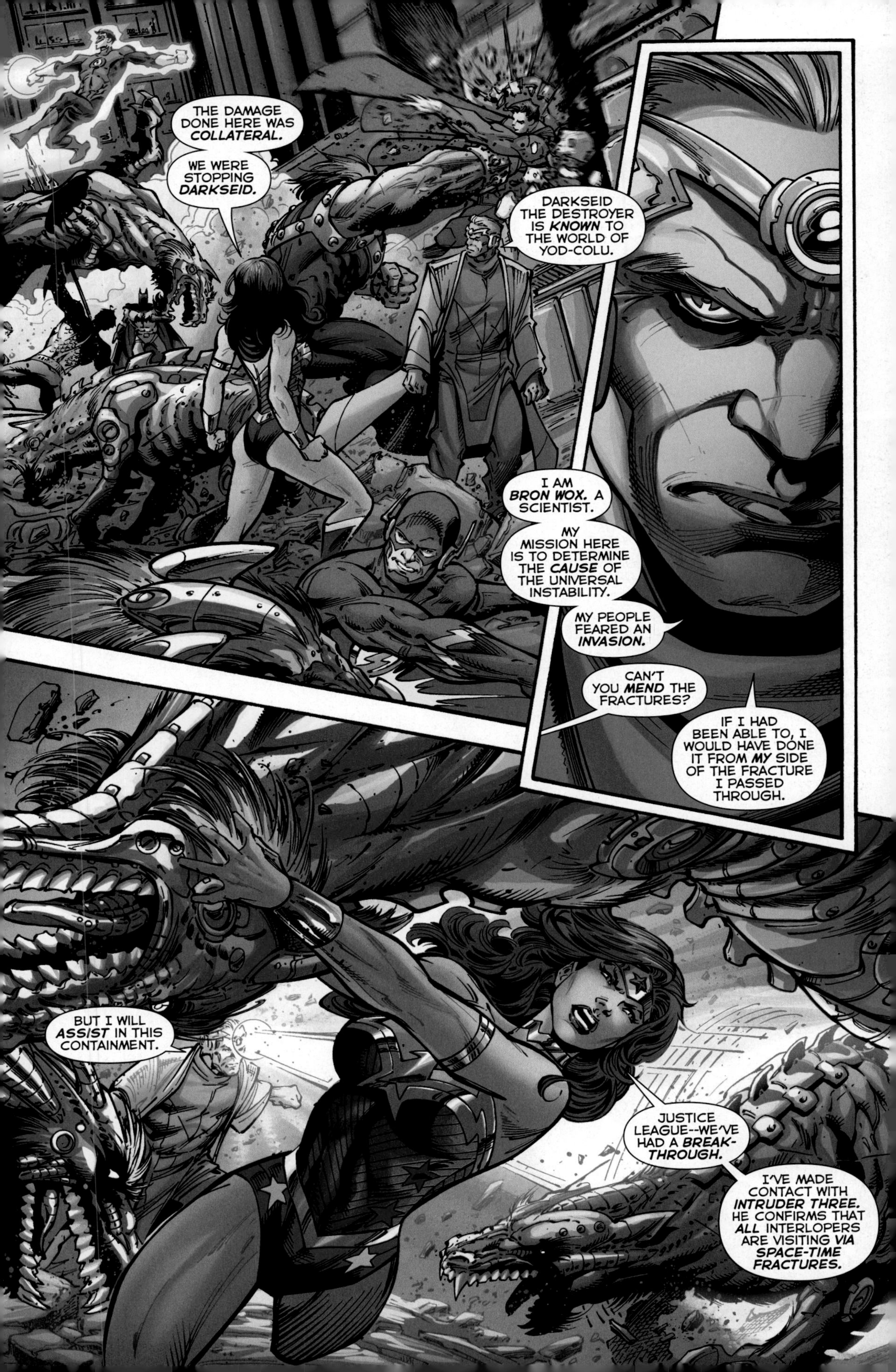
THE DAMAGE DONE HERE WAS COLLATERAL.
WE WERE STOPPING DARKSEID.
DARKSEID THE DESTROYER IS KNOWN TO THE WORLD OF YOD-COLU.
I AM BRON WOX. A SCIENTIST.
MY MISSION HERE IS TO DETERMINE THE CAUSE OF THE UNIVERSAL INSTABILITY.
MY PEOPLE FEARED AN INVASION.
CAN'T YOU MEND THE FRACTURES?
IF I HAD BEEN ABLE TO, I WOULD HAVE DONE IT FROM MY SIDE OF THE FRACTURE I PASSED THROUGH.
BUT I WILL ASSIST IN THIS CONTAINMENT.
JUSTICE LEAGUE--WE'VE HAD A BREAK-THROUGH.
I'VE MADE CONTACT WITH INTRUDER THREE. HE CONFIRMS THAT ALL INTERLOPERS ARE VISITING VIA SPACE-TIME FRACTURES.

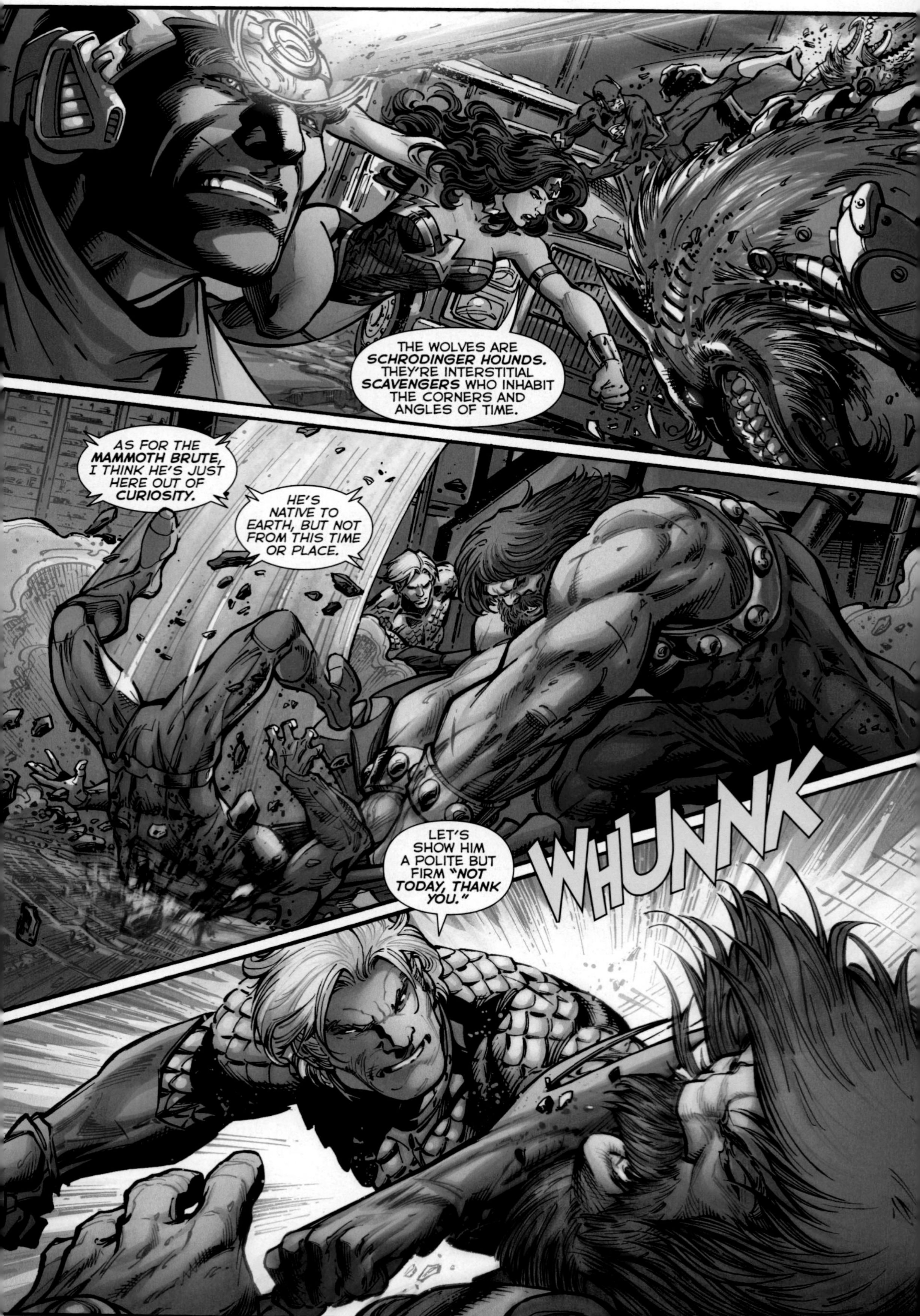

THE WOLVES ARE **SCHRODINGER HOUNDS.** THEY'RE INTERSTITIAL **SCAVENGERS** WHO INHABIT THE CORNERS AND ANGLES OF TIME.
AS FOR THE **MAMMOTH BRUTE,** I THINK HE'S JUST HERE OUT OF **CURIOSITY.**
HE'S NATIVE TO EARTH, BUT NOT FROM THIS TIME OR PLACE.
LET'S SHOW HIM A POLITE BUT FIRM **"NOT TODAY, THANK YOU."**
WHUNNK

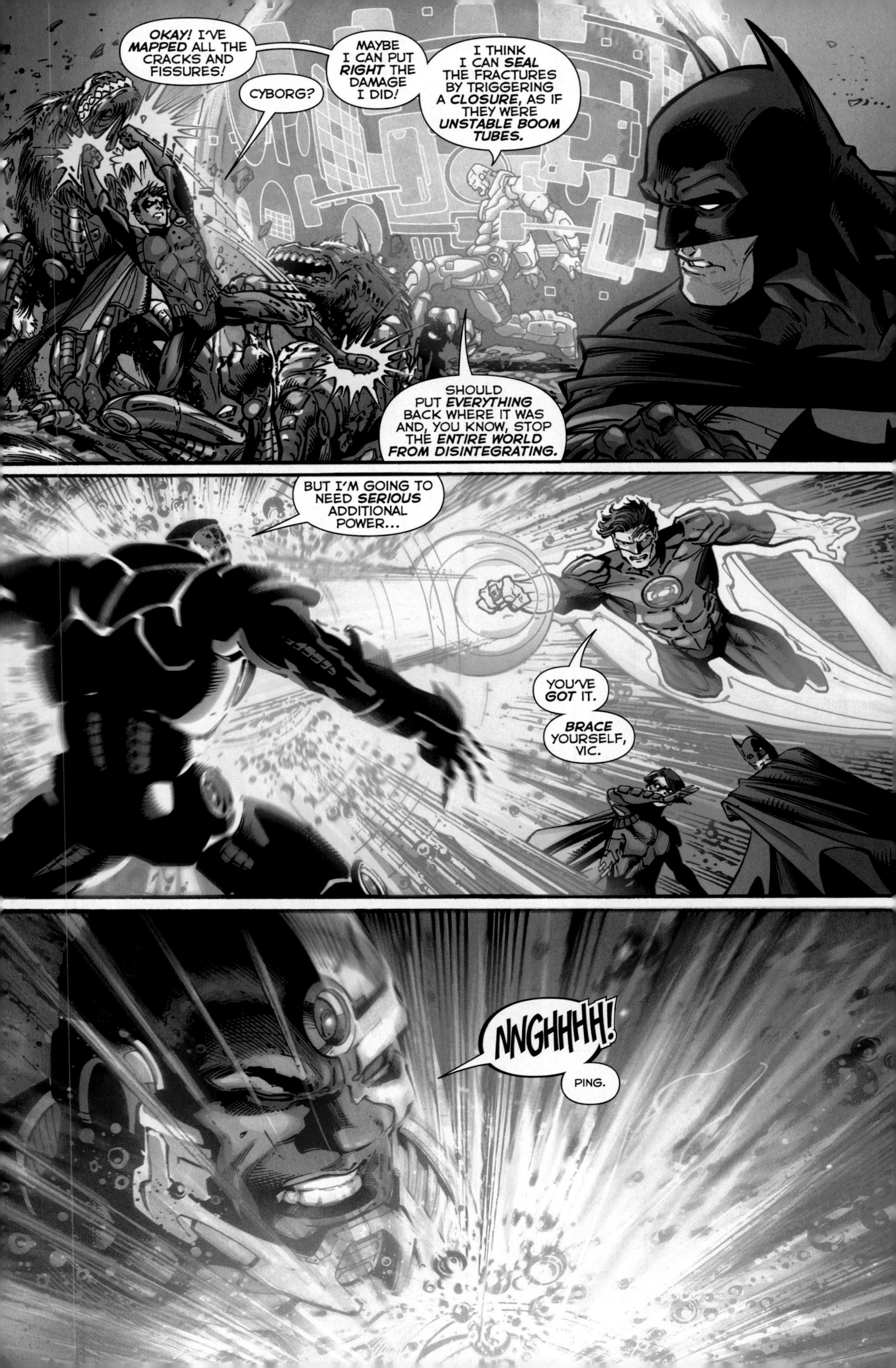
OKAY! I'VE MAPPED ALL THE CRACKS AND FISSURES!
CYBORG?
MAYBE I CAN PUT RIGHT THE DAMAGE I DID!
I THINK I CAN SEAL THE FRACTURES BY TRIGGERING A CLOSURE, AS IF THEY WERE UNSTABLE BOOM TUBES.
SHOULD PUT EVERYTHING BACK WHERE IT WAS AND, YOU KNOW, STOP THE ENTIRE WORLD FROM DISINTEGRATING.
BUT I'M GOING TO NEED SERIOUS ADDITIONAL POWER...
YOU'VE GOT IT.
BRACE YOURSELF, VIC.
NNGHHHH!
PING.

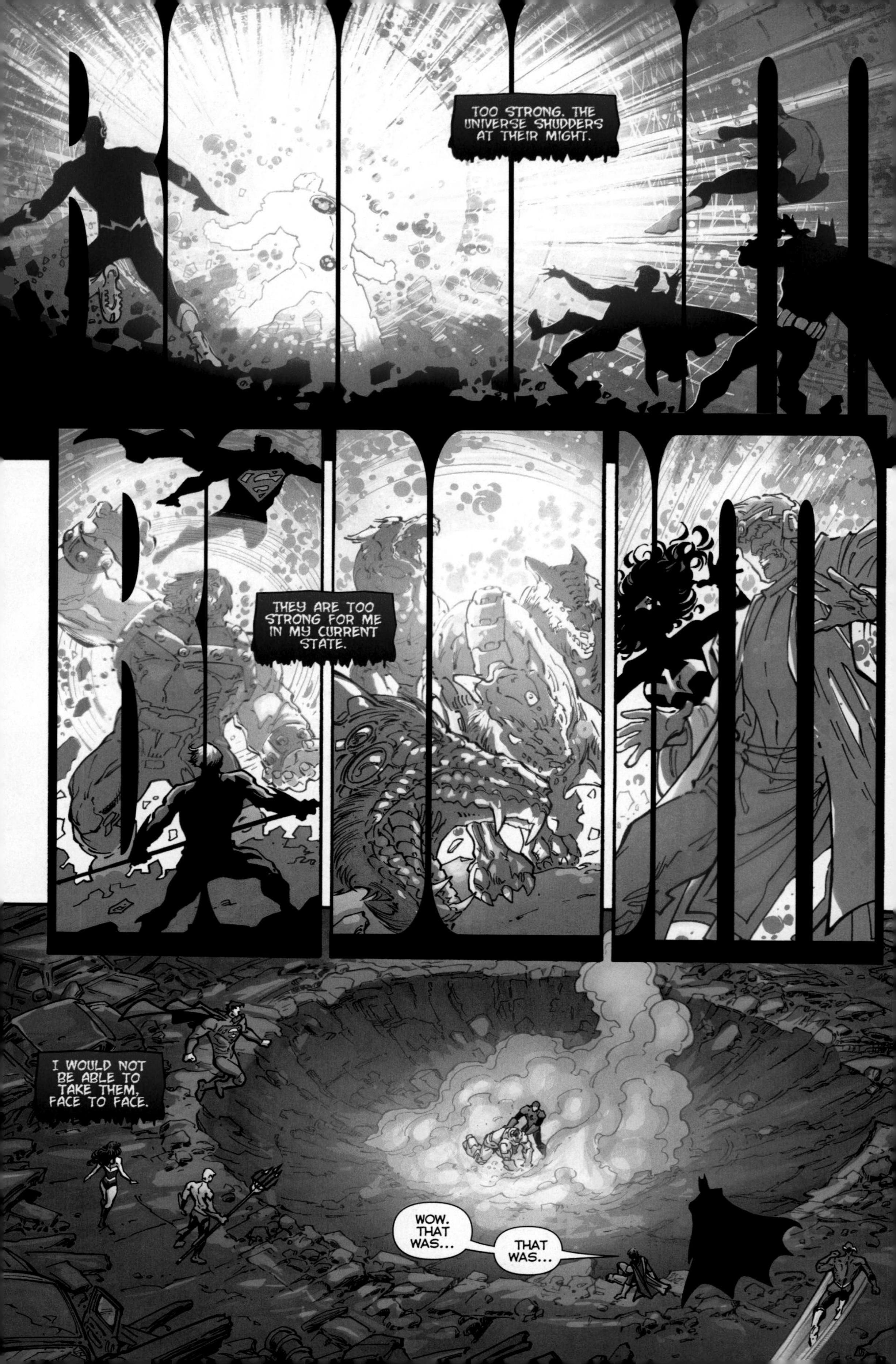
TOO STRONG. THE UNIVERSE SHUDDERS AT THEIR MIGHT.
THEY ARE TOO STRONG FOR ME IN MY CURRENT STATE.
I WOULD NOT BE ABLE TO TAKE THEM, FACE TO FACE.
WOW. THAT WAS...
THAT WAS...

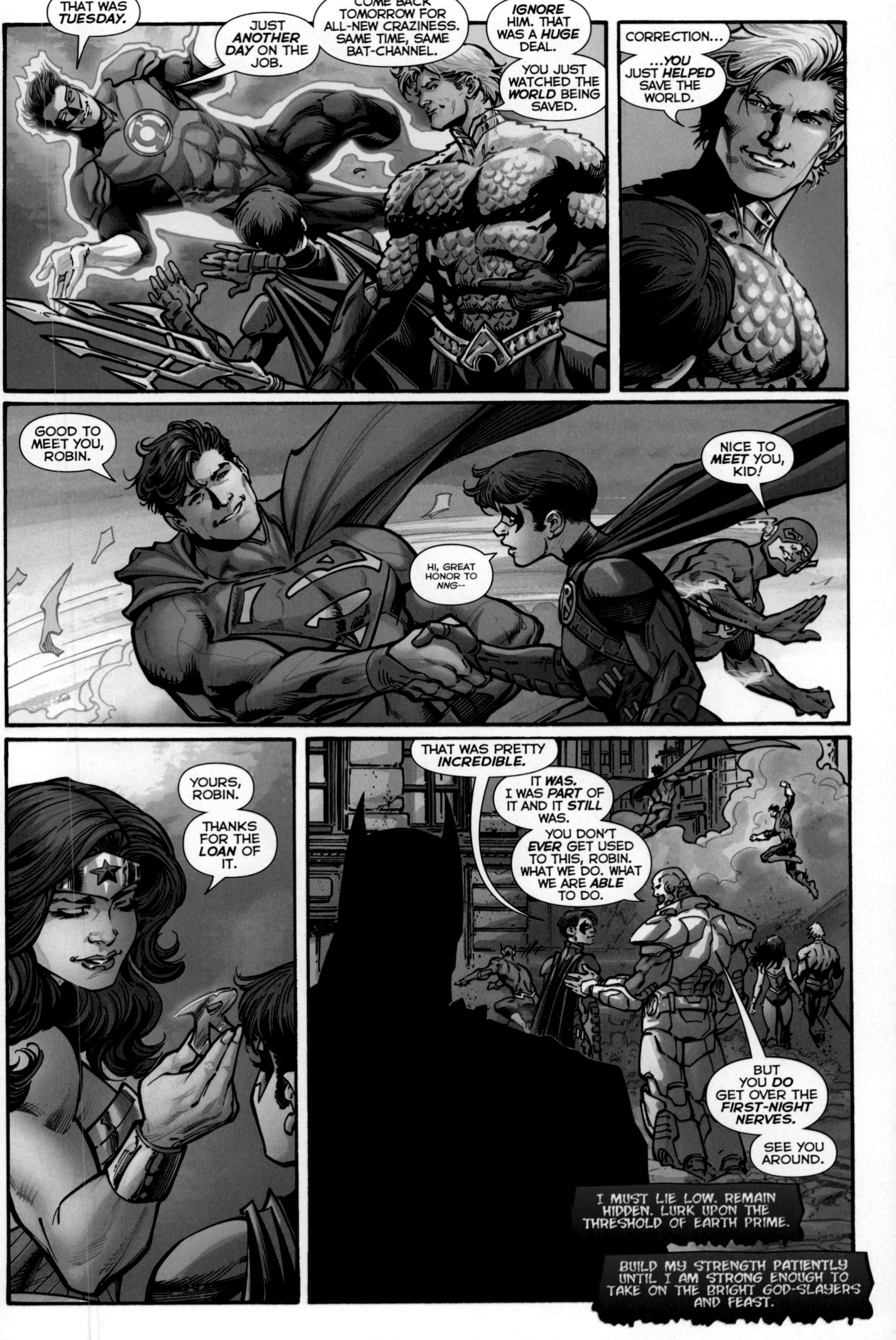

THAT WAS TUESDAY.
JUST ANOTHER DAY ON THE JOB.
COME BACK TOMORROW FOR ALL-NEW CRAZINESS. SAME TIME, SAME BAT-CHANNEL.
IGNORE HIM. THAT WAS A HUGE DEAL.
YOU JUST WATCHED THE WORLD BEING SAVED.
CORRECTION...
...YOU JUST HELPED SAVE THE WORLD.
GOOD TO MEET YOU, ROBIN.
HI, GREAT HONOR TO NNG--
NICE TO MEET YOU, KID!
YOURS, ROBIN.
THANKS FOR THE LOAN OF IT.
THAT WAS PRETTY INCREDIBLE.
IT WAS. I WAS PART OF IT AND IT STILL WAS.
YOU DON'T EVER GET USED TO THIS, ROBIN. WHAT WE DO. WHAT WE ARE ABLE TO DO.
BUT YOU DO GET OVER THE FIRST-NIGHT NERVES.
SEE YOU AROUND.
I MUST LIE LOW. REMAIN HIDDEN. LURK UPON THE THRESHOLD OF EARTH PRIME.
BUILD MY STRENGTH PATIENTLY UNTIL I AM STRONG ENOUGH TO TAKE ON THE BRIGHT GOD-SLAYERS AND FEAST.

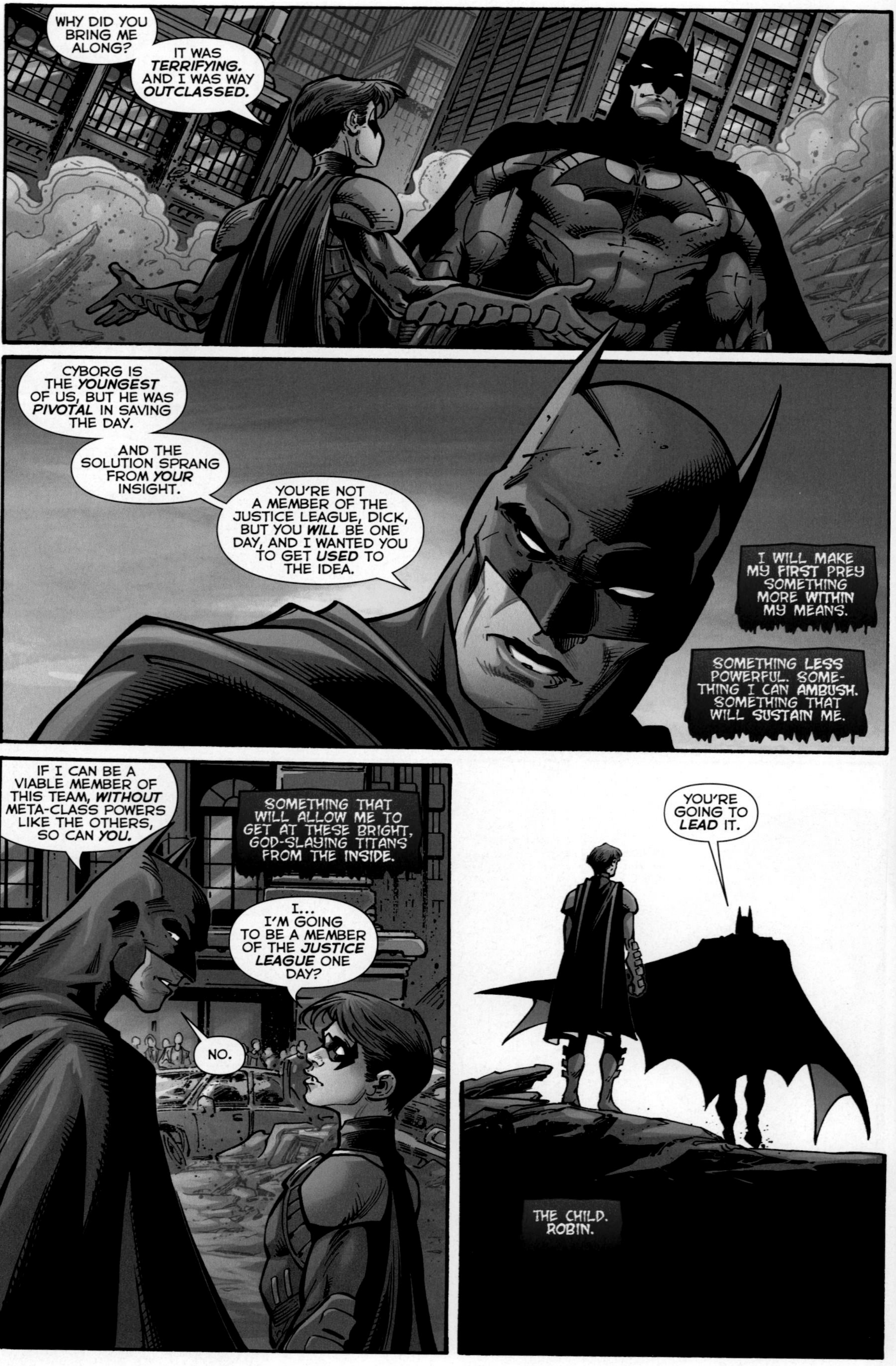
WHY DID YOU BRING ME ALONG?
IT WAS TERRIFYING. AND I WAS WAY OUTCLASSED.
CYBORG IS THE YOUNGEST OF US, BUT HE WAS PIVOTAL IN SAVING THE DAY.
AND THE SOLUTION SPRANG FROM YOUR INSIGHT.
YOU'RE NOT A MEMBER OF THE JUSTICE LEAGUE, DICK, BUT YOU WILL BE ONE DAY, AND I WANTED YOU TO GET USED TO THE IDEA.
I WILL MAKE MY FIRST PREY SOMETHING MORE WITHIN MY MEANS.
SOMETHING LESS POWERFUL. SOMETHING I CAN AMBUSH. SOMETHING THAT WILL SUSTAIN ME.
IF I CAN BE A VIABLE MEMBER OF THIS TEAM, WITHOUT META-CLASS POWERS LIKE THE OTHERS, SO CAN YOU.
SOMETHING THAT WILL ALLOW ME TO GET AT THESE BRIGHT, GOD-SLAYING TITANS FROM THE INSIDE.
I... I'M GOING TO BE A MEMBER OF THE JUSTICE LEAGUE ONE DAY?
NO.
YOU'RE GOING TO LEAD IT.
THE CHILD. ROBIN.

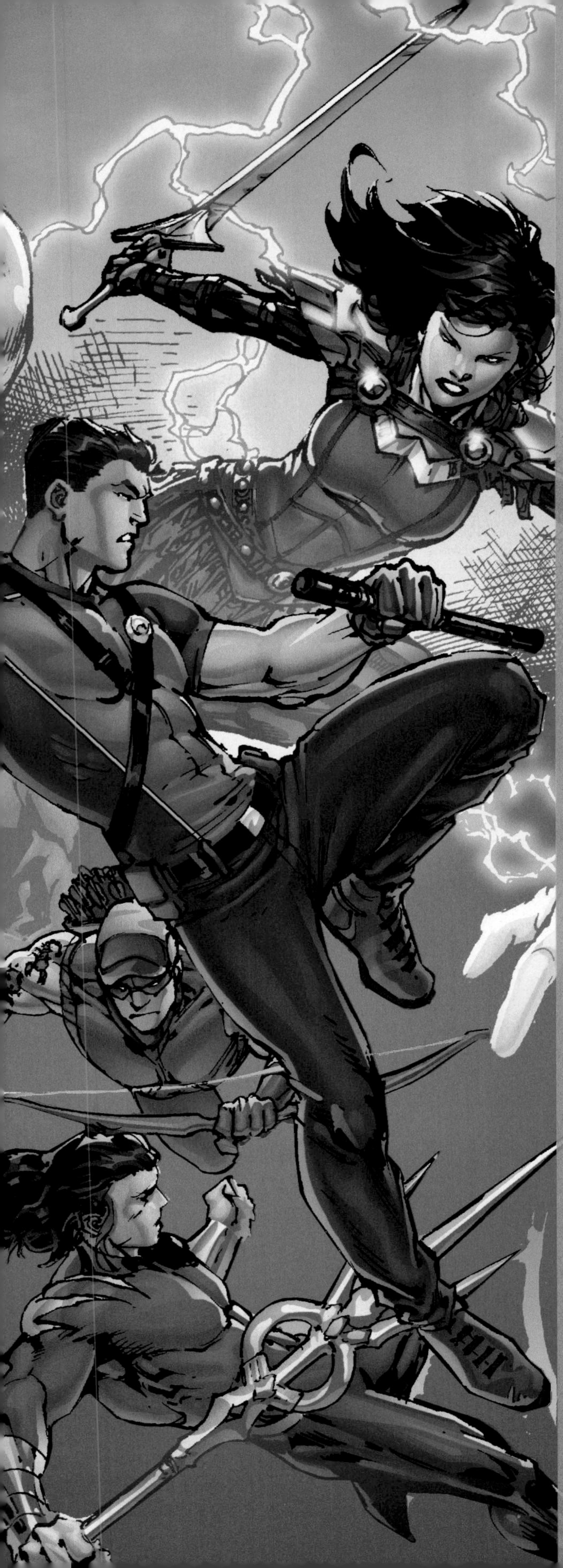

VARIANT COVER GALLERY

TITANS HUNT #1
VARIANT COVER BY
JIM LEE, SCOTT WILLIAMS
& ALEX SINCLAIR

TITANS HUNT #4
ADULT COLORING BOOK
VARIANT COVER
BY SCOTT McDANIEL

TITANS HUNT #5
VARIANT COVER BY
NEAL ADAMS, BUZZ & HI-FI

TITANS HUNT #7
VARIANT COVER BY
JOHN ROMITA JR.,
SCOTT HANNA & DAVE McCAIG

**DC COMICS PRESENTS:
TITANS HUNT 100-PAGE
SUPER SPECTACULAR**
VARIANT COVER BY RYAN SOOK

TITANS REBIRTH #1
VARIANT COVER BY MIKE CHOI

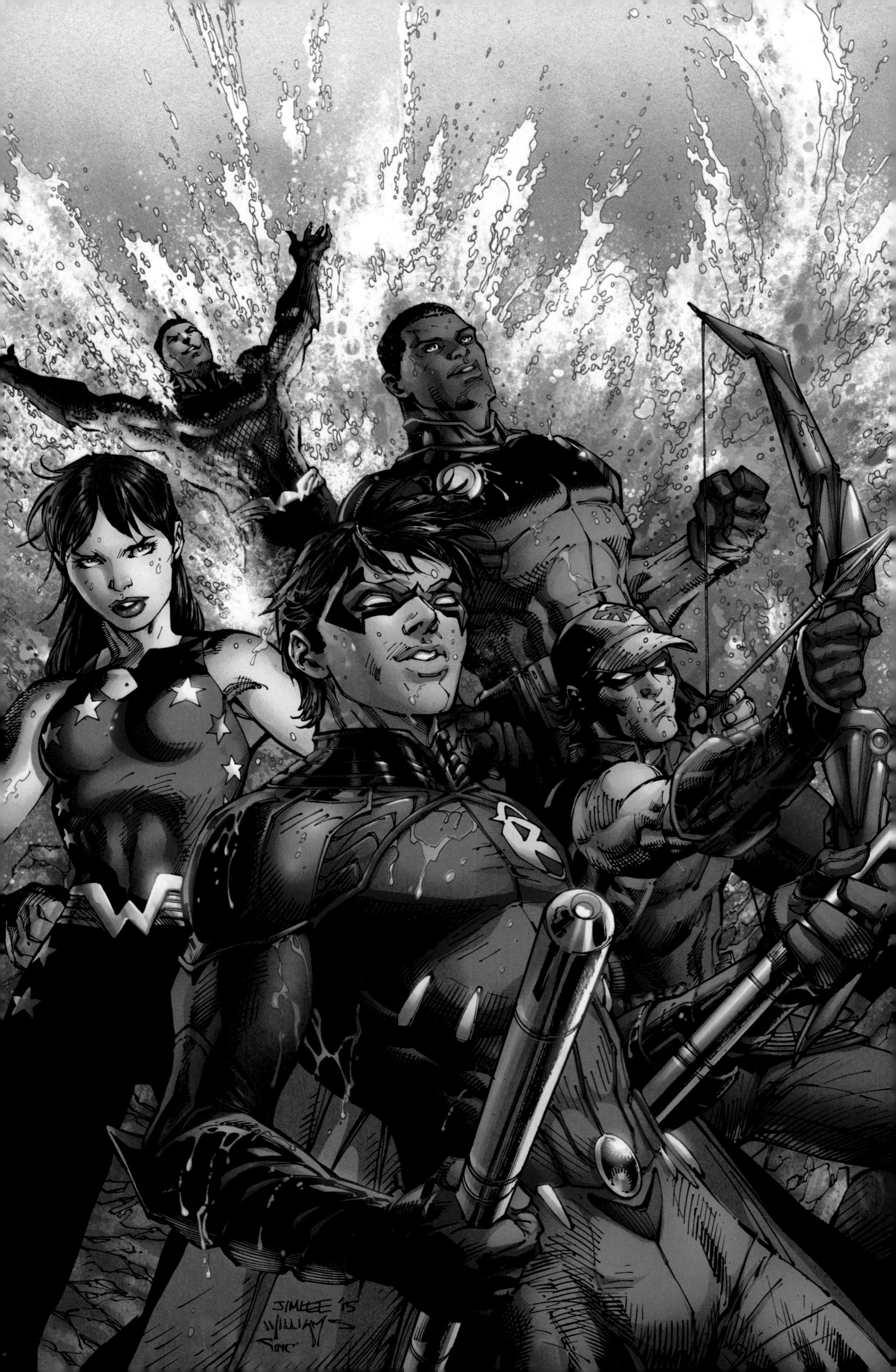
JIM LEE '15
WILLIAMS
SINC

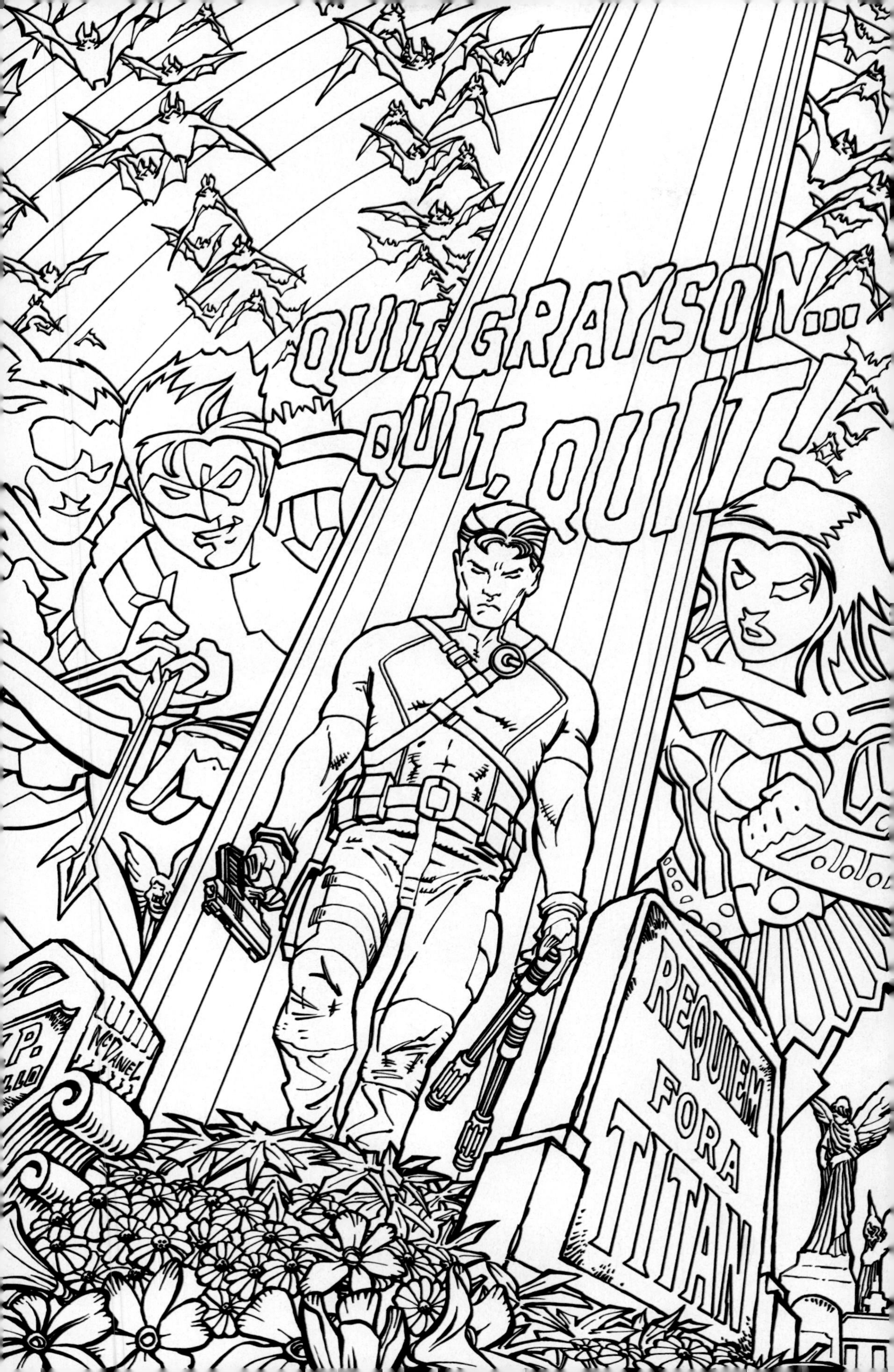
QUIT, GRAYSON...
QUIT, QUIT!
REQUIEM FOR A TITAN
McDANIEL

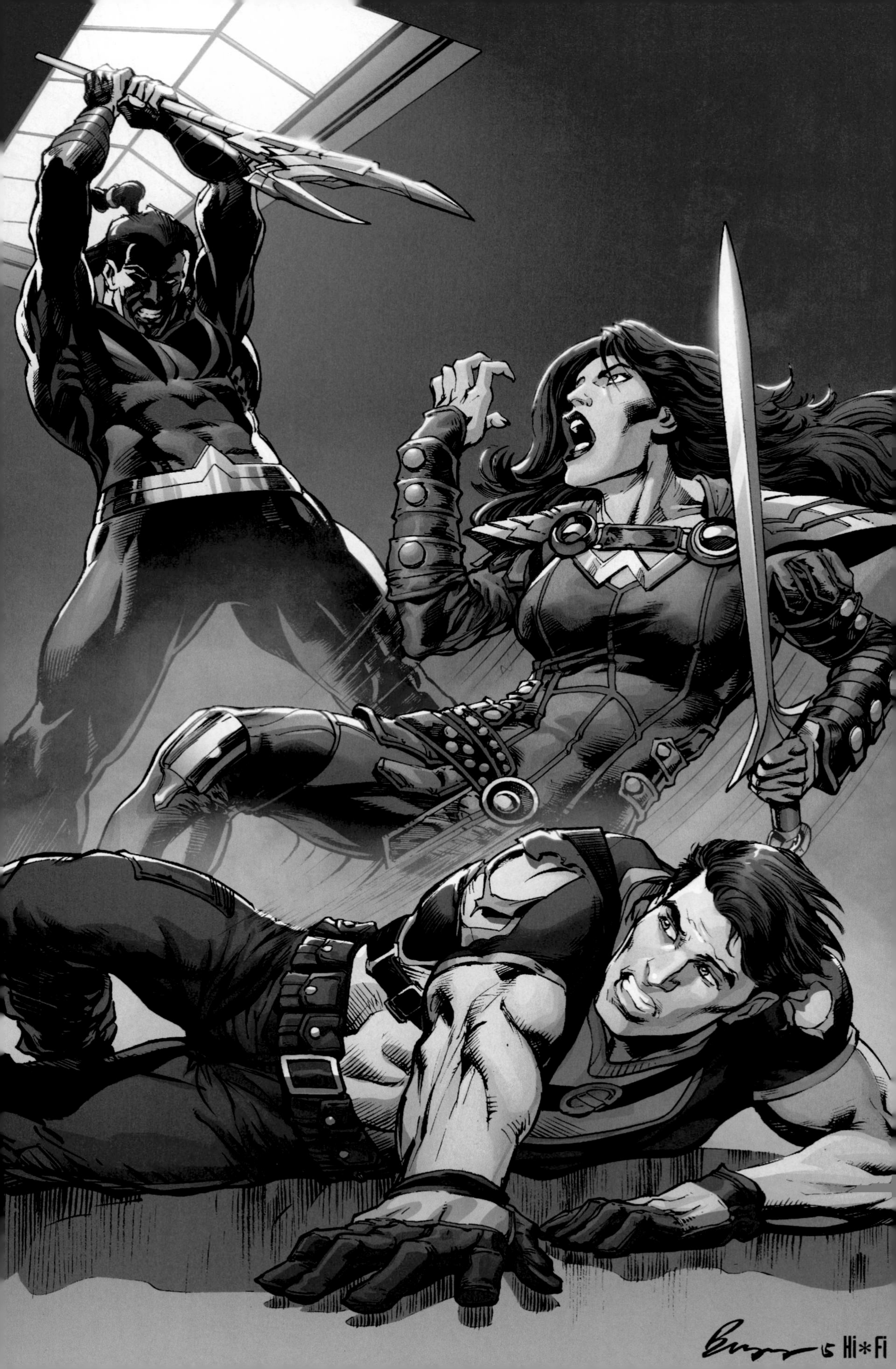
'15 Hi*Fi

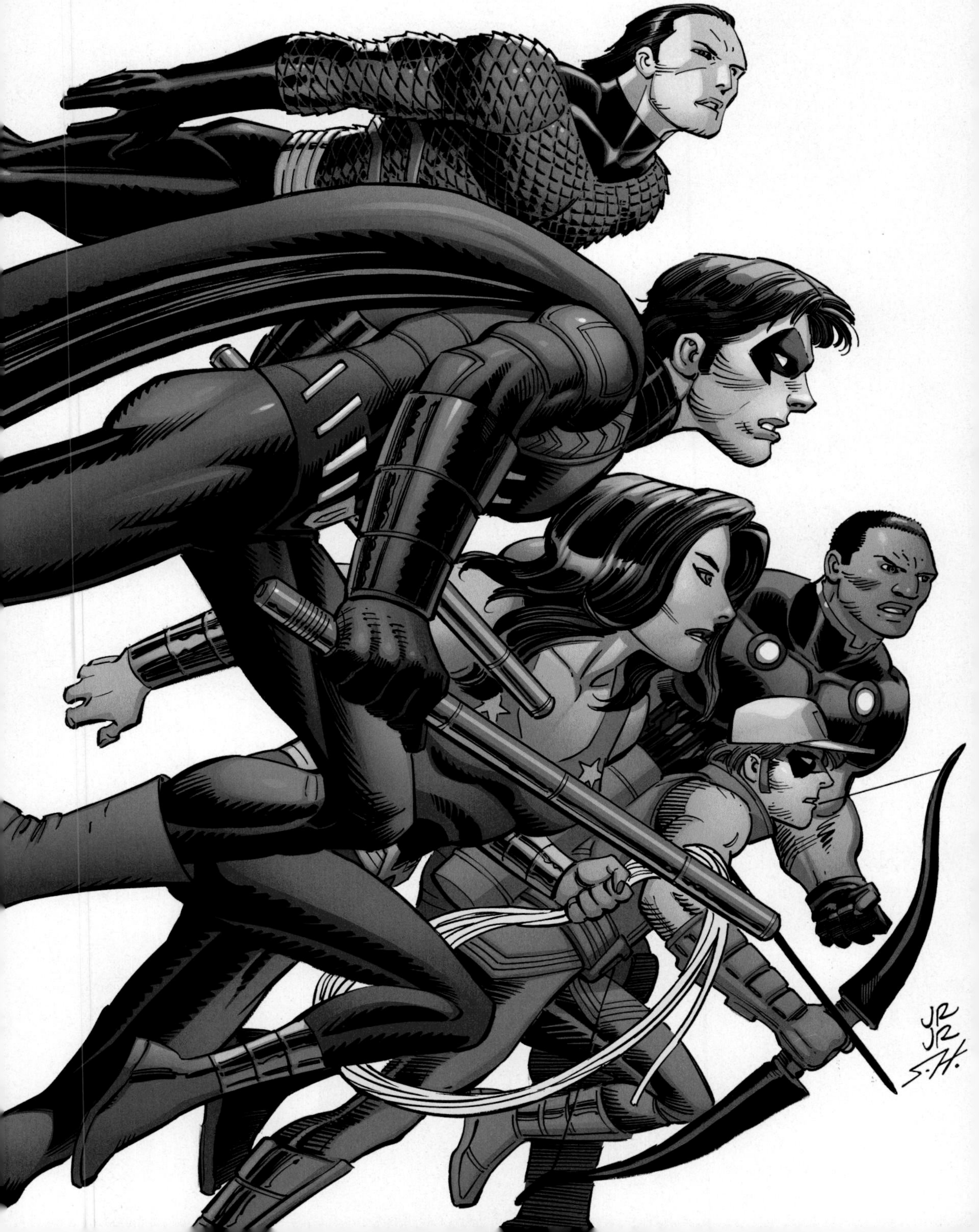

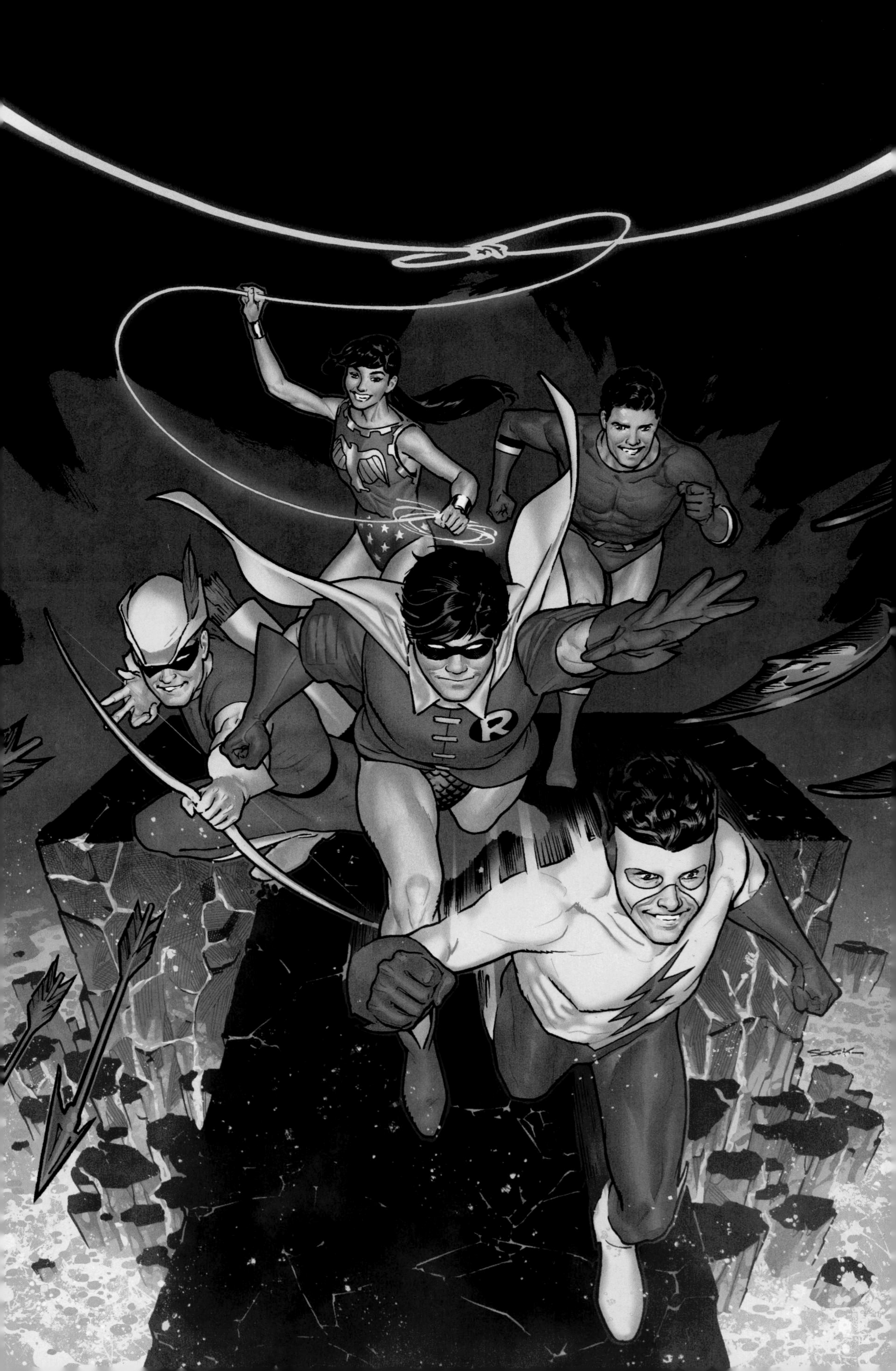

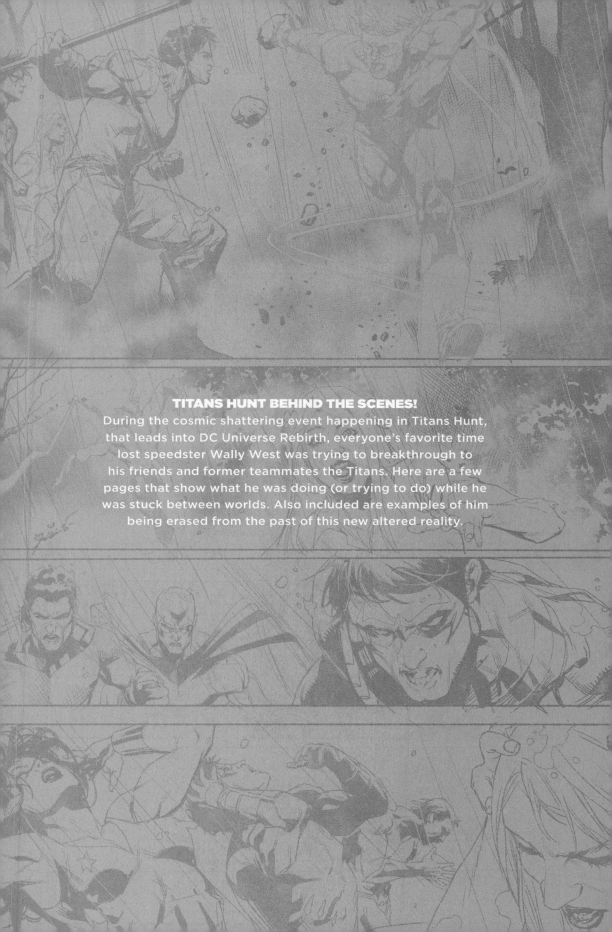

TITANS HUNT BEHIND THE SCENES!

During the cosmic shattering event happening in Titans Hunt, that leads into DC Universe Rebirth, everyone's favorite time lost speedster Wally West was trying to breakthrough to his friends and former teammates the Titans. Here are a few pages that show what he was doing (or trying to do) while he was stuck between worlds. Also included are examples of him being erased from the past of this new altered reality.

Titans Hunt 4 1

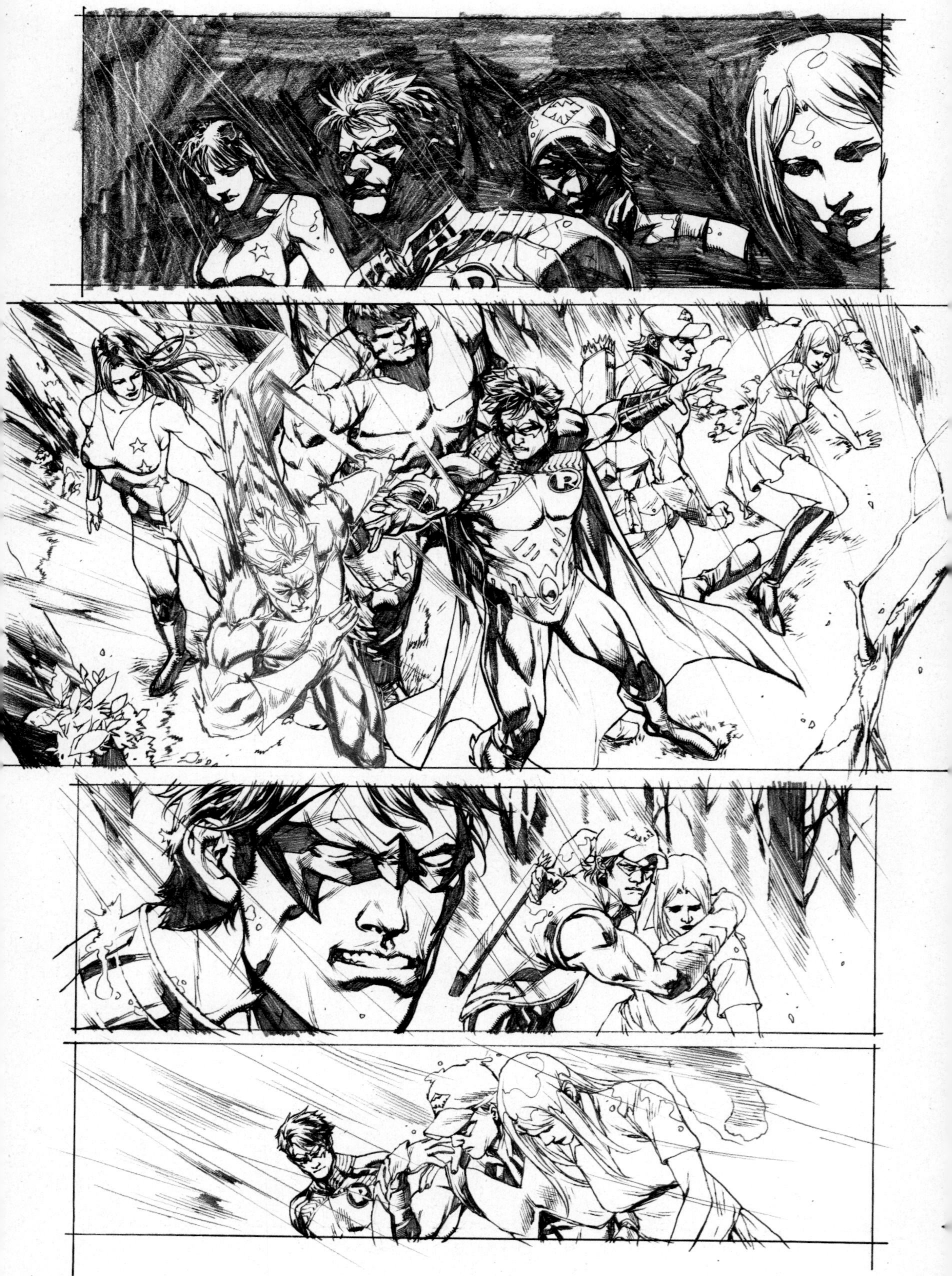

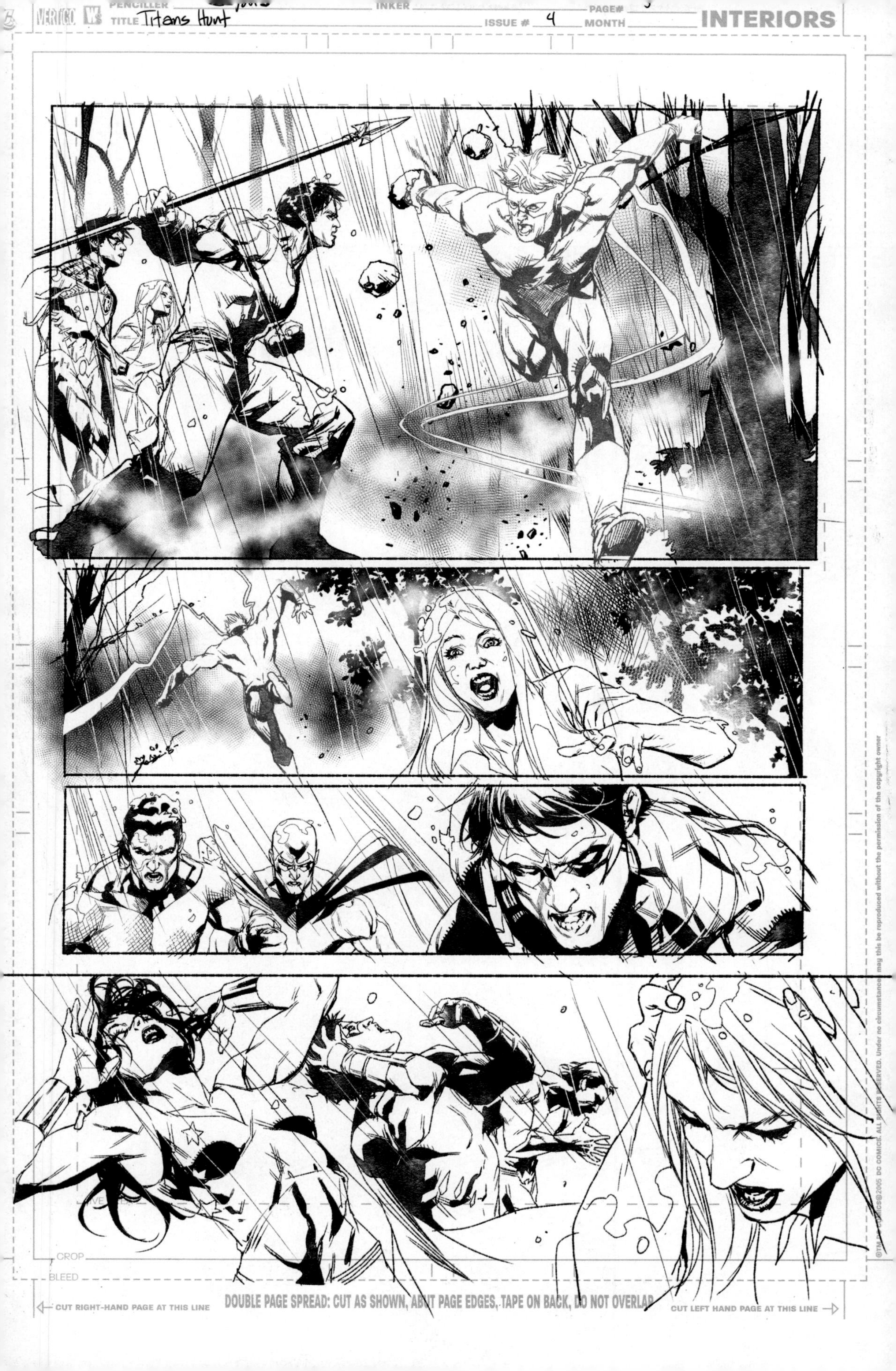
PENCILLER
INKER
PAGE#
TITLE Titans Hunt
ISSUE # 4
MONTH
INTERIORS
CROP
BLEED
CUT RIGHT-HAND PAGE AT THIS LINE
DOUBLE PAGE SPREAD: CUT AS SHOWN, ABUT PAGE EDGES, TAPE ON BACK, DO NOT OVERLAP
CUT LEFT HAND PAGE AT THIS LINE
©TM DC COMICS ©2005 DC COMICS. ALL RIGHTS RESERVED. Under no circumstances may this be reproduced without the permission of the copyright owner

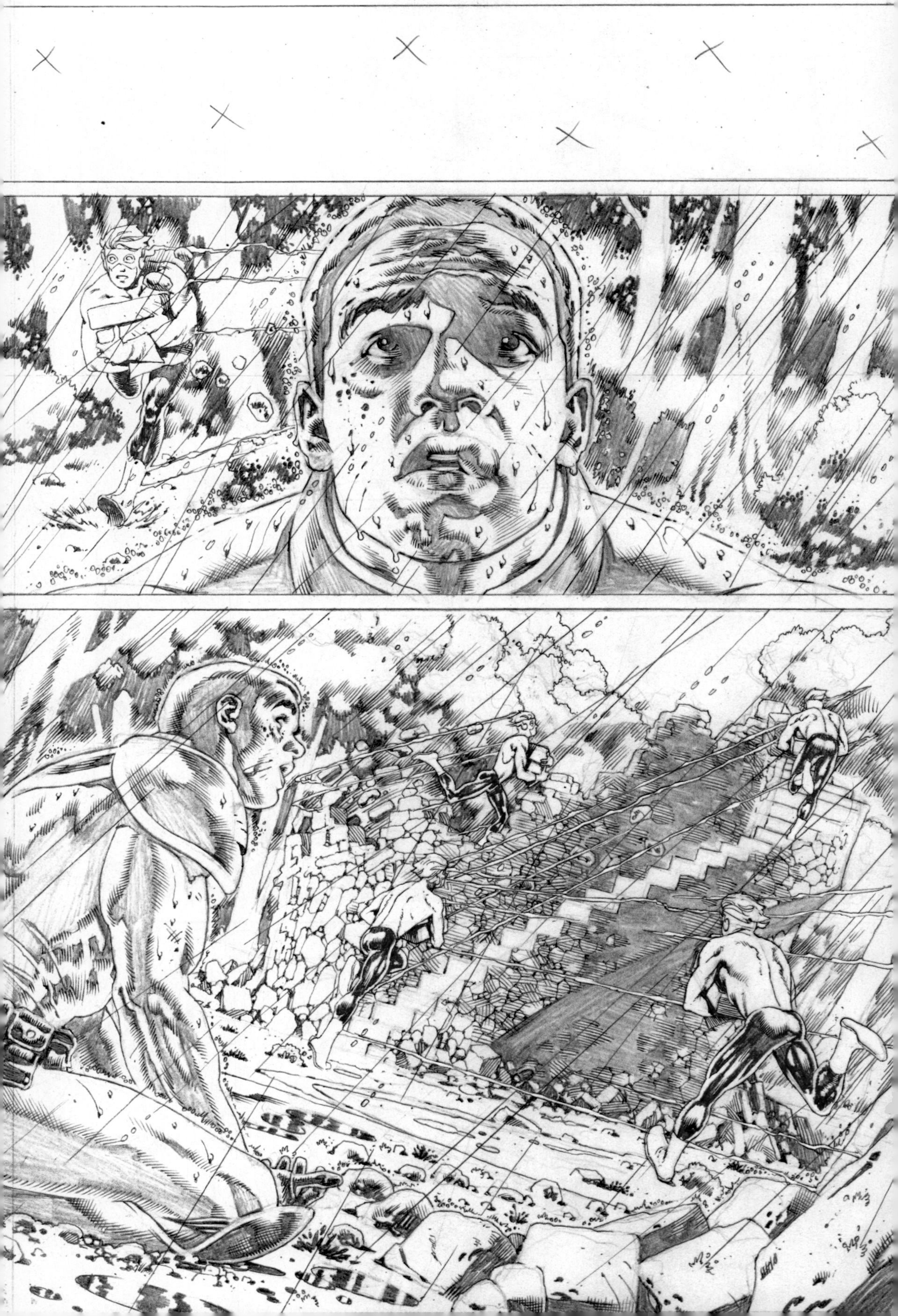

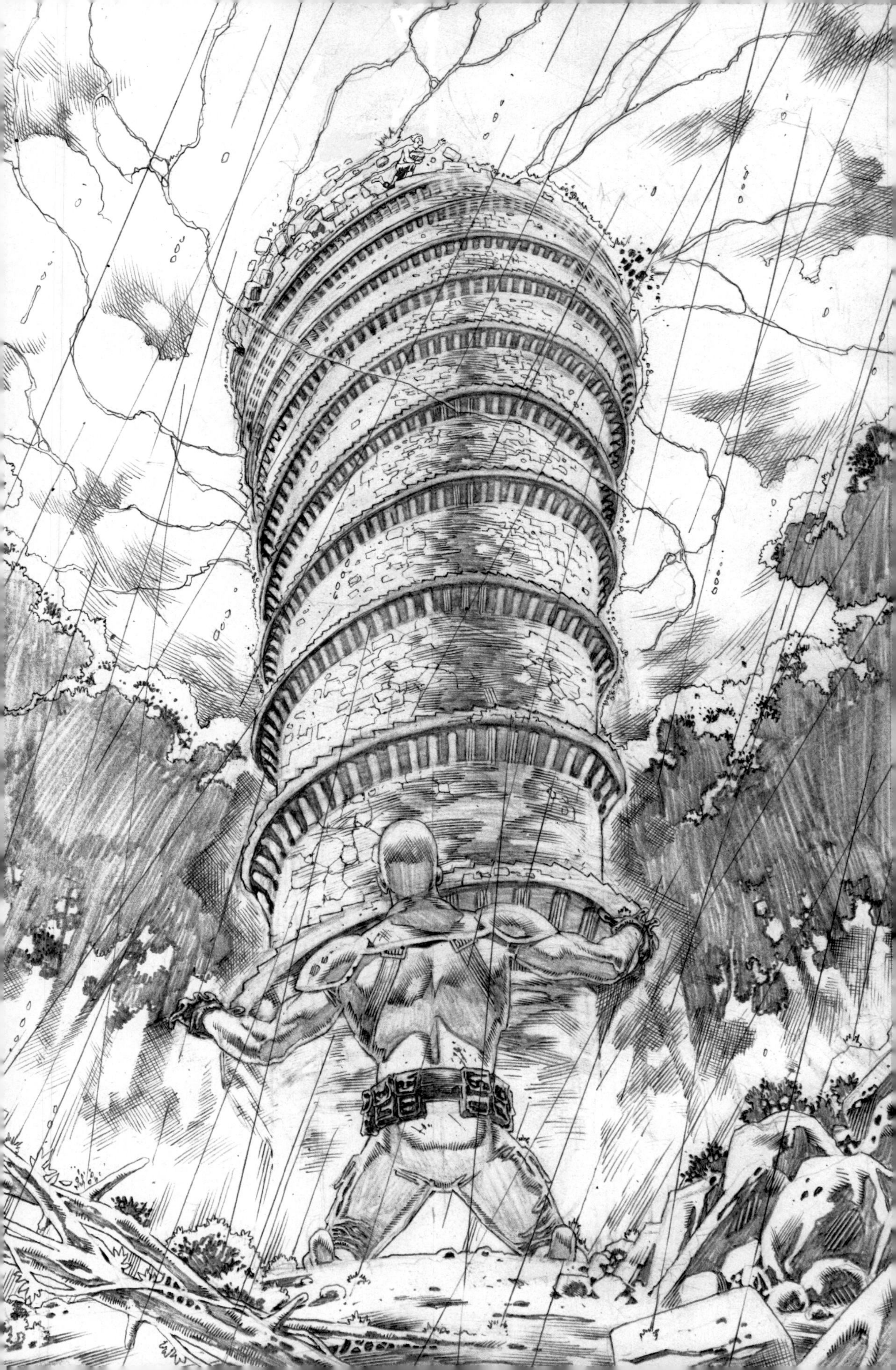

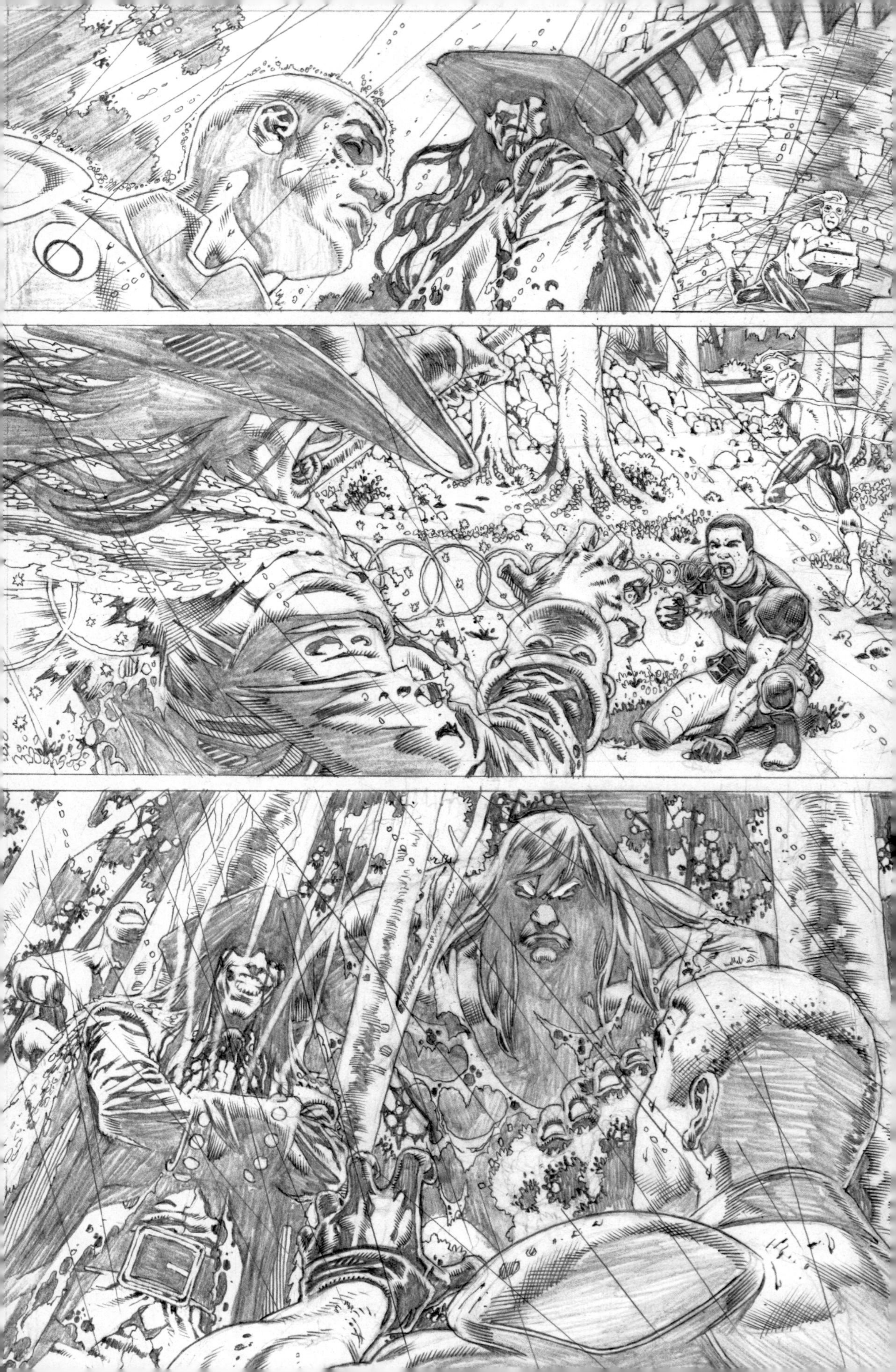

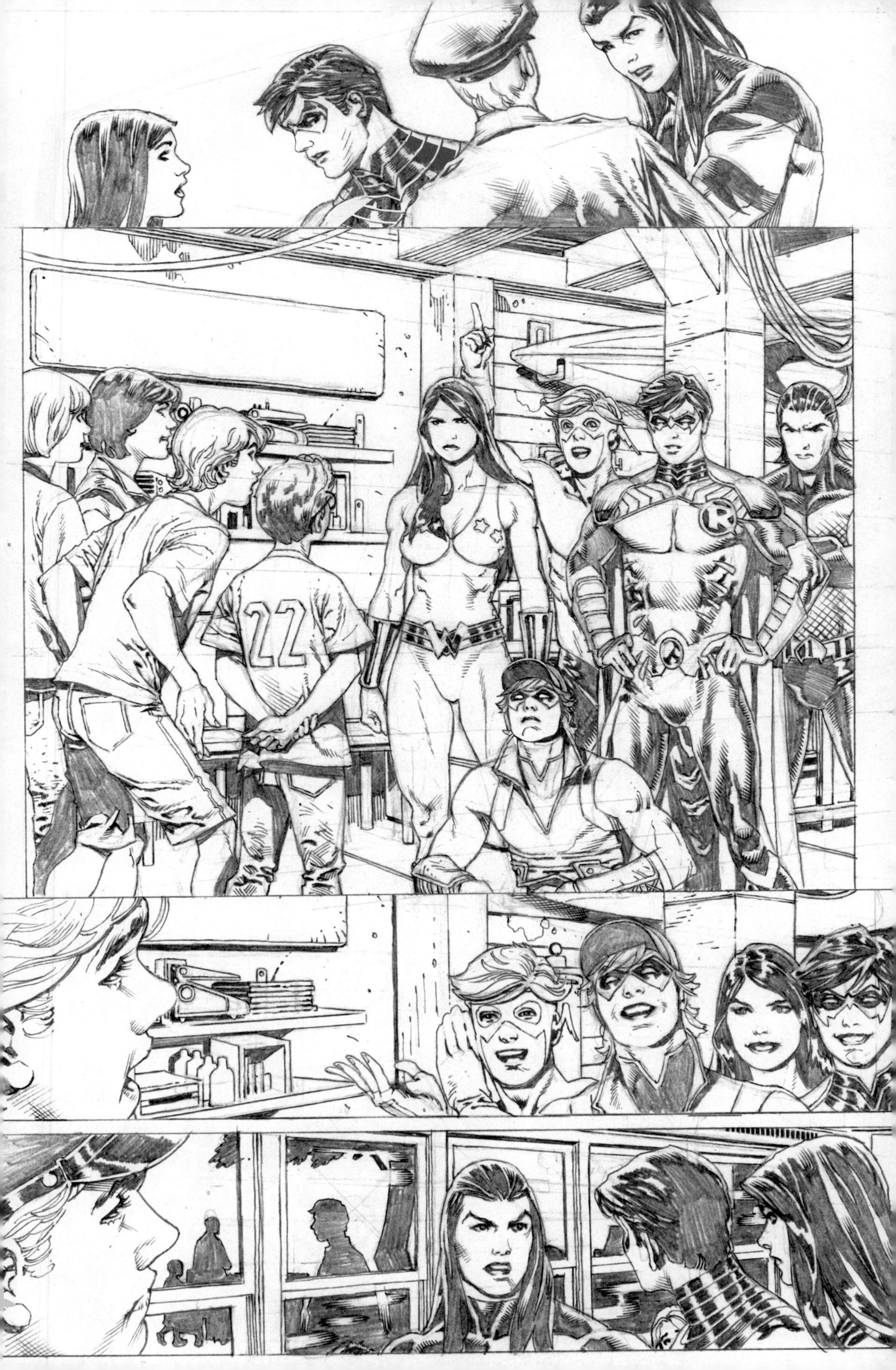
22

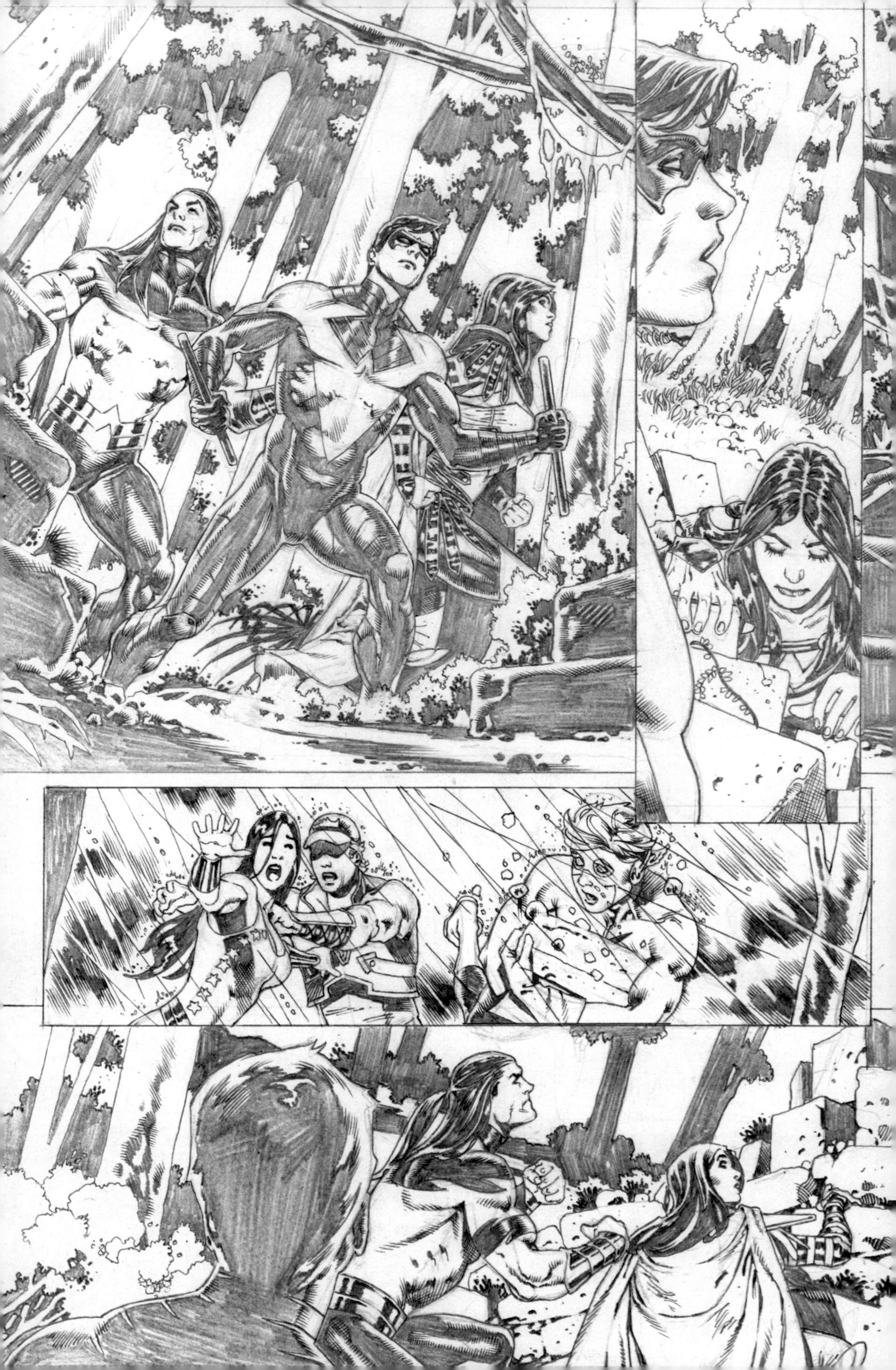

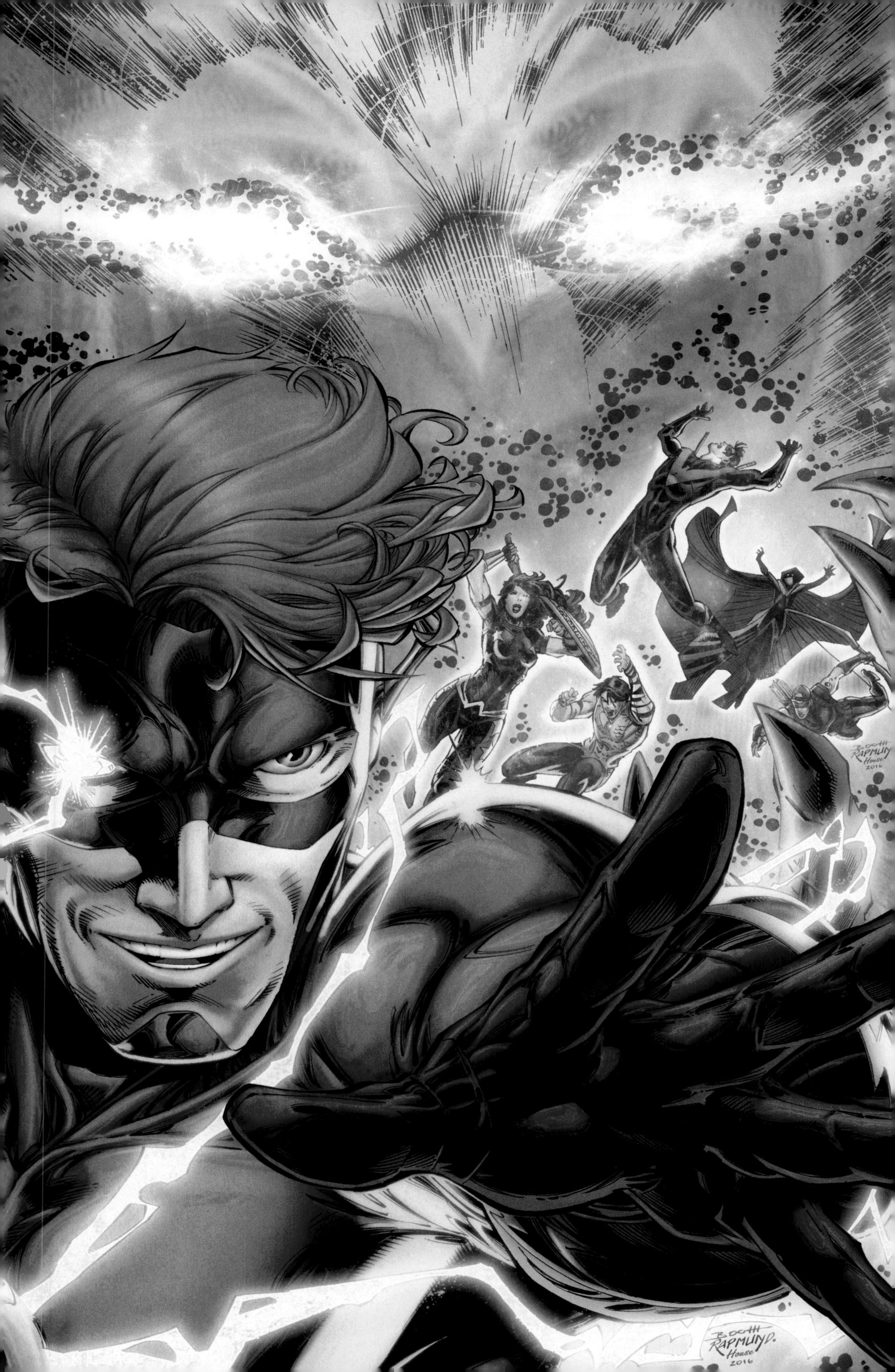
BOOTH
RAPMUND.
House
2016

The future (and past) of the DC Universe
starts with DC UNIVERSE: REBIRTH!

Explore the changing world of the Titans in this special bonus preview of **TITANS: REBIRTH #1!**

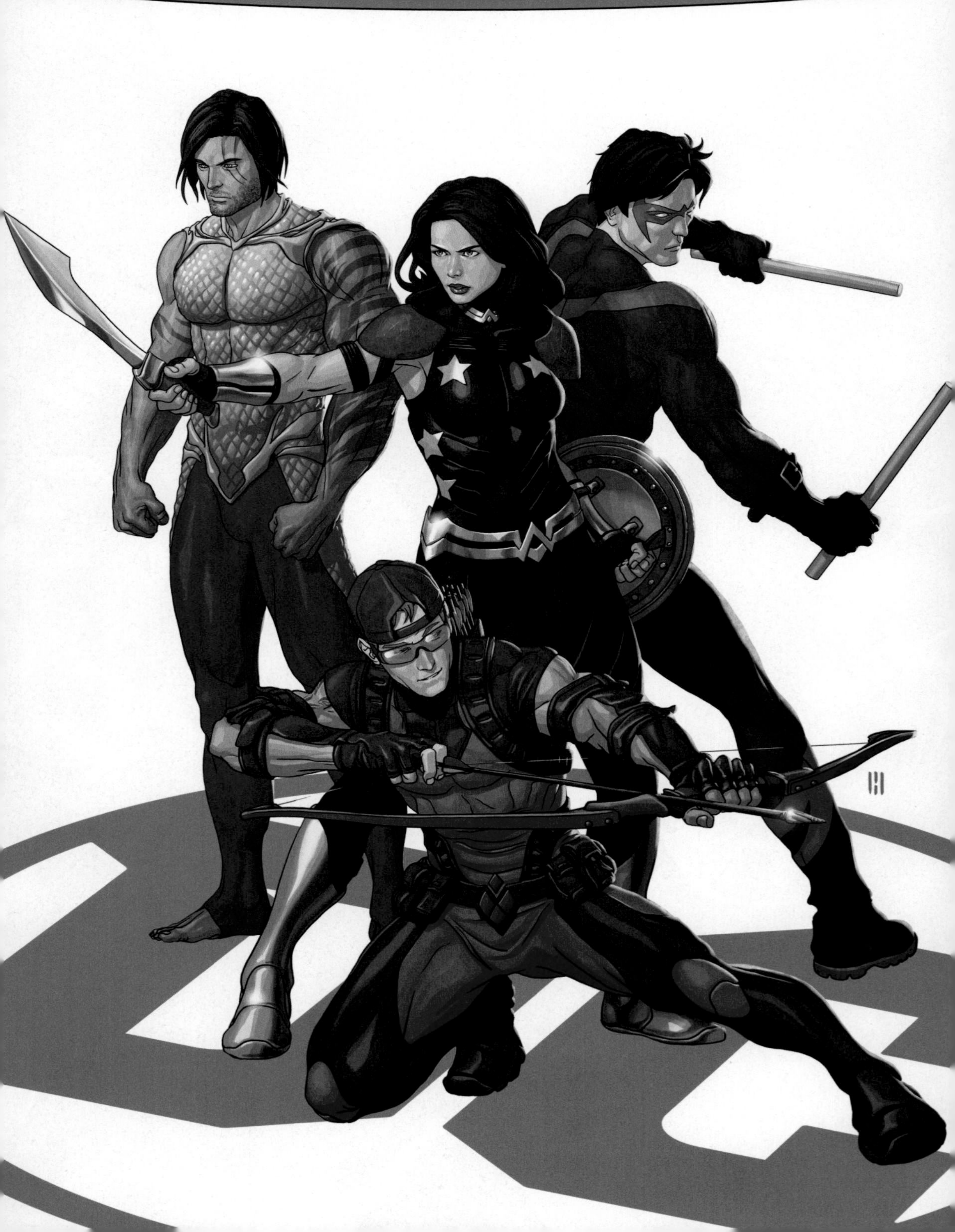

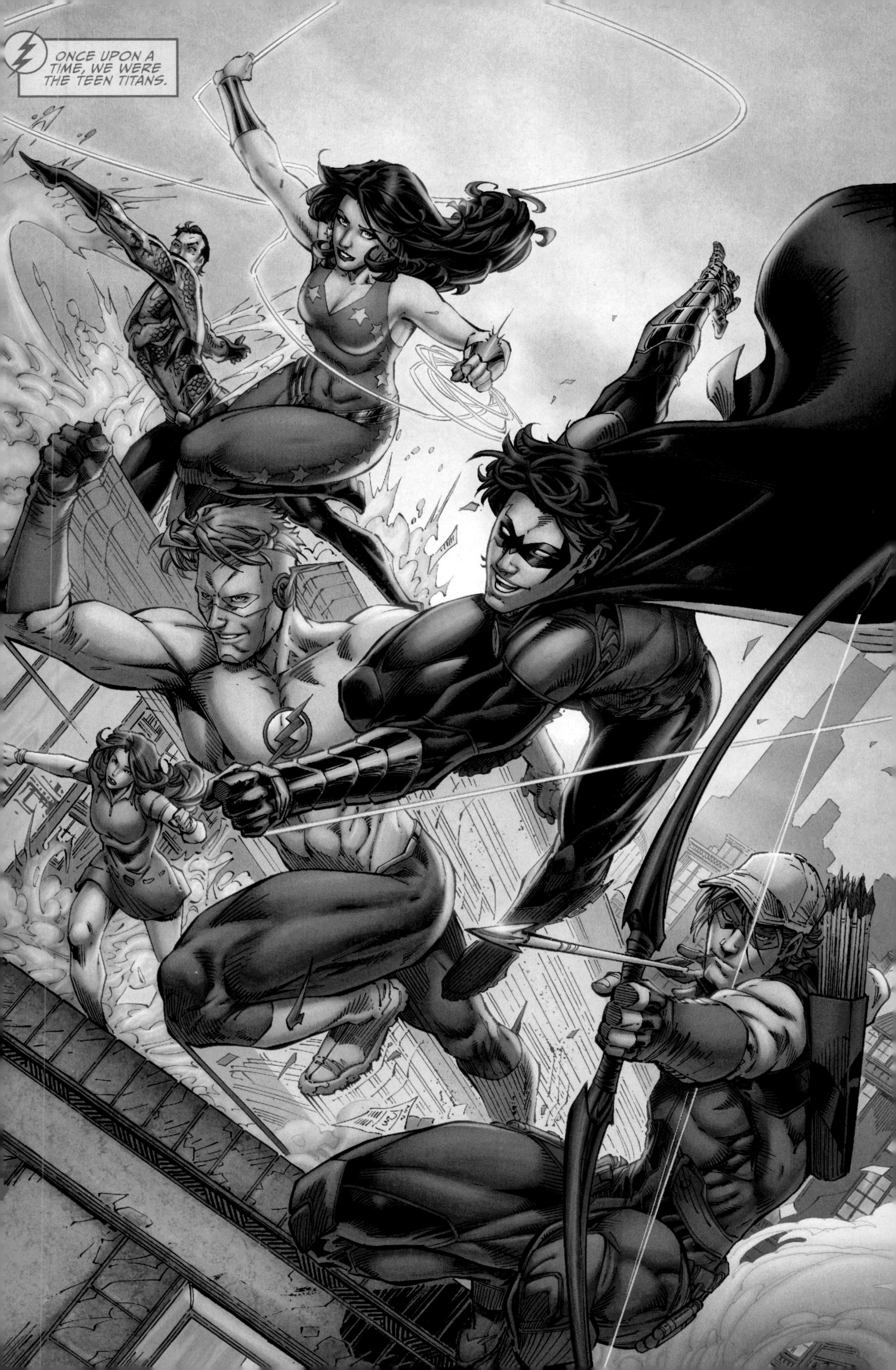
ONCE UPON A TIME, WE WERE THE TEEN TITANS.

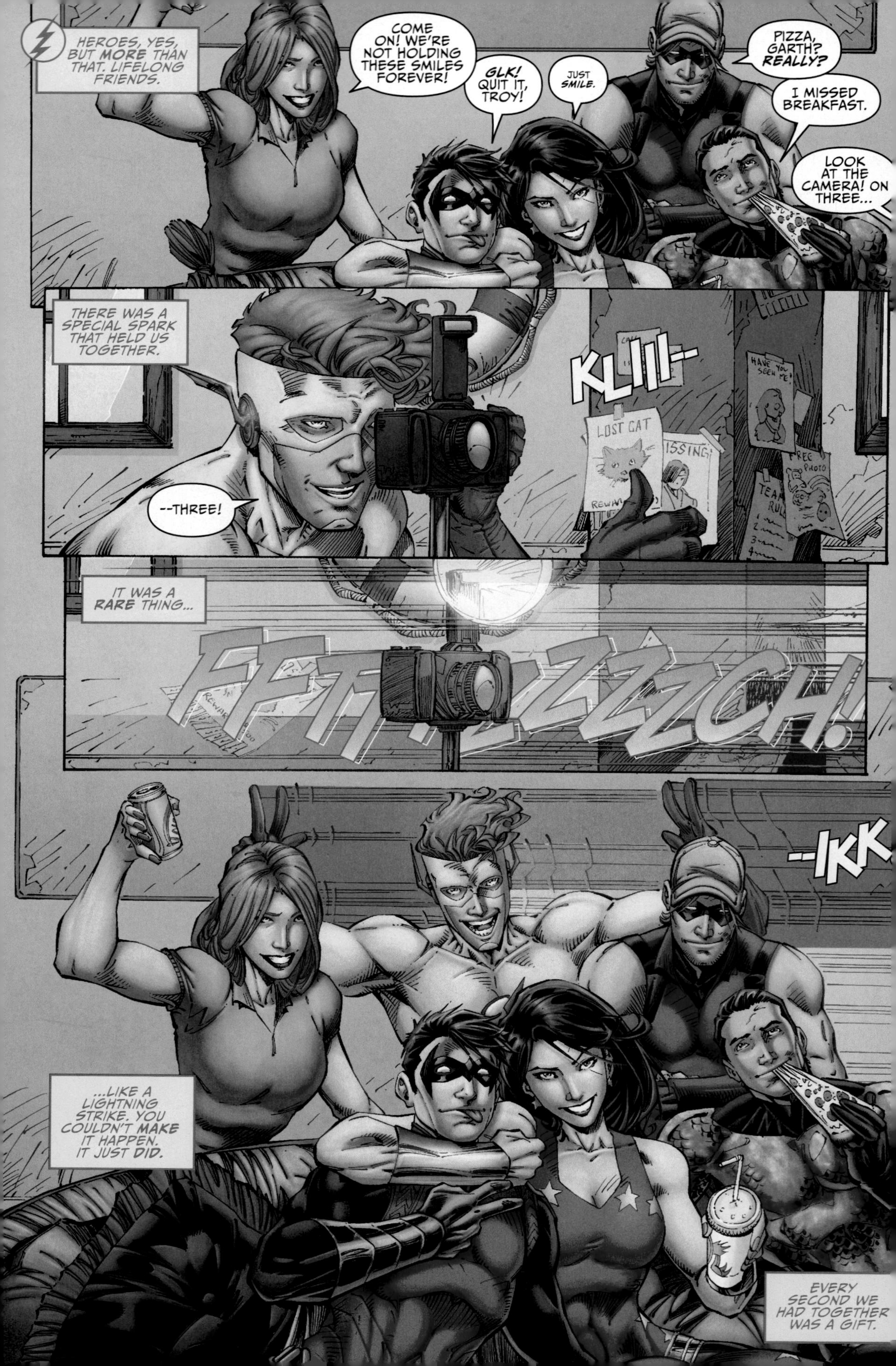
HEROES, YES, BUT **MORE** THAN THAT. LIFELONG FRIENDS.
COME ON! WE'RE NOT HOLDING THESE SMILES FOREVER!
GLK! QUIT IT, TROY!
JUST **SMILE.**
PIZZA, GARTH? **REALLY?**
I MISSED BREAKFAST.
LOOK AT THE CAMERA! ON THREE...
THERE WAS A SPECIAL SPARK THAT HELD US TOGETHER.
KLIII--
--THREE!
LOST CAT
HAVE YOU SEEN ME?
IT WAS A **RARE** THING...
FFTZZZZCH!
--IKK
...LIKE A LIGHTNING STRIKE. YOU COULDN'T **MAKE** IT HAPPEN. IT JUST **DID.**
EVERY SECOND WE HAD TOGETHER WAS A GIFT.

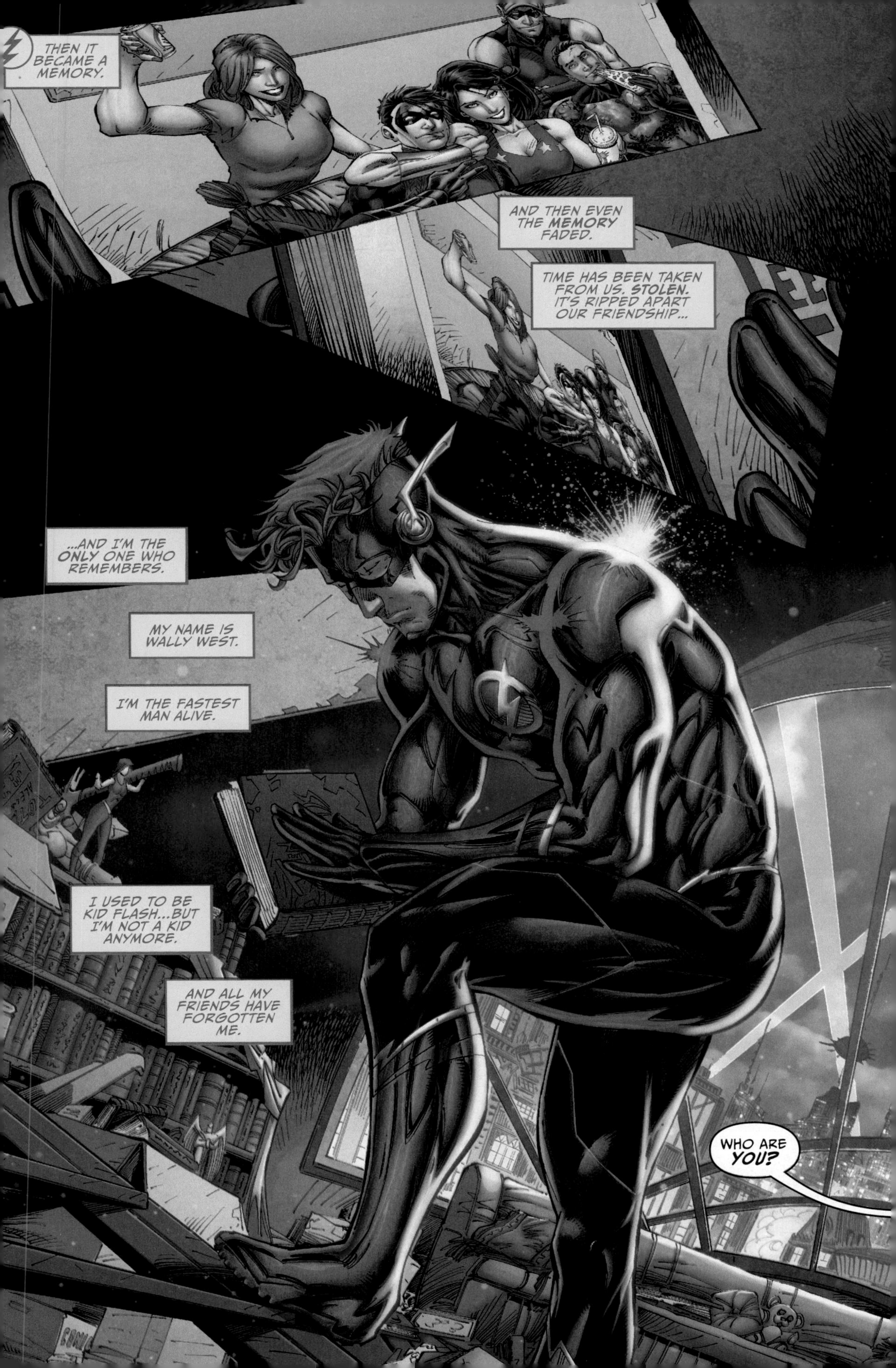
THEN IT BECAME A MEMORY.
AND THEN EVEN THE MEMORY FADED.
TIME HAS BEEN TAKEN FROM US. STOLEN. IT'S RIPPED APART OUR FRIENDSHIP...
...AND I'M THE ONLY ONE WHO REMEMBERS.
MY NAME IS WALLY WEST.
I'M THE FASTEST MAN ALIVE.
I USED TO BE KID FLASH...BUT I'M NOT A KID ANYMORE.
AND ALL MY FRIENDS HAVE FORGOTTEN ME.
WHO ARE YOU?

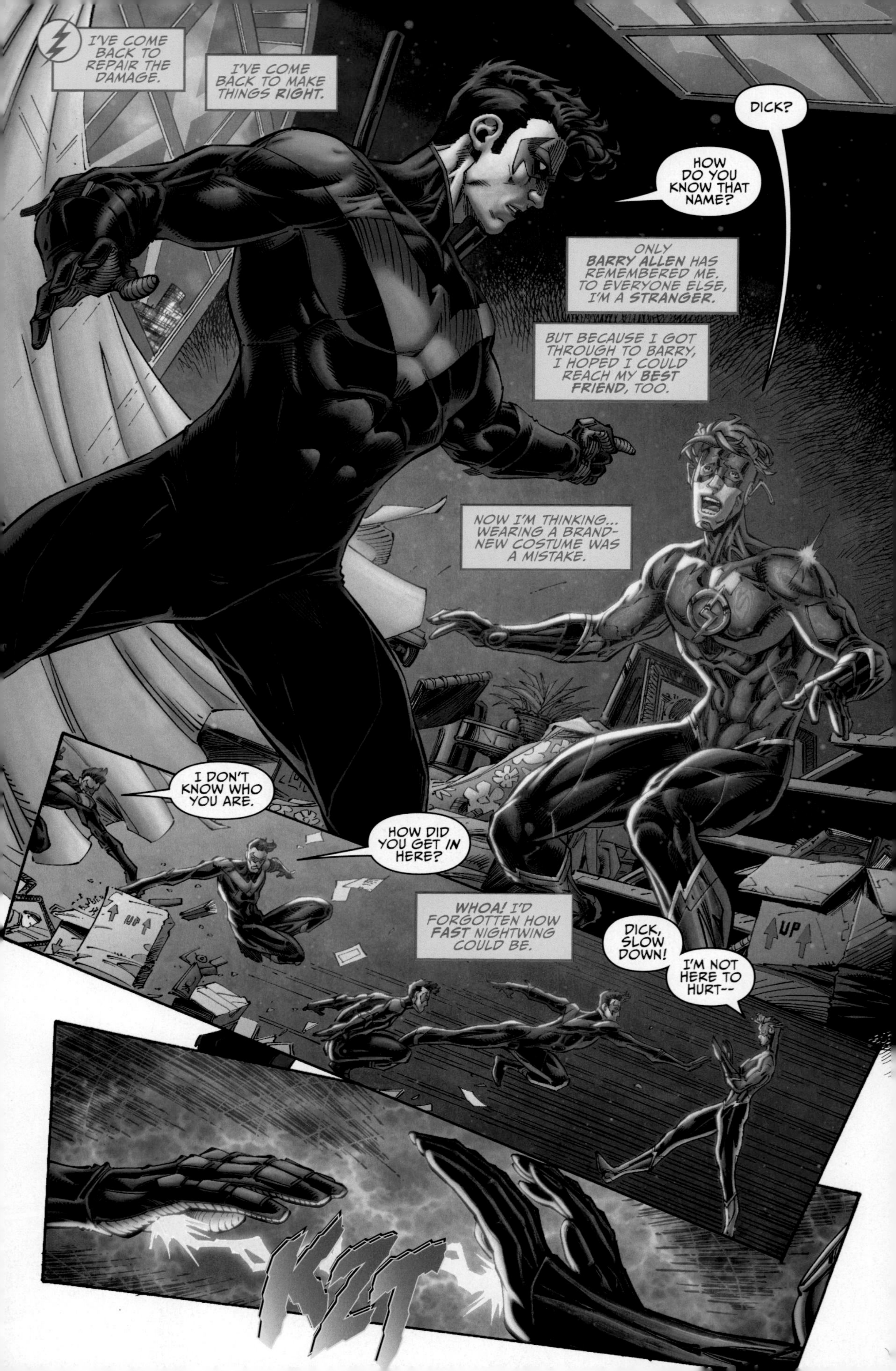
I'VE COME BACK TO REPAIR THE DAMAGE.
I'VE COME BACK TO MAKE THINGS RIGHT.
DICK?
HOW DO YOU KNOW THAT NAME?
ONLY BARRY ALLEN HAS REMEMBERED ME. TO EVERYONE ELSE, I'M A STRANGER.
BUT BECAUSE I GOT THROUGH TO BARRY, I HOPED I COULD REACH MY BEST FRIEND, TOO.
NOW I'M THINKING... WEARING A BRAND-NEW COSTUME WAS A MISTAKE.
I DON'T KNOW WHO YOU ARE.
HOW DID YOU GET IN HERE?
WHOA! I'D FORGOTTEN HOW FAST NIGHTWING COULD BE.
DICK, SLOW DOWN!
I'M NOT HERE TO HURT--
UP
KZZT

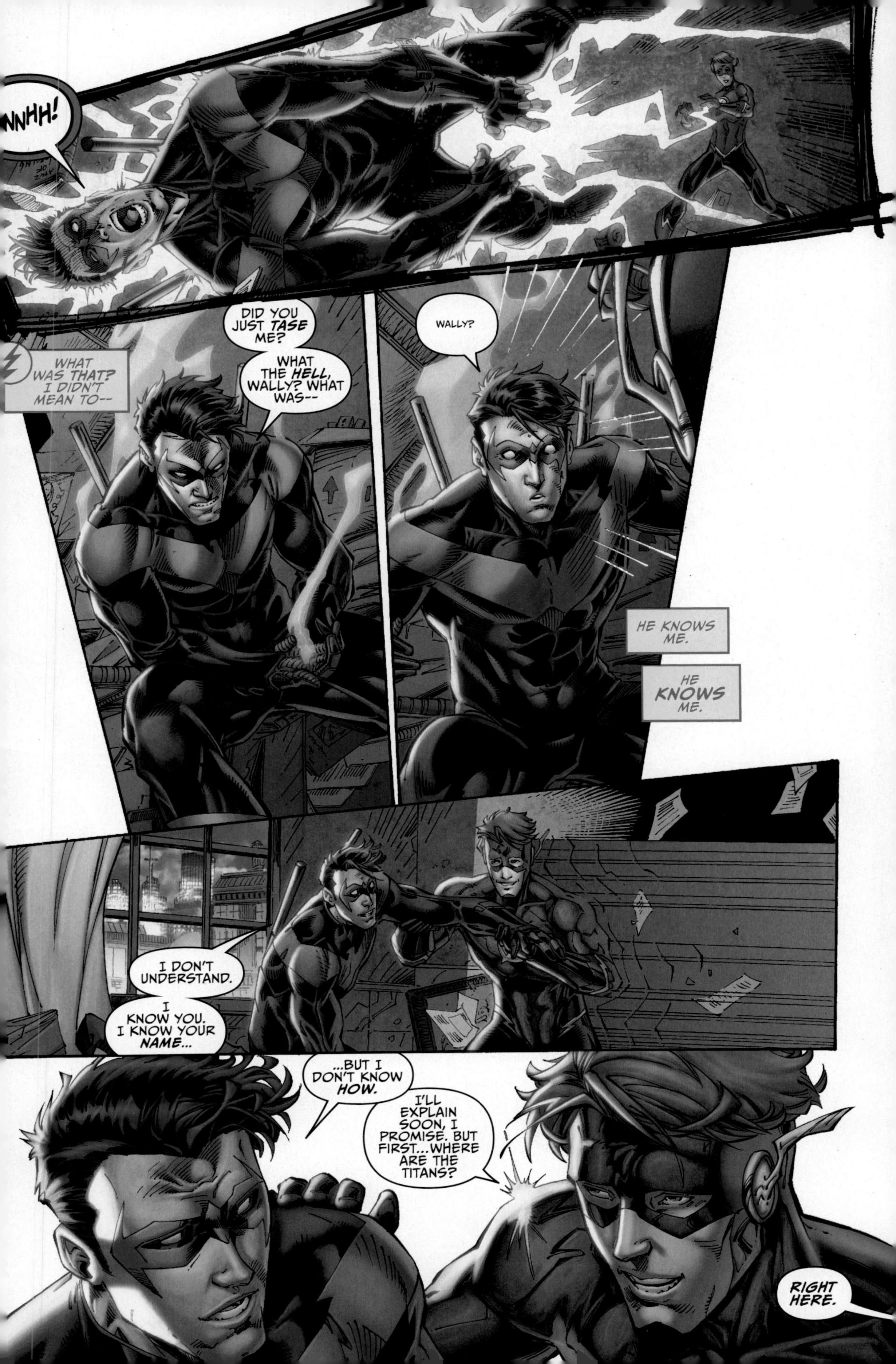
NNHH!
WHAT WAS THAT? I DIDN'T MEAN TO--
DID YOU JUST TASE ME?
WHAT THE HELL, WALLY? WHAT WAS--
WALLY?
HE KNOWS ME.
HE KNOWS ME.
I DON'T UNDERSTAND.
I KNOW YOU. I KNOW YOUR NAME...
...BUT I DON'T KNOW HOW.
I'LL EXPLAIN SOON, I PROMISE. BUT FIRST...WHERE ARE THE TITANS?
RIGHT HERE.

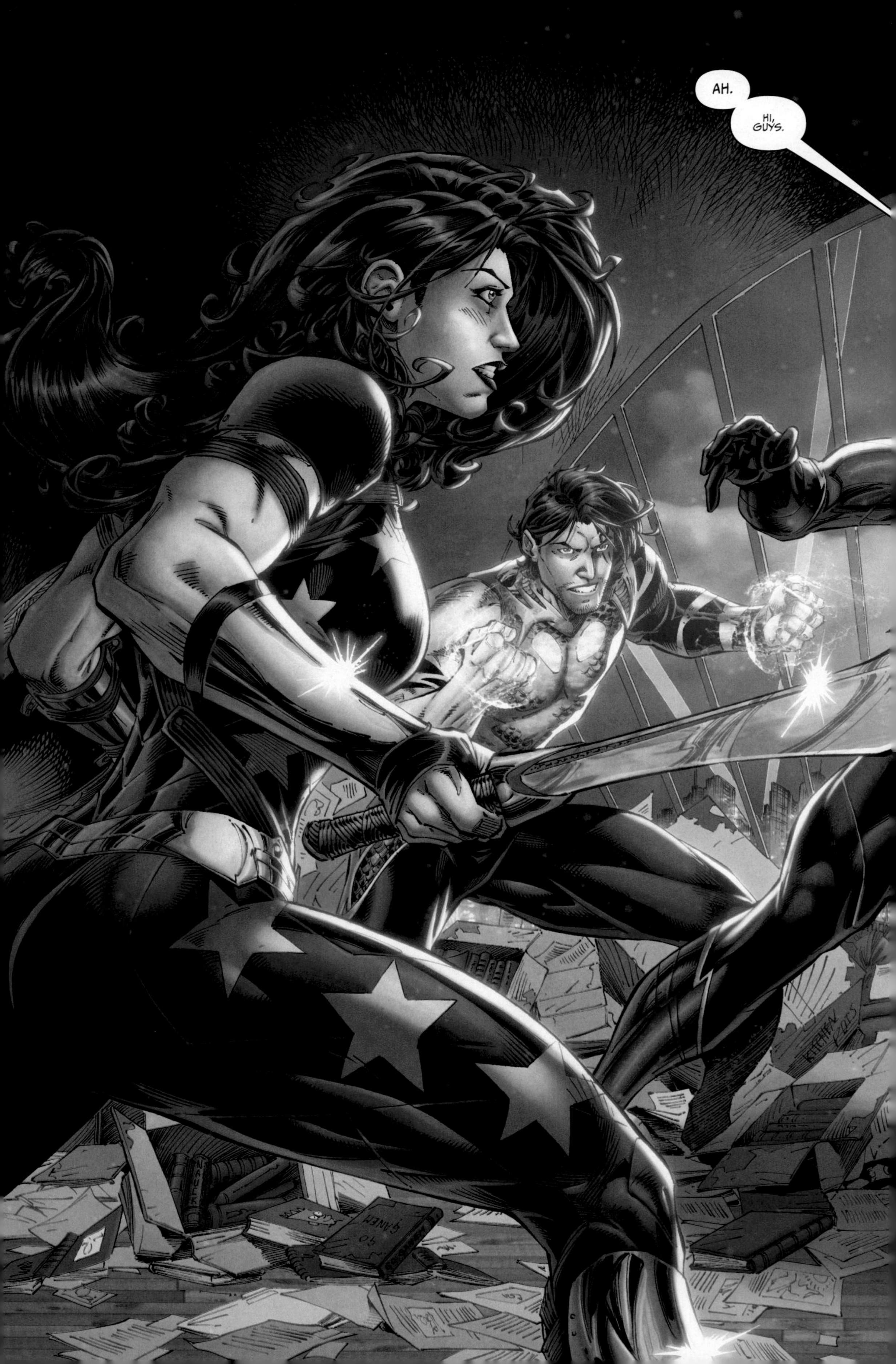
AH.
HI, GUYS.

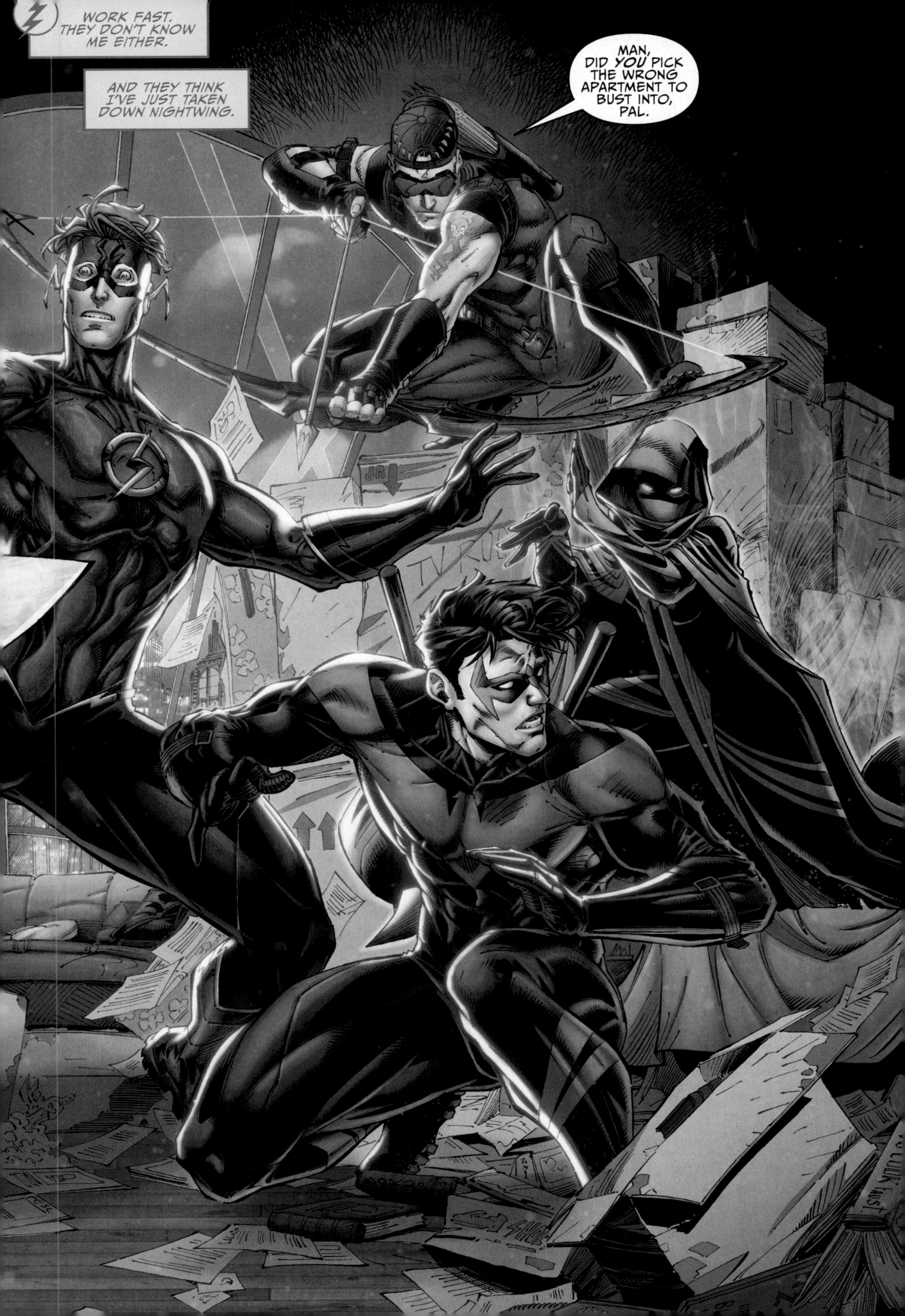
WORK FAST. THEY DON'T KNOW ME EITHER.
AND THEY THINK I'VE JUST TAKEN DOWN NIGHTWING.
MAN, DID YOU PICK THE WRONG APARTMENT TO BUST INTO, PAL.

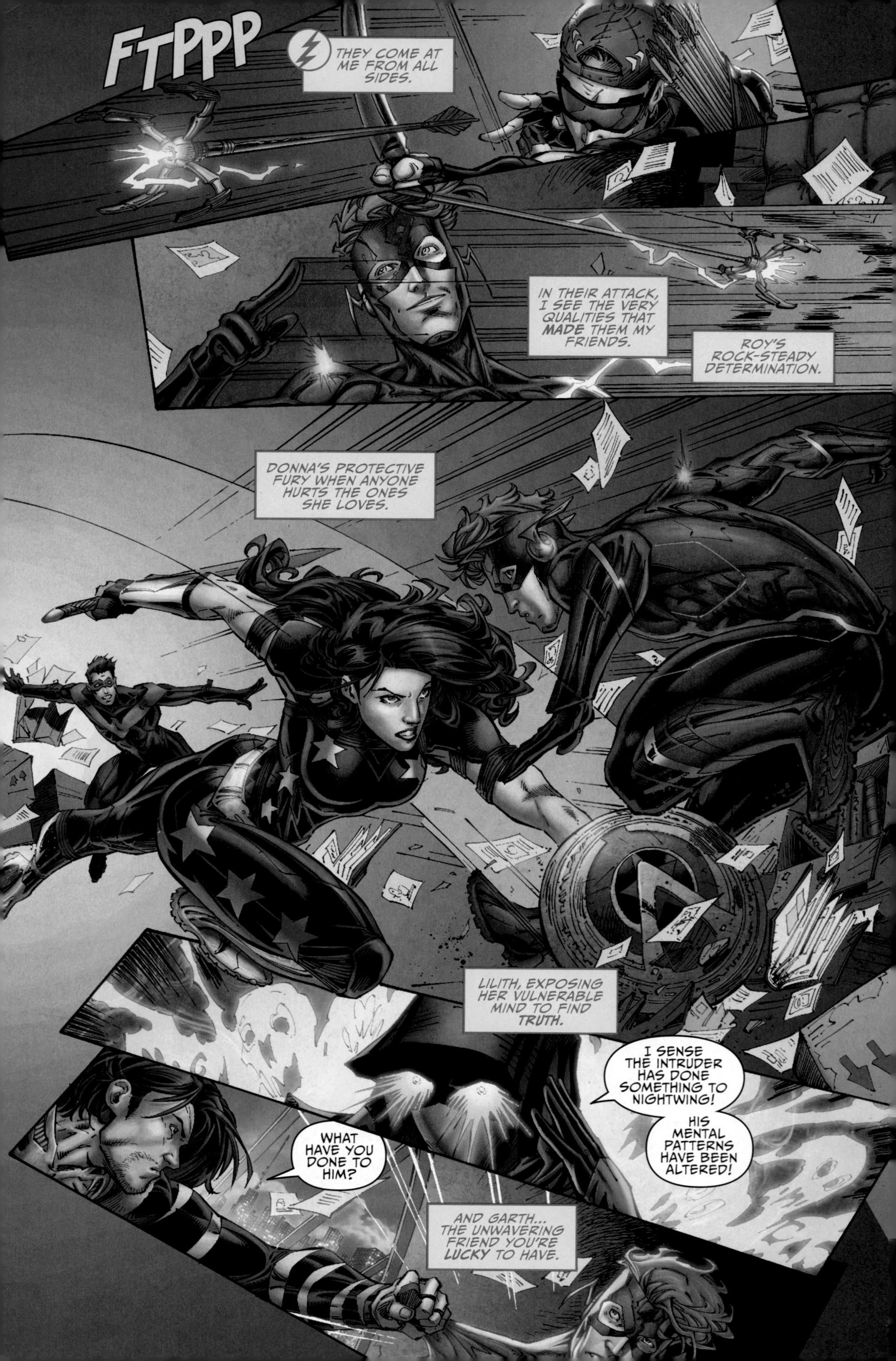
FTPPP
THEY COME AT ME FROM ALL SIDES.
IN THEIR ATTACK, I SEE THE VERY QUALITIES THAT MADE THEM MY FRIENDS.
ROY'S ROCK-STEADY DETERMINATION.
DONNA'S PROTECTIVE FURY WHEN ANYONE HURTS THE ONES SHE LOVES.
LILITH, EXPOSING HER VULNERABLE MIND TO FIND TRUTH.
I SENSE THE INTRUDER HAS DONE SOMETHING TO NIGHTWING!
HIS MENTAL PATTERNS HAVE BEEN ALTERED!
WHAT HAVE YOU DONE TO HIM?
AND GARTH... THE UNWAVERING FRIEND YOU'RE LUCKY TO HAVE.

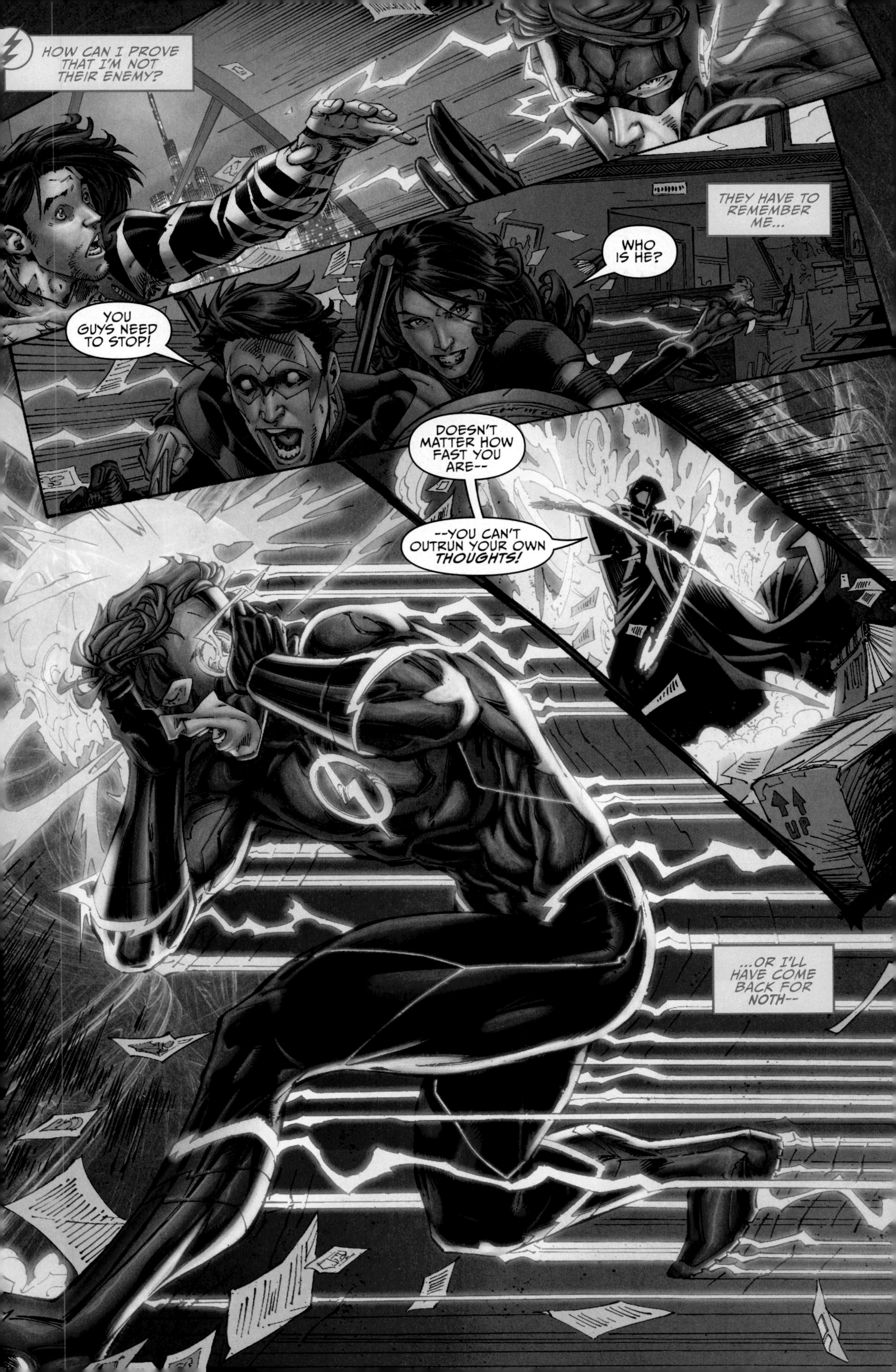
HOW CAN I PROVE THAT I'M NOT THEIR ENEMY?
THEY HAVE TO REMEMBER ME...
WHO IS HE?
YOU GUYS NEED TO STOP!
DOESN'T MATTER HOW FAST YOU ARE--
--YOU CAN'T OUTRUN YOUR OWN THOUGHTS!
UP
...OR I'LL HAVE COME BACK FOR NOTH--

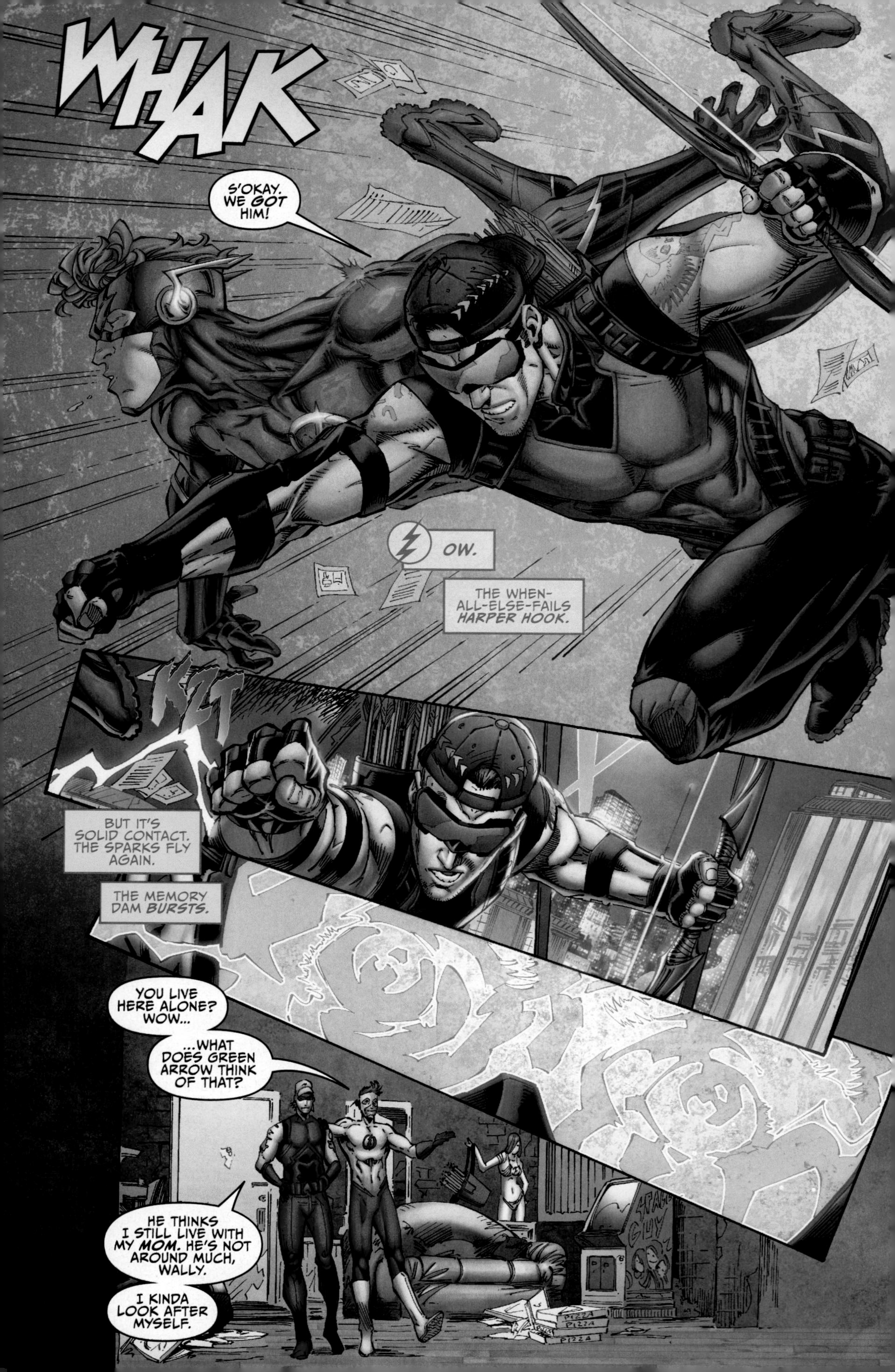
WHAK
S'OKAY. WE GOT HIM!
OW.
THE WHEN-ALL-ELSE-FAILS HARPER HOOK.
KZT
BUT IT'S SOLID CONTACT. THE SPARKS FLY AGAIN.
THE MEMORY DAM BURSTS.
YOU LIVE HERE ALONE? WOW...
...WHAT DOES GREEN ARROW THINK OF THAT?
HE THINKS I STILL LIVE WITH MY MOM. HE'S NOT AROUND MUCH, WALLY.
I KINDA LOOK AFTER MYSELF.

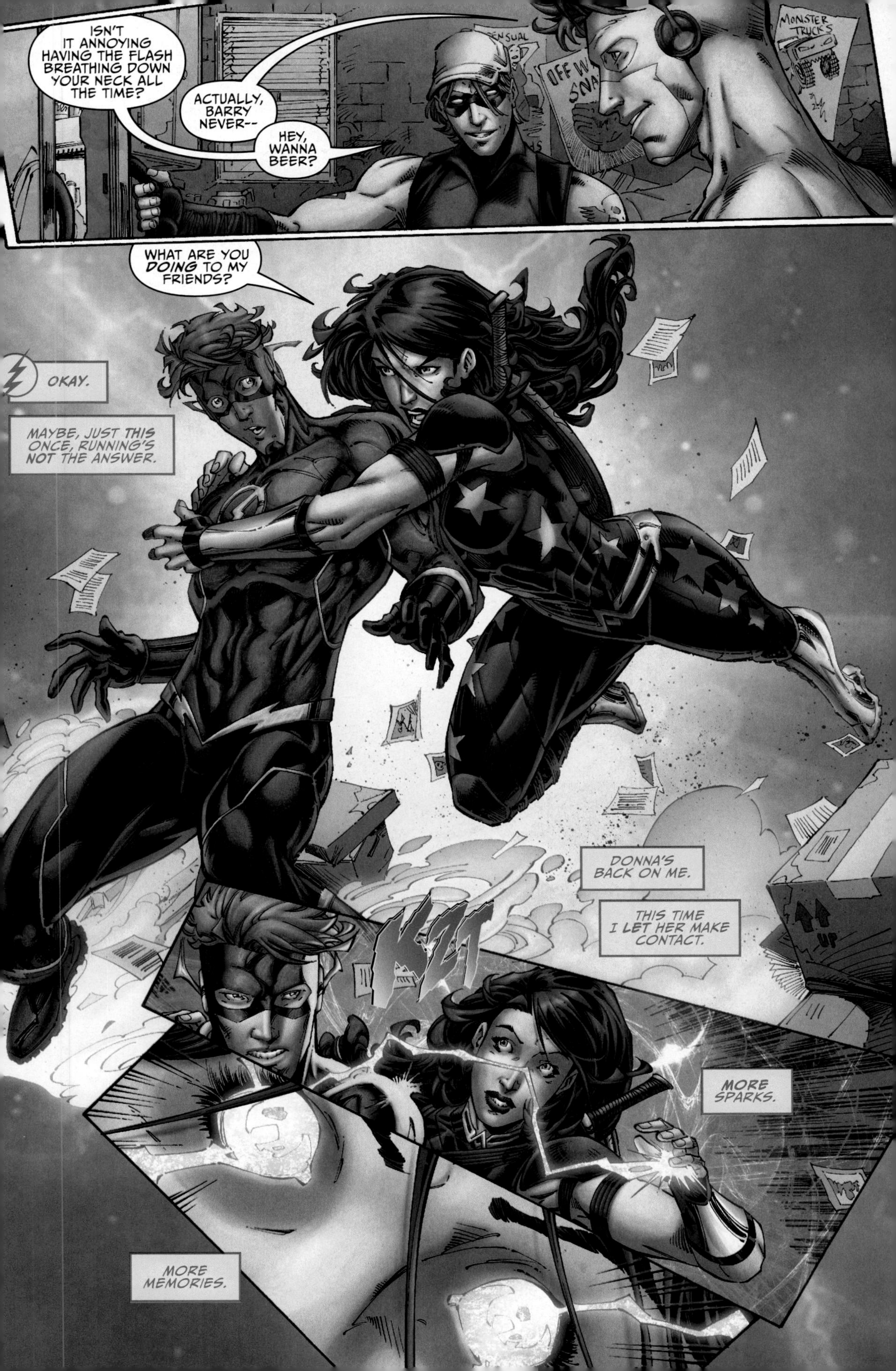
ISN'T IT ANNOYING HAVING THE FLASH BREATHING DOWN YOUR NECK ALL THE TIME?
ACTUALLY, BARRY NEVER--
HEY, WANNA BEER?
MONSTER TRUCKS
WHAT ARE YOU DOING TO MY FRIENDS?
OKAY.
MAYBE, JUST THIS ONCE, RUNNING'S NOT THE ANSWER.
DONNA'S BACK ON ME.
THIS TIME I LET HER MAKE CONTACT.
KZT
UP
MORE SPARKS.
MORE MEMORIES.

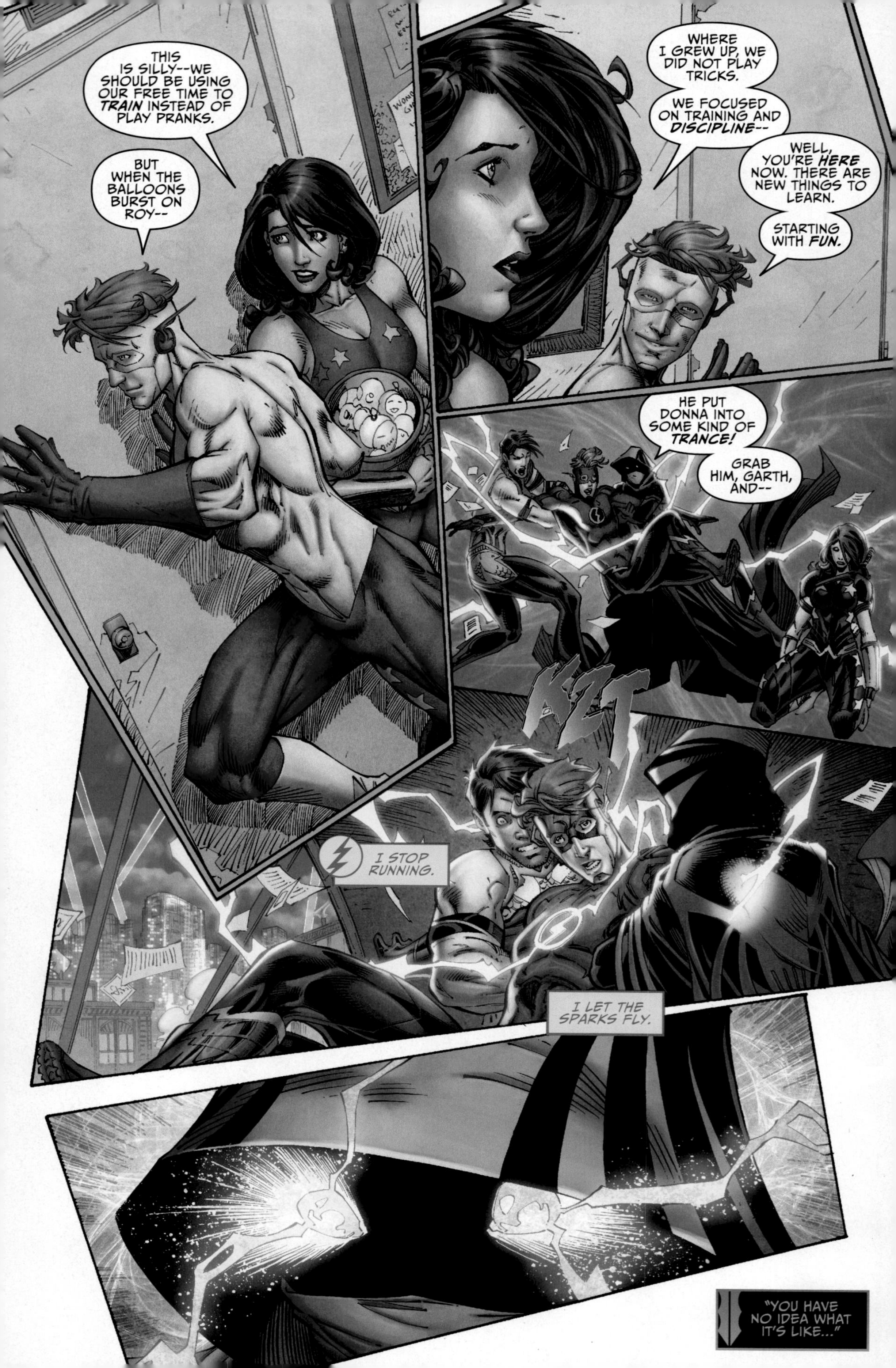
THIS IS SILLY--WE SHOULD BE USING OUR FREE TIME TO TRAIN INSTEAD OF PLAY PRANKS.
BUT WHEN THE BALLOONS BURST ON ROY--
WHERE I GREW UP, WE DID NOT PLAY TRICKS.
WE FOCUSED ON TRAINING AND DISCIPLINE--
WELL, YOU'RE HERE NOW. THERE ARE NEW THINGS TO LEARN.
STARTING WITH FUN.
HE PUT DONNA INTO SOME KIND OF TRANCE!
GRAB HIM, GARTH, AND--
KZT
I STOP RUNNING.
I LET THE SPARKS FLY.
"YOU HAVE NO IDEA WHAT IT'S LIKE..."

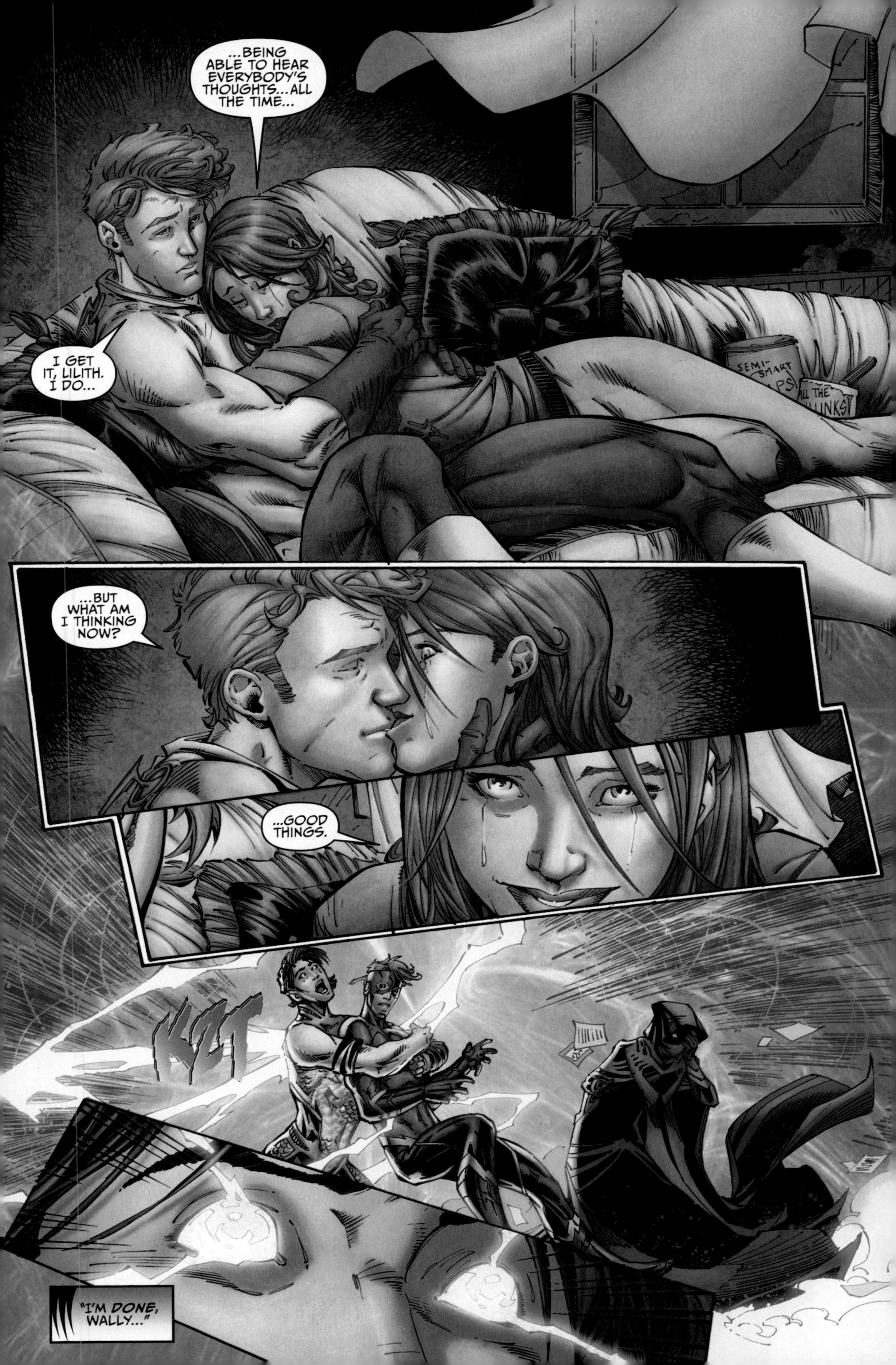

...BEING ABLE TO HEAR EVERYBODY'S THOUGHTS...ALL THE TIME...
I GET IT, LILITH. I DO...
SEMI-SMART
ALL THE
...BUT WHAT AM I THINKING NOW?
...GOOD THINGS.
KZZT
"I'M DONE, WALLY..."

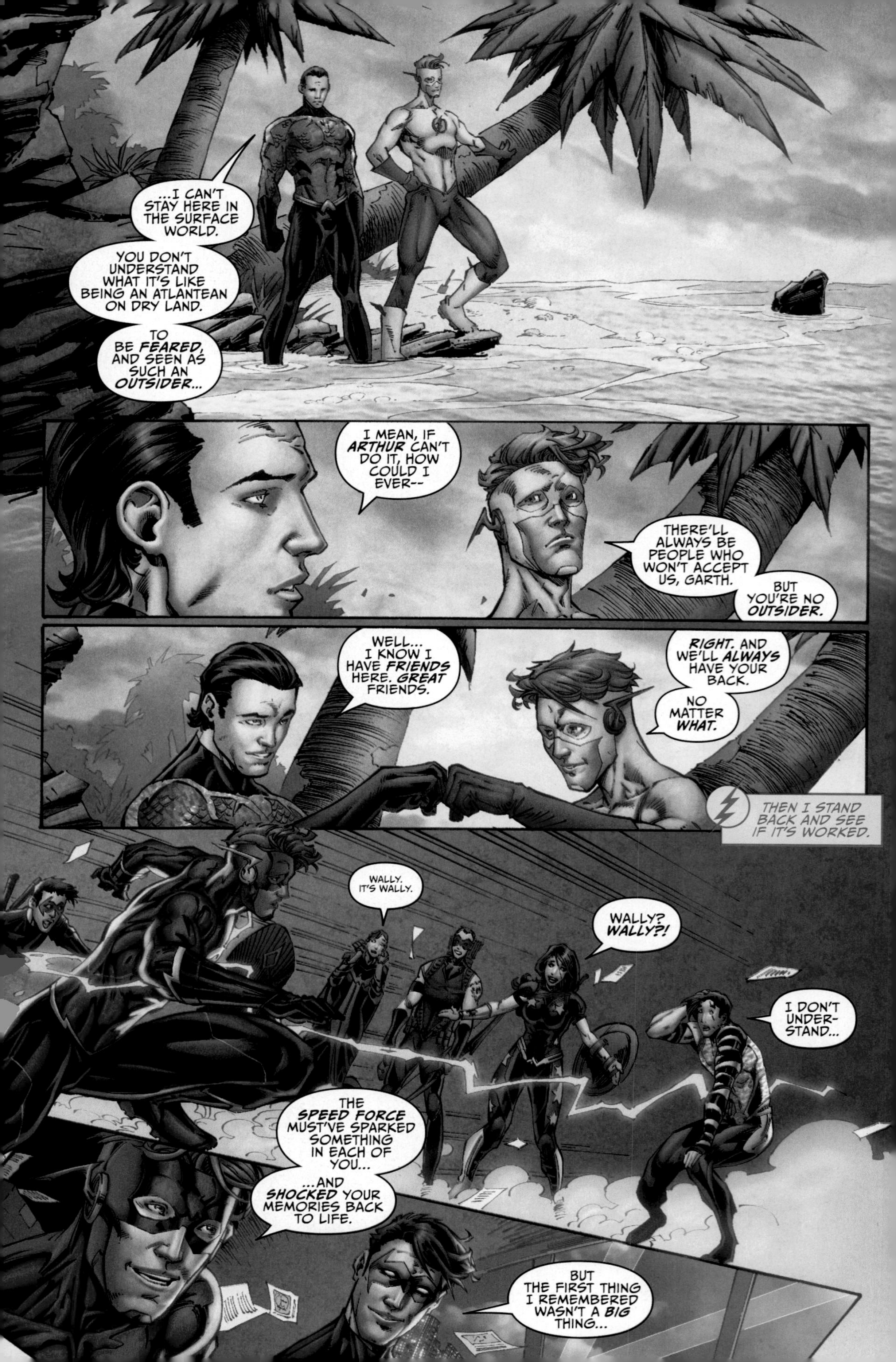
...I CAN'T STAY HERE IN THE SURFACE WORLD.
YOU DON'T UNDERSTAND WHAT IT'S LIKE BEING AN ATLANTEAN ON DRY LAND.
TO BE FEARED, AND SEEN AS SUCH AN OUTSIDER...
I MEAN, IF ARTHUR CAN'T DO IT, HOW COULD I EVER--
THERE'LL ALWAYS BE PEOPLE WHO WON'T ACCEPT US, GARTH.
BUT YOU'RE NO OUTSIDER.
WELL... I KNOW I HAVE FRIENDS HERE. GREAT FRIENDS.
RIGHT. AND WE'LL ALWAYS HAVE YOUR BACK.
NO MATTER WHAT.
THEN I STAND BACK AND SEE IF IT'S WORKED.
WALLY. IT'S WALLY.
WALLY? WALLY?!
I DON'T UNDER-STAND...
THE SPEED FORCE MUST'VE SPARKED SOMETHING IN EACH OF YOU...
...AND SHOCKED YOUR MEMORIES BACK TO LIFE.
BUT THE FIRST THING I REMEMBERED WASN'T A BIG THING...

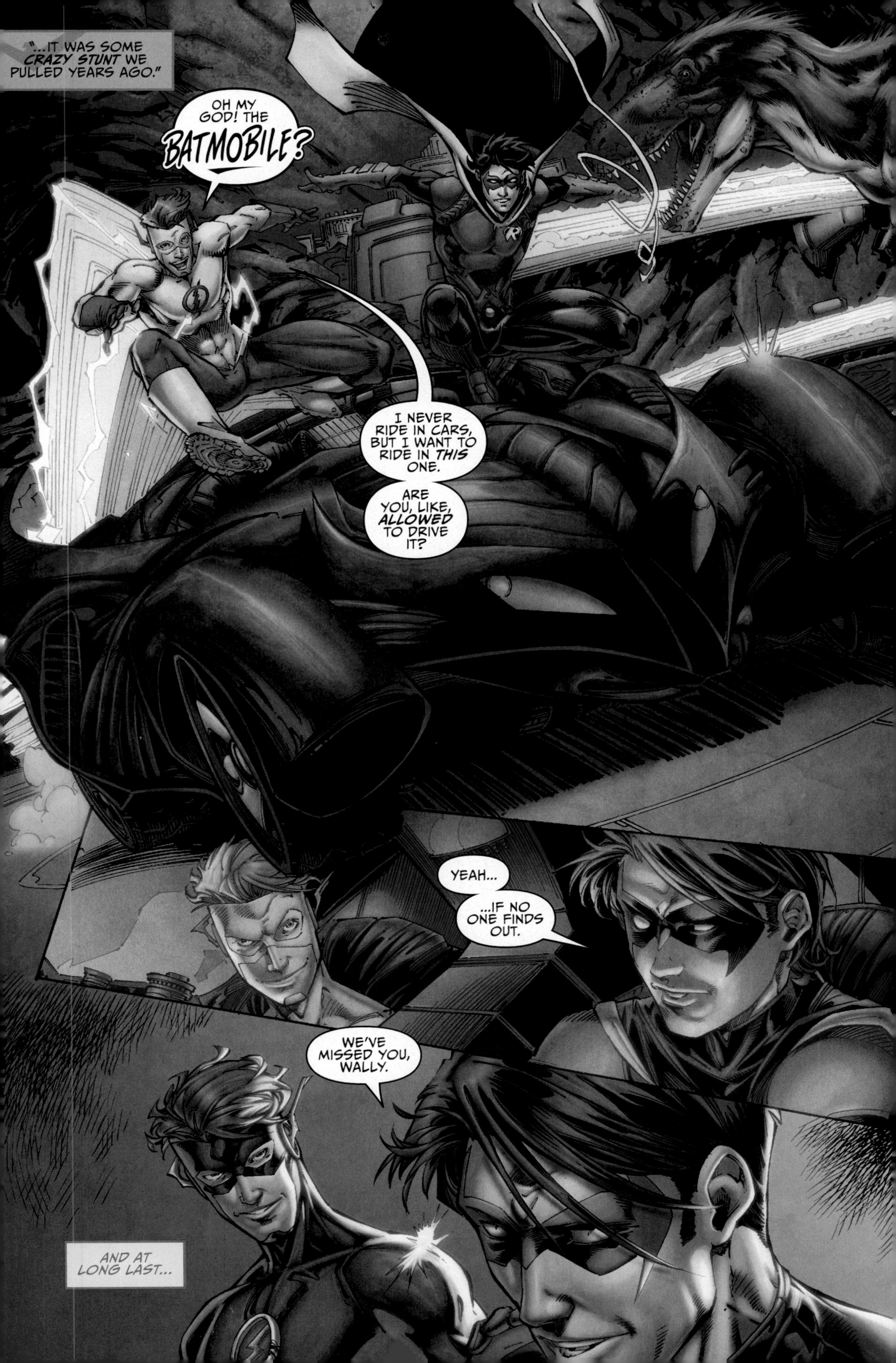
"...IT WAS SOME *CRAZY STUNT* WE PULLED YEARS AGO."
OH MY GOD! THE BATMOBILE?
I NEVER RIDE IN CARS, BUT I WANT TO RIDE IN *THIS* ONE.
ARE YOU, LIKE, ***ALLOWED*** TO DRIVE IT?
YEAH...
...IF NO ONE FINDS OUT.
WE'VE MISSED YOU, WALLY.
AND AT LONG LAST...

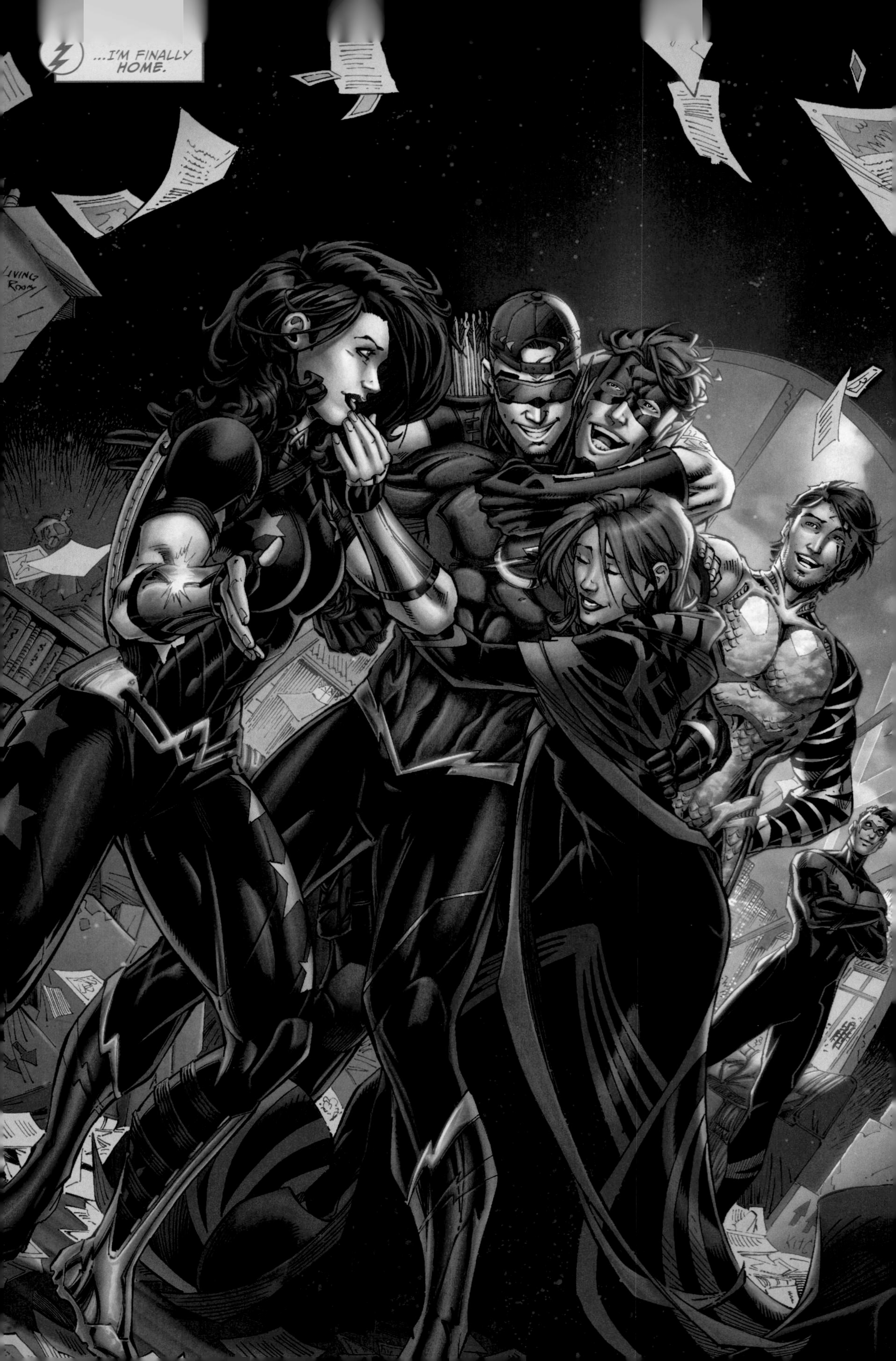
...I'M FINALLY HOME.
LIVING ROOM

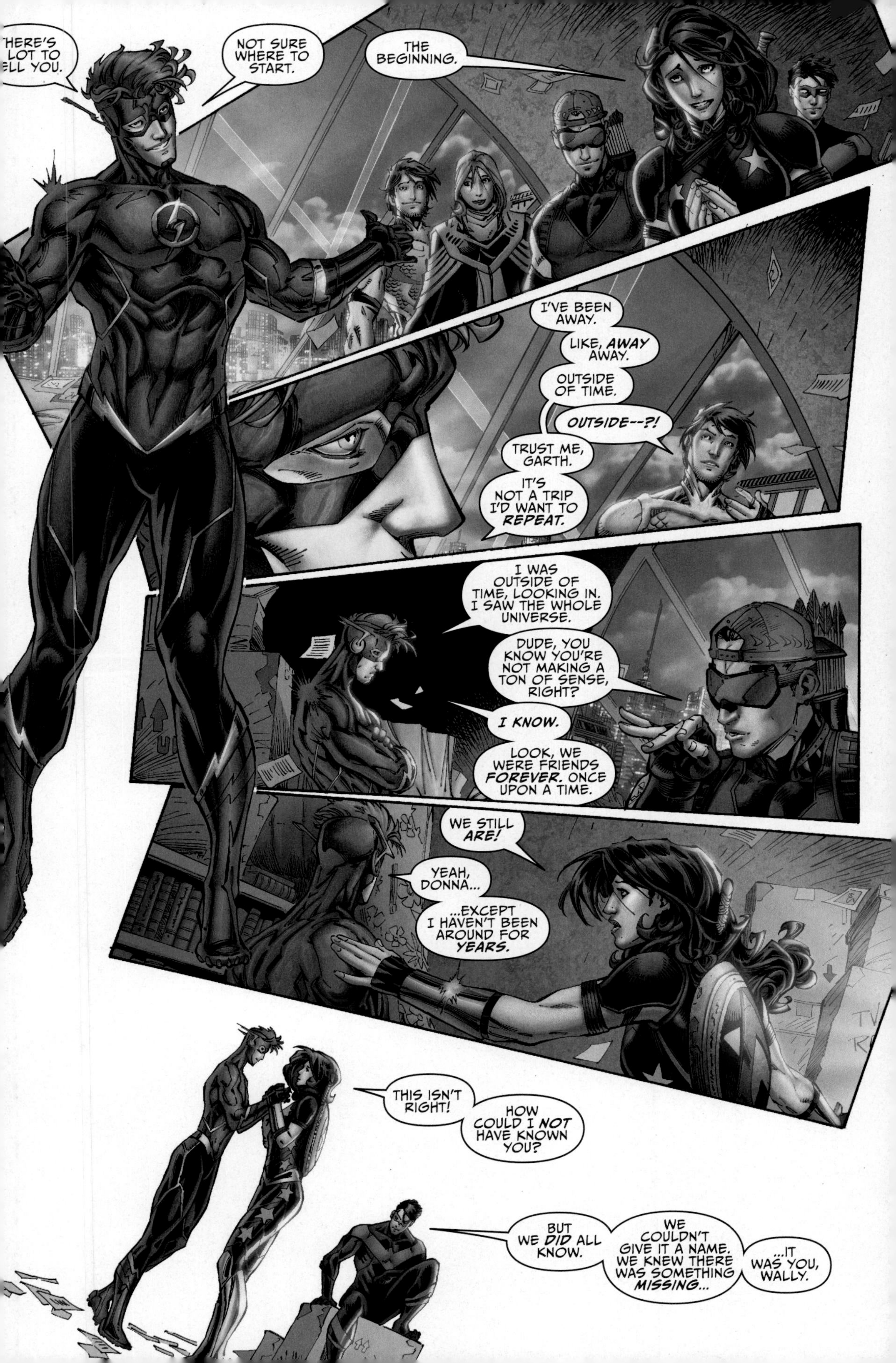
THERE'S LOT TO ELL YOU.
NOT SURE WHERE TO START.
THE BEGINNING.
I'VE BEEN AWAY.
LIKE, AWAY AWAY.
OUTSIDE OF TIME.
OUTSIDE--?!
TRUST ME, GARTH.
IT'S NOT A TRIP I'D WANT TO REPEAT.
I WAS OUTSIDE OF TIME, LOOKING IN. I SAW THE WHOLE UNIVERSE.
DUDE, YOU KNOW YOU'RE NOT MAKING A TON OF SENSE, RIGHT?
I KNOW.
LOOK, WE WERE FRIENDS FOREVER. ONCE UPON A TIME.
WE STILL ARE!
YEAH, DONNA...
...EXCEPT I HAVEN'T BEEN AROUND FOR YEARS.
THIS ISN'T RIGHT!
HOW COULD I NOT HAVE KNOWN YOU?
BUT WE DID ALL KNOW.
WE COULDN'T GIVE IT A NAME. WE KNEW THERE WAS SOMETHING MISSING...
...IT WAS YOU, WALLY.

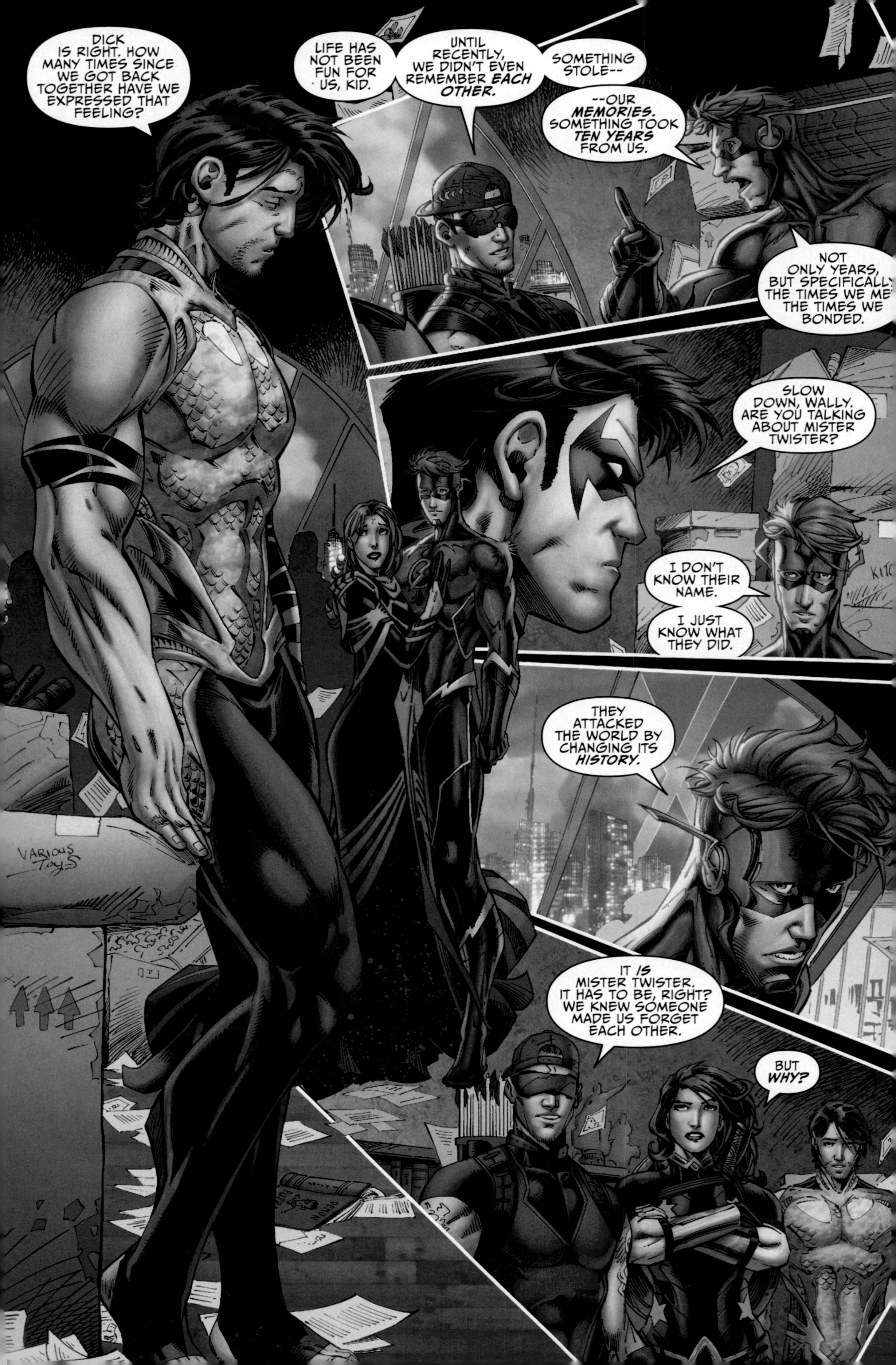
DICK IS RIGHT. HOW MANY TIMES SINCE WE GOT BACK TOGETHER HAVE WE EXPRESSED THAT FEELING?
LIFE HAS NOT BEEN FUN FOR US, KID.
UNTIL RECENTLY, WE DIDN'T EVEN REMEMBER EACH OTHER.
SOMETHING STOLE--
--OUR MEMORIES. SOMETHING TOOK TEN YEARS FROM US.
NOT ONLY YEARS, BUT SPECIFICALLY THE TIMES WE MET THE TIMES WE BONDED.
SLOW DOWN, WALLY. ARE YOU TALKING ABOUT MISTER TWISTER?
I DON'T KNOW THEIR NAME.
I JUST KNOW WHAT THEY DID.
THEY ATTACKED THE WORLD BY CHANGING ITS HISTORY.
IT IS MISTER TWISTER. IT HAS TO BE, RIGHT? WE KNEW SOMEONE MADE US FORGET EACH OTHER.
BUT WHY?

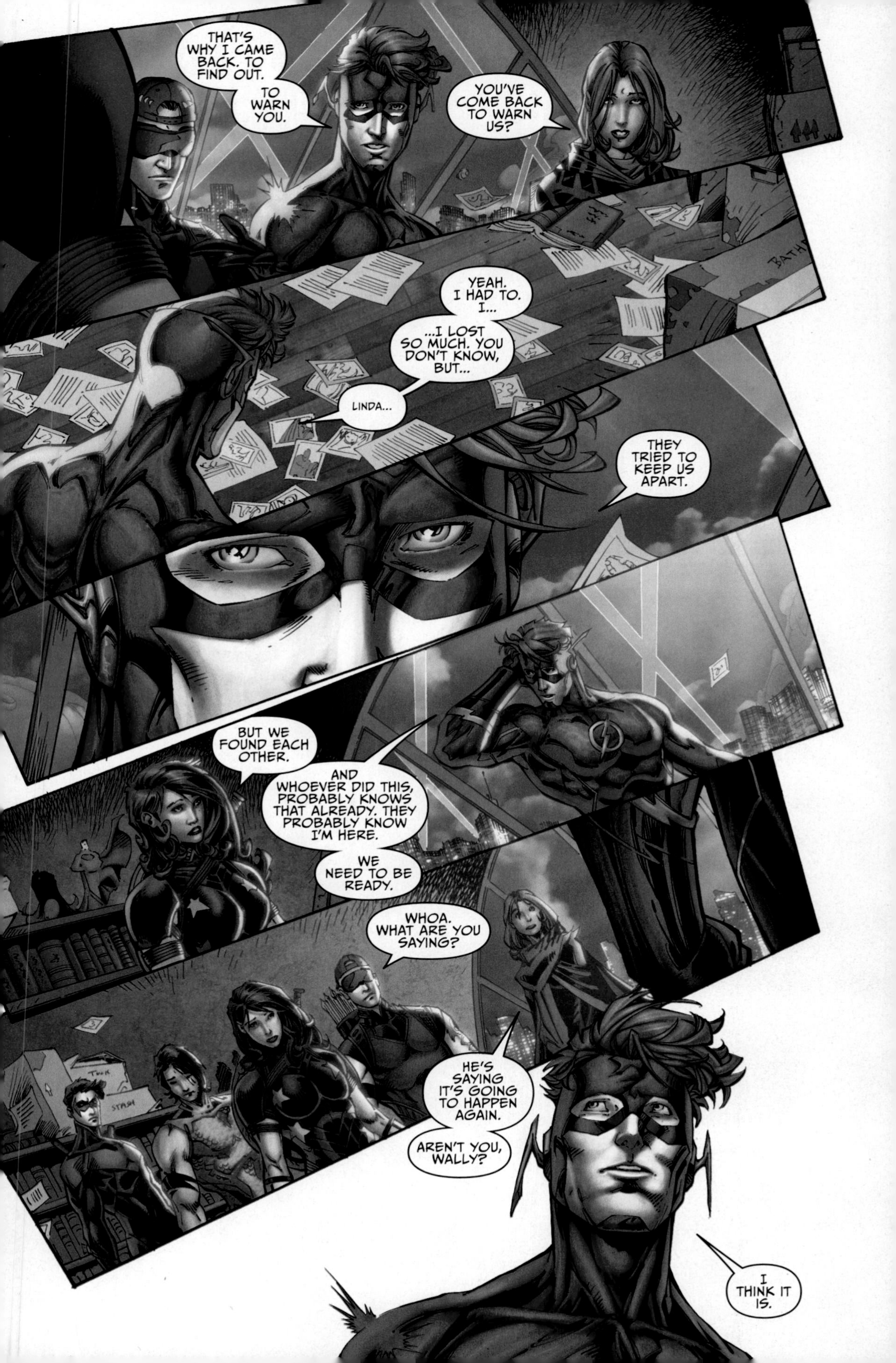
THAT'S WHY I CAME BACK. TO FIND OUT.
TO WARN YOU.
YOU'VE COME BACK TO WARN US?
YEAH. I HAD TO. I...
...I LOST SO MUCH. YOU DON'T KNOW, BUT...
LINDA...
THEY TRIED TO KEEP US APART.
BUT WE FOUND EACH OTHER.
AND WHOEVER DID THIS, PROBABLY KNOWS THAT ALREADY. THEY PROBABLY KNOW I'M HERE.
WE NEED TO BE READY.
WHOA. WHAT ARE YOU SAYING?
HE'S SAYING IT'S GOING TO HAPPEN AGAIN.
AREN'T YOU, WALLY?
I THINK IT IS.

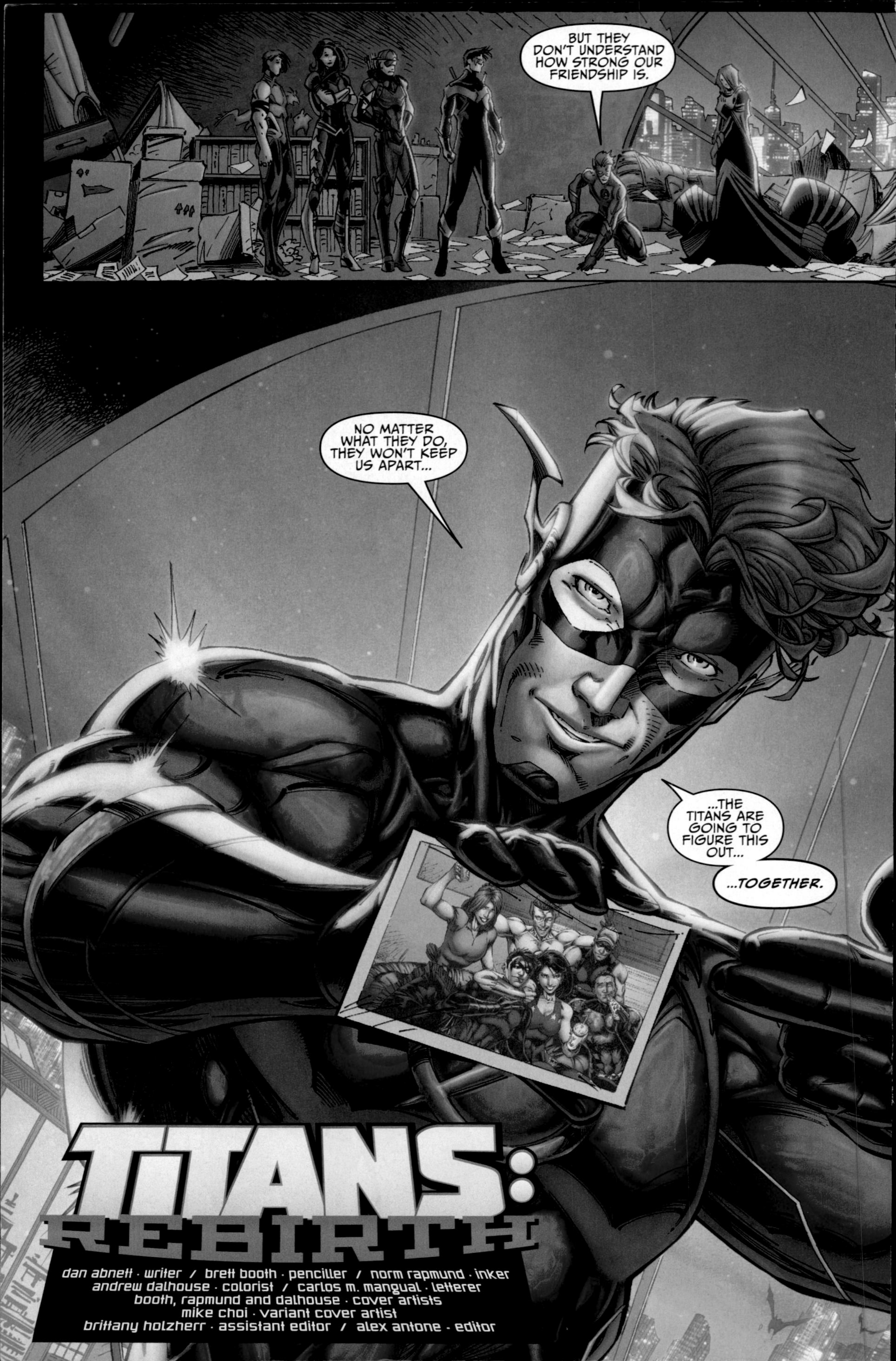

BUT THEY DON'T UNDERSTAND HOW STRONG OUR FRIENDSHIP IS.
NO MATTER WHAT THEY DO, THEY WON'T KEEP US APART...
...THE TITANS ARE GOING TO FIGURE THIS OUT...
...TOGETHER.
TITANS: REBIRTH
dan abnett · writer / brett booth · penciller / norm rapmund · inker
andrew dalhouse · colorist / carlos m. mangual · letterer
booth, rapmund and dalhouse · cover artists
mike choi · variant cover artist
brittany holzherr · assistant editor / alex antone · editor

Titans Rebirth #1 unused cover by
BRETT BOOTH, NORM RAPMUND, AND ANDREW DALHOUSE

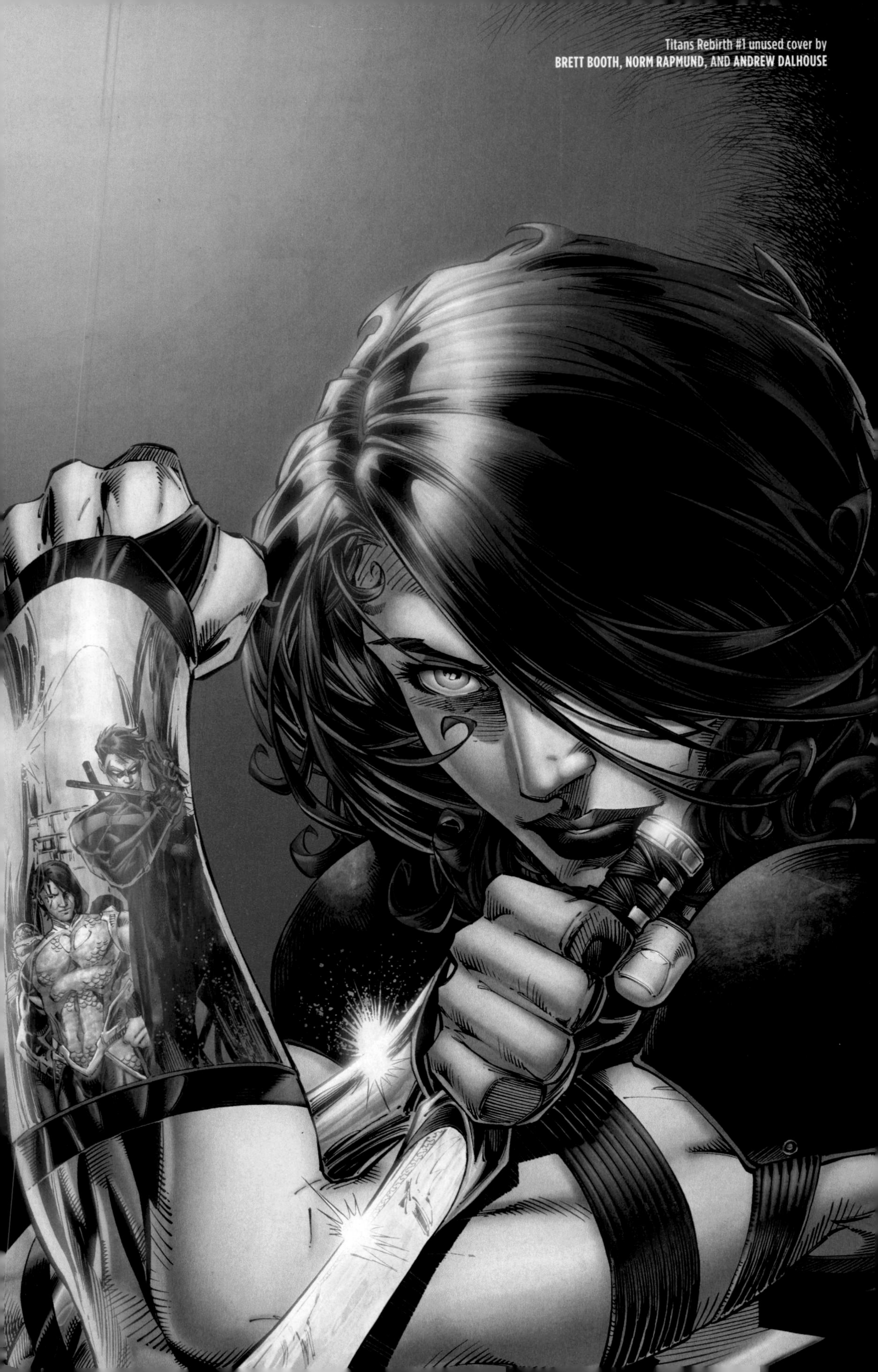

START AT THE BEGINNING!

NIGHTWING
VOLUME 1: TRAPS AND TRAPEZES

**NIGHTWING VOL. 2:
NIGHT OF THE OWLS**

**NIGHTWING VOL. 3:
DEATH OF THE FAMILY**

**BATMAN:
NIGHT OF THE OWLS**

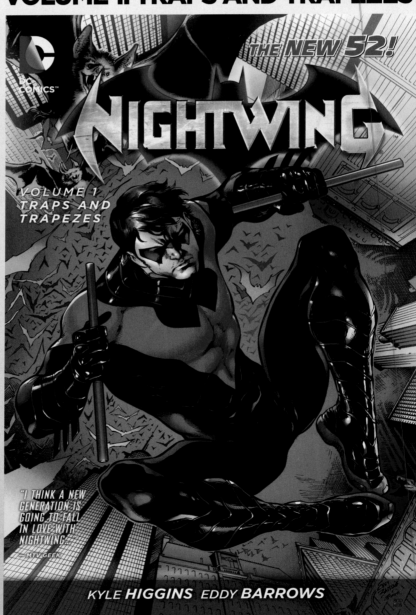

KYLE **HIGGINS** EDDY **BARROWS**